# HUNDRED GREAT MUSLIMS

# K. J. Ahmad

LIBRARY OF ISLAM

Distributor:

KAZI Publications, Inc.
3023 West Belmont Avenue
Chicago IL 60618
Tel: 773-267-7001
FAX: 773-267-7002
email: kazibooks@kazi.org

Author:

Kh. Jamil Ahmad

Hundred Great Muslims

ISBN: 0-933511-16-7

Printed in the United States of America

بِسْمِ اللَّهِ الرَّحْمَنِ الرَّحِيمِ

# CONTENTS

# FOREWORD

Khwaja Jamil Ahmad is well known in Pakistan as a journalist with long and varied experience of newspaper work, broadcasting and feature articles. He is also a good scholar, trained in my University of Allahabad, and a pupil of the savants like Dr. Ishwari Prasad and Dr. Tripathi whom, in their early years I was privileged to recruit to work in the Department of Mughal Studies which I founded. I have known Mr. Jamil Ahmad for many years through his writings; and it was with great pleasure that I was able to make his personal acquaintance while he was in Government service as Information Officer. During more than one of my visits to Pakistan as a government guest, he acted as my Conducting Officer, and helped me in a number of ways.

I was, therefore, very interested to learn that he has now written a book on *Hundred Great Muslims,* and that he is embodying in this book, among other pieces, some of his admirable biographical studies of prominent Muslim poets, philosophers, scientists, scholastics, statesmen, warriors and explorers. One of the remarkable features of the Great Men whom Islam has given birth to is the wide range of their genius. History can show many examples of warriors who have also been distinguished men of letters, of statesmen who have been excellent poets, and of scholars who have risen to the positions of great power and responsibility.

Nearly a generation ago, I edited a book entitled *Great Men of India,* in which I naturally included studies, each written by a distinguished specialist, of a number of prominent Muslims from Mughal times to our own day. This book has long been out of print, although I still receive letters asking from where copies can be obtained. Thus I am quite sure that there will be a steady demand of the book which Mr. Jamil Ahmad has written, angled as it is from the stand-point of a patriotic Pakistani, proud of his country's great tradition of Muslim culture. I have read a number of the individual biographies which will be included in this book, and am impressed with their excellence. I feel confident that the book will appeal to many readers both in Pakistan and outside.

SILCHESTER
*September 26, 1967.*

L.F. RUSHBROOK WILLIAMS

# PREFACE

Muhammad (PBUH) the Prophet of Islam and the greatest benefactor of mankind, had accomplished not only an impossible task of uniting the savage and warring Arabs tribes but also gave birth to a society which created the greatest revolution in the annals of mankind—a revolution which embraced all spheres of human activity. In less than thirty years, after the death of the Prophet, the Arabs swept over two of the mightiest empires of those times— Persians and Romans—and later became pioneers in the realm of art and learning.

The memorable words of the Holy Prophet of Islam, "Seek knowledge even unto the distant China," awakened a love of learning and a spirit of enquiry among the Muslims which hitherto lay dormant in them. They were responsible for reviving not only the dead Greek and Indian learnings but also made lasting contributions to almost all branches of sciences and arts and thus provided the necessary link between the ancient and modern civilizations. The light of learning which illuminated Cordova, the seat of Arab culture in Spain, at last dispelled the gloom that had enveloped the Mediaeval Europe, giving birth to Western Renaissance.

The Arabs, being practical people, had employed both observation and experiment in their pursuits of science—an advance over the Greek scientists who confined themselves to observation only. Their efforts in the realm of science were, therefore, crowned with greater success.

The invention of the Mariners Compass enabled the sea-faring Arab mariners to explore the distant seas. The latest research by the celebrated South African anthropologist, Dr. Jefferys, has credited the Arabs with the discovery of the New World—America—five centuries ahead of Columbus.

The teachings of the Holy Prophet of Islam had given birth to an ideal society, composed of a group of selfless people, who for thirty years successfully experimented in true democracy in the world—based on equality, fraternity and justice—which has no parallel in the annals of mankind. In that ideal democracy, there was no material distinction between the Caliph and an ordinary citizen.

Some of the most outstanding and charming personalities of Islam come from among the Companions of the Prophet, who lived during this period of ideal democracy. It is very difficult to make a selection from this group of selfless devotees to Islam, who staked their all for the glory of their New Faith.

But, the scope of the book demanded a larger canvas for selection which was provided by the outstanding scientists and scholars, historians and explorers, artists and writers, statesmen and rulers, revolutionaries and reformers of later Islam.

The inspiration to write this book I got from *One Hundred Great Lives* published by the Home Library of the Times of India Press, Bombay, in the early thirties of the present century. *Hundred Great Muslims* has been modelled on the same lines and has been divided into 12 biographical categories.

The Editors and the Publishers of the *One Hundred Great Lives* have done great injustice to the Muslims by including only two biographies of the sons of Islam—Muhammad (PBUH) the Prophet of Islam and Kamal Ataturk. It is strange that some of the greatest conquerors of the world like Timur, Khalid, Tariq and Salahuddin Ayyubi; great rulers like Harun, Mamun, Sulaiman, the Magnificent and Abdur Rahman al-Nasir; great scientists and scholars like Ibn Khaldun, ibn Sina, Baruni, Razi and Khwarizmi; great historians and explorers like Tabari, Masudi, Ibn Batuta and Sulaiman al-Mahiri; great writers and poets like Hafiz, Saadi, Firdausi, Omar Khayyam and Iqbal did not find a place in this book.

It is only to counter this utter injustice to the sons of Islam that I decided to write this book. There is another reason as well.

The ignorance of our educated class towards the achievements of their ancestors in different spheres of human activity, especially in the realm of sciences and arts impelled me to raise the curtain which hung over the glorious achievements of the sons of Islam.

The Western education is responsible for creating an inferiority complex among our educated classes who link the entire development of sciences and arts to the West. They are much familiar with Western Scientists like Newton and Stephenson, Harvey and Marconi but not with greater Muslim scientists like Khwarizmi and Ibn Sina, Baruni and Ibn Nafis. But, modern research, including some outspoken admissions by Western orientalists have brought out the truth about the achievements of Muslim scholars and scientists during the mediaeval times. These orientalists are Robert Briffault, John Draper, Phillip K. Hitti, George Sarton, Max Meyerhof, H. G. Farmer and Carra De Vaux.

Efforts have been made to provide documentary evidence for the achievements of the sons of Islam from the writings of Western orientalists, in order to save the author from a possible charge of partisanship towards Islam.

Most of the biographies included in this book have been widely published in the leading papers and periodicals of Pakistan and also of abroad.

The selection of outstanding Muslims representing different spheres of human activity was not an easy task. A number of Muslim scientists and scholars possessed encyclopaedic knowledge and versatile taste. It was found very difficult to place them in anyone category. However, this problem was solved by placing the person in a category to which he has made the most outstanding contributions.

The readers will find in this book a number of biographies from Muslim India. It is but natural as the author has more intimate knowledge of the achievements of his own countrymen, and has also sentimental attachment with them.

Absence of good libraries in Pakistan, especially in its only international city, Karachi, has greatly hampered good research work in different spheres of learning and has damped the enthusiasm of many promising scholars. The author of this book, too, had to surmount innumerable hurdles and had to sacrifice many-a-paid leave in order to have an access to the only good library in the city—Liaquat National Library—which till recently had no catalogue and was run during Central Government Office hours.

Lastly, I wish to thank all those persons who have encouraged me to write this book, including the founder-Governor of State Bank of Pakistan, late Mr. Zahid Hussain; *ex*-Managing Director of National Bank of Pakistan, Mr. Mumtaz Hasan; the *ex*-Governor-General and Prime Minister of Pakistan, Khawaja Nazimuddin; the *ex*-Speaker of Pakistan National Assembly, Moulvi Tamizuddin Khan; the novelist—Attorney General of Pakistan, late Mr. Fayyaz Ali; the renowned historian of Pakistan, late Dr. Mahmood Husain, former Vice-Chancellor of Karachi University and the outstanding Indian Urdu writer and columnist, Maulana Abdul Majid Dariyabadi.

I am particularly grateful to the celebrated British historian and writer, Professor Rushbrook Williams, who has written an illuminating and encouraging Foreword for this book.

KH. JAMIL AHMAD

# MUHAMMAD
## (P B.U.H.)
# The Prophet of Islam

# MUHAMMAD-
## (Peace be upon him)
## THE PROPHET OF ISLAM

Before the advent of Islam, Arabia was inhabited by warring tribes, whose inter-tribal feuds lasted for generations, and at times culminated in bloody conflicts in which hundreds of precious lives were lost. Idolatory was prevalent among the Arabs and the sacred house of God built by Prophet Abraham, housed hundreds of deities of demigods which were worshipped by the Arabs. They suffered from false sense of prestige and killed their female issues remorselessly. The Arabian society had degenerated to its lowest depths—feudalism was at its zenith and the poor were ruthlessly oppressed and exploited. Justice was denied to the weak and the maxim "might is right" was at no other time more applicable.

In such a gloomy atmosphere which had encompassed pre-Islamic Arabia, there glittered a light in the birth of Muhammad (Peace be upon him). Never before or after any individual placed in such adverse circumstances had so completely purged his society of the multifarious deep-seated evils, giving it a new and healthier shape, and had so much influenced the course of contemporary and future history. Muhammad's (PBUH) practical teachings had transformed a savage race into a civilized people who brought about the most wonderful revolution in the history of mankind. He was the benefactor of humanity and being the last and greatest of all the prophets, his teachings were universal and for all times to come.

Born in Makkah in 571 A.C., Muhammad (PBUH) sprang from Arabia's noblest family, Banu Hashim of Quraish, to whom had been entrusted the custodianship of Kaaba, built by Prophet Abraham and his son Ismail. Muhammad's (PBUH) father, Abdullah, the youngest son of his grandfather, Abdul Muttalib, the Custodian of Kaaba, had died before his son was born. His mother, Amina, too, died, six years later.

Young Muhammad (PBUH) was afterwards brought up by his grandfather Abdul Muttalib and on his death, two years later, by his uncle Abu Talib, the father of famous Ali, the lion-hearted.

Islam, the religion sponsored by Holy Prophet Muhammad (PBUH) through the injunctions of the sacred book of God—the Holy Quran, evolved a complete code of life, and the great Prophet translated its precepts into practice which made a lasting salutary effect on his countrymen. He stood like a rock against the surging waves of opposition and ultimately won the field. His forbearance, magnanimity., patience, and ability for organisation, stand unparalleled in the annals of mankind.

Muhammad (PBUH) proclaimed the sovereignty of God and liberated mankind from the thraldom of unholy associations with His Divinity. He upheld the dignity of man and practised the high ideals of equality, fraternity and justice he preached.

He advocated the unity of God and thereby the unity and equality of mankind. He denounced the differences of colour and race and was the "Prophet in human colour and consequently a true specimen of Islamic unity and brotherhood".

He was a great promoter of education and advocated the "pursuit of learning even unto distant China". He inculcated a love for learning among the illiterate Arabs which paved the way for their outstanding intellectual achievements, ultimately making them pioneers in the domains of science and arts during the Mediaeval times.

As a peace maker he set an example for the world to follow. The peace terms dictated by him on the conquest of Makkah stand as a landmark in the annals of treaties made among various nations of the world from time immemorial. No conqueror has ever offered more generous terms to the conquered, who were his sworn enemies and who harassed and maligned him throughout his life. Even his greatest living enemy, Abu Sufian, the leader of the nefarious Quraish group, was not touched. So much so, when his ten thousand crack troops were gasping to avenge the misdeeds of the Quraish of Makkah, the erstwhile enemies of Islam, the Prophet due to his boundless magnanimity and spirit of tolerance, gave orders not to strike anyone and declared that anyone who would take refuge in the house of Abu Sufian would be safe.

As an administrator, the Prophet accomplished what looked like an impossible task and overcame situations which would have defied the ablest administrators of the world.

The mission of Prophet Muhammad (PBUH) was to emancipate mankind from the shackles of slavery—mental or physical. He translated his noble ideas into practice by establishing a State in Medina based on equality, liberty, fraternity and justice.

The Prophet of Islam fulfilled during his lifetime the almost impossible task of knitting together the warring tribes of Arabia, who forming into an irresistible force, heralded the greatest revolution in the annals of mankind —both material and mental.

The four obligatory duties prescribed by Islam, namely Prayer, Fasting, Zakat and Haj, enabled the Prophet to realise the moral as well as material well-being of his follower :

*Prayers*—five times a day—in which the ruler and the ruled stood shoulder to shoulder, taught them the inestimable advantages of fraternity, and instilled in their hearts the spirit of equality of man.

*Fasting*—infused in them the spirit of sacrifice and abstenation from worldly pleasures. It elevated their moral standard.

*Zakat*—enabled the adherents of the new faith to evolve an egalitarian economy, as it provided a check on the rich becoming richer and the poor becoming poorer. This added immensely to the equitable distribution of wealth and to the material well-being of the poorer classes of the community.

*Haj*—Annual pilgrimage to Makkah—enabled the Muslims all over the world to meet one another and exchange views on problems facing the world of Islam.

The Prophet of Islam, being a great leader of men, both in war and peace, proved his mettle during the defensive wars fought against his enemies, including Badr, Ohad, Khandak and Khyber. His organising capacity and the spirit which he had inculcated among his warriors, won the field for him despite enemy's superiority in men and arms.

Hazrat Muhammad (PBUH) possessed innumerable, qualities of head and heart. He was a very kind-hearted man, who never abused or cursed anybody. Whenever such occasion arose and his Companions implored him to curse his torturers, he prayed for the latter's reformation. Once, while praying in Kaaba, when he prostrated, one of his opponents placed the heavy skin of a camel on his back. He remained in this condition for a pretty long time till he was rescued by some of his Companions. Even then he did not curse the miscreant. On another occasion, when he had gone to Taif, the hostile elements instigated the hooligans and children to shower stones on him and his Companions. He was badly injured and his Companions requested him to curse the children. But, kind-hearted as he was, he said instead : "O God, forgive these ignorant ones and show them the right path". Once an evil-minded Jew became his guest. He entertained him to his fill and gave him his bedding to sleep, but, out of spite, the Jew discharged faeces on the bedding and slipped away, leaving his sword behind. The Prophet, finding his guest gone, was sorry because he had left his sword behind, and began to wash the bedding with his own hands. Meanwhile, the Jew returned to fetch his sword and observed the Prophet washing the dirtied bedding. The Prophet did not utter even a word of complaint. Instead he said: "Dear friend, you had left behind your sword. Here it is". Struck by the unusual courtesy and angelic character of Muhammad (PBUH), the Jew instantaneously embraced Islam.

The teachings of the Holy Prophet of Islam created a society based on principles of equality and justice, thus demolishing all barriers between one man and the other. He was the greatest benefactor of mankind who liberated them from the shackles of race and colour bars. This spirit of equality taught by the Prophet later led to the birth of several slave ruling dynasties in Muslim countries.

The Prophet of Islam was totally impartial in his dealings with his relations and strangers. He refused a maid servant even to his dearest daughter, Hazrat Fatima, who was overworked and badly needed such a help. He, no doubt, advised his followers to help their relations, neighbours and needy persons according to their means. "No religion of the world prior to Islam", says Ameer Ali, "had consecrated charity, the support of the widow, the orphans and the helpless poor, by enrolling its principles among the positive enactments of the system". Mercy and kindness were the virtues mostly emphasised by Muhammad (PBUH) who, according to a *Hadith* in *Bukhari,* once said: "The man who plants a tree is blessed when people and birds are benefited by its fruit. A man was sent to Paradise, simply because he saved a thirsty dog from death by offering him water and the other was condemned because he tied and starved a cat to death". *(Bukhari).*

The Holy Prophet defined and prescribed the rights of individuals as set forth in the Holy Quran. He said: "It is the part of faith that you should like for your brother what you like for yourself" *(Bukhari).* He enjoined upon the faithful to show the greatest respect for one's mother after God when he said: "Paradise lies under the feet of your mother." *(Bukhari).* For other relations he said: "Anyone who is not kind to his youngsters and obedient to his elders is not from us" *(Tirmizi).* As regards Muslims as a whole, he proclaimed: "The Muslims are a single hand like a compact wall whose bricks support each other" *(Muslim).*

Even during his early life, when Hazrat Muhammad (PBUH) had not yet been bestowed the mantle of Prophethood, he was known for his piety, truthfulness and trustworthiness. He was known by the title of *"Amin"* (Trustworthy) among the Makkahans, who kept their valuables with him. When he migrated to Medina, he left behind his cousin Hazrat Ali, to return to their owners the articles kept with him as a trust. Even his sworn enemies acknowledged his truthfulness. Once he climbed the hill of Safa and addressed the Quraish, asking them. "If I tell you that there is a huge army hidden behind this hill ready to attack you, will you believe me?" All shouted with one voice: "Surely, because you have never spoken a lie." Such was the high reputation of the Prophet of Islam, even before God conferred Prophethood on him.

The generosity of the Prophet of Islam knew no bounds. Indeed, it was one of the greatest characteristics of the House of Muhammad (PBUH) that no supplicant was ever refused, and this principle was rigidly followed not only by Hazrat Fatima and her sons but even by their grand children. Once while he was grazing his herd of goats he gave the entire herd to a person who asked for it. The supplicant was surprised by his extraordinary generosity. During the last days of the Holy Prophet of Islam, the Muslims had become very prosperous. Nevertheless, he lived abstemiously contending himself with frugal diet and at times going without food.

He always resisted the temptation of power and vengeance. His was the sublimest morality of returning good for evil: to the weak and undefended he was a helper; to the defeated he showed unusual mercy. Never proud or haughty, known for his strict adherence to justice, one who undertook his share of common labour, Prophet Muhammad (PBUH) shunned no hardship and led the life of a common man.

Delivering his last address to the Muslims from Mount Arafat, the Prophet said :

"O People! Listen to my words as I may not be with you another year in this place. Be humane and just among yourselves. The life and the property of one are sacred and inviolable to the other. Render faithfully everyone his due, as you will appear before God and He will demand an account of your actions. Treat women well; they are your help-mates and can do nothing by themselves. You have taken them from God on trust. O People! Listen to my words and fix them in your memory. I have given you everything; I have left to you a law which you should preserve and be firmly attached to a law clear and positive: the Book of God and the *Sunnah*" (i.e., Practice of the Prophet).

This greatest benefactor of mankind and the last Apostle of God passed away from this world on 12th Rabiul Awwal 11 A.H., 632 AC and was buried in the room occupied of his wife, Aisha Siddiqa. He had accomplished his task.

Muhammad (PBUH) led an exemplary life. Even before he was assigned his mission, he spent his time in meditation, devotion, contemplation, fasting and service to his fellow beings. His virtuous life earned for him the title of *'Amin'* (Trustworthy). Later the Revelation commanded him to preach the faith to the people.

He taught them the unity of God and the four obligatory duties enjoined by Islam—namely Prayer, Zakat, Fasting and Haj (Annual Pilgrimage to Makkah). He himslef practised what he preached and set an example for others. He stood sometimes so long in prayers during the night that his feet got swollen. He spent the major part of night in prayers and meditation. He prayed not only for himself but for the entire creation.

His prayers and devotion to God enabled him to check such worldly desires and impulses which could distract him from the supreme goal.

Islam enjoins upon its followers to observe one month's fast in a year. This has proved to be a very effective source of controlling one's worldly desires. The Holy Prophet of Islam fasted for more than three months during a year, besides one month's obligatory fast.

His was a comprehensive life. He went through all sorts of trials and tribulations for establishing the kingdom of God on earth. Faithfully and sincerely he performed his duties to God and His creatures, to wife and children, to relations and neighbours, to friends and foes, to the needy and disabled, to allies and aliens—in fact to all human beings. An account of his comprehensive life preserved in Traditions *(Hadith)* has served as a beacon light not only for his followers but to entire humanity during the last fourteen centuries or more. His exemplary life covering different spheres of human activity continues to inspire and guide human beings for the last more than 1,400 years.

Such were the exceptional qualities of head and heart possessed by the great Prophet of Islam whose noble teachings produced a society of virtuous people who laid the foundation of true democracy in the world in which there was no distinction between the ruler and the ruled.

Writing in the *Legacy of Islam,* David De Santillana says: "The Prophet uttered some charming words with regard to neighbourly relations: "Be kind to your neighbour. Draw the veil over him. Avoid injury. Look upon him with an eye of kindness, if you see him doing evil forgive him. If you see him doing good to you, proclaim your thankfulness".

The celebrated British writer, George Bernard Shaw, in his letter to Mr. Najmi Saqib of Cyprus acknowledges that Prophet Muhammad's (PBUH) teachings on the status of women, exposure of female children and kindness to animals, were "far ahead of Western Christian thought, even of modern thought".

The great Western historian, Edward Gibbon observes: "The good sense of Muhammad (PBUH) despised the pomp of royalty; the Apostle of God submitted to the menial offices of the family; he kindled the fire, swept the floor, milked the cows and mended with his own hands shoes and his woollen garments. Disdaining the penance and merit of a hermit he observed without effort and vanity, the abstemious diet of an Arab and a soldier. On solemn occasions he feted his Companions with hospitable plenty; but in his domestic life, many weeks would elapse without a fire being kindled in the hearth of the Prophet".

"Muhammad (PBUH) was a man of truth and fidelity", says Thomas Carlyle, "true in what he said, in what he spoke, in what he thought; he always meant something; a man rather taciturn in speech, silent when there was nothing to be said but pertinent, wise, sincere when he did speak, always throwing light on the matter".

"His intellectual qualities, "says Washington Irving, "were undoubtedly of an extraordinary kind. He had a quick apprehension, a retentive memory, a vivid imagination and an inventive genius. His military triumphs awakened no pride nor vainglory as they would have done had they been effected for selfish purposes. In the time of his greatest power he maintained the same simplicity of manners and appearance as in the days of his adversity. So, far from affecting a regal state, he was displeased if on entering a room any unusual testimonial of respect was shown to him. If he aimed at universal domination it was the dominion of the faith: as to the temporal rule which grew up in his hands, he used it without ostentation, so he took no step to perpetuate it in his family.'

In his *Histoire de la Turqui,* Lamertine observes: "Philosopher, orator, apostle, legislator, warrior, conqueror of ideas, restorer of national dogmas, of a cult without images; the founder of 20 terrestrial Empires, that is Muhammad (PBUH). As regards all standards by which human greatness may be measured, we may well ask, is there any man greater than he?"

"It is impossible," says Mrs. Annie Besant, "for anyone who studies the life and character of the great Prophet of Arabia who knows how he taught and how he lived to feel anything but reverence for that mighty Prophet, one of the great messengers of the Supreme. And although in what I put to you I shall say many things which may be familiar to you, yet I re-read them as a new way of admiration, a new sense of reverence for the mighty Arabian leader."

The famous English writer and literary critic Dr. Johnson says: "His purely historical character, his simple humanity, claiming to be a man among men, his intense realism, avoiding all mystical remoteness; the thoroughly democratic and universal form under which his idea of the divine monarchy led him to conceive the relations of men, the force of his ethical appeal all affiliate Muhammad (PBUH) with the modern world".

The celebrated English writer Robert Briffault pays rich tributes to the teachings of the Holy Prophet of Islam, when he says: "The ideas of freedom for all human beings, of human brotherhood, of the equality of all men before the law of democratic government, by consultation and universal suffrage, the ideas that inspired the French Revolution and the Declaration of Rights, that guided the framing of the American Constitution and inflamed the struggle for independence in the Latin—American countries were not inventions of the West. They find their ultimate inspiration and source in the Holy Quran. They are the quintessence of what the intelligentsia of medieval Europe acquired from Islam over a period of centuries through the various societies that developed in Europe in the wake of the Grusades in imitation of the brotherhood associations of Islam. It is highly probable that but for the Arabs modern European civilization would never have arisen at all, it is absolutely certain that but for them it would never have assumed that character which has enabled it to transcend all previous phases of evolution."

# GREAT LEADERS

# ABU BAKR

Medina, the heart of Islam, was gravely threatened by the enemy hordes. The Holy Prophet of Islam appealed for funds in order to finance the defensive campaign for meeting the impending danger, Hazrat Umar being in affluent circumstances at once thought of taking advantage of this golden opportunity and thus surpassed Hazrat Abu Bakr in the service of Islam. He hurried to his home and brought a considerable portion of his wealth. The Prophet was much pleased to see it and asked him, "Have you left anything for your dependants?"

"Half of my wealth I have set aside for my children", replied Umar.

When Hazrat Abu Bakr brought his share, the same question was posed to him.

He promptly replied, "I have retained only Allah and His Prophet for my dependants."

Deeply moved by these words, Umar said, "It would never be possible for me to surpass Abu Bakr."

Hazrat Abu Bakr, the first Caliph of Islam and the most trusted as well as devoted lieutenant of the Prophet, was born in Makkah two and a half years after the year of the Elephant or fifty and a half years before the commencement of Hejira. He was known as Abul Kaab in pre-Islamic days and on conversion to Islam was given the name of Abdulla and the title of Al Siddiq (The truthful) by the Prophet. He belonged to the Quraishite clan of Bani Taim and his geneology joins with that of the Holy Prophet in the 7th generation. He was one of the most respected leaders even before and after embracing Islam. His ancestral occupation was business and occasionally he undertook commercial trips to Syria and Yemen. He visited Hazrat Muhammad (PBUH) even before, and at the time of the revelation he was in Yemen. On his return to Makkah, the leaders of Quraish including Abu Jahl, Ataba and Shoba, ridiculed in his presence the declaration of Prophethood by Muhammad (PBUH). Thereupon Abu Bakr got very much excited and exasperated and hurried to the Prophet's place and embraced Islam. According to Suyuti, the author of 'Tarikh ul Khulafa', the Prophet said, "Whenever I offered Islam to any person, he showed some hesitation before embracing it. But Abu Bakr is an exception as he embraced Islam without the slightest hesitation on his part."

It is universally admitted fact that among the grown ups, Hazrat Abu Bakr, among the youngsters, Hazrat Ali, and among the women, Hazrat Khadija, were first to embrace Islam. As stated above, Hazrat Abu Bakr, being a wealthy person, placed his entire wealth at the disposal of the Prophet. Besides, he purchased and set free a number of slaves including Hazrat Bilal, who were bitterly persecuted for accepting Islam. He had to endure all sorts of hardships, intimidation and torture in the service of the new faith. Once he was severely beaten till he became unconscious. The courage and determination exhibited by the Holy Prophet and his faithful Companions in face of bitter opposition, will always be a source of inspiration for those who strive for Truth. Hazrat Abu Bakr who had 40,000 dirhams at the time of his conversion, had only 5,000 left at the time of migration. Leaving his wife and children to the care of God, he left Makkah for Medina in the company of the Prophet.

He also fought shoulder to shoulder with the Prophet in defensive battles which the adherents of the new faith fought for their existence. Abdur Rahman bin Abu Bakr, after his conversion to Islam, told his father that in the battle of Badr he got a chance when he could easily strike him down. Abu Bakr promptly replied that he would not have spared him if he had had the opportunity.

Abu Bakr died on August 23, 634 A.C. at the age of 63 and his Caliphate lasted for two years, three months and eleven days. He was buried by the side of the Prophet.

On the death of the holy Prophet, Hazrat Abu Bakr was elected as the first Caliph of Islam After his election, at which people scrambled to offer 'bait', the Caliph delivered his memorable speech before the electorate.

Said he: "Brothers, now I am elected your Amir, although I am no better than anyone among you. Help me if I am in the right and set me right if I am in the wrong. Truth is a trust: falsehood is a treason. The weak among you shall be strong with me till (God willing) his right has been vindicated and the strong among you shall be weak with me till (if Lord will) I have taken what is due from him. Obey me as long as I obey Allah and His Prophet. If I disobey Him and His Prophet, obey me not."

Intrinsically kind-hearted, Abu Bakr stood like a rock against the disruptive forces which raised their head after the death of the Holy Prophet. It seemed then that the entire structure of Islam which had been built by the departed master-mind would crumble down. Abu Bakr, being the faithful Companion of the Prophet, proved to be an exceptionally strong man and stuck to the path shown by his master. During the illness of the Prophet an army of 700 men was mobilised under Usama bin Zaid to avenge the defeat of

Muslims at the hands of the Romans. There was a great turmoil in Arabia after the death of the Prophet, and his close associates counselled the new Caliph not to despatch forces outside Medina at such a critical juncture. Hazrat Abu Bakr was adamant on the point and replied that he would be the last person in the world to revise the orders of the Prophet. The charger of the commander Usama appointed by the Prophet was led by the Caliph himself. The army accomplished its object within forty days. The expedition had a salutary effect on the recalcitrant tribesmen who had begun to be sceptical about the inherent potentialities of Islam. The imaginative, timely and dynamic action taken by Abu Bakr, tended to establish Muslim power.

Very soon another crisis confronted Abu Bakr. On the death of the Prophet of Islam, a number of pseudo prophets i.e., imposters raised their heads in various parts of Arabia, outstanding being Aswad Asni, Talha of Bani Asad, Musailma, the liar and Sajah, a woman of Yemen. The Caliph gave at Zuhl Qassa eleven banners to equal number of commanders and assigned them various sectors. The expedition against Musailma, the liar, was the toughest and Hazrat Khalid bin Walid, after a bloody battle, routed the enemy. Musailma was killed. According to historian Tabari, "Never did the Muslims fight a more stiff battle."

Shortly after the election of the new Caliph, a large number of tribesmen pleaded with the notables of Islam in Medina to be exempted from the payment of Zakat. The situation looked so gloomy that even a person of the calibre of Hazrat Umar yielded on the point and counselled Hazrat Abu Bakr, "O Caliph of the Prophet, be friendly to these people and treat them gently." The Caliph was immensely annoyed at this unexpected exhibition of weakness, and replied indignantly, "You were so harsh during the days of ignorance, but now you have become so weak. The Divine revelations have been completed and our faith has attained perfection. Now, you want it to be mutilated during my lifetime. I swear by Allah that even if a string is withheld from Zakat, I will fight for it with all the resources at my command."

The Caliph lived up to his convictions and his integrity and strength of character, preserved the basic precepts of Islam at a very critical juncture of her history.

All the punitive expeditions directed against the apostates and rebellious tribesmen successfully terminated by the end of 11 A.H., and the spirit of revolt and dissensions which gripped Arabia was curbed for ever.

Free from the internal upheavals, the Caliph attended to the external dangers which imperilled the very existence of Islam. Kaiser and Kisra, the two most powerful emperors of the world, were lurking for an opportunity to strike at the very root of the new faith. The Persians, who for centuries ruled over Arabia as overlords, could never tolerate that the militant Arabs should unite and form themselves into a formidable force. Hurmuz, the tyrant governed

Iraq on behalf of the Kisra. His persecution of the Arabs led to the skirmishes which developed into a full blooded war. Nature willed otherwise; the Persians, who in their arrogance, had underrated the power of Muslims, could not stem the tide of their advance and had to retreat from place to place till Iraq fell into the hands of the Arabs. Muthanna, in the beginning, led the Muslim army against the Persians. He earned many laurels against his enemy. He was later on joined by the invincible Khalid bin Walid, known as the Sword of God. The decisive battle against Hurmuz was won by Muslims in which Hurmuz was killed by Hazrat Khalid and the Persians were routed with heavy losses. A camel load of chains weighing seven and a half maunds was collected from the battlefield, hence it is known as the 'Battle of Chains."

Hazrat Khalid bin Walid, who was the Commander of Islamic forces in Iraq, separated the administration of military and civil departments under different heads. Saeed bin Noman was appointed chief of the military department, while Suwaid bin Maqran was appointed chief of the civil administration of the conquered area in Iraq. Major portion of Iraq was captured during the Caliphate of Hazrat Abu Bakr and the Persians had had the sad experience of challenging of growing power of Islam. The decisive battle for Iraq was fought between Muslims and Persians during the reign of Hazrat Umar.

Heraclius, the Byzantine Emperor, who ruled over Syria and Palestine, was the greatest and most powerful enemy of Islam. He had been constantly conspiring with the enemies of Islam in an effort to annihilate it. His intrigues and secret machinations brought about several uprisings of non-Muslim tribes in Arabia. He was a constant danger to Islam. In 9 A.H., the Prophet himself had marched against the Romans and the expedition of Usama bin Zaid was also directed against the threatening Romans. Hazrat Abu Bakr despatched the flower of his army to meet the Romans and divided his forces into four armies placed under the command of Abu Ubaidah, Sharjil bin Hasanah, Yazid bin Sufian and Amr bin al-Aas and assigned them different sectors in Syria. The ill-equipped, untrained and numerically inferior army of Islam, was no match for the well equipped, well trained and numerically much superior Roman forces. Khalid was ordered by the Caliph to join the Muslim forces in Syria and his lightning march through a waterless desert added a memorable chapter to the history of military campaigns.

The opposing forces met on the plain of Yarmuk. The formidable Roman forces comprised more than 3-lakh well equipped soldiers, out of which about 80,000 were chained in order to ward off the possibility of retreat. The Muslim army was composed of hardly 46,000 men in all, which, according to the strategic plan of Hazrat Khalid, was broken up into 40 contingents in order to impress its numerical superiority upon the enemy. This memorable battle ended in the crushing defeat of the Romans who retreated, leaving a large number of dead on the battle-field. This decisive victory sealed the fate of Roman rule in Syria. The battle of Yarmuk, whose initial preparations were started during the Caliphate of Hazrat Abu Bakr was won in the reign of Hazrat Umar.

Hazrat Abu Bakr was the most trusted Companion of the Prophet of Islam. The Prophet said, "I am not aware of a person who can surpass Abu Bakr in beneficence". When the illness of the Prophet became serious, he bade Abu Bakr to lead the prayers. Accordingly, he led the prayers seventeen times during the lifetime of the Prophet.

The Prophet said : "I have paid back the obligations of all except that of Abu Bakr who will have his reward on the Day of Judgement."

According to Tirmizi, Hazrat Umar said, "O, You! (Abu Bakr) are the best of men after the Prophet of God."

According to a statement of Imam Ahmad, Hazrat Ali said, "The best among the members of this Ummat (Muslims) after the Prophet are Abu Bakr and Umar."

Glowing tributes have been paid to the character and achievements of Hazrat Abu Bakr by the contemporary and later historians. He was one of the mighty pillars of Islam who was instrumental in making the new faith a great force in the world. He was one of the great champions of the Islamic revolution which, in a short span of 30 years, brought about the greatest social, political and economic changes in the history of mankind. He was one of the founders of the true democracy that existed in the world more than 1400 years ago and never thereafter. That was a democracy in which the highest authority of the state (Caliph), who was also the most powerful monarch of his time, roamed about in the streets unguarded and unescorted, ate coarse food and wore tattered clothes. Even an ordinary citizen could approach him at any time of the day and question his actions publicly.

Hazrat Abu Bakr and Hazrat Ali were distinguished for their eloquence among the Muslims. Once he advised Hazrat Khalid bin Walid : "Try to run away from greatness and greatness will follow you. Seek death and life will be conferred on you."

He had issued instructions to his army which, according to Ibn Athir, formed the moral code that guided the conduct of the soldiers of Islam. This should serve as a model for war-ravaged world. He instructed his forces: "Don't commit misappropriations; don't deceive anybody; don't disobey your chief; don't mutilate human bodies; don't kill old men, women or children; don't cut fruit trees or burn them; don't slaughter animals except for food; don't molest Christian priests and don't forget God for His blessings that you have enjoyed." It was obligatory on the armed forces to maintain a high standard of morality even during the campaigns and to show due respect to human, animal and plant life. Any deviation from these principles was severely dealt with.

He appointed Hazrat Umar as his Grand Qazi, but people had grown so honest and their social life was so much purged of the immoralities of the pre-Islamic days that no complaint was lodged with the Qazi for one year. Hazrat Ali, Hazrat Usman and Zaid bin Sabit worked as Khatibs.

Hazrat Abu Bakr's simplicity, honesty and integrity was personified. He sacrificed everything in the service of Islam. He was a prosperous businessman owning more than 40,000 dirhams in cash when he embraced Islam, but he was a pauper when he died as the First Caliph of Islam.

He did not abandon his ancestral occupation when he was elected as Caliph and for about six months carried cloth sheets on his shoulders for selling in the markets of Medina. However, his official duties did not leave him much time for his private work, hence he was advised to accept some maintenance allowance. The Assembly of the Muslims fixed a monthly stipend which enabled him to pass the life of an ordinary citizen. He had to deposit his old clothes for replacement by new ones from the *Baitul Mal* (Public Treasury).

Before his assumption of the exalted office of Caliph, he used to milk the goats of his locality. Once while passing through a street of Medina, he heard a girl's remark's, "Now he has become the Caliph, hence he would not milk our goats." He replied instantly, "No, my daughter, I shall certainly milk the goats as usual. I hope that by the grace of God, my position will not alter my routine." He had great affection for children who used to embrace him and call him *'Baba'* (Father).

An old destitute woman lived on the outskirts of Medina. Hazrat Umar visited her occasionally to handle her household chores. But whenever he went there, he was told that someone else had preceded him in that service. Once he visited her house in the early hours of the morning and hid himself in a corner to watch the mysterious person who arrived at the usual time. He was surprised to see that he was none other than the Caliph himself.

Hazrat Abu Bakr was extremely scrupulous in drawing his stipend from the *Baitul Mal.* He charged only as much as would suffice for the barest necessities of an ordinary life. One day his wife asked for sweets, but he had no spare funds for that. She saved a few dirhams in a fortnight and gave it to him to get sweets for her. Forthrightly he gave her to understand that her savings had established that he was drawing stipend in excess of their requirements. Hence he refunded the amount to the *Baitul Mal* and reduced his stipend for the future.

He delighted in doing all his work with his own hands, and never tolerated anyone to share his domestic works. Even if the reins of the camel happened to drop from his hand, he would never ask anyone to hold it for him. He would rather come down and pick it up himself.

Whenever a man praised him in his presence he would say, "O, God! You know me more than myself and I know myself more than these people.

Forgive those sins of mine which are not in their knowledge and do not hold me responsible for their praise."

He was a man of exceptionally simple habits. A richly dressed prince of Yemen, who arrived in Medina found him putting on only two brown sheets of cloth—one wrapped round his waist and the other covered the rest of his body. He was so much touched with the simplicity of the Caliph that he, too, discarded his gorgeous dress. He said, "Under the influence of Islam, I get no pleasure in such artificialities."

On his death bed he enquired from the person incharge of *Baitul Mal* about the amount he had drawn from the *Baitul Mal* as his stipends. He was informed that he had drawn, 6,000 dirhams (roughly 1,500 rupees) during his two and a half years of Caliphate. He instructed that a particular plot of land owned by him should he disposed of and the entire proceeds be refunded to the *Baitul Mal.* His dying wish was duly complied with. He had been a camel and a piece of cloth worth Re. 1/4/- for his private use, which he ordered to be returned to the new Caliph after his death. When these articles were brought in the presence of Hazrat Umar, the new Caliph, he burst into tears and said, "Abu Bakr, You have made the task of your successor extremely difficult."

Just on the eve of his death he enquired from his daughter Hazrat Aisha, the number of the pieces of cloth used as a shroud of the Prophet. She replied, "Three". Thereupon he said that the two sheets which were on his body should be washed and used for the purpose and the third one might be purchased. With tears in her eyes she said that she was not so poor as to ill-afford a shroud for her father. The Caliph replied that the new cloth could be used more profitably for the living than for the dead.

Eloquent tributes have been paid to Caliph Abu Bakr's qualities of head and heart. Friends and foes alike have universally commended his devotion to the new faith and his simplicity, honesty and integrity of character. Jurji Zaidan, the Egyptian Christian historian writes: "The age of pious Caliphs is the real golden age of Islam. The Caliphs of this period are known for their temperance, piety and justice. When Hazrat Abu Bakr was converted to Islam, he was in possession of 40,000 dirhams, an enormous fortune at that time, but he spent the whole of it in furthering Islam including that which he earned in trade. When he died he had nothing except a dinar. He would ordinarily walk to his house in Sunh, on the outskirts of Medina and scarcely ever rode his horse. He came to Medina to conduct public prayers and return to Sunh in the evening. Each day he would go to buy and sell and had a small flock which at times he had to pasture himself. Before he became Caliph, he used to milk the sheep of his tribe and when he became Caliph, a slave girl regretted that her sheep would not be milked. But he assured her that he would continue her work of milking the sheep and dignity would cause no change in his conduct. Before his death, he ordered that a small plot of land which belonged to him should be sold and the proceeds returned to the Muslim community as set off for the sums which he had taken from them as an honorarium."

# UMAR, THE GREAT

The envoy of the Roman Emperor set out for Medina attended by a large retinue and equipped with all the pomp and pageantry which the Roman Empire could boast of. On arrival in the metropolis of Islam, he enquired of a passer-by: 'Tell me please, where is the palace of the Caliph"?.

The Arab looked around. He was surprised by this strange question, "What do you mean by a palace"? retorted the Arab." I mean the palace of Umar, the Caliph of Islam," added the envoy. "O! you want to see Umar. Come on, I will take you to his presence," replied the Arab.

The envoy was escorted to the Mosque of the Prophet, and to his utter astonishment, a person who was lying on the bare floor of the mosque was introduced to him as Caliph Umar Farooq, the greatest uler of his time, whose armies held sway over the three known continents of the world. The envoy was taken aback at such a strange sight and the report of what he observed in Medina was enough to terrorise the Roman Emperor and impress him with the invincible might of Islam.

Hazrat Umar ibn Khattab was born in Makkah in 40 B.H. (Before Hejirah). His lineage joins that of the Prophet of Islam in the eighth generation. His forefathers had held ambassadorial posts; commerce was his ancestral occupation. He was one of the seventeen literate persons of Makkah, when Prophethood was conferred on the Holy Prophet Muhammad (PBUH). He entered the pale of Islam at the age of 27. An interesting anecdote is told about his conversion to Islam. He was one of the most powerful enemies of the new faith. One day, he set out with the intention of killing the Prophet of Islam. On the way he came across one Naeem ibn Abdullah, who asked him where he was bound for. Umar told him that he had resolved to do away with Muhammad (PBUH). Naeem tauntingly asked him to reform his own house first. Umar at once turned back and on arrival in his house, found his brother-in-law reciting the Holy Quran. He got awfully infuriated and mercilessly beat him, but he and his sister refused to renounce Islam. The firm stand of his sister at last calmed him and he asked her to recite the lines of the Quran again. She readily complied. Umar was so much charmed and enthused that he hurried to the Prophet's place and embraced Islam. The small brotherhood was so much overwhelmed with joy that they raised the cry of 'Allah-o-Akbar' (God is great) and the surrounding hills resounded with the echo.

The conversion of Umar greatly added to the strength of the Muslims. He later on became the principal adviser to Hazrat Abu Bakr during his two and a half years reign. On the death of Hazrat Abu Bakr he was elected as the Second Caliph of Islam, a post which he held with unique distinction for ten and a half years. At last he was assassinated in 644 A.C., while leading the prayers in the mosque of the Prophet, by one Feroz *alias* Abu Lulu, a disgruntled Parsi (Majusi).

The teachings of the holy Prophet of Islam had transformed the warring Arab tribesmen into a united people who brought about the greatest revolution in living history. In less than thirty years the nomadic Arabs had become masters of the greatest empire of their time. Their arms held sway over the three known continents of the world and the great empires of Caesars (Rome) and Chosroes (Persia) lay tottering before their invincible arms. The Prophet had left behind a band of selfless people who dedicated themselves with singleness of purpose to the service of the new religion. One of these persons was Hazrat Umar Farooq who was great both in war and peace. Few persons in the history of mankind have displayed better qualities of head and heart than Umar in guiding their armies on the war front, in the discharge of their duties to their people and in adherence to justice. He gave detailed instructions to his armies fighting thousands of miles away and it was, to a great extent, due to his faultless judgement in the selection of the commanders and the tactics of war that Arab armies inflicted such crushing defeats on their two powerful enemies. His master mind was visible not only in planning easy victories but also in the consolidation of conquerred countries.

Islam has been charged with having been spread at the point of sword, but now it has been established through modern historical researches that Muslims waged defensive wars, during *Caliphate Rashida*. Sir William Muir, an English historian, records in his celebrated book, *"Rise, Decline and Fall of the Caliphate,"* that after the conquest of Mesopotamia, Zaid, a certain General, sought the permission of Hazrat Umar to pursue the fleeing Persian forces into Khorasan, but the Caliph forbade him saying, "I desire that between Mesopotamia and the countries beyond, the hills shall be a barrier so that the Persians shall not be able to get at us, nor we at them. The plain of Iraq sufficeth for our wants. I would rather prefer the safety of the people than thousands of spoils and further conquests." Commenting on the above Muir observes: "The thought of a world wide mission was yet in embryo; obligation to enforce Islam by universal crusade had not yet dawned upon Muslim mind."

The Romans and Persians who always looked down upon the Arabs as an uncultured race, viewed with alarm the rising power of Islam and were anxious to crush it. The Persians sent reinforcement to the rebels of Bahrain against Islam. They instigated Sajah, who pretended to be a Prophetess in Iraq, to march upon Medina. Rustam, the famous Persian General, had sworn that he would destroy the entire Arab race. Such designs and machinations of the Persians warned the Muslims of the dangers ahead, and being a spirited people, they accepted the challenge. Hence the war was actually forced upon the unwilling Muslims and they could not ignore this threat to their very existence.

The first defeat of the Persians came as a great surprise to them as they expected little resistance from the Arabs. They had already felt alarmed at their unexpected defeats during the time of Hazrat Abu Bakr. Every disaster in the battle-field only added to the flame of Persian fury. Theirs, was a vast empire, so were their resources. They recklessly deployed their forces and material in order to stem the advance of the Arabs and crush their striking power for ever. A handful of ill-equipped Arabs were arrayed against the formidable forces of Romans and Persians. One can hardly find in recorded history an instance, where, in spite of such disparities between the opposing forces, the weaker triumphed over their too powerful opponents.

The tempo of war increased when Hazrat Umar was elected as Caliph. Muslims were fighting on two fronts. In Syria, they were engaged with the powerful forces of the mighty Roman Empire and in Iraq they were arrayed against the formidable forces of Chosroes (Persians). Buran Dukht, who ascended the Persian throne, had appointed Rustam as the Commander-in-Chief of the army. All these arrangements could not check the Muslim advance and the Persians under the command of Narsi were routed at Kasker. Rustam appointed Bahman, a sworn enemy of Arabs, as the Commander of Persian forces in Iraq. A bloody battle was fought at Berait in 635 A.C. in which the Persians beat a hasty retreat leaving behind a large number of dead bodies. Muthanna, the Muslim General, declared that he had taken part in several engagements against the Persians in pre-Islamic days. Previously, 100 Persians could overpower 1,000 Arabs, but the tables had turned now.

The battle of Qadisiyah fought in 635 A.C. under the command of Hazrat Saad bin Abi Waqas, was a decisive one, inasmuch as it sealed the fate of the Persian Empire in Iraq. Rustam, the greatest war hero of Persia, had mustered a strong force against the Muslims. The Muslim commander who was ill had appointed Khalid bin Aratafa in his place and guided his movements through written instructions. A poet named Abu Mahjan Saqfi, who was in chains for his drunkenness implored the Commander's wife, Salma, to release him for a short while in order to take part in the battle. He promised to return when the battle was over. His request was granted forthwith and Abu Mahjan taking a sword in his hand went like a bolt in the thick of the battle and fought with exceptional bravery. He put himself in chains again when the battle was over, but Hazrat Saad released him on knowing his exploits. Ka'k'a had divided a portion of Muslim army into several groups which were held in reserve. These fell upon the enemy one after another. These tactics of Ka'k'a disheartened the Persians who were forced to retreat. Rustam, who tried to escape was killed. Hazrat Umar was very anxious about the result of this battle. He was a master-mind who used to issue detailed instructions for military operations in Iraq and for hours he waited daily outside Medina in the hope of good news. He actually ran behind the messenger up to Medina, who had brought the happy tidings, asking him the outcome of the battle. On reaching Medina, the people asked him: *"Amirul Momineen:* (Commander of the Faithful) what is the news"? The messenger was awe-stricken to know that the man who had been running behind him enquiring the deails of the battle was no other than Hazrat Umar himself. He implored the Caliph to be pardoned for his impertinence in not posting him with all the details before, but Hazrat Umar replied that he did not want to delay the happy news reaching the inhabitants of Medina. Thereupon, the great Caliph made a memorable speech before the Medinites. "Brothers of Islam! I am not your ruler who wants to enslave you. I am a servant of God and His people. I have been entrusted with the heavy responsibility of running the Caliphate administration. It is my duty to make you comfortable in every way and it will be an evil day for me if I wish you to wait on me every now and then. I want to educate you not through my precepts but by my practice."

The Persians made their last stand in Iraq in front of Madain, the Capital. They destroyed the bridge built on the Tigris. Such obstacles could not check Hazrat Saad, the Commander of the Muslim forces who plunged his horse into the river. The rest of the army followed suit and they crossed the river in a moment without disrupting their formations. The Persians were terrified at this unusual sight and cried out : "Demons have come", Saying this they took to flight in utter confusion. A vast treasure fell into the hands of the Muslim conquerors which included the invaluable Persian carpet. This treasure was brought to Medina and heaped in the courtyard of the Mosque of the Prophet. The great Caliph burst into tears on its sight. The audience asked him the reason for his unusual expression of grief. The Caliph replied promptly, "This wealth was the cause of the downfall of Persians and now it has come to us to bring our downfall." He ordered that the wealth be distributed among people instantaneously. Even that priceless carpet was not spared and under the advice of Hazrat Ali, it was torn to pieces and was distributed among the populace. Hazrat Umar commended the high character of his soldiers who did not touch a single thing out of this colossal booty.

Syria was another theatre of war, where the Muslims were arrayed against the formidable Roman forces. Hazrat Abu Bakr, during his lifetime summoned Hazrat Khalid bin Walid, the Sword of God, to assist the Muslims in Syria. The Syrian cities, one after another, capitulated to the Muslims. Hems, Hama (Epiphania) Kinnisrin (Chalcis), Aleppo and other important towns surrendered and opened their gates to the forces of Islam. The city of Damascus which was held by a large garrison, offered considerable resistance. One night Hazrat Khalid bin Walid who was stationed on the other side of the city scaled its walls and opened the gate. The Muslim army entered the city from the one side. Immediately the Romans offered themselves for peace to the Commander-in-Chief Hazrat Abu Ubaidah who was stationed on the other side of the city. Hazrat Khalid and Hazrat Abu Ubaidah who came from opposite directions met in the centre of the city. Hazrat Abu Ubaidah asked the Muslims not to plunder anyone as he had accepted the peace terms.

Antioch, the Capital of the Roman East, also capitulated to the Muslims after stubborn resistance. The Roman Governor named Artabin, had mustered a strong force for the defence of his province. Placing small bodies of troops at Jerusalem, Gaza and Ramleh, he had assembled a large army at Ajnadain. The Muslims who were deeply concerned at these movements of the Roman forces, withdrew their garrisons from various sectors and advanced to face Artabin. While withdrawing from Hems, Hazrat Abu Ubaidah, Commander-in-Chief of the Muslim forces, asked his treasury officer to return the *'jazia'* (Protection Tax) to the inhabitants, as they could not undertake the responsibility of the protection of their non-Muslim subjects there. The order was instantaneously carried out and the whole amount was repaid to the local inhabitants. The Christian populace was so much touched by this unusual generosity of the conquerors that they wept bitterly and cried out: "May God bring you here again." The Jews swore on Torat that they would resist the Romans to the last man if they ever ventured to caputure the city.

A bloody battle ensued in the plain of Yarmuk in 634 A.C. between the forces of Islam and the Romans. The Romans had mustered a strong army of 3 lakh soldiers, while the Muslim army comprised of 46 thousand unskilled and ill-equipped soldiers only. The Muslims fought like heroes and routed the Romans after a fierce conflict. More than a hundred thousand Romans perished on the battle-field while Muslim casualties hardly exceeded three thousand. When apprised of this crushing defeat, Caesar cried out sorrowfully, "Good-bye Syria", and he retired to Constantinople.

The few Roman soliders who escaped from Yarmuk found a refuge within the walls of the fortified city of Jerusalem. This city which was garrisoned by a heavy force, resisted for a considerable time. At last the Patriarch sued for peace but refused to surrender to anyone except the Caliph himself. Hazrat Umar acceded to his request and travelling with a single attendant without escort and pomp and pageantry he arrived at Jabia. When he arrived in the presence of the Patriarch and his men, he was leading the camel while the attendant was riding on it. The Christian priests and their associates were profoundly struck with this strange respect for the equality of man exhibited by the Caliph of Islam. The patriarch presented the keys of the sacred city to the Caliph and he entered the city along with patriarch. Hazrat Umar refused to offer his prayers in the Church of Resurrection saying, "If I do so, the Muslims in future might infringe the treaty, under pretext of following my example." Just terms were offered to the Christians whilst the Samaritan Jews, who had assisted the Muslims, were granted their properties without payment of any tax.

The subjugation of Syria was now complete. "Syria bowed under the sceptre of the Caliphs", says a well-known historian, "seven hundred years after Pompey had deposed the last of the Macedonian kings. After their last defeat, the Romans recognised themselves hopelessly beaten, though they still continued to raid into the Muslim territories. In order to erect an impassable barrier between themselves and the Muslims they converted into a veritable desert a vast tract on the frontiers of their remaining Asiatic possessions. All cities in this doomed tract were razed to the ground, fortresses were dismantled, and the population carried away further north. Thus what has been deemed to

be the work of Arab Muslim hordes was really the outcome of Byzantine barbarism". This shortsighted scorched earth policy was of no avail and could not
stem the tide of Muslim advance. Ayaz, the Muslim Commander passing through
Tauras, reduced the province of Cilicia, captured its Capital Tarsus and reached
as far as the shores of the Black Sea. His name was a terror for Romans in
Asia Minor.

After clearing Syria of the Roman forces, the Muslim army marched on
Persia and conquered Azerbaijan in 643, Bostan in 643, Armenia in 644, Sistan
in 644 and Mekran in 644 A.C. According to the celebrated historian Baladhuri,
the Islamic forces had reached as far the plain of Debal in Sind. But Tabari says
that the Caliph prevented his army making any further advances east of Mekran.
The defeated Roman forces had taken refuge in Alexandria and threatened the
Muslim-conquered Syria. Hence Amr bin al-Aas implored the Caliph to allow
him to advance on Egypt. The request was granted and Muslim forces under
Amr bin al-Aas captured Alexandria in 641-642. The Egyptian Christians called
Copts were treated with great kindness by the Muslim conquerors and were
granted landed properties. A mischievous story had been circulated by the
interested parties that the famous Library in Alexandria was destroyed by the
Muslim invaders, but it has now been established through impartial historical
researches by Western Scholars that the said library was partly destroyed by
Julius Caesar and the remaining by the Roman Emperor Theodosius, a devout
Christian who hated works written by the pagans.

A strong fleet was also built by the Arabs in order to meet the challenge
of Romans as masters of the seas. Thus the naval supremacy of Arabs was also
established and the Roman fleet fled before them to the Hellespont. A number
of islands of Greek Archipelago were captured by the Muslims.

A study of the military operations would reveal the factors which were
responsible for the sweeping victories of Muslims in such a short period. During
the reign of the Second Caliph, Muslims ruled over a vast area of land, which
included Syria, Egypt, Iraq, Persia, Khuzistan, Armenia, Azerbaijan, Kirman,
Khorasan, Mekran and a part of Baluchistan. A handful of ill-equipped and
unskilled Arabs had overthrown two of the mightiest empires of the world. The
teachings of the Holy Prophet of Islam had infused a new spirit in the adherents
of the new faith, who fought simply for the sake of God. The wise policy
followed by the Second Caliph of Islam in the selection of his generals and his
liberal terms offered to the conquered races were instrumental in the lightning
victories won by the Muslims. Hazrat Umar was a great military strategist, who
issued detailed instructions regarding the conduct of operations. A perusal of
the history of Tabari would reveal that Farooq, the Great, sitting thousands of
miles away, guided his armies on the battle fronts and controlled their movements. The great Caliph laid much stress on the moral side of the conquests by
offering liberal terms to the conquered races and by granting them all sorts of
privileges which are denied to the conquered races even in this advanced modern
age. This greatly helped in winning the hearts of the people, which ultimately

paved the way for the consolidation of the conquered countries and their efficient administration. He had strictly forbidden his soldiers to kill the weak and desecrate the shrines and places of worship. A treaty once concluded would be observed in letter and spirit. Contrary to the repression and ferocity of great conquerors like Alexander, Caesar, Atilla, Changiz Khan and Hulaku, Hazrat Umar's conquests were both physical as well as spiritual. When Alexander conquered Sur, a city of Syria he ordered a general massacre and hanged one thousand respectable citizens on the city walls. Similarly, when he conquered Astakher, a city of Persia, he beheaded its entire male population. Tyrants like Changiz, Atilla and Hulaku were even more ferocious. Hence, their vast empire crumbled to pieces after their death. But the conquests of the Second Caliph of Islam were of a different nature. His wise policy and efficient administration added to the consolidation of his empire in such a way that even today after a lapse of more than 1400 years, the countries conquered by him are still in Muslim hands. Thus Hazrat Umar Farooq is in a sense the greatest conqueror the world has produced.

The honesty, truthfulness and integrity of Muslims in general and their Caliph in particular strengthened the faith of the non-Muslims in the promises given by Muslims. Hurmuzan, a Persian chief, who was a sworn enemy of Muslims, was captured on the battle-field and was brought in the presence of the Caliph at Medina. He knew that he was sure to be beheaded for his massacre of Muslims. He thought out a plan and asked for a glass of water. The water was brought, but he was reluctant to drink it, saying that he might be killed while drinking it. The unsuspecting Caliph assured him that he would not be killed unless he drank it. The wily Hurmuzan at once threw away the water saying that since he got the assurance of the Caliph, he would not drink water any more. The Caliph kept his word and did not kill him. Hurmuzan, much struck with the honesty of the Caliph, accepted Islam.

Similarly, once the Muslim forces laid siege of Chandi Sabur. One day, the citizens opened the gate and busied themselves in their work. On enquiry, it transpired that a Muslim slave had granted them pardon. The matter was referred to the Caliph who upheld the terms granted by the slave, saying. "The word of an ordinary Muslim is as weighty as that of his commander or the Caliph."

The true democracy as preached and practised during the Caliphate Rashida has hardly any parallel in the history of mankind. Islam being a democratic religion, the Quran had explicitly laid it down as one of the fundamentals of Muslim polity that the affairs of the state should be conducted by consultation and counsel. The Prophet himself did not take momentous decisions without consultation. The plant of democracy in Islam planted by the Prophet and nourished by Hazrat Abu Bakr, attained its full stature in the Caliphate of Umar. Two consultative bodies functioned during his reign, one was a general assembly which was convened when the state was confronted with critical matters and the other was a special body comprised of 'persons of unquestionable integrity who were consulted on routine and urgent matters. Even matters relating to the appointments and dismissals of public servants were brought before this working or special committee and its decision was scrupulously adhered to. Non-Muslims were also invited to participate in such consultations. The native Parsi chiefs were frequently consulted regarding the administration of Iraq (Mesopotamia). Similarly, local leaders were consulted in Egyptian matters and a Copt had been invited to Medina as the representative of Egypt. Even the provincial governors were appointed on the advice of the people and the local inhabitants. At times, the various posts in the provinces were filled by election. When the appointment of the Tax Officers was to be made for Kufa, Basra and Syria, Hazrat Umar permitted the inhabitants of those provinces to select suitable and honest officers of their own choice. The selection of the people was later on endorsed by the Caliph. He used to say that the people must have an effective hand in the administration of the Caliphate. Even a poor old woman could publicly question the great Caliph for his various activities and he had to explain his conduct at the spot.

The Caliph had tried to inculcate true democratic spirit in the people as well as in his administrators. The public servants had been frankly told that they were paid for the service to the people and would be severely dealt with for any genuine public complaint. The Caliph himself practised what he preached. He was rather the very incarnation of true public service. Never in the history of mankind one comes across such instances of public service as one finds in the history of early Caliphate of Islam. Hazrat Umar lived like an ordinary man and every man was free to question his actions. Once he said, "I have no more authority over the *Baitul Mal* (Public Treasury) than a custodian has over the property of an orphan. If I would be well-to-do, I would not accept any honorarium; if not, I would draw a little to meet the ordinary necessities of life. Brothers! I am your servant and you should control and question my actions. One of these is that the public money should neither be unnecessarily hoarded nor wasted. I must work for the welfare and prosperity of our people." Once a person shouted in a public meeting, "O, Umar! fear God." The audience wanted to silence him but the Caliph prevented them from doing so saying: "If such frankness is not exhibited by the people, they are good for nothing and, if we do not listen to them, we would be like them." Such encouragement to the expression of public views as given by the Caliph himself ensured the efficiency and honesty of public service and state-administration. The people realised the real worth of public opinion.

The great Caliph had established separate departments for different subjects which were headed by efficient and honest officers. He had separated the judiciary from the executive, a remarkable achievement which has not yet been achieved even in the most modern states of the present day. The judiciary was free from the control of the Governors and the *Qazis* imparted justice free from fear or favour.

The success and efficiency of his administration mainly depended on his strict vigilance over the staff. When a governor was appointed, his letter of appointment which detailed his duties and privileges was publicly read, so that people could know the terms of appointment and could hold him responsible for abusing his power. Addressing a group of governors once he said, "Remember, I have not appointed you to rule over your people, but to serve them. You should set an example with your good conduct so that people may follow you."

He took particular care to emphasise that there should not be much distinction between the ruler and the ruled, and the people should have an easy and free access to the highest authority of the state. Every Governor had to sign a bond on his appointment that "he would put on coarse cloth and would eat coarse bread and that the complainant would have an easy access to his presence at any time." According to the author of the *'Futuh ul-Buldan'*, a list of the movable and immovable properties of the selected high officials was prepared at the time of his appointment which was examined from time to time and he had to account for any unusual increase in his property. All the high officials had to report to the Caliph every year at the time of *Hajj* and according to the writer of *Kitab-ul-Kharaj* every person was authorised to make complaints against the highest authorities which were immediately attended to. Even the highest officials of the state were not spared if their faults were proved. Once a person complained that a certain Governor had flogged him for no fault of his. The matter was enquired into and the Governor was also publicly awarded the same number of stripes.

Hazrat Muhammad bin Muslamah Ansari, a person of unquestionable integrity was appointed as the roving investigator, who visited different countries and enquired into public complaints. Once a complaint was lodged with the Caliph that Hazrat Saad bin Abi Waqas, Governor of Kufa, had constructed a palace there. He at once despatched Muhammad Ansari who pulled down a portion of the palace which hindered the easy entry of the public. On another complaint, Saad was deposed from his post. A report was received by the Caliph that Ayaz bin Ghanam, the *Amil* (Governor) of Egypt had kept a gate-keeper for his house. Muhammad Ansari who was immediately sent to Egypt found the report to be correct and brought the Governor to Medina. The Caliph humiliated him publicly. At times a commission was appointed by the Caliph to enquire into various charges. Such strict measures adopted by Hazrat Umar ensured an efficient and ideal administration in his vast State. Even the officials working thousands of miles away from Medina could not dare to do anything against the interests of the people and the state. None could ever contemplate incurring the displeasure of the iron Caliph. The fundamental difference between the administrations of the tyrants and his was that while the tyrants used rod for their own good, Umar used it for the good of the people.

Writing in the *Encyclopaedia of Islam* an European historian says : "But the part of Umar was nevertheless a great one. The regulation of his non-Muslim subjects, the institution of a register of those having a right to military pensions (the *diwan)*, the founding of military centres *(amsar)* out of which were to grow the future of the great cities of Islam, the creation of the office of *Kadi* (Qazi), were all his work, and it is also to him that a series of ordinances go back, religious *taravih* prayer of the month of Ramazan, the obligatory pilgrimage as well as civil and penal punishment of drunkenness and stoning as punishment of adultery."

The Caliph paid great attention to improving the state finances which was placed on a sound footing. He had established the *"Diwan"* or the finance department to which was entrusted the administration of revenues. The revenue of the commonwealth was derived from three sources: (1) *Zakat* or the tax levied on a gradual scale on all Muslims possessing means, (2) *Khiraj* or the land tax levied on zimmis, and (3) *Jazia* or capitation tax. The last wo taxes for which the Muslims have been much condemned by the Western historians were realised in the Roman and Sasanid (Persian) empires. The Muslims only followed the old precedents in this respect. The taxes realised from the non-Muslims were far less burdensome than those realized from the Muslims.

Islam which preached an egalitarian type of state laid greater emphasis on the equitable and fair distribution of wealth. Hoarding of wealth was against the teachings of Islam. The Second Caliph scrupulously followed this golden principle of Islam. He organised a *Baitul Mal* (Public Treasury) whose main function was distribution rather than accumulation of wealth.

The Caliph himself took very little from the *Baitul Mal*. His ancestral occupation was business. Naturally he had to be paid some honorarium for his exalted office. The matter was referred to the special committee in which the opinion of Hazrat Ali was accepted that the Caliph should get as much honorarium from the *Baitul Mal* as would suffice for the necessities of an ordinary citizen.

The Caliph fixed the rates of land revenue according to the type of the land. While he charged four *dirhams* on one *jarib* of wheat, he charged two *dirhams* for the similar plot of barley. Nothing was charged for the pastures and uncultivated land. In this way he systematised the fixation of revenues, which, before his time was charged haphazardly. Different rules were framed for the revenues of Egypt, whose agricultural output depended on the flood of the Nile. According to reliable historical sources, the annual revenue of Iraq amounted to 860 million *dirhams*, an amount which never exceeded after the death of the great Caliph though he was very lenient in its realisation. The main reason behind this easy realisation of the state money was that the people had become very prosperous.

He introduced far reaching reforms in the domain of agriculture, which we do not find even in the most civilized countries of the modern times. One of these was the abolition of *Zamindari* (Landlordism) and with this disappeared all the evils wrought on the poor tenants by the vested landed interests. When the Romans conquered Syria and Egypt, they confiscated the lands of the tillers of the soil and allotted these to the army, nobles, churches and the members of the royal family. Hazrat Umar, on the conquest of these countries, returned these properties to the local inhabitants who were the rightful owners of the land. The just and benevolent Caliph was exceptionally generous to the local tillers of the soil and even issued strict orders that no other persons including the Muslim soldiers who were spread all over these countries, should be granted any piece of land for cultivation purposes. Such steps taken by the Caliph not only restored confidence among the local populace but also gave a great impetus to agriculture in these countries and contributed to the enormous increase in agricultural output. The tenancy became prosperous and their standard of living was much raised. It led to the easy realisation of land revenue by the custodians of the state. According to a French historian, "The liberal policy followed by the Arabs in the fixation of revenues and their land reforms have greatly contributed to their military conquests." It was due to this liberal policy of the Second Caliph that the Christian Copts who were farmers always sided with the Muslim Arabs in preference to Roman Christians. The Caliph was not content with these reforms. He worked out beneficial schemes for the advancement of agriculture and constructed irrigation canals, wells and tanks in his vast dominions. He established a public welfare department which looked after such construction works and furthered these beneficial schemes. The celebrated historian Allama Maqrizi says that more than one lac and twenty thousand labourers were continually employed in such works throughout the year in Egypt alone. A number of canals were constructed in Khuzistan and Ahwaz during this period. A canal called "Nahr Amirul Momineen" which connected the Nile with the Red Sea was constructed in order to ensure quick transport of grain from Egypt to the holy land.

Caliph Umar is particularly known for his administration of impartial justice. Justice during his reign was administered by *Qazi* (civil judges) who were appointed by the Caliph and who were free from the control of the governors. He was the first man who separated judiciary from the executive, thus ensuring free and even-handed justice. "The judge was named and is still named," says Von Hammer, "the *Hakim ush-sharaa*, i.e., ruler though the law, for law rules through the utterance of justice and the power of governor carries out the utterance of it. Thus the Islamite administration even in its infancy, proclaims in word and in deed the necessary separation between judicial and executive power." Such separation of executive from judiciary has not been attained by some of the most civilized states in the modern times. The administration of justice during his time was perfectly impartial and he himself set an example by scrupulously carrying out the orders of the *Qazi*.

The letter written by the Caliph to Abu Musa Asha'ari detailing the fundamental principles of justice, is an invaluable piece of jurisprudence which can be favourably compared with the Roman law. The Caliph took particular care to enforce the equality of justice. In the eyes of law, all are equals. He personally visited several courts in order to have practical experience of it. Once he had to attend the court of *Qazi* Zaid bin Sabit as a defendant. The *Qazi* showed some preferential respect to him, which, the Caliph resented and warned him, "Unless you consider an ordinary man and Umar as equals, you are not fit for the post of *Qazi.*"

Jablah bin Al-Aiham Ghassani was the ruler of a small state in Syria. He was converted to Islam, and one day while he was offering *Hajj,* a part of his gown was unintentionally trampled upon by a poor Arab. Jablah gave him a slap. He too, paid him in the same coin. The infuriated Jablah hastened to the Caliph and urged him to severely deal with the Arab. Thereupon the Caliph said that he had already received the justice. Jablah retorted saying : "Had he done such an insult to me in my own land, he would have been hanged." The Caliph replied calmly: "Such was the practice here in pre-Islamic days, but now the pauper and the prince are equal before Islam.

Hazrat Umar was so strict in the enforcement of impartial justice that he did not spare even his near and dear ones if they were at fault. Once, his own son Abu Shahma was reported to have drunk wine. The Caliph flogged his son with his own hands till he died, and the remaining stripes were delivered on his grave. The history of the world cannot produce a single instance in which a state or public leader showed greater respect for justice and the rule of law.

Hazrat Umar took keen interest in the army administration. He founded many army centres including Medina, Kufa, Basra, Mosul Fustat (Egypt), Damascus, Hems and Palestine where barracks for the soldiers were constructed. He paid attention to the minutest details which were required for making an efficient army. He divided the army into regulars and volunteers or the reserve. There were big military cantonments in Armenia and Azerbaijan. The wise Caliph organised different departments of the army in such an efficient manner that one is astounded to notice the advancement he made in this sphere. Separate departments of supply and sappers and miners were attached to the army establishments. The Commander-in-Chief of the Muslim army used to lead the daily prayers. "The great superiority of Saracenic armies", says Ameer Ali, "consisted in the extreme mobility, their perseverance and their power of endurance—qualities which, joined to enthusiasm, made them invincible."

The greatness of Caliph Umar is visible in his sympathetic treatment of his non-Muslim subjects. Before the advent of Islam the rights of other races in the Roman and Persian empires were worse than those of slaves. Even the Syrian Christians had no right over their lands, so much so that with the transfer of their lands they were also transferred. When Hazrat Umar conquered these countries, he returned the lands to their tillers who were mostly non-Muslims. He granted peace to the Christians of Elia who had surrendered. The peace terms run as follows: "This is the peace, granted by Umar, the slave of God, to the inhabitants of Elia. Non-Muslims will be allowed to stay in their churches which will not be demolished. They will have full freedom of religion and will not be harmed in any way." According to Imam Shafii, once a Muslim murdered a Christian. The matter was brought to the notice of the Caliph, who allowed the heirs of the Christian to avenge the murder and the Muslim was beheaded. He consulted non-Muslims in State matters. Their voice carried much weight in the handling of affairs of special interest to them. The author of the *Kitab al Kharaj* writes that the last will of Hazrat Umar enjoined upon the Muslims to respect the assurances given to non-Muslims, and protect their lives and properties even at the risk of their own. The Caliph had been too indulgent to non-Muslims and even pardoned their treasons which no present day civilized government could tolerate. The non-Muslims were so much moved by these unusual sympathies of the Muslim conquerors that they sided with them in preference to their co-religionists. The Christians and Jews of Hems prayed for the return of Muslims. The Caliph, no doubt, imposed *Jazia,* a protection tax on the non-Muslims but such tax was not realised from those non-Muslims who joined the Muslim army. Hazrat Abu Ubaidah, the Commander-in-Chief of Muslim forces in Syria, returned the *Jazia* realised from the inhabitants of Hems, when he had to withdraw his garrison from Hems due to emergency and therefore, he could not undertake the responsibility of their protection. The people of Jarjoma refused to pay the *Jazia* on the ground of their having enlisted in the Muslim army. The Christian patriarch of Jerusalem was wonderstruck with the sense of justice displayed by the great Caliph when he refused to offer prayer in the Church of the Resurrection on the plea that his example would be followed by other Muslims thus amounting to the breach of the treaty.

Such benevolent and generous treatment of non-Muslims at the hands of the Caliph endeared him to all of his subjects, thus laying the foundation of a stable government and an efficient administration.

Hazrat Umar possessed an exemplary character and practised himself what he preached. He was intrinsically conscientious; his motto had always been the service of his people. He never favoured his own pious and learned son Abdullah bin Umar. In the fixation of monthly honorarium he gave preference to those who were close Companions of the Prophet, otherwise he observed equality even between the Quraish and the slaves. When he fixed the salary of Usama bin Zaid higher than that of his son Abdullah, the latter complained, "Usama had never surpassed me in the service of Islam." The pious Caliph at once replied, "But he was closer and dearer to the Prophet."

Unstinted service to humanity was his foremost concern. He roamed about during the night often *incognito* in order to acquaint himself with the condition of his people. One night as he was roaming outside Medina, he observed in a house a woman cooking something and two girls sitting beside her crying for food. After waiting for sometime, he asked the woman what was the matter. She told him that the children were hungry, that there was nothing in the kettle except water and a few pieces of stones and that she was lulling them to believe that food was being cooked for them. The Caliph without disclosing his identity hurried to Medina, three miles-away, brought a bag of flour on his back, cooked the food himself and was not contented until the appetite of the children was fully satisfied. The next day he called again to apologise to the old woman for his negligence and fixed dole-money for her.

The great Caliph led a very simple life. His standard of living was in no case higher than that of an ordinary man. Once the Governor of Kufa visited him while he was taking his meals comprising of barley bread and olive oil. The Governor said, *"Amirul Momineen* (Commander of the Faithful) enough wheat is produced in your dominions, why do you not take wheat bread". Feeling somewhat offended the Caliph asked him in a melancholy tone, "Do you think that wheat is available to each and every person inhabiting my vast dominions?"

"No", replied the Governor.

"Then how can I take wheat bread unless it is available to all of my people"? added the Caliph.

Honesty and integrity were the highest virtues in the character of the Second Caliph. Once, during his illness his physician prescribed honey for him. Tons of honey was kept in the *Baitul Mal,* but he did not take a drop of it unless he was permitted by the people's committee. His wife, Umme Kulsum, once presented a few bottles of perfumes to the Empress of Rome. The Empress returned the bottles filled with precious stones. When Hazrat Umar learned of it, he deposited the jewels in the *Baitul Mal.*

The Caliph had great respect for the social equality of man. The Patriarch of Jerusalem was profoundly struck by the respect for social equality shown by the esteemed Caliph when he observed the slave was riding on the camel and the Caliph was leading the camel by the string.

According to a report of Abdur Rahman bin Auf, the Caliph came to him one day and asked him to accompany him to a certain place. On enquiry, he told Hazrat Auf that a caravan had arrived in Medina and since the members must be tired, the Caliph considered it obligatory to guard them for the whole of night so that they might rest undisturbed.

Once he addressed a gathering saying, "Brothers, if I stray from the right path what will you do"? A man stood up and said, "We will behead you." Umar shouted in order to test him: "You dare utter such impertinent words for me?" "Yes, for you," replied the man. Umar was very much pleased with his boldness and said, "Thank God, there exist such bold men in our nation that if I go astray they will set me right."

"It was only to his high moral character," says a European historian, "that Umar owned the respect which he inspired, for the physical force at his command was none. Umar was not only a great ruler but also one of the most typical models of all the virtues of Islam". Tradition makes the Prophet of Islam say: "If God had wished that there should have been another prophet after me, he would have been none other than Umar."

The second Caliph of Islam occupies an outstanding place in the history of the world. One would hardly come across a ruler who led so simple a life, and dedicated himself to the service of his people and was a terror for his foes. "Of simple habits, austere and frugal, always accessible to the meanest of his subject, wandering about at night to enquire into the condition of the people without any guard or escort, such was the greatest and most powerful ruler of the time." Perhaps Dr. Iqbal, the poet of the East has said for him only :

*Jis se jigar-i-lala me thandak ho woh shabnam*

*Daryaan ke dil jis se dahel jaen woh toofan*

(Like the dew which cools the heart of lily and like the storm which shakes the heart of the rivers).

Jurji Zaidan, the celebrated Christian historian of Egypt pays glowing tribute to the achievements of Hazrat Umar in the following words :

"In his time various countries were conquered, spoils were multiplied, the treasures of the Persian and Roman Emperors were poured in streams before his troops, nevertheless he himself manifested a degree of abstemiousness and moderation which was never surpassed. He addressed the people clad in a garment patched with leather. He was himself the first to practise what he preached. He kept a vigilant eye over his Governors and Generals and enquired strictly into their conduct. Even the great Khalid bin Walid was not spared. He was just to all mankind and was kindly even to the non-Muslims. Iron discipline was maintained everywhere during his reign."

# USMAN

Ibn Saba, a Yemenite Jew converted to Islam, was the moving spirit behind a conspiracy hatched against Hazrat Usman, the third Caliph of Islam, which in reality, aimed at undermining the very foundations of Islam. His later activities proved beyond doubt that his acceptance of Islam was only a mask to cover his evil designs. The storms brewing in Fustat (Cairo), Kufa and Basrah, later burst upon Medina and culminated in the martyrdom of Usman. On smelling the foul play, Amir Muawiya, the Governor of Syria, had begged the Caliph either to move to Damascus, or to keep a strong guard for his self-protection. The pious Caliph refused both, saying that he would be the last person to leave the resting place of the Prophet and that he would never like to be guarded at public expense.

Hazrat Usman ibn Affan, known as Abu Abd Allah, was born in Makkah. Zunnurain was his epithet of honour as he had married two daughters of the Prophet one after another. He belonged to the Bani Umayyad clan of the Quraish and his ancesteral pedigree joins that of the Prophet in the fifth generation. The Bani Umayyads were only second to Bani Hashims in political importance and were entrusted with the custody of National Flag of the Quraish before the advent of Islam.

Hazrat Usman, after his early education, adopted his ancestral occupation and was one of the leading businessmen of Arabia. He was known for his honesty and integrity, piety and modesty throughout Hejaz. He was an intimate friend of Hazrat Abu Bakr Siddiq, the first Caliph of Islam. It was Hazrat Abu Bakr, who was the first man to carry the message of Islam to him. Hazrat Usman along with Talha bin Ubaidullah, accepted Islam at the hands of the Prophet. He was much tortured by his uncle Hakem for joining the new faith but he refused to renounce it, even at the cost of his life.

Hazrat Usman migrated to Abyssinia along with other Muslims under the orders of the Prophet. He was only second to Abu Bakr in rendering financial assistance to the new faith. He served Islam whole-heartedly even at the cost of his business. He took active part in the inner councils of Islam. Later on he migrated to Medina along with other Muslims, leaving his valuable properties behind. Medina had then only one well of drinking water called Bir Rumah, which was owned by non-Muslims, who charged heavy water tax from the

Muslims. The Holy Prophet wanted some Muslims to purchase it. Hazrat Usman, at once came forward, purchased it for 30 thousand *dirhams* and made it a public property. Similarly, Hazrat Usman purchased the land adjoining the Mosque of the Prophet in Medina, which could not accommodate a large number of Muslims and undertook its extension at his own expense.

Except Badr, Hazrat Usman took part in all battles fought during the lifetime of the Prophet for the defence of the new faith. At the time of Badr he was asked by the Prophet to look after his wife Ruqayya, who was on death bed.

During the caliphate of Hazrat Abu Bakr and Hazrat Umar, he occupied the position of highest trust. He was a prominent member of the inner council and his opinion was sought on all important matters of state. He was one of the two persons who were first consulted by Hazrat Abu Bakr on his death bed for nominating Hazrat Umar as his successor.

The circumstances which led to his election as the third Caliph of Islam are a controversial issue and diverse historical theories have been advanced which greatly differ from one another. But it has been established beyond doubt that Hazrat Umar, on his death bed, had nominated six persons, out of whom his successor was to be selected. The four nominees withdrew their names, leaving Hazrat Usman and Hazrat Ali, as the contestants. The two consented to accept the verdict of Hazrat Abdur Rahman bin Auf, who, on the third day, cast his vote in favour of Hazrat Usman who became the third Caliph of Islam. Thereafter, the populace of Medina vied with each other in taking the oath of allegiance on the hands of Hazrat Usman., There are certain historical sources, which state that there had been secret machinations in the election of Hazrat Usman and that of Hazrat Ali was the more popular and deserving of the two.

The first six years of the reign of Hazrat Usman are noted for great territorial expansion of the Islamic Empire as well as achievements in other spheres of life. Only six months after the election of the Third Caliph, the Persians rose in revolt against the authority of Islam. The *ex*-king of Persia, Yezdejird, who was in exile, was at the bottom of this upheaval and his agents were active throughout Persia. Hazrat Usman promptly handled the situation with a strong hand. He immediately despatched reinforcements which quelled the revolt and pursued the insurgents beyond the Persian frontiers, thus annexing extra territories. By 30 A.H., the territories lying north and east of Persia including Balkh, Turkistan, Herat, Kabul, Ghazni, Khorasan, Tus, Neshapur and Merv, fell before the invincible arms of Islam and thus were incorporated in the fast expanding Muslim Empire. Yezdejird, who had fled for his life, died in exile in 32 A.H. It led to the establishment of perpetual peace in Persia. The Muslims who encountered Turks and Romans in the North-West of Persia, inflicted crushing defeats upon their opponents. The Romans were pursued far beyond the western frontiers of Persia and the flag of Islam was firmly planted on the shores of the Black Sea.

In the second year of his caliphate, the Romans poured into Syria through Asia Minor. The garrison at the disposal of Amir Muawiya, Governor of Syria, was numerically much inferior to the invaders, and could hardly cope with the situation. The arrival of fresh reinforcements routed the Romans who were hotly pursued as far as the shores of the Black Sea. Armenia, Azerbaijan and Asia Minor fell into Muslim hands and Tiflis on the Black Sea, was also captured. In 32 A.H., Amir Muawiya laid siege to Constantinople. Strong fortifications were raised on the frontiers in order to check further Roman inroads into Muslim lands.

The Romans had set up in Egypt and West Africa spring boards for the invasion of Muslim lands. They captured Alexandria in 25 A.H. (646 A.C.) but Muslims under the command of Amr bin al-Aas soon recovered it. Gregory, the Roman Commander of Tripoli, had a strong army of 120,000 soldiers under his command. It was a constant menace to the neighbouring Muslim State. A strong contingent which included great veterans like Abdullah bin Zubair, was hurriedly despatched from Medina to face the desperate situation. The Romans offered a stubborn resistance, but, at last, with the fall of their commander at the hand of Abdulla bin Zubair, their resistance crumbled down and they were routed with heavy losses.

It was during Usman's reign that the Muslims first launched a naval warfare. Earlier, Muawiya was prevented by the Caliph to attack Cyprus, which was a Roman stronghold alongside Syria and was a constant danger for her security. It was from this strategic island that the Romans made repeated incursions on the Syrian coast. Hazrat Usman allowed Muawiya, under certain conditions, to invade the island. Muawiya built a strong naval fleet, which was the first of its kind in Islam. Curiously enough, Cyprus was occupied by the Syrians, without much resistance.

In 31 A.H. (654 A.C.), the Romans launched an invasion of Egypt with 500 ships. The Muslim Governor of Egypt met them with a small fleet. He tied his ships with one another and in a hand to hand fight inflicted a crushing defeat upon the Romans. This established the reputation of Muslim Navy in the Eastern Mediterranean.

The reasons underlying the dissensions among the Muslims which culminated in an open revolt against the authority of an elected Caliph are manifold. But the main factor at the back of this conspiracy was a hatred for Muslim power, which Ibn Saba and his followers wanted to fan from within. The democratic principles practised in Islam and the simplicity as well as the piety of Hazrat Usman who, at any cost, could not contemplate the horrid prospect of bloodshed among the Muslims, gave a free hand to the conspirators to malign and undermine his regime. The entreaties of the Administrators of affected provinces to be allowed to deal firmly with the agitators could not move the pious Caliph.

The Administration during the first six years of his Caliphate had not lost the effectiveness of his predecessor and the nation-building activities continued as before. The insurrections in Persia were put down with a strong hand; the state frontiers were extended and fortified naval warfare was introduced with great success and the state had not lost the vigour and vitality which characterised the phenomenal growth of Muslim Empire during the reign of the Second Caliph. But a large number of Christians and Jews, who had embraced Islam with mental reservation in order to take advantage of its democratic principles and who disliked the restrictions imposed by it on debauchery and general moral laxity, which they were addicted to, found an able leader in Ibn Saba, a Yemanite Jew newly converted to Islam. The Arab colonies of Basrah, Kufa and Fustat (Cairo) which were inhabited by Arabs of non-Hejaz origin fell an easy prey to the secret machinations of Ibn Saba and his henchmen. Ibn Saba spread the net of his intrigues throughout Iraq and Egypt, Kufa, Basrah and Fustat which formed the nerve centre of his nefarious activities against the Caliph.

The Caliphs adversaries charged him with following a policy of nepotism, favouritism and partisanship. But he had made no change in the old order during the first 6 years of his rule. As far as humanly possible, he was rigid and impartial in dispensing justice. This is borne out from his having awarded the required number of stripes to Waleed, a provincial Governor who was related to him and was accused of drunkenness. He dismissed several governors belonging to the Umayyad clan, when charges against them were found to be true. Moreover, Umayyad governors appointed by him justified their selection by their able administration. However, the dictates of statecraft and political acumen demanded of him to streamline his administration by drawing into it non-party elements not wanting in integrity, capabilities and dynamics. He would have been well advised to follow the example of his illustrious predecessor, who ignored even his talented son, Abdulla bin Umar for filling a particular high job. This would have deprived the insurgents of the only weapon, so skilfully used against the Third Caliph. The faulty advices of Merwan, his Secretary, were no less responsible for hastening the doom which awaited the pious Caliph.

At last the fateful hour drew near. The insurgents besieged Medina and the inhabitants of the Metropolis of Islam, who wanted to defend the Caliph with their lives, were prevented by him lest it might shed Muslim blood. Notwithstanding all this, Hazrat Ali posted his two sons at the Caliph's door to defend his person even at the cost of their lives. Others. too, followed suit. The Caliph also conceded one of the demands of the insurgents and appointed Muhammad bin Abu Bakr as the Governor of Egypt, whereupon the rebels withdrew apparently satisfied with the appointment letter in their hands and it seemed that the storm clouds which threatened Medina had melted away. But, after a few days, the rebels reappeared and laid siege of Medina. On enquiry it was given out they had intercepted a secret letter of the Caliph ordering the Governor of Egypt to behead Muhammad bin Abu Bakr as soon as he reached there. The messenger who was said to be carrying the letter was never produced.

The Caliph denied knowledge of any such letter, which was accepted by the insurgents who held his Secretary Merwan responsible for this forgery. They demanded that he should be handed over to them, but the Caliph refused to oblige them without any definite proof against him. The insurgents, however, could not give satisfactory reply to the query of Hazrat Ali. "How all of them returned together at the same time when their routes led to divergent directions." He considered the letter to be forged. The pious Caliph addressed the rebels :

"As to death, I have no fear of it and I consider it the easiest thing. As to fighting, if I wished such a thing, thousands would have come forward to fight for me. But I cannot be the cause of shedding a drop of Muslim blood."

At last the critical hour arrived. A large number of Medinites had gone to Makkah for pilgrimage. The insurgents considered it a suitable opportunity for carrying out their evil designs. They stormed the Caliph's house, as they could not dare to enter through the gate which was guarded by the valiant sons of Ali. They scaled the walls on the opposite side and slew the aged Caliph, who was reciting the Quran with extraordinary composure. The little fingers of his wife raised for his protection were chopped off. The Caliph attained his martyrdom on June 17, 656 A.C. and thus offered his life as "a sacrifice at the altar of Muslim solidarity." He was at this time 82. His Caliphate lasted 12 years.

Hazrat Usman rendered very valuable financial help to the new faith before and after his election as Caliph. He placed his entire resources at the disposal of the Prophet of Islam. His generosity knew no bounds. When he was elected to the high post of the Caliph, he did not take anything from the *Baitul Mal* (Public Treasury) and served the people even at the cost of his flourishing business. Tabari, the celebrated historian of Islam, quotes as follows from an address of the Third Caliph :

"When the reins of the Government were entrusted to me, I was the biggest owner of camels and goats in Arabia. Today I possess neither a goat nor a camel save two, which are meant for the pilgrimage. By God I have taxed no city beyond its capacity so that such a thing might be imputed to me. And whatever I have taken from the people I have spent on their own welfare. Only fifth of it comes to me (i.e., in *Baitul Mal* or in Public Treasury). Out of this, too, I consider nothing for my personal use. This is spent on the deserving people, not by me, but by the Muslims themselves, and not a farthing of public funds is misappropriated. I take nothing out of it, so that even what I eat out of my own earnings."

His financial help was indeed invaluable for the growth of a new organisation during the lifetime of the Prophet.

The greatest achievement of Hazrat Usman is the compiling of a standard copy of the Holy Quran. During his regime Islam had spread far and wide in distant lands—lands inhabited by diverse nationalities. The differences of pronunciations and dialects in Arabia led to variety of Quranic recitations. Hence, he felt the necessity of compiling a standard copy of the Quran, which might ensure uniformity in pronunciation of Quranic lines all over the world. Hazrat Abu Bakr, the First Caliph, had got compiled a standard copy of the Quran after comparing it with the help of reliable sources. This copy was in possession of Prophet's wife. Several copies of this volume were prepared by the Caliph after consultation with prominent Companions of the Prophet and despatched to centres of Islamic Empire to serve as the standard version. In order to avoid differences in versions, all unauthentic copies were burnt down. These steps were taken with the consent of all the well-known Companions of the Prophet, who formed a committee for ensuring wide circulation of the standard copy. The step taken was also in conformity with the wishes of the Holy Prophet who desired the compilation of a standard volume of the Quran.

There had been no slackening of nation-building activities during his reign. New colonies, bridges, roads, mosques and guest houses were built and new cities sprang up throughout the vast Islamic dominions. The roads leading to Medina were fully equipped with caravan serais and other amenities of life for the travellers. The Prophet's Mosque in Medina was enlarged and built of stones. Extensive arrangements for drinking water were made in Medina and other desert towns. Farms for camel and horse breeding were opened on a large scale. The Council of Consultation was maintained as before, which comprised of prominent Companions of the Prophet, who counselled the Caliph on all important matters. The Caliph, like his predecessors, was at all times accessible to the meanest of his subjects and the complaints against the highest authorities of the state were promptly attended to.

The Third Caliph of Islam was particularly known for his integrity and simplicity, piety and modesty of character. His character was above suspicion and none, not even his greatest enemies, ever doubted his sincerity. No doubt, certain people took advantage of his simplicity, but whatever he did he did with the best of intentions.

# ALI—
# THE LION HEARTED

The Qazi's court in Medina was packed to its capacity. The Qazi had summoned Hazrat Ali, the Caliph of Islam, to appear in a case filed against him by a Jew who had claimed the Caliph's armour. The Caliph arrived at the court and stood by the side of the plaintiff without caring about his own exalted position. The claimant produced several witnesses in support of his claim. The learned Qazi, then asked Hazrat Ali if he had to say anything in his defence. Ali replied in the negative. Thereupon the Qazi decided the case in favour of the Jew and awarded the armour to the Jew, which, Ali had actually purchased from him. The Jew was taken aback by the impartial judgement of the Qazi and returned the armour to the Caliph saying that the illustrious Caliph had actually purchased the armour from him. He had filed the suit in order to test the impartiality of the Caliph and his courts which had magnificently withstood the test.

Hazrat Ali, the Fourth Caliph of Islam, was a versatile genius. Few persons have ever been endowed with the unsurpassable traits of chivalry and learning, piety and clarity of thought and imagination that distinguished the illustrious son-in-law of the Prophet of Islam who had brought him up under his own fostering care and ideal guardianship. Hazrat Ali has universally been acclaimed as one of the best products of Islam. His bravery had won him the title of "Lion of God," says a well-known orientalist; "his learning, that of the 'gate of knowledge,' chivalarous, humane and forbearing as a ruler, he came before his time. Most of the grand undertakings, initiated by Umar for the welfare of the people, were due to his counsel. Ever ready to succour the weak and redress the wrongs of the injured, the accounts of his valorous deeds are still recited with enthusiasm from the bazaars of Cairo to those of Delhi."

Ali ibn Abu Talib, whose *kunniyat* was Abul Hasan, was born in the 13th year of the Year of Elephant. He was a cousin of the Prophet and his clan Banu Hashim having been entrusted with the high function of the custody of the sacred Kaaba, was held in high esteem, throughout Arabia. Abu Talib, who had a large family entrusted his son Ali to the care of the Prophet of Islam. Ali was brought up by the Prophet himself from his very childhood—a fact which greatly contributed to cultivating extraordinary virtues in him. According to reliable historical sources, Khadija was the first woman, Abu Bakr, the first man and Ali, the first child to embrace Islam. Hazrat Ali played a conspicuous role at the time of the Prophet's migration from Makkah. While Hazrat Abu Bakr accompanied the Prophet, constantly harassed and hunted by the Quraish of Makkah, on his perilous journey to Medina, Hazrat Ali was kept behind to return to the owners the valuables they had entrusted to the custody of the Prophet. It speaks volumes for the integrity of the Prophet that even his sworn enemies reposed full trust in his honesty and deposited their valuables with him. Hazrat Ali slept soundly in the house of the Prophet besieged by his enemies. The next morning he cleared the accounts and departed for Medina.

The Prophet selected the young talented Ali, as the life partner for his favourite daughter Fatima az-Zahra, the beautiful. The nuptial ceremony was performed with utmost simplicity which will serve as an example for all times to come. The dowry given to the beloved daughter of the Prophet consisted of a sheet of cloth, a few earthen utensils and a grinding stone. Three sons, Hazrat Imam Hasan, Husain and Mohsin and two daughters Zainab and Umme Kulsum were born. The lineage of the Prophet continued through Imam Hasan and Hussain, hence their descendants are called Syed (Master).

Hazrat Ali lived a humble and simple life; he earned his living through manual labour. He could not add anything to the property of the house and his beloved wife performed all household duties with her own hands. Faced with extreme poverty, the humanitarianism and the spirit of charity and self-sacrifice and self-denial of this ideal couple of Islam have hardly any parallel in the annals of mankind. They invariably preferred to go without their humble meals rather than refuse a beggar knocking at their door.

Hazrat Ali was chosen by the Prophet to carry the message of Islam to the people of Yemen, where earlier Muslim missionaries had failed. There he met with great success and the tribe of Hamdan embraced Islam the same day. His mellifluent eloquence, high intellectual and persuasive power were greatly instrumental in popularising Islam in those hostile regions.

It was in the realm of chivalry that Hazrat Ali has left ineffaceable marks in the history of early Islam. He was gifted with extraordinary daring and courage which he devoted to the service of Islam, performing wonderful deeds of heroism. In fact, he proved to be the strongest bulwark in the defence of the votaries of the new faith against the repeated hostilities of alien powers. During the lifetime of the Prophet, he took a leading part in all defensive campaigns except Tabuk, when reluctantly he had to stay back in Medina under the orders of the Prophet who said, "You stand to me in the same relation in which Aaron stood to Moses, except that there is to be no Prophet after me."

Hazrat Ali displayed his unique valour for the first time in the battle of Badr, when he overpowered Waleed and Sheba, the renowned warriors of Arabia in single combats. In the battle of Ohad, when the standard bearer of Islam fell fighting, he took hold of the standard and killed the enemy standard bearer.

This exceptional heroism made people declare, *'La Fata Illa Ali'* (There is no youth like Ali). Two years after, he met Amr ibn Abad Wudd, the greatest known warrior of Arabia in a duel and killed him. Of all his martial exploits, the most outstanding was the capture of the citadel of Khaibar which was regarded impregnable. It was strongly fortified by the Jews and withstood repeated attacks by Muslims under the command of Hazrat Abu Bakr and Umar. Thereupon the Prophet said, "Tomorrow the standard of Islam will be entrusted to a person who would capture it and who loves God and His Messenger and whom God and His Messenger also love." The next morning Ali was summoned in the presence of the Prophet. Incidentally he was suffering from bad eyesore. The Prophet applied his saliva to his eyes, and placed the standard in his hands. Ali made a dash and captured the fort by tearing asunder the huge gate which could not be moved by dozens of men.

Mercy on the defeated and overpowered foe is a part of chivalry. Hazrat Ali who had drunk enough of the milk of human kindness, pitied and pardoned the vanquished on several occasions. Once during a campaign, when his opponent fell on the ground and became naked, he left him aside. According to Ibn Saad, when his assailant Ibn Muljem was brought before him, he asked his men to treat him gently and make him comfortable.

During the reign of the first two Caliphs, Hazrat Ali as the principal adviser of the State. He solved all knotty problems and no important decision was taken by the Caliphs without his advice. His advice was sought on all matters, especially legal and religious on which he was considered an authority. His sound judgements were highly respected by friends and foes alike. After the death of the Prophet, he mostly devoted his energies to the development of the moral and intellectual life of the adherents of the new faith and seldom took part in warfare. Most of the great administrative works during the reign of Hazrat Umar were undertaken at his instance.

Hazrat Ali was elected Caliph after the martyrdom of Hazrat Usman, at a time when the world of Islam was in great turmoil and Medina, the Metropolis, was besieged by insurgents. The inhabitants of Medina and neighbouring provinces vied with one another in taking the oath of allegiance to him, as he was the most deserving person for the high post among the faithful. But Muawiya, who had gathered great power around himself, clamoured for avenging the blood of Hazrat Usman. Muawiya, being a clever person, realized that he had hardly any chance for the exalted position in the presence of Hazrat Ali, hence he devised this means of winning popular support. The insurgents were two powerful to be dealt with and a hasty step would have culminated in the disintegration of the Empire. This restrained Ali's hands. He wanted to deal firmly with the disruptionists at an opportune moment. To Talha and Zubair who insisted on the assassins of Usman being punished immediately, Hazrat Ali replied, "I am myself no less anxious about it, but I simply cannot help it. It is a critical time. If there is any disturbance of peace, the Beduins and foreigners will rise in revolt and Arabia will once more relapse into the days of ignorance. These men are yet beyond our control. Wait and see till Allah shows me some way out of the difficulty." The situation had become so critical and the political atmosphere was so much explosive, that any drastic action taken against the insurgents would have endangered the security of the new state. Ali's opponents had, however, resolved to exploit the situation to their advantage. Almost all great Muslim historians have expressed doubts about the motive behind the opposition of Muawiya. They maintain that sincerity of purpose behind the opposition of Hazrat Aisha, Talha and Zubair was lacking in the case of Muawiya.

His demand for avenging Usman's blood was not inspired by high motive. Ali explored all possibilities of amicable settlement before declaring war against Muawiya in the interest of national solidarity. Hazrat Aisha, too, was deeply stirred by the martyrdom of Usman. Accompanied by Talha and Zubair, she marched upon Basra which surrendered in October 656 A.C. Hazrat Ali when apprised of the situation hurriedly reached there. On 12th Rajab 36 A.H. Kufa accorded a royal welcome to the Caliph and made elaborate arrangements for his entertainment in the local palace. But being a saintly person, Ali shunned all pageantries and preferred to camp in an open field. The two forces lay facing each other, as Hazrat Ali and Hazrat Aisha wanted to avoid a clash and negotiate for a settlement. Obviously it would have gone against the interests of the Sabaites who formed a component part of Hazrat Ali's forces and who were all out to fan the fire of enmity between the contending parties with the ulterior purpose of undermining Islam. Hence, one night, when settlement was almost in sight, they secretly fell upon the opposing forces and started fighting. Both the parties suspected that the fighting was started by the other side. Hazrat Ali tried his best to pacify the feelings of the fighters and reminded Zubair of a prophecy of the Prophet. This induced Zubair to withdraw at once from the battle-field, while he was praying on his way back to Makkah, a Sabaite slew him. When the ruffians brought the head of Zubair to Ali for a reward, he said wrathfully, "Give the assassin of Zubair the tidings of hell". At last the forces led by Hazrat Aisha were defeated and the Caliph himself called on the reverend lady for enquiring about her health. She was respectfully sent back to Medina escorted by noble ladies and the Caliph in person saw her off for a considerable distance.

Caliph Ali now diverted his attention to Muawiya, the rebel Governor of Syria, who was threatening the solidarity of the young state. Being humane by nature, Hazrat Ali tried his level best to bring about a peaceful settlement and avoid shedding of Muslim blood. But Muawiya advanced impossible conditions. Ali offered to end the quarrel by personal combat, but the Umayyad declined the challenge. At last the fateful hour arrived and the two forces fought a bloody battle. "The rebels were defeated in three successive battles," says a well-known historian, "and Muawiya was ready to fly from the field, when a trick of his accomplice Amr, son of Aas, saved them from destruction. He made his mercenaries tie copies of the Quran to their lances and flags, and shout for quarter. The soldiers of the Caliph at once desisted from pursuit, and called on him to refer the dispute to arbitration."

The arbitration ended in a chaos in which Hazrat Abu Musa Ashari, the representative of Ali was duped by the clever Amr bin al-Aas, the representative of Amir Muawiya.

These internal dissensions within the house of Islam gave birth to a new fanatical horde called Kharijis, which proved to be a great menace for the administration of Hazrat Ali. They spread disorders throughout the domains of the Caliph, killing innocent people and converting them to their fanatical creed by force. The Caliph, who faced the turmoils and turbulence around him with extraordinary courage and patience dealt with the Khariji fanatics with a strong hand and exterminated them after a bloody battle.

The people of Kerman and Persia revolted against the authority of the Caliph. Ziad bin Abiha was despatched who soon suppressed the disorder and restored peace in that region. Instead of punishing the rebels, Hazrat Ali treated them with such kindness that the Persians recalled the rule of Nausherwan, the Just.

The Khariji insurrection to which he ultimately fell a victim, too, was handled by him firmly. Three Kharijis (fanatics) had planned to kill the three persons namely, Hazrat Ali, Muawiya and Amr bin al-Aas at an appointed time. Ibn M'aljem, who was assigned the task of killing the Caliph, struck the deadly blow at him when he was going to offer his prayer. The just and kind-hearted Caliph instructed his men to treat the assassin with all kindness. Thus died at the age of 63, one of the greatest sons of Islam. His rule lasted 4 years and 9 months and he was destined to steer the ship of Islam through the most stormy seas of internecine dissensions. He took pride in simplicity, piety, humility and kindheartedness. Being humane by nature, he loved to help the needy and forgave even his deadliest enemies. His kindness, at times, verged on the side of weakness. Worldly power and splendour had no fascination for him. "Thus died", says a celebrated writer "in the prime of his life, the best hearted Moslem, to use Colonel Osborn's words, 'that ever lived'. Mild, beneficent and humane, ready to help the weak and the distressed, his life had been devoted to the cause of Islam. Had he possessed the sternness of Umar's character he would have been more successful in governing an unruly race like the Arabs".

Hazrat Ali was elected as a Caliph in the most stormy period of Islamic history. Endowed with extraordinary daring and sound judgement, he battled against the surging waves of disruption which wanted to knock the new State off its foundation. In chivalry, he had hardly any match in the annals of early Islam. Known as the 'Lion of God', his bravery has become proverbial, and stories connected with it are still related throughout the world of Islam.

Hazrat Ali was a versatile genius. Being brought up by the Prophet himself and having had the chance of spending about 30 years in his company, Ali occupies the unique position of being the greatest intellectual among the Companions of the Prophet. Like Aristotle he is known as the father of Islamic learning. Writing in *'Izalat-ul-Khifa'*, Shah Waliullah attributes the high intellec-tualism of Hazrat Ali to the ideal training of the Prophet. He reports on the authority of Imam Hanbal that Hazrat Ali possessed the highest intellectual attributes among the Companions. This is further corroborated by the decla-ration of the Prophet: "I am the store-house of knowledge while Ali is its gate." He was a *'Hafiz'* of the Quran and a commentator of high standing. Along with Hazrat Ibn Abbas he is considered as the greatest authority on the Quran of which he arranged the chapters in order of their revelation during the first six months of the Caliphate of Hazrat Abu Bakr.

Ibn Nadim in his celebrated work *'Al Fihrist'*, has given this order of arrangement. Hazrat Ali exercised utmost circumspection in sifting reports about the traditions, so much so that the traditions reported and collected by him are universally taken to be authentic. He was the greatest *Mujtahid* and jurist of his time and one of the greatest of all times. He solved all vexing and complicated problems which defied solution. As already stated he was the principal adviser on religious and legal matters during the reign of the first three Caliphs. All knotty problems were referred to him and his verdict was considered final. Even such high personalities as Hazrat Umar and Hazrat Aisha referred their difficulties to him. All schools of religious thought regard him as the father of Islamic mysticism. The celebrated mystic, Junaid Baghdadi acknow-ledges Ali as the highest authority on the subject and according to Shah Wali-ullah, who says in *'Izalat-ul-Khifa'* that Ali devoted much time to mysticism before his being elected as Caliph. He was one of the two greatest orators of early Islam—the other being Hazrat Abu Bakr. According to Ibn Nadim, Hazrat Ali is known as the founder of Arabian grammar.

Hazrat Ali was undoubtedly the greatest jurist of early Islam. Once two women who were quarrelling over an infant child—each claiming it, were pro-duced before him. On hearing the statements of both the claimants, Hazrat Ali ordered the child to be cut to pieces. The real mother was overwhelmed with grief and weepingly pleaded to the Caliph to spare the child. Hazrat Ali awarded the child to its real mother and punished the other woman. Hazrat Umar used to say about him: "God forbid, we may be confronted with any controversial issue, which Ali might not be able to solve". According to Hazrat Abdullah bin Masood, Ali possessed the best power of judgement in Medina. The Prophet himself relied on the judgements of Ali and had appointed him the Qazi of Yemen. He had instructed him not to deliver his judgement without hearing both the contending parties. Even his opponents like Amir Muawiya referred their knotty problems to him and accepted his judgement. The early Islamic history is full of learned judgements delivered by him.

Hazrat Ali led a very simple and poverty-stricken life. His whole life was characterised by abstemiousness. He was the very incarnation of simplicity, piety and tender-heartedness. Wordly splendour had no attraction for him. The treasures of the conquered Roman and Persian Empires lay at his feet, but he never cared to cast an eye at them. Once he distributed the entire wealth kept in *Baitul Mal* among the poor. When he was accorded a royal welcome in Kufa, he preferred to stay in the open field instead of the local palace in which arrangements for his boarding had been made. He could not add to the prosperity of his house during the lifetime of Hazrat Fatima. He had only one blanket, which was barely enough to cover his head and feet when he slept. Even, during the days of his Caliphate, he did not give up his simplicity and wore tattered clothes and ate coarse food. He loathed to engage a servant for performing household chores, which were handled by his beloved wife Fatima who was the favourite daughter of the Prophet. She was accustomed to grinding the corn with her own hands.

Writing in *Izalat-ul-Khifa,* Shah Waliullah says that Hazrat Ali once received baskets of oranges from some country. Hazrat Imam Hasan and Husain picked up one orange each which Hazrat Ali snatched from the hands of his sons and distributed all the oranges among the common people. As Islam forbids accumulation of wealth, Hazrat Ali, always lived up to his convictions; neither he ever amassed wealth, nor he believed in hoarding wealth in the Public Treasury.

During his Caliphate, he had to offer even his favourite sword for sale in order to purchase a piece of cloth. In spite of being extremely poor, he never turned away in disappointment anyone who knocked at his door. One night he watered a garden of Medina and received grain as his wage. The next morning when he returned home he got a portion of grain boiled. But he gave the whole of it to a beggar who knocked at his door. This was repeated on three successive days with the result that he himself had to go without food for three days.

Unlike Muawiya who recklessly distributed the wealth of *Baitul Mal* among his own men, with ulterior motives, Hazrat Ali scrupulously followed the principles laid down by the Second Caliph and equally distributed the public money among the people. This impartial justice of the Caliph antagonised his supporters, who began to side with Muawiya. Despite surmounting difficulties Hazrat Ali faced them with courage and conviction and kept up the high traditions of the Prophet.

His Administration steered clear of partisanship, favouritism or nepotism. He was particularly severe on his Governors and kept a regular watch on their actions. Once his own cousin Ibn Abbas, the Governor of Basra, drew some money from the *Baitul Mal* for his personal expenses. Hazrat Ali questioned his action and Hazrat Ibn Abbas was so much frightened that he left Basra for Makkah. It becomes abundantly clear from this that Ali did not spare even his dear once who strayed from the path chalked out by the Prophet.

"Ali's Administration", says Ameer Ali, "was too disturbed by civil war to remedy the evils of the previous Administration; but he removed most of the corrupt Governors and restored the policy of Umar where he had the power; established a state archive for the safe custody and preservation of the records of the Caliphate; created the office of *Hajib* or Chamberlain, and of the *Sahib-ush-Shurta* or Captain of the Guard; and reorganised the Police and regulated their duties."

Notwithstanding the internecine warfare, the Muslims extended their frontiers during Ali's regime. After the suppression of revolts in Kabul and Sistan, the Arabs made a naval attack on Konkan (Bombay Coast). Being highly experienced in warfare, the Caliph established army establishments on the Syrian frontiers. He strengthened his frontiers and raised impregnable fortifications on the northern frontiers of Persia.

Contemporary and later historians have paid high tributes to Hazrat Ali's qualities of head and heart. The celebrated historian Masudi says : "If the glorious name of being the first Muslim, a comrade of the Prophet in exile, his faithful companion in the struggle for the faith, his intimate in life, and his kinsman; if a true knowledge of the spirit of his teachings and of the Book; if self-abnegation and practice of justice; if honesty, purity and love of truth; if a knowledge of law and science, constitute a claim to pre-eminence, then all must regard Ali as one of the foremost Muslims." The celebrated traditionist Shah Waliullah has discussed at length the high qualities of Hazrat Ali in his well-known work, *'Izalat-ul-Khifa'*. He concludes that, chivalry and strength of character, humanity and sincerity which are attributes of great men, were possessed in abundance by Hazrat Ali.

With the martyrdom of Hazrat Ali, ended the glorious regime of the pious Caliphs. 'Thus vanished", says a philosophical writer, "the popular regime, which' had for its basis a patriarchal simplicity, never again to appear among any *Mussalman* nation; only the jurisprudence and rules which depended on *Koran* survived the fall of the elective Government."

Another historian says : "The example of simplicity presented by the Prophet and his four successors stands unrivalled in the annals of kingship. Monarchs of vast empires, they led the lives of hermits and never cast a glance at the worldly riches which were laid in heap at their feet. Kingly palaces and robes came in their way, but the four kings, temporal as well as spiritual, ever took pride in their cottages they lived in and in the rough clothes they wore while they laboured for their daily bread. Their lives were simpler than those of the common people and like them they would go to the mosque for the five daily prayers unaccompanied by a bodyguard. For their person they had no police or guard. But for the welfare of the State they were so watchful that the smallest incident on a most distant frontier would forthwith engage their attention. Their hearts were devoted to the love of God and their bodies to the service of man."

# ABUZAR GHAFFARI

Islamic economy is, to a great extent, based on egalitarian principles which aim at maintaining the equality of man through equitable distribution of wealth, thus eliminating disparity between the rich and the poor. Islam has struck at the root of the principle of making the rich richer and the poor poorer, which has been followed in the capitalist and imperialist states since times immemorial. It has prevented the exploitation of the poor at the hands of the rich.

Islam has evolved its economic principles on such lines as to minimise these disparities and eliminate distinctions in the distribution of human fortunes. The wealthy people are to be heavily taxed through *Zakat* in order to help the poor and this taxation forms one of the cardinal principles of Islam which no true Muslim can violate. Its denunciation of "interest" and emphasis on the annual payment of *Zakat*—a religious obligatory tax levied on capital income forming one of the fundamentals of Islam, is an effective step towards non-accumulation of wealth. The Holy Quran, while enumerating the qualities of a *Momin* (true Muslim) states that he is one who distributes his wealth for Allah, among his needy brethren. The Prophet of Islam has observed that if the Muslims would faithfully pay their *Zakat,* a time would come when there would be no needy person left to receive the same.

Islam in its early days produced many zealous exponents of the egalitarian principles of Islam. They sacrificed their all for the sake of God. Instances of unparalleled generosity and benevolence are two numerous to be adduced from the life of the Companions of the Prophet. But the most vocal and fearless exponent of non-accumulation and wider distribution of private wealth was Hazrat Abuzar Ghaffari, a highly respected and trusted Companion of the Prophet.

Born in a tribe of brigands, named Ghaffar, residing near the caravan route leading from Makkah to Syria, Jundab, later known as Abuzar, soon rose to be a great leader of marauders and a terror for the surrounding country.

But Jundab possessed a live conscience and a moving heart. The ravages caused by his terrible raids and the miseries of his victims provided a turning point in his career. Introspection led to remorse, which not only made him abandon the vicious life but also dissuade others from it. This created a furore in the tribe and an unwholesome atmosphere for him which obliged him to leave the place and take shelter elsewhere.

He had now developed an extreme revulsion for his past immoral life of lust and plunder. This turning point in the life of Abuzar is of great significance as it gave the world of Islam one of its most sincere and revolutionary figures.

He, along with his mother and brother Anees, migrated to Upper Najd, where one of his maternal uncles resided. This was the first migration of Abuzar in search of truth and righteousness. Here, too, he could not stay for long. His revolutionary ideas had antagonised his tribesmen who complained to his maternal uncle. In a world of lust and vice, he seemed to be a strange figure. He left his maternal uncle's house and took refuge in a village near Makkah.

Abuzar now yearned for something else. He was in search of truth. Even before embracing Islam, he was against idol worship and considered God as one and supreme. Once he said :

"I used to say my prayers three years before I had the honour of beholding the Holy Prophet of Islam"

His brother, Anees who had gone to Makkah brought him the news of the dawn of a new horizon—Islam. It was the time when the teachings of the Holy Prophet of Islam had created a stir in Makkah and had sent a wave of resentment throughout Arabia. Abuzar was naturally drawn towards the Messenger of God and longed to see him. He arrived in Makkah, occasionally visited Kaaba and for more than a month closely studied the conduct and teachings of the Holy Prophet in the hostile environments of Makkah.

The Kaaba which, in those days, was packed with idols and was frequently visited by idol worshipers of Quraish was a popular meeting place. The Prophet of Islam, too came to offer his prayers there. Abuzar at last had a chance of meeting him. This provided him an opportunity of fulfilling his heart's desire. There and then he embraced Islam and became one of its most zealous and dauntless champions.

Now started his period of trials and tribulations. He openly offered prayer and preached the new faith in Kaaba. One day, the Quraish idolators fell upon him and had he not been rescued by Abbas, the uncle of the Prophet, who reminded the assailants that their victim was an important member of the Ghaffar clan, who happened to inhabit the area encompassing their trade route to Syria. As such, the members of the clan were in a position to put a stop to their commerce with that country. This argument cooled down their fury for the time being.

Thenceforward, Abuzar dedicated himself to the service of Islam and its founder. He soon earned an enviable and venerable place among the Companions of the Prophet and came to be recognised as one of his very close and trusted Companions.

He was deputed by the Prophet to preach Islam in his own tribe. He went to his own land and enthusiastically preached the new faith and met with tremendous success. Not only his mother and brother Anees, but almost the entire clan of marauders and brigands also embraced Islam. He was one of the foremost and rather the first missionary of Islam. Crowned with exceptional success in his difficult mission, he returned to Makkah to be all the more honoured by the Prophet and his Companions.

He was held in high esteem by the Prophet. When he later left Medina to participate in the "Battle of Rags", Abuzar was appointed as the *Imam* and Administrator of Medina. On his death bed, the Prophet sent for Abuzar and embraced him, declaring :

"Abuzar would be the same all through his life. He would not change even after my death".

The words of the Prophet proved true. Abuzar passed an utterly simple and pious life, abhorring pomp and show and denouncing the capitalists and their wealth throughout his life, specially in the time of the Third Caliph of Islam, when the members of Quraish were rolling in wealth.

Abuzar was a staunch champion of the egalitarian principles of Islam. His adherence to and interpretation of *"Aya-i-Kanz"* (verse on concentration of wealth) raised a great controversy during the time of Hazrat Usman, the Third Caliph. This *"Aya"* in *"Sura-i-Tauba"* of the Holy Quran runs as follow :

"Those who accumulate fondly gold and silver and do not spend in the path of Allah, tell them dire perdition will be their lot. On that day, their foreheads, sides and backs will be branded with the very gold and silver, made red-hot and it will be said : "This is what you had accumulated for your benefit. Now taste what you had accumulated".

Deadly opposed to the idea of accumulating wealth he considered it against the spirit of Islam. He could not reconcile himself with the growing capitalism among the Muslims in Syria governed by Muawiya. In his opinion, it was obligatory on all true Muslims to distribute their surplus wealth among their needy brethren. In substantiation he cited the following incident in the life of the Prophet :

"One day as the Holy Prophet was going for a walk along with Abuzar, the mountain of Ohad came in view, he said to Abuzar : "If I have gold equal to the weight of the yonder mountain, I would never care to look at it and have it with me on the third day except that which will be required to pay off my debts. The rest I would distribute among the slaves of Allah".

He lived up to his convictions and practised what he preached. In his attitude towards capitalism he was so uncompromising that he did not care for the highest dignitaries. Hazrat Abu Hurairah, a very renowned Companion of the Prophet, was appointed the Governor of Bahrain. He came to see Abuzar who refused to see him at first. But, on enquiry, as to why he was so annoyed with him, Abuzar replied :

"You have been appointed Governor of Bahrain".

"Yes", was the reply.

"Then you must have built a palatial house and purchased a big estate there", added Abuzar.

"Nothing of this sort", replied Abu Hurairah.

"Then you are my brother", retorted Abuzar and instantly embraced him.

His preachings were never challenged during the time of the first two Caliphs. He passed a peaceful life, and was respected by all. But the trouble arose during the time of the Third Caliph.

Abuzar had migrated to Syria, where he found Governor Muawiya living in luxury and consolidating his authority with the support of a privileged class which had amassed enormous fortunes. Abuzar's egalitarian preachings awakened the masses against this privileged class. He became a problem for the local Government. When Muawiya built his green palace, Al-Khizra, Abuzar questioned him :

"If you have built this palace out of the state funds, you are guilty of misappropriation; if out of your personal income, you are guilty of *'israf'* (extravagance)." Muawiya was stunned and could give no reply.

Muawiya tried his best to dissuade Abuzar from his egalitarian preachings but Abuzar was adamant and uncompromising on his principles. The *Ameer* arranged discussions with him by learned scholars of Islam, whose arguments cut no ice with him. People were forbidden to associate with or listen to him. Nevertheless people thronged around him for advice. At last Muawiya complained to Caliph Usman that Abuzar was preaching class hatred in Syria which might lead to serious consequences.

Thereupon, Abuzar was summoned to Medina by the Caliph. Long before his arrival in the city, the residents of Medina had come out of their houses to welcome this revered Companion of the Prophet.

In Medina, too, he could not have a peaceful life. The wealthy section of the population felt uneasy over his activities advocating equitable distribution of wealth.

The Caliph at last arranged a discussion on the subject between him and Kaab Ahbar, a learned person. The latter questioned the desirability of keeping the law of inheritance in Muslim jurisprudence when Islam did not permit the accumulation of wealth. But this was off the point. The discussion bore no result and Hazrat Usman asked him eventually to leave Medina and settle at Rabza, a small village on the caravan route from Iraq to Medina. The enemies of Islam like Abdullah ibn Saba, tried to incite him to revolt against the Caliph but he rebuked them saying :

"If Usman hangs me on the highest mountain, I will not lift my finger against him".

Like a true Muslim, Abuzar bowed before the orders of the Central Authority of Islam. He migrated to Rabza and died there on the 8th Zil-Hijja, 32 A.H. His dead body lay near the caravan route, watched by his widow. There was none to bury him. Suddenly, on the horizon appeared a caravan of *Hajis* heading towards Makkah. On being informed that the dead body was that of Abuzar, the revered Companion of the Prophet, they got down, offered funeral prayer, led by Abdulla ibn Masood, the celebrated scholar of Islam and buried him.

Thus ended the life of this trusted Companion of the Prophet who preached and practised true socialism more than a thousand years before Karl Marx. He lived and died for his principles denouncing the accumulation of wealth.

The Holy Prophet of Islam had certified him as the "most truthful", and Hazrat Ali had declared about him :

"There is now none, except Abuzar, in the world, who is not afraid of the tirade of recriminations from the side of delinquents in matters of religion. Even I am no exception".

# IMAM HUSAIN

No event in the history of mankind has, perhaps, stirred human sentiments more deeply than the tragedy of Karbala. The martyrdom of Imam Husain, grandson of the Prophet of Islam at Karbala, is being celebrated for the last 14 centuries with tears and wails throughout the world of Islam. The sacrifice of the pious Imam for the cause of truth and righteousness was so colossal and the tragedy which resulted from it was so piognant that it continues to serve as a beacon light to all fighters for freedom and truth. This has inspired not only Muslim but also non-Muslim writers, including Shelley, Chakbast, Sarshar and Nasim.

Husain was born in the 4th A.H. in Medina. His mother, Fatima, was the favourite daughter of the Prophet of Islam and his father, Hazrat Ali, was one of the most talented and outstanding personalities of early Islam. Brought up by this ideal couple under the fostering care of the Prophet, Husain soon distinguished himself as a promising scholar, warrior and saint. The ideal training which he received from his parents and maternal grandfather made him as one of the noblest sons of Islam. Even in his early teens, he was noted for his piety and nobility, chivalry and scholarship.

The two brothers, Imam Hasan and Husain, continued to flourish during the time of the first four Caliphs. They commanded great respect of all classes of Muslims for their sterling traits. They were shown great consideration even by the successive Caliphs. It was during the Caliphate of their father, Ali, that trouble arose when Ameer Muawiya revolted against the Central authority of Islam which led to the division of Muslim Caliphate into two—one led by Hazrat Ali and the other by Ameer Muawiya. The martyrdom of Hazrat Ali left the field open for Ameer Muawiya. Imam Hasan, who succeeded his father compromised with and abdicated in favour of Ameer Muawiya in the larger interests of Islam. He was soon poisoned to death.

Muawiya dealt the greatest blow to the democratic spirit of Islam during the closing years of his reign when, on the advice of Mughira, the Governor of Basra, he nominated his son Yazid as his successor. The democratic spirit of Islamic Caliphate degenerated into monarchy. It was also a breach of contract with Imam Husain. He obtained the oath of fealty to Yazid through questionable means. He himself visited Medina for the purpose and was successful in his efforts to some extent. But the four notable personalities of Islam who took exception to his un-Islamic practice were Husain, the son of Ali, Abdulla, the son of Umar, Abdur Rahman, the son of Abu Bakr and Abdulla, the son of Zubair. "Two men threw into confusion the affairs of the Muslims", says Imam Hasan of Basra, "Amr, the son of Aas, when he suggested to Muawiya the lifting of the Koran on the lances and Mughira, who advised Muawiya to take the covenant of allegiance for Yazid. Were it not for that, there would have been a Council of Election till the day of resurrection, for those who succeeded Muawiya followed his example in taking the covenant for their sons" *(History of Saracens)*.

Yazid, the most cursed personality in the annals of Islam, ascended the throne of Damascus in April 683 A.C. He was a tyrant who revelled in vicious pleasures of life. He hated and took delight in persecuting Muslim divines. He tried to obtain the allegiance of the four notable Muslims including Imam Husain through intrigue and force. But, Husain, who had inherited the virtuous and chivalrous disposition of his father, Ali, was not a man to be won over by force or favour. He remained adamant and refused to acknowledge such a vicious and dissolute person, as the Caliph, supposed to be the spiritual as well as political Head of the world of Islam.

Immediately after his accession, Yazid ordered Waleed ibn Utaba, the Governor of Medina, to force Imam Husain for the oath of fealty to him. Meanwhile, Husain received messages from the citizens of Kufa imploring him to free them the tyrannical Omayyad rule. He received hundreds of such letters from the residents of Kufa offering him their allegiance. The kind hearted virtuous Husain considered it his duty to respond to the call of the oppressed. He sent his cousin Muslim ibn Aqeel as his emissary to Kufa. Thousands of Kufis rushed to swear fidelity to Husain on Muslim's hands. The reports sent by Muslim from Kufa were highly heartening. He invited Husain to come to Kufa.

But the Kufis were soon won over through force and favour and turned their backs on Muslim, the emissary of Husain. He met a pitiable death. In the meantime, Imam Husain, along with his family members, relations and companions left for Kufa. When he approached the borders of Iraq, he was surprised at the absence of the promised Kufi soldiers. A few stages from his destination he learned the tragic end of his emissary. Eager, fierce and impetuous, the Kufis were utterly wanting in perseverance and steadfastness. "They knew not their minds from day to day. One moment, ardent as fire for some cause or person, the next day they were as cold as ice and as indifferent as the dead." He was confronted with a strong detachment of Omayyad army under the command of Hur, who, under the orders of Ubaidullah ibn Zayad, forced Husain and his party to march towards Karbala, a place about 25 miles north—east of Kufa. Here, close to the bank of the Euphrates, Husain encamped along with his companions. The circle of steel formed by the Umayyad soldiers closed in around him. The Umayyad Governor, Ubaidullah ibn Zayad wished to persuade or force Husain to surrender. He cut off all access to the Euphrates, hoping to reduce him to thirst. But Husain, the son of Ali was made of a different metal. He remained obdurate and firm in his resolve not to acknowledge a vicious tyrant as the Caliph of Islam.

This small band of 72 souls which included respectable ladies, men and children of the House of Fatima, encamped on the western bank of the Euphrates at Karbala surrounded by a powerful Umayyad army of 4,000 soldiers commanded by Amr bin Saad. A showdown seemed imminent as Husain was determined to shed the last drop of his blood for the sake of truth and righteousness and Ubaidullah was also bent upon preventing the flower of Muslim nobility escaping from his hands. Diabolical forces had arrayed themselves against the few members of the Prophet's house-hold. Husain, therefore, allowed his companions to leave him and go to places of safety. But who could bear to leave the grandson of the Prophet in the lurch!

Now started a period of trials and tribulations for the descendants of Muhammad (PBUH). For days, the vicious army of Ibn Saad surrounded their tents but dared not come within reach of Husain's sword. They immediately cut off their water-supply with a view to reducing them to hunger and thirst, thus forcing them to surrender. For four days, commencing from the 7th to the 10th Muharram not a drop of water entered the mouth of Imam Husain and his companions who were dying of thirst in the grilling heat of the Arabian desert, without their fortitude and perserverance for a noble cause being impaired in the least. Faced with this dire catastrophe which would have made the stoutest heart shudder and, strongest feet stagger, Husain and his companions did not wince at all. The restraint and patience and the power of endurance exhibited by this heroic band of Karbala were indeed superhuman. These noble qualities of theirs stand unrivalled.

At last the fateful hour arrived. This was on the 10th of Muharram, a memorable day in the history of Islam. One of the enemy's chief named Hur, horrified at the miserable plight of the grand children of the Prophet, deserted along with thirty followers to meet the inevitable death. None could dare face the Fatimides in single combats. But the enemy archers picked them off from a safe distance. One by one the defenders fell—friends, cousins, nephews and sons—until there remained the grandson of the Prophet and his infant son, Asghar. He was crying with thirst. Carrying him in his arms he drew near the enemy positions and delivered a memorable sermon. But, instead of giving water to the crying child, they transfixed him with a dart. Husain brought the dead child smeared with blood and placed him in the lap of his mother.

He knew that the end was near. During his last moments Husain demonstrated the highest spiritual and moral greatness by praying for the very persons who had killed his infant child and other family members. Coming out of the tent, he made a desperate charge. The enemy soldiers fell back as they could not stand up against fierce attack of Husain, the son of the "Lion of God". But he was too much exhausted due to loss of blood and excessive thirst. The valiant Imam got down from his horse and offered his last prayers to his Creator. As he prostrated, the murderous crew rushed upon him and Saran ibn Uns struck the fatal blow. "They cut off his head, ruthlessly trampled on his body, and with savage ferocity subjected it to every ignomiy". His tents were pillaged. His head was carried to the inhuman Obaidullah, who struck his lips with a cane. "Alas"! exclaimed an aged Muslim, "On these lips have I seen the lips of the Apostle of God". "In a distant age and climate", says Gibbon, "the tragic scene of the death of Husain will awaken the sympathy of the coldest reader."

Thus, fell on the 10th Muharram 61 A.H., one of the noblest personalities of Islam and along with him perished the members of the House of Fatima, the flower of Muslim nobility, piety and chivalry. The only male survivor was sickly Zainul Abedin, son of Husain who escaped general massacre at the intervention of Husain's sister, Zainub.

The female members of Husain's family were despatched to Damascus along with Zainul Abedin. Their pitiable condition evoked sympathy even from alien quarters and Yazid, fearing an outburst in his capital in favour of the oppressed and persecuted family, hurriedly sent them back to Medina.

The massacre of the Prophet's family at Karbala sent a wave of horror and indignation throughout the world of Islam. Medina rose in revolt against the Umayyad Caliph. Abdullah ibn Zubair installed himself as the Caliph in Makkah. It gave birth to a new movement in Persia which ultimately brought about the doom of Omayyad rule and paved the way for the establishment of the Abbasside Caliphate.

The martyrdom of Husain at Karbala provided the moral victory of virtue over vice. It was a triumph of good over evil. It continues to serve as a beacon light for all strugglers for truth and righteousness. It leaves behind the message that it is glorious to die for a just and noble cause. It also establishes the moral victory of right over might. It revived the virtues of Islam, which were slowly being enveloped by evil. Maulana Muhammad Ali, the celebrated Muslim patriot, has rightly observed :

*"Katl-e-Husain asl main marg-e-yazid hai*
*Islam zinda hota hai her Karbala ke bad."*

"The martyrdom of Husain actually means the death of Yazid, as every such Karbala leads to the revival of Islam."

How truthfully says a Persian poet :

بنا کردند خوش رسمے به خاک و خون غلطیدن
خدا را رحمت کند این عاشقان پاک طینت را

"They initiated a noble example of tossing in dust and blood May God bless these well-intentioned lovers (of His)."

# UMAR BIN ABDUL AZIZ

Hazrat Umar bin Abdul Aziz, the celebrated Umayyad Caliph whose empire stretched from the shores of the Atlantic to the highlands of Pamir, was sitting in his private chamber examining a pile of State documents. The dim light of the room was adding to the serenity and sombreness of the place and the Caliph could scarcely feel the arrival of his wife, Fatima, till she addressed him :

"Sire! Will you spare a few moments for me? I want to discuss some private matter with you."

"Of course", replied the pious Caliph, raising his head from the papers, "But, please put off this State lamp and light your own, as I do not want to burn the State oil for our private talk."

The obedient wife, who was the daughter of Abdul Malik, the mighty Umayyad Caliph and the sister of two successive Umayyad Caliphs, Waleed and Sulaiman, complied accordingly.

The short rule of Hazrat Umar bin Abdul Aziz was like an oasis in a vast desert—a benevolent rain which had fallen on an arid soil. It was the brightest period in the 91-year Caliphate of the Umayyads, which, though short lived, had transformed the outlook of the State and had released such powerful democratic forces that after his death the attempts for the restoration of autocracy under Hisham failed miserably and ultivately culminated in the fall of the Umayyads at the hands of the Abbasides.

Hazrat Umar bin Abdul Aziz, surnamed 'al Khalifat as Saleh' (The pious Caliph) was the son of Abdul Aziz, the Governor of Egypt, and his mother, Umme-Aasim was the grand daughter of Caliph Umar. He was born in 63 A.H. i.e. 682 A.C. in Halwan, a village of Egypt, but he received his education in Medina from his mother's uncle, the celebrated Abdulla ibn Umar. Medina, which in those days was the highest seat of learning in the world of Islam, was greatly instrumental in moulding his life to a pattern quite distinct from those of other Umayyad Caliphs. He remained there till his father's death in 704 A.C., when he was summoned by his uncle Caliph Abdul Malik and was married to his daughter Fatima. He was appointed Governor of Medina in 706 A.C. by Caliph Waleed. Unlike other autocratic governors, immediately on arrival in Medina, he formed an advisory council of ten eminent jurists and notables of the holy city and carried on the administration with their consultation. He empowered them to keep a watchful eye over his subordinates. This step had a salutary effect on the residents of Medina, who hailed his beneficent Administration. He successfully strove to erase the signs of ravages, committed in the holy cities of Islam under Yazid and Abdul Malik. During his two-year stay as the Governor of Medina, he repaired and enlarged the Mosque of the Prophet as well as beautified the holy cities with public structures; constructed hundreds of new aqueducts and improved the suburban roads leading to Medina. "Moderate, yet firm", says Ameer Ali, "anxious to promote the welfare of the people whom he governed, Umar's rule proved beneficent to all classes." His patriotic rule was for the good of his subjects.

His just administration attracted from Iraq a large number of refugees who were groaning under the oppression of Hajjaj bin Yusuf. But, according to Tabari, this migration highly enraged the tyrant who prevailed upon Waleed to transfer him from Medina which he left amidst 'universal mourning.'

The Umayyad Caliph Sulaiman ibn Abdul Malik who had great respect for Umar bin Abdul Aziz nominated him as his successor. On his death the mantle of Caliphate fell upon Umar bin Abdul Aziz who reluctantly accepted it. Giving up all pomp and pageantry the pious Caliph returned the royal charger, refused the police guard and deposited the entire equipment meant for the person of the Caliph in the *Baitul Mal.* Like a commoner he preferred to stay in a small tent and left the royal palace for the family of Sulaiman. He ordered that the horses of the royal stables be auctioned and the proceeds be deposited in the Treasury. One of his family members asked him why he looked downhearted. The Caliph replied instantly, "Is it not a thing to worry about? I have been entrusted with the welfare of such a vast empire and I would be failing in my duty if I did not rush to the help of a needy person." Thereafter, he ascended the pulpit and delivered a masterly oration saying: "Brothers! I have been burdened with the responsibilities of Caliphate against my will. You are at liberty to elect anyone whom you like." But the audience cried out with one voice that he was the fittest person for the high office. Thereupon the pious Caliph advised his people to be pious and virtuous. He allowed them to break their oath of allegiance to him, if he wavered from the path of God.

His short rule was noted for great democratic and healthy activities. He waged a defensive war against the Turks who had ravaged Azerbaijan and massacred thousands of innocent Muslims. The forces of the Caliph under the command of Ibn Hatim ibn Ali Naan Al Balili repulsed the invaders with heavy losses. The Caliph permitted his forces to wage a war against the notorious Kharijis, but under conditions that women, children and prisoners would be spared, the defeated enemy would not be pursued, and all the spoils of war would be returned to their dependents. He replaced corrupt and tyrannical Umayyad administrators with capable and just persons.

His first act after assuming office was the restoration to their rightful owners the properties confiscated by the Umayyads. He was hardly free from the burial ceremonies of Caliph Sulaiman and wanted to take a short respite when his son asked him if he would like to take rest before dealing with cases pertaining to confiscated properties. He replied "Yes, I would deal with these after taking rest."

"Are you sure that you would live up to that time?" asked the son. The father kissed his dear son and thanked God that he had given him such a virtuous son. He immediately sat up to deal with this urgent matter and first of all returned all his movable and immovable properties to the public treasury. He deposited even a ring presented to him by Waleed. His faithful slave, Mazahim was deeply moved at this uncommon sight and asked, "Sir, what have you left for your children"?

"God", was the reply.

He restored the possession of the garden of Fidak to the descendants of the Prophet which had been appropriated by Marwan during the Caliphate of Usman. He bade his wife Fatima to return the jewellery she had received from her father Caliph Abdul Malik. The faithful wife cheerfully complied with his bidding and deposited all of it in the *Baitul Mal.* After her husband's death, her brother Yazid who succeeded him as Caliph offered to return it to her. "I returned these valuable during my husband's lifetime, why should I take them back after his death", she told him.

The restoration of Fidak provoked mixed reaction from the people. The fanatical Kharijis who had become hostile to the Caliphate soon softened towards Umar bin Abdul Aziz, proclaiming that it was not possible for them to oppose a Caliph who was not a man but an angel.

The house of Umayyads accustomed to luxuries at the expense of the common man, revolted against this just but revolutionary step taken by the Caliph and bitterly protested against the disposal of their age-long properties.

One day, the Caliph invited some prominent members of the House of Umayyads to dinner, but advised his cook to delay the preparation of food. As the guests were groaning with hunger, the Caliph shouted to his cook to hurry up. At the same time he asked his men to bring some parched gram which he himself as well as his guests ate to their fill. A few minutes later the cook brought the food which the guests refused to take saying that they had satisfied their appetite. Thereupon the pious Caliph spoke out, "Brothers! when you can satisfy your appetite with so simple a diet, then why do you play with fire and usurp the properties and rights of others." These words deeply moved the notables of the House of Umayyads who burst into tears.

In general, he laid great stress on compensating the victims of illegal extortion in any form.

His administration of impartial justice went against the interests of the Umayyads who were accustomed to all sorts of licences and could hardly tolerate any check on their unbounded freedom. They plotted against the life of this virtuous member of their clan. A slave of the Caliph was bribed to administer the deadly poison. The Caliph having felt the effect of the poison sent for the slave and asked him why he had poisoned him. The slave replied that he was given one thousand dinars for the purpose. The Caliph deposited the amount in the Public Treasury and freeing the slave asked him to leave the place immediately, lest anyone might kill him. Thus died in 719 A.C. at the young age of 36 at a place called Dair Siman (The convent of Siman) near Hems, one of the noblest souls that ever lived in this world. His martyrdom plunged the Islamic world into gloom. It was a day of national mourning; the populace of the small town came out to pay their last homage to the departed leader. He was buried in Dair Siman on a piece of land he had purchased from a Christian.

Muhammad ibn Mobad who happened to be in the Durbar of the Roman Emperor at that time reports that he found the Emperor in drooping spirits. On enquiry he replied, "A virtuous person has passed away. This is Umar bin Abdul Aziz. After Christ if anyone could put a dead person to life it was he. I am hardly surprised to see an ascetic who renounced the world and gave himself to the prayers of God. But I am certainly surprised at a person who had all the pleasures of the world at his feet and yet he shut his eyes against them and passed a life of piety and renunciation."

He reportedly left behind only 17 dinars with a will that out of this amount the rent of the house in which he died and the price of the land in which he was buried would be paid.

"Unaffected piety," says Ameer Ali, "a keen sense of justice, unswerving uprightness, moderation, and an almost primitive simplicity of life, formed the chief features in his character. The responsibility of the office with which he was entrusted filled him with anxiety and caused many a heart searching. Once he was found by his wife weeping after his prayers; she asked if anything had happened to cause him grief, he replied, "O! Fatima! I have been made the ruler over the Moslems and the strangers, and I was thinking of the poor that are starving, and the sick that are destitute, and the naked that are in distress, and the oppressed that are stricken, and the stranger that is in prison, and the venerable elder, and him that hath a large family and small means, and the like of them in countries of the earth and the distant provinces, and I felt that my Lord would ask an account of them at my hands on the day of resurrection, and I feared that no defence would avail me, and I wept."

His honesty and integrity have few parallels in the history of mankind. According to *Tabaqat ibn Saad,* he never performed his private work in the light of a lamp which burned the State oil. On every Friday, Farat ibn Muslama brought State papers for his perusal and orders. One Friday the Caliph brought a small piece of State paper in his private use. Muslama who was aware of the exceptional honesty of the Caliph thought that he had done it out of sheer forgetfulness. The next Friday when he brought back home the State papers, he found in them exactly the same size of paper which was used by the Caliph.

Out of the funds of *Batul Mal,* a guest house was founded for the poor. Once his servant burned the firewood of the guest house to heat water for his ablution. He forthwith got the same quantity of firewood deposited there. On another occasion, he refused to use the water heated from the State charcoal. A number of palatial buildings had been constructed in Khanasra out of the funds of *Baitul Mal* which were occasionally used by other Caliphs when they visited that place, but Umar bin Abdul Aziz never used them and always preferred to camp in the open.

According to the author of *'Tabaqat ibn Saad'* he got his articles of luxury and decoration auctioned for 23 thousand dinars and spent the amount for charitable purposes.

His diet used to be very coarse. He never built a house of his own and followed in the footsteps of the Prophet. Allama Siyuti in his well-known historical work *'Tarikh ul Khulafa'* (History of the Caliphs) states that he spent only two dirhams a day when he was the Caliph. Before his election as Caliph his private properties yielded an income of 50 thousand dinars annually but immediately after the election he returned all his properties to the public coffers and his private income was reduced to 200 dinars per annum.

In spite of the fact that Umar bin Abdul Aziz was a loving father, he never provided his children with luxuries and comforts. His daughter Amina was his favourite child. Once he sent for her, but she could not come as she was not properly dressed. Her aunt came to know of it and purchased necessary garments for his children. He never accepted any presents from anyone. Once a person presented a basket full of apples. The Caliph appreciated the apples but refused to accept them. The man cited the instance of the Prophet who accepted presents. The Caliph replied immediately, "No doubt, those were presents for the Prophet, but for me this will be bribery."

Ibn al Jawi, his biographer, writes that "Umar wore clothes with so many patches and mingled with his subjects on such free terms that when a stranger came to petition him he would find it difficult to recognise the Caliph. When many of his agents wrote that his fiscal reforms in favour of new converts would deplete the Treasury, he replied, "Glad would I be, by Allah, to see every body become Muslim, so that thou and I would have to till the soil with our own hands to earn a living." *(Encyclopaedia of Islam).* According to Fakhri, "Umar discontinued the practice established in the name of Muawiya of cursing "Ali from the pulpit in Friday prayers" *(Encyclopaedia of Islam).*

He was very kind-hearted. Once he was moved to tears on hearing a tale of woe related by a villager and helped him from his private purse. He was kind to animals even and several stories concerning this are found in the early historical records.

He had complete faith in God and never cared for his life. Unguarded, he roamed about in streets listening to the complaints of the common man and assisting him as much as he could.

He introduced a number of reforms; administrative, fiscal and educational. A reformer appears in the world when the administrative, political and ethical machinery is rusted and requires overhauling. This unsurpassable reformer of the Umayyad regime was born in an environment which was very gloomy and necessitated a change. His promising son, Abdul Malik a youth of 17 advised his father to be more ruthless in introducing his beneficial reforms, but the wise father replied, "My beloved son, what thou tellest me to do can be achieved only by sword, but there is no good in a reform which requires the use of the sword."

Under his instructions, As Samh, his Viceroy in Spain, took a census of the diverse nationalities, races and creeds, inhabiting that country. A survey of the entire peninsula including those of her cities, rivers, seas and mountains was made. The nature of her soil, varieties of products and agricultural as well as mineral sources were also carefully surveyed and noted in records. A number of bridges in southern Spain were constructed and repaired. A spacious Friday Mosque was built at Saragossa in northern Spain.

The *Baitul Mal* (Public Treasury) which was one innovation of Islam and had proved a blessing for poor Muslims during the regime of 'Pious Caliphs,' was freely used for private purposes by the Umayyad Caliphs, Umar ibn Abdul Aziz stopped this unholy practice and never drew a pie from *Baitul Mal.* He separated the accounts for *'Khams,' 'Sadqa'* and *'Fi'* and had separate sections for each. He immediately stopped the practice of richly rewarding the authors of panegyrics of the royal family from the *Baitul Mal.*

One of the most important measures was his reform of taxation. He made adequate arrangement for easy realisation of taxes and administered it on a sound footing. He wrote a memorable note on taxation to Abdul Hamid ibn Abdur Rahman which has been copied by Qazi Abu Yusuf; "Examine the land and levy the land tax accordingly. Do not burden a barren land with a fertile one and vice versa. Do not charge the revenue of barren land." His generous reforms and leniency led the people depositing their taxes willingly. It is a strange paradox that in spite of all oppressive measures adopted by the notorious Hajjaj bin Yusuf for the realisation of taxes in Iraq, it was less than half of the amount realised during the benevolent regime of Umar bin Abdul Aziz.

He paid special attention to the prison reforms. He instructed Abu Bakr ibn Hazm to make weekly inspection of jails. The jail wardens were warned not to maltreat the prisoners. Every prisoner was given a monthly stipend and proper seasonal clothing. He advised the jail authorities to inculcate love for virtue and hatred for vice among the prisoners. Education of the prisoners led to their reformation.

The public welfare institutions and works received much stimulus All over his vast empire thousands of public wells and inns were constructed. Charitable dispensaries were also opened. Even travelling expenses were arranged by the Government for the needy travellers. A large number of inns were constructed on the road leading from Khorasan to Samarkand.

Umar ibn Abdul Aziz was a capable administrator well versed in his duties towards this world and the hereafter. He was extremely hardworking and when people urged him to take rest, he never heeded them. He had set before himself Caliph Umar's administration as a model to be copied. According to the well-known Imam Sufian Suri, there are five pious Caliphs namely Abu Bakr, Umar Farooq, Usman, Ali and Umar bin Abdul Aziz. The outstanding feature of his Caliphate was that he revived Islam's democratic spirit which had been suppressed after the accession of Yazid. In a letter addressed to the Prefect of Kufa, he exhorted his governors to abolish all unjust ordinances. He wrote, "Thou must know, that the maintenance of religion is due to the practice of justice and benevolence; do not think lightly of any sin; do not try to depopulate what is populous; do not try to exact from the subjects anything beyond their capacity; take from them what they can give; do everything to improve population and prosperity; govern mildly and without harshness; do not accept presents on festive occasions; do not take the price of sacred book (distributed among the people); impose no tax on travellers, or on the marriages, or on the milk of camels; and do not insist on the poll tax from anyone who has become a convert to Islam"

The pious Caliph disbanded 600 bodyguards, meant for guarding the person of the Caliph. He received lesser salary than his subordinates. He attracted around him a galaxy of talented men who counselled him on State matters.

That Umar bin Abdul Aziz was very kind and just towards non-Muslims has been acknowledged by the *Encyclopaedia of Islam.* As a devout Muslim he was not only graciously tolerant to the members of other creeds but also solicitous towards them. Christians, Jews and fire worshippers were allowed to retain their churches, synagogues and temples. In Damascus, Al-Waleed had taken down the 'basilika' of John, the Baptist, and incorporated the site in the mosque of Umayyads. When Umar became Caliph, the Christians complained to him that the Church had been taken from them, whereupon he ordered the Governor to return to the Christians what belonged to them. While he endeavoured to protect his Muslim subjects from being abused, he was also anxious that his Christian subjects should not be rushed by oppressive taxation. In Aila and in Cyprus the increased tribute settled by treaty was reduced by him to the original amount.

Once a Muslim murdered a non-Muslim of Hira. The Caliph, when apprised of the event, ordered the Governor to do justice in the case. The Muslim was surrendered to the relations of the murdered person who killed him. A Christian, filed a suit against Hisham ibn Abdul Malik who later on succeeded as Caliph. The just Caliph ordered both the plaintiff and the defendant to stand side by side in the court. This annoyed Hisham who abused the Christian. Thereupon the Caliph rebuked him and threatened him with dire consequences.

Umar bin Abdul Aziz laid great emphasis on the ethical aspects of education in order to turn the hearts of people towards charity, forbearance and benevolence. He relentlessly discouraged and punished laxity of morals.

All these beneficial measures added to the stability of the State and the prosperity of the people who lived in peace and tranquility. During his short reign of two years, people had grown so prosperous and contented that one could hardly find a person who would accept alms. The only discontented people were the members of the House of Umayyads who had been accustomed to a life of vice and luxury and could hardly change their heart.

Umar bin Abdul Aziz did not lay much stress on military glory. He paid greater attention to internal administration, economic development and consolidation of his State. The siege of Constantinople was raised. In Spain, the Muslim armies crossed the Pyrennes and penetrated as far as Toulouse in central France.

His short reign was like a merciful rain which brought universal blessings. One of its special features was that almost all Berbers in Northern Africa as well as the nobility of Sind embraced Islam of their own accord. "Umar, however, by no means felt obliged to spread Islam by the sword," adds the *Encyclopaedia of Islam* "He rather sought peaceful missionary activity to win members of other creeds to the faith of the Prophet."

Umar bin Abdul Aziz was a unique ruler from every point of view. The high standard of administration set by him could only be rivalled by the first four Caliphs of Islam. "The reign of Umar II," writes Ameer Ali "forms the most attractive period of the Umayyads" domination. The historians dwell with satisfaction on the work and aspirations of a Ruler who made the weal of his people the sole object of his ambition." His short but glorious reign has no match thence after. "As a Caliph, Umar stands apart," acknowledges a European orientalist. "He was distinguished from his predecessors and successors alike. Inspired by a true piety, although not entirely free from biotry, he was very conscious of his responsibilities to God and always endeavoured to further what he believed to be right and conscientiously to do his duty as a ruler. In his private life he was distinguished by the greatest simplicity and frugality."

# GREAT WOMEN

# KHADIJA'T AL-KUBRA

The Prophet of Islam, Hazrat Muhammad (PBUH) had been devoting most of his time in meditation in the seclusion of cave Hira. One day, when he was absorbed in it, he had his first revelation. Angel Gibrael revealed to him the first commandment of God, contained in Sura *Iqra* of the Holy Quran.

Muhammad (PBUH) was highly excited with his new experience and came home trembling with fear. He lay down on his bed with an attack of fever.

His wife, Khadija, was much concerned with his unusual condition. She attended to him and enquired the reason of his excitement. Muhammad (PBUH) narrated the whole story relating to the strange experience of his first revelation.

Elated, Khadija congratulated him on being elevated to the highest position of Prophethood saying, "Be consoled, God will never forsake you". She was the first to embrace the new religion, Islam.

Khadija, daughter of Khuwailid of Quraish family of Abd-al-Uzza, had the distinction of being the first wife of Muhammad (PBUH).

She was a rich widow endowed with exceptionally good qualities of head and heart. In the pre-Islamic days, due to her virtuous life, she was known by the name of Tahira. According to *Tabaqaat ibn Saad*, she was the richest woman of Makkah.

Muhammad (PBUH) who had been doing business independently, was known throughout the Hejaz for his honesty, integrity and morality. In recognition of his good qualities, the people began to call him *"Ameen"* (Trustworthy).

Khadija, too, was attracted by the brilliant qualities of young Muhammad (PBUH) and took him in service. He was sent to Busra with her merchandise. On return, after three months, she proposed the marriage. Muhammad (PBUH) was 25 and Khadija was 40 years old at that time.

Arab women in those days exercised free volition in respect of matters pertaining to their marriage, therefore Khadija held a direct talk with Muhammad (PBUH) on the matter. On the appointed day, Muhammad's (PBUH) relatives, who included his uncle Abu Talib and Hamza assembled at the house of Khadija. Abu Talib delivered the nuptial address.

The Prophet did not marry any other woman during her lifetime. She lived for 25 years after her marriage with Muhammad (PBUH) and died three years before the Hejirat.

Khadija bore him six children—two sons, Qasim and Abdullah, who died in infancy and four daughters, namely Fatima Zahra, Zainab, Ruqayya and Umme Kulsoom. It was with reference to Qasim that the Prophet was sometimes addressed as Abul Qasim (Father of Qasim).

Khadija's daughter Zainab was married to her cousin. Her daughters, Ruqayya and Umme Kulsoom were married to the Third Caliph Usman one after the death of the other. Khadija's daughter Fatima Zahra who was the dearest daughter of the Prophet was married to Hazrat Ali. The lineage of the Prophet progressed through her sons Hasan and Husain.

The Prophet had all his issues by Khadija except Ibrahim who also died young.

The house in which Khadija lived was purchased by Ameer Muawiya and converted into a mosque which still bears the name of the great lady.

The Prophet cherished greatest regard and love for Khadija. Even after her death, he remembered her frequently with love and gratitude. "When all other persons opposed me", he said, "she supported me, when all were infidels, she embraced Islam. When none was my helper, she helped me."

Her great wealth and high status proved very useful for the propagation of Islam. The majority of Muslim religious leaders acclaim Khadija, Fatima and Aisha as the three greatest women in Islam. They class Fatima as the first, Khadija as the second and Aisha as the third highest and greatest woman in Islam.

According to Hafiz ibn Qayyim, a disciple of Imam ibn Taimiya, if one considers the relationship with the Prophet, Fatima stands on the top, if one takes into account the priority in accepting Islam and the moral as well as the material support given to the new religion, Khadija to the first position, but in matters of learning and service rendered occupies the propagation of the Prophet's teachings, none stands in comparison to Aisha.

A number of traditions of the Prophet of Islam are in praise of Khadija. According to *Sahih Muslim,* there are two women occupying the highest position in the eyes of God : Mariam (Mary) and Khadija.

# AISHA SIDDIQA

Small care-free girl, nine years old, was playing merrily with her mates. Her hair had gone disarray and her face was covered with dust. Suddenly a few elderly persons emerged on the scene from a neighbouring house. They took the girl home with them, dressed her neatly and the same evening she was married to the greatest of men, the Prophet of Islam a unique honour that ever fell on a woman.

Hazrat Aisha was the beloved daughter of Hazrat Abu Bakr, the faithful Companion of the Prophet who succeeded him as the first Caliph of Islam. She was born in Makkah in 614 A.C., eight years before the commencement of the Hejira era. Her parents had already embraced Islam. They brought up and trained her from her very childhood in conformity with the highest traditions of the new religion which fully prepared and entitled her to her later exalted position.

She remained with the Prophet for ten years. She was very young, when betrothed to the Prophet, but she acquitted herself extremely well and proved herself an intelligent, faithful and loving wife of the greatest benefactor of mankind. She is universally recognised as the most authentic reporter of the traditions of the Prophet and the teachings of Islam, as propounded by him. She was blessed with a proverbial memory and retained whatever questions were asked by the female callers to the Prophet and the replies given by him. She retained fully the lectures delivered by the Prophet to the delegations and congregations in the Mosque of the Prophet as Hazrat Aisha's room adjoined the Mosque. She attentively listened to the addresses, lectures and discussions of the Prophet with his Companions and other people. She also made queries to the Prophet on delicate and intricate matters relating to the tenets of the new religion. These immensely contributed to her becoming the greatest and most authentic scholar and reporter of the traditions of the Holy Prophet and the tenets of Islam.

Hazrat Aisha was not destined to live with the Prophet for long. The union lasted ten years only when the Prophet died in 11 A.H., 632 A.C. and was buried in the room occupied by her.

The Prophet was succeeded by his faithful Companion, Hazrat Abu Bakr, as the first Caliph of Islam. Hazrat Aisha continued to enjoy the position of the first lady and after Hazrat Fatima's death in 11 A.H., she was universally recognised as the most important woman in the Muslim world. But her father, Hazrat Abu Bakr, too, did not live long and died 2½ years after the death of the Prophet.

During the reign of Hazrat Umar Farooq, the Second Caliph, Hazrat Aisha enjoyed the status of the first lady of the rapidly expanding dominions of Islam and her wise counsels were sought and respected on all important matters. The martyrdom of Hazrat Umar, the second Caliph, and later of Hazrat Usman, the third Caliph, shook the foundations of the new State and led to a tragic division among the Muslims. It proved extremely harmful for the fast expanding and developing religion, which by this time had spread up to the confines of the Atlas Mountains in the West and the heights of Hindu Kush in the East.

Hazrat Aisha could not remain a silent spectator to the disintegrating factors. She sincerely sided with those who were clamouring for avenging the martyrdom of the Third Caliph. In the 'Battle of Camel' fought against the Fourth Caliph Hazrat Ali, her forces were defeated and she had to retreat to Medina under a guard provided by the Caliph's sons themselves.

A number of interested historians, Muslims and non-Muslims alike, have criticised Hazrat Aisha's role in fighting against the Fourth Caliph, but none have doubted her sincerity of purpose and her conviction in avenging the blood of Hazrat Usman.

Hazrat Aisha witnessed the vicissitudes through which the new religion passed during the thirty years of the Pious Caliphate. She died in 678 A.C., during the reign of Amir Muawiya. The Amir, under whom the Islamic Caliphate was giving place to a temporal power, was extremely afraid of Hazrat Aisha and her outspoken criticism of the politically changing state of Islam.

The First Lady of Islam was distinguished for her multifarious qualities— piety, learning, wisdom, simplicity, generosity and the care with which she safeguarded and faithfully reported the traditions of the Prophet.

Her simplicity and modesty continue to serve as a guiding light to all Muslim ladies thereafter. She lived in a room hardly 12 x 12 feet along with the Prophet of Islam. The room had a low roof covered with date leaves and branches plastered with mud. The only entrance to the room had no shutters and an ordinary curtain was hung over it. There were hardly three successive days during the lifetime of the Prophet, when Hazrat Aisha had a full diet. The night when Prophet breathed his last, she had no oil to light her lamp, nor anything to eat.

During the Caliphate of Hazrat Umar when the important Companions of the Prophet and his wives were sanctioned substantial monthly honorarium, Hazrat Aisha seldom kept the money and gifts she received for the second day and promptly distributed these among the needy. Once, during the month of Ramzan, when Hazrat Abdullah ibn Zubair presented her a purse of one lakh dirhams she distributed these before breaking her fast.

Hazrat Aisha was a well-known orator of her time. Her services to popularies and promote the knowledge of traditions and *fiqh* (Islamic jurisprudence) have few parallels in the annals of Islamic history. Whenever a difficult problem of tradition or *fiqh* was encountered which defied solution, the matter was ultimately referred to her and her word was final. Apart from Hazrat Ali, Hazrat Abdulla ibn Abbas and Hazrat Abdulla ibn Umar, she is regarded as the greatest intellect of early Islam.

The great lady of Islam breathed her last on 17th Ramzan, 58 A.H. July 13, 678 A.C. Her death cast a gloom over Madina and the entire Islamic world.

Hazrat Aisha has been bracketed with Hazrat Khadija and Hazrat Fatima-az-Zahra as a most distinguished woman of Islam. Most of the religious scholars and theologians place Hazrat Fatima on the top, followed by Hazrat Khadija with Hazrat Aisha as last. Allama ibn Hazm ranks her only second to the Prophet of Islam—above all his wives, Companions and relations. According to Allama ibn Taimiya, Hazrat Fatima occupies the highest place, being the most beloved daughter of the Prophet. Hazrat Khadija is great because she was the first to embrace Islam. But there is none to rival Hazrat Aisha in her role in popularising the teachings of the Prophet.

# FATIMA AZ-ZAHRA

Once while Prophet Muhammad (PBUH) was in his mosque at Medina, surrounded by his Companions, suddenly his beloved daughter, Fatima, wedded to the famous warrior-scholar of Islam, Hazrat Ali, arrived there. She implored her father to lend her a servant who could assist her in household work, as she, with her frail constitution and poor health, could not perform the strenuous duties of grinding corn and bringing water from the distant well, besides looking after her children. The father, ostensibly moved by her pleading hesitated for a moment, but repressing his emotion, he told her solemnly: "My dearest daughter! I cannot spare anyone from among those who are engaged in the service of *Ashab-e-Suffa.* You should be able to bear the hardships of this world in order to get the reward of the world hereafter". The daughter went back, well satisfied with the reply of the Prophet and never sought any servant again during her lifetime.

Fatima az-Zahra, the beautiful, was born 8 years before Hejira in Makkah. Her mother Hazrat Khadija, was the first and most respected wife of the Prophet. He did not marry any other woman during her lifetime. Fatima was the fourth and the youngest daughter of her mother. Others were Zainab, Ruqqaya and Umme Kulsoom. The last two were married to Hazrat Usman, who became the Third Caliph of Islam.

Fatima was brought up under the fostering care of her father, the greatest teacher and benefactor of mankind. Unlike other children she possessed a sober and somewhat melancholy temperament. Her weak constitution and frail health kept her away from the children's get-togethers and games. Her great father's teachings, guidance and inspiration, developed her into an extremely cultured, amiable, sympathetic and enlightened lady.

Fatima who greatly resembled her father in countenance and saintly habits was his most beloved daughter and had been immensely devoted to him after her mother's death. In this way, she, to a great extent, made up the loss of her mother.

The Prophet, on several occasions, gave expression to his extreme fraternal love for Fatima. Once he said: "O Fatima! God will not like a person who displeases you and will be pleased with a person who wins your favour".

On another occasion, the Prophet is reported to have said: "Fatima is my child. One who distresses her, distresses me and one who comforts her comforts me."

Hazrat Aisha, the beloved wife of the Prophet, once said: "I have never come across a greater personality than that of Fatima except that of her father, the Prophet of Islam."

On an enquiry she once replied: "Fatima was the one whom the Prophet loved most. She was dearest to him."

Hazrat Abu Bakr and Hazrat Umar both sought her in marriage but the Prophet kept quiet. Hazrat Ali, who was brought up by the Prophet himself and who combined in him the rare virtues of chivalry and bravery, piety and scholarship, hesitated to seek Fatima in marriage due to his poverty. But, at last he took courage to put forward the proposal which was readily accepted by the Prophet. Ali sold his beautiful cuirass which he had won in the battle of Badr for 400 dirhams and made arrangements for the nupital ceremony, which was extremely simple. Evidently the primary object underlying the celebration of the great event with simplicity, was to impress upon the Muslims the need for celebrating marriages unostentatiously.

Fatima was hardly 18 years old at the time of her marriage with Ali. All that she got in her dowry from her illustrious father was a leather water carrier, an earthen pitcher, a mat and a corn grinding stone.

Addressing his daughter, the Prophet said, "My daughter, I have married you to a person who had stronger faith and is more learned than others and one who is distinguished for his morality and virtues."

Fatima's married life was smooth and simple. Indefatigable and persevering as he was, Ali laboured hard all day long to earn his livelihood, while his industrious, frugal and devoted wife laboured at home, performing her household duties which included grinding of corn and carrying of water from the well. This ideal couple was known for their piety and generosity. They never turned away a beggar from their door without giving him whatever they had. At times, they gave away their entire food to a beggar and themselves remained hungry.

The humanitarian and benevolent nature possessed by the House of Prophet has few parallels in the annals of mankind. Fatima Zahra, the youngest daughter of the Prophet of Islam, was known for her benevolence.

Once a person belonging to the Bani Salim tribe, who was reputed to be a magician, came to the Prophet of Islam and exchanged hot words with him. The Prophet, on the other hand, returned the strangers abuse, with kind words. The magician was so much moved by this unusual behaviour that he embraced Islam. The Prophet asked him if he had anything to eat. On the stranger replying in the negative, the Prophet asked the Muslims present there if there was anyone who could present him a camel. Hazrat Sa'ad ibn Ibada offered him a camel. The Prophet was much pleased and asked if anyone could offer his brother in Islam a cloth to cover his bare head. Hazrat Ali, instantly, took off his turban and placed it on the stranger's head. Thereafter, the Prophet directed Hazrat Salman to take him to some Muslim who could feed him as he was hungry.

Salman led the new convert to several houses but none could feed him at this unusual hour. Suddenly, Salman came upon the house of Hazrat Fatima and, knocking her door, informed her the purpose of his visit. With tears in her eyes the daughter of the Prophet informed him that she had nothing to eat in her house for the last three days. Still the daughter of the Prophet was reluctant to refuse a guest saying:

"I cannot send back a hungry guest without satisfying his hunger". Taking off her sheet of cloth, she gave it to Salman imploring him to take it to Shamoon, a Jew, and in its return bring some corn. Salman as well as the new convert were much moved by the angelic behaviour of the daughter of the Prophet. The Jew, who was also highly impressed by the benevolence of the Prophet's daughter, embraced Islam, saying that *"Torat* has informed us about the birth of this virtuous family".

Salman brought corn to the Prophet's daughter, who herself grinded and baked loaves of it. On a suggestion by Salman that she should keep some loaves for her hungry sons, the Prophet's daughter replied that she had no right over it as she had given her cloth for the sake of God.

The Prophet's beloved daughter was blessed with five children—three sons, Hasan, Husain and Mohsin and two daughters, Zainab and Umme Kulsoom. Hasan was born in the 3rd and Husain in the 4th year of Hejira. Mohsin died young. Both Hasan and Husain were the favourites of the Prophet who often carried them on his shoulders. They even sat on his back during his prostration in prayer. These two sons of Fatima and daughter Zainab later played a significant and memorable role in the history of Islam.

Fatima tended her father's wounds in the battle of Ohad. She also accompanied him during his conquest of Makkah and also during his farewell pilgrimage towards the end of 11 A.H.

The Prophet fell seriously ill soon after his return from the farewell pilgrimage. Fatima stayed at his bedside. He whispered something in her ears which made her weep and later whispered something which made her smile. After his death in 11 A.H., she related the incident to Hazrat Aisha, saying that when her father told her that he was going to die, it made her weep, but when he told her that she would be the first person to join him in the next world, it made her happy.

Fatima could not survive the Prophet long; she passed away during the same year, six months after his death. She was 28 at the time of her death and was buried by Ali in Jannat-ul-Baqih (Madina) amidst universal mourning.

Fatima who represents the embodiment of all that is divine in womanhood—the noblest ideal of human conception was proclaimed by the Prophet to be the "Queen of Women in Paradise."

# RABIA BASRI

Rabia Basri is one of the earliest mystic saints of Islam. She renounced her worldly life and devoted herself entirely to praying God.

Both in a humble family of Basra in 713 A.C., she was the fourth daughter of her parents. A strange story is related about her birth. On the night of her birth, there was nothing in the house—not even oil to light the house, or a small rag to swaddle the newly born child. Her mother implored her father to borrow some oil from a neighbour. This was a moment of trial for the poor father, who had promised to God not to extend his hand for help before any mortal being. Reluctantly he went to a neighbour's house, tapped his door, but there was no reply. He thanked God for being able to keep his promise. He came back and went to sleep. That night he had a dream in which the Prophet of Islam congratulated him on his newly born child who was destined to rise to a great spiritual position in Islam.

Rabia lost her parents at an early age. Her three sisters also died in a famine which ravaged Basra. She fell into the hands of a tyrant who sold her as a slave for a paltry sum. Her new master was no less a tyrant.

Little Rabia spent most of her time in carrying out the orders of her master. She spent the nights in praying. One night her master detected signs of her spiritual greatness. She was praying to God: "Almighty, You have made me the slave of a human being and I am duty bound to serve him. Had I been free I would have devoted every moment of my life to praying to You". Suddenly a halo of sacred light encircled her head and her master was awe-stricken to see this sight. The next morning he set her free.

Rabia, being free, retired to a secluded place, for a life of meditation. Later she moved to a cell near Basra. Here she led a strictly ascetic life. A worn out mat, an earthen pot and a brick formed her entire belongings.

She wholly devoted herself to prayers, had only a wink of sleep before the dawn and regretted even that much.

A number of good offers of marriage were made to her. These included those from the Governor of Basra and the celebrated mystic saint, Hasan Basri.

But Rabia was so much devoted to God that she had little time for worldly affairs, hence she declined them.

Rabia had many eminent desciples including Malik bin Dinar, Raba-al-Kais, Shaikh al-Balkhi and Hasan of Basra. They often called on her to seek her counsel or prayers or listen to her teachings.

Once Hazrat Sufian Soori, a respected and devout Muslim came to Rabia, raised his hands and prayed: "Almighty, I seek worldly welfare from Thee". Rabia wept over it. When asked for it, she replied: "The real welfare is acquired after renouncing the world and I find that you seek it in this world only".

A person once sent forty dinars to her. She wept and raised her hand towards the sky: "You know it well that I never seek worldly welfare from you, although You are the Creator of the world. How can I then accept money from a person who is not the real owner of it?"

She enjoined her disciples not to disclose their good work to anyone and to conceal it just as they conceal their evil deeds.

Considering illness as her Lord's will, Rabia always bore it with exemplary courage and fortitude. No pain however severe ever disturbed or distracted her in devotion to God. She often remained unaware of the injury, until pointed out by others. One day she struck her head against a tree and started bleeding. Someone drew her attention to it saying, "Don't you feel pain"? "I am entirely devoted to God. I am fully in communion with Him: He has made me occupied with things other than you generally perceive," she replied calmly.

Rabia was the foremost mystic to preach disinterested love for God—a concept which was later adopted by other mystics. She would often urge: "I do not serve God for any reward—have no fear of hell or love of paradise. I will be a bad servant if I serve for material benefit. I am duty bound to serve Him only for His love."

Once someone asked her whether she hated Satan. She replied: "No, the love of God has left no room for the hatred of Satan."

She was a mystic of a very high stature and belonged to the first group of Muslim mystics. She enriched Islamic literature by expressing her mystical experiences in high class verses.

She died in Basrah in 801 A.C. and was buried in the house in which she lived. Her funeral was attended by a large number of saints, sufis and devout Muslims.

There are many things and sayings attributed to

When questioned by someone as to why she did not seek help from her friends, she replied, "I should be ashamed to ask for this world's good from Him to Whom it belongs, then why should I seek anything from those to whom it does not belong."

"Will God forget the poor because of their poverty or remember the rich because of their riches? Since He knows my state, there is hardly any need for me to pin-point His attention to it. What He Wills, we should also will".

Miracles were attributed to her as to other Muslim saints. Food was supplied to her guests by miraculous means. It was said that when she was dying, she bade her friends to depart and leave the way free for the messengers of God. As they went out, they heard her making confession of faith to which a voice responded: "O Soul be at rest, return to thy Lord, satisfied with Him, giving satisfaction to Him".

Among the prayers recorded of Rabia, is one which she offered at night upon her roof. "O, my Lord, the stars are shining and the eyes of men are closed and the kings have shut their doors and every lover is along with his beloved and here am I alone with Thee".

Again she prayed: "O, my Lord, if I worship Thee from the fear of hell, burn me therein, and if worship Thee for hope of paradise, exclude me therefrom, but if I worship Thee for Thine own sake, then withhold not from me Thy Eternal Beauty".

# RELIGIOUS TEACHERS, LEGISTS AND TRADITIONISTS

# IMAM JAFAR SADIQ

The durbar of the majestic Abbaside Caliph, Al-Mansur, was packed to its capacity. The venerable Fatimid Imam Jafar Sadiq had been summoned by the Caliph who was afraid of his growing popularity and sought some pretext to denigrate and punish him.

At last a haggard and slim person entered the durbar and without making the customary obeisance advanced towards the Caliph. To the great astonishment of the entire audience, which expected some harsh words from the Caliph, the latter stood up to pay respects to the learned Imam and seated him by his side.

Incidentally the Caliph was pestered by a fly which kept teasing him. He enquired from the Imam :

"What is the purpose of creating flies?"

"Simply to humble the pride of despots," was the prompt reply.

The hot-tempered Caliph was all courtesy to the reverend Imam and when he was leaving, Al Mansur asked him if he could be of any service to him. Imam Jafar Sadiq replied: "The only service I seek from you is that I should not be given the trouble to attend your durbar again."

Imam Jafar Sadiq, son of Imam Muhammad Baqir, was the great grandson of Hazrat Ali. His mother was the great grand daughter of Hazrat Abu Bakr. He is recognised as the sixth Fatimid Imam (Spiritual Leader).

He was born in Medina on 7 Rabiul-Awwal, 53 A.H. (699/700 A.C.) at a time when the world of Islam was passing through a critical time. Spiritual as well as moral values of this great religion had reached their lowest ebb. The great intellectual and spiritual luminaries who had lit the world of Islam had disappeared, a number of them were eliminated by the degenerated and tyrannical Umayyad rulers.

Imam Jafar was brought up by his pious and learned grandfather, Imam Zainul Abdeen and his talented father, Imam Muhammad Baqir who gave him the best possible spiritual as well as intellectual training.

He was born in the reign of the Umayyad Caliph, Abdul Malik, son of Marwan and witnessed the reign of 10 Umayyad and two Abbaside Caliphs.

Imam Jafar Sadiq rose to be one of the greatest intellects of Islam who dedicated his life to the spiritual and intellectual development of the community. He played no part in politics and was celebrated for his piety and knowledge of tradition, alchemy, astronomy and other sciences. His *Madrassa* (School) at Medina attracted people from all over the Islamic world. Amongst his pupils were some of the greatest intellectuals—jurists and scientists—including outstanding legists like Imam Abu Hanifa and Imam Malik; traditionists like Sufian Suri and Saidul Ansari and also Jabir bin Hayyan, the greatest chemical scientist of Islam.

The *Madrassa* of the Imam which played a historical role in educating some of the greatest intellectual giants of Islam occupied a high place among the great educational institutions of early Islam. In Medina, the Imam's house and the Prophet's mosque were great educational and research centres. These housed a very simple-looking university, where students ensconced on mattresses, received all sorts of spiritual, moral and material education. They were taught theology, metaphysics and astronomy and all other sciences known to the world. Names of more than 4,000 students who attended the Imam's *Madrassa* are mentioned in records. According to historians, students from all parts of the world of Islam were attracted towards this great seat of learning in Medina. After receiving education from the great Imam, they went back to their places and diffused the light of learning throughout the known world.

"These are four: Firstly, none should be allowed to do my work, which I can do myself. Secondly, I know that God sees everything I do. This keeps me modest and always terror-stricken from doing anything repugnant to the tenets of Islam. Thirdly, it is a part of my faith that no one can deprive me of my subsistence which God has granted me. Therefore, I am fully satisfied and do not worry for my livelihood. Fourthly, I know that I have to die one day, I am, therefore, always prepared for it."

Imam Jafar Sadiq is distinguished for reporting cent per cent authentic traditions of the Prophet. It is on account of his truthfulness and sincerity in reporting traditions that he has been given the surname of *Sadiq* (Trustworthy) by the Muslims.

Being highly self-respecting and principled he never curried favour with the Umayyad and Abbaside Caliphs who always tried to seek his favour and goodwill.

He was endowed with tremendous patience and forbearance. He always returned good for evil and in this way followed the example of the Prophet of Islam. In piety and generosity, he was the true son of his great family and kept up its high traditions. No amount of trial or temptation could deflect him from the right path.

The great Imam breathed his last in Medina in 756 A.C. and was buried in Jannat-ul-Baqih. He was succeeded by his son Musa al-Kazim who is recognised as the 7th Fatimid Imam.

His death cast a gloom over the world of Islam. Answering a question, the Abbaside Caliph Mansur said: "The real leader of Muslims, the most learned man and theologian has left this world." According to Imam Abu Hanifa, "He was the greatest scholar of Islamic theology and jurisprudence." Imam Malik says: "My eyes have not seen a more learned, pious, God-fearing man than Imam Jafar Sadiq". Sheikh Kamaluddin Muhammad bin Talha Shifai admits that "he was an ocean of learning and was the stream of Quranic teachings". Allama Momin observes that "Imam Jafar's attributes are innumberable which cannot be described in words." According to Jabir bin Hayyan: "There can hardly be a better teacher than him in the world"

Some of his recorded adages are :

"The greatest quality of a virtue is that one should make haste to perform it, should try to surpass it and should not disclose it."

"One should try to do good to others in order to save himself from domination by Satan."

"People are recognised by their families in the world, but in the next world one's good deeds will only be recognised."

"One who is contented with his lot and what God has given him will always feel satisfied, while one who is greedy of others' wealth will always remain a beggar."

# IMAM ABU HANIFA

The glorious period of the Caliphate Rashida lasting 30 years will go down in the history of mankind as the most successful experiment of democratic rule in the world, in which there was hardly any distinction between the ruler and the ruled. Notwithstanding his being the Head of the mightiest Empire of his time, Umar the Great refused to taste wheat unless it was available to every citizen of his vast dominions. This golden epoch of Islamic democracy was, however, shortlived and the evil forces which lay dormant under the exemplary rule of the Iron Caliph, raised their head during the reign of Yazid. The noble descendants of the Prophet had to make supreme sacrifice without precedent in history in order to hold aloft the banner of truth and virtue in the world. Brutal political persecution of his opponents started by Yazid, was relentlessly continued by tyrant Hajjaj bin Yusaf. Even such venerable persons as Hasan Basri and Anas bin Malik could not escape the wrath of the Umayyad rulers and their lieutenants. The two and half years' rule of Umar bin Abdul Aziz, who endeavoured to revive the traditions of his maternal grandfather Farooq-e-Azam, was only a glimmer in the vast gloom of evil, which at last prevailed over it.

In such a dark atmosphere was born Hazrat Imam Abu Hanifa who valiantly braved the persecution by the ruling class and never budged from the right path.

Abu Hanifa Al-Numan ibn Tabit, the greatest authority on Muhammadan canon law, was born in Kufa in 80 A.H. (699 A.C.), in the reign of Abdul Malik bin Merwan. He was a non-Arab of Persian extraction. His grandfather, Zauti, embraced Islam and presented Tabit, his son, to Hazrat Ali, who prayed for the glorification of his family which ultimately took shape in the form of Imam Abu Hanifa. The Imam saw the reign of ten Umayyad Caliphs including that of Umar bin Abdul Aziz who ruled when the Imam was eighteen years of age. He also saw two Abbaside Caliphs Saffah and Mansoor. The notorious tyrant Hajjaj bin Yusuf, the great persecutor of Muslims died when Imam Abu Hanifa was 15 years of age.

During his childhood, Hajjaj was the Umayyad viceroy of Iraq. The venerable Imams and religious leaders who wielded great influence with the Arabs were made the main targets of his persecutions. Primarily occupied with his commercial occupations during the Caliphate of Waleed, the Imam paid little attention to education. But during the reign of Sulaiman, when education received state patronage and people showed greater inclination towards learning, Abu Hanifa developed a penchant for acquiring religious knowledge. An interesting story is told about the beginning of his studies. One day while he was passing through the Bazaar he came across Imam Shebi, a well-known Kufi Divine, who casually questioned him about his literary pursuits. Receiving the reply in the negative, Imam Shebi felt sorry and advised young Hanifa to devote his time to studies. Imam Abu Hanifa took the advice to his heart and whole-heartedly plunged himself into studies and soon amassed knowledge of theology and jurisprudence. In those times, literature, *Fiqh* and *Hadith,* were the only subjects taught. The associations with Persian, Syrian and Egyptian savants enlarged the scope of Arabian studies. Philosophy and logic entered the sphere of religious doctrines which is termed as *'Kalaam'.* Abu Hanifa, who was gifted with a keen sense of reasoning and exceptional intelligence, acquired great fame as interpreter of religious doctrines. Hammad, who was one of the greatest Imams of the time, owned the biggest school in Kufa. Abu Hanifa joined his school. Hammad was impressed by the intelligence, perspicaciousness and extraordinarily retentive memory of the new pupil who soon became his favourite. Out of great regard for his learned teacher, Abu Hanifa did not open any school during the lifetime of Hammad, in spite of his great reputation as a unique jurist. Makkah and Medina, Kufa and Basra were the great centres of learning in those times. The venerable Companions of the Prophet and their illustrious associates resided in these cities and adorned their literary circles. Kufa, which was founded during Umar's Caliphate as an Arab colony, had the distinction of being the Capital of Ali. It was inhabited by more than one thousand Companions of the Prophet, including twenty-four who had participated in the battle of Badr. It grew to be the famous centre of *Hadith,* and Imam Abu Hanifa took full advantage of the presence of the celebrated *mohaddis* (teacher of *Hadith)* there. According to Abul Mahasin Shifai, Imam Abu Hanifa had learned *Hadith* from as many as 93 teachers. He attended the lectures of Ata bin Abi Rabah and Imam Akrama who were reputed teachers of *Hadith.* They held Abu Hanifa in high esteem.

The Imam went to Medina in 102 A.H., in pursuit of knowledge and attended the lessons of seven top theologians. The celebrated Imam Musa Kazim and his illustrious son Imam Jafar Sadiq the descendants of the House of the Prophet, were the greatest authorities in Islamic learning of their times and Imam Abu Hanifa took full advantage of their society in Medina. He was highly impressed with erudition of Imam Jafar Sadiq whom he acknowledged as the most learned man in the world of Islam. Imam Abu Hanifa also attended the classes of Imam Malik who was thirteen years younger to him. It was his good fortune that Umar bin Abdul Aziz had organised the study and recording of *Hadiths* on a sounder footing. Before the Caliphate of Umar bin Abdul Aziz, the record of *Hadiths* was confined to the memory of the people. In a letter addressed to the learned men of Medina in 101 A.H., he requested them to preserve in writing the record of *Hadiths.* Imam Zahri furnished the first collection of *Hadiths.* The teaching of *Hadiths,* too, had undergone a revolutionary change. From his pulpit the learned teacher discoursed on the subject of which the pupils assembled round him with pen and paper carefully took down the notes. Imam Abu Hanifa had learnt *Hadiths* from more than four thousand persons.

It redounds to the credit of Imam Abu Hanifa that he left behind the greatest number of pupils in the world of Islam, including Qazi Abu Yusuf, Imam Muhammad, Hafiz Abdur Razzaq, Abdullal bin Al Mubarak, Abu Neem Fazal, and Abu Asim who acquired great fame in their days. Qazi Abu Yusuf rose to be the Grand Qazi of Abbaside Caliphate during the time of Haroon-ar-Rashid.

Imam Abu Hanifa was deeply impressed by the reformatory ideas of Umar bin Abdul Aziz, who had, to a great extent, revived the pristine glory of Islam.

The principal occupation of Imam Abu Hanifa was business. He carried on a flourishing trade of textile goods. His success in commercial enterprises was largely due to his absolute honesty in business transactions. He was so much trusted by all that even non-Muslims deposited their wealth with him. He did not believe in excessive profits. and never tolerated to earn money through illegal and questionable means.

Once he sent a few pieces of cotton goods to one Hafs bin Abdur Rahman with a word that some of the pieces were defective of which the customer should be apprised. Hafs forgot to do so and disposed of all the pieces. This deeply shocked the Imam who by way of atonement gave away the entire sum amounting 30 thousand dirhams in charity.

Once a woman brought to him a piece of *Haz* (costly cloth) for disposal. She demanded hundred dirhams as its price. She was wonderstruck with his honesty when he paid her five hundred dirhams for the piece.

The prices of commodities kept in his shop were fixed. Once in his absence, some of his pupils unknowingly sold certain articles at relatively higher prices. When he learned about it on return, he resented it very much, saying they had cheated the customer. Meanwhile the customer who was an inhabitant of Medina, had left Kufa. It is stated that the Imam himself undertook a journey to Medina and paid him the balance.

Contrary to the general tendencies prevalent among the wealthy class of people, Imam Abu Hanifa was exceedingly kind-hearted. It is stated on the authority of celebrated mystic saint Shafiq Balkhi that once while he was accompanying Imam Abu Hanifa they sighted a person who suddenly turned to another lane. Thereupon the Imam called him out why he was turning to the other side. The man stopped; he was in a flurry of spirits. On being accosted, he said that he could not face the Imam as he owned him ten thousand dirhams which he could not afford to pay back. Being deeply moved, the Imam, told the debtor that he need not bother to pay him back. Not only that, he apologised to the borrower for causing him so much distraction. Such was the humanitarianism of our Imams, which is unparalleled in the annals of the world.

The Imam was very popular among the masses who loved and respected him. This greatly irritated and upset the lieutenants of the Umayyad Government, who hired hooligans in order to tease and malign him. Once a mercenary hoodlum intruded in the social gathering of the Imam and began to criticise and abuse him. His pupils wanted to oust him forcibly, but he prevented them from doing so. When he started for home, the hooligan followed him and went on abusing him to the very door steps of his house. Halting at the gate, he addressed him, "Brother, I am entering my house; you will not be able to get in. Please abuse me to your heart's content before I step in."

The Imam was very much annoyed with a drunkard neighbour, who used to call names the whole night in a drunken state. His neighbours were fed up with his objectionable behaviour. One day, the police caught hold of him and put him behind the bars. In the evening, when the Imam got back home, he inquisitively asked as to why the drunkard had assumed silence. On learning that he was imprisoned for his misbehaviour, he at once called on the Governor who was taken aback at the unexpected visit of the Imam. The Imam apprised him of the whole matter and secured the release of the drunkard on his surety. On being free, the Imam said to the drunkard, "Brother, we do not want to lose you at any cost." The drunkard was so much struck with the angelic behaviour of the Imam that he abstained from wine for ever and became one of the famous pupils of the Imam.

The powerful Umayyad and Abbaside rulers tried to win his favour, but he always kept away from them. He scrupulously avoided association with corrupt and tyrannical administrators. Mansur, the Abbaside Caliph, once offered him a high sum as a gift which he declined, saying that it was repugnant for him to share the money of *Baitul Mal* which was public property and should go to the needy.

Mansur offered him the high post of Grand Qazi of his vast Empire, bluntly replied, "Supposing a complaint is lodged against you in my court and you want it to be decided in your favour, otherwise I would be thrown into the river: then please rest assured that I would prefer to be drowned in the river rather than tamper with justice." This outspoken curt reply of the Imam silenced the Caliph for the time being.

Imam Abu Hanifa possessed exceptional qualities of head and heart. He could never be purchased or cowed down by the ruling power. Ibn Hubaira, the Umayyad Governor of Kufa, once requested him to pay him occasional visits for which he would be highly grateful to him. Since he abhorred corrupt rulers, he frankly replied, "Why should I meet you? If you favour me, I would be associating myself with your evil. If you persecute me you would add to my insults. I do not aspire for any position or wealth. Whatever God has given me am content with it."

There had been some dispute between the Abbaside Caliph Mansur and his wife Hurra Khatun. The Khatun wanted the matter to be referred to Imam Abu Hanifa. The Imam was summoned by the Caliph and his wife also sat behind the curtain; The Caliph asked the Imam, "How many wives at a time are allowed in Islam?" The Imam replied, "Four." Mansur cried out to his wife, "Did you listen what the Imam said? The Imam at once said, "But this is subject to one condition. A man is empowered to marry more than one provided he is capable of doing equal justice to all of his wives." The last part of Imam's reply went against the interests of the Caliph. On reaching home in the evening he found a man waiting for him with a bag of guineas and a letter of thanks from the wife of the Caliph. The Imam returned the money with the remarks that it was his duty to speak the truth without any fear or favour.

The Imam lost his father in his childhood, but his mother survived till his old age. He respected and served her devotedly.

Yazid bin Umar bin Hubaira, Governor of Kufa, during the Caliphate of Merwan II, persuaded the Imam to accept some respectable job in the Government which he refused. The Governor swore that he would have to do his bidding, but the Imam stuck to his words. Thereupon he was put behind the bars, and was flogged everyday under orders of the Governor. He was released after a few days, and left Kufa for Hejaz where he stayed for 2½ years, until the Umayyad Caliphate was replaced by the Abbasides.

Hakam, son of Hisham, the Umayyad Caliph, once said, "Our Government offered two alternatives to Imam Abu Hanifa—either to accept the keys of our treasuries or to get his back flogged, but the Imam preferred the latter."

The Imam pinned rosy hopes on the Abbaside Caliphate. On the accession of Safah, the 1st Abbaside Caliph he had returned to his native town Kufa from Hejaz. But soon he was disillusioned for the Abbasides, turned out to be equally bad, if not worse for him. They stepped up his persecution. On transferring his Capital from Hashmiya to Baghdad, Mansur, the second Abbaside Caliph offered him the post of Grand Qazi. The Imam flatly declined it saying that he was not fit for it. The Caliph indignantly shouted, "You are a liar." The Imam retorted, "You have upheld my contention. A Liar is unfit for the post of a Qazi." The Caliph became non-plussed and swore that he would have to accept the post of the Grand Qazi. The Imam too swore that he would not. The whole Durbar wondered at the boldness of the Imam. Rabi, a courtier explained, "Abu Hanifa, you have taken the oath of allegiance to the Amirul Momineen." The Imam promptly replied, "But it is easier for the Caliph to compensate for his oath."

Thereupon the Imam was thrown into a dark prison in 146 A.H. There he was poisoned. Under the effect of poison he prostrated in prayer and died. The news of his death soon spread throughout Baghdad. The whole citizenry came out to pay their last homage to their greatest Imam. More than fifty thousand people participated in his first funeral prayer. His funeral prayer was offered six times. According to the historian Khatib, the funeral prayers of the Imam were offered for twenty days after his burial. Commenting on his death, Sheba bin Hajjaj said, "Night has settled over Kufa."

His grave for a long time was a place of pilgrimage for the Muslims. Sultan Alp Arslan Suljuki built a tomb over it as well as an attached school to it. Ibn Batuta, the celebrated explorer of Asia saw this school when he visited Baghdad and was highly impressed by its good management as well as its boarding facilities.

Imam Abu Hanifa has the distinction of being the greatest legist of Islam. Being the highest authority of Islamic canon law, his disciples and followers from a majority in the Islamic world. He has left behind him three works namely (1) *Fiqh Akbar*, (2) *Al Alim Wal Mutaam* and (3) *Musnad*. *Fiqh Akbar* is a brief magazine, which is very popular.

He founded a body of intellectuals, of which he was the President, to counsel on the codification of Islamic doctrines and to transform the Islamic Shariat in the form of law. According to Khwarizmi, "The number of sections of Islamic law framed by him is more than 83 thousands of which 38 thousands are related to religious matters and 45 thousands dealt with worldly affairs."

Though the Imam has not left behind any collection of *Hadith,* he occupies a high place as a *Muhaddis.* Imam Malik is the author of *'Muwatta',* a book of *Hadith* which is well-known in the Islamic world. Imam Ahmed bin Hanbal was also a celebrated *Muhaddis* of his time.

The exponents of *Hadith (Muhaddis)* were divided in two groups—Those who collected the *Hadith* (sayings of the Prophet) from various sources and those who critically examined the authenticity of those sources and interpreted them according to their knowledge. The second group was called the *Mujtahid* and Imam Abu Hanifa belonged to this group. The Imam was the greatest legist of Islam who gave a sounder basis to *Fiqh.* Imam Abu Hanifa and Imam Malik have laid down similar conditions for appraising the authenticity of *Hadith.* It is said that *Muwatta,* the celebrated work of Imam Malik originally contained more than ten thousand *Hadith,* but the number of *Hadith* was reduced to seven hundred only on subsequent revision of the book by Imam Malik. Once Imam Shafii said, "Hazrat Abu Bakr had reported only seventeen *Hadith* from the Prophet, Hazrat Umar reported about fifty, Hazrat Usman and even Hazrat Ali who was so closely related to the Prophet had reported very few *Hadith. "* The *Hadith* which are against commonsense should not be accepted. This was the criterion which Imam Jozi in the 6th century A.H., followed for distinguishing between authentic and non-authentic *Hadith*. During the time of Imam Abu Hanifa too much reliance on commonsense for distinguishing between the authentic and non-authentic *Hadith* was resented, but the Imam followed this principle to a great extent and during the later centuries his principles were universally accepted.

Imam Abu Hanifa has left behind scores of wise sayings some of which are as follows :—

(1)    No person has sustained greater loss than that whose learning could not restrain him from indulging in vices.

(2)    A person who talks of religion and does not think that he will have to account for what he says, does not know the meaning of religion and his conscience.

(3)    If the religious people are not the friends of God then God has no friends in this world.

(4)    A person who attains knowledge for the benefit of the world, his knowledge does not take root in his heart.

(5)    To have learned discourses with a person who has no sense of knowledge is to annoy him unnecessarily.

The greatest contribution of Imam Abu Hanifa is to *Fiqh* or Islamic jurisprudence. He is the most outstanding legist of Islam, whose *Fiqh* Hanafi is followed by the majority of Muslims of the world, including those of Turkey, Egypt, Turkistan, Afghanistan and Indo-Pakistan sub-continent. He rejected most of the traditions as untrue and relied solely on the Quran. By 'analogical deductions' he endeavoured to make the simple Quranic verses applicable to every variety of circumstances. Writing in *"The Spirit of Islam"*, Ameer Ali, the celebrated historian says: "He was a speculative legist, and his two disciples, Abu Yusuf, who became Chief Qazi of Baghdad under Harun, and Muhammad Ash-Shaibani, fixed Abu Hanifa's conception on a regular basis."

The Imam occupies the same place in *Fiqh* which Aristotle occupies in Logic. Actually he formulated the Islamic jurisprudence in a scientific manner. Shah Wali Ullah of Delhi has written a fine article describing the history of *Fiqh*. According to him, the Companions of the Prophet of Islam never enquired from him about his action. Ibn Abbas says that the associates of the Prophet did not ask the explanation of more than 13 doctrines from the Prophet during his lifetime. The Prophet was scrupulously and faithfully followed by his Companions. After the death of the Prophet the conquests of the Arabs spread over the three continents and new problems in religious matters cropped up, which had to be solved through the commonsense of the learned Muslims.

The Hanafi *Fiqh* being too liberal and practical soon gained much popularity among the masses. It also received the patronage of Abbaside, Saljuki and other Muslim ruling dynasties. The pupils of the Imam, who held important posts of Qazi during the Abbaside Caliphate also immensely contributed to its propagation.

Besides the above, there are other inherent factors which made Hanafi *Fiqh,* so popular among Muslim masses as well as among the intelligentsia. The secret of its popularity lies in its being more rational, intelligible, liberal and universally applicable.

# IMAM MALIK

During his visit to Medina, the celebrated Abbaside Caliph Haroon-ar-Rashid, wished to attend the lectures on *Muwatta* (collection of Traditions) delivered by Imam Malik. He sent for the Imam who sermonised him: "Rashid, Tradition is a learning that used to be patronised by your forbears. They had utmost regard for it. If you don't venerate it as Caliph, no one else would. People come in search of knowledge but knowledge does not seek people." At last the Caliph himself came to attend the lectures of the Imam, which were attended by all classes of people. Haroon wanted others to leave the class, but the Imam opposed it saying, "I cannot sacrifice the interest of the common man for that of an individual". Hence the great Caliph as well as his sons had to sit alongside the common people and listen patiently to the Imam's illuminating discourse on the Traditions of the Prophet.

Medina, the seat of Islamic learning in those times, boasted of some of the greatest intellectuals of the age. One of them was Imam Malik, a great traditionist, who left behind him ineffaceable marks in the sphere of Arabian learning. His *Muwatta* occupies an outstanding place among the rare collections of Traditions. Being a teacher of exceptional merits, Imam Malik occupies a unique place in the Islamic history as the originator of Maliki School of Jurisprudence which exercised great influence on the contemporary and later generations of Islam, particularly those inhabiting Africa and Spain. With his indomitable will, courageous and incorruptible soul, which never yielded even to the highest authorities of the state, the Imam belonged to a class of early Muslims, whose life would always serve as a beacon light for those who strive for the realisation of nobler and higher virtues in the world.

Malik ibn Anas, belonged to a respectable Arab family which held important social status before and after the advent of Islam. His ancestral place was Yemen, but after the birth of Islam, his ancestors who were converted to Islam migrated to and settled in Medina. His grandfather, Abu Aamir was first in his family to embrace Islam in 2 A.H. The date of Imam's birth is a disputed point among the historians. Ibn Khalikan has given 95 A.H., but as universally believed the Imam was born in 93 A.H., and he was 13 years younger to his illustrious counterpart Imam Abu Hanifa. He received his education in Medina, which in those times was the highest seat of learning in the vast Islamic Empire and housed most of the distinguished Companions of the Prophet. He, therefore, had no need to go out of Medina in quest of knowledge. His grandfather, father and uncle were all Traditionists, who coached the young Imam in traditions and other branches of knowledge. Other illustrious intellectual luminaries who taught the young Imam were Imam Jafar Sadiq, Muhammad bin Shahab Az Zahri, Nafeh, Yahya bin Saeed and Rabi Rayi.

Imam Malik continued to serve the noble cause of education for 62 years. He died on 11th Rabi-ul-Awwal 179 A.H., at the age of 86.

Teaching, which was looked upon as the noblest profession, was adopted by some of the greatest intellectuals that the world has produced, including Aristotle and Plato, Ghazzali and Ibn Khaldun, Imam Abu Hanifa and Imam Malik. The high reputation of Imam Malik as a scholar and teacher attracted people from the four corners of the vast Islamic Empire. Perhaps no other teacher ever produced such talented scholars who ascended the pinnacle of glory in different walks of life. Among the persons who benefited from his learning were Caliphs like Mansur. Mehdi, Hadi, Haroon and Mamun; legists like Imam Abu Hanifa, Imam Shafii, Sufian Suri and Qazi Muhammad Yusuf; scholars like Ibn Shahab Zahri and Yahya bin Saeed Ansari; mystics like Ibrahim bin Adham, Zunnun Misri and Muhammad bin Fazil bin Abbas. According to reliable historical sources, the number of his students who acquired great name in life was more than 1,300. His classes were characterised by their serenity, discipline and high sense of respect, exhibited by the students for their learned teacher. He never tolerated any indiscipline when he lectured on the traditions of the Prophet. Once, the Abbaside Caliph, Mansur who was discussing certain traditions with the Imam spoke a bit loudly. The Imam rebuked him saying, "Don't talk stridently when the Traditions of the Prophet are under discussion." He refused to discourse on the Traditions in the camp of the Caliph.

The Imam left behind him more than a dozen works including his world famous *Muwatta,* which is considered as second to the Holy Quran. His treatises deal with religious, ethical matters and Islamic jurisprudence. *Muwatta* is universally acknowledged as the most important book in the Library of Islam after the Holy Quran. According to Shah Waliullah, it is a collection of the most authentic traditions of the Prophet selected by Imam Malik after thorough investigation of their sources. The Imam compiled his book after a thorough verification and sifting of the Traditions and included only those which he considered correct. The reliability of the reports and reporters were his chief consideration and he took pains to ensure that no incorrect report found place in his book. Formerly, *Muwatta* included ten thousand Traditions, but in the revised edition, the Imam reduced the number to 1,720 only. This book has been translated into several languages and has sixteen different editions.

As a traditionist he occupies a unique place among the galaxy of talented scholars like Imam Bukhari and Muslim who are well-known for collecting the Traditions of the Holy Prophet of Islam. He is said to have always avoided the company of a person who was not highly learned. According to Imam Hanbal, he was the only person to have such a distinction, never reported a tradition from a person unless he had fully satisfied himself. He was held in such high esteem by the later scholars that once someone enquired from Imam Hanbal about a certain reporter. He replied that the reporter must be reliable because Imam Malik had reported from him. Imam Malik experienced great hardship in quest of knowledge. Like Imam Bukhari, who had once to live on herbs and roots for three days, he too, had to sell the beams of his house in order to pay his education dues. He used to say that one could not attain the heights of intellectual glory, unless faced with poverty. Poverty was the real test of man; it awakened in him the hidden energies and enabled him to surmount all difficulties.

His contemporaries and later traditionists and religious scholars have formed very high opinion about his intellectual attainments. According to Abdur Rahman ibn Mahdi, there is no traditionist greater than Imam Malik in the world. Imams Ahmad bin Hanbal and Shafii speak very highly of him as a Traditionist. The learned Imam was also a great legist; for more than 60 years he gave *Fatwas* in Medina.

Imam Malik was known for his integrity and piety. He always lived up to his convictions. Neither fear nor favour could ever deflect him from the right path. He was among the members of the glorious society of early Islam who could not be purchased and whose undaunted courage always proved as a guiding star for the freedom fighters.

When he was aged 25, the Caliphate passed into the hands of the Abbasides. Caliph Mansur who was his colleague highly respected him for his deep learning. The Imam, however, favoured the Fatimid Nafs Zakriya for the exalted office of Caliph. When he learned that the people had taken the oath of fealty to Mansur, he said that since Mansur had forced people to do so, the oath was not binding on them. He quoted a Tradition of the Prophet to the effect that a divorce by force is not legal. When Jafar, a cousin of Mansur, was posted as Governor of Medina, he induced the inhabitants of the Holy city to renew their oath of allegiance to Mansur. The Governor forbade him not to publicise his *Fatwa* in respect of forced divorce. Highly principled and fearless as he was, he defied the Governor's orders and courageously persisted in his course. This infuriated the Governor, who ordered that the Imam be awarded 70 stripes, as punishment for flouting his authority. Accordingly, seventy stripes were inflicted on the naked back of the Imam which began to bleed. Mounted on a camel in his bloodstained clothes, he was paraded through the streets of Medina. This brutality of the Governor failed to cow down or unnerve the noble Imam. Caliph Mansur, when apprised of the matter, punished the Governor and apologised to the Imam.

Once, Caliph Mansur sent him three thousand Dinars as his travelling expenses to Baghdad, but he returned the money and refused to leave Medina, the resting place of the Prophet.

In 174 A.H. Caliph Haroon-ar-Rashid, arrived in Medina with his two sons Amin and Mamun. He summoned Imam Malik to his durbar for delivering a lecture on *Muwatta*. The Imam refused to comply with his orders. Arriving in the durbar, he told the Caliph, "Rashid! Tradition is a learning cultivated and patronised by your ancestors, if you don't pay it due respect, no one else would." This argument convinced the Caliph, who preferred to attend the class taken by the Imam along with his two sons.

The Imam was reputed throughout the world of Islam for his self-control and great patience. Once a band of Kharijis armed with swords forced their way into a mosque of Kufa, where he was praying. All persons scampered away from the mosque in panic but he stayed there undismayed. It was customary with all those who waited on Caliph Mansur in his durbar to kiss his hands but Imam Malik never stooped to this humiliation. On the other hand, he paid highest respects to the learned people and once, when Imam Abu Hanifa came to see him, he offered him his own seat.

Muslims inhabiting Western Arabia, exclusively subscribe to the Maliki sect.

# IMAM SHAFII

The Third Imam, Abu Abd Allah Muhammad bin Idrees, better known as Imam Shafii, who is the founder of Shafii School of *Fiqh* (Islamic jurisprudence), belonged to the Kuraish tribe, was a Hashimi and remotely connected with the Prophet of Islam. He was born in 767 A.C. in Ghazza. He lost his father in his childhood and was brought up in poverty by his talented mother.

In Makkah, the young Imam, learnt the Holy Quran by heart. He spent considerable time among the bedouins and acquired a thorough grounding in old Arab poetry. Later, he studied Tradition and *Fiqh* from Muslim Abu Khalid Al-Zinjii and Sufyan ibn Uyaina. He learnt *Muwatta* by heart when he was only thirteen.

When about 20, he went to Imam Malik ibn Anas at Medina and recited the *Muwatta* before him which was very much appreciated by the Imam. He stayed with Imam Malik till the latter's death in 796 A.C.

His poor financial condition obliged him to accept a government post in Yemen, which was a stronghold of Alids who were much suspected by the Abbaside Caliphs. He was involved in Alid intrigues and was brought as a prisoner along with other Alids before the Abbaside Caliph, Haroon-ar-Rashid, to Rakka in 803 A.C.

The Caliph, on learning the Imam's arguments in his defence set him free with honour. In Baghdad, he became intimate with the celebrated Hanafi Scholar Muhammad ibn al Hasan al Shaibani.

Later, in 804 A.C., he went to Syria and Egypt *via* Harran. He was given an enthusiastic welcome in Egypt by the pupils of Imam Malik. He spent six years in teaching jurisprudence in Cairo and arrived in Baghdad in 810 A.C. where he set up successfully as a teacher. A large number of learned scholars of Iraq became his pupils. In 814 he returned to Egypt but, as a result of disturbances, was soon compelled to leave for Makkah.

He returned to Egypt in 815/16 A.C. to settle down finally there. He died on January 20, 820 A.C. (29 Rajab 204 A.H.) and was buried in the vault of Banu Abd al Hakam at Fustat amidst universal mourning.

His tomb which was built by the Ayubid Ruler al Malik al-Kamil in 1211/12 A.C. is a favourite place of pilgrimage.

Like his predecessors, Imam Abu Hanifa and Imam Malik, Imam Shafii too refused to become Qazi (Judge) of the Abbaside regime. The years spent by him in Iraq and Egypt were the periods of his intensive activity. He spent most of his time in writing and lecturing. He was very methodical in his daily life and had systematically divided his time for different types of work and he seldom deviated from this routine.

"Al Shafii", states the *Encyclopaedia of Islam*, "may be described as an eclectic who acted as an intermediary between the independent legal investigation and the traditionalism of his time. Not only did he work through the legal material available, but in his *Risala,* he also investigated the principles and methods of jurisprudence. He is regarded as the founder of *'Usual al Fikh'.* Unlike Hanafis, he sought to lay down regular rules for 'Kiyas', while he had nothing to do with 'istihsan'. The principle of 'ishtibah', seems to have been first introduced by the later Shafiis. In al-Shafii two creative periods can be distinguished, an earlier (Iraqi) and a later (Egyptian)".

In his writings he made a masterly use of dialogue. He elucidates the principles of jurisprudence in his *Risala* and has tried to adopt a mean between the Hanafii and Maliki jurisprudence. The collection of his writings and lectures in *"Kitabul Umm"* reveals his master intellect.

The main centres of his activity were Baghdad and Cairo. First of all he follows the Quran, then the Sunnah. The most authentic Traditions of the Prophet are given the same consideration by him as Quran. He was very popular among the traditionists and the people of Baghdad called him the *"Nazir-us-Sunnat"* (exponent of the Traditions of the Prophet).

Imam Shafii who combined in himself the principles of Islamic jurisprudence as well as the fluent language of the people of Hejaz and Egypt was matchless both in conversational and written language. His writings can favourably be compared with those of the best writers of Arabic language of his time, including Jahiz.

The teachings of Imam Shafii spread from Baghdad and Cairo to distant parts of Iraq, Egypt and Hejaz. The most notable of his pupils were al-Muzani, al-Buwaiti, al-Rabib Sulaiman, al-Maradi, al-Zafarani Abu Thawr, al-Humaidi, Ahmad ibn Hanbal and al-Karabisi.

During the third and fourth century A.H., the Shafiis won more and more of adherents in Baghdad and Cairo. In the fourth century, Makkah and Medina were the chief centres of Shafiite teachings besides Egypt.

The Shafiite School became predominant under Sultan Salahuddin Ayyubi. But Sultan Baibars gave recognition to other Schools of *Fiqh* also and appointed judges of all the four Schools.

Before the advent of the Ottoman power, the Shafiites held absolute pre-eminence in the Central lands of Islam. During the beginning of the 16th century A.C. the Ottomans replaced Shafii with Hanafi Imams. Nevertheless Shafiite teachings remained predominant in Egypt, Syria and Hejaz. It is still largely studied in Al-Azhar University of Cairo. The Shafiite *Fiqh* is still largely followed by the Muslims in South Arabia, Bahrain, Malay Archipelago, part of East Africa and Central Asia.

# IMAM HANBAL

The grand Durbar of the greatest of the Abbaside Caliphs, Mamun ar-Rashid, at Tarsus, was packed to its capacity. A frail bodied person, with a resolute look and a calm countenance, was carried forward by the guards, through a long row of distinguished courtiers, officials and religious scholars. The person was Ahmad ibn Hanbal who had been summoned by the Caliph, an exponent of the Mutazellite doctrine of the creation of Quran.

The Caliph asked him if he accepted the Mutazellite doctrine about the creation of Quran.

"No", replied Ahmad ibn Hanbal firmly, "The Quran is the world of God. How can it be treated as a creation?"

The Caliph tried to argue with Ahmad bin Hanbal supported by several religious scholars but the Imam was adamant and refused to change his views, which were in conformity with the faith of the Prophet and his Companions. He was, therefore, put behind the bars.

Imam Ahmad ibn Muhammad ibn Hanbal, the founder of the Hanbali School of Muslim jurisprudence, is one of the most vigorous personalities of Islam, which profoundly influenced both the historical development and modern revival. The celebrated theologian, jurist and traditionist, Ahmad ibn Hanbal, was "through his disciple Ibn Taimiya, the distant progenitor of Wahabism. He inspired also in certain degree the conservative reform movement of the Salafiyya" *(Encyclopaedia of Islam)*.

Born at Baghdad on the 1st of Rabi-ul-Awwal, 164 A.H. (December 780 A.C.) Ahmad ibn Hanbal was an Arab, belonging to Bani Shayban of Rabia, who had played an important role in the Muslim conquest of Iraq and Khorasan. His family first resided at Basra. His grandfather Hanbal ibn Hilal, Governor of Sarakhs, under the Omayyads had his headquarters at Merv. Ahmad's father Muhammad ibn Hanbal, who was employed in the Imperial Army in Khorasan, later moved to Baghdad, where he died three years later.

Ahmad who had become an orphan at a very early age, inherited a family estate of modest income. He studied jurisprudence, Tradition and lexicography in Baghdad. There he attended the lectures of Qazi Abu Yusuf. His principal teacher was Sufyan bin Uyayna, the greatest authority of School of Hejaz. Later, he was much influenced by Imam Shafii and became his disciple. From 795 A.C., he devoted himself to the study of Tradition and made frequent visits to Iran, Khorasan, Hejaz, Yemen, Syria, Iraq and even to Maghrib in quest of authentic Traditions of the Prophet. He made five pilgrimages to the holy cities.

According to Imam Shafii, who taught *Fiqh* (Islamic jurisprudence) to Ahmad ibn Hanbal, the latter was the most learned man he had come across in Baghdad.

The way Imam Ahmad ibn Hanbal withstood the trials and tribulations of the Abbaside Caliphs for 15 years on account of his opposition to the officially supported Mutazillite doctrine of the creation of Quran, is a living tribute to Imam's high character and indomitable will which has immortalised him as one of the greatest men of all times.

The Abbaside Caliph, Mamoon ar-Rashid, was, in his last days, much influenced by the rationalist doctrines of Mutazillites, including that of the creation of Quran, and gave an official support to it. The distinguished religious leaders and divines, one after another, succumbed to the views of the Caliph. It fell to the lot of Imam Ahmad bin Hanbal to oppose this doctrine vigorously and suffer for it, which immensely added to his popularity and immortalised him as one of the greatest exponents of the true faith.

The Abbaside Caliph, Mamoon ar-Rashid died shortly after the imprisonment of Imam Ahmad. He was succeeded by Al-Mutasim, who summoned the Imam and asked the same question about the creation of Quran. Still strongly refusing to accept this Mutazillite doctrine, he was severely flogged and thrown into prison. He was, however, allowed to return home after two years. During the reign of the succeeding Abbaside Caliph, Wasiq, he was not permitted to preach his faith and was compelled to live in retirement. All these hardships failed to detract him from the righteous path.

The sufferings of the Imam ended when Al Mutawakkil became the Caliph and returned to the old traditional faith. The Imam was invited and enthusiastically welcomed by the Caliph who requested him to give lessons on Traditions to the young Abbaside Prince, al-Mutazz. But the Imam declined this offer on account of his old age and failing health. He returned to Baghdad without seeing the Caliph and died at the age of 75 in Rabi-ul-Awwal of 241 A.H. (July 855 A.C.). He was buried in the Martyrs' cemetery, near the Harb gate of Baghdad. "His funeral was attended by millions of mourners and his tomb was the scene of demonstrations of such ardent devotion that the cemetery had to be guarded by the civil authorities and his tomb became the most frequented place of pilgrimage in Baghdad" *(Encyclopaedia of Islam)*.

Imam Ahmad laid greater emphasis on Traditions. His monumental work is

*Musnad,* an encyclopaedia containing 28,000 to 29,000 Traditions of the Prophet in which the Traditions are not classified according to the subject as in the Sahihs of Muslim and Bukhari, but under the name of the first reporter. His other notable works are: *"Kitab-us-Salaat* (Book on Prayer); *"Ar-radd alal-Zindika"* (a treatise in refutation of Mutazillites, which he wrote in prison); and *'Kitab-us-Sunnah"* (Book in which he expounds his creed).

Though the fundamental purpose of the Imam's teaching may be seen as a reaction against the codification of *Fiqh,* his disciples collected and systematised his replies to questions which gave birth to the Hanbali *Fiqh,* the fourth School of Muslim jurisprudence.

The Hanbali School which was exposed throughout its history to numerous and powerful opponents came into prominence under the teachings of its greatest exponent, Imam ibn Taimiya, who denounced the veneration of saints and worshipping of tombs. Later, it was further renovated by the Saudi Arabian reformer, Abdul Wahab, who greatly popularised it in Saudi Arabia.

# IMAM BUKHARI

Few persons in the world have ever been endowed with a proverbial memory. One of these was Imam Bukhari, the greatest Traditionist that Islam has produced. He is said to have retained in his memory one million Traditions with full details of all the different sources and reporters of each Tradition which came down to him. His *Sahih Bukhari* (Collection of Traditions) is universally recognised as the most authentic collection of Traditions of the Holy Prophet of Islam.

Abu Abdullah Muhammad ibn Ismail, later known as Imam Bukhari, was born in Bukhara on Shawwal 13, 194 A.H. (July 21, 810 A.C.) He was the grandson of a Persian, named Bradizbat.

The newly-born child had scarcely opened his eyes in the world when he lost his eyesight. His father was immensely grieved by it. His pious mother wept and prayed to God to restore the eyesight of her newly-born child. During her sleep, she dreamt Prophet Abraham, who said: "Be pleased, your prayer has been accepted by God." When she got up, the eyesight of the newly-born child was fully restored.

He lost his father when he was still a child. He was brought up by his illustrious and virtuous mother.

He began his study of the Traditions at the early age of eleven. In his 16th year he made pilgrimage of the Holy places along with his mother and elder brother. There he attended the lectures of the great teachers of Traditions in Makkah and Medina. He was still 18 years old, when he wrote a book, *"Kazayai Sahaba wa Tabain."*

His elder brother, Rashid ibn Ismail reports that the young Bukhari used to attend the lectures and discourses of learned men of Balkh along with him and other pupils. But, unlike other pupils he never took notes of these discourses. They criticised him for not taking notes of the lectures and thus wasting his time. Bukhari did not give any reply. One day, being annoyed by their consistent criticism of his carelessness, Bukhari asked his fellow pupils to bring all they had noted down. By that time, his fellow pupils had taken down more than 15 thousand Traditions. Young Bukhari, to the amazement of all, narrated all the 15 thousand Traditions from his memory with minutest details which were not noted down by the pupils.

He, then started on a study pilgrimage of the world of Islam, which lasted 16 years. Of this period, he spent five years in Basra, visiting Egypt, He_1az, Kufa and Baghdad several times and wandered all over Western Asia in quest of knowledge and learning. During his travels he reported Traditions from 80,000 persons and with the help of his exceptional memory he could retain these Traditions with all their sources in his mind to be penned down at an opportune time.

The fame of young Bukhari had soon reached the distant parts of the Islamic world and wherever he went he was received with great veneration. People were wonderstruck by his deep learning and extraordinary memory.

A large number of learned and pious men throughout the world of Islam became the disciples of young Bukhari. These included Sheikh Abu Zarah, Abu Hatim Tirmizi, Muhammad ibn Nasr, Ibn Hazima and Imam Muslim.

Imam Darami, who was a spiritual teacher of Imam Bukhari admits that his learned pupil had deeper insight into the Prophet's Traditions. He was the wisest among the creation of God during his time.

Imam Bukhari devoted not only his entire intelligence and exceptional memory to the writing of this momentous work, *"Sahih Bukhari"*, he attended to the task with utmost dedication and piety. He used to take bath and pray whenever he sat down to write the book. A part of this book was written by the learned Imam, sitting by the side of Prophet's grave at Medina.

Imam Bukhari returned to his native place, Bukhara, at last and was given a rousing reception by the entire populace of this great cultural city. But he was not destined to live here for long. He was asked by the Ruler of Bukhara to teach him and his children the Traditions of the Prophet at his Palace. This he declined and migrated to Khartanak, a town near Samarkand. Here he breathed his last on Ramzan 30, 256 A.H. (August 31, 870 A.C.).

The entire populace of the town and the vicinity came out to pay their last homage to one of the greatest sons of Islam, whose *"Sahih Bukhari"*, ranks only second to the Holy Quran. His grave in Khartanak is still a favourite place of Muslim pilgrimage.

His monumental work, *Al Jami-al-Sahih,* popularly known as *Sahih Bukhari* established his reputation as the greatest Traditionist in Islam. It is recognised as the most authentic source material on Sunnah.

It is said that Imam Bukhari had retained in his memory one million

Traditions of the Holy Prophet of Islam with all the details of their sources and reporters. Once his religious teacher, Sheikh Ishaq ibn Rahu urged that some-one might collect in a book, the most authentic Traditions of the Prophet of Islam. Imam Bukhari promised to fulfil his teacher's wish. Out of the million Traditions which he had learnt from 80,000 reporters, he selected 7,275 Traditions and, according to Ibn Hajar, 9,082, for his monumental work, *Sahih Bukhari*. He took 16 years to complete it.

This monumental work of Imam Bukhari has been acclaimed by thousands of traditionists, and erudite theologians as the best work on Prophet's Traditions. More than 53 commentaries, some of these in 14 volumes, have been written on *Sahih Bukhari*.

This book is divided according to the chapters of *Fiqh*, for which he had planned a complete scheme. In his selection of traditions, he showed the greatest critical faculty and in the editing of the text he tried to obtain the most scrupulous accuracy. Yet he did not hesitate to explain the material, at places, in short notes, which is quite distinct from the text and throws light on the environment obtaining at that time.

Imam Bukhari is the author of about two dozen other books on religion, Islamic philosophy and history. But his monumental work is *Sahih Bukhari*, whose hundreds of commentaries and translations have appeared in different languages during the last more than one thousand years. It is respected and recognised as the most important and essential book in the world of Islam after the Holy Quran.

# IMAM MUSLIM

The third century of the Hejira has been the most congenial period for the collection and development of Prophet's Traditions in the Muslim world. During this period as many as six well-known collections of Traditions, popularly called as 'Sahih' (authentic collections) saw the light of day. These included the 'Sahih' Bukhari and Sahih Muslim.

During this period, conditions were extremely favourable for the collection of Traditions. A certain unanimity had been attained on all disputed points, particularly on questions of law and doctrine and a definite opinion regarding the value of most Traditions had been formed by the well-known Muslim scholars. It was, thus, possible to proceed and collect all such Traditions which were generally accepted as reliable.

The most outstanding reporters of the Traditions had been Hazrat Aisha, Hazrat Abu Horaira, Hazrat Abdullah ibn Abbas, Hazrat Fatima az-Zahra, Hazrat Abdulla ibn Umar, Hazrat Abdulla ibn Masood, Hazrat Zaid ibn Sabit, Hazrat Uns ibn Malik and Hazrat Saeed ul Maseeb al-Makhzoomi. Several collections of Traditions were prepared by different scholars through these reporters. In the beginning, Traditions were arranged according to their transmitters and not according to their contents. The best known of such collections is the Musnad of Imam Ahmad ibn Hanbal. The best collection of Traditions of this period is the Muwatta of Imam Malik.

But, later the collections of Traditions were arranged according to their contents, more scientifically and conveniently. Such collections arranged according to chapters are called Musannaf (arranged). Six such collections of Traditions universally recognised by the learned Muslims as Sahih (authentic) appeared during the Third century A.H. These are the collections of (1) Imam Bukhari (died in 256 A.H.–870 A.C.), (2) Imam Muslim (died in 261 A.H.–875 A.C.), (3) Al Dawood (died in 275 A.H.–888 A.C.), (4) Al Tirmizi (died in 279 A.H.–892 A.C.), (5) Al Nasai (died in 303 A.H.–915 A.C.), and (6) Ibn Maja (died in 273 A.H.–886 A.C.). These books are recognised as authentic Traditions. Of these, the Sahih Bukhari and Sahih Muslim are held in high esteem in the Muslim world, ranking only second to the Holy Quran.

The merit of the collections of Imam Bukhari and Muslim lies not in the fact that they had been able to sort genuine Traditions out of a mass of circulating material on the subject, but because their collections were universally acclaimed as genuine, particularly by the learned and orthodox Muslims. The *Sahih Muslim* (authentic collection of Traditions by Imam Muslim) is considered only second to *Sahih Bukhari.*

Al Hajjaj Abul Husain Al Kushairi Al Nishapuri, better known as Imam Muslim, was born at Nishapur in 202 A.H., 817 A.C. or 206 A.H., 821 A.C. and died in 261 A.H., 857 A.C., and was buried at Nasarabad, a suburb of Nishapur.

After completing his education, Muslim set out to collect Traditions for his memorable work on the subject. He travelled extensively to collect Traditions in Arabia, Egypt, Syria and Iraq and consulted some of outstanding authorities on the subject, including Imam Ahmad ibn Hanbal and Ishaq ibn Rahuya. His *Sahih* is said to have been compiled out of more than three lakh Traditions collected by him. He also wrote a number of books on *Fiqh* traditionists and biographies, which are not extant at present.

His outstanding collection of Traditions, *Sahih Muslim,* is distinguished from other such collections in the matter that it is sub-divided into chapters. It is not difficult to trace in the order of Traditions in Muslim's *Sahih* a close connection with corresponding ideas of *Fiqh.*

Secondly, Muslim has paid particular attention to *Isnads* (chain of authentic reporters) which "serve as an introduction to either the same or to slightly different *Matn* (text). Muslim has been praised for his accuracy regarding this point." In other respects Bukhari's *Sahih* is superior to Muslim's, a fact which has been accepted by his great admirer, Al-Nawawi, who has written a copious commentary on Muslim's *Sahih,* which itself is a work of immense value on Muslim Theology and *Fiqh.* '

Imam Bukhari has added copious notes to his chapters, which are not found in Muslim's book. But both contain Traditions not only relating to the canon law, but also many ethical, historical and dogmatic traditions.

Muslim has written a learned introduction dealing with the Science of Traditions to his outstanding work, *Sahih Muslim.* The work, consisting of 52 chapters, deals with common subjects of Traditions—the five pillars of religion, marriage, barter, slavery, hereditary law, war, sacrifice, manners and customs of the Prophet and the Companions and other theological subjects. The book opens with a chapter, giving a complete survey of the early theology of Islam and closes with a short but comprehensive chapter on the Holy Quran.

# IMAM GHAZALI

Abu Hamid Al-Ghazali known as 'Algazel' in the West is one of the most eminent thinkers of Islam. He had the rare distinction of being appointed as the Principal of Nizamiah University of Baghdad, the greatest university in that period at an early age of 34 and later on turned into a sceptic and roamed about for 12 years in search of truth and mental peace, ultimately finding solace in "Sufism."

Al-Ghazali was born in 1058 A.C. in a small town of Khorasan called "Toos." His father was a yarn seller, hence he was nicknamed as "Ghazali," which is an Arabic word meaning yarn maker. Allama Samyani's contention that 'Ghazal' is a village of Toos where Ghazali resided does not stand the test of historical research.

In those days education was too liberal amongst common people. The highest type of education was within the reach of the humblest members of the society and all sorts of facilities for free education were provided for the common man. Out of the lowest societies have risen such intellectual giants of their age, like Imam Abu Hanifa who was a petty cloth merchant, Shamsul Aima who was a sweetmeat seller, Imam Abu Jafar who was a coffin stitcher and Allam Kaffal Morazi who was a blacksmith. Unfortunately, Ghazali's father was illiterate, and on his death bed, he entrusted his two sons to an intimate friend imploring him to give them proper education. The friend carried on the education for a certain period, but the funds deposited with him by Ghazali's father were soon exhausted and he was obliged to ask them to make their own arrangements. In those days there was no dearth of private institutions which were addressed by learned men. The expenses of the students including lodging and boarding were borne by the eliters of the place, hence, contrary to our times, when higher education is out of bounds of the poor, even the humblest had equal opportunities for obtaining highest education in those days. Ghazali also took full advantage of these golden opportunities and got his elementary religious education from a local teacher Ahmad ibn Muhammad Razkafi. Therefrom, he went to Jarjan where he received education from Abu Nasar Ismaili. An interesting story is related regarding the circumstances which served as an incentive for his educational progress. Once, on his way to his home town, he was robbed of his valuable lecture notes. Ghazali implored the leader of the robbers to return those papers, whereupon he laughed heartily and taunted that he had wasted all his energies if his education depended on a few papers only. These words had a salutary effect on Ghazali and he memorised all his lecture notes within three years.

Ghazali had to leave his home town for higher education. In those times Baghdad and Neshapur were the highest seats of learning in the East, which had the privilege of accommodating the two most celebrated teachers of Islam, namely Imamul Harmain who adorned the literary circles of Neshapur and Abu Ishaq Shirazi who glittered on the literary firmament of Baghdad. As Neshapur was nearer of the two, Ghazali became a pupil of Imamul Harmain.

Neshapur was a great centre of learning and Madrasa-e-Bakiath of Neshapur had the privilege of being the first University of the world of Islam. Nizamiah of Baghdad is wrongly believed to be the first university of the East as, long before its existence, several universities like Bakiath, Sadia and Nasiria founded by the brother of Mahmood Ghaznavi were functioning in Neshapur.

Ghazali was the most brilliant pupil of Imamul Harmain and soon acquired so much knowledge that he used to assist his teacher in his educational pursuits. He left Neshapur after the death of his celebrated teacher and by this time when he was hardly 28 he had acquired so much knowledge that he had no equal in the entire world of Islam.

The Caliphate of Abbasides was tottering, culminating in the formation of several Turkish principalities, including that of Saljuks who had founded the most powerful state of their times. The dynasty of Saljuks was distinguished for a succession of brilliant monarchs like Tughril, Alp Arsalan and Malik Shah who had kept aloft the dwindling candle of Islamic civilization. Malik Shah owed his historical greatness to his far-sighted Minister, Nizamul Mulk Toosi, one of the greatest administrators of all ages—one who was a great patron of learning and had the distinction of being the founder of the celebrated Nizamiah University of Baghdad. More than twenty million rupees were budgeted for education by the wise Minister. Hardly any ancient or modern state can boast of spending such a large portion on education out of the public exchequer. Ghazali's fame by this time had travelled to the distant corners of the Islamic world and he too attended the grand durbar of Nizamul Mulk whom he knew as a friend of men of learning. He was respectfully received by the eminent Vazier and he proved his mettle in scholastic discussions with learned men who had thronged the court of Nizamul Mulk, whereupon he was appointed as the Principal of the famous Nizamiah University of Baghdad at an early age of 34.

Ghazali was highly respected in both the great durbars of the Islamic World—the Saljuks and the Abbasides, which were the centres of Islamic glory and splendour. In compliance with the request of Abbaside Calip* Al-Mustazhar Billah, who, to some extent, was responsible for the emancipation and reorientation of Islamic religious thought, Ghazali wrote a book in reply to the dogmatic beliefs of *"Batinia'* cult and named it as *"Mustazhari"* after the name of the

Caliph. Shaikh Syed bin Al Faris, his favourite pupil, compiled the daily lectures of Ghazali in two volumes and it was named as *"Majalis-i-Ghazalia."*

*Spiritual Pilgrimage:* Ghazali was at last fed up with the artificiality and pomp and pageantry which pervaded the social life of Imperial Baghdad. He yearned for something else which was not available in the theoretical knowledge of enormous volumes which he came across in the highly literary circles of the city. He resolved to make a spiritual pilgrimage which, in itself, presents a fascinating story deserving to be better known in its details. He severed his connection with the social and Imperial circles, resorted to partial hunger strike, preserved a forced silence and even shunned the medical advices. His health began to fail him and rejecting all counsels, he left Baghdad wrapped in a rough blanket. The populace of the great Metropolis which had witnessed the pomp and the costly garments of their learned Imam were wonderstruck to observe him in his saintly attire. Ghazali had renounced his worldly pleasures and his inner self revolted against the futility of human life and the paucity of human knowledge. The story of his conversion to mysticism, as told by himself is a classic of its kind. He was a sceptic in his earlier life, but a mystical experience cured him of this malady and caused him to devote all his powers to the search of absolute truth. He did not get any light in the study of philosophy and scholastic theology, nor did the *'Talimis'* with their doctrine of an infallible religious authority, come off any better when put to the test. So he had to turn his attention to mysticism as revealed in the writings of *'Harith-al-Muhasbi,"* and the earlier mystics, and as he read, the truth dawned upon him. "I saw plainly," he says, that what is most peculiar to them (The Sufis) cannot be learned from books, but can only be reached by immediate experience, ecstacy and inward information," in other words, by leading the mystical life. He saw, too, that his own salvation was at stake, but his worldly prospects were brilliant, and it cost him a hard struggle to give them up. His health broke down under strain and at last he surrendered himself entirely, taking refuge with God, "as a man in sore affliction who has no resource left." He was not yet forty when he quitted Baghdad with the resolve never to return again.

Earlier, he had studied the works of the great mystic saints like Hazrat Junaid, Shibli and Bayazid Bustami, but, as this knowledge lies more in practice than in precept, he resolved to undergo the different phases of renunciations practised in mysticism. It was Ghazali's personal experience of this truth which he incorporated in his brilliant work *"Ihya-ul-Uloom,"* that inspired the great religious revival brought about in circles hitherto unfriendly to mysticism. Henceforward, he brought about a definite change in the mystic outlook towards Islam and he insisted that sainthood is derived from prophecy and constantly appealed to the supreme authority of Hazrat Muhammad (PBUH) whose law, according to him, must be obeyed both in letter and spirit.

Leaving Baghdad, Ghazali reached Damascus, the old capital of Umayyads and retired to a life of seclusion and prayer. He stayed there for two years and at times he returned to mystical topics in *Jamai Umayya* (the Grand Mosque of

Umayyads) which was virtually the University of Syria. Here he became the disciple of Shaikh Farmadi, the greatest mystic saint of his age who was highly respected throughout the length and breadth of Islamic world.

An interesting story is related about the cause of his leaving Damascus. One day he visited the *"Madarasa-i-Aminia"* of Damascus, where a lecturer who did not recognise Ghazali was profusely quoting from his books in his lecture. Ghazali left the city at once, lest he might not be recognised and bestowed honours which might arouse a sense of pride in him, a feeling which is strongly suppressed by mystics.

He arrived in Jerusalem and, therefrom he visited the eternal abode of Prophet Abraham and by the side of his grave, he resolved to stick to three things. Firstly, he would never attend the durbar of a king; secondly, he would never accept a present from a king; and thirdly, he would never take part in unnecessary scholastic discussions. He actually lived up to his determination and convictions. Therefrom, he set out on the pilgrimages of Makkah and Medina and stayed there for a long time. Leaving Hejaz, he toured Alexandria and Egypt. Ghazali roamed about for more than ten years visiting sacred places scattered over the vast Islamic domains.

According to Ibn-ul-Asir, Ghazali, during his tour wrote *"Ihya-ul-Uloom,"* his masterpiece which revolutionised and profoundly influenced the social and religious outlook of Islam in diverse ways. His intense prayers and devotion to God had purified his heart and revealed the divine secrets hitherto unknown to him.

Despite the incessant messages by the Abbaside Caliph and the durbar of Saljuks, requesting him to guide the literary and educational pursuits in their dominions, Ghazali refused to have any truck with the Ruling class and carried on his teaching activities in his home town till his death. He met a dramatic end in 505 A.H. (1111-A.C.) at Tehran. As usual, he got up early on Monday, offered his prayers and sent for his coffin. He rubbed the coffin with his eyes, and said: "Whatever may be the order of my Lord, I am prepared to follow." Saying this he stretched his legs, and when people looked at him, he was dead.

Ghazali set himself to study afresh the several systems of philosophy and theology and embodied his results in his works which were later translated into several European languages, especially in Latin. His books on Logic, Physics and Metaphysics became known through the translators of Toledo in the twelfth century A.C. According to Alfred Guillaume, "The Christian West became acquainted with Aristotle by way of Avicenna, Al Farabi and Alghazel, *Gundisalvus's Encyclopaedia of Knowledge* relies in the main on the information he has drawn from Arabian sources."

It is rather strange that Europe has paid greater attention to the works of Alghazali and preserved his invaluable literary and philosophical treasures.

His celebrated work, *Makasid ul Falasifa* (the purpose of philosophy) in which he has nicely arranged the problems of Greek philosophy is not traceable in Islamic countries. A copy of it is available in the Imperial Library of Spain, which has also been translated in the Spanish language. The book deals with different branches of philosophy namely logic, physics, ethics and metaphysics. Goshi, a German professor, has written a book about Alghazel in the German language, published in Berlin in 1858, in which he has quoted several pages out of Ghazali' *Makasid-ul-Falasifa*. A second book, entitled *Al Mankad min Alzalal*, in which Ghazali has penned the changes of his religious ideas and the facts about prophethood, was published in Arabic alongwith its French translation in France and M. Pallia and M. Schmoelder wrote commentary on it.

*Ihya-ul-Uloom* is the masterpiece of Ghazali. It is a classic by itself. Hardly any book can compete it in sincerity and effectiveness. Its every word, every thought, pierces the heart. Ghazali wrote this book at a time when he was intoxicated with the wine of mysticism and had forgotten his worldly existence, hence he expressed his experiences and sentiments without fear or favour. Allama Naudi writes in *Bustan* that Ghazali was a prolific writer and despite his exceptionally busy life, he maintained an average of writing 16 pages a day. According to Mohaddis Zainul Abadin, *"Ihya-ul-Uloom"* is the nearest approach to the Holy Quran. Al-Ghazali did not content himself with intermingling philosophy and ethics, but he expounded the ethical science to such an extent that in comparison to it the Greek Ethics pales into insignificance and looks like a drop in an ocean. In *"Ihya-ul-Uloom"*, he has freely dealt with and exposed the so-called philanthropists and social workers whose charitable and social actions are generally guided by selfish motives. He says: "A number of people build mosques, schools and inns and think they have done virtuous deeds. But the funds out of which the building in question was erected was obtained through questionable means and, even if the money invested was earned through moral sources, the motive behind the construction was popularity and not the service of humanity."

Ghazali diverted his attention towards the moral reformation of the nation. He tried to find out causes of social degeneration. He had a wide personal experience of the inner life of the ruling class as well as that of the religious heads and he has drawn his conclusions in these memorable words: "The morals of the subjects have deteriorated because the life of the ruling class has much degenerated which is ultimately, the result of the moral weakness of the religious leaders. The "Ulema" have sold their conscience in the lust of wealth and power."

Islam has laid the foundations of politics, culture and ethics on religion. This is why the religious leaders in the 1st century A.H. used to rule over the diverse sects comprising the Muslim Nation and thus people maintained their high sense of morality.

This high prestige of "Ulemas," to a certain extent, continued even up to the time of Ghazali and when Nizamul Mulk Toosi tried to obtain from the

"Ulema" certificates for his services to Islam, Abu Ishaq Shirazi complimented only so much, "Nizamul-Mulk is somewhat better than other tyrants." Ghazali tried to infuse the spirit of truth and straightforwardness in people's hearts. He freely and boldly propagated that it is the duty of the subjects to correct their ruler. Such interference in the affairs of the ruling class is not justified if it imperils the very existence of the state. If it endangers one's life only, it is virtuous. Such a person if killed for a noble cause will be a martyr.

The entire ethical philosophy of Ghazali rests on the foundation of mysticism. He had himself experienced the different aspects of worldly life, namely scholastic discussions, pride of high office, popularity among people and pomp and wealth. He had realised the effects of such contacts on one's character. He has described these experiences in *Ihya-ul-Uloom.* The writings of Ghazali influenced such great writers like Maulana Room, Shaikhul Ashraq, Ibn Rushd and Shah Waliullah, who have reflected the rational ideas of Ghazali in their works. Even the eminent Persian poets like Attar, Roomi, Saadi, Hafiz and Iraqi derived their inspiration from the writings of Ghazali and he was mainly responsible for infusing mysticism in Persian poetry and directing it towards right channels. He tried to reconcile the tenets of Islam with the teaching of prevailing philosophy and science. His masterpiece *"Ihya-ul-Uloom"* was widely read by Muslims, Jews and Christians and influenced Thomas Aquinas and even Blaise Pascal.

Ghazali, undoubtedly, is one of the greatest thinkers of Islam who has immensely contributed to cultivating the social, cultural, political, ethical and metaphysical outlook of Islam.

# IMAM IBN TAIMIYA

The thirteenth century A.C. is a period of great calamity in the annals of Islam. The Muslim world had hardly recovered from the ravages of the long-drawn-out Crusades, when it experienced a worst catastrophe. The Muslim countries were overrun by the Mongol hordes, destroying the intellectual and cultural treasures amassed during centuries of Muslim rule, and massacring millions of Muslims. Baghdad, the dream city of the famous Arabian Nights, which was the intellectual and cultural Metropolis of Islam, nay of the whole world—was sacked by Hulaku Khan, the Mongol, in 1258 A.C. and its entire cultural and intellectual heritage was burnt to cinders or thrown into the Tigris.

In such period of turmoil and holocaust was born Ibn Taimiya, a great religious thinker, who substantially and significantly influenced the subsequent Muslim thought. An independent thinker and an ardent believer in the freedom of conscience, one who was disputed by some but venerated by all, his life and works have since been a source of inspiration to all. His was a heroic life, which punctuated with trials and tribulations, sorrows and sufferings, was dedicated to the cause of religion, truth and the supremacy of individual conscience.

Young Ibn Taimiya, born in Harran, fled from the fear of Mongol hordes and arrived along with his parents in Damascus in 1268 A.C. He was hardly six years old at this time. Endowed with exceptional intelligence, penetrating intellect and wonderful memory, Ibn Taimiya mastered, at an early age, all the existing sciences, religious and rational jurisprudence, theology, logic and philosophy. This gave him the lead among all his contemporaries. In this, he was assisted and educated by his father, an eminent scholar of Hanbali *Fiqh*. Besides, he benefited from the learned discourses of Zain-al-Din Ahmad, al-Muqaddasi.

In 1282 A.C. when his father died, Ibn Taimiya succeeded him as the Professor of Hanbali Law and occupied this post with rare distinction for about 17 years. But his independent thinking, later won him the hostility of Shafite scholars and cost him his post. But, by this time, he had acquired immense popularity in the world of Islam and was commissioned to preach *jihad* against the Mongols who had overrun Syria and captured Damascus. His preachings galvanised the populace and obliged the Sultan of Egypt, Sultan al-Nasir, to take up arms against the so-called invincible Mongols. In a fierce battle at Marj-as-Safar, in 1302 A.C. in which Ibn Taimiya fought valiantly, the Mongols were routed with heavy losses.

Thenceforward, till his death, began a period of severe trials and tribulations for him. His independent views proved the bane of his life. He provoked opposition from many quarters and antagonised many divines. In 1307 A.C. he was imprisoned for four years along with his two brothers for attributing human characteristics to God. On release he was appointed Professor in a Cairo school founded by the Sultan of Egypt.

He' was, however, allowed to return to Damascus after seven years and reinstated in the post of Professor of which he had been relieved. But soon his serious differences with the Sultan on religious matters again led him to prison in 1320 A.C. for a few months.

A believer in the supremacy of the individual conscience, his independent thinking was not palatable to the orthodox and conventionalist Muslims. His virulent denunciation of the practice of worshipping saints and those who followed them resulted in the wrath of the Sultan who imprisoned him in the citadel of Damascus in 1326 A.C. Here he devoted himself to writing a commentary on the Holy Quran and other pamphlets on a number of controversial issues. He died in 1327 A.C. in prison. The news of his death cast a gloom over Damascus, and some 200,000 people including 15,000 women participated in his furneral. The funeral prayer was led by Ibn-al-Wardi.

The greatness of Ibn Taimiya lay in his selflessness and independent thinking. He was one of the greatest *mujtahids* Islam has produced, one who rejected *'taqleed'* and even *'Ijma.'* Belonging to the Hanbali School, he faithfully followed the Quran and Sunnah and like his religious ancestor, Imam Hanbal, he was uncompromising and an inveterate anthropomorphist.

The Greek sciences and arts were translated during the Abbasside period. Their problems were reconciled by Ibn Taimiya with the Islamic doctrines under the pressing demands of the new converts to Islam.

His greatest service to Islam lay in his impressing upon the people the necessity of their adopting the simplicity and purity of early Islam and implicitly following the Quran and the Sunnah. The basic principles of Ibn Taimiya's thoughts were :—

(1)   Revelation is the only source of knowledge in religious matters. Reason and intuition are but dependable sources,

(2)   The consensus of opinion of competent scholars during the first three centuries of Islam also contributed to the understanding of the fundamentals of Islam besides the Quran and Sunnah, and

(3)   Quran and Sunnah are the only authentic guides in all matters.

He discarded and emphatically denounced the corrupting foreign influence, which polluted the purity and simplicity of early Islam. It was from Ibn Taimiya that Muhammad ibn Abdul Wahab, a great thinker of the 18th Century, and the al-Manar Reform School in Egypt, took inspiration in this matter.

His hostility to the Muslim exponents of Greek philosophy was most pronounced. Philosophy, according to him, engendered scepticism and caused schisms in Islam. He subjected Ibn-al-Arabi's doctrine of the Unity of Being to a most severe criticism. In his opinion, Ibn-al-Arabi's conclusion in this respect was not only contrary to the teachings of the Prophet but also not in conformity with the doctrine of the Unity of God as contained in the Quran and Sunnah.

Ibn Taimiya stands as one of the most controversial figures in Islam. An independent thinker, who believed in the supremacy of individual conscience and one who wanted to see Islam in its pristine glory, he subjected all later impurities and foreign influences which had crept into Islam to most scathing criticism. For this he was denounced, beaten, lashed, imprisoned and put to all sorts of mental and physical tortures. But his was a daring spirit which lived up to his convictions, notwithstanding the persecution to which he was subjected from time to time.

# SUFIS AND SAINTS

# ABDUL QADIR JILANI

A caravan bound for Baghdad from Gilan (Iran) encountered a band of robbers. There was exchange of fire for a while but the members of the caravan were soon overpowered by the superior might of the brigands. Then search and looting followed. One by one each member of the caravan was relieved of his valuables. A few robbers at last came upon a simple looking poor boy sitting quietly at one side. They enquired from him: "Have you got anything with you?"

"Yes", replied the boy, "I have forty dinars." The robbers searched him thoroughly, his bedding and clothes, but found nothing. They thought that the boy was bluffing and went forward to search other persons.

After the search was over the robbers reported the strange boy to their Chief. Immediately, he was summoned before the Chief who asked him: "You say, you have forty dinars with you." "Yes," replied the boy.

"Where are they?", demanded the Chief.

Instantly, the boy tore open a portion of his jacket and took out forty dinars to the utter surprise of the robbers.

"Why did you disclose your precious property? If you had told otherwise, none would have suspected you," enquired the Chief.

"I was instructed by my mother, who had stitched these dinars in my jacket, never to speak a lie," replied the boy.

The Chief of the robbers was stunned by the strange behaviour of the boy, who carried out the wish of his mother by speaking the truth. This was a novel experience for him, and became a turning point in his life. He thought: "This boy is so obedient to his mother, while I am disobedient even to my Creator." The Chief was moved to the inner-most depth of his heart and tears rolled down his eyes.

He returned all the looted property to the members of the caravan and renounced the life of a robber.

The name of this strange boy was Abdul Qadir. He rose to be the greatest saint in the world of Islam and is known by the title of "Bare Pir Sahib" (The Great Saint) among the Muslims. He is universally recognised as the "Purifier of religion" of the evil influences which had crept into Islam after the "Pious" Caliphs and one who in his person reflected a delightful harmony of *"Shariat"* (Tenets of Islam) and *'Tariqat'* (Spiritualism).

The Muslim world, during the later part of the 11th century A.C., was passing through a period of great turmoil and turbulence. It was a period of political as well as moral decadence.

The golden days of Abbaside Caliphate were over and Government had passed into the hands of weak and effete Caliphs who had given themselves to a life of pleasure and luxury.

The diabolical Carmathian sect was engaged in their murderous activities and chased the high personages of Islam with their daggers. A number of great Muslims including Nizam-ul-Mulk Toosi had fallen victims to their daggers but no Muslim ruler was powerful enough to stop their nefarious activities.

The rationalism of Mutazellites in religious matters, which was earlier patronised by powerful Abbaside Caliphs, Mamoon and Mutasim, had dealt a grievous blow to Islamic spiritualism.

In such a gloomy atmosphere was born Abdul Qadir Jilani who, with his extraordinary abilities, brought harmony between *Shariat* (tenets of Islam) and *Tariqat* (Spiritualism) which restored to the misguided Muslims of his time both the form and spirit of Islam.

Abdul Qadir was born on the first of Ramazan, 471 A.H., in a pious Syed family of Gilan (Iran). His father, Abu Swaleh, an extremely virtuous person, was married to the equally saintly daughter of Syed Abdullah Saumai, a well-known divine of his time.

An interesting story is narrated about their marriage. It is said that Abu Swaleh was sitting by the side of a river. He had not eaten anything for several days. He sighted an apple floating down the stream. He caught hold of it and ate it. But immediately afterwards, he repented it and thought that he had no right to eat an apple without the permission of the garden-owner to whom it belonged. He set out to find out the garden-owner and obtain his pardon. After covering about eight miles up the stream, he came across an apple garden belonging to Saint Syed Abdullah Saumai, to whom he begged his pardon for the unauthorised eating of the apple. The Saint Saumai, himself a pious person, was astounded by the exhibition of such piety and promised to pardon him if Abu Swaleh would marry his blind, dumb and paralytic daughter. Abu Swaleh had to agree to it.

But, when he entered the bride's apartment he found a charming healthy girl instead of the reported crippled daughter of Syed Saumai. He, therefore, abstained from approaching her until assured by his father-in-law that the description he had given was only allegorical, explaining that his daughter was blind because she had never cast her eyes on any undesirable object; she was dumb because she had never uttered any undesirable word and she was paralytic because she had never set her foot outside her house.

Fatima, the pious wife of Syed Swaleh, gave birth to a son in 471 A.H., when she was 60 years old. The birth of the child, named Abdul Qadir, at the advanced age of his mother was considered a great Divine blessing. It is said that the newly-born child did not suck the milk of his mother during the day time in the month of Ramazan (Month of Fasting).

Abdul Qadir lost his father at an early age. He was brought up and given elementary education by his venerable maternal grandfather and saintly mother. When he was 17 years old, he was sent to Baghdad for higher studies.

In Baghdad, a great centre of Islamic learning in those days, Abdul Qadir became the favourite pupil of Allama Abu Zakariya Tabrezi, Principal of the *Jamia Nizamiah*. He studied there for 8 years and acquired mastery in all branches of learning. During this period, young Abdul Qadir had to pass a life of trials and tribulations. Though languishing under starvation he loathed begging food from anyone.

Having completed his education, Syed Abdul Qadir set out to acquire spiritual training. He spent scores of years, undergoing the rigours of spiritual life, and passing his time in meditation and search of truth and God. He, at last, became a disciple of Sheikh Abu Saeed Mukhzumi, a renowned saint of his time.

The great Saint settled down in Baghdad and devoted the rest of his life to the service of Islam and mankind. He was endowed with the fluent tongue of a great orator. His lectures, enriched by his worldly education and spiritual insight attracted large gatherings, numbering 70 to 80 thousand people at a time. These lectures were attended by high dignitaries of the Abbaside Caliphate, including the Caliph himself, and also by non-Muslims who embraced Islam in large numbers.

The conflict between the exponents of *Shariat* (tenets) and *'Tariqat'* (spiritualism) assumed alarming proportions after the Pious Caliphs and a balance could not be maintained between the two. The religious rationalism of Mutazilla struck at the spirit of Islam. The patronage and championship of Mutazilla doctrines by the powerful Abbaside Caliphs, Mamoon and Mutasim, threatened the religion of the Prophet of Islam. This led to the persecution of Imam Ahmad bin Hanbal by the Abbaside Caliph.

The celebrated Imam Ghazali, after his spiritual transformation, tried to strike a balance between the tenets and spiritualism of Islam. But, he was more a scholar than a spiritual thinker and, therefore, confined himself more to the precepts than to the practice of spiritualism.

It was Syed Abdul Qadir Jilani who struck a middle course between-the two extremes—spiritualism of Mansur Hallaj and rationalism of Mutazilla. In him *Shariat* (tenets) and *Tariqat* (Spiritualism) have their fullest expression. His person contained a delightful balance between the two. He is, therefore, called "Mohiuddin," meaning purifier of religion. In *Fiqh*, he followed Imam Ahmad bin Hanbal.

His writings are as effective and remarkable as his speeches. His *"Fatuh-al-Gheyb,"* is a remarkable book on mysticism. It was translated by Shah Abdul Haq Dehlavi into Persian and by several scholars into Urdu. His other well-known book in *"Ghinyat-ul-Talibin"* which has also been translated into Urdu. It is a comprehensive book dealing with the principles of *Shariat* and *Tariqat*. His third book *"Fath-al-Rabbani"* containing summaries of his lectures and discourses has been translated into Persian. His verses are replete with Divine love.

Syed Abdul Qadir Jilani passed a simple, pious and regulated life. He spent his days in preaching the true principles of Islam and nights in prayers and meditation. His life was a model of simplicity, selflessness and truthfulness. He used to take very simple food, consisting of barley bread and vegetables, cooked without any kind of fat. He was kind to the common people and translated into practice the saying of the Prophet of Islam: "The best person is one who loves and serves mankind most."

This greatest of all divines and mystic saints of Islam breathed his last on the 11th Rabi-us-Sani, 561 A.H., at the age of 91 years. His death cast a gloom over the world of Islam but his life and teachings will ever illuminate the hearts of Muslims.

# BAYAZID BUSTAMI

The rays of Islam which had illuminated Arabia had begun to penetrate into the distant parts of Iraq, Syria, Persia and even Turkistan. A new sect of sufis (mystics) who believed in renunciation of worldly pleasures by cultivating Islamic spiritualism through self-mortification, had sprung up and had produced some eminent Sufis in Iraq and Persia like Rabia Basri, Hasan Basri, Abdul Wahid and Bayazid Bustami. These sufis carried the message of Islam to the distant parts of the world and were, to a great extent, responsible for attracting the heathens to the new faith (Islam).

Hazrat Imam Jafar Sadiq, the great grandson of Caliph Hazrat Ali, was a versatile genius, who combined in him the worldly as well as spiritual learning. He is universally recognised as the fountain head of sufism, from whom spring different sects of sufism. He had entrusted the robe of *Naqshbandia* sect of sufism to Bayazid Bustami.

Abu Yazid Taifur bin Isa bin Adam bin Surushan was born in 128 A.H. 746 A.C. in the town of Bustam. His great grandfather was a Zorastrian who had embraced Islam.

The young Abu Yazid Taifur had a touch of future greatness in him and unlike all other children, he did not take part in games and frivolities. He passed most of his time in seclusion and meditation. When he grew up, he renounced the world and roamed about in quest of inner peace and spiritualism. He obtained guidance and inspiration from 113 spiritual teachers of his time which included Imam Jafar Sadiq and Shafiq Balkhi.

He led an ascetic life and was the first to introduce the doctrine of *Fana* (Nirvana). His followers are called *Tifuriya* or *Bustamiya.*

He studied Hanifite law before subscribing to the tenets of *sufism.* He taught some parts of it to Abu Ali al-Sindi, from whom in return he had instructions in the highest precepts of sufism and the doctrine of *Fana.*

Bayazid is universally recognised as one of the greatest sufis. "He combined strict ascerticism and reverence for religious law with an extra-ordinary power of intellectual and imaginative speculation. His attempt to reach absolute unity by a negative process of abstraction, *Fana Fil. Tauhid,* is pursued relentlessly to a point where, having denunded himself of personality like a snake which casts off its skin, he assumes Divine attributes and cries: Glory to me." *(Encyclopaedia of Islam).*

His sayings are "Twelve years I was the smith of myself and five years the mirror of my heart."

He breathed his last in 877 A.C., at the age of 131 years and was buried at Bustam. A magnificent tomb was erected on his grave in 1301 A.C. by the Mongol Sultan, Uljaitu Muhammad Khudabanda, whose spiritual teacher, Sheikh Sharfuddin was a descendant of Bayazid Bustami. His tomb is a popular place of pilgrimage of Muslims drawn from all parts of the world.

His disciples and followers, known as *Taifuris* formed a school of Sufism which, according to Hazrat Hujwairi, the author of *"Kashf al-Mahjoob,"* was opposed to the sect of Junaid Baghdadi, in preparing mystical intoxication *(Sukr)* to mystical sobriety *(sahw).*

Hazrat Bayazid, one of the greatest sufis, is held in great reverence by Muslims all over the world. According to another well-known sufi, Hazrat Junaid Baghdadi, "Bayazid occupies the same status among sufis which Gibrael occupies among angels."

# DATA GANJ BAKHSH

Ghazni, the Queen of the East; presented a gala appearance, when Sultan Mahmood, after his memorable victory against the combined Hindu forces at Somnath in 1026 A.C. returned to his Capital. He was accompanied by a large retinue loaded with treasures of Hindustan, including the sandal wood gate of the famous temple at Somnath. The populace of the Ghaznavide Metropolis had come out to accord an unprecedented welcome to the great conqueror.

The Sultan held a grand Durbar in which some of the rare exhibits brought from Hindustan were exhibited to the excited populace of the Capital city. These included a Hindu Savant (philosopher) who was known for his deep knowledge and erudition. There seemed hardly anyone in the Ghaznavide Court who could challenge him. At last, a young man of 20 years, stepped forward to challenge the Hindu philosopher and in the presence of the Sultan, he "utterly discomfited him by an exhibition of miraculous powers". The young man was Syed Ali Hujweri, better known as Data Ganj Bakhsh, who was destined to play an important role in the spiritual life of the sub-continent.

Syed Abul Hasan ibn Osman ibn Ali al-Jullabi al-Ghaznavi al-Hujweri, surnamed as "Data Ganj Bakhsh," was born in 1009 A.C., at Hujwer, a suburb of Ghazni. He was a Hasani Syed, whose family had migrated from Arabia during the Omayyad regime and settled down in Iran and later in Afghanistan.

He was given a thorough education in different branches of learning. His teachers included Abul Abbas bin Muhammad Shaqani, a learned pious Muslim. He received his spiritual education and training from Abul Fazal Muhammad bin Hasan Khatli who belonged to the *Junaidia* order of the Sufis.

Syed Abul Hasan, during his early life, undertook an extensive tour of the world of Islam in search of truth and spiritualism. He visited Iraq, Iran, Turkistan, Egypt, Syria and Hejaz, offered *fateha* at the tombs of well-known pious Muslims and met several living Sufi saints.

Data Saheb in his well-known work *Kashful Mahjub* has given some details of his spiritual experience of *Kashf.* Once, during his travels he came across in a village of Khorasan a convent of Sufis. Data Saheb who was wearing a rough dark gown with a staff in his hand and a leather bottle hung across his shoulder did not present a respectable appearance to the Sufis. He was lodged on the ground floor while the Sufis made merry in a comfortable upper floor room, eating sweet smelling food, giving only crumbs to their guest, and they also pelted him with skins of melons which they ate. This was to impress upon Data Saheb how lightly they thought of him. This strange behaviour of the so-called 'Sufis' taught Data Saheb humility and forbearance and the meaning of *kashf* which are the essential attributes of Sufis.

Data Saheb, who was a disciple of Abul Fazal Muhammad bin Hasan Khatli belonged to *Junaidia* sect of Sufis. He was much benefited from the long line of saints of this sect who inspired and thus shaped his spiritual life.

Once, Data Saheb saw the Holy Prophet of Islam in a dream. He implored the Prophet to give him a word of advice. The Prophet said: "imprison your tongue and your senses". Acting on this invaluable advice, Data Saheb reached the heights of spiritualism. According to him, the imprisonment of tongue means complete self-mortification. Imprisoning of senses meant shutting the door to all sorts of impurities and the subordination of physical senses to spiritual well being. This enabled him to distinguish between pure and impure, virtue and evil and climb the heights of spiritual glory.

Having accomplished the spiritual maturity through extensive travels in Islamic countries, meeting a number of Sufi saints and undergoing rigorous spiritual discipline, he was directed by his Pir (Spiritual Teacher), Hazrat al-Khatl to proceed to Lahore. According to Hazrat Nizamuddin Aulia, as stated in *Fuad-ul-Fawad,* Data Saheb expressed surprise at the order as his spiritual brother Shaikh Zanjani was already there, but his Pir asked him to comply with the order without questioning. Data Saheb, therefore, reached Lahore probably in 1034 or 1035 A.C. and the first thing he came across at Lahore was the funeral of Shaikh Zanjani. He led the funeral prayer of his brother disciple and at that moment it dawned upon him why his Pir (Spiritual Teacher) had directed him to proceed to Lahore.

The exemplary spiritual life led by Data Saheb and his impressive discourses brought a large number of non-Muslims into the fold of Islam. These included Rai Raju, who was the Administrator of Sultan Maudud ibn Masood Ghaznavi at Lahore. He was given the nickname of Shaikh Hindi and his descendents continued to be the keeper of the Tomb of Data Saheb at Lahore till 1960. In January 1960 it was taken over by the Auqaf Department, Government of the Punjab, Lahore.

Data Saheb did not like the un-Islamic practices which had been creeping into the fold of Sufism. He strictly adhered to the *Shariat* of Islam and purified Sufism from unhealthy un-Islamic trends. The conception that a beggar was a parasite on society was opposed by Data Saheb who held that paying of alms was obligatory on well-to-do persons and the beggar who received the alms, in fact, relieved a brother Muslim of his obligation, and thus should be thanked rather than condemned.

Data Saheb who was also a poet has written a number of books including *Kashful Mahjub, Minhajuddin, Kitab Al-Fana-wal-Baqa* and *Bahr-ul-Kulub*. But, of these, the most outstanding is *Kashful Mahjub* (The Revelation of Mystery) which is recognised as the first book on Sufism written in Persian. This has been translated into several languages, including English and Urdu. Professor Reynold A. Nicholson rendered the first English translation of the book which was published in 1911. A number of Urdu translation of this book were published, including one by Moulvi Ferozuddin, founder of Ferozsons Ltd., in 1893 and another by Shaikh Muhammad Iqbal.

A number of eminent Sufi saints, including Nizamuddin Aulia and Syed Jehangir Ashraf Samnani speak highly of this book. The book, which is divided into 25 Chapters deals with the multifarious spiritual experiences of the learned author. In the first chapter, he defines knowledge and classifies it into human and Divine. The second chapter deals with poverty, the third with Sufism, the fourteenth discusses various orders of the Sufis and their doctrines and at the end of the book he justifies *Sama* (audition). He says, if audition produces, a lawful and healthy effect on the mind, it is permitted.

Writing in the Preface of *Kashful Mahjub*, Prof. Nicholson says: "The object is to set forth a complete system of Sufism, not to put together a great number of sayings of different Shaykhs, but to discuss and expound the doctrines and practices of Sufis.

The author's attitude throughout is that of a teacher, instructing a pupil . . . . His exposition of Sufi doctrine and practice is distinguished not only by wide learning and first hand knowledge but also by strongly personal character impressed on everything he writes".

The author of *Punjab-men-Urdu*, Mr. Mahmud Sherani has credited Data Saheb with the origination of Urdu language, by bringing about a synthesis between Persian and the local dialects.

Data Saheb, died at Lahore in 465 A.H. or 1072 A.C., as given by most of the historians and was buried there.

Data Saheb, an eminent Sufi saint, scholar, poet and philosopher has contributed towards bridging the gulf between orthodox theology and Sufism. The celebrated Saint of Ajmer, Khwaja Moinuddin Chishti, known as Sultan-ul-Hind spent forty days of seclusion and meditation at the Shrine of Data Saheb and it was there that he got the spiritual illumination. The Saint of Ajmer, standing at Data Saheb's grave expressed himself in verses.

"Thou art Ganj Bakhsh, the bestower of treasures in both the worlds;

"Thou art the manifestation of the glory of God;

"Thou art an accomplished guide for those who are perfect; and

"Thou showeth the way to those who stray."

# KHWAJA MUEENUDDIN CHISHTI

The Indo-Pakistan sub-continent ruled for about a thousand years by the Muslims has witnessed many vicissitudes. Great empires have risen and fallen, pompous emperors and mighty conquerors have appeared on the Indian soil and have gone. Their mortal remains enshrined in magnificent tombs scattered all over the sub-continent have become relics of the past. But the tomb of Khwaja Mueenuddin Chishti, the saint of Ajmer and the uncrowned spiritual monarch of the sub-continent who still reigns over the hearts of millions of people, is the popular place of pilgrimage of the Muslims drawn from all parts of the world.

Khwaja Sahib, popularly known as "Gharib Nawaz" (Benefactor of the Poor), had earned this title due to his service to humanity and love for the poor and downtrodden. A man of indomitable will and dauntless courage, he dedicated his life to the love of God and His creatures. He achieved his mission despite insuperable obstacles and insurmountable difficulties.

Khwaja Mueenuddin Chishti was born in Siestan (Southern Iran) on Rajab 14, 530 A.H. i.e. 1142 A.C. He was a Husaini Syed from his father's side and a Hasani Syed from his mother's side. His father, Syed Ghiasuddin Ahmad was a very learned devout person. He carried on a modest business and owned an orchard. His father who had migrated to Khorasan, died at Neshapur in 545 A.H. leaving behind him an orchard and a flour mill. Khwaja Mueenuddin was then hardly 15 years old.

The Muslim world at this time was passing through a critical period of its history. The Abbaside Caliphate of Baghdad was tottering. The Caliph, sunk in a life of pomp and pleasure exercised little hold over the once vast empire, whose far-flung parts were getting independent of the Central control. Baghdad, however, the Metropolis of the Caliphate, was still the cultural, spiritual and educational centre of Islam.

The young Khwaja soon came under the influence of Sufi Ibrahim Qandozi. He sold his orchard and the mill, distributed the money among the poor and embarked up on a spiritual pilgrimage which in itself makes a fascinating story, deserving to be better known in detail.

He set out on his noble mission to establish the kingdom of God on earth. His life provides a beacon light to all those struggling for a noble cause. In this difficult task, he was assisted in the end by a few disciples but throughout he was without any worldly means whatsoever.

In the Shawwal of 560 A.H., the Khwaja became a disciple of Hazrat Usman Harooni, follower of Khwaja Ishaq Ghani Chishti, founder of the *Chishtia* Order. Khwaja Sahib served his teacher for 20 years, spending most of his time in prayers and meditation. This was the period of his preparation for the great mission lying ahead of him.

Thereafter, taking leave of Khwaja Ishaq Ghani, he proceeded to the Holy cities of Makkah and Medina for pilgrimage. On accomplishing this task, he went to Sanjar and met Sheikh Najmuddin Kubra and stayed with him for 2½ years. Thence he proceeded to Gilan, where he paid his respects to the celebrated Saint Hazrat Abdul Qadir Jilani, founder of the *Qadiria* Order, and along with him came to Baghdad. Here he met Sheikh Ziauddin and Shahabuddin Suhrawardy (founder of the *Suhrawardia* Order), the two well-known spiritual luminaries of Baghdad.

Passing through Hamdan and Tabrez and meeting men like Khwaja Yusuf Hamdani, Abu Saeed Tabrezi and Sheikh Mahmood Isfahani, he arrived in Isfahan, where he came across Khwaja Qutbuddin Bakhtiyar Kaki, who later became his chief lieutenant and after his death, accomplished his mission in India.

From Isfahan, Khwaja Sahib proceeded to Astrabad. Here he met Sheikh Nasiruddin, a learned Saint of the area. Leaving Astrabad, he arrived in Herat, where he tackled and reformed the tyrant Governor, Yadgar Muhammad, who oppressed his people.

From Sabzwar he arrived in Balkh where he met the celebrated Muslim scholar Hakim Ziauddin, who eventually became his disciple. From there, Khwaja Sahib went to Ghazni and waited for the call. Earlier, he had seen the Holy Prophet in his dream who blessed him and ordained him to go to India.

Khwaja Sahib arrived in Lahore, in about 586 A.H., where he performed *Chilla* (meditation and prayers) at the Shrine of Hazrat Sheikh Abul Hasan Ali Hujwiri, popularly known as Data Ganj Bakhsh. Leaving Lahore, he went to Multan, in those days the seat of Islamic learning in India and stayed there for five years to learn Sanskrit and Prakrit. From there, he proceeded to Delhi, arriving there in 1193 A.C. and from there he went to Ajmer, where he settled down for the rest of his life and which later formed the nerve centre of his activities. He died at Ajmer in 1236 A.C.

Ajmer in those days was the Capital of the most powerful Hindu State of the sub-continent ruled by Prithvi Raj Rathore. He was ordained to strike against the strongest citadel of autocracy in India. At first no notice was taken of the great Muslim Saint, but, soon his piety and love of mankind began to attract large number of people who vied with each other in embracing Islam. This was an alarm signal for the Hindu Raja.

Khwaja Sahib paid a deaf ear to the temptations and threats of the autocratic Hindu ruler designed to deflect him from the righteous path. He was not made of ordinary human metal. At last the celebrated Hindu magician, Jogi Jai Pal was sent to combat him. But his magical acrobats were of no avail before the spiritual power of Khwaja Sahib, and these only recoiled upon his own head. Overawed, he embraced Islam and became a well-known disciple of the Saint.

Alarmed at the success of Khwaja Sahib and his growing popularity among the masses, the autocratic Ruler of Ajmer ordered him to leave his territory. His reply was: "Give us time and we will see", and when questioned by his anxious companions he said: "We are going to hand over this arrogant ruler as a prisoner to a neighbouring King." It is said that Shahabuddin Ghauri, who, a year before, had sustained a crushing defeat at the hands of Prithvi Raj Rathore, the ruler of Ajmer, saw Khwaja Sahib in a dream who ordered him to invade India and assured him of victory.

Accordingly, Shahabuddin Ghauri made preparations, invaded India, defeated Prithvi Raj and captured him alive.

Khwaja Sahib carried on his proselytising activities from Ajmer for about half a century. During his lifetime, the Slave Dynasty had established its rule in Northern India which also included Ajmer and the celebrated Slave Kings, Sultan Qutbuddin and Sultan Iltimush who were devotees of Khwaja Sahib held him in great esteem.

The great Muslim Saint breathed his last on the 6th of Rajab, 633 A.H. (March 1236 A.D.) at the ripe age of 97. He was buried at Ajmer and mourned by the Muslims and Hindus alike. His sacred tomb, since that time, forms the popular place of pilgrimage of kings and commoners alike.

Khwaja Sahib was acclaimed as the spiritual head of the sub-continent, loved and adored by all. The glory of Islam in India, was to a large extent, due to the spiritual teachings of Khwaja Mueenuddin and his disciples.

Khwaja Sahib was known for his piety, simplicity and humanitarianism. Once a non-Muslim came with the intention of killing him. Khwaja Sahib got fore-knowledge of it through his mystic power. As soon as the intending assassin stepped in, he asked him to take out his dagger and kill him. Utterly non-plussed, the man threw off the dagger and implored Khwaja Sahib to punish him for his evil intentions. Khwaja Sahib told him that it was customary with sufis to return evil with good. Thereupon, Khwaja Sahib prayed for him and he lived and died as a good pious Muslim.

Khwaja Sahib had greatest regard for his neighbours. Whenever a neighbour died, he attended his funeral prayers and prayed for his soul.

The Muslim rulers of India had great love and regard for this illustrious Muslim Saint. When Salim (Jahangir) was born, Akbar, the famous Mughal Emperor, went on foot from Agra to Ajmer to offer his thanks-givings to the Saint of Ajmer. Mughal Emperors Jahangir, Shah Jahan and Aurangzeb visited Ajmer several times and lavished their bounty on the residents of this sacred city. Jahangir used to walk in Ajmer barefooted. Jahan Ara, the talented daughter of Shah Jahan, considered herself a spiritual disciple of the Saint and never slept on a cot while in the city. She wrote a book : *'Moonis-ul-Arwah'*, describing the lineage of *Chishtia* Saints in which she states that she used to apply the dust lying near the grave of the Saint to her eyes.

Khwaja Sahib is the author of several books including *'Anisul Arwah,* (giving details of his 28 meetings with his spiritual teacher Sheikh Usman Harooni) and *'Dalil-ul-Arfin'.*

Among his recorded sayings are :

A true Muslim befriends three things, namely—

"Abstinence, disease and death".

"One who helps the needy is a friend of God".

"The highest spiritualism is to remember one's death".

# IBRAHIM BIN ADHAM

The royal bed of Ibrahim bin Adham, Ruler of Balkh, was carpetted with roses each night.

One night, the maid servant, entrusted with the work, was tempted to lie down on it for a while. Unfortunately she soon fell asleep and was shaken out of her slumber, on experiencing the whips inflicted by the Ruler.

The maid servant stood up staggering.

"What made you sleep on the royal bed"? cried King Ibrahim.

She was speechless for a moment and then burst into sardonic laughter.

The King became furious and enquired the cause of her unusual laughter.

"Sir", replied the maid servant, "I had hardly slept for a while on the royal bed, when I received three or four whips on my tender body. I wonder what punishment you will get from God for sleeping on this bed every night".

Ibrahim bin Adham was much struck by the blunt and satirical reply of his maid servant. He was mentally upset and disquieted; and brooded over the provocative, spontaneous remark of his maid who lashed him at his weakest spot. Under the impact of this eye-opener he gave up many of his royal comforts and pleasures. Henceforward, he devoted much of his time to the welfare of his people and prayers to God.

One night, when he was praying, he felt someone walking on the roof of his palace. He went upstairs and found a person searching something there.

"What are you searching here?" enquired King Ibrahim.

"My camel", was the instant reply.

Ibrahim laughed! "Are you mad?

"You are searching your camel on the roof of the royal palace".

"For your part, you are searching God in the Royal Palace", retorted the stranger.

The incident produced a deep effect on the mind of King Ibrahim. He renounced his throne, became a hermit, and set out in quest of spiritual peace and Divine truth. All that he carried with him was a tumbler, a blanket and a pillow. He had hardly gone a few miles when he observed a man drinking water with his scooped hands. Instantly, he threw off the tumbler, thinking it to be useless.

When he went further, he found a man sleeping, using his arms as a pillow. He cast away the pillow, carried by him, considering it to be equally useless. A little further, he saw, another man sleeping without covering his body with a blanket. Ibrahim, thereupon, gave away his blanket as well.

Now he had no worldly belongings left with him. He roamed about in different countries in quest of Divine truth. He now yearned for a spiritual teacher who could lead him to the path of Divine Reality.

At last he called on the famous Sufi Saint, Hazrat Bayazid Bustami, and requested him to accept him as his disciple.

Hazrat Bayazid told him that he would have to undergo a period of prayers and severe test. Ibrahim readily agreed.

He was asked by the Sufi Saint, to bring logs of firewood from the forest. One day, the Saint instructed his maid servant to inform Ibrahim that the firewood he brought was not dry and caused a lot of smoke while cooking food.

This embittered Ibrahim and he cried, "Had you been in my State, I would have flogged you to death for this impertinent complaint".

When Bayazid came to know of Ibrahim's reaction to the complaint, he observed that he had not forgotten his regal life and required further test.

A few months later, the Sufi Saint asked his maid servant to give coarser food to Ibrahim.

Ibrahim took this food without grumbling but his dislike for it was visible from his facial expressions.

The maid servant reported the incident to the Saint, who remarked that Ibrahim required further training.

After a few months, the Saint observed that a person unknowingly threw a basket of dust on Ibrahim, but he did not protest to it. Bayazid Bustami was much pleased with the transformation of Ibrahim and conferred on him his robe of *Khilafat*.

After his conversion to Sufism, Ibrahim migrated to Syria and until his death worked and lived by his labour.

The anecdotes and sayings of Ibrahim recorded by his biographers show that he was an ascetic, but believed in earning his living through hard labour and not living on charity.

Like ancient Sufis, he took every care that his food was not impure in the religious sense of the word. He condemned begging as a means of livelihood and, on the other hand, supported himself by gardening reaping, and grinding wheat, etc. He did not carry the doctrine of *Tawakkul* to the point of refusing to earn his livelihood. He said! "There are two kinds of begging. A man may beg at people's doors, or he may say, 'I frequent the mosque and pray and fast and worship God and accept whatever is given to me'. This is the worse of the two types. Such a person is an importunate beggar".

Some of his sayings are :

(1) "Poverty is a treasure which God keeps in Heaven and bestows on those whom He loves".

(2) "This is the sign of one who loves God that his chief care is goodness and devotion and his words are mostly in praise and glorification of God".

In a reply to Abu Yazid al Djudhami, who declared that Paradise is the utmost that devotees can hope to attain from God hereafter, Ibrahim said: "I deem that the greatest matter, as they consider it, is that God should not withdraw from them His gracious countenance".

He found greatest peace and joy in self-mortification and renunciation of the world.

Ibrahim bin Adham died in 894 A.C. while he was taking part in a naval expedition against the Greeks. According to Yakut, he was buried at Sukin, a fortress in Rum.

# NIZAMUDDIN AULIA

Sultan Alauddin Khilji, one of the greatest Muslim rulers of India, was a great admirer of Sufi Saint, Hazrat Nizamuddin Aulia. On several occasions, he sought the Saint's blessings for his difficult military campaigns in Southern India and every time his armies came out with flying colours.

On the conquest of Warrangal, the Sultan sent a purse of 500 gold sovereigns to Hazrat Nizamuddin Aulia, which the latter forthwith gave to a Khorasani *'dervish'*, who happened to be with him at the moment.

The Sultan detailed his two sons, Khizr Khan and Shadi Khan to serve the Saint and be always at his beck and call.

The Sultan was very anxious to see the Saint personally and once sought his permission to present himself to him. But Hazrat Nizamuddin, who shunned the society of monarchs, declined to oblige him and sent him a message : "I have two doors in my house. If the Sultan enters the house through the front door, I shall leave it by the back door".

Syed Muhammad ibn Syed Ahmad, later known as Nizamuddin Aulia Mahboob Elahi (the beloved of God), Sultan-ul-Mashaikh (King of Saints) was born in Badayun (U.P.) in 634 A.H. Migrating from Bukhara, his ancestors arrived at Lahore and later settled down at Badayun. His father died, when he was only five years old. He was brought up by his illustrious and saintly mother. He received his early education from Maulana Alauddin. Later he went to Delhi along with his mother and received a thorough education from Maulana Shamsuddin and Maulana Kamaluddin Zahid.

Hazrat Nizamuddin Aulia arrived in the presence of his spiritual teacher, Hazrat Baba Fariduddin Ganj Shakar on 15 Rajab, 655 A.H. and remained with him till 3 Rabiul-Awwal 656 A.H. He, along with his other companions, passed an extremely rigorous life at the *'Khanqah'* (monastery) of Hazrat Ganj Shakar at Ajodhan (Pakpattan). The inmates of the *Khanqah* helped to prepare their daily meal. Maulana Badruddin Ishaq brought firewood. Another *dervish*, Shaikh Jamaluddin Hanswi brought a wild fruit, 'Vela', from the forest which was boiled into water and taken as a drink by the inmates of the monastery. One day, no salt was available. Nizamuddin bought one piece of salt from a grocer's shop on credit. When the inmates of the monastery together with their spiritual Teacher, Fariduddin Ganj Shakar sat down for their meal, the latter felt reluctant to take the food. "I smell extravagance from this food", he said. On enquiry, he was told that the salt was obtained on credit from the grocer's shop. On this information, he observed that it was better for a *dervish* to die rather than obtain anything on credit. From that day, Nizamuddin resolved never to take anything on credit.

On completing his strenuous training from his spiritual teacher, Fariduddin Ganj Shakar he settled down at Ghiaspura near Delhi. In the beginning, he passed a very hard life. Sometimes days passed without Nizamuddin and his family having anything to appease their hunger. On such occasions, his pious mother declared that they were the guests of God. Nizamuddin felt an immense inner pleasure at such moments.

Once, the King of Delhi, Jalaluddin Khilji, requested Nizamuddin to accept a few neighbouring villages for meeting the expenses of his *Khanqah*, but he refused to accept any such gift.

The teachings of Nizamuddin Aulia had a sobering effect on the pleasure-loving society of the Imperial city of Delhi. Persons attached to the royal court who revelled in pleasure, abstained from it. A number of such dignitaries, including some members of the royal family were attracted towards the Saint of Ghiaspura and became his disciples. Their life underwent a strange transformation. Two of these were the sons of Sultan Alauddin Khilji—Prince Khizr Khan and Shadi Khan. But the greatest of Nizamuddin's disciples was Ameer Khusroe, a versatile genius-poet, musician, writer and mystic—greatest master of fine arts that the thousand years of Muslim rule in India has produced.

Khusroe, a highly respected member of the royal court of Delhi, was a great admirer of his spiritual teacher, Nizamuddin Aulia. In fact he was always prepared to sacrifice his all for his sake. Once a supplicant came to Nizamuddin and begged for alms. The Saint had nothing with him. He gave his wooden shoes to the supplicant, who went away from there satisfied.

The supplicant had hardly gone out of Delhi, when Ameer Khusroe, who was returning to the Capital along with the King, met him, and said to him: I feel the sweet smell of my spiritual teacher from your body. Have you any token from him?". The supplicant took out the wooden shoes of Nizamuddin from his cloak. Ameer Khusroe kissed those shoes and cried out: "Do you want to sell these?" Ameer Khusroe had five lakh Tunkas (silver coins) with him which the Sultan had awarded him in appreciation of his poem. Khusroe gave the entire money in lieu of his teacher's shoes. Appearing before Hazrat Nizamuddin, with his shoes upon his head, Khusroe observed: "The *dervish* agreed to accept five lakh tunkas as the price of the shoes. Had he asked for my entire property and even my life as the price of it, I would have willingly given these to him."

Nizamuddin shunned the society of Kings. Sultan Ghiasuddin Khilji was very anxious to meet him and requested him through Ameer Khusroe to grant him an interview but the latter declined to oblige him. He also refused to see Sultan Alauddin Khilji.

Sultan Qutbuddin Mubarak Shah Khilji, who ascended the throne of Delhi, after assassinating Khizr Khan and Shadi Khan, the favourite sons of Sultan Alauddin Khilji and the disciples of Nizamuddin Aulia, objected to his nobles visiting the *Khanqah* of the Saint. He had become inimical towards the Saint and even ordered him to attend his Durbar. The Saint refused to obey the King's order, adding: "I can see what is going to happen". The same night the King was assassinated by one of his nobles named Khusroe Khan (not Ameer Khusroe).

Hazrat Nizamuddin Aulia was known for his piety and benevolence. He passed his nights in prayers and when he came out of his room in the morning, his eyes were often swollen. He was accustomed to breaking his fast with a handful of coarse food.

He delivered his lectures after the morning prayers which the audience listened to with rapt attention. The audience felt as if they were listening the words of God which went straight into their hearts.

He was extremely kind to the poor and the needy, and always held himself in readiness to alleviate the suffering of those in distress. None had ever left his door disappointed and dissatisfied. Once he observed: "Anyone who relates his sorrows to me makes me doubly sorrowful. It rends my heart. I deplore and pity those callous persons who see the miseries and sad plight of their brethren and yet do not help them".

He never thought ill of any person and was forgiving and benevolent even to his enemies. Jhajjoo, a resident of Ghiaspura, was instigated by certain mischief mongers to tease Hazrat Nizamuddin who never coaxed or reprimanded the miscreant for his misdeeds. His magnanimity and indulgence tended to win over Jhajjoo. When the latter died, Hazrat Nizamuddin led his funeral prayers.

The great Saint died full of years. Forty days before his death, he dreamed the Prophet showing anxiety to see him. He died on 18 Rabiul Awwal, 725 A.H. and was buried at Ghiaspura, now known as Nizamuddin (Delhi). His tomb was built by Sultan Muhammad Tughlaq of Delhi.

His lectures and anecdotes have been recorded in four books, namely (1) *Fawaidul Fawad*, (2) *Fazlul Fawad*, (3) *Rahatul-Muhibbeen* and (4) *Siratul-Aulia.*

The first book was compiled by Khwaja Hasan Sanjari. It carries the lectures and aphorisms of his spiritual guide from 707 A.H. to 719 A.H.

The last one deals with the life and achievements of mystic saints.

The following few authentic anecdotes about the great Saint may be mentioned for the interest of the readers:—

(1) One droughty summer when the people of Delhi, languished under sizzling heat, some of Khwaja Sahib's ardent disciples waited on him with the request to pray to God for rainfall. He sardonically asked them if they actually needed it. And then he addressed a letter to an elderly Hindu grocer directing him to invoke God for early showers and bade his disciples to deliver it to him. Getting the 'letter' the grocer reverently kissed it and then lifting his scales, he pronounced God's name in all humility, and as he supplicated that ever since he started wielding it he never under-weighed any commodity sold to his customers there suddenly appeared a cloud no bigger than a man's hand. In a few moments the sky was overcast and the downpour came, inundating the town. As long as the grocer held aloft the scales, the downpour continued. He asked his spiritual mentor's disciples if it was enough, or they wanted more. On their saying that it was more than enough he gradually laid it down. Miraculously, simultaneously the rain ceased. Thanking the grocer, the disciples left with their hearts brimming with devotional feelings for the great Khwaja.

On another occasion, some of his followers implored him to rid the town of mighty hordes of flies that had invaded it and plagued the people's life. Khwaja Sahib issued an order to the flies to leave the town forthwith. As soon as the order was pasted on the gates of the town, large swarms of flies started quitting the town till all of them disappeared.

Once, one of his devotees complained to him that his shoe in good condition had incidentally been replaced by someone's worn out one at the Khwaja's mosque. The illustrious Saint advised his devotee to be of good cheer and to offer next day his morning prayers at Qutabuddin Aibek's mosque where the shoe would be restored to him. The devotee did so. After the morning prayers, as he came to collect the worn out replaced shoe, he was utterly aghast to find that it had been replaced with his own new one.

In the course of a *'qawwali'* being held on the bank of the Jamuna, in honour of Khwaja Sahib who sat wearing his cap aslant, a *'qawwal'* began singing Amir Khusroe's lyric containing the couplet:

هر قوم راست راهے ، دینے وقبله گاهے
من قبله راست کردم بر طرف کج کلاهے

Every people have a straight path of rectitude, a specific faith to follow and a direction to turn their face in praying.

I have fixed my 'Qibla' at one who is wearing his cap aslant.

The *'Qawwal'* made the couplet burden of his song. It terribly enthralled the audience and drove them into fits of spiritual ecstasy so much so that one man in a deep ecstatic state rolling close to the river plunged himself into it and was swallowed by the waves.

# THINKERS AND SCIENTISTS

# MUHAMMAD BIN
# MUSA AL-KHWARIZMI

Of all the great thinkers who have enriched the diverse branches of knowledge during the era of early Islam, Muhammad bin Musa Khwarizmi occupies an outstanding place. Being one of the greatest scientists of all times and the greatest of his age, Khwarizmi was a versatile genius, who made lasting contributions to the field of Mathematics, Astronomy, Music, Geography and History. "Khwarizmi was the principal figure in the early history of Arabic Mathematics", writes Phillip K. Hitti in his well-known work, *The History of the Arabs*. "One of the greatest minds of Islam, he influenced mathematical thought to a greater extent than any other mediaeval writer."

Muhammad bin Musa al-Khwarizmi (780--847 A.C.) was born in Khwarizm (Modern Khiva) situated on the lower course of Amu Darya. His forefathers had migrated from their native place and settled in Qutrubulli, a district West of Baghdad. Little is known about his early life. According to H. Suter, he died between 835 to 844 A.C., while C. A. Nallino is more definite when he puts his death in 846-47 A.C. Khwarizmi soon acquired a prominent place in the *Darul Hukama* founded by Mamoon, the celebrated Abbaside Caliph. He was entrusted with the astronomical researches conducted under the patronage of the talented Caliph.

As a mathematician, Khwarizmi has left ineffaceable marks on the pages of the mathematical history of the world. Undoubtedly he was one of the greatest and most original mathematicians that the world has produced. Apart from compiling the oldest astronomical tables, he had the rare distinction of composing the oldest works on arithmetic as well as on algebra. Writing about his celebrated work on algebra entitled *'Hisab al Jabr wal Muqabala'*, the author of the *History of Arabs* says: "Translated in the 12th century in Latin by Gerard of Cremona, the work of Al-Khwarizmi was used until the 16th century as the principal mathematical text-book in European Universities and served to introduce into Europe the science of algebra, and with it the name of Al-Khwarizmi's works were also responsible for the introduction into the West of the Arabic numerals called "Algorism" after him." The mathematical works of Khwarizmi influenced such well-known mathematicians as Umar Khayyam, Leonardo Fibonacci of Pisa and Master Jacob of Florence.

His mathematical works were the principal source of knowledge on the subject to the world for a pretty long time. George Sarton pays him glowing tributes when he considers him, as "one of the greatest scientists of his race and the greatest of his time". He systematised the Greek and Hindu mathematical knowledge. The oldest arithmetic composed by him was known as *Kitab ul-Jama-wat-Tafriq,* which has disappeared in Arabic, but its Latin translation, *"Frattati d' Arithmetica,"* edited by Bon Compagni in 1157 A.C. at Rome is extant. Al-Khwarizmi was the first exponent of the use of numerals including Zero, in preference to letters. It was through him that Europe learnt the use of zero or cipher, whose employment facilitated the application of arithmetic in everyday life. His work on the Indian method of calculations was translated into Latin by Adelard of Bath in the 12th century and was named as *De Numero jndico* which has survived, though the Arabic original was lost. According to J. Ruska, this Latin translation corresponds to his work on Hindi numeral, *Kitab ul-Jama-wat Tafriq bi Hisab al Hind.* The *Fihrist* of Al Nadim, perhaps due to the mistake of the copyist has attributed to Sarad bin Ali, the three well-known mathematical works of Khwarizmi, namely (1) *Hisab al Hindi,* (2) *Al Jama-wat Tafriq,* and (3) *Al Jabr wal Muqabla.*

Al Khwarizmi is the author of *Hisab al Jabr wal Muqabla,* an outstanding work on the subject which contains analytical solutions of Linear and Quadratic equations. He has the distinction of being one of the founders of algebra, who developed this branch of science to an exceptionally high degree. His great book contains calculations of integration and equations presented through over 800 examples. He also introduced negative signs which were unknown to the Arabs and illustrated his point with six different examples. He also gives geometric solutions with figures of Quadratic equations, e.g. $x^2$ $10^x=39$, an equation which was repeated by later mathematicians. Robert Chester was first to translate his book in Latin in 1145 A.C. which introduced algebra to Europe. Later on, this book was translated by Gerard of Cremona, too. This Algebra written by Al-Khwarizmi is lucid and well arranged. After dealing with equations of the second degree, he has dealt with algebric, multiplications and divisions. Writing in the *Legacy of Islam,* Carra De Vaux says: "In 18th century Leonardo Fibonacci of Pisa, an algebraist of considerable importance says he owed a great deal to Arabs. He travelled in Egypt, Syria, Greece and Sicily and learned the Arabic method there, recognised it to be superior to the method of Pythagoras, and composed a *Liber Abaci,* in 15 Chapters, the rest of which deals with algebraic calculations. Leonardo enumerates the six cases of quadratic equations just as al-Khwarizmi gives them." The translation of Khwarizmi's algebra by Robert Chester marks an epoch for the introduction and advancement of this branch of science in Europe. "The importance of Robert's Latin translation of Khwarizmi's algebra," says a modern orientalist, "can hardly be exaggerated, because it marked the beginning of European algebra."

Khwarizmi has made an invaluable contribution to trigonometry also. His trigonometrical tables which deal with functions of sine and tangent were translated into Latin in 1126 A.C. by Adelard of Bath.

Khwarizmi was an astronomer of outstanding ability. Mamoon got a degree of meridian measured by him in the plain of Sanjar, North of the Euphrates, his astronomers employing a method superior to that of the Greeks. This was one of the most delicate geodatic operations successfully undertaken by a number of astronomers headed by Musa al-Khwarizmi. The idea behind these astronomical operations was the determination of the size and sphericity of earth. The measurement was carried out at Sanjar as well as at Palmyra, which "yielded 56 3/4 Arabic miles as the length of a degree of meridian—a remarkably accurate result exceeding the real length of the degree at the place by about 2,877 ft.", says C. A. Nallino. "This would make the diameter of earth 6,500 miles and its circumference 20,400 miles." Muhammad bin Musa Al Khwarizmi, a versatile genius of the Islamic history, had translated *Sidhanta,* or Indian Tables and had written commentary on it. He had written a valuable treatise on astronomy and had compiled his own tables *(Zij)* which was after two centuries revised by the Spanish astronomer Majriti (d/1007) and was translated into Latin by Adelard of Bath in 1126 A.C. This formed the basis of later astronomical pursuits in the East and the West, which replaced all earlier tables of Greek and Indian astronomers. This table was also adopted in China. It included values of trigonometrical sine and tangent functions, which was in conformity with the tendency of the earlier writers when trigonometry was not considered a separate subject.

He wrote two books on astrolable namely *'Kitab al Amal bil Asturlab',* and (2) *Kitab Amal al Asturlab'.* The former dealt with the manner of using the astrolabe and the latter dealt with the art of making astrolabe. Kifti has mentioned the first book. He also wrote *"Al Rukhama",* a book on Sundials which is non-extant.

Khwarizmi also dealt with the practical side of astrology. According to the celebrated astrologer Abu Mashar, he "investigated how far the conjunction at the time of Hazrat Muhammad's (PBUH) birth indicated his future as a Prophet."

His mathematical treatise in which he has discussed his theory of music was translated by Adelard of Bath in the 12th Century and named as *Liber Ysagogarum Alchorism.* This contains a section on music. His views on music were conveyed to Europe through this Latin translation, which, according to Phillip K. Hitti, was one of the first to introduce Arab music to the Latin world.

Khwarizmi was also a Geographer of repute. His *Kitab Surat al Ard* (The work on the shape of the earth) laid the foundation of geographical science in Arabic. The manuscript of this book is preserved in Strassburg (Germany). Abul Fida, the celebrated Geographer, calls it *Kitab Rasm al Rub al Mamur.* (The book of drawing of the inhabited parts of the globe). This book was illustrated with maps, whose Latin translation was edited by C. A. Nallino, who declared "that this is a work, like of which no European nation could have produced at the dawn of its scientific activity." Later on H. Von Mazik translated and edited this book as well as annotated the part dealing with Africa. This book corrected and completed earlier geographical facts and notions stated by Ptolemy.

Khwarizmi wrote a book on history known as *Kitab al-Tarikh*, which served as a source for Masudi and Tabari. The history written by Tabari contains a passage about the return of Caliph Mamoon to Baghdad which was probably taken from this book.

# JABIR IBN HAYYAN

Chemistry is one of the sciences to which Muslims have made the greatest contribution. They developed it to such a high degree of perfection that they were considered authority in this specific branch of science. Till the end of the 17th century A.C. Jabir and Zakriya Razi have the distinction of being the greatest chemists that mediaeval times have produced. Writing in his illuminating *History of the Arabs,* Phillip K. Hitti acknowledges the greatness of the Arabs in this branch of science. He says. "After materia medica, astronomy and mathematics, the Arabs made their greatest scientific contribution to chemistry. In the study of chemistry and other physical sciences, the Arabs introduced the objective experiment, a decided improvement upon the hazy speculation of the Greeks. Accurate in observation of phenomena and diligent in the accumulation of facts, the Arabs nevertheless found it difficult to project proper hypotheses." Another well-known historian, Robert Briffault frankly admits the debt which modern chemistry owed to the Muslim scientists: "Chemistry, the rudiments of which arose in the process employed by Egyptian metallurgists and jewellers— combining metals into various alloys and "tinting" them to resemble gold processes long preserved as a secret monopoly of the priestly colleges, and clad in the usual mystic formulas, developed in the hands of the Arabs into a widespread, organised passion for research which led them to the invention of distillation, sublimation infiltration, to the discovery of alcohol, of nitric and sulphuric acids (the only acid known to the ancients was vinegar), of the alkalis, of the salts of mercury, of antimony and bismuth, and laid the basis, of all subsequent chemistry and physical research."

"Jabir would still remain a very impressive personality." Writes George Sarton, "at once because of his own achievements and because of the glamour traditionally attached to him. The most famous alchemist of Islam, Jabir ibn Hayyan, seems to have good experimental knowledge of a number of chemical facts."

Jabir ibn Hayyan-al-Azdi, called as Sufi (Mystic) known as Geber in the West flourished in Kufa about 776 A.C. and is reputed as the father of modern chemistry. Along with Zakariya Razi, he stands as the greatest name in the annals of mediaeval chemical science. His father was a druggist in Kufa who died a "martyr" to the Shiite propaganda. Jabir received his education from the Umayyad Prince Khalid ibn Yazid ibn Muawiya and from the celebrated Imam

Jafar al-Sadiq. In the beginning he practised as a physician and was closely attached to the house of Bermakides, whose members occupied the high posts of viziers during the reign of Haroon ar-Rashid. Jabir, too, had to share the misfortune of Bermakides at the time of their downfall in A.C. 803 and died in exile at Kufa. His famous laboratory was found in ruins about two centuries later.

Jabir is credited to have composed more than 100 works of which 22 chemical works are still extant. He introduced experimental research in chemical science which immensely added to its rapid development. The latest research of a few Western scholars has confused the issue and has revealed that the chemical works ascribed to Jabir were composed during the 10th century A.C. by a Secret Society similar to the so-called *'Ikhwan-as-Safa'* (Brethren of Purity) as the 'Greek references quoted by Jabir had not been translated by the end of the 8th century. But the overwhelming historical evidences found in the Arabic language falsify this contention of the few Western scholars who must have based their conclusion on inadequate data.

The fame of Jabir rests on his alchemical writings preserved in Arabic. Five of his works namely *Kitab al Rahmah* (Book of Mercy), *Kitab al Tajmi* (Book of Concentration), *Al Zilaq al Sharqi* (Book of Eastern Mercury), *Book of the Kingdom* and the little *Book of Balances*, have been published. "We find in them remarkably sound views on method of chemical research," writes George Sarton "A theory on the geologic formation of metals; the so-called sulphur, mercury theory of metals (the six metals differ essentially because of different proportions of sulphur and arsenic and antimony for their sulphides). Jabir deals also with various applications of refinement of metals, preparation of steel, dyeing of cloth and leather, varnishes to waterproof cloth and protect iron, use of manganese dioxide in glass making, use of iron pyrites for writing in gold, distillation of vinegar to concentrate acetic acid. He observed the imponderability of magnetic force." He worked on the assumption that metals like lead, tin and iron, could be transformed into gold by mixing certain chemical substances. It is said that he manufactured a large quantity of gold with the help of that mysterious substance and two centuries later when a road was laid in Kufa, a large piece of gold was unearthed from his laboratory. He laid greater emphasis on the importance of experimentation in his researches, hence he made great headway in the chemical science. The Western writers credit him with the discovery of several chemical compounds, which are not to be found in his twenty-two extant Arabic works. According to Max Meyerhof, "His influence may be traced throughout the whole historic course of European alchemy and chemistry." As already stated in the foregoing pages, he is the author of more than 100 chemical works. "Nevertheless, the works to which his name was attached," says Phillip K. Hitti, "were after the 14th century, the most influential chemical treatises in both Europe and Asia." He explained scientifically the two principal functions of chemistry; 'calcination and reduction, and registered a marked improvement in the methods of evaporation, sublimation, distillation, melting and crystallization.' Jabir modified and corrected the Aristotelian theory of constituents of the metal, which remained unchanged till the beginning of the modern chemistry in the 18th century A.C. He has explained in his works the preparation of many chemical substances including "cinnabar" (Sulphide of Mercury) and arsenious oxide. It has been established through historical researches that he was conversant with the preparation of nearly pure vitriols, alums, alkalis and the production of the so-called liver and milk of sulphur by heating sulphur with alkali. He prepared mercury oxide and was thoroughly conversant with the preparation of crude sulphuric and nitric acids. He knew the method of the solution of gold and silver with this acid. Al-Razi has classified alchemical substances as vegetables, animals or minerals, whereas Jabir and other Arabian chemists have divided mineral substances into bodies (gold, silver, etc.), souls (sulphur, arsenic, etc.) and spirits (mercury and sal-ammoniac). Jabir is also the author of a book on astrolabe and has written several treatises on spherical trigonometry.

His chemical treatises have been translated into several European languages including Latin and had a deep influence over the entire course of the development of modern chemistry. Several technical scientific terms coined by Jabir found their way in various European languages through Latin and were adopted in modern chemistry. Among these technical words and terms are realigar (red sulphide of arsenic) tutia (Zinc Oxide), alkali, antimony (Arabic-Ithimid), alembic for the upper and aludel for the lower part of distillation vessel. Sal ammoniac, a new chemical substance which has been explained in the works of Jabir was unknown to the Greeks. The ammonium referred to in the writings of Greek scientists was in fact a sort of rock salt.

A real estimate of Jabir's achievements is only possible when his enormous chemical works including the *Book of Seventy* are published. Richard Russel (1678), an English translator, ascribes a book entitled *Sun of Perfection* to Jabir. He considers Jabir as the "most famous Arabian prince and philosopher." A number of his chemical works have been published by Bertholot, which, according to him, are anthropomorphic and animistic. His works translated into English are *Book of Kingdom, Book of Balance* and the *Book of Eastern Mercury*. Latin was the first European language in which the works of Jabir were translated. In 1144 A.C., Englishmen Robert of Chester made the first translation of Jabir's book on the *Composition of Alchemy*. His *Book of Seventy* was translated into Latin by Gerard of Cremona (d/1187 A.C.) the celebrated translator of Arabic Scientific Works.

Jabir has been recognised as the Master by the later chemical scientists, including Al Tughrai and Abu Al-Qasim Al-Iraqi who flourished during the 12th and 13th centuries A.C., respectively. These Muslim chemists made little improvement on the methods of Jabir. They confined themselves to quest of the legendary *"elixir" (Al-Iksir)* which they could never find out. During the 12th century hardly any monumental creative scientific work was added to the long list of Arab scientific works. The writers during this period confined themselves to the reproduction, summarization and writing commentaries on the works of Razi (Rhazes) ibn Sina (Avicenna) and Jabir (Geber). The works of great Muslim scientists, including Alhazen, Geber, Avicenna and Rhazes have been expounded by the celebrated English scientist Roger Bacon and his rival Albert of Bollstaedt (Albertus Magnus). The influence of Alhazen's *'Thesaurus opticae'* may be traced to the optics written by Roger Bacon. Similarly, Albert incorporated the alchemical teachings and formulas of Jabir in his *De Mineralibus.* "The influence of Geber is very pronounced," writes an European writer in the *Encyclopaedia Speculum Naturale* by Vicent de Beauvais. "The alchemical tracts ascribed to Arnold of Villanova and to Raymond Lull are full of quotations from Geber. Arabic alchemy, associated as it was with astrology, predominated throughout the 13th and 14th centuries."

# ABU ISHAQ KINDI

The ninth century A.C. forms the golden period of the development of Islamic learning, when the Arabs were the real standard bearers of civilization. They not only saved Greek learning from total extinction but also made lasting contributions to almost all branches of knowledge and made considerable advancement in diverse spheres of human activity. The distinguished scientists during the first half of the IXth century were Al Kindi, Al Khwarizmi and Al Farghani.

Al Kindi, an encyclopaedist and a versatile genius was regarded by Cardan, a philosopher of Renaissance as 'one of the 12 subtlest minds.' According to Abu Maashar, the author of *Mozakkarat,* Al Kindi was considered among the four greatest translators that the Muslim world had produced.

Abu Yusuf Yaqub ibn Ishaq al Kindi, who belonged to the South Arabian tribe of Kinda was born in Basrah in the beginning of the 9th century A.C. He is known as Al Kindus in the West. His father, Ishaq ibn Saleh, was posted as the Governor of Kufa during the reigns of three Abbaside Caliphs Mehdi, Hadi and Haroon ar-Rashid. Young Kindi, who was of pure Arab descent, was entitled as the 'Philosopher of Arabs.' He received his education in Basrah and Baghdad where he served in various capacities under three Abbaside Caliphs Mamoon, Mutasim and Mutawakkil. He was a favourite of Caliph Mamoon ar-Rashid and was given every kind of state patronage. He was, however, persecuted under the orthodox reaction led by Al Mutawakkil (847–861 A.C.). He had acquired great knowledge in medicine, philosophy, mathematics, occult sciences, astronomy, music and logic. He had mastered Persian, Greek and Indian learning and was well versed in Hebrew, Greek and Arabic languages. First of all, he was appointed as translator and editor of Greek works during the reign of Mamoon. He also served as a tutor of a son of Mutasim and was later on attached as an astrologer to the Abbaside Court. He was persecuted by Mutawakkil and his library was confiscated. He died in 873 A.C.

Al Kindi, an encyclopaedic scientist, made invaluable contributions to mathematics, astrology, astronomy, physics, optics, music, medicine, pharmacy, philosophy and logic. Authorship of no less than 265 works is ascribed to him, of which only a few have survived in original language. But, a good deal are still extant in Latin translations made by Gerard of Cremona. According to historical records, out of his 265 works, 22 dealt with philosophy, 19 with astronomy, 16 with astrology, 7 with music, 11 with mathematics, 22 with numerals, 22 with medicine, 21 with politics, 33 with physics, 9 with logic and the rest with other branches of knowledge. He wrote four books on the use of Hindu numerals. He made and revised a number of translations of Greek works into Arabic. He wrote a number of invaluable treatises dealing with precious stones. He considered alchemy as an imposture and has dealt with this subject in one of his treatises.

He is the most dominating figure in Mediaevel science and one of the greatest Muslim scholars in physics. Over and above he was an astrologer, philosopher, mathematician, alchemist, optician and musical theorist. Of his hundreds of works, fifteen are on meteorology, several on specific weight, on tides, on optics and on reflection of light. Two of his most important scientific works are :

(1)   *De Aspectibus,* a treatise on geometrical and physiological optics which influenced Roger Bacon, Wirelo and other Western scientists.

(2)   *De Medicinarum Compositarum Gradibus* is an exceptional treatise in which an attempt has been made to establish posology on a mathematical basis. "His principal work on geometrical and physiological optics," writes Phillip K. Hitti, "based on the optics of Euclid in Theons, recension, was widely used both in East and West until superseded by the greater work of Ibn al-Haitham. In this invaluable optical work, Al Kindi has dealt with the passage of light in straight lines; direct process of vision; the process of vision by looking glass and the influence of distances and angle of vision or sight along with optical delusions. He says that light takes no time to travel and vision takes place through a bundle of rays, which, sent out from the eye expanding in the form of a cone, embrace the object. While the other four senses receive impression from things, the sense of sight grasps its object in an active and instantaneous manner."

One of his treatises translated into Latin deals with the causes of the blue colour of the sky: According to him, this 'colour is not really special to heavens but arises from the mixture of the darkness of the sky with the light of the atoms of dust, vapour, etc. In the air illuminated by the light of the Sun.' He had composed a remarkable work on ebb and flow which has been translated into Latin. He incorporated his theories in this book after personally testing them through experiments. He wrote several small treatises on iron and steel to be used for weapons. He applied mathematics not only to physics but also to medicine. He thought that gold and silver could only be obtained from mines and not through any other process. He endeavoured to ascertain the laws that govern the fall of bodies, hence he may be considered as the forerunner of the Theory of Gravity, propounded by Newton.

He was a reputed astrologer and during his lifetime he could forestal the duration of about 450 years for Abbaside Caliphate which was then threatened by Carmathians. He was considered among the nine Judicas of astrology.

The reign of the Abbaside Caliph Mamoon constitutes the most glorious epoch in Islamic history, and has rightly been called the Augustan age of Islam. Al-Kindi founded the *House of Wisdom*, in which philosophy acquired its real progress. He translated and wrote commentaries on a number of philosophical works of Aristotle. His theory of the Universe is similar to the theory of Aristotle. Being a natural philosopher he has extensively discussed the doctrine of soul and intelligence. The divine intelligence is the cause of the existence of the world. According to him, "the world as a whole is the work of an externally active cause, the Divine intelligence, whose activity is transmitted in many ways from above to the world. Between God and the world or bodies is the world of soul, which created the world of heavenly spheres. In so far as the human soul is combined with the body, it is dependent on the influence of heavenly bodies, but in its spiritual origin and being it is free." Both immortality and freedom could only be acquired in the world of intelligence. If anyone attains these two, his intellectual power is developed to such an extent that he may acquire true knowledge about God and the Universe. Thus in *De Intellectu* the Latin translation of the philosophical work of Al Kindi which was edited by Nagy, the Western world found for the first time the doctrine of Intelligence.

Al Kindi is one of the greatest musical theorists who has written more than half a dozen treatises on music. "In one of which," says George Sarton, "we find the first definite use of notation among the Arabs. He is the earliest writer on music whose work has come down to us." His works contain notation for the determination of the pitch. Out of his seven treatises on music, three have been preserved up to the present time, namely, *"The Essentials of Knowledge in Music; On the Melodiesi* and *"The Necessary Book on the Composition of Melodies."* In one of his treatises, Al Kindi describes rhythm *(iqa)* as constituent part of Arabian music. "Measured song or mensural music," writes Phillip K. Hitti, 'must, therefore, have been known to the Muslims centuries before it was introduced in Europe." Ahmad ibn Muhammad Al Sarakhsi (d 899 A.C.) and Mansoor ibn Talha ibn Tahir who were disciples of Al Kindi wrote a number of books on musical theories. The former has to his credit at least half a dozen books on the subject.

The writings of Al Kindi deeply influenced the Eastern and Western thinkers in diverse spheres of knowledge. A number of his works were first translated into Latin by Gerard of Cremona, whose study obliged Cardan to consider him as one of the 12 greatest minds born in the world since the creation of the universe till the middle of the 16th century A.C. His writings on optics greatly influenced Roger Bacon and other Western scientists who considered him along with Alhazen and Ptolemy as one of the three greatest authorities on the subject.

# ZAKARIYA AL-RAZI

Zakariya Al-Razi, better known as Rhazes in the West, is universally recognized as the most outstanding scientist of the mediaeval times, who influenced the course of thought in diverse branches of knowledge. "Rhazes," says Max Mayerhof, "was undoubtedly the greatest physician of the Islamic world and one of the greatest physicians of all times." He wrote several remarkable manuals of medicine which are characterised by striking originality and brilliance. A number of his works were translated into several European languages and according to *Encyclopaedia of Islam,* "Down to the Seventeenth Century A.C., the authority of Razi was undisputed. . . . . . . In the field of medical practice he surpasses the knowledge of the ancients." Writing in his well-known book *Arabian Medicine,* Edward G. Browne recognizes Razi as "the greatest and most original of all the Muslim Physicians and one of the most prolific as an author. He was the most eminent thinker of the ninth century A.C., which is known as the golden period of Islamic learning." "The Persian Al-Razi," admits George Sarton, "was not simply the greatest Clinicians of Islam and of the whole of Middle Age; he was also a Chemist and Physist. . . . . . He may be considered one of the forerunners of the latrochemists of the Renaissance . . . . . Galenic in theory, he combined with his immense learning true Hippocratic wisdom." Together with Ibn Sina (Avicenna), Razi forms the two most brilliant luminaries on the firmament of Islamic Medicine. While Razi excelled in the clinical side of medicine, Ibn Sina surpassed in the theoretical side. "Influence of Rhazes and Avicenna upon Western Thought was equally great," writes Cyril Elgood in the *Medical History of Persia and the Eastern Caliphate.*

Abu Bakr Muhammad ibn Zakariya Al-Razi (865–925 A.C.) was a Persian Muslim who was born at Rayy near modern Tehran. He studied mathematics, philosophy, astronomy and alchemy at Baghdad under a disciple of Humayun ibn Ishaq who was well versed in Greek, Persian and Indian medicines. He had had a chance of visiting the famous Muqtadari hospital, whose intimate practical experience prepared the ground for his medical expression. He practised as an alchemist in his youth and very soon he earned a high reputation which attracted patients and pupils from distant parts of Western Asia. He entered the service of the Ruler and was appointed the Administrator of the newly built hospital at Rayy. Soon after he shifted to Baghdad in the same capacity and worked for a considerable period as the Administrator of the well-known Muqtadari hospital of Baghdad. His high reputation as a Physician took him from one court to another. His unsettled life was due to his constant demand even in distant cities and was also the result of the fickle-mindedness of the Rulers and the uncertainties of political situations. He returned several times to Rayy where he died in 925 A.C.

Razi practised medicine for not more than 35 years. During this period he travelled widely and was entrusted with duties both clinical and administrative.

Razi was a prolific writer who left behind him immortal works on medical science, chemistry, physics, music, philosophy, mathematics, astronomy and ethics. "His erudition was all-embracing," says Max Mayerhof, "and his scientific output remarkable, amounting to more than 200 books, half of which are medical." In spite of his enormous practice as the greatest practising physician of his time, he could find time to write such monumental and gigantic medical works as *Al Hawi, Kitab Al Mansuri* and *Al Judari Wal Hasbah*. His excessive devotion to studies impaired his eye-sight. In his young age he practised as an alchemist and later on he devoted himself exclusively to the development of medical science both in theory and practice. He wrote a monumental work *Kitab Al-Mansuri* (called *Liber Almansoris* in Latin) dedicated to his patron Mansoor ibn Ishaq al Salmani, the Governor of Rayy, which ran into 10 volumes and dealt with Greek medicines. Its first Latin translation was published in Milan in the last quarter of the 15 century. It was later on published into several European languages, including German and French. His writings on medicine included many short treatises on lighter topics like, *'On the fact that even skilful physicians cannot heal all diseases.; 'Why frightened patients easily forsake even the skilled physician;' 'Why people prefer quacks and charlatans to skilled physicians;' 'Why ignorant physicians, laymen, and women have more success than learned medical men.'* He also contributed to gynaecology, obstetrics, ophthalmology. His other valuable works deal with some of the common diseases in the East including stone in bladder and kidneys. His treatise *'Barr-ul-Saat,'* or 'cure within an hour,' was widely read and was translated into Persian and French languages. He wrote a pamphlet entitled *'Of Habit which becomes Natural',* and thus was the forerunner of Sherrington's 'conditioned Reflex Theory.' His monograph on 'Diseases in Children, earned him the title of the Father of Paediatrics. A number of his treatises on medicine were translated into Latin and printed together under the title of *'Opera Parva Abubetri.'*

His outstanding work, *'Al Judari Wal Hasbah,'* a book dealing with small-pox and measles, is the earliest and one of the most authentic books on the subject even up to the present times. It was translated into Latin and other European languages and was published for more than forty times between 1498–1866 A.C. It was translated into Latin and printed in Venice in 1489; in Basle in 1549; in London in 1747 and in Gottingen in 1781 A.C. This invaluable work provides the first description of smallpox as a clinical entity, hence according to Neuburger, "In every land and with justice it is regarded as an ornament to the medical tradition of the Arabs." It contains detailed information regarding treatment of pustules after full development of smallpox. This remarkable work is reputed for its originality and until the 18th century was prescribed as a text-book in most of the universities, both in the East and the West. "This treatise," writes Phillip K. Hitti in his *History of the Arabs,* "served to establish Al-Razi's reputation as one of the keenest original thinkers and the greatest clinicians not only of Islam but of the middle ages." The symptoms and treatment of smallpox as detailed by the celebrated physician provide ample testimony of his medical abilities. He says; "The outbreak of smallpox is preceded by continuous fever, aching in the back, itching in the nose and shivering during sleep. The main symptoms of its presence are backache with fever, stinging pain in the whole body, congestion of the face, sometimes shrinkage, violent redness of the cheeks and eyes, a sense of pressure in the body, creeping of the flesh, pain in the throat and breast accompanied by difficulty of respiration and coughing, dryness of the mouth, thick salivation, hoarseness of the voice, headache and pressure in the head, excitement, anxiety, nausea and unrest. Excitement, nausea and unrest are more pronounced in measles than in smallpox, whilst the aching in the back is more severe in smallpox than in measles." The modern medical science could hardly add to these symptoms.

The greatest achievement of Al-Razi in the realm of medical science is his monumental work, *Al-Hawi* (Latin-Continents) the most comprehensive Encyclopaedia of Medicine ever written by a medical man which runs into 20 volumes. According to historical records, Al-Razi could not finish this work during his lifetime and actual form was given to it by his disciples after his death. This book was translated into Latin by the Sicilian Jewish physician, Faraj ibn Salim in 1279 A.C. under the orders of Charles I, King of Sicily, and was named as *Continens.* It was repeatedly printed from 1486 onwards. *Al-Hawi* is the largest medical encyclopaedia in Arabic, which Razi took 15 years to complete. He compiled it in the light of personal experience and knowledge. For every disease he furnished Greek, Syrian, Arabic, Persian and Indian sources and at the end he gave his own opinion. "Printed when printing was still in infancy," writes a Western Orientalist, "these medical works of Al-Razi exercised for centuries a remarkable influence over the minds of the Latin West." "Its *(Hawi's)* influence on European medicine was very considerable," says Max Mayerhof. "The work was gigantic and not many copies were made. Only fifty years later, Haly Abbas could find only two copies of this book and, according to him, "As to his (Razis') book which is known as *'Al-Hawi.'* I found that he mentions in it everything the knowledge of which is necessary to the medical man, concerning hygiene and medical and dietetical treatment of diseases and symptoms. He did not neglect the smallest thing required by the student of this art concerning treatment of diseases and illness."

Al-Razi, being a versatile genius left behind him invaluable works on medicine, natural science, mathematics, astronomy, ethics, philosophy, theology and music. His contribution to natural sciences is lasting. It includes alchemy, optics, matter, time, space, motion, nutrition, putrefaction, growth and meteorology. He wrote *Kitab al-Asrar* in chemistry (Book on the art of Alchemy) dealing with preparation of chemical substances and its appliances. His great work on the art of Alchemy was recently found in the library of an Indian Prince. This book was translated into Latin as *'Liber Experimentorum'* by Constantine. Razi proved himself to be a greater expert than all his predecessors including Jabir in the exact classification of substances. His description of chemical experiments as well as their apparatus are distinguished by their clarity which is not visible in the writings of his predecessors. Jabir and other Arabian chemists have divided mineral substances into bodies (gold, silver, etc.); souls (sulphur, arsenic, etc.) and spirits (mercury and sal-ammoniac), while Razi has classified his mineral substances as vegetables, animals and minerals. The class of minerals he divided into spirits, bodies, stones, vitriols, boraxes and salts. 'In chemistry Razi rejecting all occultist and symbolic explanations of natural phenomena, confined himself exclusively to the classification of substances and processes as well as to the exact description of his experiments. Pseudo Majriti in his *'Kitab Rutbat Al-Hakim,'* endeavoured to reconcile the Alchemy of Razi with that of Jabir.'

Razi investigated the determination of specific gravity by means of hydrostatic balance, called by him *Mizan-al-Tabii.* Most of his works on physics, mathematics, astronomy and optics have perished. In physics his writings deal with matter, time, space and motion. In his opinion the matter in this primitive state before the creation of the world was composed of scattered atoms, which possessed extent. Mixed in various proportions with the articles of void, these atoms produced these elements which are five in number, namely earth, air, water, fire and celestial element. Fire is created by striking iron on the stone.

During his ealy life he was much interested in practical as well as theoretical music. He was an artist of repute and was a skilled vocal and instrumental musician. He was an expert in playing on the lute. He wrote *Fi Jamal il Musuqi,* an encyclopaedia of music, but in later years he lost interest in music. Most of his metaphysical, philosophical and ethical works have perished and only a few fragments are available. Al-Biruni who wrote a complete *Risala* (treatise) on the life and works of Al-Razi frequently quoted him in his writings. Al-Razi professes the existence of five eternal principles in metaphysics namely (1) Creator, (2) Soul, (3) Matter, (4) Time and (5) Space. The eternity of the world is, according to Razi, the necessary corollary to the concept of God, the unique and immutable principle . . . . . .When the human souls have obtained liberation (from body) the world will dissolve and matter deprived of forms will return to primitive state.' He is against excessive asceticism in spite of his pessimistic metaphysics and like Socretes he believes in taking active part in life and in working for the welfare of the people. Following the maxim of Aristotle he does not blame the human passion but its excessive indulgence. His theory of pleasure and pain dominates his ethical teaching. 'Pleasure is not something positive but the simple result of a return to normal conditions, the disturbances of which causes pain'.

He believed in the evolution of scientific and philosophical knowledge and in this respect he was much ahead of ancient philosophers.

The high reputation of Al-Razi as a teacher of medicine attracted students from distant parts of the Islamic world. So great was the attendance of students in his lectures that he was inaudible to those sitting far away. So the near one passed on his words to the outer circle of students. He was the greatest practising physician of his time and had the distinction of being the head (Director or *Mutawalli)* of two of the biggest hospitals of his time situated at Rayy and Baghdad. According to Ibn Abi Usabiyah, he selected a new site for the great hospital of Baghdad by hanging pieces  of raw meat in various localities, prefering the place where it showed least symptoms of putrefaction. He was an eminent surgeon of his time and was the inventor of *Seton.* He also introduced the 'use of animal gut as a ligature for surgical operations and was the first to recognize the reaction of the pupil to light'.

The influence of Al-Razi and Ibn Sina (Avicenna) on Western as well as Eastern medicine was overwhelming. Razi's book on Alchemy, *'Kitab Al-Asrar* (the *Book of Secrets)* translated and edited by Gerard of Cremona was the principal source of medical knowledge in the West till 14th century. It has been profusely quoted by Roger Bacon, one of the principal figures, of Western Renaissance. "In Vienna in 1520 and in Frankfurt on the Oder in 1588," writes Max Mayerhof, "the medical curriculum was still largely based on Avicenna's *Canon* and on the ninth book *'Ad Almansorem'* of Rhazes. The two universities of Europe, Montepellier and Bologna specialised in the teaching of Arab learning. "From these two centres," writes Cyril Elgood, in *A Medical History of Persia and the Eastern Caliphate,* "the teaching and influence of the Arabs spread to every medical school of Europe. From the 12th to the 17th century Rhazes and Avicenna were held superior even to Hippocrates and Galen . . . . The popularity of the Arabs was thus established and among them Rhazes and Avicenna were considered prominent. So great was their popularity and so long did it endure that we find Montagna, Gentile da Fabriano and other artists decorating the edge of the Madonna's robe with Arabic letterings and two Arab doctors, Cosmas and Damian, raised to the altars of the Church."

# ABU ALI SINA

Nooh ibn Mansur, the Samanid king of Bukhara (976–97 A.C.) was lying in a precarious condition on his sick bed, and the court physicians had given up all hopes of his recovery. In consequence, a boy of 17 years was summoned and ushered into the Chamber of the sick King, passing through a congregation of astonished dignitaries composed of distinguished courtiers and talented physicians. This boy was Ibn Sina who was finally entrusted with the treatment of the King. The marvellous boy cured the dying Ruler, to the great astonishment of all and was accorded due honour and prestige at the Court. He was given the privilege of using the Ruler's remarkable Library, which, in fact, could be the highest award for his great work.

Ibn Sina, the greatest intellectual giant of the Middle Ages and one of the greatest of all times, was a versatile genius who influenced the course of thought in diverse ways. Being an outstanding encyclopaedist, he made lasting contributions to medical sciences, philosophy, logic, occult sciences, mathematics, astronomy, music and poetry. He was an eminent rational philosopher, whose invaluable discoveries in varied branches of knowledge forestalled many later discoveries and won for him an immortal place among the galaxy of eminent scientists and thinkers of the world. "He is important as Universal Encyclopaedist," adds the *Encyclopaedia of Islam*, who fixed the system of learning for centuries following".

Abu Ali Husain ibn Abdullah ibn Hasan ibn Ali ibn Sina, known as Shaikh-ur-Rais (Prince of all Teachers), was born in 980 A.C. at Afshinah near Bukhara (Turkistan). His father Abdullah who hailed from Balkh was appointed as a Samanite Governor and was later posted at Bukhara, where the young Abu Ali received his early education. From the very beginning he showed such an extraordinary intelligence and made so remarkable progress in his education that at the early age of 10, he was well versed in Quran and different branches of literature.

Being brought up in an Ismaili family, he was deeply influenced by Ismaili proselytism and developed a taste for philosophy which enabled him to study Greek, Islamic and other material on the subject. Meanwhile Abu Abdullah, an Natili, a leading philosopher of his time, visited Bukhara and stayed at his house. Ibn Sina studied logic, geometry and astronomy from him. The intelligent boy soon surpassed his teacher and studied by himself medicine, physics and metaphysics. He gained a deep insight into these categories of knowledge. He acquired deep knowledge of medical science and established such a high reputation as a practising physician, that reputed physicians consulted him in difficult cases. Metaphysics he learnt from the works of al-Farabi. The metaphysical and logical speculations of al-Farabi, determined the direction of his thought. He mastered all these subjects before he was 17 years of age.

Endowed with extraordinary powers of assimilating, absorbing and retaining knowledge, he soon mastered all the varied intellectual material found in the Imperial Library, which later enabled him to undertake his monumental works. "I went there," writes Avicenna,' "and found a large number of rooms filled with books packed up in trunks. I then read the catalogue of the primitive authors and found therein all I required. I saw many books the titles of which were unknown to most people, and others which I never met with before or since." He started writing at the age of 21. His style is clear and comprehensive. After the death of his father, he had to leave Bukhara due to political disturbances and reached the city of Gorgan which was noted for its high culture. His fame had travelled faster than him and he was accorded a hearty welcome by the King of Khwarizm, a great patron of art and learning. It was at this famous seat of learning that he met his great contemporary Abu Raihan al-Biruni. He had hardly set his foot there, when Sultan Mahmood of Ghazni, demanded from the King of Khwarizm to send these intellectual luminaries to Ghazni. Reluctantly the King of Khwarizm, had to comply with the request of the great conqueror, Mahmood Ghaznavi and despatched Al-Biruni, Abu Nasr Arraq and Abul Khair Khammar to Ghazni. But Ibn Sina and Abu Sahl Masihi refused to go to Ghazni and set out for Gorgan. At Gorgan he practised as a physician and engaged himself in the teaching and writing of books. It was here that he met his sincere friend and pupil Abu Ubaid Jawaz Jami. Lack of patronage and appreciation of his deep erudition, forced him to leave Gorgan and reach Rayy. Here he was welcomed by the Dalamite Ruler Majdul Dawlah. His stay at Rayy was brief and shortly afterwards he went to Hamadan. At Hamadan he stayed for a longer period and he was closely associated with its ruler Shams-ud Dawlah, whom he had cured of a painful colic. It was here that Ibn Sina completed his monumental work on medicine called, *'Al Qanun Fit Tib.'* Majdul Dawlah, the Dalamite Ruler, had appointed him his Minister for a brief period. The army threatened a mutiny as it suspected Ibn Sina to be in correspondence with the Ruler of Isfahan. At last he hurried to Isfahan, where he was heartily welcomed by its Ruler, Alaud Dawla. Ibn Sina got some respite in Isfahan and carried on the task of completing most of his immortal works here. Repeated travels and exacting political and intellectual preoccupations, had undermined his health. He was suffering from colic and he made some special efforts towards his own treatment and probably overdid it which produced intestinal complications. He became bed-ridden at Hamadan, and having realised that his end was approaching, he took bath, offered repentence and began reciting Quran till his end came. Thus died the greatest thinker of the Mediaeval times at the age of 57 in 1037 A.C. being victim of a disease in which he was a specialist. His grave in Hamadan is yearly visited by a large number of pilgrims and admirers.

His was a chequered career and his life was a struggle not without a lesson for the common man. He lived in a period when the Muslim world was passing through great revolutionary times and his restless soul could not provide him the peace and tranquillity which is ordinarily essential for undertaking such gigantic intellectual works as he did. It is a great tribute to his genius that in such disturbed conditions and with a distracted state of mind, he could compile a number of monumental works on diverse subjects. He was the greatest encyclopaedist of the middle ages, a versatile genius who has left behind him ineffaceable marks in diverse branches of knowledge. His works embraced a wide range of subjects, including logic, medicine, philosophy, psychology, mathematics, astronomy, theology, ethics, politics, mysticism, tafseer, literature and music. He is said to have written 50 pages a day at an average and is the author of no less than 238 books and treatises. His literary works commenced at Bukhara at an age of 21 and continued at Gorgan, Rayy, Hamadan and Isfahan in spite of his political pre-occupation and disturbed environments. The last 13 years of his life at Hamadan and Isfahan was a period of his greatest intellectual activities in which he completed most of his gigantic works. His chief works on philosophy *'Ash-Shifa* and *An-Najat* were written here. He also concluded his works on ethics and *Al Magest* and added 10 chapters to the later. He wrote treatises on geometry, arithmetic and music. He made new additions to arithmetic and disproved a number of theories advanced by Euclid. He wrote two books on zoology and botany during a trip to Shahpur Khwast along with his patron, Alaud Dawlah. During the same journey he wrote his *'Kitab an-Najat'*. At Isfahan he wrote his *'Danish Namai Alai'*, *Kitab al-Insaf* and works on literature and lexicography. He is considered as the father of the science of geology, on account of his invaluable book on mountain in which he discussed the matters relating to the earth's crust and gave the scientific cause for earthquakes.

His chief contribution is to the realm of medicine and philosophy. He wrote at least eight large medical treatises, which occupy the most outstanding place in the history of mediaeval medical science. One of these deals with treatment of colic in which he was a specialist. Another contains a chapter on the possibility of the production of exceptional psychical phenomena. The medical traditions of Galen, Hippocrates, Aristotle, Zakariya Razi and Al-Majusi reached their climax in the *Canon* of Ibn Sina. His gigantic work *'Al Qannun Fil Tib'* known as *Canon* in Latin is the culmination and masterpiece of Arab systematisation. Written in five volumes it is a medical encyclopaedia, dealing with 760 drugs besides general medicines, simple drugs and diseases affecting all parts of the body from head to foot. This book particularly deals with pathology and pharmacopoeia and was translated in the 12th century by Gerard of Cremona. An appendix dealing with clinical observations was lost. He treats acute and chronic diseases and prescribes methods of treatment and preventive measures. He has distinguished mediastinitis from pleurisy and has discovered the contagious nature of diseases which spread through water and soil. "Translated in Latin by Gerard of Cremona in 12th Century", writes Phillip K. Hitti, "This *Canon* with its encyclopaedist contents, its systematic arrangements and philosophic plan, soon worked its way into position of prominence in the medical literature of the age, displacing the works of Galen, Al-Razi and Al-Majusi and becoming the Text for medical education in the schools of Europe. From the 12th to 17th century this work served as the chief guide to the medical science in the West and it is still in occasional use in the Moslem East". In the words of Dr. Osler it has remained, "a medical Bible for a longer period than any other work." The popularity of this great book may be gauged by the fact that during the last 30 years of the 15th century it was published 16 times and was published 20 times in the 16th century in various European languages. The publication of its parts as well as commentaries in various languages of the East and the West are innumerable. According to a celebrated European writer, "Probably no medical work ever written has so much been studied. Hence Avicenna's influence on European medicine has been overwhelming." "This book was started when Avicenna was in Gorgan," writes the author of the *Medical History of Persia,* "and finished at Rayy. When it became known to the medical world, it at once superseded all previous works on medicine". Sir Jadu Nath Sircar, the well-known Indian Historian pays eloquent tributes to Ibn Sina when he says: "Avicenna has the greatest intellectual giants of the middle ages." Avicenna was responsible for elevating Islamic medicine to its zenith, and his portrait as well as that of al-Razi still adorn the Grand Hall of the Faculty of Medicine in the University of Paris.

Avicenna is considered by many as the greatest philosopher of Islam, whose rationalist philosophy tried to explain religious dogmas in the light of reason and invited severe criticism of Imam Ghazali. Like his predecessors he tried to harmonise the abstract forms of philosophy with the Islamic religious faith. His outstanding philosophical works are *'Kitab as-Shifa' Al-Najar* (The Salvation) and the *Isharaat* (Instructions). His *'Kitab as-Shifa.'* which contains valuable knowledge on logic, physics and metaphysics, had a deep influence over Western as well as Eastern philosophy. Persian writers class this book along with *Almagest,* of Ptolemy and treat it as a work devoted to a branch of astronomy, but the sections dealing with medical properties of stones and other chemical matters were included in the book, because all these subjects were included in philosophy in those days. His philosophical works reflected a conflict between materialism and idealism. He expounded the doctrines of Farabi and followed him in logic and epistemology. "Avicenna made for himself and posterity a problem which taxed his ingenuity to the utmost", writes a celebrated orientalist. "He laid down the principle that from the one and indivisible only one being can originate. Therefore, it is not possible to assert that form and matter spring directly from God, for that would involve the assumption that there are two different modes in the Divine essence. Matter, indeed is not to be thought of as coming from God, because it is the very principle of multiplicity and diversity." He has more clearly brought out the dualism of mind and matter, God and the world than Farabi. The doctrine of the immortality of soul is more definitely laid down by him. His philosophy in fact brings out his scientific and progressive outlook. His rationalistic and materialistic outlook which was quite natural, being shaped by the philosophical trends of his times, was severely criticised by Ghazali. His compromise with Muslim theology did not find favour with the orthodox circles and his philosophical works were put to fire in Baghdad. He explains the moving, changing and developing matter. Similar is his approach to the process of knowledge. His philosophy is the necessary link between the philosophy of Farabi and Ghazali on one hand and that on Ibn Rushd (Averroes) on the other. His book *'Shifa,'* according to Ibn Ali Usabiya was completed by him in 20 days in Hamadan. But Nizami states that the books was written in Isfahan with great deliberation. In logic, he has followed Farabi and has expanded as well as supplanted the deductions of Aristotle. His logical treatise *'Nafia'* was translated in French and was published in 1658 in Paris.

Being a materialist, Avicenna is one of the greatest scientists of the middle ages. He has given his own classification of sciences, which is based on materialism. He differed from Aristotle regarding classification of sciences. He acknowledges the reality of the outer world and found an inter-relation between time and movement. Time can be conceived only in relation to movement. According to him, where there is no movement there is no time. He refuted the Theory of Aristotle that the sources of motion is the invisible force who is God while Avicenna asserts that natural laws operate in the world with which Providence does not interfere. Hence the outlook of Avicenna is more modern and scientific than that of Aristotle. According to the celebrated orientalist R. Briffault, "an air thermometer is said to have been employed by Ibn Sina".

Ibn Sina ranks only next to Farabi as the greatest musical theorist of Islam. His *'Kitab as-Shifa,'* a philosophical encyclopaedia of repute also contains much original work on music. He also wrote an introduction to the art of music, whilst a few definitions regarding music are found in his *'Division of Science'.* The work of Ibn Sina considerably influenced the West on the subject and Roger Bacon recognises his contribution to therapeutic value of music. According to a Western critic of music, "Both Farabi and Ibn Sina are claimed to have added to what the Greeks taught."

Avicenna, who was a versatile genius, made contributions to the field of astronomy also. He was entrusted by Alaud Dawlah, with the work of improving the existing calendar and the arrangement for the establishment of an observatory. "In proving the falsity of astrology", says a Western writer, "he opposed the fallacious contention of the Greek, Arabian and Hindu astronomers who maintained that the obliquity of the ecliptic diminishes gradually towards the Celestial Equator."

He is considered as the father of the science of geology and in his well-known treatise published in Latin, as *'De Conglutiatione lapidum',* he deals with the formation of mountains and the earth crust. He gives the scientific cause of earthquakes. His literary works, *Hal, the son of Yakzan* and *Al Tair,* directed the course of literary development in Iran, Afghanistan, Central Asia and Arabian countries. His best poetical contribution is the *Ode* describing 'the descent of the soul into the body from the higher spheres', which is still learnt by heart by the Arabic students.

Avicenna's influence over the Eastern as well as Western thought has been overwhelming. He not only assimilated the Greek and Eastern sciences, but improved upon them. His exhaustive biography was written by his favourite disciple Jurjani which was translated in Latin and several other languages. "His works", according to *Encyclopaedia of Islam*, "were much read, annotated and translated into Western languages." Acknowledging Avicenna as one of the greatest men that this world has seen, Cyril Elgood writes in his monumental work, *'Medical History of Persia:* "Here is a man who starting with none of the advantages of life (except perhaps an appreciative father) becomes, while still a youth, the Adviser and confident of his ruler, who, changes his city though he may, yet always becomes the leading within a few months and whose writings influenced all Europe, although he died before he was sixty and never travelled outside the semi-desert of Central Asia. He was hailed by his countrymen as the Second Teacher, the chief master; he has been seen by Dante in Paradise along with the greatest intellects of the non-Christian world; and William Harvey will say 600 years after his death to his friend Aubrey; 'Go to the fountainhead and read Aristotle, Cicero and Avicenna."

# AL-BIRUNI

Mahmood Ghaznavi, the great Muslim conqueror of the 11th century A.C. occupies an outstanding place amongst the patrons of learning. He drew to his court two of the greatest luminaries of the Islamic world, namely Firdausi and Biruni. Firdausi became the author of the world famous *Shahnama*, while Biruni, was a versatile genius of the age who ranks amongst the greatest thinkers of Islam and in whose lifetime the greatest intellectual giant of the middle ages, Ibn Sina, is said to have taken to flight due to fear of competition with Al-Biruni. According to the celebrated Indian historian, Sir J. N. Sircar, "Few know physics and metaphysics. Amongst those few, the greatest in Asia was Al-Biruni, at once a philosopher and a scientist and pre-eminent in both of these two seemingly incompatible fields." A contemporary of the renowned Avicenna, Biruni occupies a distinguished place among the intellectual wizards produced by the world of Islam. "Abu Rayhan Muhammad Al-Biruni called the Master," says Max-Mayerhof, "a physician, astronomer, mathematician, physicist, geographer and historian, is perhaps the most prominent figure in the galaxy of universally learned scholars who constitute the golden age of Islamic science."

Abu Raihan Muhammad ibn Ahmed, better known as Al-Biruni was born near the town of Khwarizm or Khiva, situated on lake Aral in Central Asia, in September 973 A.C. Little is known of his early life and education. He had acquired in his youth a good reputation as a scholar. When his native state was conquered by Mahmood, he joined the court of the celebrated Conqueror and had a chance to visit India along with him. Mahmood's conquests had opened North—Eastern India to Islam and Biruni taking advantage of these golden opportunities, travelled for twenty years throughout the length and breadth of the sub-continent, learning Hindu philosophy, science and religion from the learned Pandits and imparting Arabic and Greek sciences to them in return. He took pains to learn the difficult Sanskrit language in advanced age in order to have an access to the vast storehouse of Indian knowledge. He spent more than forty years visiting different parts in quest of knowledge. He died in 1048 A.C. at a matured age of 75 years.

Al-Biruni was a prolific writer, whose versatility enabled him to attempt with outstanding success such diverging subjects as philosophy and mathematics, geography and astronomy, physics and metaphysics. His earliest biographer writes: "He never had a pen out of his hand, nor his eye ever off a book and his thoughts were always directed to his studies". His keen sense of observation and accuracy of experiments*pervade through his illuminating works, which have baffled even the modern scientists. He had incorporated the results of his studies in India in his outstanding work, *"Tahqiq al-Hind"* (Facts about India) which contains a comprehensive and accurate account of the history, geography, philosophy, science and social conditions of India in the 11th century. This book provides the missing link regarding the life and customs of the subcontinent between the periods ranging from the visit of the Chinese Buddhist pilgrims in the 7th century and the writing of *Ain-i-Akbari* in 1590, A.C., Dr. Sachau (1888) translated the book into English. An English critic of the 19th century pays glowing tributes to Al-Biruni when he says, "Abu Raihan is the only Arabic writer who investigated the antiquities of the East in a true spirit of historical criticism." This book contains an account of Hindu numerals which is the best on the subject recorded in mediaeval times.

He was the first Muslim who introduced Indian chess to Islamic countries; and explained the problems of advanced trigonometry in this book. At the end of the book *"Tahqiq-al-Hind"*, Al-Biruni says, "I have translated into Arabic two Indian works (Sanskrit books), one entitled *"Sankhya"* which discusses the origin and quality of the things that exist, and the other *"Patanial'* (Yoga Sutra) which treats of the deliverance of the soul from the trammels of the body". This book on India gives an accurate and authentic history of the invasion of Mahmood and the origin of Somnath. Despite the entire resources of the state being at his disposal, Abul Fazal's *Ain-i-Akbari* written about six centuries later is poor in comparison to Al-Biruni's book. Abul Fazal borrowed the idea and the arrangement of his work from his great predecessor. On his return from India, he wrote *"Qanun al-Masudi* in 421 A.H. (1030 A.C.), an astronomical encyclopaedia, which he dedicated to his patron, Sultan Masood. The following anecdote recorded by his biographer testifies to his strength of character and his utter disregard for wealth. "Sultan Masood on receiving, *"Qanun al-Masudi"* presented to the author an elephant load of silver, which Al-Biruni returned to the royal treasury". His outstanding achievement in the realm of physics is the accurate determination of the weight of 18 stones. He also discovered that light travels faster than sound. His most brilliant work is *Asrar al-Baqiya*, a chronology of ancient nations, containing the minute and accurate details of geographical and historical information. The subject of calendar and era of ancient races has been specially dealt within this book, which also discusses the current theory of the rotation of earth on its axis. Longitudes and latitudes have been accurately determined by the famous author in this book. Besides the above, he has immensely added to the geological knowledge by providing a correct explanation of the formation of natural springs. He suggested that formerly the Indus valley was a basin filled with alluvial soil. Baihaqi, the Court historian of the Sultan of Ghazna said, "Abu Raihan was beyond comparison, superior to every man of his time in the art of composition and in scholarly accomplishments. He had a most rigid regard for truth."

One gets a glimpse of the wide range of his scientific knowledge, when he comes across such books as *Kitab-al-Saidana* (Materia Medica) dealing with medicine, the *Kitab-al-Jawahar* discussing different types of gems and their specific gravity and *Al-Tafhim*, a treatise which was translated into English by Wright in 1934.

Thus Al-Biruni figures in history as a subtle-minded mathematician whose accuracy in astronomical calculations had earned for him the nickname of "Magician" He was much respected by his great patron Mahmood. According to George Sarton, "His critical spirit, toleration, love of truth and intellectual courage, were almost without parallel in mediaeval times." Of such intellectual curiosity tirelessly pursued through a long life, there is hardly any other example recorded in the annals of Islam.

# IBN AL-HAITHAM

The Arabs who were pioneers in diverse branches of mediaeval sciences have made invaluable contribution to the field of optics. Of all the sciences that have received the imprint of Arab genius, optics stands on the top. The highest authority in optics during the mediaeval times whose brilliance outshone that of the Greek thinkers, was Ibn Al-Haitham, better known as Alhazen in the West. "The glory of Muslim science," writes Max Meyerhof," is in the field of optics. Here the mathematical ability of Alhazen and Kamal-a-Din outshone that of Euclid and Ptolemy. Real and lasting advance stands to their credit in this department of science".

Abu Ali Al Hasan ibn Al-Haitham, was one of the most outstanding mathematicians, physiologists and opticians of Islam. He was born at Basrah in 965 A.C. and received his education in Basrah and Baghdad which were great centres of learning in those days. Later, he moved to Egypt and entered into the service of the celebrated Fatimid Caliph Al-Hakim (996–1020 A.C.) and was entrusted with the task of discovering the method of controlling the annual floods caused by the Nile. But, having been unsuccessful in this mission, he remained underground and also assumed madness till al-Hakim's death. He also visited Spain. During this period he got ample time for his intellectual pursuits and composed a number of works on medicine, which was his original profession. He died in Cairo in 1039 A.C.

Alhazen, a versatile genius, made lasting contributions to optics, mathematics, physics, medicine and philosophy. The author of 'Uyunul Ariba fi Tabaqaat il Atibba', a well-known biographical work quoted the names of 200 scientific works written by Alhazen on diverse subjects, including optics, mathematics, medicine, physics and philosophy. Alhazen is best known to Europe through his optical works, which were translated into Latin.

His main work on optics, which was lost in Arabic, still survives in Latin. In it, Alhazen has corrected the conception of Ptolemy and Euclid that the eye sends out visual rays to the object of vision. "He was the first to correct the Greek misconception as to the nature of the vision", observes John Wil' am Draper in his *History of the Intellectual Development of Europe*, "showing hat the rays of light come from external objects to the eye, and do not issue forth from the eye, impinge on external things, as, up to his time, had been supp sed.

His explanation does not depend upon mere hypothesis or supposition, but is plainly based upon anatomical investigations as well as geometrical discussion".

His works on optics influenced the greatest Western scientists and paved the way for later discoveries and developments in the field of optics. He has examined the refraction of light rays through transparent objects, including air and water. In experimenting with spherical segments (glass vessels filled with water) he has forestalled the theoretical discovery of magnifying lenses, which was made three centuries later in Italy. He also prepared the ground for Snell and Descartes to establish the law of sines, six centuries later.

Among other things he discussed was the 'propagation of light and colours, optic illusions and reflection, with experiments for testing the angles of incidence and reflection'. His 'Alhazen Problems' in optics are still known throughout the West. 'In a spherical concave or convex, a cylindried or conical mirror to find the point from which an object of given position will be reflected to an eye of given position. It leads to an equation of the fourth degree which Alhazen solved by the use of a hyperbola.

He made a number of monumental discoveries in the field of optics, including one which locates retina, as the seat of vision. This discovery falsified the earlier contention of the Greek scientists that eye sends out visual rays to the object of the vision.

According to him, the impression made by light on 'retina is conveyed to the brain through optic nerves. He also explained how only one object is visible when seen from both the eyes, because the 'visual images are formed on symmetrical portions of the two retinas'. The optical illusions, according to him, are due to rays of light suffering from reflection or refraction. "He is perfectly aware", writes a Western orientalist, "that the atmosphere decreases in density with the increase of height, and from that consideration he shows that a ray of light, entering it obliquely, follows a curvilinear path which is concave toward the earth, and that, since the mind refers the position of an object to the direction in which the ray of light from it enters the eye, the result must be an illusion as respects the starry bodies; they appear to us, to use the Arabic term, nearer to the zenith than they actually are, and not in their true place." He has found out a wonderful optical illusion in the twilight when he sees stars. Sun and Moon before they have risen and after they have set. He has explained that greater the density of atmosphere, the greater the curvature of a ray of light. "To this refraction he truly refers the shortening, in their vertical diameter, of the horizontal Sun and Moon; to its variations he imputes the twinkling of the fixed stars". He quite accurately determined the height of the atmosphere as nearly 58½ miles. Describing his lasting contribution to optics, John William Draper states; "All this is very grand. Shall we compare it with the contemporary monk miracles or the monkish philosophy of Europe? It would make a profound impression if communicated for the first time to a scientific society in our own age". Commentaries on Alhazen's optics were written by oriental writers and his views were to some extent shared by Al-Biruni and Avicenna. His book on optics *'Kitab Al Manazir'* was translated into Latin by F. Risner and published in Basle in 1572 A.C. His other work on twilight was translated into Latin and published in the same year. His optics has immensely influenced the Western scientists, including the celebrated Roger Bacon and Vitelo.

Al Hazen has written several treatises on physical optics, including one on light. He thinks that light is a sort of fire which is reflected at the spheric limit of the atmosphere. In another treatise entitled, *'On Twilight Phenomena'*, he has calculated this atmosphere to be about 10 miles in height. Some of his treatises on physical optics deal with the halo, the rainbow, and with spherical and parabolic mirrors. He has fully explained the factors which cause a rainbow. He has also written treatises dealing with shadow and eclipses. All of these invaluable treatises are of a highly mathematical character. "Most of his works were products of the last ten years of his life", writes Max Meyerhof, "as was his fundamental study on the burning glass, in which he created a dioptric far superior to that of the Greeks. The work exhibits a profound and accurate conception of the nature of focussing, magnifying, and inversion of the image, and of the formation of rings and colours by experiments." The Muslim scientists were always particular in supporting their hypothesis with experiments. So was the case with Alhazen. During lunar eclipses, Alhazen observed the semi-lunar image of the Sun on a wall which was opposite to a small hole made in the window shutters. This was the first record of the 'camera obscura'. Alhazen has also written commentaries on the optical works of Ptolemy and Euclid and on the physics and problemata of Aristotle.

His *'Mizanul Hikma'* deals with the density of the atmosphere in which he has established a connection between the height of the atmosphere and its increasing density. He demonstrated that the weight of body increases in proportion to the increasing density of the atmosphere. He explains the force with which bodies will rise out of heavier media, in which these are immersed and also 'discussed the submergence of floating bodies as ships upon the sea'.

He has discussed the problem regarding the centre of gravity and has successfully applied it to the investigation of balances and steelyards, explaining the relations between the centre of gravity and the centre of suspension. He recognised gravity as a force, a theory which was later on developed by Newton. He knows correctly the relation between the velocities, spaces and time of falling bodies, and has very distinct idea of capillary action. "The determination of the densities of bodies", observes a Western writer, "as given by Alhazen, approach very closely to our own; in the case of mercury they are ʾu more exact than some of those of the last century."

His treatise on *'Configuration of the Universe* was translated into Latin. A Hebrew translation of it was made by the Jew Jacob bin Mahir, which was again translated into Latin by Abraham de Balmes in the latter half of the 15th century. This book was again translated in Spanish by Abraham de Toledo in the latter half of the 13th century A.C.

The optical works of Alhazen had a deep influence on the mediaeval scientists both in the East and the West. His writings on the subject paved the way for later researches on optics in the West. His works on optics and treatises on physics were translated into several European languages. A book on the balance of Wisdom, said to be written by Alhazen, translated by M. Khanikoff, the Russian Consul General at Tabriz, contained some useful mechanical theories and conceptions which have been propounded with exceptional clarity. About his views on human evolution, John William Draper observes: "Though more than seven centuries part him from our times, the physiologists of this age may accept him as their compeer, since he received and defended the doctrine now forcing its way, of the progressive development of animal forms. He upheld the affirmation of those who said that man, in his progress, passes through a definite succession of states; not however, "that he was all once a bull, and was then changed to an ass, and afterwards into a horse, and after that into an ape, and finally became a man." "This," he says, "is only a misrepresentation by people of what is really meant." His progressive ideas on the evolution of man led to the development of this theory by modern scientists, including Darwin.

The abbreviated translations of a large number of Alhazen's treatises have been published in German, by E. Weidemann, together with critical notes. The celebrated American historian George Sarton has given a large list of his works in his *'Introduction to the Study of Science'*. According to Phillip K. Hitti, "Roger Bacon, Leonardo da Vinci and John Kepler, show traces of his influence. His *'Kitab Al Manazir'* (The Book on Optics) influenced all the mediaeval writers on the subject, who borrowed their ideas from him. "Roger Bacon" (13th century), admits Max Meyerhof, "and all mediaeval writers on optics—notably the Pol Witelo or Vitello, base their optical works largely on Alhazen's *'Opticae Thesaurus*. His work also influenced Leonardo da Vinci and John Kepler. The latter modestly entitled his fundamental work on dioptrics *'Ad Vitellionem Paralipomena* (Frankfurt 1604)"*.

# IBN AL-BAITAR

Observation and experiment are the two sources for acquiring scientific knowledge. Aristotle, the father of Greek sciences, made imperishable contributions to physics, astronomy, biology, meteorology and other sciences. The Greek method of obtaining scientific knowledge, it may be noted, was mainly speculative, hence science as such could make little headway in Greece.

The Arabs who were more realistic and practical in their approach adopted the experimental method for harnessing scientific knowledge. Observation and experiment formed the vehicle of their scientific pursuits, hence they gave a new orientation to science of which the world was totally unaware. Their achievements in the field of experimental science added a golden chapter to the annals of scientific knowledge of the world and opened a new vista for the growth of modern sciences. Al-Ghazali was the follower of Aristotle in logic, but among Muslims Ishraqi and Ibn-Taimiya were first to undertake the systematic refutation of Greek logic. Abu Bakr Razi criticised Aristotle's first figure and followed the inductive spirit which was reformulated by John Stuart Mill. Ibn-Hazm in his well-known work *'Scope of Logic'*, lays stress on sense perception as a source of knowledge and Ibn-Taimiya in his *'Reformation of Logic'*, proves beyond doubt that induction is the surer form of argument, which ultimately gave birth to the method of observation and experiment. It is absolutely wrong to assume that the experimental method was formulated in Europe. Roger Bacon, who, in the West is known as the originator of the experimental method, had himself got training from the pupils of Spanish Moors, and had learnt everything from Muslim sources. The influence of Ibn Haitham on Roger Bacon is clearly visible in his works. Europe was too slow to recognise the Islamic origin of her much advertised scientific (Experimental) method. Writing in the *'Making of Humanity'*, Briffault admits: 'It was under their successors at the Oxford School that Roger Bacon learned Arabic and Arabic science. Neither Roger nor his later namesake has any title to be credited with having introduced the experimental method. Roger Bacon was no more than one of the apostles of Muslim science which he transmitted to Christian Europe. As a matter of fact he never wearied of declaring that the knowledge of Arabic and Arabic science was for his contemporaries the only way to true knowledge. Discussions as to who was the originator of the experimental method are part of the colossal misrepresentation of the origins of European civilization. The experimental method of Arabs was by Bacon's time widespread and eagerly cultivated throughout Europe. . . .Science is the most momentous contribution of Arab civilization to the modern world, but its fruits were slow in ripening. Not until long after Moorish culture had sunk back into darkness, did the giant which it had given birth to raise his might. It was not science only which brought Europe back to life. Other and manifold influences from the civilization of Islam communicated its first glow to European life. . . .For although there is not a single aspect of European growth in which the decisive influence of Islamic culture is traceable, nowhere is it so clear and momentous as in the genesis of that power which constitutes the permanent distinctive force of the modern world, and the supreme source of its victory—natural science and the scientific spirit. . . .The debt of our science to that of the Arabs does not consist in startling discoveries or revolutionary theories; science owes a great deal more to Arab culture. it owes its existence. The ancient world was, as we saw, pre-scientific. The astronomy and mathematics of Greeks were a foreign importation never thoroughly acclimatized in Greek culture. The Greeks systematised, generalised and theorised, but the patient ways of investigation, the accumulation of positive knowledge, the minute methods of science, detailed and prolonged observation and experimental enquiry were altogether alien to the Greek temperament. Only in Hellenistic Alexandria was any approach to scientific work conducted in the ancient classical world. What we call science arose in Europe as a result of a new scientific inquiry, of new methods of investigation, of the method of experiment, observation, measurement of the development of mathematics in a form unknown to the Greeks. That spirit and these methods were introduced into the European world by the Arabs". In his outstanding work, *'The Reconstruction of Religious Thought in Islam',* Dr. Muhammad Iqbal, the poet of Islam writes: 'The first important point to note about the spirit of Muslim culture then is that for purposes of knowledge, it fixes its gaze on the concrete, the finite. It is further clear that the birth of the method of observation and experiment in Islam was due not to a compromise with Greek thought but to a prolonged intellectual warfare with it. In fact the influence of Greeks who, as Briffault says, were interested chiefly in theory, not in fact, tended rather to obscure the Muslim vision of the Quran, and for at least two centuries kept the practical Arab temperament from asserting itself and coming to its own." Thus the experimental method introduced by the Arabs was responsible for the rapid advancement of science during the mediaeval times. This experimental method was universally applied by the Arabs to their scientific investigations, also by Ibn al-Baitar, the greatest Muslim natural scientist.

Abu Muhammad Abdullah ibn Ahmad ibn al-Baitar Diya al-Din al-Malaqi was the last of the great Muslim scientists who had undertaken an extensive tour of the Mediterranean littoral in quest of rare botanical herbs grown there. Born in Malaga (Spain) towards the end of the 12th century A.C. he rose to be the celebrated Spanish *Muslim* botanist and pharmacist, who, according to George Sarton, was 'the greatest (botanist) of Islam and the Middle ages'. Ibn al-Baitar means son of a horse doctor or farrier. His father was a farrier. He received his early education from Abul Abbas al Nabati, who was a renowned herbalist of his time and collected plants around Seville (Spain) along with his teacher. He greatly owed his interest and knowledge of botany to his illustrious teacher. He set out from Spain about 1219 A.C. travelling in North Africa and passing through Bugia, Constantine, Tunis, he sailed to the southern coast of Asia Minor reaching Adalia in 1224 A.C. Later he entered the service of the Ayubid King, Malik al-Kamil as his Chief Herbalist at Cairo and was called *'Rais ala Sairi-i-Ashshabin'*. In 1237, when the rule of Malik al-Kamil was extended to Damascus also, Ibn Baitar moved to that city along with his patron. At last he settled down in Damascus and remained in service of Malik al-Saleh (1240—49) who succeeded Malik al-Kamil. Occasionally he made extensive tours of Arabia, Syria, Palestine and Iraq in search of herbs grown there. He had made a thorough study of the plants growing in countries bordering the Mediterranean sea. He died in Damascus in 1248 A.C.

He roamed about in search of plants and collected herbs on   the Mediterranean littoral, from Spain to Syria. His main work, a collection of simples known as *'Kitab al Jami fi Adwiya al Mufrada'*, is the most outstanding botanical work in Arabic. According to a well-known Western critic, "This book, in fact, is the most important for the whole period extending from Dioscorides down to the 16th century". It is an encyclopaedic work on the subject. Describing more than 1,400 medical drugs and comparing them with the records of more than 150 ancient and Arabian authors, this book deals with about 200 novel plants which were not known up to that time. It is an invaluable book containing simple remedies regarding animals, vegetables and minerals. Being a methodical compilation based on personal observations, it deals with simples, drugs and various species of food. Besides its own original contributions, the book contains the whole of Dioscorides and Galens knowledge on the subject. Al-Razi and Ibn Sina have also been frequently quoted by him. The synonyms of plant names have received his special consideration, and he has given the names of the plants not only in Arabic and Greek but also occasionally in Latin, Persian, Berber and Arabic dialect of Spain. His *'Jami'* is acclaimed by Meyer *(Gesch der Botanik)* as "a monument of industry". According to Max Meyerhof, "It is a work of extraordinary erudition and observation and is the greatest of the Arabic books on botany". Latin version of his *Simplicia* was published in 1758 at Cremona.

His second monumental work *"Kitab al Mughani fil Adwiya al-Mufrada"* is a materia medica dealing with medicine. It is almost the reversion of the first book. Though dealing with the same simples and vegetables it is arranged in therapeutical order instead of alphabetical one. This book contains 20 chapters including those dealing with simples for diseases of head, ear, eye, cosmetics, simples against fevers, antidotes and most common drugs. His *'Mughani'* is a materia medica and not a natural history. In this book, the authorities quoted also differ from the first one and the celebrated surgeon Abdul Qasim has been too frequently quoted in it. The sources of quite a few items of this book may be traced to al Idrisi and al Ghafiqi. Both of his well-known works which were completed during the first quarter of the 13th century were dedicated to his patron Malik al-Saleh Ayubi. Ibn al Usaibia who was a disciple of Ibn Baitar accompanied him during his botanical execursions around Damascus.

The influence of Ibn al-Baitar may be traced to the eastern as well as Western writers on the subject. His two monumental works which were considered authority on the subject influenced the contemporary and later botanists. Andrea Alpago (latter half of 15th century) made use of it to enrich his glossary of Ibn Sina's *Qanun*. His article on Lemons was translated from Al-Baitar's *'Jami'*. The first Western orientalist who was considerably influenced by al-Baitar's writings was Guillaume Postal (1510–1581 A.C.). The first complete translation of *Jami* in any Western language, appeared in 1758 A.C.

Ibn al-Baitar is undoubtedly the greatest botanist of Islam and of the Middle ages whose writings prepared the ground for the development of botanical science during the modern times.

# IBN RUSHD

Muslim Spain has produced some of the brightest intellectual luminaries of the Middle ages. One of them was Ibn Rushd, better known as Averroes in the West who is universally acknowledged as the greatest philosopher of Islam and one of the greatest of all times. Being a versatile genius, he influenced the course of thought both in the East and the West in more than one domain of knowledge. According to George Sarton, "He was great because of the tremendous stir he made in the minds of men for centuries. A history of Averroism would include all the essential elements of a history of thought from the end of the 12 century to the end of the sixteenth—a period of four centuries which would perhaps deserve as much as any other to be called the Middle ages, for it was the real transition between ancient and modern methods."

Abul Waleed Muhammad ibn Ahmed ibn Muhammad ibn Rushd, known as Averroes in the West was born in Cordova, the Metropolis of Muslim Spain in 1126 A.C. He came of an illustrious Muslim family of Cordova which held the high office of the Grand Qazi for the last two generations, Ibn Rushd himself occupying the same post in the third generation. His grandfather Abul Waleed Muhammad ibn Rushd (1058—1126) was an eminent Maliki Theologian, who was the Imam of the Grand Mosque of Cordova. His father also occupied the high office of Qazi. The young Ibn Rushd received his education in his native city which was the highest seat of learning in the West. He was taught Tradition by Abul Qasim, Abu Marwan ibn Masarrat Abu Jafar ibn Aziz and Abu Abdullah Marzi. He learnt 'Fiqh' from Hafiz Abu Muhammad ibn Rizq. Abu Jafar, a reputed scholar, taught him medicine. Ibn Rushd, soon acquired great scholarship in literature, law, philosophy and medicine. He was a contemporary of some of the outstanding thinkers of Muslim Spain, including Ibn Zuhr, Ibn Baja and Ibn Tufail. Ibn Rushd was a juris-consult of the first rank and was appointed Qazi of Seville in 1169-70 A.C. In 1182-83 he was invited by the Almohade Caliph Abu Yaqub (1163—84) to Morocco and replaced Ibn Tufail as the Court Physician. In the beginning, he was patronised and respected by the succeeding Almohade Caliph Yaqub al-Mansur (1184—99 A.C.), but, when the pent-up Berber fanaticism burst forth, he fell victim to religious fanatics who were jealous of his genius. The Caliph had to banish him to Lucena, a Jewish colony near Cordova. His entire library consisting of invaluable books except the scientific ones was reduced to ashes in 1194-95. In 1198, when the religious fanaticism subsided, Ibn Rushd was recalled to Morocco by the Almohade Ruler

Yaqub al-Mansur, but he did not live long to enjoy the favour of his patron and died on December 10, 1198 A.C. at the age of 75.

Ibn Rushd was known for his humility and hospitality. Being pensive by nature, he abhorred position and wealth. As a judge, he was very kind-hearted and never awarded corporal punishment to anyone. He passed most of his time in study and, according to Ibn al-Abar, during his long life there had been only two nights when he could not study—one was the night of his marriage and the other was the night of his death. He did not make any distinction in his treatment towards friends and foes. He was a great lover of his native land. Like Plato who in his *'Republic'* has highly praised Greece, Ibn Rushd has claimed his native land, Spain, to be the rival of Greece. According to Ptolemy, Greece possessed the best climate in the world but Ibn Rushd claims the same distinction for Cordova, the Capital of Muslim Spain.

Averroes, who was considered Avicenna of the West, applied himself to philosophy, mathematics, medicine, astronomy, logic and Islamic jurisprudence. His works have been given to the world by Renan. "He was one of the profoundest commentators," says Munk, "of Aristotle's works." According to Ibn al-Abar, his writings are spread over more than 20 thousand pages, the most important works being on philosophy, medicine and *'Fiqh'* (Islamic jurisprudence). He was an eminent legist of his time and worked as a Qazi for a considerable period. His *'Hidayat al Mujtahid wa Nihayat al Muqtasid'* which deals with Maliki *Fiqh,* is, according to Abu Jafar Zahbi, the best book ever written on this subject. Renan has given a detailed list of his writings in his 'Averroes' (Edition III, pages 58—79). The list totals 67 works of Ibn Rushd, including 28 on philosophy, 5 on theology, 8 on law, 4 on astronomy, 2 on grammar and 20 on medicine. He was an astronomer of repute, who wrote *'Kitab fi Harkat al Falak,'* a treatise dealing with the motion of the sphere. He also summarised the *'Almagest'* of Ptolemy which was translated into Hebrew by Jacob Anatoli in 1231 A.C. He is credited with the discovery of sunspots.

Muslim Rulers had had the reputation of being the greatest patrons of learning in the world. Writing in his well-known book the *"Making of Humanity,"* Robert Briffault admits: "The incorruptible treasures and delights of intellectual culture were accounted by the princes of Baghdad, Shiraz and Cordova, the truest and proudest pomps of their courts. But it was not a mere appendage of their princely vanity that the wonderful growth of Islamic science and learning was fostered by their patronage. They pursued culture with the personal ardour of an over mastering craving. Never before and never since, on such a scale, has the spectacle been witnessed of the ruling classes throughout the length and breadth of a vast empire given over entirely to a frenized passion for acquirement of knowledge. Learning used to have become with them the chief business of life. Khalifa and Amirs hurried from their Diwans to closet themselves in their libraries and observatories. . . . . . . Caravans laden with manuscripts and botanical specimens plied from Bukhara to Tigris, from Egypt to Andulusia; embassies were sent to Constantinople and to India for the purpose of obtaining books and teachers; a collection of Greek authors or a distinguished mathematician was eagerly demanded as the ransom of an Empire." The Umayyad Caliph of Spain, Al-Hakam had founded a magnificent library containing about half a million books. He had accumulated a rare collection of books on eastern philosophy and was instrumental in creating a taste for philosophy in Spain which in later years produced some of the greatest Muslim philosophers in the West, including Ibn Rushd. About two centuries later another Muslim ruler of the West, Abdul Momin who was himself a great scholar had drawn to his Court a galaxy of talented thinkers, including Ibn Tufail and Ibn Rushd. The learned Averroes owed his knowledge in philosophy to Abu Jafar Haroon, a well-known rationalist and according to Abi Asibiyah, to Ibn Baja who is recognised as the Aristotle of Andulusia. But the philosophy of Ibn Baja reached its climax in Averroes who surpassed his teacher and rose to be the greatest commentator and exponent of Aristotalian philosophy in the world. Together with Ibn Masarra and Ibnul Arabi, Ibn Rushd forms the trio of the greatest Arabian thinkers of Spain. The first two were essentially mystic, while the third (Averroes) was a rationalist.

His chief philosophical work is *'Tahafut al-Tahafut'* (The Incoherence of the Incoherence) which was written in refutation of Al Ghazali's work, *'Tahafut al Falasifa* (The Destraction of Philosophy). This work of Averroes evoked severe criticism and stirred bitter reaction throughout the Muslim world. A strong refutation of Ibn Rushd's arguments in *Tahafut al-Tahafut* was made by a Turk, Mustafa ibn Yousuf al Bursawi, commonly known as Khwaja Zada (d/1487-88) who wrote a third destraction.' This 'indicated once more the weakness of human understanding and the strength of faith. But, contrary to Muslim reactions, the philosophical writings of Averroes produced a great impact on Christian Europe and still he continues to be the most popular Muslim philosopher in the West. Alfred Gillaume in his article on philosophy and theology in the *'Legacy of Islam,'* writes that Ibn Rushd "belongs to Europe and European thought rather than to the East . . . . . . .Averroism continued to be a living factor in European thought until the birth of modern experimental science. Latin is said to have preserved more than one of Ibn Rushd's works which Arabic had lost." His *Tahafut al-Tahafut* is essentially a reply of Al Ghazali's attack on rationalism. His fame as a philosopher specially in the West both in Christian and Jewish circles is based on his three commentaries of Aristotle's works known as the *'Jami'* (Summary), the *'Talkhis'* (Resume) and a long *'Tafsir* or *Sharah'* (Commentary). These commentaries were translated into Hebrew by Samuel ibn Tibbon in the first half of the 13th century, by Jacob Anatoli in 1232 A.C. and by Michael Scott and Hermann, the German into Latin. These translations were later revised in the 15th and 16th centuries. Among his other philosophical treatises are *'Kitab Fasl al Maqal'* and the *'Kitab al Kashf al Manahij,* which were edited by M. J. Muller and published in Munich in 1859 A.C.

Regarding predestination, Ibn Rushd maintained that man was 'neither the absolute master of his destiny nor bound by fixed immutable decrees, but, that, the truth lay in the middle, i.e., *'Al Amr Bain al Amarin.'* 'Human actions depend partly on his free-will and partly on outside causes. These causes spring from general laws of nature, God alone knows their sequence.' According to him, man should make utmost efforts to attain perfection which implies complete identification with the active universal intellect. This human perfection can only be attained through study, speculation and negation of desires specially those relating to the senses.

Ibn Rushd considered the Caliphate Rashida (Pious Caliphs) as the model Republic in which the dreams of Plato were realised. He claimed women to be equal of men in all respects and possessing equal capacities to shine in war and peace. He has cited women warriors among Greeks, Arabs and Africans.

Ibn Rushd was the most learned commentator of Aristotelian works and was more Aristotelian than Ibn Sina. He corrected some of the misconceptions of Ibn Sina about the rational philosophy of Aristotle. A number of his invaluable works perished when the Christian conquerors set fire to the intellectual treasures of the Moors (Spanish Muslims) amassed after centuries of intellectual activities. More than 80 thousand rare manuscripts were reduced to ashes in Granada alone. Muslim thinkers like Ibn Sina and Ibn Rushd formulated their ideas with logical precision and in the latter, 'Arabic philosophy reached its apogee.' It is all the more creditable for the learned Averroes that he compiled his varied and invaluable works in such a distracted state of mind and disturbed conditions.

In the beginning, philosophy was considered to be an irreligious subject in Muslim Spain where the society was formulated on true Arabic lines. Ishaq ibn Umran, a physician of Baghdad was first to introduce philosophy in Spain, which flourished thereafter, specially during the reigns of Al Hakam and Yousuf ibn Momin. The ideas of Ibn Rushd, were incompatible with the religious sentiments of orthodox Muslims and he was accused of being an atheist. But, according to Phillip K. Hitti, "He was a rationalist and claimed the right to submit everything save the revealed dogmas of faith to the judgement of reason, but he was not a free thinker or unbeliever. His views of creation of God were evolutionary: not a matter of days but eternity." George Sarton also holds similar views. "Ibn Rushd was not by any means less honest and sincere, nor was he necessarily less pious, than the other schoolmen; but he was more intelligent, and his deeper vision enabled him to reconcile statements which seemed irreconcilable to others." Ibn Rushd, being a rationalist wanted to explain religion in the light of reason. His contemporary Abdul Kabir, a highly religious person, describes him as a person anxious to establish a harmony between religion and philosophy. In his well-known book, *'Averroes and Averroism,'* Renan writes: "There is nothing to prevent our supposing that Ibn Rushd was a sincere believer in Islamism, especially when we consider how little irrational the supernatural element in the essential dogmas of this religion is, and how closely this religion approaches the purest Deism."

Ibn Rushd, a versatile genius, is the author of about 20 medical treatises including his encyclopaedic work, *'Kitab al Kulliyat fil Tibb'* (General Rules of Medicine), better known as *'Colliget'* in Latin. This book was written before 1162 A.C. comprises of seven volumes, treating respectively of anatomy, physiology, general pathology, diagnosis, materia medica, hygiene and general therapeutics. He considered that none suffers twice from smallpox. He also fully understood the function of retina. But his 'Colliget' stands no comparison to 'Continents' of Rhazes and *'Canon'* of Avicenna. Actually his fame as a physician was eclipsed by his fame as a philosopher. His *Kulliyat (Colliget)* was first translated into Latin by the Jew Bonacosa in the latter half of 13th century A.C. It was again translated into Latin by Syphorien Champier about 1537 A.C. It was twice translated into Hebrew. "In Spain, the philosophical bias predominated among medical men," remarks, Max Meyerhof. "The prototypes of this combination are the two Muslims, Ibn Zuhr (Avenzoar) and Ibn Rushd (Averroes)."

Muslim Spain has produced some talented musicians both theorists and practical musicians. Ibn Bajja (d. 1138) known as Avempace, who as musical theorist, occupies the same place in the West which Farabi occupies in the East. Ibn Rushd has also made invaluable contribution to musical theory by writing a commentary on Aristotle's *'De Anima,'* 'dealing perspicuously with the theory of sound.' This was translated into Latin by Michael Scot (d. 1232).

A number of his biographies have appeared in different languages but the most elaborate account of his life and works is found in *'Averroes et j'averroisme'* written by Ernest Renan published in Paris in 1852 A.D. "This admirable work," says Georgs Sarton, "has justly become a classic; it is a penetrating study which every student of mediaeval philosophy ought to read, but it must be used with caution." About the autocratic rule, Ibn Rushd has said, "The tyrant is he who governs for himself and not for his people."

It has been customary with the Western writers to minimise the intellectual attainments of Muslim thinkers, but now the less partial researches have lifted this veil and their achievements stand in all their glory. Alfred Guillaume says, "We may be sure that those who accuse the Muslim scholars of lack of originality and of intellectual decadence have never read Averroes or looked into Algazel but have adopted second hand judgements. The presence of doctrines of Islamic origin in the very citadel of Western Christianity, the *'Summa'* of Aquinas, is a sufficient refutation of the charge of lack of originality and sterility."

The works of Ibn Rushd (Averroes) which were very popular in the West were translated into several European languages including Latin, Hebrew, German and English. It was through his commentaries that the West learned about Aristotle and other Greek thinkers. The Latin *'Editio Princeps'* of Aristotle with Averroes' commentaries was published for 50 times in Venice alone. Andrea Alpago of Belluno in Italy (d. 1520) translated into Latin, Avicenna's *'Canon'* and the minor works of Averroes. The Italian Emperor Frederik, the

Great, who, on account of being a great patron of Muslim culture, was accused by the Bishops to have embraced Islam, was instrumental in getting translated a number of Arabic books, including those of Averroes.

Thus, the works of Averroes which were not so popular in Islamic countries wielded considerable influence in the Western thought, both Christian and Jewish. "He deeply influenced Jewish philosophy through many translations and disciples," writes George Sarton, in his monumental work, *An Introduction to the Study of Science.* "Jewish Averroism reached its zenith under Levi ben Gershon in the first half of the fourteenth century, and it continued to prosper until the end of the fifteenth century. The Christian schoolmen were influenced as the Jewish, and in various ways." According to Phillip K. Hitti, "Last of the great Arabic writing philosophers, Ibn Rushd belonged more to Christian Europe than to Muslim Asia or Africa. To the West he became the commentator as Aristotle was 'The Teacher.' From the end of the 12th to the end of the 16th century Averroism remained the dominant school of thought, and that in spite of the orthodox reaction it created first among the Muslims in Spain, then among the Talmudists and finally among the Christian clergy . . . . . After being purged of objectionable matter by ecclesiastical authorities, his writings became prescribed studies in the University of Paris and other institutions of higher learning. With all its excellence and other misconceptions collected under its name, the intellectual movement initiated by Ibn Rushd continued to be a living factor in European thought until the birth of modern experimental science". Writing in the Chapter 'Crusades' of *Legacy of Islam,* Ernest Barker admits: "The philosophy of Cordova and its great teacher Ibn Rushd (Averroes) penetrated to the University of Paris".

# AL-MAWARDI

The glorious Caliphate of the Abbasides provided the most congenial atmosphere for the advancement of learning and is rightly known as the golden period of Islamic civilization. It was during this Regime that the celebrated Caliph Mamoon ar-Rashid founded his *Darul Hukama* (House of Wisdom) which served as the laboratory for translation and research work that paved the way for future advancement of knowledge. It was this period which gave birth to legists like Imam Abu Hanifa, Imam Malik, Imam Shafii and Imam Abu Yusuf; philosophers like Ishaq al-Kindi, Imam Ghazali and Abu Nasr Farabi; scientists and mathematicians like Musa Khwarizmi, Jabir ibn Hayyan and Zakriya Razi; Sufis like Hazrat Abdul Qadir Jilani, Hazrat Junaid Baghdadi and Hazrat Shibli; musicians like Ishaq Mausili and Zalzal and administrators like Yahya Bermaki and Hasan ibn Sahl. Intellectual development during the epoch attained a standard without any precedent in the history of Islam. The Caliphs and their Amirs vied with one another in literary pursuits and patronage of learning. One of the great intellectual luminaries of this age was Al-Mawardi, who is distinguished as the first political thinker of Islam and ranks amongst the greatest political thinkers of mediaeval times, including Nizamul Mulk Toosi, Ibn Khaldun and Machiavelli. From the post of a Qazi, he rose to be the Roving Ambassador of the Caliph and solved many knotty political tangles of his State. "Al-Khatib of Baghdad". writes an orientalist, "on the authority of Abu Ali Hasan ibn Da'ud, relates that the people of Basrah always took pride in their three learned countrymen and their works viz., Khalid ibn Ahmad (d. 175 A.H.) and his work, *'Kitab-ul-Amin'*, Sibawayh (d. 180 A.H.) and his *'Kitab-un-Nahw';* Al-Jahiz (d. 225 A.H.) and his *Al-Bayan-wat-Tabiyan*. To this may be added the name of a fourth scholar Al-Mawardi, the learned jurisconsult and political economist of Basrah, whose monumental work *"Al-Ahkam-us-Sultaniyah'*. is a master-piece of politico-religious literature of Islam.

Ali ibn Muhammad ibn Habib, Abul Hasan Al-Mawardi was born at Basrah in 364 A.H./1058 A.C. into an Arab family which manufactured and carried on trade in rose water, hence the sobriquet 'Al-Mawardi'. He received his early education at Basrah, studying jurisprudence from the well-known Shafiite jurist, Abul Qasim Abul Wahid As-Saimari. Later he proceeded to Baghdad for higher studies and learnt jurisprudence, grammar and literature from Abdullah al-Bafi and Sheikh Abdul Hamid al-Isfraini. Soon he was well versed in Islamic studies including *Hadith* and *Fiqh* as well as in politics, ethics and literature.

He served as Qazi (Judge) at various places and was appointed the "Qazi al-Quzat" (Supreme Judge) of Ustuwa, a district of Nishapur. In 429 A.H. he was elevated to the highest judicial post of "Aqb-al-Quzat" (Grand Qazi) of Baghdad, a post he held with distinction until his death.

He was an eminent practical politician and a prolific writer on diverse subjects like religion, ethics, literature and politics. The Abbaside Caliph al-Qadir Billah (381–422 A.H.) held him in high esteem and Qa'im bin Amrillah (391–460 A.H.), the 26th Abbaside Caliph of Baghdad posted him as his Roving Ambassador and sent him on several diplomatic missions to the neighbouring and satellite States. His wise statesmanship was, to a great extent, responsible for maintaining the prestige of the dwindling Caliphate of Baghdad among her too powerful and almost independent Seljuk and Buwayhid Amirs. He was heavily loaded with valuable presents by the Seljuk, Buwayhid and other Amirs whom he proffered wise counsels which were in conformity with the dignity of the Caliphate of Baghdad. According to Jalal-ud-Dawlah, he surpassed other men of his class in wealth. A few persons charged him with professing Mutazili creed but later writers have refuted it. He died in 1058 A.C. after a successful career.

Al-Mawardi, being an exponent of the Shafi'ite school, was a prominent traditionist. Unfortunately none of his works on the subject have survived. No doubt a number of *Hadiths* from him have been quoted in *'Ahkam-us-Sultaniya'*, *'A'lam-un-Nubuwa-t'*, and *'Adab-ud-Dunya-wad Din'*. His hold on *Hadith* can be gauged from his *'A'lam-un-Nubuwat'*. His explanation of the difference between miracle and magic in the light of the sayings of the Prophet is according to Tash Kopruizadah the 'best recorded until that time.'

As a Jurisconsult, Al-Mawardi occupies an eminent place amongst Muslim scholars on the subject. He had specialised in the subject and was universally recognised as one of the greatest jurists of his time. He propounded the Shafi'ite *Fiqh* (Jurisprudence) in his masterly work *'Al Hawi'* which served as an invaluable reference book on Shafi'ite Jurisprudence for the later jurists, including Al-Isnavi who speaks very highly of it. This book of 8,000 pages was condensed by Al-Mawardi into an epitome comprising of 40 pages and was named *'Al Iqna.'*

Al-Mawardi enjoys high reputation among the old commentators of the Holy Quran. His commentary entitled *'Nukat-wa'l-Uyum'* has a place of its own amongst the classical commentaries of Al-Qushairi, Al-Razi, Al-Isfahani and Al-Kirmani. The charge that his certain commentaries bear germs of Mutazilite views does not stand to reason and such outstanding divines as Ibn-Taimiya has classed it among the good books on the subject. His commentary of the Holy Quran had been very popular and it was abridged by a writer. A Spanish Muslim scholar named Abul Hasan Ali came all the way from Saragossa in Spain to read this book from the author himself.

Al-Mawardi also wrote a book on the Quranic similitudes, which, in the opinion of As-Suyuti was the first book on this subject. Emphasising the importance of this book Al-Mawardi writes, "one of the main Quranic sciences is the science of parables or similitudes. People have neglected it as they have confined their attention to similitudes only and have lost sight of the similars mentioned in the similies. A similitude without a similar is a horse without a bridle, or a camel without a rein".

Al-Mawardi, though not a regular student of political science, was a high class political economist and his speculative political writings are of much value. His monumental work, *'Al Ahkam-us-Sultaniyah'* occupies an important place amongst the political treatises written during the mediaeval times. He wrote four books on political science namely: (1) *'Al Ahkam-us-Sultaniyah'* (Laws concerning Statecraft), (2) *'Adab-al-Wazir'* (Ethics of the Minister), (3) *'Siyasat-ul-Malik'* (Kings' Politics), and (4) *'Tahsil-un-Nasr-wat-Ta'jit-uz-Zafar'* (Facilitating conquest and hastening victory). Of these, the first two books have been published. His *'Al-Ahkam-us-Sultaniyah'*, which has been translated into several languages including French and Urdu is an invaluable work on Islamic public laws. In the contents of this book, he has followed the *Kitab-ul-Umm* of As-Shafi'i. the *'Adab-al-Wazir'* (Ethics of the Minister) which deals with the functions of the Prime Minister and lays down sound advice on public administration. A vast literature dealing the duties and privileges of the Prime Minister has been produced in Islamic countries, but Al-Mawardi's *'Adab al-Wazir'* is the most comprehensive and important work on the subject which embraces almost all phases on this intricate matter.

The political as well as religious writings of Al-Mawardi wielded considerable influence over the later writers on the subject, specially in Islamic countries. His influence may be traced into the *'Siyasat Nama'* of Nizamul Mulk Toosi and the *'Prolegomena'* of Ibn Khaldun. Ibn Khaldun, who is recognised as the founder of Sociology and is an outstanding writer on political economy, no doubt, excelled Al-Mawardi in many respects. Enumerating the necessity of a ruler, Ibn Khaldun says: "The sovereign exists for the good of the people . . . . The necessity of a ruler arises from the fact that human beings have to live together and unless there is someone to maintain order, society would break into pieces." He observes: 'There is a constant tendency in an oriental monarchy towards absolutism, towards unlimited power, so undoubtedly the tendency of the oriental governors was towards greater and greater independence of central authority." Earlier, Al-Mawardi had pointed out the unlimited powers of governors during the decline of Abbaside Caliphate when the governorship was acquired through usurpation and the central authority had little control over them.

Thus Al-Mawardi stands out as the first great political thinker in Islam whose writings as well as practical experience in politics have gone a long way in moulding the political outlook of the later writers.

# NASIR AL-DIN TOOSI

The citadel of Almut standing amidst the lofty Caucasus was the stronghold of the Ismailis, where Hasan ibn Sabha and his followers (Assassins) had built their earthly paradise. This inaccessible stronghold which for centuries had successfully defied the successive invasions was at last captured by Hulaku Khan, the Mongol in 1256 A.C. A long line of prisoners tied with one another was paraded before the Mongol tyrant. Among them was a middle aged man peculiarly dressed, who being ushered in Hulaku's presence impressed him with his great eloquence and extraordinary intelligence. The man introduced to him was Nasir al-Din Toosi, a versatile genius and above all, a capable astrologer, who could foretell the fortune of the Mongol conqueror. Hulaku, finding Nasir al-Din to be a very useful person took him in his retinue and kept him as his trusted Adviser throughout his life.

Nasir al-Din Toosi, one of the great thinkers of Islam, was a man of towering ability whose encyclopaedic work embraced almost all branches of knowledge, including astronomy, mathematics, sciences, optics, geography, medicine, philosophy, logic, music, mineralogy, theology and ethics.

Abu Jafar Muahmmad ibn Muhammad al Hasan Nisar al-Din al-Toosi al-Muhaqqiq (the Investigator) was born on February 18, 1201 A.C. in Toos, a city of Khorasan where he received his early education. His principal teacher was Kamal al-Din ibn Yunus. His fame as a versatile scholar and astrologer soon spread to the distant parts of Persia and he was kidnapped by Nasir al-Din Abd al-Rahman ibn Ali Mansur, the Ismaili Governor of Kohistan, who despatched him to Almut, where he remained as an unwilling guest for a long time. In 1256 A.C when Almut was captured by Hulaku Khan, he entered the service of the Mongol conqueror and remained his trusted Adviser. In February, 1258, when Baghdad capitulated to the Mongols and was sacked by them, Nasir al-Din Toosi who accompanied them was greatly instrumental in influencing Hulaku, to spare a part of its population as well as the Shiite sanctuaries in Southern Iraq.

Hulaku appointed Toosi as his Wazir and Supervisor of Wakf Estates. It was under his orders that Toosi at the age of sixty set about building in 1259— one year after the sack of Baghdad, on the fortified Maragha Hill, the world famous observatory popularly known as the Maragha observatory. It was equipped with the best available instruments and staffed by some of the prominent astronomers of the age who carried on most important astronomical researches under the direction and supervision of Toosi.

Toosi retained his influence in the Mongol Court even under Abaka without interruption until his death on June 26, 1274 A.C. in Baghdad.

Nasir al-Din Toosi was an outstanding encyclopaedist with a fine synthetic brain. He was a prolific writer; not less than 56 of his works are listed by Brockalmann. A large number of his treatises are not included in this list. He had made a thorough study of Greek learning and had translated as well as edited a number of Greek works, into Persian. This collection of translations is called *'Kitab al Mutawassitat Bain al Handasa wal Hai-a'* (The middle books between geometry and astronomy). He discussed scientific matters with the celebrated Sufi poet Jalaluddin Rumi through correspondence, and with Najam al-Din Katibi orally. He dedicated his *"Talkhis Muhassal"* to the historian Alaud-din and his *"Awsaf al Ashraf"* to Sahib Diwan Shamsuddin. His fame as one of the greatest intellects of Islam rests on his researches in astronomy, astrology, mathematics, physics, medicine and exact sciences.

It is in astronomy that Nasir al-Din Toosi acquired great fame and made lasting contributions. His practical work and invaluable researches in the subject owed much to the interest of Mongol Rulers, especially Hulaku. He took 12 years to complete his new *'Planetary Tables"* known as *'Ilkhanian Tables.'*

He wrote a number of astronomical treatises of which the most important is *'Kitab al Tazkira al Nasirya'* or *"Tazkira fi Ilm a hai'a"* (Memorial of Astronomy) a survey of the whole field of astronomy on which numerous scholars have written commentaries and which has been translated into several Eastern as well as Western languages. The book was named after his first patron Nasir al-Din, Governor of Kohistan. Hence the book which had two editions was written before 1256 A.C. *"Tazkira,"* which forms a landmark in the development of astronomy, won great popularity throughout the East and the West. A large number of its commentaries were written by renowned scholars, including *"Bayan Maqasid Tazkira"* (Explanation of the Aims of *Tazkira)* by Muhammad ibn Ali Husain al Himadhi, with notes by Mahmood ibn Masud Qutbuddin al-Shirazi (d. 1310-11); the *"Tanzih al Tazkira"* (Illustration of the *Tazkira)* written in 1311-12 by al Hasan ibn Muhammad Ali Nishapuri. A commentary in Turkish language was written by Fath Allah Sherwani in 1414 A.C. A large number of commentaries assisted in the assimilation of *"Tazkira"* which is very condensed. This book is divided into four large chapters dealing with (1) 'Geometrical and cinematical introduction with discussions of rest, simple and complex motions', (2) 'General astronomical notions—secular change of the obliquity of the ecliptic, trepidation of the equinoxes'. A part of this chapter which was translated by Carr De Vaux, bristles with scathing criticism of *Almagest* written by Ptolemy. The learned Toosi corrected the views regarding the anomalies of the Moon and the motion in latitude of the planets as contained in *Almagest*, (3) 'Earth and the influence of celestial bodies on it. It also contains accounts of seas, winds, tides and how these are caused', and (4) 'The size and distances of the planets'.

His forceful criticism of Ptolemic astronomy paved the way for the Copernican reform. He has written a large number of astronomical treatises including (1) *'Zubdat al Hai'a* (The Cream of Astronomy); (2) *'Kitab al Tahsil fil Najum'* (The Stars made Easy); (3) *'On the Trajectory, Size and Distance of Mercury';* (4) *'Parts of Mutawassit';* (5) *'Rising and Setting';* (6) *'On the Moving Sphere';* (7) *'On the Size and Distances of Sun and Moon';* *'Phenomena';* (8) *'On the Ascension of Stars';* (9) *'Spherics';* (10) *'Days and Nights';* (11) *'Habitations';* and (12) *'Tahzir al Majisti'.* This book contains criticism of Ptolemy's views. His *'Zubdat al Hai-a'* is extant in Arabic and Persian.

The fame of Nasir al-Din Toosi in astronomy rests chiefly on his astronomical researches carried on in the Maragha observatory. The destruction wrought by the Mongol hords served as a death blow to all cultural and intellectual movements in the world of Islam. Their cultural treasures amassed during centuries of intellectual pursuits were reduced to ashes on the fall of Baghdad. Together with *'Darul Hukame* of Baghdad, founded by Mamoon ar-Rashid in the first half of the 9th century and *'Bait-ul-Hukama* of Cairo, established by the Fatimid Caliph Al-Hakam in the first half of the 11th century, the observatory of Maragha was the third greatest centre of literary and astronomical research in the East. This Khaniz observatory was completed in 1259 A.C. Its remains are still extant. This observatory was equipped with the best available instruments, including an "armillary sphere, the mural quadrant and a solstitial armil," which were probably brought from Baghdad and Almut. It also housed a big library, which, according to Ibn Shakir, contained more than 400,000 books, collected by the Mongol armies from Syria, Iraq and Persia. The Khaniz observatory of Maragha functioned under Nasir al-Din Toosi who was its first Director and was later on succeeded by his two sons. It was staffed by some of the eminent astronomers of the age, including Mohi al-Din al-Maghribi and the illustrious Abul Faraj. The instruments used in this observatory have been described by al Urdi and Khwandmir which included *'Tamathil-i-Ashkal-i-aflak';* *'Hawamil'* *(deferents);* *'Dawairi Mauhuma wa Suwar wa Buruj-i-duwaz'* (Imaginary Circles, Constellations and Signs of the Zodiac).

He is reputed as the inventor of the "Turquet (Torquetum), an instrument containing two graduated circles in two perpendicular planes, which became very popular in the West during the 15th and 16th centuries, towards perfecting their instruments. "They endeavoured to make their instruments as large as possible," writes Carra De Vaux, "In order to minimise error; they then began to make special instruments, each being devoted to special class of observations. In the observatory at Maragha there were instruments made of rings for special purposes; ecliptical, solstitial and equatorial armillaries. The ecliptical, which were very much used, had five rings, the largest of which was some 12 feet across. It was graduated in degrees and minutes. When Alfonso of Castilla wanted to construct an armillary sphere, which would be finest and best that had yet been made, it was to the Arabs that he turned for information"

The principal research carried on in the Maragha observatory which lasted for two generations only, related to the compilation of *"Al Zij-al-Ilkhani"* better known as *"The Ilkhanian Tables"*, which earned great popularity throughout the East, including China. This Table was compiled by Nasir al-Din Toosi after 12 years of hard research and was completed in 1272 A.C. The original text was probably written in Persian. This work is divided into four books namely, (1) *Chinese, Greek, Arabic and Persian Chronology*, (2) *Motions of the Planets*, (3) *Ephemerides*, (4) *Astronomical Observations*. This Table was translated into Arabic and several commentaries were written on it.

His other important astronomical works regarding calendar are (۴) *'Mukhtasar fi Ilm al Tanjim wa Marifat al-Taqwim'* (Summary of Astrology and of the Calendar) which is extant in Persian; and (2) *'Katab al-Barifi Ulum al-Taqwim wa Harakat al Aflak wa-Ahkam al Nujum'* (The excellent book on the Calendar, the Movement of the Spheres and Judicial Astrology). This Astrological treatise *'Kitab-i-si-Fasl,'* is a work of high order.

Only next to astronomy stands Nasir al-Din's contribution to mathematics. He has left behind him immortal works on geometry and trigonometry. He edited most of the ancient mathematical works numbering 16, which included four books of the Muslim period. He wrote four treatises, on arithmetic and algebra, including *"Al Mukhtasar bi Jami al Hisab bil Takht wal Turab"*, (Summary of the whole of Computation with Table and Earth) and *'Kitab al Jabr wal Muqabala'* (Treatise on Algebra). The first one is extant in Arabic and Persian.

He is equally important as a geometer. He wrote no less than fifteen treatises on geometry, which included his *'Al Usul ul Maudua'* (Treatise on Euclids Postulates); *'Qawaid-al-Handasa'* (Principles of Geometry) and *"Tahrir al Usual"* (the two Reductions of the Elements of Euclid) in which, contrary to the principle followed by Euclid, he multiplied the special cases

Nasir al-Din Toosi played no small part in the advancement of trigonometry. His works on trigonometry marked the culmination of the progress in the subject. He is the author of the *'Kitab Shakl al Qatta'* (A treatise on Quadrilateral) an extremely original work in which trigonometry has been treated independently of astronomy. The book dealing with spherical trigonometry is very comprehensive and perhaps the best work on the subject written during the mediaeval times. It was translated into French and edited by Alexandre Cara Theodory Pasha in 1891. Writing in the *Legacy of Islam*, Carra De Vaux says, "Trigonometry, plane or spherical, is now well established and finds in this book its first methodically developed and deliberate expression". This treatise of Nasir al-Din had a deep influence over the mathematicians of both the East and West who based their trigonometrical researches on this book.

"To appreciate Nasir al-Din's achievements", admits George Sarton", it will suffice to realise that his *"Shakl al-Qatta"* was almost the Arabic equivalent of 'Regiomontanus', *'De Triangulis Omnimodis Libri Quinque,* posthumously printed in 1533'.

Being a versatile genius, Nasir al-Din Toosi has made lasting contributions to optics, occult sciences, mineralogy, medicine, geography, music, philosophy, theology and ethics. In optics he has left behind three treatises namely *"Tahrir Kitab al Manazir,' Mabahith Fin'ikas al Shu'aat wa in Itafiha'* (Research on the Reflection and Deflection of Rays) and reply to Ali ibn Umar al Qazwini. All these treatises have been translated into the German language by Eilhard Wiedemann.

He wrote probably two treatises on music, namely *'Kitab fi Ilm al Mausiqi'* which was written in Arabic and *'Kanz al Tuhaf',* written in Persian. His musical theories were elaborated and enlarged by his celebrated disciple Qutab al-Din al-Shirazi. He is said to have invented a flute known as *"Mahtar Duduk"* (Chapel Flute).

A chapter of his *Tazkira* deals with geodesy describing the seas, winds the tides. His medical works are of no less scientific importance. He wrote *'Kitab al Bab Bahiya fil Tarakib al Sultaniya,* a regimen divided into three parts which deal with diets, health rules and sexual intercourse. This book was translated into Turkish language.

His two treatises deal with logic. These are *'Kitab al Tajrid fi Ilm al Mantiq* (Compendium of Logic) and commentary on the *'Katab Alisharat wal Tanbihat',* written by Ibn Sina. His *'Akhlaq-i-Nasiri'* classifies knowledge into speculation and practical. The speculative knowledge he has subdivided into *(a)* Metaphysics and Theology; *(b)* Mathematics (including music, optics and mechanics), *(c)* Natural Sciences which included Elements, Science of Transformations, Meteorology, mineralogy, botany, zoology, psychology, medicine, astrology and agriculture. The practical knowledge included *(a)* ethics, *(b)* domestic economy, and *(c)* politics.

In order of importance, his large number of philosophical, metaphysical and theological treatises rank only next to his works on astronomy and mathematics. In orthodox circles of his sect, his fame chiefly rests on these treatises. His *'Kitab al Fusul'* dealing with metaphysics was written in Persian which was translated into Arabic by Al-Jurjani. His monumental philosophical work *"Tajrid al Aqaid' (Al Kalam)* is his most popular work on which a large number of commentaries have been written in Arabic, Persian and Turkish languages. The best commentary was written by Ali ibn Muhammad Al-Jurjani. His outstanding work on ethics entitled *'Akhlaq-i-Nasiri'* (Nasirian Ethics) is one of the best books written on the subject which still serves as a text-book in Arabic schools throughout the Islamic world. This was written before 1256 and translated into Arabic as *Risala fil Tahqiq-al Ilm.* Together with *Akhlaq-i-Jalali,* this invaluable ethical treatise of Nasir al-Din Toosi, is one of the two most popular works on the subject in the East. Several editions of this book were printed in India and parts of it were also translated and published in the English and German languages.

# ABUL QASIM AL-ZAHRAWI

Muslim Spain has produced some of the greatest intellectual giants and scientists of the mediaeval times, including Ibn-Rushd (Averroes), Ibn Khaldun, Ibn-Zuhr, Ibn-Baitar, Ibn-Khatib, Dinawari and Abul Qasim Al-Zahrawi, whose works, when translated into European languages, brought about the Western Renaissance as well as provided the firm ground on which the imposing edifice of European culture was built. "It was under the influence of Arabian and Moorish revival of culture", acknowledges Robert Briffault in his well-known work, *'The Making of Humanity'*, "and not in the 15th century that the real Renaissance took place. Spain, not Italy, was the cradle of the rebirth of Europe. After steadily sinking lower and lower into barbarism, it had reached the darkest depth of ignorance and degradation when the cities of the Saracenic world, Baghdad, Cairo, Cordova, Toledo, were growing centres of civilization and intellectual activity. It was there that the new life arose which was to grow into a new phase of human evolution. From the time when the influence of their culture made itself felt, began the stirrings of new life".

Al-Hakam II (961–976), better known as Mamoon of the West, was one of the most talented, learned and enlightened rulers of the Middle ages. He ruled over Muslim Spain in the later half of the 10th century. His love for learning knew no bounds and his patronage had attracted to his Court, the intellectual luminaries from all parts of the world of Islam. Abul Qasim Zahrawi was one of them. He had founded a chain of higher educational institutions in Spain and had built a library containing four lakh books catalogued in 44 bulky volumes. The talented Caliph had gone through a sizeable number of them and had written marginal notes in them. According to Ibn Khaldun, he had purchased the first edition of the book of Farghani for ten thousand dinars. Mr. S. P. Scot writes in his *History of Moorish Empire in Spain:* "He (Al-Hakam II) was worthy representative of the advanced culture, the scientific attainments, the poesy and the art of Hispano-Arab civilization, as contrasted with the intellectual darkness, the disgusting immorality, the revolting filth, the abject superstition which characterised the contemporaneous society of Europe. His tireless industry and prodigious erudition were the marvels of his time".

Abul Qasim Khalef ibn al-Zahrawi, better known as Abulcasis or Albucasis or Alsabaravius in the West, was one of the talented figures who adorned the court of Al-Hakam II, the Spanish Caliph. He is recognised as the greatest

Muslim surgeon who was the personal physician of the Caliph. He was nick-named Al-Zahrawi because he was born at Al-Zahra, a suburb of Cordova in 936 A.C. He died in 1013 A.C.

Abul Qasim al-Zahrawi, the greatest surgeon of Islam and of the Middle ages, was a versatile genius. He was a talented surgeon, medical theorist and physician. The book on which his fame rests in *"Al-Tasrif"*, an encyclopaedic work in 30 sections dealing with medical science, whose most important last three volumes deal with surgery. These volumes, introduce or emphasise such new ideas as cauterization of wounds, crushing a stone inside the bladder and the necessity of vivisection and dissection". *Al-Tasrif* contains interesting and elaborate method of preparing drugs through sublimation and distillation. A portion of his surgical volumes is devoted to obstetrics and the surgical treatment of eye, ear and teeth. This monumental work, was first translated into Latin by Gerard of Cremona, published in Venice (Italy) in 1497, at Strassburg (Germany) in 1532, at Basle (Switzerland) in 1541 and at Oxford (England) in 1778 A.C. It was also translated in Provencal and Hebrew. Thus this work of repute earned great popularity in the West and held its place for centuries as a manual of surgery at Salerno, Montepellier and other early schools of medicine in Europe. It was illustrated with pictures and sketches of surgical instruments. According to George Sarton, 'the Muslim prejudices against surgery stifled Abul Qasim's fame in Islam but in Christian world his prestige was soon immense'. *Al-Tasrif* laid the foundation of the development of surgery in the West. An elaborate account of Al Zahrawi's surgical work with 100 surgical instruments sketched in it is found in the *German History of Surgery, "Geschichte der Chirurgie,* written by E. Grait and published in Berlin in 1898. Capar Wolph in his *Collection Gynaeciorum"* has published the portion of *Al-Tasrif* dealing with gynaecology.

Abul Qasim al-Zahrawi is said to have invented many surgical appliances which were not known to the world. Of his several instruments the three most useful were : "(1) The sponge tipped probang which he used to remove foreign bodies from the upper end of the respiratory canal, (2) The grooved probe meant for internal examination of the urethral passage, (3) The ear springs".

Al-Zahrawi was a reputed physician as well as surgeon. In his invaluable work *Al-Tasrif* he has elaborately dealt with the preparation of several drugs, obstetrics and female diseases. His description of the surgical treatment of teeth, ears and eyes is of exceptionally high order. It immensely benefited the West. He was an outstanding dentist and his book is illustrated with numerous dental instruments meant for shaking, loosening and extracting the teeth. His book contains the earliest type of the turn key extraction of roots, vulsella for removal of portions of the jaw and the gold and silver wire which he used to bind a loose tooth with a sound one. He also dealt with the operation for correcting the projecting teeth which disfigures human face. He has very ably discussed the "oval deformities, dental arches and formation of tartor". He was an expert dentist who could very successfully set an artificial tooth in place of a diseased one.

As a physician and surgeon Al-Zahrawi occupies an outstanding place in the history of medical science. He was rather first to explain the deadly disease, Haemophilia in which due to the absence of the clotting property, the incessant flow of blood cannot be stopped. He was specialist in treatment of diseases with the help of fire and gives a list of fifty such diseases. "He made cautery the nautical instruments of the Arabs", which according to Dr. Campbell, "led to the widespread use of this means of treatment throughout Western Europe during the Middle ages".

His influence on European medicine, specially on European surgery, was overwhelming. In fact, the study of his immortal illustrated work, *Al-Tasrif* which was translated into several European languages laid the foundation of Western surgery. The natural dislike for surgery in Islamic medicine prevented *Al-Tasrif* to win the same popularity in the Islamic world which it earned in the West. Writing in his well-known work, *History of Arabian Medicine,* Dr. Campbell acknowledges the great influence which Abul Qasim Al-Zahrawi produced on the development of Western medicine and surgery. He observes: "His lucidity and method of presentation awakened prepossession in favour of Arabian literature among the scholars of the West. His method eclipsed those of Galen and maintained a dominant position in Mediaeval Europe for five hundred years. He helped to raise the status of surgery in Europe. . . . . . . . His descriptions of operations are clear and particularly valuable because they portray the figures of surgical instruments used by him in the long course of his own surgical practice".

Thus Abul Qasim Al-Zahrawi deserves to be ranked among the greatest surgeons of the world, one who was not only the father of surgical science during the Mediaeval era but also developed it to a high degree of perfection.

# SIR SHAH MUHAMMAD SULAIMAN

The Special Court room of the Allahabad High Court was packed to its capacity. The front rows were occupied by a galaxy of eminent lawyers who had come from all parts of India to defend the accused in the famous Merrut Conspiracy Case, the greatest conspiracy unearthed against the British Government since the national upheaval of 1857. The lawyers who had volunteered themselves to defend the highly educated accused, numbering more than 100, included Sir Tej Bahadur Sapru, Mr. Bhola Bhai Desai, Sir Srinavasa Iyengar, Mr. B. K. Das, Mr. P. L. Bannerji, Mr. Asif Ali and Dr. Kailash Nath Katju. The Court was presided over by the Chief Justice of the Allahabad High Court, Sir Shah Muhammad Sulaiman, assisted by Justice Young.

The case which had taken two years in the Magistrate's Court and four in the Sessions Court, was expected to last for months in the High Court. But, to the astonishment of all, the hearing of the appeal and the judgement was all over in eight days. The judgement delivered by Sir Shah Muhammad Sulaiman stands out as a landmark in the history of judicial administration in India. Speaking of this judgement in Federal Court case No. 1 of 1938, Mr. H. J. Morgan KC, an outstanding constitutional lawyer of Britain, while delivering the Tagore Law Lectures at the Calcutta University said:

"Now I have just been reading the judgement of the Federal Court at Delhi in that important case. One of those judgements stands out conspicuous and pre-eminent and may well prove to be the *"Locus Classicus"* of the law on the subject. It is a judgement worthy of the highest traditions of the House of Lords as an Appellate Tribunal and of the Privy Council itself. I refer to the brilliant judgement of Mr. Justice Sulaiman. In depth of thought, in breadth of view, in its powers alike of analysis and of synthesis, in grace of style and felicity of expression, it is one of the most masterly judgements that I have ever had the good fortune to read. Everyone in India interested in future development of the constitution should study it."

Shah Muhammad Sulaiman was born into a distinguished family of lawyers and scientists of Jaunpur district (U.P.). One of his ancestors was Mulla Mahmood, a notable physicist, author of *Shams-i-Bazigha,* and a contemporary of Newton in India. Shah Sulaiman's father, Muhammad Usman, was a leading member of the Jaunpur Bar.

Young Sulaiman was immensely devoted to his studies. He graduated from the Allahabad University in 1906 and topped the list. He was awarded the Provincial Government Scholarship to study abroad. He joined the Cambridge University and obtained Mathematical Tripos in 1909 and Law Tripos in 1910. In 1909 he sat for the Indian Civil Service examination and was luckily not selected, otherwise the boredom of the Civil Service would have deprived India of one of its greatest legal and scientific talents. He did not make a second attempt to appear in the Civil Service examination and prepared to be called to the Bar. He was awarded, LL.D. by the University of Dublin (Ireland) in 1910.

Shah Muhammad Sulaiman retu. ned to India in 1911 and started his legal practice as a junior to his father in Jaunpur. In 1912, he shifted to Allahabad to practise in the High Court. Here he embarked on his meteoric career which remains unique in the annals of Indian jurisprudence. He was endowed with a proverbial memory, and an extraordinary sense of understanding things. He possessed a keen eye and a rare grasp of subjects which made him successful in whatever field of activity he took part. He achieved distinction in many spheres of life and his career, in fact, is a catalogue of great achievements. At Allahabad High Court where he had to compete with such legal giants as Pandit Moti Lal Nehru, Sir Tej Bahadur Sapru, Maulvi Ghulam Mujtaba, Sir Sunder Lal, Sir Ross Alestan and Pandit Ajodhya Nath Kunzuru, he soon made his mark. The Rani of Sherkot's case, the Bamrauli case, the Dharampur case and the Bhilwal case, were his early legal triumphs. He impressed the English Chief Justice of Allahabad High Court so much that he was offered a seat on the Bench at an early age of 34.

Sir Shah Muhammad Sulaiman acted as Chief Justice of the Allahabad High Court when he was 43 and at the age of 46 he was made the Permanent Chief Justice of this Court. Five years later, he was elevated to the Federal Court, "a record in the British Commonwealth and perhaps in the judicial world". As Chief Justice, he delivered that memorable judgement in the Meerut Conspiracy Case which stands out as a landmark in the history of jurisprudence.

Sir Shah maintained the independence of the judiciary in those troubled times when the British bureaucracy was considered supreme. He never allowed the Government and the legislature to intervene or interfere with the independence of judiciary which he guarded with enviable jealousy.

Sir Shah was a versatile genius and he distinguished himself in diverse fields of human activity and different aspects of learning. He was an institution by himself. He was an outstanding educationist who took keen interest in the administration and advancement of several educational institutions where he left distinctive marks. He was founder President of several educational institutions and a member of the Courts and Executive Councils of Allahabad and Aligarh Muslim Universities for a number of years. As President of the United Provinces Educational Conference at Badaon in 1924, he revived the conference. In 1928, he presided over the All-India Muhammadan Educational Conference at Ajmer and in his address he advocated a revolutionary and progressive change in the educational system by stressing the practical, technical and vocational sides of education. He delivered masterly convocation addresses at the universities of Dacca, Aligarh, Hyderabad and Agra, which are characterised by their lucidity of expression and clarity of practical thinking.

Sir Shah was elected Vice-Chancellor of the Aligarh Muslim University at a critical period of its history and held that post in honorary capacity with distinction. He introduced several beneficial reforms and laid down policies of far reaching importance which extricated the University out of its financial and administrative crisis and placed it on the road to progress. He gave an impetus to education of women in the University and introduced Urdu as an independent subject in B.A. classes. He improved the finances of the University, helped execution of scheme concerning Water Works, Agricultural and the Technological Institutes. His dynamic leadership infused a healthy spirit of competition among the students in beneficial spheres of educational activity which enabled the Aligarh Muslim University to compete successfully in the All-India competitive examinations in larger numbers. He made the University a centre of higher scientific research.

Sir Shah had agreed to become Vice-Chancellor of the Aligarh University at a considerable inconvenience to himself. He was a Judge of the Indian Federal Court at Delhi and used to visit the University at the weekend without any remuneration. At the University he took the ordinary food served in the hostels on payment.

His association with Aligarh Muslim University gave a fresh impetus to higher scientific and historical research in this highest Muslim educational institution of India and established it on a sound footing, educationally and financially.

Sir Shah was also the President of the famous Anglo-Arabic College of Delhi for a number of years. In his inaugural address at the Hindustani Academy, Allahabad, and in his Presidential Address at the All-India Adult Educational Conference at Delhi, he dealt with the practical solution of problems facing the subcontinent in the spheres of educational activity.

Sir Shah Muhammad Sulaiman was a litterateur of great stature. He had a keen sense for poetry and presided over a number of All-India Poetical Symposiums. His delightful remarks as well as his enlightened Presidential addresses at these gatherings of poets and intellectuals drawn from different parts of the country were highly appreciated. He edited and wrote an enlightened introduction to the *"Alam-e-Khiyal"*, the immortal *Masnavi* of Shauq Qidwai. But, it is in the realm of mathematics and sciences that he has left an ineffaceable impress of his unique and versatile personality. He challenged the validity of Einstein's Famous Theory of Relativity. He carried out valuable mathematical research to correct certain misconceptions and miscalculations in Newton's

Theory of Gravity and Einstein's Theory of Relativity. In this, he was supported by a number of outstanding scientists from all over the world and the later observations of phenomenon justified his initial conclusions. But, unfortunately he did not live to complete his research in the matter.

Sir Shah Muhammad Sulaiman as a man was much greater than Sulaiman as a scientist, judge, educationist and litterateur. He was the very incarnation of courtesy and humility. He always took precedence to pay respects to his juniors, subordinates and even to his peons. He made no distinction between the highest dignitary and a clerk who came to see him.

It was really a sight to see him embracing high dignitaries and poor peons alike, on the Eid Day and personally serving sweets to them. He followed the injunctions of the Prophet of Islam about the equality of man, both in letter and spirit.

Sir Shah breathed his last after a brief illness, on March 13, 1941 at Delhi at the prime of his achievements. He was only 52. His irreparable loss was mourned all over India and in many foreign countries. A large number of mourners, including Quaid-e-Azam Muhammad Ali Jinnah, Sir Muhammad Yaqub and Sir Akbar Hydri accompanied his funeral. He was buried at Nizamuddin.

# POETS AND WRITERS

# MUTANABBI

Saif al-Dawla, the Hamanid Ruler of Aleppo was a great patron of arts and learning. He attracted to his Court some of the greatest intellectual luminaries of his time, including the encyclopaedist Abu Nasar Farabi and poet Mutanabbi.

Mutanabbi, one of the greatest panegyrists of all times came to the Court of the Hamanid Chief in 948 A.C. and stayed there for about nine years. He accompanied the Ruler during his campaigns against the By-Zantines and Bedouins add wrote some of his best panegyries personifying him as the ideal Arab Chief—courageous, magnanimous and generous.

Saif al-Dawla never treated the over-sensitive poet with arrogance and frequently loaded him with gifts.

But, Mutanabbi's difficult character and over-sensitive nature soon earned him many enemies at the Hamanid Court. Their leader was his rival, the celebrated poet Abu Firas. Saif al-Dawla who, at first paid no heed to these complaints, soon got wearied and Mutanabbi, finding his life not safe there, secretly left Aleppo for Damascus in 957 A.C.

Abu Taiyib Ahmad bin Al Husain, Al Mutanabbi was born in al-Kinda quarters of Kufa in 915 A.C. His family originated from Yemen, hence he always claimed the linguistic superiority of the Southern over the Northern Arabs.

Mutanabbi was brought up in humble circumstances, receiving education only in his native town. But he soon distinguished himself by his keen intelligence, prodigious mermory and supremacy as a poet. When Kufa was sacked by Carmathians, his family migrated to Samawa, where they remained for two years. This short stay among the Bedouins, enabled the young Mutanabbi to have a profound knowledge of the Arabic language.

On return to Kufa in 927 A.C. Mutanabbi decided to devote himself entirely to poetry, to which he had a natural inclination. He was much impressed by the works of the celebrated panegyrists, Ibn Tamim and al-Buhturi.

A born poet as he was, Mutanabbi found in poetry a good means of earning fame and wealth. Abul Fazal of Kufa was his first patron and the poet dedicated a short piece to him.

Mutanabbi had a chequered career. His over-sensitive nature and vanity did not permit him to stick to one place. He was a convert to Carmathicism and later adopted a stoic and pessimistic philosophy, "The world is made of seductions which the death destroys".

He found himself completely out of harmony with the world which he contacted. The consciousness of his talent increased his vanity to an inconceivable degree and created a bitterness in his works. He coveted all his life the riches and power which he scorned in his heart. But, despite this apparent contradiction in his nature, he stands out from his contemporaries for his rigid morality and austerity.

He set out to Baghdad in 928 A.C. in order to conquer the world with his poetic talents and became a panegyrist of Muhammad Ubaidullah Alawi. He did not stay there for long and soon left for Syria where, for two years, he led the life of a wandering troubadour. His poems of this period, though not of lasting value, carry the imprint of his genius.

Lack of recognition of his exceptional merit produced despondency and irritation in his nature. He forsook the work of paid panegyrist for sometime and led the life of a religious revolutionary. He was, therefore, put behind the bars for two years being regarded as a Carmathian agitator.

The poems composed by him during this period are distinguished for the flight of imagination, spontaniety and vigour of their expression. The poet took much liberty with poetic forms.

He got the epithet of Mutanabbi and was fully convinced that poetry alone could lead him to glory and realise his ambitious dream of prosperity.

On release from the prison, he resumed his profession of panegyrist, getting at first little success. For several years he led a wandering life, obtaining a precarious existence on the subsistence of minor officials of Damascus, Aleppo and Antioch.

His fame continued to grow and the brightness in him yearned for an opportunity to show his greatness as a poet. This he got in 939 A.C. when he became the Court poet of Amir Badr al-Kashani, Governor of Damascus. He regarded Badr as the Maccenes for whom he was waiting so far. His poems written in praise of Badr bristled with sincerity of thought and spontaniety of expression.

But Mutanabbi's stay with Badr lasted hardly for 1½ years and was disturbed by the intrigues of his jealous rivals. The poet had to take refuge in the Syrian desert and returned to Damascus, soon after Badr had left the place.

The fame of Mutanabbi had by this time travelled far and wide. He was invited by the Hamanid Ruler of Aleppo, Saif al-Dawla, a great patron of learning. Here the poet stayed for nine years and passed the best period of his life. He earned the sincere admiration of his patron who fully recognised his greatness as a poet.

Mutanabbi wrote some of his finest panegyrics in the praise of his patron, Saif al-Dawla whom he idealised as the best Arab Ruler. But the difficult nature of the poet, obliged him to flee from the Hamanid Court to Damascus.

His poems of this period reveal his supremacy as a poet and place him among the greatest panegyrists of all times. In flight of imagination and sublimity of thought, in spontaniety of expression and grandeur of diction, he ranks high among his contemporaries. His poems are fuller and epic in style than those of Abu Firas.

He arrived in Egypt from Damascus and obtained the patronage of Ikhshidid Kafur, whom he did not like at heart. He did not stay there for long and secretly left for Iraq after writing a biting satire of Kafur.

Hereafter, he was constantly on move. He visited Kufa and settled down in Baghdad for sometime. Later went to Susiana, where he was welcomed by the Buyid Minister, Ibn al-Amid. In 941, he went to Shiraz where he obtained the patronage of Buyid Ruler, Adud al-Dawla and wrote some of his best panegyrics in praise of his new patron.

He was returning to Baghdad from Shiraz when he was attacked by the marauding Bedouins and was killed in August 955 A.C.

Thus ended the chequered career of Mutanabbi, one of the greatest panegyrists of all times, who exercised considerable influence over the later Arabic poetry, which owed much to him.

# FIRDAUSI

The three leading poets of the Court of Mahmood were one day conversing together in a garden of Ghazna. They were Unsari, Asjadi and Farrukhi. A stranger from Nishapur arrived there and desired to join their conversation. Unsari resenting this untimely intrusion said to him: "Brother! we are the Court poets and none but a gifted poet may participate in our conversation. Each of us will compose a verse in the same rhyme and if you could supply the fourth hemistich of the quatrain, you will be welcomed in our company, otherwise not. The stranger who was no other than Firdausi readily consented to this amazing condition and Unsari intentionally choosing a rhyme wherein three hemistiches could be composed but not the fourth one, started:

"Thine eyes are clear and blue as sunslit ocean"

Asjadi said:

"Their glance bewitches like a magic potion"

Farrukhi stated:

"The wounds they cause no balm can heal, nor lotion"

Instantly Firdausi alluding to a scarcely known legend of the ancient kings of Persia concluded:

"Deadly as those Give's spear dealt out to Poshan." Explaining the allusion, Firdausi exhibited such a rich knowledge of the ancient history of Persia, that the three Court poets were astounded by his poetical superiority as well as by his historical knowledge and readily admitted him to their society.

Firdausi, the author of the immortal *Shah Nama,* was the greatest of all the great Persian poets. Persia, the land of poetry, learning and culture in the East, has produced some most outstanding poets in the world, including Rumi, Saadi, Hafiz, Anwari and Firdausi. Firdausi towering high above them is universally recognised as one of the greatest epic poets of all times.

Hassan ibn Ishaq ibn Sharf *alias* Firdausi was born in Toos. The *Tarikh Guzida* (Select History) written by the historian Hamdullah Mustawfi in 1330 A.C., gives the name of Firdausi as Abul Qasim Hassan Ali of Toos. His birth place is a controversial issue among historians. According to *Chahar Maqala,* it was Baz, a village of Bostan. The preface of *Shah Nama* gives it as Shadab. But it has now been established by modern reliable research scholars that he was born in the District of Toos, the place which produced renowned scholars of Islam like versatile Imam Ghazali and the encyclopaedist Nasiruddin Toosi.

It is related that on the birth of Firdausi, his father dreamt that the newly born child climbing the upper storey of the house raised a strident cry which was reponded from all sides. Elaborating on the dream Najibuddin predicted that the boy would one day become a great poet who would win a world-wide recognition. Firdausi, when he grew up, received thorough education.

Mahmood of Ghazna, the well-known Muslim conqueror, was a great patron of art and learning. Being a renowned scholar himself, he had drawn to his Court such well-known intellectual luminaries of Islam as Biruni, Firdausi, Unsari, Farrukhi and Daqiqi. He had built a magnificent college and a big museum at Ghazna, which rivalled Baghdad and became the highest seat of learning in the East. He contemplated having a thorough research conducted into the ancient history of Persia and was in search of a competent poet who could undertake this gigantic work, but no such versatile poet was available.

According to one source, he summoned Firdausi for this task. Firdausi on his way to the Court of Mahmood, met the three leading poets, referred to above, in a suburban garden of Ghazna. Unsari was so much impressed by the genius of Firdausi that he introduced him to the Sultan saying that he was the most competent and pre-eminently fit person to undertake the task of versifying the national epic.

This account is based on the research of Daulat Shah. Other historians maintain that Firdausi first appeared in the Court of Ghazna, where the above-mentioned poetic competition was held.

Mahmood entrusted this important assignment to Firdausi, and allotted him an apartment in the Royal Palace, fully equipped with all sorts of weapons and paintings depicting battle scenes and palace life in ancient Persia.

Mahmood offered to pay him one gold coin for each couplet, apart from one thousand gold coins on completion of one thousand couplets. But Firdausi declined to accept the payment piecemeal and consented to receive full payment on the completion of the assignment.

It may be noted that the *Shah Nama* was begun long before Firdausi's arrival in the Court of Mahmood. It took 35 years for its compilation as stated by Firdausi in one of his couplets and Mahmood's reign lasted for 31 years only.

Hence Firdausi had begun it in his native town under the patronage of Abu Mansoor, the Governor of Toos. Salan Khan succeeded Abu Mansoor as the Governor of Toos. By this time, the fame of *Shah Nama* had reached Mahmood who summoned Firdausi to his Capital. At first Firdausi declined this offer but soon he recollected the prophecy of Shaikh Mashooq and consented to go to Ghazna.

Firdausi immediately applied himself to the most arduous task and after labouring on it unremittingly for over a decade, he completed the monumental epic poem comprising sixty thousand couplets. But, according to one version, contrary to the agreement, Firdausi was paid in silver instead of gold coins. This broke his heart and obliged him to write a touching satire of Mahmood. In fact, his exclusiveness had offended Ayaz, the favourite of Mahmood.

Moreover, there was an influential group in the Court of Mahmood constantly working against Firdausi and his admirer Prime Minister, Hassan Memandi. This rival group was greatly instrumental in the breach of the earlier offer made to Firdausi.

The great poet, broken-hearted and friendless, left Ghazna and roamed about in the neighbouring dominions in search of a peaceful place. But as ill-luck would have it, no neighbouring ruler was prepared to give him a lasting asylum, being afraid of incurring the hostility of Mahmood, who was offended by Firdausi's satire. At last he reached Baghdad, where he was welcomed by the Abbaside Caliph. Here he wrote his another long poem *'Yusuf and Zulaikha.*

Stung by remorse and qualms of conscience, Mahmood at last softened towards Firdausi and despatched the agreed money to him. But it was too late. When the camels carrying the award of *Shah Nama* were entering Toos through one gate, the funeral of Firdausi appeared from the other. Browne in his *Literary History of Persia (Vol. II, page 137)* quotes one Nizami of Samarqand *vide Chahar Maqala* by Daulat Shah, compiled a century after the death of the poet, as saying "In the year 514 A.H. (1120-21 A.C.) when I was in Nishapur, I heard Amir Muizzi say that he had heard Amir Abdur Razzaq of Toos relate as follows: Mahmood was once in India, returning thence towards Ghazna. It chanced that on his way there was a rebellious chief possessed of a strong fortress. Next day, Mahmood encamped at its gates and despatched an Ambassador to him, bidding him come before him on the morrow to do homage and pay his respects at the Court, where he should receive a robe of honour and return to his place. Next day, Mahmood rode out with the Prime Minister on his right hand. The Ambassador had turned back and was coming to meet the King. "I wonder," said the King to the Minister, "what reply he will have given?" The Minister answered :

"And should the reply with my wish not accord,
Then Afrasiyab's field, and the mace and the sword."

"Whose verse is it", enquired Mahmood? "For he must have the heart of a man". "Poor Abul Qasim Firdausi composed it", answered the Minister, 'he who for five and twenty years laboured to complete such a work and reaped for it no advantage". "You speak well", said Mahmood, "I deeply regret that this noble man was disappointed by me. Remind me at Ghazna to send him something". So, when the Sultan returned to Ghazna, the Minister reminded him and Mahmood ordered that sixty thousand dinar worth of indigo should be given to Firdausi, and that this indigo should be carried to Toos on the King's own camels and that apologies should be tendered to Firdausi.

"For years the Minister had been manoeuvring till at last he achieved his end. So now he caused the camels to be loaded and the indigo safely reached Tabaran."

But even as the camels were entering through the Rudbar gate, the funeral of Firdausi emerged from the gate of Razan. Outside the gate there was a garden belonging to Firdausi, and there they buried him and there he lies to this day.

They say that Firdausi left a very high spirited daughter, to whom they would have given the King's gift: but she would not accept it, declaring that she did not need it.

"The postmaster wrote to the King who ordered that the money should be given to Imam Abu Bakr ibn Ishaq for the repair of the Serai at Chaha, which stands on the road between Merv and Neshapur at the confines of Toos. When this order reached Toos and Nishapur, it was faithfully executed and the restoration of the rest-house at Chaha was effected with this money."

"When the famous traveller Nasir Khusroe visited Toos in 430 A.H. he found a big caravan serai there, which, he was told was built out of the money awarded to Firdausi. According to *Farhang Rashidi* and *Chahar Maqala* this was named as *"Chah"*.

But modern research has established that the story of Sultan Mahmood  .iling from his commitment to pay 60,000 gold coins is more a fib than a fact. It was least expected from such a generous patron of learning like Sultan Mahmood.

Firdausi's works include *"Shah Nama, Yusuf and Zulaikha* and a considerable number of lyrical fragments, collected, translated and edited by Dr. Etha.

It is on *Shah Nama* universally recognised as one of the best epic poems in the world, that Firdausi's reputation as a poet rests. In their high estimate of this monumental poem, the Western as well as Eastern writers and critics are unanimous, with the exception of Professor Browne, who, ignorantly considers it to be inferior to the Arabic *Muallaqat*.

Maulana Shibli Nomani, the author of the famous *Sherul Ajam,* has refuted this underestimate of Firdausi most convincingly. Professor Browne has based his conclusions regarding the value of *Shah Nama* on minor flaws. He has failed to appreciate its sublimity of thought, its beauty of expression, its thoroughness of description, its faithful portrayal of difficult situations and emotions in which the minutest details have not escaped the imaginative eye of the great poet.

The combat and battle scenes as pictured in *Shah Nama* can very favourably be compared with the great Greek Classics *Iiliad* and *Odessy.* Firdausi has out-matched Homer, his Greek counterpart, in this vital department of epic poetry.

The *Shah Nama* which was completed in 400 A.H. took 35 years for its completion. It was begun by Firdausi 20 years before his arrival at Ghazna, and not at the behest of Mahmood as wrongly contended. Firdausi has very faithfully versified the events of the ancient history of Persia. A German Professor has written a book detailing the sources of *Shah Nama.*

The outstanding qualities of *Shah Nama* have enabled it to rank among the greatest poems in the world are many. The poet has an unrivalled hold over the Persian language and in his long poem comprising sixty thousand couplets he has very rarely used Arabic words at a time when Arabic had become almost the literary language of the Islamic world, including Persia. Thus, he succeeded where Ibn Sina had failed.

One who reads *Shah Nama* is struck by the thoroughness of the poet's description. He has very faithfully portrayed scenes of life in ancient Persia. He has a deep insight into the secrets of human nature and has very sincerely pictured subtle human emotions both on the occasions of war and peace. In this respect, he has outmatched not only all oriental but also Western poets.

He is a master-craftman who has faithfully versified diverse and difficult situations and emotions. Brevity and lucidity of expression, thoroughness of description and flawless portrayal of emotions as well as true picturing of battle scenes have made *Shah Nama* an immortal epic poem in the world.

Homer is acclaimed as the greatest epic poet of the West, while Viyas, the author of *Mahabharat* is known as the greatest Indian epic poet, but Firdausi is far greater of the two. How splendidly he begins the story of Sohrab and Rustam !

The story of Sohrab and Rustam now hear !
Other tales thou hast heard : to this also give ear.
A story it is to bring tears to the eyes,
And wrath in the heart against Rustam will rise.
If forth from this ambush should rush the fierce biast.

And down in the dust the young orange should cast.
Then call we it just, or unkind and unfair.
And say we that virtue or rudeness is there?

*Shah Nama* became a very popular poem throughout the world of Islam. For centuries its couplets were on lips of everybody and were oft quoted in literary discourses and pursuits for Khorasan to Baghdad.

Firdausi has been universally acclaimed as a great poet both in the East and the West. Anwari, another renowned Persian poet, says about him :

Aan ki Ustad bood o ma Shagird
Aan Khudwand bood o ma Bandah

(He was my teacher and I am his pupil. He was the god of poetry and I am his worshipper).

The celebrated historian Ibn Athir states that the Arabic language despite its phenomenal development could not produce anything which could rival *Shah Nama*. Sir Gour Osley has compared Firdausi with Homer. Maulana Shibli Nomani in his monumental work *Sherul Ajam* has classed Firdausi among the greatest poets of the world.

# SAADI

The main thoroughfare of Tabriz was thronged with her populace. The inhabitants of the metropolis of Mongol conqueror Hulaku Khan had come out of their homes and lined both sides of the main road to witness the imperial procession which was passing along it. The procession was attended by all the Ministers, Courtiers and high dignitaries of State, including the celebrated Prime Minister, Khwaja Shamsuddin and his talented brother Khwaja Alauddin, who were greatly instrumental in converting the son of Hulaku Khan to Islam. Suddenly the imperial procession came to a halt and Prime Minister, Khwaja Shamsuddin and his brother alighted from the royal coach and hurriedly advanced towards a frail bodied old man, who was standing among the spectators. They respectfully bowed before him and kissed his hands :

"Sire ! How are you here? You should have graced our humble residence with your benevolent presence," remarked the Prime Minister.

"I have just arrived in Tabriz and was on my way to your residence when I happened to come across this procession and did not want to disturb you here", replied the old man.

The two brothers came back to their royal coach. The Imperial son of Hulaku Khan was highly surprised at the unusual respect paid by his celebrated Prime Minister to the betattered frail bodied old man, and enquired.

"Who is he that received so high respects from you learned brothers?"

"He is our father," the Prime Minister.

"But your father died long ago?" retorted the Emperor.

"He is our spiritual father," replied the Prime Minister. "Sire, you would have heard the name of Saadi, the well-known poet, moralist and sage of Persia. It was he".

The Emperor expressed his great desire to meet Sheikh Saadi. Next day the Prime Minister and his brother called on the Sheikh and implored him to accompany them to the Emperor. The pious Sheikh shunned Imperial Society but, on the imploration of the two brothers who were his disciples, he consented to visit the Emperor. On arrival at the Imperial palace Sheikh Saadi was respectfully received by the Emperor and at the end of their prolonged meeting he requested the Sheikh to give him some advices. The Sheikh replied, "After death, only good deeds will help you. Now it is up to you to collect and carry good or bad deeds with you". The Emperor was highly impressed by the spiritual advice of the Sheikh and requested him to compose it in verse, which he did instantly. The recitation of these couplets moved the Emperor to tears.

Muslehuddin Saadi, the originator of Persian lyric and the greatest ethical writer that the world has produced, was one of the three prophets of Persian poetry, the other two being Firdausi and Anwari. "No Persian writer enjoys to this day", writes Browne, "not only in his own country but also wherever his language is cultivated, a wider celebrity or a greater reputation".

His date of birth is a disputed point among the historians, but according to majority of them he was born at Shiraz about 1184 A.C. and died more than a centurian in 1291 A.C. His father, whom he lost at an early age, was in service of Atabek Saad bin Zangi, ruler of Shiraz, hence he took 'Saadi', as his pen name.

His parents played a great part in his early education which moulded his character. On his father's death, he was taken under the protection of Atabek Saad bin Zangi and was sent to Baghdad where he joined the famous Nizamiah University. Here he received education from Ibn Jauzi. His long life, which, according to several reports, lasted for 120 years, has been divided into three distinct periods. The first period lasting up to 1226 A.C. was the period of study, spent mostly at Baghdad. Even during this period he made several trips including one mentioned in Book V of Gulistan to Kashgar in 1210 A.C., when Sultan Khwarizm Shah had made peace with Cathay (The ancient name of China). In Baghdad he came under the influence of the celebrated Sufi Saint Sheikh Shahabuddin Shurawardy, an event which was greatly instrumental in building up his role as a great moralist. In one of his anecdotes in *'Bostan'*, Saadi speaks highly of the deep piety and humanity of the Sufi Saint. Ibn Jauzi was another learned figure of Baghdad whose deep erudition greatly benefited young Saadi.

The second period lasting up to 1256 A.D. was a period in which Saadi made extensive travels in the world of Islam. Leaving his native city of Shiraz in 1226 due to unsettled conditions in Fars, he wandered from India in the East to Syria and Hejaz in the West, gaining rich experience which he incorporated in his two immortal books *'Gulistan'* and *'Bostan'*. To his departure from Shiraz he alludes in the preface to *Gulistan* :

"O Knowest thou not why, an outcast and exile,

In land of the stranger a refuge I sought?

Disarranged was the world like the hair of a negro

When I fled from the Turks and the terror they brought."

He travelled in a true *dervish* fashion, mixing with all sorts of people, at times wandering miles in trackless deserts, at others carrying a water bag on his back in Jerusalem, sleeping by roadside, and seeing life in all its nakedness. He observed the diversities of life and studied the characteristics of different nationalities, societies and regions from different angles. The "Pilgrim's Progress" was not confined to a particular region. It was extensive and spread over a large part of the Islamic world. He visited Balkh, Ghazna, Punjab, Somnath, Gujarat, Yemen, Syria, Iraq, Baalbak, Damascus, Baghdad, Egypt, North Africa and Asiatic Turkey. He wandered through the great educational and cultural centres of Islam, including Baghdad, Damascus, Balkh, Ghazna and Cairo. He has incorporated his rich first hand experiences in his momentous books: *Gulistan,'* and *Bostan,'* which have made them the most popular ethical works in the world. "In his own writings (specially in *Gulistan)'',* writes Browne", he appears now painfully stumbling after the pilgrim caravan through the burning deserts of Arabia, now, bandying jests with a fine technical flavour· of grammatical terminology with school boys at Kashghar, now a prisoner in the hands of Franks, condemned to hard labour in the company of Jews in the Syrian town of Tripoli, now engaged in investigating the mechanism of a wonder-working Hindoo idol in the temple of Somnath".

Saadi was a good humourist who excelled in quick repartees. Writing in his well-known work, *'Sheruj Ajam'* (The Oriental Poetry), Maulana Shibli Nomani describes an incident in Sheikh's life, when, wandering through the Syrian forests he was caught by the Jews and was assigned the digging of a ditch in Tripoli. A few days after, an old friend of Saadi, happened to pass that way and was astonished to find him in such a plight. On enquiry, Saadi recited two couplets asking him to realise the condition of a person who shunned the society of human beings to be made to live among animals. The friend was deeply moved by his couplets, paid 10 dinars for freedom and married his daughter to Saadi for 100 dinars. His wife was very arrogant and haughty. One day, she taunted him that he should not forget that he was freed by her father. The Sheikh replied instantly, "Yes, he freed me for 10 dinars but enslaved me for 100 dinars."

According to some sources Saadi had met Amir Khusrou in India. He returned to Shiraz after the death of Saad Zangi.

Saadi was in fact a *dervish* who was greatly loved and respected by the rulers, administrators, nobles and people of his time. The rulers and their administrators, vied with each other to please the Sheikh and sent to him large sums of money to be distributed among the poor. Once Khwaja Shamsuddin, the celebrated Grand Vizier of Hulaku Khan's son sent 50 thousand gold coins for the Sheikh, which he was reluctant to accept. But the Grand Vizier, who was a disciple of the Sheikh persuaded him to accept the money for God's sake. At last the money was accepted and a magnificent caravan sarai was built with it.

During the last days of his life, Saadi retired to a secluded hut built in the suburb of Shiraz. He spent his time in prayers and fasting. Here the rulers and the ruled often assembled to pay their respects to the great moralist.

Saadi combined in him the rare qualities and capabilities of a poet, a sufi, a jurist and a moralist. He had observed life from diverse angles. On his return to his native town, Shiraz, in 1256 A.C. he settled down to literary work. This marks the beginning of the third period of his life lasting till his death, being the most important period of his life mainly devoted to literary creations. In 1257, he wrote his famous *'Bostan'* (Orchard) in verse, and a year later in 1258, he completed his well-known *'Gulistan'* (Garden) in prose, a collection of anecdotes, drawn from rich stories of observation and experience, based on ethical reflections and maxims of worldly. wisdom. "Both the books are so well-known", writes Browne, "and have been translated so often in so many languages that it is unnecessary to discuss them at length". His *'Gulistan'* and *'Bostan'* are the first classics to which the student of Persian is introduced. In Persian lyric, he occupies a place only second to Hafiz.

His *Gulistan* and *Bostan* are undoubtedly the most popular ethical works in the world. These have been widely translated into Western as well as Eastern languages including English, French, German, Russian, Latin, Polish, Turkish, Arabic, Urdu and Hindi. The oldest copy of the *'Kulliyat-i-Sheikh'* (The works of Saadi) exists in the London Museum Library. This was copied by Abu Bakr ibn Ali ibn Muhammad, 36 years after the death of Saadi. It contains *'Gulistan',* *'Bostan',* Arabic and Persian panegyrics, elegies, lyrics, quatrains, etc. But the works which have established his fame and immortalised his name among the men of letters in the world are *Gulistan, Bostan* and his *Persian lyrics.* Saadi is very popular in Europe. His book *'Bostan',* was published in Vienna in 1850 and in London in 1891. The German translation of the book was published in Jena in 1850 and in Leipzing in 1882; the French translation was published in 1880 and the English translation was published in London in 1879. His other book in prose, *'Gulistan',* was even more popular than *'Bostan'.* The book was published in English in Calcutta in 1806, in Hertford in 1850 and again in 1863, in London in 1823, 1852, 1880 and 1890; in French it was published in 1631, 1704, 1789 and 1858; in Latin it was published in 1651 and again in 1655; in German it was published in 1654, 1822 (in Hamburg), 1846 (in Stuttgart) and 1806 (in Leipzig); in Russian it was published in Moscow in 1857; in Polish it was published in Warsaw in 1879; in Turkish it was published in Constantinople (Istambul) in 1874 and again in 1876; in Arabic it was published in 1263 A.H. and in Urdu it was published in Calcutta in 1852. *(Sherul Ajam* of Maulana Shibli Nomani).

Saadi, as noted before, had a many-sided personality. But his real fame rests on his ethical writings. Both in verse and prose he is matchless and unique as a moralist and ethical teacher. Even before Saadi, ethical poetry existed in Persian and produced such well-known poets as *Sinai,* Khayyam and Attar, but Saadi carried it to a height where none could reach. His ethical writings do not suffer from the insipidity of a missionary. Ethical teachings when deprived of imaginative touches become philosophy rather than poetry. Saadi has drawn valuable morals from ordinary tales created out of his observation or imagination. His favourite ethical subjects are justice, kindness, love, generosity, hospitality, contentment and thankfulness. In his teachings regarding contentment he has emphasised on self-respect rather than on the negative ascetic attitude of inactivity, leaving everything to fate. He states, "By God it is better to dwell in Hell rather than go to Paradise with the help of one's neighbour". Again, he remarks that if you would adopt contentment you would not find any difference between the king and the beggar. Why do you bow before a king, leave your lust and you are yourself a king. He is very outspoken in his criticism of bad rulers and their ministers. His approach has always been free from all prejudices and partisanship.

Saadi represents the half pious and half worldly side of Persian character. Worldly wisdom rather than mysticism are his chief characteristics. The secret of his popularity as the greatest ethical teacher in the world rests on his catholicity. "His work *Gulistan*", writes Browne, is matter of every taste, the highest and the lowest, the most refined and the most coarse, and from his pages sentiments may be called worthy, on the one hand, of Eckhardt or Thomas. A Kampis or, on the other, of Caesar, Borgia and Heliogabalus. His writings are a microcosm of the East, alike in its best and its most ignoble aspects, and it is not without good reason that, whenever the Persian language is studied, they are, and have been for six centuries and half, the first book placed in the learner's hands." In his ethical writings, pious sentiments abound but these are predominantly practical. He has exposed the fickle nature of autocrats. "Wise men", states Saadi, "have said that one ought to be much on one's guard against the fickle nature of kings, who will at one time take offence at a salutation, and at another bestow honours in return for abuse."

Saadi is a great champion of downtrodden, destitute, orphans, widows and all those who should be helped on humanitarian grounds. His repartees and ethical writings have melted many a tyrant's heart. He has a soft corner specially for orphans, because he had himself tasted the pangs of losing his father at an early age. In *'Bostan'* he states :

"Protect thou the orphan whose father is dead;
Brush the mud from his dress, ward all hurt from his head.
Thou knowest not how hard his condition must be;
When the root has been cut; is there life in the tree?
Caress not and kiss not a child of thine own
In the sight of an orphan neglected and alone.
If the orphan sheds tears, who his grief will assuage?
If his temper should fail him, who cares for his rage?
O ! see that he weeps not, for surely God's throne
Doth quake at the orphan's most pitiful moan !
With infinite pity, with tenderest care,
Wipe the tears from his eyes, brush the dust from his hair."

As a lyrist, Saadi occupies a place only second to Hafiz. But Hafiz, too, has acknowledged the greatness of Saadi as a lyrist known for the simplicity of his diction and the sincerity of his ideas. Hafiz has stated, "Saadi had been the master of lyric". Another great Persian lyrist and versatile genius Amir Khusrou has admitted that he has followed Saadi in his lyrics. Browne is reluctant to admit that Saadi was inferior to Hafiz. But, according to Maulana Shibli Nomani, an authority on the subject, Saadi ranks only second to Hafiz as a lyrist. The chief characteristics of his lyrics are his sincerity of ideas, simplicity of diction and originality of expression. He is the father of Persian lyric, whose sincerity and naturalness has added much poetic appeal to his lyrics. But the exuberance and sentimentalism of Hafiz distinguishes him from the simplicity and sincerity of Saadi.

Saadi has also written some fine panegyrics and elegies. In panegyrics he followed the Arab panegyrists and confined himself to facts and even fearlessly giving the praised person his valuable advice. In elegies, he introduced national elegies. On the destruction of Baghdad in 1258 A.C., at the hands of Hulaku Khan he wrote a pathetic elegy mourning the loss sustained by the metropolis of Islam, which went against the interest of his patron Abu Baky Zangi who had allied himself with the Mongol tyrant.

Saadi, the sage of Persia, loved and respected by all, passed away in 691 A.H. at a ripe age of 120 years. He was buried in the suburbs of Dilkusha, now called Saadiya, which is a favourite resort of pilgrims drawn from distant parts of the Islamic world.

# HAFIZ SHIRAZI

On his arrival in Shiraz the great Tamerlane, who had conquered a substantial part of the known world, sent for Hafiz Shirazi, and equired from him:

"Have you composed this couplet?"

"If my beloved could conquer my heart I would bestow Samarkand and Bukhara for her mole".

"Yes," replied Hafiz.

"Do you know that I have overrun the entire world in order to build up Samarkand and Bukhara, which are my native places, and you are prepared to give them away in return of a mole only," asked the awe-inspiring monarch.

Hafiz remained unmoved and retorted: "This is on account of such extravagances that I have been reduced to this state of poverty". The great conqueror, in whose presence mighty rulers used to tremble with fear was much amused with the reply of Hafiz and sent him back loaded with presents and wealth.

Hafiz Shirazi, the immortal Persian lyrist and one of the four pillars of Persian poetry, is called by his admirers *'Lisanul Ghaib'* (The Tongue of the Unseen) and *'Tarjumanul Asrar'* (The Interpreter of Mysteries).

The grandfather of Hafiz, who resided in the suburbs of Isfahan, had migrated to Shiraz during the time of Atabeks of Shiraz. His father, Bahauddin, a wealthy merchant, died a premature death, leaving behind three sons, who squandered his wealth in frivolities. Hafiz, the youngest among his brothers, remained with his mother, and due to extreme poverty was obliged to work in a baker's shop. Hafiz had great passion for learning. Whatever time he could spare from his master's work, he spent in learning. He gave one-third of his wages to his mother, the other one-third to his teacher and the rest one-third to the needy persons. Thus he obtained a respectable education and learnt the Quran by heart, hence he adopted his poetic pen name as 'Hafiz,' a term commonly applied to those who learn the Quran by heart.

Hafiz's was the age of poetry and romance. There was a cloth merchant in his locality, who was an admirer of poets. Poets from different parts of the city gathered every evening at his shop and recited their poems. It served as an incentive to young Hafiz, who also began to compose and recite poems, but with little success. People made fun of him. One night, being highly disappointed with his failure as a poet, he visited the shrine of Baba Kuhi, situated on a hill north of Shiraz. He wept and prayed for his success and in a vigil it is said he was visited by Hazrat Ali, who gave him to eat some mysterious heavenly food and told him that henceforth the gates of poetry as well as knowledge would remain open for him. When he woke up the next morning he composed a poem, which surprised everybody. Henceforward, Hafiz was unparalleled in the realm of Persian lyrics and his fame as an immortal lyrist soon reached the distant parts of the Muslim world.

Hafiz received letters from the Royal Houses of Iraq, India and Arabia inviting him to visit their countries, but he was not prepared to leave his beautiful land at any cost. High praise of the rose garden, fascinating description of lovely scenes and bracing salubrious climate of Shiraz pervade his numerous pieces.

Maulana Shibili Nomani, in his monumental work: *'Sherul Ajam'* (The Poetry of the East), refers to several rulers whose favour and patronage Hafiz enjoyed. One of these was Sheikh Abu Ishaq Inju, a semi-independent ruler of Shiraz. Himself a reputed poet, the pleasure-loving Abu Ishaq was a great patron of arts and learning who pursued culture at the cost of the affairs of the State. One day, when he was persuaded by his favourite Sheikh Aminuddin to pay attention to the Muzaffari hosts, who were invading his Capital, Abu Ishaq simply remarked that 'the enemy must be a fool to waste the pleasant spring season in such a fashion'.

Hafiz saw several rulers of Shiraz, who succeeded one another. All were impressed by his poetic genius and favoured and placated him. It was during the reign of Zainul Abdin that Tamerlane (Taimur) visited the city and met the famous poet. Daulat Shah has described in detail the meeting of these two outstanding figures of the era—one, the greatest conqueror of his time and the other, the greatest poet.

Sultan Ahmed ibn Owais-i-Jalair, the talented II Khani ruler of Baghdad, requested Hafiz to visit Baghdad, but the poet declined saying :

"The Zephyr—breeze of Musalla and the stream of Ruknabad.
Don't permit me to travel or wander afield."

Invitations were also received by him from two rulers of India, who tried their best to induce him to visit their courts. One of these, Mahmood Shah Bahmani, a great patron of arts and culture, even sent the travelling expenses and a ship to bring Hafiz to India. He sent his favourite Mir Fazalullah along with money and presents to escort the immortal poet from Shiraz to Gulbarga. Hafiz spent a considerable part of the money in Shiraz and on arrival on the Persian Gulf gave the rest to a destitute friend. Two Persian merchants bound for India offered to meet the entire travelling expenses of the poet. When they reached Hurmuz, a ship was waiting to convey the poet to India. Hafiz got on the ship, but, when the ship was about to set sail a tempest arose and Hafiz got ashore. Instead of going to India he sent the following few couplets written on the occasion to King Mahmood :

> Not all the sum of earthly happiness
>     Is worth the bowed head of a moment's pain,
> And if I sell for wine my *dervish* dress
>     Worth more than what I sell is what I gain!
> The Sultan's crown, with priceless jewels set,
>     Encircles fear of death and constant dread;
> It is head dress much desired—and yet
>     Art sure 'tis worth the danger to the head?
> Down in the quarter where they sell red wine
>     My holy carpet scarce would fetch a cup
> How brave a pledge of piety is mine,
>     Which is not worth a goblet foaming up!
> Full easy seemed the sorrow of the sea
>     Heightened by hope of gain—hope flew too fast?
> A hundred pearls were poor indemnity,
>     Not worth the blast.
> (Translated by Miss Gertrude Lowthian Bell—Poems from *"Diwan"* of Hafiz).

Another Indian ruler, Sultan Ghyasuddin of Bengal also implored Hafiz to visit his Court, but the poet, instead sent him an ode.

Hafiz had a good knowledge of the Arabic language, which is evident from his billingual poems.

Hafiz is universally recognised as one of the four pillars of Persian poetry and one who is matchless in the realm of the lyric. His successors, including Saib, Urfi, Salim have acknowledged his incomparable skill in this branch of poetry. He, not only expanded the scope of the Persian lyric through his Epicurian philosophy, which was earlier expanded by Umar Khayyam in his famous quatrains, but also immortalised, Persian lyric through his inimitable style, his sincerity and sublimity of thought and exuberance of expression and melliflousness. Before him Saadi and Khusrou had beautified the Persian lyrics through their sincerity of thought and simplicity of diction and Salman Sauji and Khwajoo Kirmani beautified it through ornamentation of language as well as with rhetorical artifices. Hafiz, combined in himself the merits of all those poets as well as added a charm of his own. His lyrics have been fascinating to all lovers of Persian poetry during the last six centuries, that have elapsed since his death in 793 A.H. Having a tinge of humour, his couplets brim with an optimistic note. Being a man of cheerful disposition, he observes life with a smiling countenance and preaches Epicurian philosophy with greater success than Khayyam.

As a panegyrist, he is distinguished from the great Persian panegyrist Zahir Faryabi, Anwari and Salman of Sawa, as he never employed mean and despicable ways to extort money, hence his praise lacks the high sounding words and excessive flights of imagination so essential for good oriental panegyrics. He is a devotee of Shiraz, and is never wearied of singing the praise of the stream of Ruknabad and the rose gardens of Musalla.

"Bring, cup bearer, all that is left of thy wine !
    In the garden of Paradise vainly thou 'It seek
The life of the fountain of Ruknabad
    And the bowers of Musalla where roses twine".

He sings of spring, rose, nightingale, wine, youth and beauty which at times elevate him to the realm of eternal beauty and bliss of which all these fair things are a pale reflection.

According to Sir Gore Ouseley, "his style is clear, unaffected and harmonious, displaying at the same time great learnings and matured sciences, and intimate knowledge of the hidden as well as the apparent nature of things; but above all a certain fascination of expression unequalled by any other poet".

Miss Gertrude Lowthian has given a correct estimate of Hafiz when she states: "To Hafiz, on the contrary, modern instances have no value; contemporary history is too small to occupy his thought. . . . But some of us will feel that the apparent indifference of Hafiz (to his environments), lends to his philosophy a quality which Dante does not possess. The Italian is bound down within the limits of his philosophy, his theory of universe is essentially of his own age, and what to him was so acutely real is to many of us merely a beautiful of terrible image. The picture that Hafiz draws represents a wider landscape, though the immediate foreground may not be so distinct. It is as if his mental eye endowed with wonderful acuteness of vision, had penetrated into those provinces of thought, which, of later age, were destined to inhabit. We can forgive him for leaving for us so indistinct a representation of his own time, and the life of the individual in it, when we find him formulating ideas as profound as the warning that there is no musician to whose music both the drunk and the sober can dance".

The poetry of Hafiz has a universal appeal. His philosophy is the same as that of Khayyam, but in his it has been more vigorously and fascinatingly expressed. He states that man is hardly aware of the secrets of nature. This idea had earlier been propounded by Socrates, Farabi, Ibn Sina and Khayyam, but in Hafiz, it has attained greater force and charm of expression. In his opinion the presence of the Eternal Being (God) is visible from every particle, every leaf and everything found in this world, and only the spiritual eye can see Him. Through the words of 'Saqi' (cup bearer), wine, rose, garden, he has conveyed the praise of Eternal Beauty, which has charmed the Sufis (Mystics) and commoners alike. His poetry also contains high class moral philosophy, through which he has exposed such preachers who do not practise what they preach.

Hafiz is undoubtedly one of the most popular poets of the East. His fame as an immortal lyrist, one who has painted some lively pictures of the optimistic side of life, has transcended the barriers of Persia and reached the distant parts of the East and the West. Numerous biographies as well as commentaries on his works have been written after his death. Beginning from Daulat Shah, who wrote his biographical work a century after the poet's death, there is a long list of biographies down to quite modern compilations like Raza Quli Khan's *"Majmaul Fusaha"* and *"Riyazul Arfeen"*.

But his best critical study is found in Shibli's *"Sherul Ajam"*, written in Urdu. Among the notable Persian biographies of Hafiz are Daulat Shah's *"Memoirs of Poets"*, Jami's *'Baharistan'* Lutf Ali Beg's *'Atishkada'* (Fire Temple) and a quite modern biography *"Majmaul Fusaha"* (Assembly of the Eloquents).

The number of commentaries on the poems of Hafiz in Persian, Turkish and Urdu languages, is considerable. The three best commentaries in Turkish language are those of Sururi, Shami and Sudi.

The poems of Hafiz, 693 in number have been translated into several Western languages, including English, German, French and Latin. A translation of his complete work in German verse has been done by Rosenzweig Schwannan and in English prose by Willberforce Clark. Of English verse translations of Hafiz, the largest is that of Herman Bickwell. But the greatest European poet influenced by Hafiz was Goethe (German) who dedicated a number of poems to Hafiz.

There has been a general practice in Persia and India of taking out auguries from 'Diwan-i-Hafiz' which have often proved to be true. Instances are common. Shah Abbas II, the Safavi Ruler of Persia (1642—67 A.C.) obtained the following augury from 'Diwan-i-Hafiz' regarding his intended campaign against Azerbaijan Province, of which Tabriz was the Capital.

"Thou has captured Iraq and Fars by thy verse, O Hafiz!
    Come, for it now the turn of Baghdad and the time of Tabriz."

The king at once decided in favour of the campaign which turned out to be completely successful.

The Mughal Emperor Jahangir has been a number of instances in his well-known *"Memoirs"*, in which the auguries taken out by him from 'Diwan-i-Hafiz' turned out to be true.

Hafiz died in 793 A.H. and was buried in a green orchard in the suburbs of Shiraz, which was later called after him as *"Hafiziya"*. His tomb was built by Abul Qasim Babar, the great grandson of Tamerlane (Taimur) and further beautified by later rulers. It is now a place of recreation and pilgrimage for the visitors drawn from distant countries. The poet's words have come out to be true :

"When thou passest by our tomb, seek a blessing, for it shall become a place of pilgrimage for the libertines of all the world".

Ralph Waldo Emerson in his essay on Persian Poetry, pays blowing tributes to Hafiz :

"Hafiz is the Prince of Persian Poets, and in his extraordinary gifts adds to some of the attributes of Pindar, Anacreon, Horace, and Burns, the insight of a mystic, that sometimes affords a deeper glance at Nature than belongs to either of these bards. He accosts all topics with an easy audacity". "He only", he says, "Is fit for company, who knows how to prize earthly happiness at the value of a nightcap. Our father Adam sold Paradise for two kernels of wheat; then blame me not, if I hold it dear at one grape-stone". He says to the Shah, "Thou who rulest after words and thoughts which no ear has heard and no mind has thought, abide firm until thy young destiny tears off his blue coat from the old greybeard of the sky".

# MAULANA JALALUDDIN RUMI

Two persons were exchanging hot words in a street of Konya. Both were abusing each other. One was saying, "O! cursed, if you would utter a single abuse against me, you would get ten in return". Maulana Rumi, who happened to pass by, heard their altercation. Addressing them he said: "Brothers! whatever store of abuse you have, shower on me. You may hurl thousands of abuses on me, but you would not get anything in return". The two persons forgot all their abuses, fell on the feet of the great Maulana, and reconciled themselves.

Maulana Jalaluddin Rumi, the greatest mystic poet that the world has produced, whose renowned *Mathnavi* is known as the Quran in the Persian language, was born in Balkh in 1207 A.C. He came of a family of great religious scholars, descending from the first Caliph of Islam. His grandfather Husain Balkhi, a great mystic scholar, was so much respected that Sultan Muhammad Khwarizm Shah married his daughter to him. Hence the ruler of Khwarizm was the maternal grandfather of Jalaluddin Rumi.

Sheikh Bahauddin Balkhi, the father of Jalaluddin Rumi, was acknowledged as one of the greatest scholars of his time in the world of Islam. Muhammad Khwarizm Shah became a disciple of Sheikh Bahauddin and frequently visited him. He imparted education and lectured on all subjects. But due to the Court rivalry, Sheikh Bahauddin left Balkh and followed by hundreds of his disciples and followers migrated westward. He passed through Nishapur and in 1212 visited Sheikh Fariduddin Attar, who, according to chroniclers, took Jalaluddin in his arms, predicted his greatness and gave him his blessings and a copy of his poem '*Asrar Nama*'. From Nishapur, the Sheikh arrived in Baghdad, where he stayed for a number of years, lecturing on religious subjects. The Ambassador of the Seljuk Ruler, Kaikobad, who also attended his lectures, apprised his Ruler of the deep learning of the Sheikh. King Kaikobad also became a disciple of the Sheikh. From Baghdad the Sheikh and his party went to Hejaz and thence of Zanjan, where he remained for one year, and thence to Larinda (Kirman) where he stayed for seven years. Here he married his son Jalaluddin to a lady named Gauher, who bore two sons, Sultan Veld and Alauddin. The Seljuk Ruler, Alauddin Kaikobad, an admirer of the Sheikh, invited him to stay in the capital. Accepting the invitation, the Sheikh went to Konya (Iconium), the Capital of Seljuk State. The Seljuk King along with his courtiers, went out of the city to receive the Sheikh, and followed him on foot. Here Sheikh Bahauddin, the father of Maulana Jalaluddin, died in 1231 A.C.

Jalaluddin received his early education from his learned father. Among the disciples of his father was a renowned scholar, named Syed Burhanuddin Muhaqqiq. The Maulana was entrusted to his care; he taught him all worldly subjects. At the time of the death of his father, Jalaluddin who was 25 years of age, went to Damascus and Aleppo, great centres of learning for higher education in those days. Syed Burhanuddin also instructed him in the mystic lore. After his death, Jalaluddin came under the influence of and received teaching from Shams-i-Tabriz, a "weird figure", as Nicholson calls him "wrapped in coarse black felt, who flits across the stage for a moment and disappears tragically enough".

Maulana Jalaluddin Rumi, who had become a great scholar, a worthy son of his learned father, was surrounded by scholars and followers attracted from distant parts of the Islamic world. Here, in 642 A.H. he met Shams-i-Tabriz. The meeting, proved a turning point in his life. From a worldly teacher, Rumi became a recluse. Discarding all worldly pomp and pleasures, he retired to a life of prayers and devotion to his spiritual teacher, Shams-i-Tabriz. This sudden change in his life created restiveness among his disciples, and Shams-i-Tabriz in order to calm their uneasiness, slipped away, from Konya one night. This separation from his teacher, utterly disquieted the Maulana, who reacted to the incident by renouncing the world. It caused deep perturbation to his family. Therefore, his eldest son was deputed to search Shams-i-Tabriz. He brought him back to Konya from Damascus. The teacher and his disciples remained together for sometime, and one day, being annoyed by certain followers of the Maulana, Shams-i-Tabriz again disappeared from Konya never to return. A thorough search for the Saint, in which the Maulana himself participated, ended in a fiasco.

The disappearance of his spiritual teacher brought a great change in Maulan's life and gave an edge to his sentiments and his inspirational poetical instincts which hitherto lay dormant in him. This revolutionary spiritual transformation was climaxed by a spurt of poetical effusion. The beginning of his immortal *Mathnavi* (long poem) was made during this period.

Maulana Jalaluddin Rumi gave birth to a line of mystics called Jalalia. The celebrated Sheikh Bu Ali Qalander of Panipat remained with the Maulana for a number of years and was much influenced by him. Another well-known Saint, Sheikh Shahabuddin Suhrawardy had also benefited from him. Sheikh Saadi, the famous Persian poet and moralist, according to the author of *"Manaqib-ul-Aarfeen"* had also visited the Maulana at Konya.

Maulana Jalaluddin Rumi has left behind him two works on which his fame rests—his *Diwan* and his immortal *"Mathnavi"*. His *Diwan* containing 50 thousand couplets, mostly mystical lyrics, is wrongly considered to be composed by his spiritual teacher Shams-i-Tabriz, due to the latter's poetic name being frequently used in the last couplet. The bulk of this work was composed by Rumi after the disappearance of his spiritual teacher, while Rida Quli Khan regards the major part of this work to have been composed in his memoriam. According to Nicholson, a "part of *Diwan* was composed while Shams-i-Tabriz was still living, but probably the bulk of it belongs to a later period".

The Maulana's lyrics are replete with sincerity and sublimity, deep emotionalism and a spirit of forgetfulness which characterise the works of mystic poets of Persia, including Sinai and Attar. His lyrics are free from ornamentation and passivity prevalent in the lyrics of Salman, Khakani and Anwari.

It was a time when great panegyrists flourished in Persia, so much so that poets of the calibre of Saadi and Iraqi, too, could not abstain from dabbling in panegyrics, but Maulana Rumi steered clear of this growing social evil. He confined his poetry to sincerely translating his true sentiments into verse. Instinct with exuberance of feelings, his lyrics have immense poetic appeal which elevates one to the higher world. He appeals more to the higher and nobler sentiments of man.

With the decline of Seljuk power in Persia, the patrons of poets disappeared, hence the poets paid greater attention towards lyrics instead of panegyrics. The poets who refined lyrics and made it a vehicle of sincerity of feelings, were Rumi, Saadi and Iraqi. The Maulana himself a great mystic, has faithfully painted the diverse phases of love, which he had experienced in his life.

His immortal, *"Mathnavi"* is undoubtedly the most popular book in the Persian language. It has been translated into several Eastern and Western languages and has given him a distinguished place among the few immortal poets of the world. According to the author of *'Majma-us-Safa'*, the four outstanding books in the Persian language are *Shahnama-i-Firdausi*, *Gulistan-i-Saadi*, *Mathnavi of Rumi* and *Diwan-i-Hafiz*, but the *Mathnavi* of Rumi is the most popular of all. It has always been a favourite book of intellectuals and religious men. A number of commentaries have been written on it.

This immortal work of Maulana comprising 6 books and containing 26,660 couplets, was completed in 10 years. According to the author, the *Mathnavi* contains, "the roots of religion and the discovery of the mysteries of nature and divine knowledge". (Arabic Preface to Book I). "It contains great number of rambling anecdotes" writes Browne in his *'A Literary History of Persia'*, of the most various character, some sublime and dignified, others grotesque, interspersed with mystical and theosophical digressions, often of the most abstruse character, in sharp contrast with the narrative portions, which though presenting some peculiarities of diction, are, as a rule, couched in very simple and plain language". The book is further remarkable as beginning abruptly, without any formal doxology, with the well-known and beautiful passage translated by the late Professor E. H. Palmer, under the title of the "Song of Reed".

The *Mathnavi* (long narrative poem) as a form of poetry owes its growth to Mahmood of Ghazni under whose patronage Firdausi made it a vehicle of narrating the ancient history of Persia in his immortal *Shah Nama.* Later Hakim Sinai wrote *'Hadiqa',* the first mystic poem in the Persian language. He was followed by Khwaja Fariduddin Attar, who wrote several *Mathnavis* alive with mystic thoughts. But the *Mathnavi* of Maulana Jalaluddin Rumi marks the climax of mystic poetry and ranks among the immortal poems of the world.

Among the factors which have contributed to the popularity of this matchless massive work are the sublimity of thought and subtlety of complex ideas versified in an extremely simple manner, hardly found in any other language. The ethical and mystic values have been beautifully explained through intelligent stories and parables drawn from everyday life. The way in which the Maulana has explained the intricate ethical and mystic problems through realistic stories, amply brings him out to be a person who has a keen insight into the secrets of human nature. With him, the art of teaching morality through life-like stories, has reached its climax. He points out to hidden evils of humanity in such a manner that one feels he knew it beforehand.

The main characteristic of this poem is the sublimity of thought and the simplicity and spontaneity of its expression. Contrary to the pessimism and the life of resignation practised and preached by the mystics in general, the Maulana preached a healthy optimism and a life full of action. In one of his stories he argues that it is self-evident what a master means when he places a shovel in the hands of his servant. In the same way, God who has given us hands and feet, wants us to make use of them. Hence the life of renunciation and resignation is against the will of God. The Islamic teaching is that one should try his best and leave the result to God. Man proposes but God disposes. In this way, among all the mystics, the Maulana made the most practical, realistic and Islamic approach towards life and became the forerunner of Iqbal, the poet of Islam.

Before his meeting with Shams-i-Tabriz, the Maulana passed a life full of pomp and splendour. Wherever he went, he was accompanied by a large number of scholars and disciples. Thereafter, he spent his time in prayers and speculation. Mostly he spent the whole night in prayers.

He was very humane and generous. The neighbouring rulers and their courtiers sent valuable presents which he always distributed among the poor. Whenever there was nothing to eat in his house, he was much pleased and exclaimed: "Today our house is like those of saints", He was so generous that he used to offer to the supplicant whatever he had on his body.

He shunned the society of rulers and their courtiers. The rulers and their ministers vied with each other in order to win his favour and visited him at times, but he avoided them as far as possible.

That Maulana Jalaluddin Rumi was gifted with supernatural powers from his very childhood, will be evident from the following anecdote:

As a child of eleven, while Rumi was playing one day with his friends on the roof of his house, the former suggested they might now shift to the opposite house to resume their play there. Rumi refused to accompany his playmates giving them to understand that he would jump over to the said house in spite of a wide lane between the two houses, rather than go there through the stairs. "How could that be possible? You are not a Jinn, nor have you Alladin's wonderful lamp to summon one to transport you to the opposite house lying across the lane, over the roof", they asked jeeringly. On reaching the roof of the other house they were flabbergated to find Rumi already present there.

The Maulana died in 1273 A.C. and was buried in the mausoleum erected over his father's grave at Konya by Alauddin Kaikobad, the Seljuk Ruler. People of all communities and sections followed his funeral crying and wailing. The Christians and Jews were reciting their scriptures. The Seljuk King who also accompanied the funeral procession asked them what relation had they with the virtuous Maulana. They replied, "If the deceased was like your Muhammad (PBUH) he was like our Christ and Moses". The entire population had turned out to pay their last homage to the departed Saint.

Maulana Jalaluddin Rumi was an eminent poet, an outstanding mystic and above all a great man. "He is undoubtedly the most eminent Sufi poet that Persia has produced", writes Browne, "while his mystical *Mathnavi* deserves to rank amongst the great peoms of all times".

# UMAR KHAYYAM

Muslim Persia has produced some of the greatest luminaries of the Islamic world, who have immensely contributed to the intellectual development of mediaeval times and were mainly instrumental in bringing about the renaissance of the Western world. Their invaluable works procured the necessary link in the evolution of mankind and have left their ineffaceable marks on the pages of world history.

In the development of Islamic literature, the Persians formed the vanguard of all cultural and literary movements and a number of their literatures acquired international reputation. The four pillars of Persian poetry are Firdausi—the author of *Shah Nama,* the world famous epic poem; Saadi—the great moralist; Hafiz—the celebrated lyrist and Maulana Jalaluddin Rumi, author of the well-known *'Mathnavi'* which is held as the 'Quran in the Persian language'.

Umar Khayyam, one of the intellectual giants of the Middle ages—a man of versatile taste and a sceptic by nature who is not much known in Persia as a poet but as a mathematician and an astronomer. "Umar Khayyam is a name more familiar in England and America than in Persia", writes H. A. R. Gibb in the *Legacy of Islam.*

Ghyasuddin Abul Fateh ibn Ibrahim Al Khayyam, better known in the world as Umar Khayyam, was born in 1048 at Nishapur, the capital of Khorasan which is a province of Persia. His place of birth is a disputed point among historians. Muhammad and Saharazuri hold that he was born in Basang, a village of the district of Astrabad, but their contentions do not stand the test of later historical researches. Actually he was born and educated at Nishapur where he passed the major part of his life and ultimately died and was buried then. "His tomb at Nishapur is in itself sufficient proof of the identity of his birth place", says a writer. "For in Iran the custom in Umar's days as in ours, was to bury the dead in the place of their nativity".

Though Umar has universally been accepted as a Persian national, some historians hold that he originally belonged to an Arabian tribe, "Al-Khayyami", who were tent makers and had migrated and settled in Persia long after her conquest by the Arabs. Not much is known about the early life of the celebrated poet, but being the son of a well-to-do father he was given the best education available in those days and became the pupil of the learned Imam Mowakkif, a well-known teacher of the Islamic world. Here he met and made intimate friendship with Hasan Ali ibn Ishaq, better known in history as Nizamul Mulk Toosi, the Grand Vizier of Malik Shah Seljuki and Hasan bin Sabah who later on became the founder of the fanatical sect of Ismailies, called "Assassins".

The three class-fellows, who, in their later life, earned immortal places in the pages of history and were intimate friends, had entered into a remarkable bond of friendship—that being the pupils of Mowakkif who were mostly successful in life, if anyone of them got ahead of the others, he would try his level best for the advancement of the remaining two, to the extent of sharing his wealth and honour. Nizamul Mulk who was the most brilliant among the trio and topped the list in the examination, was invited to undertake the education of Alp Arsalan, the Seljuk Prince. On the accession of Alp Arsalan as the Emperor of Seljukide Empire, Nizamul Mulk was elevated to the high rank of the Grand Vizier and proved himself as one of the ablest administrators the Islamic world has produced. In the midst of his many preoccupations Nizamul Mulk did not forget his former friends and in spite of being fully aware of the evil propensities of Hasan, kept his promise and installed him in a post of considerable responsibility—but the crafty Hasan involved himself in several court intrigues and left the service to become the founder of the notorious sect of Assassins, which was later on responsible for the assassination of his illustrious friend and benefactor, Nizamul Mulk.

Umar Khayyam, a sceptic by nature, had, on the other hand, declined a lucrative government job and preferred an annual pension of 1,200 gold pieces paid out of the revenues of Nishapur, where he had settled to devote the rest of his life to literacy pursuits.

Umar Khayyam was a high class poet, whose worth as a poet was not fully realised during his lifetime and whose immortal Quatrains *(Rubaiyat)* have been better appreciated in the West during the last one century. The best part of his poems were composed during his youth in the quiet and beautiful landscape of Nishapur. Under the shade of sweet-scented trees that shed their lovely flowers at his feet, Umar often sat sipping his cold 'Sharbat' from the hands of *'Saki'* and smoke his fragrant *'Hookkah'*. He watched the dark-eyed maidens roaming about—and as he watched, he forgot all the anxieties of worldly life.

The translated version of his famous *Rubaiyat* (Quatrains) was first published by E. Fitzgerald in 1859, which made him famous throughout the Western world. "If the moods expressed in the famous Quartrains", says Gibbs, "is not the most heroic or exalted, none-the-less they caught the exact tone of the age, and voiced it as perfectly as eight centuries earlier they had voiced the polished hedonism of the cultured society of Isfahan".

His verses are clothed in beautiful and chaste Persian which is much suited and add charm to his favourite theme. Like Hafiz, Umar Khayyam used the metaphors and figures of Sufism to add colour to his works.

Alongside the ecstatic spiritualism of the Sufis lies the colder pessimistic scepticism of Umar Khayyam, who, to a great extent, followed the line toed by Avicenna. He has impressively portrayed the transient character of human life.

> Think, in this battered carvan-sarai
>> Whose portals are alternate night and day
> How Sultan after Sultan with his pomp
>> Abode his destined hour, and went his way.

The wise man is he who passes the few moments of his uncertain transitory life in pursuit of pleasure, free from all worldly cares and anxieties. Here his ideas follow the lines of Epicurian philosophy, namely: "Eat, drink and be merry" and come very close to the Hedonistic theory of "Pleasure as the End of Life".

> Ah, my beloved, fill the cup that clears
>> Today of past regret and future fears
> Tomorrow! why, tomorrow I may be
>> Myself with yesterday's seven thousand years.

In his poetry he is typically Persian. In it he shows himself as the chief and the foremost of that group of free thinkers, who ridiculed the limitations of the dogma and taught the futility or piety and orthodoxy. He would prefer to enjoy the pleasures of this world than to aspire for the enjoyment of the next.

> Some for the glories of this world, and some
>> Sigh for the Prophet's Paradise to come,
> Ah, take the cash and let the credit go,
>> Nor heed the rumble of a distant drum!

It is not to be wondered that the philosophy of Umar was very much repugnant to the conservative class of people. The question of *"Jaza"* and *"Saza"* has been agitating the minds of our thinkers who could hardly procure a satisfactory solution of this controversial issue. Umar has taken advantage of this point of Muslim religious philosophy.

> Oh, thou who didst with pitfalls and with gin
>> Beset the route I was to wander in
> Thou wilt not with predestined evil round
>> Enmesh, and thou impute my fall to sin.

It is needless to search for a carefully reasoned system of philosophy in the works of a poet—so was the case with Umar, whose verses record certain moods. The dominant note of his verses is to cast off the cares and anxieties of the worldly life by sipping a cup of wine. A few drops of liquor would free one from all sorts of miseries and would transport him to the realm of ecstasy and bliss.

The verses of Umar were composed at various periods of his life and the contradictions in his writings are due to the progress of his ideas as he passed through various stages of life—from pious Muslim to avowed sceptic. His sole consistency lies in his praise of wine, to which in his moments of depression he turns for oblivion and perhaps for exaltation. His love for wine is so intense that he wishes that his body may be washed with wine after his death.

> Ah, with grape my fading life provide,
>     And wash the body whence the life has died,
> And lay me, shrouded in the living leaf,
>     By some not unfrequented garden side.

He says that he tried to give up wine and swore not to taste it again—but when spring came he scattered penitence to the winds.

> Indeed, indeed, repentence oft before
>     I swore—but was I sober when I swore
> And then, and then came spring, and rose in hand
>     My thread—bare penitence apieces tore.

Umar has also left behind him three metaphysical treatises—namely, the manuscript of the treatise, *"On Existence"* exists in Berlin; manuscript of a small Persian treatise titled *"Dar ibn Qulliyat"* has been preserved in a library of Paris and *"Nauroz Nama"* has recently been revealed by F. Rosen.

After completing his studies, Umar visited Samarkand, Bukhara, Isfahan and Balkh which were the intellectual centres in those times and added to his astronomical knowledge by exchanging views on the subject with some of the eminent intellectuals residing in those cities. He united with his scientific pursuits the study of medicine and won a high reputation as a healer.

Khayyam's fame in the Muslim countries mainly rests on his outstanding mathematical and scientific researches and not on poetry. In Europe, too, he was known for his scientific achievements long before as a poet. His works on *Algebra* were translated in 1851 while his *"Rubaiyat"* were first published in 1859. The manuscripts of his principal works exist in Paris and in the India Office, London; *"Masadrat"* researches on Euclid's axioms and *Mushkilat-al-Hisab,* dealing with complicated arithmetical problems have been preserved in Munich (Germany). According to V. Minorsky, "he was the greatest mathematician of the mediaeval times". His primary contribution is in *Algebra* in which he has registered much advance on the works of the Greeks. His *Algerba* is an advance on that of Khwarizmi, too in degree of equation—as the greater part of Umar's book is devoted to cubic equations while Khwarizmi dealt with quadratic equations only. His *Algebra* deals with geometric and algebraic equations of second degree, an admirable classification of equations, including the cubic. His classification of equations is based on the number and different terms which they include. He recognises thirteen different forms of cubic equations. His solution of cubic and quadratic equations with the help of conic sections is probably the most advanced work of Arabic mathematics that he left for us. "His skill as a geometer", says Max Mayerhof, "is equal to his literary erudition and reveals real logical power and penetration".

In Physics, Umar's researches are devoted to specific weight of gold and silver. The *Tarikhul Fi* gives the *Mizamul Hukama* which determines the method of ascertaining the weight of objects studded with precious stones without taking out such stones.

During the reign of Malik Shah Seljuki, his illustrious Grand Vizier, Nizamul Mulk Toosi, a great patron of learning, had invited a body of savants to carry out astronomical observations which was headed by Umar Khayyam and Abdur Rahman Hazini. Their efforts led to the reform of Calendar which was in advance of the *Gregorian* by 600 years and, according to Sedillot, an authority on the subject, "it is more exact". The famous observatory where Umar carried out his astronomical researches was constructed at Ray and the Calendar formulated by Umar is known as *At Tarikh-al Jalali.*

According to the latest research conducted by Soviet orientatists, the *Code of Rules on Astronomy,* a hitherto anonymous treatise, is now definitely attributed to Umar Khayyam, an outstanding Persian poet and scientist of the Middle Ages.

The authorship of the treatise has been established by Nuriya Hairetdinova, a young mathematician from the Teachers' Training Institute in Ferghana, Uzbekistan. Her conclusions have been supported by prominent Soviet orientalists.

She has analysed the *Code of Rules* which consists of a preface, six preambles and three books, by using a photostat copy of the manuscript kept at the Istanbul Library.

Her research has helped glean new information on the development of spherical trigonometry in the mediaeval Orient, and the scientific views of Umar Khayyam, the initiator of a reforms of the old Arabic calendar and the author of famous treatises on mathematics and other fields of knowledge.

The treatise kept in Istanbul was re-written in 1235. A searching textual analysis helped the Uzbek mathematician to establish that Umar Khayyam finished this treatise in 1094 A.C.

Of his death the following story is told by *Nuzhatul-Arwah.* "On the day of his death, Umar was attentively reading the *Book of Healing,* a metaphysical work of Avicenna. When he came upon the chapter titled, *'One and Many'*, he put aside the book, stood up, offered his prayers and made his last injunctions to his friends and relations. Since then he neither ate nor drank till the evening and after the evening prayers he prostrated and cried out, 'O, Almighty, verily I have tried to realise Thee to the extent of my abilities. I beg Your Forgiveness', Saying· this he sank to death and was widely mourned by his friends and admirers. He was buried according to his life-long desire in a beautifully shaded grove".

Such was the end of Umar Khayyam, a great poet, philosopher, astronomer and mathematician.

# MIRZA ASADULLAH KHAN GHALIB

Ghalib was born in a period when India was passing through one of the most revolutionary and turbulent times of her history. The great Mughal Empire lay tottering and Bahadur Shah, the last Mughal Emperor, was a monarch in name only. The War of Independence in 1857 had shaken the fabric of the entire Indian society and served as death-knell to Muslim civilisation in India. The British rulers tried to efface all traces of Muslim culture.

Born in Agra in 1797, Mirza Asadullah Khan Ghalib, originally of Tatar descent, later settled down in Delhi, the Capital of the tottering Mughal Empire.

He traced his descent from the House of Turan, son of Faridun. His grandfather had migrated from Transoxiana (Central Asia) to India and sought employment with the Mughal Emperor Shah Alam II. His father, Mirza Abdullah Khan, had a chequered career, serving one royal court after another. He served with the Nawab of Oudh, the Raja of Alwar and the Nizam of Hyderabad.

Young Asadullah Khan was hardly five years old, when his father died and he was brought up by his maternal uncle, Mirza Nasarullah Khan, a Risaldar in the British army. He was given good education by teachers like Moazzam and Nazir Akbarabadi.

At the age of 13, Ghalib was married to a noble lady of the Loharu ruling family. Born and brought up in a rich and cultured family, Asadullah Khan's later life was far from happy.

India at that time was passing through the worst period of her history. The Muslims who had ruled for about a thousand years had reached the lowest level of their decadence. The last vestige of the Muslim power, the Mughal Emperor, was no better than the king of a chessboard.

The politico-economic condition of the Muslims had much deteriorated and the British were slowly but surely replacing the Muslim power in the subcontinent. In such an atmosphere, surcharged with uncertainty and economic depression, especially for Muslims, Ghalib had to struggle for the rest of his life.

Ghalib's married life was not happy. His early marriage was followed by the death of several children in infancy. In the absence of his own children, he had developed great attachment to one of his nephews, named Arif. But, unfortunately, Arif, too died in youth. Ghalib wrote a touching elegy on his death which guided his disciple, Hali, to pave the way for the introduction of modern elegy in Urdu poetry as opposed to the conventional elegies on the martyrdom of Karbala, written by Mir Anees and Dabir and other Lucknow poets.

Ghalib's domestic and financial worries kept on multiplying till his death; these shattered his nerves and eventually reconciled him to his fate.

His misfortune did not leave him alone. A pension of Rs. 500 per year granted by Wajid Ali Shah, last Ruler of Oudh, was stopped two years after its inception due to the annexation of Oudh by the British. A personal brawl with a British Inspector of Police in Delhi, landed him in prison for three months. He could not get a job of Professor of Persian in the newly-founded Delhi College as the British Secretary did not show him normal courtesy when he called on him for an interview. A salary of Rs. 50 per month granted to him by the last Mughal Emperor, Bahadur Shah Zafar, for writing the history of the Timur dynasty was discontinued after the War of Independence in 1857.

The post-War of Independence period proved to be the culminating point of his miserable life—all his near and dear ones had perished, the Imperial city of Delhi was in ruins and the literary gatherings in the Red Fort of Delhi were no more. He struggled for life till his death in 1869.

Despite all these hardships, Ghalib never thought of stooping below his dignity. He bore these trials and tribulations cheerfully.

Ghalib was much influenced by the happenings of his time, which are deeply reflected in his poetry. Like Mir, he also passed a life full of woes and sorrows, but unlike him he did not wail for his sufferings; his contentment and cheerful disposition enabled him to face all these miseries with a smiling countenance. Says he:

رنج کا خوگر ہوا انساں تو مٹ جاتا ہے رنج
مشکلیں اتنی پڑیں مجھ پر کہ آساں ہو گئیں

(Sorrows disappear if one gets accustomed to them; I had to face so many troubles that these have ceased to be troublesome to me).

"No poet can ascend the summit of greatness, unless he has a deep insight into philosophy", says Coleridge. Ghalib is one of the two great philosopher poets that Urdu has produced. Iqbal is more a philosopher than a poet while Ghalib is more a poet than a philosopher.

Some westernised people have compared Ghalib with a host of European poets like Shakespeare, Wordsworth and Milton, without reflecting deeply into his poetical attributes. Salahuddin Khuda Bakhsh has compared Ghalib with the German poet, Heine, who was simply a poet of love, while Ghalib depicts the multifarious phases of human life in his verses and soars high in the realm of imagination. Dr. Iqbal, being himself a great poet, has made in the following couplet a correct appraisal of Ghalib when he compares him with the celebrated German poet Goethe. Both have reached the limits of human imagination and have mirrored almost all aspects of human life.

آہ تو اُجڑی ہوئی دِلّی میں آرامیدہ ہے

گلشنِ ویمر میں تیرا ہمنوا خوابیدہ ہے

Iqbal was a great admirer of Ghalib. He paid him compliments by placing him in the Heaven alongwith Mansur-al-Hallaj. The famous Urdu critic and writer, Dr. Abdur Rahman Bijnori has equated Ghalib's *"Diwan"* with Vedas, considering them as the only two Divine books in India. In his preface to his work on Ghalib, Dr. Bijnori says: "O Ghalib: if the art of poetry were a religion, this book would form the divine gospel of that religion".

Ghalib had a singularly rich personality. It has many facets like that of the great German poet Goethe.

Aristotle considers poetry a sort of photography. Ghalib's verses are matchless from this point of view and on every page of his *Diwan* one comes across such lines which may be converted into living pictures and sketches. Ghalib has painted the sentiments of love in their most natural forms, which require a command over the language as well as a deep insight into human nature.

نیند اس کی ہے دماغ اس کا ہے راتیں اس کی ہیں

جس کے شانوں پر تیری زلفیں پریشان ہو گئیں

Nature is a hidden reality. The secrets of nature hidden from our eyes are exposed to the eyes of the poet who unfolds them in his verses. He sees a new light in every sight. Ghalib, like Wordsworth, observes life from different angles and paints it in all its varied shades. Like Shakespeare and Wordsworth, he sees nature through an imaginative eye and his natural scenes are marked with brevity.

Ghalib takes a non-materialistic view of life and the world around. He denies the existence of matter and in this respect his philosophy is similar to that of Hume.

ہستی کے مت فریب میں آ جیو اسد

عالم تمام حلقۂ دامِ خیال ہے

In Urdu poetry, metaphysical conceptions have hardly been so beautifully portrayed as in Ghalib. He says:

سے کہاں تمنّا کا دوسرا قدم یارب
ہم نے دشتِ امکاں کو ایک نقشِ پا پایا

(Where is the second footstep of the heart's desire, O Lord? This wilderness of being appeared to be a mere footprint).

He was an outstanding philosopher-poet who combined in himself the genius of a poet with the art of a skilful artist. He expresses the views of the celebrated Averroes in his couplet when he says that "one does not complain of the sorrows of life when the secrets of existence are unfolded to one's eyes and he thinks life and miseries as two sides of the same picture".

قیدِ حیات و بندِ غم اصل میں دونوں ایک ہیں
موت سے پہلے آدمی غم سے نجات پائے کیوں

At times Ghalib has broken the bonds of grammar and let loose his imagination. But grammar is the objective phase of logic and poetry is free from logic. According to Abdur Rahman Bijnori, "Shakespeare and Ghalib are too great to care for the dogmatism of grammar and diction. Rather grammar should be moulded according to their writings". He has coined a variety of new words, phrases and idioms and made them vehicles of his lofty ideas. He was an expert in the art of forming beautiful phrases. He has maintained an individuality of his own, inventing new similes and metaphors. One great quality of Ghalib which is hardly found in any other poet is that some of his couplets contain a store of knowledge.

کوئی ویرانی سی ویرانی ہے
دشت کو دیکھ کے گھر یاد آیا

The poet had the real taste of life in love only.

عشق سے طبیعت نے زیست کا مزا پایا
درد کی دوا پائی درد لا دوا پایا

In love I found the ecstasy of life,

A remedy to my pain

A remedy which is nothing

But an eternal pain.

The entire edifice of his poetry stands on the foundation of originality—originality of thought and expression, similes and metaphors, allusions and array of words. This exceptional adherence to originality had made him somewhat unpopular in his days, but he never cared for it. Once he said:

نہ ستائش کی تمنّا نہ صلہ کی پرواہ
گر نہیں ہیں مرے اشعار میں معنی نہ سہی

I have neither longing for praise nor yearning for compensation. I do not care if my couplets are meaningless.

But the immense popularity of Ghalib among future generations has fully brought out the worth of his verses. Ghalib struck a different line for himself. He is undoubtedly one of the greatest poets of the world, who instead of being carried away by conventionalism, created a world of his own and influenced later poets. His departure from traditionalism in Urdu literature was followed by Hali, his worthy disciple, who incorporated these progressive ideas, in his famous work of Urdu criticism, *'An Introduction to Poetry'*, which served as a turning point in Urdu Poetry. Paying rich tribute to Ghalib for his sublimated thought, Iqbal says in *Bang-i-Dara:*

فکرِ انساں پر تیری ہستی سے یہ روشن ہوا
ہے پرِ مرغِ تخیل کی رسائی تا کجا

Your life clarified it to human thought—

How far are the reaches of man's imagination.

# MAULANA ALTAF HUSAIN HALI

Maulana Altaf Husain Hali who died on December 31, 1914 is one of the greatest figures of Urdu litterature. Born in 1837, at Panipat, and bred in the most stormy period of Indian History. Hali, was destined to play an important role in shaping the modern Urdu literature. Being a high class biographer, an eminent poet and above all an outstanding literary critic, he was, to a great extent, responsible for preparing the ground on which the grand edifice of modern Urdu poetry was built. In fact he was the first to strike at the roots of conventionalism in Urdu poetry. He was a literary genius who greatly contributed towards social, cultural and political awakening of the Muslims of the Indo—Pakistan Subcontinent.

The great catastrophe of 1857 had shaken the entire social and political structure of India. The tottering Muslim Kingdoms of Delhi and Oudh were unprooted for ever, and the well-known literary centres of Delhi and Lucknow which were established under the patronage of their Rulers disappeared with their patrons. But it served as an essential factor to reorientate the outlook of our litterateurs. The occasional contacts with English literature, gave birth to same tendencies in Urdu literature, which the "Renaissance" in the 16th century and the urge for "Romance" in the 18th century, had brought about for English literature. The persons first to respond to this call were Muhammad Husain Azad and Altaf Husain Hali. Hali, the famous disciple of Gahlib, inspired by the lead given by his celebrated teacher in the sphere of Urdu lyric and affected by the growing influence of Western thought proved to be the greatest exponent of modern Urdu poetry.

Far from being a conservative, he was liberal enough to accept and introduce the modern trends of Western literature. He provided the turning point in Urdu literature, especially in the spheres of poetry and literary biography and the difference in the Urdu literature produced before and after Hali is very pronounced.

Urdu language flourished during the decline of Muslim power in India, hence its old literature contains germs of a decadent society. The old Urdu poetry, which, in fact, was a child of Persian poetry suffered from hackneyed ideas, sophisticated and unnatural love themes.

Before the emergence of Hali on the literary horizon of India, only half-hearted effort was made at Fort William College, Calcutta, to simplify Urdu prose and Mir Amman's *Bagh-o-Bahar* was a commendable effort in this direction. Ghalib, with his originality in thought and diction, had also struck at conventionalism in Urdu literature. But, it was Hali, who proved to be the real crusader against the deep-rooted conventionalism of Urdu literature and successfully accomplished this task during his lifetime.

Literary criticism was unknown in Urdu liteature before Hali, who wrote the first book on literary criticism in which he discussed the nature and evaluation of poetry which paved the way for modern Urdu poetry.

The publication of his *Introduction to Poetry,* stands as the grearest landmark in the annals of Urdu literary criticism which was mainly instrumental in changing the course of Urdu poetry, particularly of the lyric. Hali, himself being an eminent poet, translated into practice what he preached. He widened the field of Urdu lyric and made it the vehicle of his diverse ideas. His lyrics are distinguished for sincerity and sublimity of thought as well as simplicity of diction.

Hali introduced natural poem into Urdu poetry which was later developed by Iqbal, Chakbast, Akbar and Josh. His *"Mosaddas Maddo-Jazr-i-Islam".* (The poem relating to the Rise and Fall of Islam) is recognised as a classic of Urdu poetry and is the most widely read Urdu poem. This poem, which beautifully portrays the rise of Islam in the world and the causes of its downfall, is one of the masterpieces of Urdu poetry. Sir Syed Ahmad Khan who had requested the poet to write such a poem says:

"Of course it was I who persuaded him to take up this task and I think it to be one of my good deeds so that when God would ask me, "what have you brought with you, I would reply that I have got the *Musaddas"* written".

Being deeply influenced by his environments, Hali wails the futility and misfortunes of human life. Like Saadi, Hali too, was a great moralist, but his preachings, at times, suffer from the passivity of professional missionaries.

In elegy, too, Hali has given a lead to other Urdu elegists. Till his time, elegies in Urdu were confined to the conventional theme of the tragedy of Karbala. He was the first to write a personal elegy in Urdu poetry. His elegy on the death of his well-known teacher, Ghalib, fulfills all the conditions of modern elegy. The elegies written by Milton and Gray are criticised for being devoid of the personal touch, but Hali mournfully relates the loss which he suffered with the death of his great teacher.

The Aligarh School of thought led by the celebrated Sir Syed Ahmad Khan which included such intellectual luminaries of the age as Hali, Shibli, Mohsinul Mulk, Wiqarul Mulk, Nazir Ahmad and Maulvi Chirag Ali, proved to be the greatest modernising force in the sphere of Urdu literaure. But, of all these intellectual giants, Hali was the greatest reformer. It was he who translated into action the revolutionary ideas of his school and played a dominant role in shaping the trends of modern Urdu literature.

He introduced literary biographies in Urdu and wrote three voluminous as well as brilliant biographies, namely, *'Hayat-e-Sadi'* (Life of Saadi), *'Yadgar-i-Ghalib'*, (The Reminiscence of Ghalib) and *'Hayat-i-Javed* (Life of Sir Syed Ahmad Khan).

His style in prose bristles with simplicity, spontaneity and sincerity. He discarded the flowery and high sounding language used in Urdu prose and adopted simple, lucid and straightforward language for expressing his ideas. He, at times, makes use of suitable English words in his writing and has thus enriched the Urdu vocabulary. Although not well versed in English language, he had fully understood the trends of English literature and has very creditably applied them to his critical study of Urdu poetry.

As a man, Hali was the very embodiment of humility and simplicity, hospitality and humanitarianism. In one of his interesting articles, Maulvi Abdul Haq, who was a close associate of Hali, speaks very highly of him as a man and enumerates many qualities of his head and heart. His reforms, no doubt, evoked country-wide criticism, but whoever came in contact with him was received with a smiling countenance and a magnanimous heart. His severest critics, were disarmed by his affability and accommodating spirit.

Thus, Maulana Altaf Husain Hali, who, though brought up in a conservative environment, was endowed with all the qualities of a reformer and with the efficient use of his modernising weapons brought about the greatest revolution in the *History of Urdu Literature.*

# MAULANA SHIBLI
# NOMANI

Shibli Nomani was one of the greatest luminaries who glittered on the literary firmament of Urdu literature and the brilliance of whose achievements outshone those of his contemporaries as well as predecessors in diverse branches of knowledge. Few writers in the 19th century could achieve the versatility of the genius of Shibli.

The impact of Western civilisation brought about a reorientation in the outlook of Urdu writers which culminated in the creation of the same atmosphere for Urdu literature ·in India, as the Renaissance in the 16th century and the zeal for Romance in the 18th century had developed for English literature. Azad, Hali and Shibli were the torch-bearers who heralded this revolution and paved the way for later writers. Azad left behind him some good specimen of natural poetry, while Hali introduced the revolutionary changes in Urdu literature, especially in Urdu Poetry. Shibli, though not destined to be as great a poet, yet he outmatched his two rivals as a critic, historian, biographer and philosopher.

Shibli was born in a conservative family of Azamgarh district (U.P.), India, in the stormy year of 1857 and got his education from the learned teacher Maulana Muhammad Farooq Chirayyakoti. He was later employed as Professor of Arabic in the Anglo-Muhammadan College, Aligarh. He was an associate of Sir Syed Ahmad Khan. He devoted himself to the service of Urdu literature and had the distinction of being the founder of *Darul Musannafeen* (The House of Authors) at Azamgarh which is still functioning and which had drawn within its portals a galaxy of talented scholars, such as Maulanas Sulaiman Nadvi, Abdus Salaam Nadvi and Masood Nadvi who enriched Urdu literature by their invaluable contributions. Maulana Shibli died in 1914. He was a profilic writer and has dozens of high class books to his credit.

The Maulana had cultivated a unique style for the conveyance of his ideas which embodied the elegance of Azad, the colloquialism of Nazir Ahmad and the simplicity of Hali. He believed in moderation and his style with slight modification could successfully be employed in scientific, poetic, critical, historical and philosophical themes. He elevated Urdu literature to an eminence so that it may easily compete with the advanced literatures of the world. He initiated the spirit of research in Urdu; some of his outstanding works are distinguished for thorough research on those subjects and may be classed with the best works of the world. Hardly any other Urdu writer had been so popular and beneficial to the educated class. His style is characterised by clarity, simplicity, lucidity and amplification of points. A logical sequence pervades his writings, which never suffer from the complexities of expression, and are distinguished for the vigour and spontaneity of expressions. Complimenting him on his immaculate style, Sir Syed Ahmad Khan once said, "Both Delhi and Lucknow should be proud of you".

The Maulana was one of the leading figures of his time. One hardly comes across a person with a greater range of ideas and diversities of taste. He embodied in himself the attributes of a remarkable historian, a successful critic, a high class biographer and an efficient reformer. He occupies a high position as a litterateur, historian and a scholar of literary research. His principal historical contributions are *Al-Farooq, Al-Mamun, Al-Ghazali, Al-Noman* and *Aurangzeb Alamgir.* In *Al-Farooq*, he deals with the life and achievements of the redoubtable Farooq-i-Azam, the Second Caliph of Islam who was known for his piety, jusitce, simplicity and indomitable will. Few books on Caliph Umar in oriental literature may reach the authenticity and fluency of Shibli's book. *Al-Mamun* narrates the achievements of Mamun, the Great, whose reign is known as the golden age of Islamic culture. Mamun was a great patron of learning and during his reign Muslims made invaluable contribution to the advancement of knowledge and various sciences and arts registered phenomenal progress. According to a European writer, "To the Islamic world, Christians had conceded and that grudgingly—only a military superiority. Now they realised with shame that it was also the intellectually superior". *Al-Ghazali* deals with the life and teachings of Imam Ghazali, the greatest religious teacher that Islam has produced and who is better known as "Hujjat-ul-Islam". Shibli has clearly brought out the different phases of the philosophy and mysticism of the great teacher, which ultimately revolutionised the Islamic religious thought in more than one way. The Maulana has excellently portrayed the brilliant reign of the greatest of the Mughal Emperors, *Aurangzeb Alamgir,* who passed a truly Islamic life. The example set by the pious Emperor would serve as a beacon light to those who want to build their state on the foundations of Islamic polity. Shibli, undoubtedly is the greatest historian in Urdu language and his historical works are distinguished for their authentic research and lucidity of expression. He has clothed the past grandeur of Islam in modern attire.

Maulana Shibli has earned for himself an immortal reputation by writing the *"Seerut-un-Nabi"* (The Life of the Holy Prophet) (PBUH) which is one of the best achievements on the subject in oriental languages. It runs into several volumes. At places the description of events is too graphic and one comes across good specimen of poetic prose, reminiscent of the passages of the celebrated *Aab-i-Hayat* of Azad; The chapter dealing with the philosophy of sacrifice and the story of Hazrat Ismail is vivid in description and superb in presentation. Besides the above, he also wrote the *"Sawaneh Maulana Rum"* (The Biography of Maulana Rum) who was a great mystic poet of Persia and was the spiritual mentor of the late Allama Iqbal. His work *Hayat-i-Khusrou* (The Life of Khusrou) deals with the many-sided personality and poetical achievements of this celebrated Indian savant. Khusrou was a disciple of Hazrat Nizamuddin Aulia and is supposed to be one of the greatest lyrists of Persian literature and the pioneer of Urdu poetry.

The real fame of Shibli rests on his role as an outstanding literary critic. His *"Sherul Ajam"* (The poetry of the Orient) dealing with the principles of criticism and the brilliant criticism of Persian Poetry may be ranked as one of the best works on literary criticism in any language. According to the famous British orientalist Professor Browne, *Sherul Ajam* is undoubtedly the best literary estimate of Persian poetry written up to the present day. It is in this book that the Maulana has displayed his masterly hold over the literary study of literature and his depth of knowledge. It combines the high class research with the fluency and lucidity of expression. The fifth chapter of the book elaborately deals with the principles of criticism, on which he has based the poetical estimate of Persian poets. *"Moazina Anis-o-Dabir"* (The Comparison between Anis and Dabir) is another standard book of literary criticism in which he has compared the achievements of the two greatest elegists of Urdu poetry. Anis, no doubt, was greater of the two; the Maulana has fully proved with examples the superiority of Anis, both in thought and expression. The poetry of Anis was known for its purity of language, simplicity of diction, novelty and originality of ideas and graphic descriptions. Dabir, on the other hand believed in the verbosity of language and excessive flights of imagination.

The Maulana wrote some excellent essays in *"Makalat Shibli"* (The Essays of Shibli) on various topics. His book *Philosophy of Islam* and *Al-Kalaam* are valuable contributions to Islamic philosophy and religion.

Shibli belongs to the modern school of Urdu Poetry. Had he exclusively devoted himself to the service of the Muse, he would have been the second Iqbal. Hali simply lamented the decline of the Muslim power, but could not seriously contemplate the remedies for saving Islam from falling into the abyss. Shibli's poetical career may be divided into two parts. During the first period, when he was employed at Aligarh, he was a close associate of Hali and Sir Syed Ahmad Khan. His outstanding achievement of this period is his well-known poem *Subh-i-Ummeed* (The Morn of Hope) in which he has chosen the theme of *Mosaddas Hali*. The only difference between the two is that Hali's poem bristles with pessimistic ideas, while a sort of optimism pervades the poem of Shibli which concludes with a forecast of the bright future for Islam. But the poem of Hali is superior of the two, as it maintains uniformity in standard which Shibli's poem so badly lacks. This poem of Shibli comes very close to the healthy optimism preached by Iqbal in a later period. The second part of his poetical career starts from the time, when, due to ideological differences, Shibli had to sever his connection with the Aligarh Muhammadan College and henceforward he devoted himself solely to the betterment of Muslim India. He was not an opponent of Aligarh College, but he did not like the principles of its Education for its excessive liberalism. Wordsworth, the celebrated English poet, was at one time a great supporter of the French Revolution, but when he awarded of its unhealthy developments he became its great opponent. The deep insight of Shibli helped him cultivate his point of view regarding Western civilisation, which was ultimately adopted by Akbar and Iqbal. Unlike the blind imitation of the West as propagated by the Hali group, Shibli adopted a via media and his clear insight enabled him to shun the harmful influences of Western culture and adopt the beneficial objects found in it. Hali and Shibli both lamented the decline of Muslim power—but Hali ascribed it to their dissociation from the materialism of the West, while Shibli attributed it to their estrangement from Islamic principles. Shibli has given graphic description of events in his poem *'Adl-i-Jahangir* (The Justice of Jahangir) and *Hamari Tarz-i-Hukoomat* (Our System of Government)'. He wrote a pathetic poem lamenting the premature death of his younger brother Ishaq, which fulfills all the conditions of modern elegy.

Shibli devoted the major part of his life to literary pursuits. He is, undoubtedly, one of the main pillars on which the grand edifice of Urdu literature rests. He, on the whole, was a versatile genius, who occupies a prominent place amongst the men of letters in this subcontinent.

# IQBAL

On the death of the Mughal Emperor Aurangzeb in 1707 A.C., there set in the process of disintegration of Muslim power in India which touched its lowest depths during the second half of the 19th century, when the British rulers, along with the Hindus conspired to oust the Muslims from the political and economic life of the country. Sir Syed Ahmad Khan and his worthy companions successfully planned to stem the deterioration in the politico-economic life of Muslim India. But the awakening of Muslim masses in the subcontinent owes primarily to the poetry of Iqbal, the writings of Maulana Muhammad Ali and Sulaiman Nadvi and the selfless services of Maulana Hasrat Mohani, Maulana Muhammad Ali, Muhammad Ali Jinnah, Nawab Badadur Yar Jang, Maulana Shaukat Ali, Maulana Zafar Ali Khan and Maulana Shabbir Ahmad Usmani. It was they who, through Muslim mass contact movement, prepared the ground for Pakistan which was ultimately established under the capable and inspiring leadership of Quaid-e-Azam Muhammad Ali Jinnah.

Iqbal, the poet of Islam is, in fact, the poet of humanity in the wider sense, as Islam transcends all political, sectarian and colour barriers. He was born in a middle class family of Sialkot on November, 9, 1877. His grandfather, Muhammad Rafiq had migrated from his ancestral home in Kashmir to settle down in Sialkot. His father, Sheikh Noor Muhammad was a Sufi and a man who attached considerable importance to spiritual values. It was under the spiritual guidance of his learned father and the inspiring supervision of his celebrated teacher Maulvi Mir Hasan that the initial growth of Iqbal's mind had taken place. From the very inception Iqbal was an abnormal child. He was an exceptionally bright student. He started writing verses even during his school days and sent some of his earlier lyrics to the celebrated Urdu poet, Dagh for correction. But after sometime, Dagh wrote back to Iqbal that his verses needed no correction.

In 1895, after passing his first University Examination from the Scotch Mission College, Sialkot, Iqbal migrated to Lahore, the intellectual centre of north-western India, for higher studies. Here he came into contact with Sir Thomas Arnold, who introduced him to all that was best and noblest in Western thought. Iqbal obtained his M.A. in Philosophy in 1898.

During this period he recited his well-known poem, *"Himala"* at a literary gathering of Lahore. It was published in the *"Makhzan"* in 1901. It introduced him to the outside world. His recital of "*Nala-i-Yateem*" (Wails of an Orphan) at an annual function of Anjuman-i-Himayat-i-Islam created a stir in literary circles of Lahore and acclaimed him as a rising poet on the literary horizon of the subcontinent whose brilliance, later, dazzled the eyes of people living in distant countries and won for him an honourable place amongst the galaxy of immortal poets of the world.

Iqbal later became a Reader in Philosophy in the Government College, Lahore. In 1905, he went to Europe for higher studies. His three years stay in Europe greatly contributed to the development of his thought. He joined the Lincoln's Inn for Bar. He was admitted as an advanced student of Philosophy at the Cambridge University and wrote his thesis on the *Development of Metaphysics* in Persia. The University of Munich (Germany) conferred on him the degree of Ph.D. for this thesis. He was called to Bar in 1908. He returned home in August, 1908. The same year he joined the Government College, Lahore, as a part-time Professor of Philosophy and English Literature. He was allowed to practise Law. But, later, he resigned his Professorship and wholly concentrated on Law.

Iqbal's stay in Europe enabled him to study Western learning and civilisation closely and he formulated an outlook on life, modern as well as ancient. Contrary to the westernised persons of the East, who are dazzled by the glamour of Western civilization, he could see it in all its nakedness and instead of being an admirer, became its critic. His study of Western nationalism totally changed his views on the subject. Hitherto, he was a great exponent of Indian nationalism. But now he became its opponent and an exponent of Internationalism and Pan-Islamism.

During his stay in Europe, Iqbal wrote some excellent romantic poems in which he depicted romantic scenes giving in them imaginative touches which brought him very close to the celebrated English poet Wordsworth. There is a personal note in his treatment of Nature. Describing the advent of the Spring he states :

"Arise ! for on hills and dales
    The Spring has arrived
        Mad in singing are nightingales
Cuckoos, partridges and quails,
    Along the banks of the brook
        Have sprung roses and poppy,
Come out and see,
    Arise ! for on hills and dales
    The spring has arrived".

(Translated by S. A. Vahid).

Like Wordsworth, Iqbal was a lover and worshipper of Nature in the beginning. He says :

In each thing glows some spark of beauty immortal :
Mankind has speech, and buds with all hues dazzle;
A secret union lurks within dispersal;
One are the firefly's glitter, the flower's sweet phial

(Translated by V. G. Kiernan).

A common theme of Iqbal's lyrics of this period is his concept of beauty and love. He sees beauty in everything which is powerful and perfect. For him, beauty is a mental experience. His concept of beauty has cultivated a robust vitality in his poem which is conspicuous by its absence in the oriental lyrical poetry. He widened the scope of Urdu *"ghazal"* (lyric) and made it a vehicle of expressing his diverse ideas. His lyrics are distinguished for lucidity of expression and musical harmony.

Some of his well-known romantic and Nature poems of this period are :

*Love. End of Beauty. The Star of Dawn. The Bud. A Glimpse of Beauty. An Evening and Separation.*

But it was the transitory period of Iqbal's poetic career. His ideas were being matured.

It was after his return from Europe that started his real poetic career. His transitory period was over. His ideas had matured in Europe and he had formulated his outlook on different aspects of life which lasted throughout his life. He composed his epoch-making poems *"Shikwa"* (Complaint) and *"Jawab-i-Shikwa"* (Reply of the Complaint) within a few years of his return from Europe. In 1915 he wrote his long Persian poem *"Asrar-i-Khudi"* (Secrets of Self) which thrilled the literary circles of the East and the West. It deals with the fundamental principles leading to the development of human personality. It was translated into English by Professor R. A. Nicholson of the Cambridge University. Writing in the introduction of the book, Professor Nicholson remarks:

"The artistic quality of the book is remarkable when we consider that the language is not author's own."

Hailing the development of ego, Iqbal states :
   "Appear, O rider of Destiny
      Appear, O light of the dark realm of Change !
         Silence the tumult of the nations,
            Imparadise our ears with thy music !
      Arise and tune the harp of brotherhood.
         Give us back the cup of the wine of love !
      Bring once more days of peace to the world
         Give a message of peace to them that sue out battle !
   Mankind are the corn-field, and thou the harvest,
      Thou art the goal of Life's Caravan.

(Translated by R. A. Nicholson)

The book created a storm in the pseudo-mystic circles. Iqbal vehemently attacked the so-called mystic philosophy and its exponents like Hafiz who preached a life of inaction. He was deadly opposed to the negative and pessimistic Platonic philosophy which he considered as against the spirit of Islam. In 1917, Iqbal wrote his another well-known Persian poem *Rumuz-i-Bekhudi* (Mysteries of Selflessness) the counterpart of his first poem *Secrets of Self*.

These two poems deliver the message he has for mankind. The *Asrar-e-Khudi*, deals with the doctrine of the development of individual self, while the *Rumuz-i-Bekhudi* deals with problems an individual faces as a member of the society. In formulating his outlook about self, society and life, he was much influenced by the teachings of Maulana Jalaluddin Rumi who, in his well-known *Mathnavi*, preached the Islamic mysticism. His mysticism did not preach a life of idleness but a dynamic life full of vitality and activity. His robust optimism was opposed to the pessimistic Platonic and inactive mystic philosophy.

In the meantime, Iqbal published a collection of his Urdu poems, *Bang-e-Dara* (Call of the Caravan) containing some of his well-known Urdu poems which created a stir throughout the Subcontinent. This was followed by his another Persian poem, *Payam-i-Mashriq* (The Message of the East) which was written in response to Goethe's *West-Ostlicher Divan*. Two years later he wrote *Zubur-i-Ajam* containing his "mystic, vitalizing and ennobling" Persian verses. This was followed by *Javed Nama*, a long Persian poem, universally acknowledged as the masterpiece of Iqbal. This is a counterpart of Dante's *Divine Comedy*, in which Iqbal has travelled through Heavens accompanied by Rumi meeting there some of the historical personalities who express their views on diverse problems confronting humanity in the present-day world. The Hindu sage Jetan Dost (Vishwamitra) tells that the salvation of humanity today lies in the synthesis of Eastern and Western Cultures. East has been concentrating too much on spiritualism neglecting materialism, while the West is concentrating on materialism caring little for spiritualism. He says :

"The East saw God but failed to see the world of matter
The West got embroiled in the world and neglected God".
                                        (Translated by S. A. Vahid)

Jamaluddin Afghani asks the poet to inform the communists that without God their progress will come to naught.

Ahmad Shah Abdali was alarmed at the growing tendency of blind imitation of the West in Eastern countries.

Thus Iqbal's *Javed Nama* ranks among the world classics.

In 1935 appeared another collection of his Urdu poems, *Bal-i-Jibreel* which vibrates with dynamism. Another such collection, *Zarb-i-Kalim* was published in 1936. He published a Persian poem, *Musafir* (Traveller) in 1934

another Persian peom *Pas Che Bayad Kard in 1936*. His best, collection of Urdu as well as Persian poems entitled, *Armughan-i-Hejaz*, appeared after his death. His monumental work in English, *Reconstruction of Religious Thought in Islam*, a collection of six lectures delivered by him in Madras, Hyderabad and Aligarh, was published by the Oxford University Press. In this book, he elucidates the dynamic philosophy of Islam which is the only religion which has preached a healthy practical life. In it he exposed the pessimistic Platonic and inactive mystic philosophy as the very negation of the teaching of Islam. On the basic of this book he was invited by the Oxford University to deliver the Rhodes Lectures, but his failing health did not permit him to complete this assignment.

Iqbal suffered from a prolonged illness between 1934 and 1938. He breathed his last on April 21, 1938. His death cast a gloom all over the East.

Iqbal was, undoubtedly, the greatest Islamic thinker of the modern times and one of the greatest of all times. He was, in fact, a versatile genius-poet, philosopher, lawyer, educationist, politician and reformer. As a thinker and philosopher, he has made a lasting contribution to human thought. Through his immortal poetic works, he has earned an honourable place amongst the greatest poets of the world. As a *politician,* he was the dreamer of Pakistan, and in 1930 elaborated his scheme of an independent Muslim State in the Subcontinent in his Presidential Address of the All India Muslim League Session at Allahabad. His views on education have been creditably explained by Mr. K. G. Saiyidain in his well-known work, *Iqbal's Educational Philosophy.*

Iqbal gave a message of hope and action to mankind. "For Iqbal", observes Mr. S. A. Vahid in his work, *An Introduction to Iqbal,* "the two powerful impulses to artistic expression are his faith in human capacity for limitless development and man's unique position in the Universe; and both these impulses serve to impart an unparalleled charm to his poetry. . . . . . . Life, according to Iqbal, is nothing but a progressive succession of fresh ends, purposes and values".

The patriotic poetry of Hali, Shibli, Akbar, Chakbast, Jauhar and Hasrat found its culmination in the poetical works of Iqbal. There are two phases of Iqbal's patriotic poetry—Indian and Islamic. Young Iqbal was highly impressed by the Indian National Movement waged against the domination of a Foreign Power over the Subcontinent. In those days Muslims and Hindus worked side by side for the liberation of their country from alien yoke. During this period of his poetic career, Iqbal wrote some beautiful poems depicting the Indian scenes, pleading for communal harmony and reminding the people of their past glory. In *Himala,* he has painted fascinating landscapes of the mountains giving imaginative touches here and there. He concludes this poem with a beautiful couplet.

> *"Han dekha de ai tasawwar phir woh subho sham tu*
> *Daur peeche ki taref taref aiy gardish-i-ayyam tu."*

The poet yearns for the good old days. His another immortal poem, *Taswir-i-Dard* (The Picture of Agony) is a masterpiece in which he has made an impassioned appeal to his countrymen to sink their differences and fight unitedly against the common enemy. At places, he has used allegorical language to bring home his view-point which has added to the charm of the verses. He warns the people not to be lethargic but beware of the machinations of the West, which is bent upon their annihilation.

> *"Ghhupa kar aastin men bijlian rakkhi hain gardoon ne*
> *Anadil bagh ke ghafil na bathen ashiyanon men."*

The similies and metaphors, the excellent setting of words, the unique turn of phrases and the fine touches of imagination, have made this poem one of the masterpieces of Urdu poetry.

His National Anthem is still the most popular poem sung in India. He paints some lively pictures of the Indo—Pakistan Subcontinent. Its running streams, its verdant meadows, its emerald mountains crowned with milky white peaks have been immortalised in this poem through the masterly pen of Iqbal.

His *Naya Shiwala* (New Temple) marks the culmination of his national feelings. He is a worshipper of his country and, therefore, preaches communal harmony.

Being an idealist, he wants to build a temple in his heart, which would be the highest place of worship and whose pinnacles would reach the sky :

> *"Sooni pari hui hai muddat se dil ki basti*
> *Aa ik naya shiwala is des me banaden*
> *Duniya ki teerathon se uncha ho upna teerath*
> *Daman-e-asman se iska kalas miladen."*

Iqbal was profoundly influenced by his environments. His change over from the Indian nationalism to Islamic poetry marks the growth of his poetic career and the growth of his personality. In Europe, his ideas on nationalism had undergone a great change. It was but natural. His first hand knowledge of modern nationalism in Europe exposed it in all its nakedness. He saw with his own eyes that nationalism had divided into warring nationalities which resulted in two of the bloodiest wars in living history. This mad passion for nationalism has contributed to international conflicts and instead of being a blessing has proved a curse for humanity. He had to change his views. Moreover, his foresight enabled him to realise the dangers of Hindu dominated nationalism in India. The advent of such a nationalism in the subcontinent would have amounted to delivering a death blow to Islamic culture and civilization in the subcontinent. He had to dissociate himself from such a nationalism which was far from being the panacea for the ills of humanity.

Wordsworth, the celebrated English poet was, at one time, a great admirer of French Revolution. But, when he studied it fully and from close quarters, he totally changed his views and became its opponent. Iqbal's stay in Europe greatly contributed towards the maturity of his political ideas on the subject. A learned European critic has said that Laws of Nature are universal and not national, hence nationalism is against Nature. Another Western writer says that God has created man while Satan has divided them into nationalities. According to Renan, Islam frees humanity from nationalism, caste, creed and colour bars. All such divisions based on national and colour bars, are, therefore, un-Islamic in character. Islam transcends all geographical and sectarian barriers and Muslims residing in any part of the globe are Muslims first and last. Iqbal realised the dangers of modern nationalism and found in Islam the solution of all problems facing humanity. He became a poet and preacher of Islamic patriotism. Now he began to say about modern nationalism.

*"Akwam men makhlooq-i-Khuda bat-ti hai is se,*
*Kaumiyati—Islam ki jar Kat-ti hai is se."*

(Nationalism divides the creation of God into groups and strikes at the root of Islamic brotherhood).

Realising the futility of modern nationalism which was responsible for many tragedies and strifes during the present times, Iqbal became a preacher of Pan-Islamism. Islam which transcends all barriers, according to him, is the panacea of all ills facing humanity today. Thereafter, Iqbal devoted himself to write his classical poems on Islam, reminding its followers of their past glory and their virtues which enabled them to bring about in a short span of 30 years, the most amazing political and social revolution recorded in the annals of mankind. He wants Muslims to read the same old lesson of truth, justice and valour which had made them the leaders of the world. He strikes an optimistic note when he says that Muslims would once again lead the world.

*"Sabaq phir parh sadaqat ka, adalat ka, shujat ka,*
*Liya jayega tujh se kaam duniya ki imamat ka."*

He wants to restore the same self-confidence among Muslims which led them to the heights of glory in the past.

A true Muslim, in his eyes, is all-powerful and none can visualise the strength of his arms as well as the depth of his character. His inner self is so bright that his mere look can change human destinies.

*"Koi andaza kar sakta hai uske zore bazu ka*
*Nigah-i-marde momin se badal jati hain takdirein."*

(Who can visualise the strength of a Momin's arms whose mere look changes human destinies).

While returning from Europe in 1908, he was moved at the sight of Sicily, once the cradle of Arab civilization and their important naval base.

*"Role ab dil khol kar ai deedai khoonaba bar*
*Woh nazar aata hai tahzib-e-Hejazi ka mazar. "*

(My eyes . . ! shed tears of blood as I behold before me the ruins of Hejazi civilization).

*"Ghalgalon se Jinki Lazzat geer abtak gosh hai*
*Kiya woh takbir ab hamesha ke liye khamosh hai. "*

(Has the cry of Allah-o-Akbar been silenced for ever which is still resounding in my ears). He implores the land of Sicily to disclose its agony to the poet :

*"Dard apna mujh se kah main bhi sarapa dard hoon*
*Jiski too manzil tha main us karwan ki gard hoon. "*

(Divulge your agony to me as I am too full of anguish. I am the last dust of the Caravan whose destination you were).

On his return from Europe, his message took a definite shape. He gave the message of action, hope and struggle to suffering humanity.

*"Razi hayat poonch le Khizri khajasta gam se*
*Zinda har ek chiz hai koshish-e-natamam se. "*

(Ask the secret of life from Khizr, the untiring traveller. Everything lives by vainly and constantly striving for it).

His *Islamic Anthem* is rather the most popular poem sung by the Muslims of the subcontinent. In a very impressive language, the poet recalls the past glory of Islam. Islam is an universal religion and the entire world is the native-land of Muslims.

*"Cheeno Arab hamara Hindostan hamara*
*Muslam hain ham watan hai sara jahan hamara. "*

(Ours is China, India and Arabia. We are Muslims and the whole world is our nativeland). Then he recalls the great achievements of Muslim arms.

*"Maghrib ki wadiyan men goonji Azan Hamari*
*Thamta na tha kisi se sail-e-rawan hamara. "*

(Our call for prayer echoed in the valleys of the West and none could check the current of our storm.)

A Muslim, according to him, can never be cowed down by falsehood.

*Batil se dabne wale ai aasman nahin ham*

*Sao bar karchuka hai tu imtehan hamara.*

(We are not among those who can bow down to falsehood. In this respect we have been tested hundreds of times).

His poems *Shikwa* (Complaint), *Jawab-i-Shikwa* (Reply of the Complaint) and *Tuloo-i-Islam* (The Dawn of Islam) provides the culmination of Iqbal's poetry. In *Shikwa,* the poet boldly complains to God for the decadence of Islam in the present day world. He reminds God that it was the Muslims who carried His true faith to the four corners of the world.

*"They Hameen ek tere marka aaraon men*

*Khushqion men kabhi larte kabhi dariyaon men*

*Din Azanen kabhi Europe ke kalisaon men*

*Kabhi Africa ke tapte hue saharaon men*

*Shan Aankhon men na junchti thi jahandaron ki*

*Kalima parhte the hami chhaon men talwaron ki."*

(We were the sole warriors of Yours. We fought for You on land and rivers. We sounded the call of Your prayer in the churches of Europe and the hot deserts of Africa. We were never impressed by the pomp of the rulers and recited the '*Kalima*' even under the shadow of sword).

In *Jawab-i-Shikwa* (Reply to the Complaint) God replies to the Complaints of the poet and gives reasons for the decline of Muslims. But a ray of hope illuminates the sombre picture. The poem ends on an optimistic note in which God reminds the poet that the Muslims can regain their past glory by faithfully following the principles of Islam.

In his immortal poem, *Shama-o-Shair* (The Candle and the Poet) Iqbal gives the message of hope. It vibrates with healthy optimism.

*"Aasman hoga saher ke noor se aaina posh*

*Aur zulmat rat ki seemab pa hojaye gi."*

(The Sky will be brightened by the first streaks of Dawn and the darkness of the night will disappear).

He wants to revive the self-confidence of Muslims which they have lost.

*"Kiyun giriftar-i-tinseme hech miqadari hai tu*

*Dekh to poshida tujh men shaukat-i-toofan bhi hai"*

(Why are you suffering from inferiority complex? Behold, you have the power to raise a storm.)

His another patriotic poem is *Tuloo-i-Islam* (The Dawn of Islam) in which he preaches a life of action for Muslims. He gives a message of hope and puts forward certain invaluable principles which may lead Muslims to regain their past glory.

> *"Yaqeen mohkem, amal paiham, mohabbat fatahe alam*
> *Jihad-e-zindgani men hain yeh mardon ki shamsheeren. "*

(Iron Faith, Incessant action and the all conquering love are the means of the valiant in the struggle of life).

He wants to restore self-confidence among the Muslims.

> *"Gulami men na kam aati hain shamsheerain na tadbirain*
> *Jo ho zauq-e-yaqeen paida to kat jati hain zangirain.*

(The swords and plans are of no avail in slavery. The chains break up if one possesses self-confidence).

The chief distinction of Iqbal's patriotic poetry lies in the spirit of optimism which runs through his verses. He is an idealist who takes the reader to a dreamland, the land of his glorious past. He is the chief herald and embodiment of national renaissance of Muslims India.

Iqbal's patriotic poetry deeply influenced the younger generations of today and produced a host of Urdu poets who tried to follow him and wrote some patriotic poems, relating to Islam and Pakistan. Among such poets are Josh Malihabadi, Zafar Ali Khan, Faiz, Mahir, Asad Multani, Nazar and Anwar Sabri.

Iqbal's fame transcended the national barriers during his lifetime and reached the distant corners of the civilized world. Articles were written on his life and works in almost all the progressive languages of the world. His well-known poetic works were translated into Arabic, English, Turkish, Latin, French, German and Russian languages by well-known scholars. Professor R. A. Nicholson of Cambridge University translated his *Asrar-i-Khudi* into English. Professor A. J. Arberry translated his *Rumuz-i-Bekhudi* into the English language. His well-known Urdu poems *Shikwa* and *Jawab-i-Shikwa* were translated into English by Mr. Altaf Hussain, Dr. Abdul Wahab Azzam, Professor of Al Azhar University, Cairo, translated his *Payam-i-Mashriq* and *Zarb-i-Kalim* into Arabic. *Payam-i-Mashriq* was translated into Turkish language by Dr. Ali Ganjeli. Mr. Bahrum Rangkuti, rendered his *Asrar-i-Khudi* into Indonesian Language. The Quotations of *Payam-i-Mashriq* were translated into the German language by Professor Hell, of Erlangen University. Madame Eva Meyerovitch of Paris has translated *Iqbal's Reconstruction of Religious Thought in Islam* in French. His well-known work, *Javed Nama* was translated into Italian by Professor Alessandor Busani under the title "II Poema Celeste" and into English by Professor Arberry.

Iqbal was one of the greatest thinkers and intellectuals of the modern times. Like Goethe, he was a seer and humanist. His poetry has a mission behind it. His dynamic philosophy will continue to inspire mankind to hope and action.

# MAULVI ABDUL HAQ

The mighty Indian National Congress and its undisputed leader, Mahatama Gandhi, had championed the cause of Hindi as the National Language of India. He had brushed aside Urdu, as the language of Muslims, written in the Quranic script. But a frail-bodied, resourceless man took up this challenge to prove that Urdu, born and bred in India, having been developed by Muslims and Hindus alike, cannot be treated as a language of one community only. This man was Maulvi Abdul Haq whose devotion to his cause at last compelled the great Mahatma to change his view and admit in the Bhartiya Sahitya Parishad meeting held at Nagpur that Hindustani, written both in Arabic and Devanagri scripts, was the national language of the subcontinent.

Dr. Maulvi Abdul Haq, who was later popularly known as Baba-e-Urdu, lived, laboured and died for Urdu. There could be few parallels to his devotion to a mission, which will continue to inspire all those who struggle and make sacrifices for a noble cause.

He was the last in the galaxy of Urdu luminaries that glittered during the 19-20 century. These included Sir Syed, Azad, Hali, Shibli and Dr. Nazir Ahmad. Abdul Haq was born in March 1870 in a middle class family of village Sarawan, Tehsil Hapur, District Meerut (U.P.). His father's name was Sheikh Ali Hasan.

He received his early education in his home village and later moved to Aligarh for higher studies. Here he came under the influence of Sir Syed Ahmad Khan who inspired him with his perseverance, unlimited energy and lucid Urdu prose-qualities which were creditably acquired by Abdul Haq himself.

Abdul Haq graduated from Aligarh in 1894 with High Proficiency in Mathematics. He competed for Honours in Mathematics with no less a person than the late Dr. Ziauddin Ahmad. In Aligarh he came under the influence of Sir Syed Ahmad who kindled in him the flame of Urdu which burnt in his heart till his last breath.

He moved to Hyderabad in 1895 as a teacher in the Madrassa-e-Asafiah. Here he started his magazine *Afsar*. He was appointed Honorary General Secretary of the Anjuman Taraqqi-e-Urdu in 1912 and it was then that people could discover his devotion, drive and energy. The Anjuman created in 1903 by the Muslim Education Conference was hitherto a lifeless body. Maulvi Abdul Haq's association with it as Secretary soon made it a virile organization charged with a noble mission. The Head Office of the Anjuman remained at Aurangabad with its Secretary for 25 years. He served in the Education Department of Hyderabad State for a considerable time and retired from the State Service as the Principal of Aurangabad College.

Immediately afterwards, he was offered the Chair of Urdu at the Osmania University. But he did not occupy it for long and moved to Delhi after resigning it.

During his stay in Hyderabad which lasted for about 45 years, he made valuable contribution to the establishment of Osmania University and the organisation of the Translation Bureau which under his supervision as *Nazim* translated hundreds of technical and classical books from foreign languages into Urdu.

The Anjuman Taraqqi-i-Urdu was set up by the All-India Muhammadan Educational Conference in 1903 to check the rising tide of Hindi. Its first Secretary was Maulana Shibli Nomani. He resigned in 1905 and was succeeded by Habibur Rahman Khan Sherwani and later by Aziz Mirza. Maulvi Abdul Haq, who was appointed Secretary of the Anjuman, was greatly instrumental in making it a virile organisation. His association with the Anjuman lasted for 50 years, till his death in 1961.

The Head Office of the Anjuman moved to Delhi along with him in the early thirties. This was the time when the Indian National Congress flushed with success at the polls had taken up the cause of Hindi as the national language of the subcontinent. Mahatma Gandhi and his associates had openly declared that Urdu was the language of the Muslims written in Quranic script. The Vidiya Mandir and Wardha schemes sponsored under the patronage of Mahatma Gandhi and his associates had given Hindi a privileged place at the cost of Urdu which, long before, during the British regime had been declared the Court language of Northern India.

It was this challenge of the powerful All-India Congress, with its unlimited financial and other resources, that the Secretary of the Anjuman with his limited resources had to face. He travelled widely from 1939 to 1947, in every nook and corner of the country, advocating the cause of Urdu. He fought with courage and conviction with the powerful Congress both on the platform and through the Press. His fortitude and unlimited energy at last obliged the great Mahatma to yield and accept Hindustani—written both in Devanagri and Arabic scripts—as the Lingua-Franca of the subcontinent.

The All-India Muhammadan Educational Conference had long suspended its financial assistance to Anjuman. But Maulvi Abdul Haq gave the Anjuman his life earnings. He made it a dynamic organisation which had branches all over the country. At the time of the partition of the Indian subcontinent, the Anjuman had assets worth Rs. half a million. More than 250 books were translated and compiled by it.

The most ambitious programme of the Anjuman was the Compilation of the Dictionary of Scientific Terms which was started in 1917 and was completed under his supervision in 1925, when the Anjuman published this invaluable dictionary. The Anjuman, under his Editorship, started three journals, including the quarterly *"Urdu"*, which was launched by Maulvi Abdul Haq at Aurangabad in 1921 and was soon recognised as the best literary journal in the country.

Most of the literary researches about Urdu, conducted under the auspices of the Anjuman, specially about the early Urdu literature, were done by Maulvi Abdul Haq himself. He had taken up the early development of Urdu literature of a period several hundred years before Wali.

With the assumption of power by the All-India National Congress, first in the Provinces, and later at the Centre, Urdu–Hindi controversy had taken a serious political turn and assumed an unusual importance. Hindi was patronised by the Hindu Congress and backed by its unlimited financial resources and powerful press. Urdu, which was backed by the Muslim League had one man behind it, Maulvi Abdul Haq—who had made it as his life mission. It was at this stage that he came in contact with Quaid-e-Azam Muhammad Ali Jinnah, who extended him his whole-hearted support.

In September 1947, when Delhi was in the grip of communal frenzy, the Head Office of the Anjuman Taraqqi-i-Urdu in Dariyaganj, was set on fire and many invaluable manuscripts were reduced to ashes. This has only one parallel, though on a much bigger scale, in the burning of the invaluable literary treasures of Baghdad by Hulaku Khan in 1258, of the magnificent library of Tripoli (Syria) by the Crusaders, and of the famous library of Alexandria (Egypt) by Julius Caeser.

This act of vandalism broke Maulvi Abdul Haq's heart but not his indomitable spirit. He had to migrate to Pakistan, to start his work afresh in the newly-born country.

He settled down at Karachi and started the Anjuman Taraqqi-i-Urdu, Pakistan, which founded the Urdu College, a unique experiment in the country of teaching all sciences and arts through the Urdu medium. In this, he was very successful as was abundantly clear from the splendid results of the Urdu College in the University examinations which brought home the fact that students could learn difficult subjects better through the medium of their mother tongue, and that Urdu was capable of teaching all subjects. His ambition was to establish a Urdu University in Pakistan on the lines of the Osmania University of Hyderabad, but he did not live to realise this ambition.

In Pakistan, he had no easy task. He had to work hard for the recognition of Urdu as the State Language of Pakistan and its introduction as the medium of instruction in educational institutions and as the official language in the Government and other offices. As expected, he had to encounter stiff opposition from the regional languages of Pakistan and serious resistance from the 'English-minded' civil servants of the country. The oft-repeated changes in the Government in Pakistan which ultimately led to the political domination of civil servants in the country, marred the progress of Urdu and the realisation of the dream of Maulvi Abdul Haq to make Urdu as State language of Pakistan in the practical sense, applicable to all spheres of life. The anti-national narrow-mindedness of the "English-minded" civil servants, stood in the way of Baba-e-Urdu realising his dream during his lifetime.

Maulvi Abdul Haq has made a lasting contribution to literary research in Urdu. He has creditably edited many unknown and rare Urdu *Tazkiras* and *Diwans*. These included *'Malukars Shuara-i-Bijapur Ka Kalam-o-Halaat Ka Jaiza aur Tabsara, Mulla Nusrati, Marhatti Zaban Par Farsi Ka Asar, Urdu Ki Nasho Numa Men Sufia-i-Kiram Ka Kaam, Muqaddmaat* (Two Volumes), *Tanqeedaat* (Two Volumes), *Khutbaat, Chand Ham Asar, Intikhab-i-Kalaami-i-Mir, Intikhab-i-Dagh, Hali–Halaat-o-Afkar, Mazameen-i-Abdul Haq,* and *Alam-i-Islam.* He has also edited and published scores of manuscripts, including *Sabras.*

He has also compiled Urdu Grammars, namely, Urdu *Sarf-o-Nahv* and *Qawaid-i-Urdu.* He has compiled English into Urdu dictionaries, namely, *Standard English–Urdu Dictionary* (for students), *Popular English–Urdu Dictionary* (for school children) and *Qadeem Urdu Lughaat.* But his monumental work was the *Urdu Dictionary of Scientific Terms* which had enabled the teaching of technical and scientific subjects through Urdu medium in Osmania University, Hyderabad (Daccan). His other imperishable work is *Chund Ham Asar* (A few contemporaries) in which he has very lucidly and accurately given the pen portraits of some of his famous contemporaries.

His prose is distinguished for its simplicity, brevity and lucidity, devoid of verbosity and unnecessary ornamentation.

As a writer, Maulvi Abdul Haq is one of the stylists of modern Urdu prose which include Hasan Nizami, Abul Kalam Azad, Niaz Fatehpuri, Abdul Majid Dariyabadi, Rashid Ahmad Siddiqi and Qazi Abdul Ghaffar.

Maulvi Abdul Haq died in Karachi on August 16, 1961. With him passed away an inimitable stylist of Urdu prose, an ardent devotee of learning and literature who symbolised in his person a whole century of Muslim culture prevailing in the Indo–Pakistan subcontinent. He was the greatest figure in Urdu literature after Sir Syed Ahmad Khan—and one who lived and died for Urdu.

The people and the Government of Pakistan, deeply mourning his death, paid rich tributes to him for his erudition and dedication to the cause of Urdu.

# SYED SULAIMAN
# NADVI

The Annual Convocation of *Nadvat-ul-Uloom* was being held in a packed Hall at Lucknow in 1907. The conferring of degrees in this well-known institution of religious education was to be followed by *Dastar Bandi* (Investiture of academic gowns and turbans) ceremony, which was being presided over by Khwaja Ghulam-us-Saqlain, a renowned scholar and son-in-law of Maulana Altaf Husain Hali and was attended by Mohsinul Mulk and other intellectual luminaries of the time.

Meanwhile, someone got up from amongst the audience and addressing Maulana Shibli Nomani, questioned the scholarship of the students who had graduated from the Institution and their proficiency in modern Arabic. The Maulana, being a celebrated historian, accustomed to confront his adversaries with incontrovertible facts, asked a young graduate to deliver a speech on any given topic. The student got up and delivered a masterly speech in chaste Arabic on certain aspects of modern philosophy. His command over the language, the sublimity of his ideas and his excellent delivery, astounded the President and all those present there. The speaker was the young Sulaiman, who was destined to become one of the greatest historians and the greatest biographers of the Prophet of Islam during his time.

Syed Sulaiman was born in 1885 in a well-known Syed family of Desna, a village in the district of Patna (Bihar, India). His father, Hakim Syed Abul Hasan, known for his learning and piety was highly respected in the locality.

The young Sulaiman received his early education from his elder brother. Then he joined the Arabic Madrassa at Phulwari Sharif and later he enrolled himself in the Madrassa-e-Imdadia, Darbhanga.

In 1901 he joined the Darul-Uloom of Nadva, Lucknow, which was recognised as the foremost institution of religious and Arabic education in the subcontinent. Here he completed his seven years' Arabic course and came in contact with such eminent scholars as Maulana Farooq Chirayyakoti, Syed Muhammad Ali of Monghyr, Maulana Hafizullah and Allama Shibli Nomani who were much impressed by his talent, intelligence and diligence.

In 1904, when Allama Shibli Nomani joined the staff of Nadva, Syed Sulaiman came under his direct tutorship, a relationship which turned into a life-long companionship between the two great scholars of modern India.

In 1906, he joined the staff of *An-Nadva,* a magazine brought out by the Darul-Uloom. In 1908, he was appointed a lecturer in the Darul-Uloom, and for two years worked as an Assistant to Allama Shibli Nomani, who was engaged in the preparation of his well-known work, *Seerat-un-Nabi* (Life of the Holy Prophet), the major part of which, in fact, was completed in six volumes by Syed Sulaiman himself after the death of his illustrious teacher.

The international political situation was becoming extremely explosive at this time. The European powers were conspiring for dividing the Turkish Empire and wanted to fnish this "Sickman of Europe". In 1911, when Italy launched an unprovoked attack on Tripoli, a port of the Turkish Empire, young Sulaiman gave up his literary and educational pursuits and joined *Al Hilal,* Calcutta, edited by Maulana Abul Kalam Azad, another pupil of Shibli Nomani. Together with Azad, Syed Sulaiman made '*Al-Hilal*' a powerful organ of young Muslims which ultimately played a dominant role in the awakening of Muslim India.

The association of Syed Sulaiman with *Al-Hilal* could not last long. In 1912, Allama Shibli Nomani got him appointed as Assistant Professor of Persian at the famous Deccan College, Poona. Here, too, he could not stay for long. The death of his illustrious teacher, Shibli Nomani, two years later, obliged him to return to Azamgarh and take up the unfinished literary work of his master.

Syed Sulaiman Nadvi hereafter settled down at Azamgarh to a peaceful life of research and study, which later won for him an immortal place as a historian and scholar.

Sulaiman Nadvi, whose life had been an un-interrupted devotion to scholarship and literary pursuits, was called upon to devote his energies to the service of Islam and his country. The first quarter of the present century was a period of trials and tribulations for the Indian Muslims in particular. The political scene was tense, surcharged with revolution. The Caliphate held by the Turkish Sultan was at stake. The Western powers were conspiring to do away with this "Sickman of Europe". The wars in the Balkans and Tripoli and ultimately World War I, were all pointing to this end. In India, too, the Indian National Congress and especially the All-India Khilafat Committee, under the dynamic and inspiring leadership of Maulana Muhammad Ali, had created a stir throughout the length and breadth of the Subcontinent which led to an unprecedented awakening of the masses. Syed Sulaiman Nadvi, too, could not resist responding to the national call. In 1920, he joined a Khalafat Delegation, headed by Maulana Muhammad Ali, to London, for securing equitable and just treatment to Turkey at the hands of the victorious Allies.

In 1924, when the Sharif of Makkah and King Ibn Saud of Najd were at war, Sultan ibn Saud sought the help of the Khilafat Committee to settle the dispute. A delegation, headed by Syed Sulaiman Nadvi, which included Maulana Muhammad Ali and Shoaib Qureshi went to Hejaz in 1926 and fearlessly placed the views of Indian Muslims before Sultan ibn Saud for establishing a truly democratic rule in the Holy land. In 1926, Syed Sulaiman presided over the memorable annual session of Jamiat-ul-Ulema at Calcutta, which considered the deteriorating Hindu—Muslim relations in the subcontinent due to the Shuddhi—Sanghattan Movement started by the Shardhanand—Malaviya Group. The same year, the Maulana at the invitation of King Ibn Saud headed a delegation of celebrated Muslim leaders including Maulana Muhammad Ali and Shaukat Ali to Makkah to participate in the *Motamar-i-Alam-i-Islami.* Delegations of almost all Muslim countries had participated in the conference and Syed Sulaiman Nadvi had been elected the Vice-President of the Conference *(Motamar).* On his return from Makkah, he retired from active politics and decided to devote his heart and soul to literary pursuits only.

Syed Sulaiman Nadvi had started his career as the Sub-Editor of *An Nadva,* a well-known magazine devoted to religious research. In 1910 he joined as an Assistant Editor and leader writer of the celebrated *'Al Hilal'* of Maulana Abul Kalaam Azad. He wrote some of its best editorials, including one on Cawnpur Mosque incident which electrified the Indian Muslims. But his association with *Al Hilal* lasted two years only. In 1914, when the *Shibli Academy* was established and its official organ, the *'Maarif'* started publication, he became its founder Editor. This magazine, during the last 44 years of its existence has maintained an enviable record of high class articles. It introduced in Urdu journalism short notes and second leaders on important men and matters, called *"Shazrat".*

The greatest achievement of Syed Sulaiman Nadvi was the establishment of *Darul Mosannafeen* (House of Writers) also known as the *Shibli Academy* at Azamgarh which became the pioneer in the field of literary and historical research in the subcontinent. He attracted around him a large number of talented scholars who carried on the literary mission of his illustrious teacher, Shibli Nomani, with unabated zeal. This institution of learning founded in 1914 continues to spread its lustre throughout the subcontinent and during the last 48 years of its existence has published some outstanding works on diverse branches of knowledge. Maulana Sulaiman Nadvi dedicated his life to the service of learning and kept his uninterrupted association with the Shibli Academy, Azamgarh. During this period he spent an austere life at Azamgarh, busy in writing books which inspired an entire generation.

Syed Sulaiman Nadvi was a prolific writer who wrote books on history, biography, literature and travel. His greatest work is the *Seerat-un-Nabi* (Life of the Prophet of Islam) in six volumes which has hardly any parallel in any language of the world. This outstanding work on the life of the Holy Prophet of Islam was started by Shibli Nomani, but the major part of it was completed by his pupil,

Syed Sulaiman. This has since been translated into several languages and is the most widely read book on the life and teachings of the Great Prophet of Islam. He has made 'Seerat' a new and separate subject in Islamic studies.

His first book was *Durus-ul-Adab,* an Arabic reader in two parts. In 1912 he compiled a Dictionary of New Arabic Words. In 1915 he brought out the first volume and in 1918 the second volume of *Arzul Quran* (the lands of Quran) which is a priceless piece of historical research. This is the only book of its kind in Urdu which has made great impression of his scholarship on the orientalists.

In 1910, he wrote another very important biographical work, *Seerut-e-Aisha* which is the most authentic book on the life of Hazrat Aisha, wife of the Prophet of Islam.

His other widely read book is *Arbon ki Jahazrani* (Arab Navigation) dealing with the great voyages undertaken by the Arab navigators during the mediaeval times who, with the help of Mariners' compass, which they invented, roamed about in open seas reaching as far as the Bering Strait, East and West Indies and even touched the New World.

The *Khayyam,* which appeared in 1933 deals with the life and work of Umar Khayyam. It is yet another popular work of his. Dissipating a popular misconception about Khayyam being a dreamer, steeped in wine, he brought out Khayyam's great contribution to mathematics, astronomy and science.

His *Khutbaat-e-Madras* is a collection of his lectures delivered at the invitation of the Muslim Educational Conference at Madras on the life of the Holy Prophet of Islam. This has been translated into English and has since been published into several editions.

In 1939, he published a collection of his essays on diverse subjects, known as *Naqoosh-e-Sulaiman.* These essays known for the sublimity of thought and lucidity of diction are a living testimony to his scholarhsip and mastery over the language.

His yet another monumental work *Hayat-e-Shibli* was published in 1943. It deals not only with the life and works of his teacher, Allama Shibli Nomani, but, in fact, is a detailed history of literary and educational activities of Muslim India during the last 100 years.

Syed Sulaiman Nadvi had developed a style which was sober and lucid but at the same time convincing and impressive. It was essentially suitable for his historical writings. He is scholarly and objective in his treatment of history which appeals more to the head than to the heart.

The brutal persecution of Muslims in India by the Hindu majority community compelled him to migrate to Pakistan in 1950. The pleadings of the

Prime Minister of India not to leave India could not dissuade him from going to Pakistan where he was immensely needed for guiding the framing of a truly Islamic constitution. On arrival in Karachi, he was made President of the Islamic Talimaat Board, attached to the Constituent Assembly. He had come to Pakistan with an ambitious plan in his mind of establishing an Academy of Islamic Studies in Karachi which could rival the Shibli Academy of Azamgarh (U.P.). But he was not destined to live here long and died three years after, in 1953. His death was mourned throughout the world of Islam and the loss of this great scholar, historian and religious writer was universally acknowleged. His death has created a void in the literary life of the subcontinent which cannot be easily filled.

Syed Sulaiman Nadvi was a great scholar, historian, religious writer but above all he was a great man. Like all truly great scholars he was the embodiment of humility and simplicity. He was unostentatious and never took pride in his greatness.

The services of Syed Sulaiman Nadvi were recognised and his greatness as a great scholar was acknowledged during his lifetime. The Muslim University, Aligarh, conferred on him the degree of D. Litt. in 1941. A number of Universities and institutions, including the Aligarh Muslim University, the Hindustani Academy of Allahabad, the Jamia Millia, Delhi, the Nadvat-ul-Ulema, Lucknow, and the Hindustani Committee of the Government of Bihar, had associated him with their work.

# ARTISTS AND MUSICIANS

# ABU NASR FARABI

Saifuddawlah, the Hamdanite monarch who ruled over Aleppo and the neighbouring country, was presiding over a congregation of learned men summoned from different parts of the Islamic world. A manikin with sparse beard, attired in Turcoman dress and heelless shoes with painted toe called 'zerbul', was ushered into the meeting hall. This was Farabi. Saifuddawlah requested him to take his seat.

"Where should I sit", asked Farabi. "Should I sit according to my status or yours?"

"No, according to yours", replied the Ruler.

Thereupon Farabi went forward, and pulling the Ruler aside, sat down in his place. Saifuddawlah was a bit annoyed and told his servant in a secret dialect that he would put certain questions to Farabi and if he could not give correct replies he should be severely dealt with. None seemed to be conversant with this dialect except the Ruler and his servant. But, to his utter astonishment, Farabi replied in the same dialect, "Master, have patience. The end will justify the means". The Ruler asked him, "Do you also know this dialect?" "Yes, I am conversant with seventy languages", replied Farabi. Thereafter the meeting was addressed by Farabi in a hushed silence. His masterly exposition of diverse subjects and his brilliant eloquence made the audience spell bounded. The meeting was later on dispersed by the Ruler who asked Farabi if he would eat or drink anything. "No", replied Farabi. He, however, consented to musical entertainment. The best troupe of his musicians was summoned by the Ruler. The demonstration did not move Farabi at all. Taking out his 'ud' ('lute) he started playing over it. His performance cast a spell over the audience; he directed their sentiments as he liked. They were so much enchanted that all of a sudden they began to laugh. He changed the tune and they burst into tears. He again changed the tune and now they fell asleep.

The above account of the entry of Farabi into the Durbar of Saifuddawlah has been given by the famous historian Allama ibn Khalikan. The virtues and the versatility of Farabi had a deep impression on Saifuddawlah who highly respected him and did not part with him till his death. Farabi, the Muslim Neo-Platonist and encyclopaedist was, according to George Sarton, "conversant with the whole scientific thought of his day".

Muhammad ibn Muhammad ibn Tar Khan Abu Nasr Farabi (Latin—Alpharabius), one of the greatest intellectual giants of the mediaeval times, was born towards the end of the IXth century A.C. in Wasij, a small town in Farab (Turkistan). His father was a General in the army. Jurji Zaydan asserts in his *History of Islamic Civilisation* that his parents were Persians but reliable historical records reveal his Turkish origin. Farabi never gave up his Turkish dress wherever he went. He received his early education in Farab and Bukhara, and later on settled down in Baghdad for 42 years (901 to 942). He acquired a command over the Arabic language and a thorough knowledge of various branches of learning. During the period, he saw six Caliphs and passed his time in solitude in pursuits of poetry, music and philosophy. He wrote *'Al Taleem al Sani'* at the behest of Ali Salman, the Ruler of Turkistan whom he visited while he studied at Baghdad.

He visited Damascus, Egypt and finally settled down at Aleppo, which was ruled by Hamdanite monarch Saifuddawlah, a great patron of scholars. His Durbar was adorned by some of the greatest intellectuals of the age, including Farabi and Mutanabbi.

He was a sufi and in spite of the repeated persuasions of the Ruler who held him in highest esteem, Farabi consented to accept only four dirhams a day for his expenses. He died in 950 A.C. (339 A.H.) at the ripe age of 80 in Damascus whither he had accompanied the King on a campaign.

By nature he was very sensitive and simple minded and passed a secluded life. He was thoroughly versed not only in philosophy, logic, politics, occult sciences and sociology but also in mathematics and medical sciences. It has been recorded that he could speak 70 languages, but it has been established beyond doubt that he was fully conversant with Turkish, Persian, Arabic, Greek and Hebrew languages.

Farabi was a versatile genius and encyclopaedist, an outstanding mathematician and physician, an occult scientist and a distinguished musician. According to reliable historical sources, he left behind him more than hundred works in Arabic on different subjects, but only 15 or 20 more are extant. The list of his works given by Kifti and Ibn Abi Saibah contains 17 commentaries, 15 treatises and 60 books on diverse branches of knowledge.

He wrote a large number of original works, including psychological, polititical and metaphysical treatises of great importance, such as *On the Intelligence, Intelligible, On the Soul, Faculties of Soul, One and the Unity, Substance, Time, Empty Space* and *Space and Measure.* He was first to speak of evolution in psychology and thus influenced later writers.

He also wrote several treatises explaining and elaborating the philosophical theories of Plato and Aristotle. The most important is *'Risala Fusus of Hikam'* (The Bezels of Philosophy or Wisdom).

Of his scientific treatises, the most useful is *'Kitab Ihsal Ulum'* which deals with the fundamental principles of science. The Arabic originals of his treatises translated into Latin as *'De Scientus'* and *'De Ortu Scientiarum'*, have been lost. In 1890 Dieterici had edited and published in German 12 small treatises of Farabi, mostly scientific.

Farabi made a lasting contribution to sociology by writing his memorable work *'Risalah fi Ara Ahl al-Madinah al Fadilah* (Epistle on the Opinions of People of Superior City) and thus paved the way for the immortal *'Prolegomena* of Ibn Khaldun'. It was translated and published by Dieterici as *'Philosophia de Araber'* and later on as *'Der Mustarstaat von Alfarabi'*. Farabi has presented his conception of a model city in his well-known work *'Al Siyashat al Madniyah'* (Political Economy) in which he seems to be inspired by the *Republic* of Plato and *Politica* of Aristotle. His ideal city is to be governed by wise men who are perfect morally and intellectually. He lays great importance on the happiness and high morality of the citizens of his model city. The book in 34 chapters, translated and edited by Dieterici, is of great sociological interest.

His book *'Musiqi al-Kabir'* is the most outstanding book on oriental music and is regarded an authority on the subject. His works were published in translations into German, Latin, French and Hebrew which began to appear in the last quarter of the 19th century. Some of his books including *'Ihsa al Ulum'*, an encyclopaedic work, have greatly influenced the Western writers. A complete bibliography of his works has been prepared by Hazmi Tura and B. Ahmad Atas which is preserved in the libraries of Istambul.

Farabi is also known for simplifying logic. He made two divisions of logic— imagination and proof. According to Kazi Syed, the author of *At Tausif al Tabajat ul-Umam,* Farabi outmatched all previous philosophers in logic.

Farabi is known as the commentator of Aristotle which won him the title of *Moallim-e-Sani* (Second Teacher). His commentaries as well as those of Averroes popularised the works of Aristotle in the West, which was awakened to his greatness. Farabi commented on *'Categories'*, *'Hermenuties'*, *'Analytics'*, *'Sophistics'*, *'Rhetoric'* and *'Poetics'*. He also wrote commentaries on the 'soul' and physics of Aristotle as well as on the *'Almagest'* of Ptolemy. He is one of the great Muslim thinkers who saved the Greek thought from oblivion and it is due to him that the West came to know of Aristotle.

During a period of intellectual stagnation in Europe which lasted from 5th to 10th centuries A.C., Islamic thinkers kept aloft the candle of knowledge, which ultimately dispelled the gloom that had enveloped Europe. One of these intellectual luminaries was Farabi, whose philosophical system, according to George Sarton, "is a syncretism of Platonism, Aristotelianism and Sufism". Farabi is the founder of the Turkish School of Philosophy. He is an exponent of Muslim Neo-Platonic Philosophy, a system which was originated by Al-Kindi and acquired its full growth in Avicenna. Apparently there is a marked difference in the philosophical approach of Farabi and Zakariya Razi (Razes) who was his contemporary. "While Farabi's system is deductive, rational and built entirely on abstract logic". Writes a Western orientalist, "Razi's philosophy is experimental, inductive and is more specially concerned with the concrete—but they are two aspects of a more general system and not opposed to one another. Razi, who was a physician and naturalist, emphasises the concrete side of the system, while Farabi who had more inclination towards logic, mathematics and mystic speculation, presents the abstract side of it. In Avicenna we find the two forms reunited". Avicenna is no doubt clearer and more methodical in his approach. The difference between Farabi and Avicenna is more pronounced on the question of the immortality of soul which is accepted by the former and rejected by the latter.

Like Plato, Farabi is a mystical thinker, whose reasoning leads him finally to mysticism and metaphysics. With him, like all mystics, contemplation dominates action.

He interpreted a number of religious dogmas and concepts in a philosophical manner. He tried to find the reasoned and logical explanation of such intricate problems as prophecy, inspiration, heavens, destiny and celestial throne. Prophecy, according to Farabi, is a form of moral perfection rather than an innate gift. In this way, he is considered as the founder of philosophical theology which later on found its great exponent in Fakhruddin Razi. He was also first to preach practical morality by recognising that the faculty of discerning good from evil is possessed by oneself. Avicenna, thus, borrowed the idea of his mysticism of right or reason from Farabi.

Farabi was the greatest musical theorist that the Muslim world has produced. He composed several outstanding works on music. Among them were the *Kitab Mausiqi al-Kabir* (Grand Book of Music), *Styles in Music,* and *On the Classification of Rhythms.* Besides the above, he has also dealt with musical topics in two of his voluminous works on the science: *The Classification of the Sciences,* and *The Origin of Sciences.* His Grand Book of Music is universally recognised as the highest authority on the oriental music and, according to Farmer, a well-known writer on music, this work of Farabi, "deserves to be ranked as one of the greatest works that has been written on music". Out of the several works of Farabi on music, *Kitab Musiqi al Kabir* has survived, which in the words of Sarton, "is the most important oriental treatise on the theory of music". According to Farabi, he wrote this book, because he found that the earlier books written by Greeks, Romans and Persians were full of obscurities and shortcomings. H. G. Farmer pays glowing tribute to this immortal work of the great musician, saying, 'Al Farabi's treatment of physical and physiological principles of sound and music is certainly an advance on that of Greeks". Farabi has given a detailed account of musical instruments which is non-existent in the musical works of Greeks. He invented the musical instruments called *'Rabab'* and *'Qanun'.* He also knew mensural music and recognised the major third $(4:5)$ and the minor third $(5:6)$ as consonances. Farabi made a valuable contribution to physiological acoustics which was not touched by the Greeks. He was an outstanding practical musician of his time and when he played on his flute in the presence of his patron Saifuddawlah he is said "to have cast his hearers into a fit of laughter, drew tears from their eyes or set them all asleep, including even the door-keepers". The Mawlawi darveshes still sing ancient chants composed by him. The musical works of Farabi had a universal appeal and influenced the musical theories of the West as well as those of Muslim Spain. "Al-Farabi still continued to attract the attention of the scholars until the 17th century A.C."; says H. G. Farmer. According to Kazi Sayad, "Farabi had attained a perfection both in theoretical and practical sides of music".

The musical theories of Farabi had a great influence over the writings of the West. The *'De Divisione Philosophiae'*, written by Gundislaves has a section on music, much of which has been reproduced from Farabi's *'De Scienties'* and *'De Ortusceintiarum'*. In the musical treatise entitled *'De Musica'* and the *'Speculum Doctrinale* of Vicent de Beauvais (d. 1264), Farabi has been frequently quoted along with other theorists.

A number of well-known Western writers like Robert Kilwardley (d. 1279), Raimundo Lull (d. 1315). Simon Tunstedo (1300—69), and Adam de Fuldo were influenced by Farabi. Even up to the end of the 17th century, his theories on music continued to influence the Western writers which may be ascertained from the *"De Expetendis et Fugiendis Rebus"*, written by George Valla (1497—1501) the *Margarita Philosophica'* (1508) of George Reish and the republication of *'De Scientus'* by Camerarius in 1638.

The influence of Farabi on the later writers and thought was tremendous. All philosophers coming after Farabi were influenced by this great thinker. He is the foremost encyclopaedist of Islam who is credited with the evolution of Islamic logic. "His rational philosophy", says a Western orientalist, "had made him the forerunner of the German Philosopher Kant; his theory of the great man and the little savant of the Englishman Spencer. By saying that knowledge is not acquired only by intellectual effort but it flows from a superior soul to men, he was the precursor of the theory of philosophic intuition of the Frenchman Bergson. He, thus introduced the theory of social contract of Rousseau, by stating that social union comes about through the will of the individual". Among the orientals his influence may be traced in the works of such eminent thinkers as Avicenna, Averroes, Ibn Khaldun, Fakharuddin Razi, Ibn Haytham, Ibn Miskawayh, Jalaluddin Rumi and Al-Ghazali.

After paying glowing tribute to his achievements, Allama Ibn Khalikan, the celebrated historian says: "No Muslim ever reached in the philosophical sciences the same rank as al-Farabi, and it was by the study of his writings and by the imitation of his style that Ibn Sina attained the proficiency and rendered his own work so useful".

# AMIR KHUSROU

Muslims and music are generally considered poles apart. Few people know the part played by Muslims in the development of fine arts, specially music. The contribution of Muslims to the development of theoretical as well as practical music is indeed great and a number of songs and musical instruments adopted by various countries of the world owe their origin to the genius of Muslim musicians. The *'Mausiqi-al-Kabir'* written by Abu Nasr Farabi, is according to H. G. Farmer, one of the greatest books ever written on music. The influence of this book on Western music has been overwhelming. The Arabian music, according to Farmer, entered Europe *via* Spain and reached China through Baghdad. The Muslim world can boast of such great musicians as Farabi, Momin, Ishaq Mosli, Zalzal and Ziryab who have left ineffaceable marks on the pages of musical history of the world. One of these master artists was Amir Khusrou, a versatile genius who has made lasting contributions to the domains of poetry, music and mysticism.

The enlightened West has considered all people inhabiting the vast Indo—Pakistan subcontinent as Hindus—hence Indian music has wrongly been taken to be entirely a speciality of the Hindus. Unfortunately, the Western historians being inspired by their Hindu counterparts have not only ignored the cultural, political and artistic enterprises and achievements of Muslim India, but also formed a biased opinion in favour of Hindus. Notwithstanding their stupendous efforts in under-rating the cultural achievements of Muslims, well-known historians and critics such as Sir William James, Lt.-Col James Tod, Augustus, W. Hunter, Surendra Mohan Tagore, Anand Kumar Swami and Prof. Ranade, had to admit, though half heartedly, the valuable part played by Muslims in the development of Indian music. The Muslims since the time of Amir Khusrou who live in the reign of Alauddin Khilji, formed the vanguard of all cultural movements in India and were pioneers in the domains of music. The Muslim rulers of India had always been the great patrons of art and culture. Besides Amir Khusrou, who flourished during the days of Khiljis and Tughlaqs, Tan Sen adorned the Court of the Mughal Emperor Akbar. Jahangir, the cultured Mughal Emperor, had an exceptionally fine taste for music. During his reign, all cultural movements recorded phenomenal advancement. Writing in *"Ghubar-i-Khatir"* Maulana Abul Kalam Azad says: "The first dynasty which patronised and cultivated music as an art was the Sharqi dynasty of Jaunpore. It was during their reign that *'Khiyal'* became very popular and replaced *'Dhurpad'*. Round about this time, the Nizam Shahi dynasty and the Adil Shahi of Bijapur exhibited a fine taste for music. "Ibrahim Adil Shah", according to Zahoori, "was a master musician, whose patronage had lighted the lamp of music in each and every house of Bijapur. The romantic land of Malwa during the reign of Baz Bahadur had become the cradle of theoretical as well as practical music".

Amir Khusrou, born in 1253 A.D. at Patiali near Kanauj (U.P.) was a master musician—a man possessing extraordinary abilities and versatile taste. His father, Saifuddin Mahmood, who was among the nobles of Balkh, migrated to India due to devastations wrought by Chengiz Khan in Turkistan. Farishta and Daulat Shah have corroborated the above statement. According to Abul Fazal, the celebrated author of *Aeen-i-Akbari* and the historian Badayuni, Patiali where Khusrou was born, was a small town on the bank of the Ganges which was also called Mominabad. When Khusrou was born, his father carried his infant son to a *'Darvesh'* (saint) who blessed him, saying that he would, one day, outmatch Khakani. The father died when Khusrou was only seven. He had a natural taste for music and poetry and had acquired a thorough knowledge of different branches of learning before he was fifteen years old. He died at a ripe age of 71 in 1324 A.C., and lived to enjoy the favour of the five successive Kings of Delhi.

Amir Khusrou was a disciple of Hazrat Khwaja Nizamuddin Aulia, the famous saint of Delhi. Hazrat Khwaja had conferred on him the title of 'Tarkat Allah'. The society of Khwaja Nizamuddin had brought a revolutionary change in the life of Khusrou, who dedicated himself to the service of his great teacher. Once a darvesh begged something from Hazrat Khwaja, who had at the moment nothing to give him. He bade him to see him the next day. That day, too, he had nothing to give him. However he presented him his shoes. Accidentally, the darvesh came across Khusrou outside the city. He enquired the welfare of his master from the darvesh, saying, "I find a token of my saint with you, would you like to sell it?" The darvesh consented to sell the shoes to Khusrou at half a million Tankas, which he had been awarded for a poem by the king. Placing the shoes upon his head he appeared before Hazrat Khwaja Nizamuddin and said, "The darvesh was contented with the price paid to him for the shoes, otherwise if he had demanded my entire property and even my life, I would have readily given him".

Hazrat Khwaja Nizamuddin, too, deeply loved Khusrou. He used to say, "If God would enquire on the Day of Judgement as to what I have brought, I would present Khusrou".

Khusrou was in Bengal, when Hazrat Khwaja died in Delhi. On hearing the sad news, he distributed his entire wealth among the poor and hurried to Delhi. Seeing the grave of his teacher he cried out convulsively, "O God! The Sun has gone down the earth and Khusrou is still alive." Thereafter, he became a recluse and died within six months of the passing away of his spiritual teacher.

Khusrou was a great intellectual wizard—the greatest intellectual luminary that had shone so resplendently on the literary firmament of Muslim India. He has left behind him immortal achievements in the fields of poetry and music, mysticism and politics.

In 686 A.H., Sultan Balban died and contrary to his will, his drunkard grandson Kaikobad, was installed on the throne of Delhi. A clash between Kaikobad and his father Bughara Khan which seemed imminent was averted at the last moment. Khusrou described the whole incident in a long poem called *Qaranus Sadain.* The Slave dynasty was soon replaced by the Khiljis. Jalaluddin Khilji who was a well-known patron of learned men, selected Khusrou as one of his trusted companions. Khusrou had given poetic form to Jalaluddin's conquests and named it as *Tajul Futuh.* Alauddin Khilji who succeeded his uncle was one of the greatest rulers that Muslim India has produced. He conquered almost the whole of Southern India. He held Khusrou in great esteem. The poet described the military exploits of Alauddin Khilji in his well-known work *Khazain ul Futuh* (The Treasure of Conquests). When Khusrou's mother and brother Hissamuddin passed away in 698 A.H., he wrote a touching elegy entitled Laila Majnoon. A *Mathnavi* (long poem) which he wrote in 701 A.H. was *Hasht Bahisht* (The eight paradises). He was awarded an elephant load of silver coins by King Qutbuddin Mubarak Shah for his *Mathnavi Neh Sipahr* (Nine skies) which he completed in 718 A.H. The weak and lingering Khilji dynasty was replaced by the Tughlaqs. Ghyasuddin Tughlaq, the first king of this dynasty, was a great admirer of Khusrou, who in his *Tughlaq Nama* wrote an elaborate history of the period.

Jami in his *Nafhat ul Uns* has given a list of 92 books written by Khusrou. According to the poet's own statement, he composed about half a million verses. Ohdi in his *Urfat* writes that Khusrou has left behind more verses in Hindi than in Persian. In his celebrated work *Matla-e Anwar* he has dealt with the intricacies of mysticism. His *Aejaz-i-Khusravi* in three volumes deals with the principles of prose writing. The detailed history of Delhi is found in his *Manaqib Hind.*

As a poet, Khusrou occupies a high place in the galaxy of Persian poets. He is master of different forms of Persian poetry. Usually certain poets have attained the height of fame in particular forms of Persian poetry, Firdausi and Nizami are on the top in *Mathnavi, Anwari* and *Khaqani* are known for their panegyrics, Hafiz and Saadi are famous for their lyrics—but Khusrou has scaled considerable heights in all these forms of Persian poetry. He was enormously productive. Daulat Shah credits him with nearly half a million verses. Of these, Mirza Baysunqur after ceaseless efforts, succeeded in collecting 120,000, but having subsequently discovered 2,000 more from his lyrics; he concluded that it would be very difficult for him to collect the complete work of the poet, and gave up the idea for ever.

Amir Khusrou was conversant with several languages, including Persian, Turkish, Arabic, Hindi and Sanskrit and has left his works in most of these languages. His verses in Hindustani language except those found in *Khaliq Bari* are non-extant. This subcontinent has hardly produced such a versatile genius as Khusrou.

Khusrou, was, undoubtedly, the greatest musician that mediaeval India produced. He won the title of Nayak which none could get after him during the last 629 years. He wrote enchanting songs and composed many new ones in place of *dhurpad* which acquired great popularity even during his lifetime. He also invented a new type of *sitar*. He enriched Indian music through his compositions and innovations of *Khiyal, Kaul Kalbana, Zelf, Ghaza, Kedar* and *Tarana*. *Sazgiri* and *Khiyal* composed by him formed the culmination of his achievements which have earned an outstanding place in the domain of Indian music. Professor Ranade, writes in his book *Indian Music*: "At the close of the 13th century when Muslims conquered Deccan by overthrowing the Devagiri Ruler, Islamic music began to influence the *Indian Music*. The originator of new trends in the North Indian music was Amir Khusrou whose keen sense enabled him to raise it to a high degree of perfection." According to the latest historical researches, too, the originator of the new type of music in Northern India was Amir Khusrou, who, not only found new avenues but also developed it to a high standard. Even after a lapse of more than 600 years, he is considered an authority on diverse branches of theoretical and practical music.

During his time, there was one Nayak Gopal who had 1,200 disciples, and who carried their master seated on a wooden chair from place to place on their shoulders. The fame of Nayak Gopal reached Sultan Alauddin Khilji. He was summoned by the King. The Nayak gave, display of his music in six different meetings. In the seventh, Khusrou too, participated. Nayak was also aware of the greatness of Khusrou in Indian music. He requested the Amir to give the performance of his vocal music. The Amir replied that since he was a Turk, he was not much conversant with the Indian music. When Nayak sang a song. Khusrou said that he himself was the composer of that song and he sang it in a far better way emphasising all its peculiarities. Whatever Gopal sang, Khusrou repeated it in a much better manner. In the end Khusrou added whatever performance of vocal music was given by Gopal was of ordinary class. Thereafter he gave performance of his typical songs, which simply charmed Nayak Gopal and he became a disciple of Khusrou. Khusrou who being master of both Persian and Hindustani music, had created a pleasant mixture by intermingling both.

Muhammad Husain Azad writes in *Abi Hayat*: "Amir Khusrou possessed much originality of approach. He had a special aptitude for music. He invented *Khiyal, Kaul* and *Kalbana* which easily replaced *Dhurpad* and became exceedingly popular throughout India.

Writing in *Ghubar-i-Khatir* Maulana Abul Kalaam Azad says: "The birth of such a great musician as Amir Khusrou in India during the 7th century A.H. proved beyond doubt that Muslims acquired a hold over Indian music. The innovation of such immortal songs as *Sazgiri, Uljan* and *Khiyal* by Amir Khusrou has earned for him an outstanding place in the history of Indian classical music".

According to the celebrated musician Hakim Muhammad Akram Khan, the author of *Maadan Mausiqi* (The Treasure of Music), "Amir Khusrou was considered *Nayak* of his time. He invented seventeen tunes of *Dholak*, and is looked upon as the originator of *Purbi Rag* (Eastern Tune) which was the favourite of Hazrat Nizamuddin Aulia".

Writing in his well-known book, *The Life and Works of Amir Khusrou,* Mirza Mahmood Ahmed says: "The natural inclination which Amir had for music pervades all his writings. The originality inherent in his nature revolted against the dogmatism of traditional school of Indian music. There had not been a greater artist in the history of classical music of India".

Herbert A. Poplay pays glowing tribute to the genius of Amir Khusrou when he acknowledges in his celebrated work, *Music of India* that Amir Khusrou was not only a renowned poet and musician but also a great soldier and statesman.

The following few anecdotes pertaining to Amir Khusrou will be found of great interest:

Once Amir Khusrou called on a Sufi Saint. At the door he was stopped by the *durban* (doorman) who would not let him in without the permission of the Saint. This very much offended and angered Amir Khusrou who, on the spur of the moment, wrote on a scrap of paper the following hemistich extemporaneously:

در درویش را دربان نباید

A dervish requires no doorman.

The doorman delivered it to the Saint who instantaneously added to it the following hemistich:

باید ، تا سگِ دنیا نہ آید

(There should be (posted) one, so that no worldly dog may intrude).

This evoked a sardonic chuckle from Amir Khusrou and, at the same time, amused him. He was forthwith admitted to the presence of the Saint.

It is said that on one occasion a few guests who came to dine with Amir Khusrou, were not inclined to leave long after the dinner was over. He began to be bored by their prolonged presence and wanted them to quit. Meanwhile the kettle-drum sounded the near midnight hour. Thereupon, satirically addressing the guests, he asked if they knew what it implied and before anyone of them could reply, he laughingly observed that the kettle-drum said it was time for them to depart. Simultaneously, he recited the following couplet composed impromptu in Persian chiming with the number of hours struck by the kettle-drum:

نان که خوردی ، خانه برو ، خانه برو ، خانه برو

ناکه بدست تو کردم، خانه برو ، خانه برو ، خانه برو

Since you have done with supping, you (had better)
Leave for home, now, leave for home,
Leave for home, leave for home, leave for home,—
I haven't mortgaged to you my house,
I haven't mortgaged to you my house,
I haven't mortgaged to you my house.

# MIAN TAN SEN

Akbar, the Great Mughal, was a great patron of art and learning. He had drawn to his Court some of the greatest intellectual and artistic luminaries of the age. Being a contemporary of Sulaiman, the Magnificent of Turkey and Queen Elizabeth of England, his brilliant rule was distinguished for internal peace and prosperity—qualities which are greatly instrumental in preparing the ground for the development of arts and sciences. Tan Sen, the celebrated vocal musician, whose name has become a household word in the realm of music, was one of the brightest gems that adorned the Durber of Akbar, the Great. The stately edifice of modern Indo-Pakistani music has been raised on the foundations laid by the genius of Tan Sen.

Abul Fazal, the author of the well-known *Aeen-e-Akbari*, pays glowing tribute to the matchless art of Tan Sen when he says: "A singer like him had not appeared in India for the last thousand years—such a genius in music might not be born again".

Tan Sen was born in a Brahmin family of Benares in 1506 A.C. His father Mukundaram, himself a good singer, led an unhappy life in spite of being extermely rich. Several sons were born to him, but none had survived. Mukundaram had learnt of a Muslim Saint Hazrat Muhammad Ghaus residing at Gwalior, whose fame as a spiritualist had reached the distant corners of the subcontinent. Mukundaram went to pay homage to the celebrated Saint who gave him an amulet for his wife intimating him that all rites being strictly observed, he would be blessed with a gifted son. The words of the Saint bore fruit and shortly after a son was born to him who was named Ramtanu.

Ramtanu had no charm for academic pursuits and possessed a romantic nature. He was blessed with a wonderful natural gift of possessing a perfect voice and in his childhood he could successfully imitate the voices of animals and birds. By a strange coincidence, he came into contact with his professional Guru, Swami Haridas, a hermit of Bindraban, who was on his way to Benares along with his disciples. All of a sudden the companions of the hermit were terrified by the roar of a nearby lion. But he was satisfied that no lion was found in those parts of the country, and a search led to the discovery of Ramtanu, who was roaming about in the suburbs of the Holy city. Ramtanu was taken as a disciple of Swami Haridas and taken to Bindraban, where he developed his art of vocal music to such a high degree, where none could reach during the last thousand years or more. Just like Plato, the teacher of Aristotle, Haridas will go down in musical history of the world as the teacher of inimitable Tan Sen.

The Sen remained in Bindraban for about ten years. Therefrom he went to Gwalior to fulfil the last wish of his dead father who had instructed him to devote his life to the service of his spiritual 'Guru', Hazrat Muhammad Ghaus. Tan Sen had an access to the Court of Maharaja Man Singh of Gwalior and his talented Queen Mriganayani. There he fell in love with Husaini Brahmani (a Muslim convert) and embraced Islam having been named Ata Ali Khan. After the death of Hazrat Muhammad Ghaus, Ata Ali Khan (Tan Sen) again migrated to Bindraban and completed his course in music.

By this time, the fame of Tan Sen as a vocal and classical musician had reached the distant corners of India. Maharaja Raja Ram of Rewa, invited him to join his Court as his Court musician. Emperor Akbar who once visited Rewa had an opportunity of listening to the matchless songs of Tan Sen and was charmed by the melodies of the immaculate artiste. The Maharaja of Rewa grasped the opportunity of winning the favour of the Emperor by offering his celebrated Tan Sen to Akbar in 1556 A.C. and thus opened the most glorious chapter in the life of the famous musician. The Durbar of Akbar was adorned, besides his nine gems, with experts of arts and learning. Out of a host of vocal and instrumental musicians, who warmed the meetings of the Emperor, Mian Tan Sen and his four sons, namely, Surat Sen, Sarat Sen, Taranga Sen and Bilas Khan, won a high reputation in the world of music.

Hazrat Amir Khusrou, the most talented and versatile genius that Muslim India has produced had the distinction of being the originator of a new style in Indian music which was a sweet fusion of Hindu and Muslim elements. He was the master artist who is known in the annals of Indian Music as the inventor of *Khiyal, Kaul* and *Qalbana.* Tan Sen, comig later on, popularised and improved upon the innovations of the earlier master, opening new vista for Indian music. His innovations in vocal music are known as *Mian Ka Rag* (The Song of Mian Tan Sen). Of his direct descendants and disciples, his son Bilas Khan and his son-in-law Misri Singhi, kept aloft the high reputation of their immortal teacher. Bilas Khan is known as the originator of *Bilas Khan Todi*–a song which acquired immense popularity throughout the subcontinent. One of his descendants, brought about beneficial changes in the *Sitar* by increasing its strings. Niyamat Khan Shah Sadarang a descendant of Misri Singhi, living in the reign of the last Mughal Emperor, improved upon the *Khiyal* songs.

Mian Tan Sen had become a legendary figure in the realm of music and many interesting stories are current in this subcontinent about his musical performances–which though apparently incredulous cannot be lightly brushed aside and, on the other hand, bear ample testimony to the hold of music over the elements of nature. Like all great men, Tan Sen, too, had his enemies who were jealous of his unique success. They conspired against his life by instigating the Mughal Emperor to persuade Tan Sen to give a performance of *Dipak* song, which the Emperor had not listened so far. Tan Sen contended that the singing of such a song would endanger his life, but this plea only added to the curiosity of the Emperor who struck to his order. Tan Sen was obliged to consent to and requested for 15 days time in order to make necessary preparations. Within this period he taught his talented daughter the art of Megh Raga. The appointed day at last came and the Emperor along with his Courtiers waited impatiently for the commencement of the fateful song. Tan San began singing the *Dipak Raga*. His eyes became blood shot and at the end of the fourth song, the entire hall was lit and afire. The audience ran helter skelter and Tan Sen himself hurried home crying with burning sensations. His daughter started her Megha Raga. Suddenly the sky was overcast with clouds and rain began to pour down in torrents. The cool breeze and the refreshing rain soothed the burning sensations caused by the Dipak Raga in the body of Tan Sen. The injurious effects of the *Dipak* song did not disappear completely and Tan Sen was confined to bed for more than a quarter year.

Tan Sen, having grown too old, was permitted by Emperor to lead a retired life at Gwalior on a pension of Rs. 2,000/- a month. His four sons were taken as Court musicians by Akbar on handsome salaries. He died at a mature age of 80 years in 1585 A.C. and in compliance with his last wish was buried by the side of his spiritual teacher Hazrat Muhammad Ghaus in Gwalior. A tamarind tree casts its shade over his grave and it is said that chews the leaves of this tree is blessed with a melodious voice.

# SINAN

Muslims are known as the greatest builders in history. Some of the finest and most splendid buildings in the world including the Alhamra and the Mosque of Cordova in Spain; the Taj Mahal of Agra and the Jami Mosque of Delhi; the Mosque of Ibn Tulun in Cairo; the Friday Mosque of Isfahan and the Sulaimaniya and Salimiya Mosques of Istanbul, have been built by Muslims. A large number of magnificent palaces built by Muslims in Cordova, Cairo, Baghdad, Istanbul and Samarkand, have perished due to the ravages of time, or razed to the ground by the later invaders.

The history of architecture is full of the achievements of Muslim architects who raised splendid monuments in different parts of the world. But the greatest among the Muslim architects was Sinan who is credited with erecting 343 magnificent buildings throughout the Ottoman Empire.

Sinan, usually called 'Khudai-Memar Sinan', is universally recognised as the greatest architect of his time and of the Ottoman Empire. He was born on April 15, 1489, in Kaisariya (Anatolia). He was the son of Abdal-Mannan. He became a Janissary in Istanbul. As a Janissary in the Ottoman army, he distinguished himself for bravery in the campaigns against Belgrade in 1521 and Rhodes in 1522. Later he was promoted to the post of Chief Fire-work Operator in the Ottoman army.

During the Persian war, fought by the Ottomans in 1534 A.C., he devised ferries for crossing Lake Van which were very effective and led to the victory of the Turks.

When the Ottoman Sultan Salim I, advanced on Wallachia, Sinan hastily built a bridge across the River Danube which laid the foundation of his rising fame.

Henceforward, he was assigned the task which suited his genius. He was extensively engaged in erecting monumental buildings on orders from the Sultan and the grandees of the great Ottoman Empire.

After the death of Salim I, he built the Salimiya Mosque on the top of a hill overlooking Istanbul.

Sulaiman, the magnificent, the successor of Sultan Salim I, is credited with raising some of the best monuments throughout the vast Ottoman Empire. These monuments were built by Sinan under orders of Sulaiman.

These include the Mosque of Roxelana (Khasseki Khurram) built in 1539, the Princes' Mosque built in 1548, the Sulaimaniya Mosque built in 1550—56, and the Salimiya Mosque of Adrianople built on the orders of Salim II. These are considered to be his best efforts.

In addition to these, Sinan is credited with erecting numerous mosques, palaces, schools, bridges and baths, etc. His biographer, poet Mustafa Sai, gives a list of 81 mosques, 50 chapels, 55 schools, 7 Quran Schools, 16 kitchens for the poor, 3 infirmaries, 7 aqueducts, 8 bridges, 34 palaces, 13 rest houses, 3 store houses, 33 baths, 19 domed tombs, totalling 343 buildings built by the famous architect, Sinan, during a period of three quarters of a century in a region extending from Bosnia to Makkah.

Sinan displayed an incomparable lightness of touch in his construction of domes. "On a square, hexagonal octagonal base he developed his interiors, always striving at the effect of a great ceremonial hall, a uniform architecture enclosing the worshipping rulers and their hosts".

Sinan is mostly concerned with the interior of his buildings, sometimes at the cost of their exterior. "But everywhere", says Gurlitt, "appears the peculiarity of Turkish character. Everywhere he creates models which are as little Byzantine as they are Persian, as little Syrian as they are Saljuk, but all the more Turkish". He had a large number of pupils who attained great fame as architects. These included Ahmad Agha Kamal al Din, Daud Agha, Yatim Baba Ali, Yusuf and Sinan, the junior. Yusuf, his favourite pupil, is reputed to be the architect of the palaces at Delhi, Lahore and Agra built by Akbar.

This great Muslim architect, Sinan, breathed his last on July 17, 1578 at the age of 90 years and was buried under the shadow of his masterpiece, Sulaimaniya Mosque of Istanbul.

# BEHZAD

The Mongols who rose from Central Asia and swept over most parts of Eurasia, razing cities, destroying civilizations and massacring a large number of people, later became well-known patrons of art and culture. Samarkand and Bukhara became great centres of art and learning. The Maragha observatory set up by Hulaku Khan, the Mongol, under the guidance of the Encyclopaedist Nasir al-Din Toosi, did much useful researches in astronomy and other branches of science.

The Mongol influence found its way in different branches of Persian art and culture, particularly in painting. The Mongols not only took keen interest in promoting art in the Muslim countries but also brought it into contact with the highly developed painting of the Far East and directed it towards new subjects, thus enlarging the painters' outlook. The main tendency was now the pictorial reproduction of historic events, specially the great national epic of Firdausi and similar poems of Nizami and Kirmani as well as the sentimental lines from Shirin-Farhad, Laila-Majnoon. The captions were no longer Arabic but Persian. The acquaintance of Persian painters with. the work of the Chinese masters resulted in enhancing the feeling of landscape among them.

The enthusiasm which the Persian painters displayed for the pictorial reproductions of important events in their national history and the beauty of their native countryside, gave the Persian painting of the Mongol period a romantic pattern. In this period, the harmony between picture and text reached the highest degree of prefection.

But, "an undeniable weakness of Perso—Mongol painting lies in the diagrammatical conventionalising of figures, the spiritless treatment of the heads and the absence of expression in the movement", observes the Encyclopaedia Britannica. Strangely enough, no progress in this respect was observed in the development of Persian art and a revolutionary personality was needed to make up this deficiency and set things right. This personality was found in the genius of Kamaluddin Behzad who rose to be the greatest master of Persian painting. Behzad was the greatest miniaturist in Persia who reached the summit of his glory and was universally recognised as the greatest master of Persian painting during his lifetime.

Kamaluddin Behzad was born in Herat before 1450 A.C., and died after 1520 A.C. He is said to be a disciple of Amir Ruhullah *alias* Mir Naqqash of Herat. According to another version, Behzad, who had lost his father in his childhood, was a disciple of Pir Syed Ahmad Tabrizi. First of all, he was employed with Mir Ali Sher, Minister of Sultan Husain Mirza. Later he got employment with Sultan Husain Mirza, the last of the Timurid monarchs who, himself possessing versatile taste, was a great patron of artists and scholars. He was made Head of the Herat Academy.

When Tabriz was taken over by Shah Ismail, he invited Behzad to Tabriz and employed him. The Shah was very kind to him, appointed him his Chief Librarian in 1522 and covered him with honours. He was equally honoured during the reign of Shah Tahmasp, successor of Shah Ismail.

He died in Tabriz in 1546-47 and was buried there.

Behzad who represents the zenith of the Mongol and the beginning of the Safawid period in Persian painting was a reformer in treatment of landscapes which are more real and natural in his works. In the choice of subjects, too, he is more realistic than his predecessors. He "understood, how, even in the most populous compositions, to differentiate every single figure in countenance and bearing; his palette was extraordinarily rich, especially in warm, full tones, and this enabled him to individualise his portraits by the employment of numerous colours—nuances for costumes and even for flesh" *(Encyclopaedia Britannica)*. He revolted against the dictates of the calligraphers and admitted no text at all. At times he has given only a few lines of verse at one corner of the illustrated pages.

His works also contain exquisitely drawn double-page miniatures. According to Khan Damir, Behzad possessed great refinement, minute perfection and power of life-like representation. Kazi Ahmad marks his sense of proportion and mentions the excellence of his bird images and avers that he was fluent in charcoal drawings.

Behzad was universally acclaimed as the greatest master of Persian art during his lifetime. He was a great miniaturist. He excels in drawing living figures. He has illustrated many masterpieces of Persian poetry, including that of Nizami. According to the Mughal Emperor Babar, Behzad's art was exceptionally fine. He excelled in drawing bearded faces but not the beardless ones as he exaggerates the length of double chin. *(Babar Nama)*.

The Mughal Emperors of India were great admirers of Behzad's art. They had adorned their libraries and palaces with Behzad's works. They paid Rs. 3,000 to Rs. 5,000 for each picture drawn by Behzad. Emperor Jahangir particularly has great liking for Behzad's art, specially those depicting battle scenes. He adds that Behzad's creations are full of life and his battle scenes are extremely vivid and lively.

Behzad is known for his colour sense and has exquisitely used fine and deep colours in his pictures. He has generally preferred cool colours, namely green and blue particularly in interior scenes but these are always balanced by comparatively warm colours, specially a bright orange. He superbly completes each unit of the design in their proper and natural setting, which fit into a decoratively conceived all-over picture, which is perfectly executed. The branches of trees in bloom, the richly decorated title patterns and the designs on the carpet reveal in particular the artist's decorative sense and the delicacy of his work. Its realism distinguishes it from paintings of previous period.

Behzad has, thus, very faithfully followed nature, giving imaginative touches here and there. He has mostly used green and blue which are nature's colours. He, no doubt, balances these at times, with maroon and orange colours. In the reproduction of human and other figures, he tries to be as natural as possible. But he is not a blind imitator of nature and uses his imagination to make his figures more effective and lively. Kazi Ahmad ranks him above Mani.

His works have mostly been lost. Among his few undisputedly extant works are the *History of Taimur*, illustrated by him in 1467, which was formerly in Schulz collections but later taken to America; an edition of Saadi's *Bostan*, dated 1478 is in the Cairo library and his illustrations of *Leila and Majnun* are kept in the Leningrad Library.

Behzad deeply influenced the realm of painting, particularly in Persia. He had a large number of disciples, both in Herat and Tabriz who carried his style in Persia, Western Turkistan and India. During the 16th century, his fame had travelled far and wide. His art was imitated by all and even the pages of most various origins were furnished with his signature to enhance their value.

Behzad was undoubtedly a genius whose art reached the summit of glory which will continue to inspire generations to come.

# IBN AL-BAWWAB

The absence of figural representation in Islamic art led to an unprecedented development of calligraphy as a decorative art throughout the world of Islam. In almost all periods of Muslim rule, calligraphy has been the favourite art, which has been developed in numerous patterns and floral designs.

The Muslim Rulers and Emperors have taken keen interest in the development of calligraphy, which, besides being used in writing books, has been a favourite art of decoration, especially of architectural monuments. Such monuments, particularly mosques and mausoleums, built throughout the Muslim world, bear exquisite calligraphic inscriptions and floral designs.

Two of the well-known Muslim Rulers of India, Nasiruddin Mahmud (1246–1266 A.C.) and Aurangzeb Alamgir (1656–1705 A.C.), were good calligraphists who used to transcribe the Holy Quran for their livelihood.

The Mughal rule is particularly known for the development of calligraphic art in India. Almost all the splendid monuments erected by the great Mughals, including the world famous Taj Mahal, the famous Juma Mosque of Delhi, the Pearl Mosque in the Delhi Fort, the Badshahi Mosque of Lahore, the tombs of Mughal Emperors Humayun, Akbar, Jahangir and Shah Jahan, bear exquisite patterns of calligraphic art.

The history of calligraphy in the Muslim world dates back to earliest period of Islamic era when Arabic was written in *Kufic* script. *Kufic* character originated two centuries before Islam and was used in oldest Arabic documents, coins and inscriptions. For nearly five centuries, the *Kufic* script was popular, though it was artificial as well as awkward. The Holy Quran of early period has been written in *Kufic* script which continued up to the 10th century A.C.

From the beginning of the 11th century, *Naskh,* a rounded script of rather level ductus with orthographic marks was introduced in transcribing the Holy Quran. This script received the final shape by the beginning of the 10th century and was perfected a hundred years later. By and by it was developed to such a degree of perfection that it outclassed and later replaced the *Kufic* script.

The third and the most popular script *Nastaleeq*, was developed by the Iranian calligraphers during the 13th century A.C. It was used mostly for writing Persian works. The *Nastaleeq* script, was developed in Persia with rounded circles and a more formal and correct symmetry. The *Nastaleeq* style was beautiful and fluent, but the scribes needed much time and patience to give full shape and form to circular letters.

It, therefore, gave birth to another variation called *'Shikasta'* which is broken in style and later on to another form, *Shafia*, named after the scribe of that name. *Shikasta* was also called *Khatt-i-Diwani* (Civic script) in India. Urdu adopted the *Nastaleeq* and Sindhi the *Naskh* script. These attained great popularity during the reign of the Mughal Emperor Jahangir, whose Court calligrapher Mirza Muhammad Husain won great fame in it and has left behind many masterpieces.

Almost all ruling Muslim dynasties had their own calligraphers but the greatest among them has been Ibn al-Bawwab, Ahmad Suhrawardy and Yaqut al Mustasimi whose works are recognised as marvels of this art.

Abul Hasan Aladin Ali ibn Hilal, better known as Ibn al-Bawwab, the celebrated Arab calligrapher was a porter's son of the Audience Hall of Baghdad. He was also called Al-Sitri and died in 1022 A.C.

He was buried beside the tomb of Imam Ahmad ibn Hanbal.

Ibn al-Bawwab is recognised as one of the greatest Arab calligraphers, whose works are viewed with great admiration and considered marvels of the Calligraphic Art.

He had wide knowledge of Islamic law, had learnt the Holy Quran by heart and wrote out 64 copies of the Holy Book. One of these copies, he wrote in *Kihani* script which is preserved in the Laleli Mosque of Constantinople (Intanbul). It was presented to this mosque by the Ottoman Sultan Salim I.

The *Diwan* of the pre-Islamic Poet Salma ibn Jandal, copied by him, is extant in the Library of Aya Sofia (Istanbul).

Ibn al-Bawwab had invented the *Kihani* and *Muhakkik* scripts. He founded a School of Calligraphy in Baghdad which survived to the time of Yaqut al-Mustasimi, another great Arab calligrapher, who died in 1298 A.C.

# BUNDOO KHAN

The spacious hall of the Muir Central College of Allahabad University was packed to its capacity. Musicians as well as listeners from all parts of the subcontinent had assembled to participate in the All-India Music Conference held in 1935. The stage was occupied by a galaxy of outstanding musicians *(Ustads* and *Kavis)* including Faiyyaz Khan, the Sun of Indian Music, Abdul Karim Khan, Mushtaq Husain and Bare Ghulam Ali Khan, the star singers and Alauddin Khan, the talented *Sitar* player. Ustad Faiyyaz Khan had finished a solo recital of vocal music and the atmosphere in the Hall was tense with excitement. Meanwhile, an unimpressive, frail-bodied musician with a small wooden instrument hung across his shoulders, was seen climbing up the platform. He squatted on the carpet and started tuning his small stringed instrument. Those who did not know him, laughed at his coming after Faiyyaz Khan, the Star musician of the subcontinent. He started playing on his *Sarangi* (a stringed wooden instrument) in low tones, steadily raising it, till he reached the zenith of his performance. His hand holding the bow moved with mechanical rapidity and the instrument began to emit fire all around. The entire audience seemed to be spell bound. The old enchantment hovered over the stage casting a mesmeric spell over the listeners, who were brought to their senses only when the performance came to an end. This instrumentalist was Ustad Bundoo Khan, whose solo performance of *Sarangi* thrilled the audience and according to Wordsworth:

"The music in my heart I bore
Long after it was heard no more."

It was Bundoo Khan's unique performance long remembered by the listeners' as Shelley has righly observed :

"Music when soft voices die?
Vibrates in the Memory !

Among the luminaries in the realm of classical music in the subcontinent during the present century who could draw and keep huge audiences spell bound for hours together, Ustad Bundoo Khan occupies an eminent place. From a gifted *Sarangi* player living in penury once, he became one of the most talented instrumentalists of the subcontinent. Bundoo Khan's is a dramatic life story. Endowed with many attributes essential for a successful musician, he combined in him the rare qualities of musical lineage, inherent taste, intelligence, musician-ship, devotion and determination, which enabled him to rise to the great heights of professional ability and popularity.

The classical music in the subcontinent is passing through a transitional stage. The era of the great legendary *Ustads,* the princely patronage and of marathon recitals lasting for hours, is giving place to concerts and film music. But this vanishing era is of colour and romance in which the musicians brought to the art of music a dedication and a great deal of gracefulness. It is hard to forget the performances of the late Abdul Aziz Khan of Patiala, the great *vichitra-veena* player, of Inayat Khan *Sitaria* of Faiyyaz Khan, the vocalist and above all of Bundoo Khan, the veteran *Sarangi* player. They gave the vocation of music a heroic mould and trailed clouds of glory wherever they went.

Born in a family of traditional musicians of Delhi in 1882, Bundoo Khan got his early training in music from his father Ali Jan Khan, a well-known *Sarangi* player. But the man who was mainly instrumental in raising Bundoo Khan to such great heights of instrumental music was his maternal uncle and later father-in-law, Mamman Khan, the veteran *Sarangi* and *Sursagar* player.

The story of the musical training of Bundoo Khan is a story of devotion, perseverance and endurance for the sake of art. He made pilgrimages throughout the country learning the art wherever available. A glance at his life shows his mastery by a rare combination of talent and perseverance. Starting his training at an early age of 8, his musical gifts were evident at an amazingly early age. According to his maternal uncle Mamman Khan, the musical training in his family started from the day a child was born. Their family house used to be a conservatory of music wherein one corner a vocalist was seen singing and in another an instrumentalist was found practising on his musical instrument. This practice continued throughout the day and these strange sounds reached the ears of the newly-born child, who developed a taste for music from his very infancy.

Bundoo Khan started his training in music at an early age of 8 and completed it at the age of 20. He states: "I practised hard day and night at the cost of my sleep. Music became the sole aim of my life. All my miseries and joys were engrossed in music".

The young Bundoo Khan once demonstrated his skill before a selected gathering of family members. Flushed with success, the young musician expected praise from his *ustad* (master), but Mamman Khan remained unmoved. This non-appreciation disheartened him momentarily, but soon led him to greater efforts towards perfection of his art. He practised hard and a few months after, when he gave a solo performance of instrumental music before a special audience, he thrilled his master beyond imagination. Mamman Khan embraced the young musician with joy saying, "My son! now you have learnt the intricacies of this art. Music requires refinement of taste. However expensive a dish may be, unless it is tasty, it is useless". Bundoo Khan was hardly 13 at the time.

Bundoo Khan attached to the princely Court of Indore and remained there for 27 years. He studied Sanskrit in order to have access to classical music of ancient India. His devotion to music had impaired his health. The only thought which haunted him consistently was—How to attain perfection in his art. He had lost his sleep. Whenever he passed through the streets of Delhi, he had his *Sarangi* hung across his shoulders hidden under a sheet worn by him. In the way he continuously moved his thin fingers over the strings of the little instrument.

Bundoo Khan was a maestro, universally respected by all classes of musicians. He accompanied all the great singers of his time, including Aladiya Khan, Allabande Khan, Abdul Karim Khan, Bare Ghulam Ali Khan and Faiyyaz Khan. They considered it a privilege to be accompanied by him. He would never let a soloist down. It was a pleasure to watch him playing on his instrument. A stream of music seeming to emanate from his little instrument flowed into the hearts of the listeners, transporting them to a state of ecstasy in which they lost all sense of time and space. He seemed to be so much absorbed in his art that in moments of deep exultation, he partially closed his eyes and instinctively sung with the instrument. His dreamy eyes together with the enchanting music cast a spell over the listeners.

Music demonstrates diverse moods—sorrow or delight, fury of serenity, exultation or ecstasy. An experienced musician demonstrates these diversities to his advantage at different moments. Bundoo Khan knew this secret of success, hence his demonstration was never boring. Every time he played the same tune in a different way, which gave freshness to his art. Once questioned about the secret of his success, he said : "Each *rag* mirrors a different feeling. If it is a good piece of music, do not expect it to mean the same thing to you each time you listen to it". The change of his tunes was at times deceptive, involving among other intricacies the sudden switching from slow ones to incredibly fast ones.

He introduced many musical innovations. He introduced what is known as *'Meendh soot ki Sargam'*, in which the musician in the midst of recurring moledy shifts from one note to another with bewildering alacrity.

Bundoo Khan was a mobile encyclopaedia of music. He had mastered more than 500 *rags* (tunes), with their intricacies and differences, while hardly any oriental musician could master more than 50 *rags*. Bundoo Khan's achievement in this sphere of musical art looks extraordinary. He possessed a brilliant memory and explained the differences of the *rags* in special musical demonstrations.

But the greatest achievement of the maestro lay in his making an insignificant instrument like *Sarangi* into *Sau-rangi* (hundred tuned instrument) a powerful musical instrument which could produce diverse tunes. This wonderful instrument in which he combined different musical instruments and could produce all sorts of tunes, bear the unmistakable stamp of his genius. Like harmonium and piano, he introduced tapping in this new instrument. He used an incredibly small *Sarangi* with steel strings instead of gut. Once questioned by a Hindu vocalist about the usefulness of the insignificant instrument carried by him, Bundoo Khan retorted, "I can make any piece of wood speak, if I so desire".

There was hardly a musical form he did not attempt on his little instrument whose tune was smooth and silvery, which cast a hypnotic spell over the listeners. "His name will always be associated with the *Sarangi*", says a well-known writer on classical music, "as the name of Casals is associated that of *cello,* of Segovia with the *guitar,* of Wande Landowska with *harpsichard,* of Lionel Tertis with the *viola*". Each one of the abovementioned musicians was responsible for the emancipation of his instrument. Bundoo Khan, too, raised the insignificant *Sarangi* from a position of subservience to human voice into an important *solo* instrument. Throughout his life his dear *Sarangi* rarely left him. At home in his daily outings and even during his sleep this little instrument was always found beside him. Even during the closing years of his long life he devoted a major part of his leisure time in practising on sarangi.

Bundoo Khan was also a musical theorist. His book, *Jauhar-i-Mausiqi* known in Hindi as *Sangeet Vivek Darpan,* was published both in Urdu and Hindi languages in June 1934. Dealing with classical music of the subcontinent, it elicited high appreciation from all classes of classical musicians.

As a man, Bundoo Khan was gentle, amicable and unassuming. He was simple like a child and humble like a saint. He was generous to a fault. Unlike most of the assuming orthodox musicians who are reluctant to part with the secrets of their art, Bundoo Khan gave out his art and his mind freely. Throughout his life he never missed an engagement.

He was a man of sterling qualities. Unlike other artists of his class, he never cared for worldly wealth and prosperity. Despite the persuasions of the late Sardar Patel, Home Minister of India, and the offer of Rs. 1,200 a month made by the All-India Radio, he preferred a life of poverty in Pakistan, the land of his dreams, living as a refugee in a small house in Lalu Khet, Karachi, till his death on January 13, 1955. With him snapped another link with the past. His death created a void in the classical music of the subcontinent which would hardly be filled in the near future.

# REFORMERS, REVOLUTIONARIES AND PATRIOTS

# THE SAINT OF SIRHIND

The Durbar Hall of the Mughal Emperor Jahangir was packed to its capacity. The Emperor was seated on his golden throne studded with precious stones, placed on a raised marble platform, attended by his Ministers and Courtiers flanking the passage leading to the Throne. All eyes were directed impatiently towards the entrance. The Emperor had summoned to his presence a person known as a dangerous religious reformer. At the appointed hour a slim and lanky person in the attire of a dervish advanced in measured steps towards the Throne. All eyes turned towards him till he reached the Throne and did not make the customary obeisance of kissing the floor before the Emperor, whereupon the Vizier standing beside the Emperor cried out :

"Make obeisance and kiss the floor. You are in the august presence of Emperor Jahangir."

"No", replied the visitor firmly. "This head which bows before Almighty God can never bow before any mortal."

A wave of resentment swept the audience and after a few cross questionings, the Emperor ordered the visitor who was no other than the Saint of Sirhind himself to be thrown into the Gawalior prison.

Sheikh Ahmad Farooqi of Sirhind, better known as Mujaddid Alif-i-Sani, also styled as Imam Rabbani, lived at a time when Islam faced the greatest threat to its existence in India due to the irreligious practices of the Mughal Emperor Akbar who, with his grotesque religious innovations, including the introduction of "Deen-i-Elahi", had considerably weakened Islam, thus striking at its very foundation. In such an atmosphere was born Sheikh Ahmad who boldly faced the mighty Emperor and his misguided associates, and restored Islam to its pristine glory. His courageous stand for the purification of Islam by ruthless and fearless campaigning against the irreligious practices introduced by Akbar, set an example to the future generations of Muslims to fight against any encroachment on their great religion.

Sheikh Ahmad Farooqi, Reformer of the Second millenium of the Hejira Era and universally acclaimed as the Saint of Sirhind, was born in 1564 at Sirhind, a town in East Punjab. His family originally belonged to Madina and his great ancestor was Hazrat Abdullah ibn Umar Farooq. From Madina his ancestors migrated to Kabul and thence to Samana in the Patiala State. His father Sheikh Abdul Ahad was reputed for his high learning and religious background. Sheikh Ahmad was his fourth son. After receiving his early education from his father, he proceeded to Lahore and Sialkot for higher education. At Sialkot he obtained religious education from such reputed scholars as Maulana Kamaluddin Kashmiri and Maulana Yaqub Kashmiri. Another well-known scholar of the time, Qazi Bahlol Badakhshani taught him jurisprudence. *Sirat* and history.

Having been well versed in worldly education at an early age of 17, Sheikh Ahmad diverted his attention towards spiritual education. He was initiated into the Qadiriya System by his father and later by Shah Sikandar. On his father's death in 1007 A.H. he became the disciple of Khwaja Baqi Billah, a great mystic saint of Delhi, who appointed him his lieutenant in Sirhind.

In one of his letters, the Saint writes about Sheikh Ahmad : "In Sirhind is a person Sheikh Ahmad by name whose knowledge is extensive and whose will power is immense. For a few days he was with me. I chanced to observe very strange things from the way he behaved and passed his days. I hope he would prove such a shining light as would illumine the entire world. He is sure to attain perfection in mysticism and spiritualism which further leads me to confirm what I have said above".

Sheikh Ahmad, too, had great regard for his illustrious teacher. In one of his works, the *Mabda wa Ma'ad*, he writes: "It is my conviction that the company like that of Khwaja Baqi Billah and a training and guidance like the one imparted to us during the time of the Holy Prophet, has not been possible. This is a fit occasion of thankgiving. Although it has not been my good fortune to have been present in the days of the Prophet, yet I have not been deprived of the company of Khwaja Baqi Billah".

Later, Sheikh Ahmad went to Akbarabad (Agra), the seat of the Mughal Empire, where he came into close contact with Faizi and Abul Fazal, the two intellectual luminaries of the Imperial Court, who were highly impressed by his deep knowledge. It is said that once Faizi got stuck up and could not find suitable words for certain Quranic verses in connection with his *Swati-al-Ilham*, the dotless commentary of the Holy Quran. His further progress in this connection had come to a standstill when perchance the Sheikh happened to arrive there and solved the problem without much difficulty. Abul Fazal in his momentous work, *Aeen-e-Akbari*, considers Sheikh Ahmad as one of the intellectual giants of the age. Once Abul Fazal, in his discussion with the Sheikh, used disrespectful language about Imam Ghazali. The Sheikh lost his temper and openly rebuked the powerful Prime Minister for using objectionable remarks against such a well-known *Savant* and until Abul Fazal apologised for his conduct, the Sheikh did not visit him.

The frequent contacts of the Sheikh with the two talented brothers enabled him to acquire first-hand knowledge of the scepticism and irreligiosity pervading the Mughal Court and the two brothers, too, realised the high intellect and indomitable courage of the Sheikh. During his stay at Agra, he wrote several treatises in Arabic and Persian including, *Mabda wa Ma'ad* and *Radd-i-Rawafiz.*

He married the daughter of Sheikh Sultan, a nobleman of Thanesar. He built a Stately Mosque out of the Dowry brought by his wife. He had seven sons from his wife.

He died on December 10, 1624 and was buried in the small town of Sirhind.

During the reign of Mughal Emperor Akbar, Islam in India was at its lowest ebb and its tenets were openly violated. People were encouraged to adopt anti-Islamic ways. The Emperor himself, surrounded by irreligious courtiers, was more inclined towards Hinduism and had promulgated *Deen-e-Elahi* as the state religion which was the negation of some of the basic principles of Islam. The celebrated historian Badayuni in his well-known historical work *Muntakhabat-Twarikh* throws ample light on the un-Islamic activities of Akbar and some of his courtiers. He says: "Public prayers and the *Azan* which was called five times a day for prayer in the state hall, were stopped. Names like Ahmad, Muhammad and Mustafa, etc. were offensive to His Majesty, who thereby wished to please the infidels outside and the princesses (Hindu women) inside the harem till after sometime those Courtiers who bore such names changed them; and names like Yar Muhammad, Muhammad Khan were altered to Rahmat. *(Muntakhabat-Twarikh* by Abdul Qadir Badayuni, Vol. II, page 314). Badayuni further states: "During the Nauroz festivities most of the Ulema, pious men and Qazis were forced to participate in carousals . . . . A separate quarter was built for this legalised adultery in a land of Islam and was named Shaitanpura. He appointed a Keeper, a Deputy and a Secretary for the quarter so that anyone wishing to associate with those wenches or take them home or hire, may do so with the full knowledge of the government officials . . . . . . . The killing of animals on the first day of the week was strictly prohibited, because this day was sacred to the Sun (Vol. II, page 322). A second order was issued by the Emperor that the Sun should be worshipped four times a day. A thousand names of the Sun were diligently collected and Akbar devoutly read them over standing with his face towards the Sun . . . . . The accursed Birbal tried to persuade the Emperor that since the Sun gives light to all and ripens grains and fruits as well as supports human life, therefore this heavenly body should be the object of worship and veneration, that face should be turned towards the rising and not towards the setting Sun, i.e. the West as the Muslims do. He was further told to venerate fire, stones and trees and all other objects of nature even down to the cows and their dung, so sacred to the Hindus . . . . He smeared his forehead with the Hindu marks of tilak at noon and at midnight".

It would be seen that Akbar's policies and way of life were extremely detrimental to the healthy growth of a society based on Islamic principles. Islam met its greatest threat from within during his reign. Its basic principles were not only defied but ridiculed. All opposition was suppressed either by money or by force. This was the proper occasion for the appearance of a reformer who could have the courage to face the onslaughts of a degenerated Imperial system aimed at wiping out all traces of Islamic culture and religion from India. The great reformer who appeared on the scene was Sheikh Ahmad Sirhindi. He boldly faced Akbar. With his indomitable will and incessant efforts, he once more firmly implanted Islam on the Indian soil and established a society based on equality, fraternity and justice preached by Islam. It was primarily due to the great moral and religious influence which Sheikh Ahmad wielded during his lifetime and thereafter, that the Mughal Emperors Jahangir, Shah Jahan and Aurangzeb and the ruling class as a whole came closer and closer to Islam.

The early period of the reign of Jahangir was troublesome for the Sheikh. His increasing popularity in the army and high personages alarmed the Emperor, who was systematically prejudiced against the Sheikh by interested persons. A showdown looked imminent. The Emperor was advised to summon the Sheikh and question him about his views, which, according to the informers, were slowly sowing the germs of revolution and indiscipline in the Imperial army. Accordingly, the Sheikh was summoned by Jahangir who, not being satisfied with the explanation offered by the Sheikh, cast him into Gwalior prison. Earlier, Shah Jahan, a sincere disciple of the Sheikh, had advised him through his associates to perform the customary obeisance before the Emperor, but the dauntless Sheikh flatly refused to do so, saying that such a bow was permitted for Almighty only.

Sheikh Ahmad remained in the Gwalior prison for a year. His exemplary character and teachings revolutionised the life of the criminals who came into contact with him in the jail and became pious Muslims. Sir Thomas Arnold says: "In the reign of Emperior Jahangir (1605—1628), Sheikh Ahmad Mujaddid who was kept in prison converted to Islam several hundred idolators who were his companions in the same prison" *(Preaching of Islam)*.

This solitary confinement of the Sheikh was, according to his own confessions in a letter to one Mir Muhammad Noman, a blessing in disguise which gave him time for meditation and cultivation of other spiritual as well as moral virtues. The haughty Mughal Emperor, at last realized his mistake, set the Sheikh free and bestowed all honours on him. Writing in his *Memoirs* on the 15th anniversary of his accession, Jahangir says: "I called to my presence Sheikh Ahmad who had spent sometime in the prison and set him free. I gave him a *Khilaat* (Robe) and one thousand rupees, with the option to stay at the Court or return to his home. He was fair enough to admit that the chastisement had done him good".

Jahangir abolished the Deen-i-Elahi of Akbar and restored the practice of Shariat Law throughout his realm. Henceforward, Sheikh Ahmad was adviser of the State in all religious matters and was free to preach his Islamic principles among all classes of people including the Imperial forces. His moral teachings had greatly influenced the army and the nobles, who now came closer to the true spirit of Islam.

Jahangir, the Mughal Emperor, had himself requested the Sheikh to remain with the Imperial army. The Sheikh complied and preached true Islam among the troops which greatly contributed to enhancing the morale of armed forces as well as prepared them for their duties towards Islam and the State.

Sheikh Ahmad, the Saint of Sirhind, was an outstanding religious reformer, who amended and rectified some of the wrong doctrines as well as practices introduced among Muslims by sufis. His father had succeeded Abdul Quddus Gangohi as the Chief of the Chishtiya Sect, an office which later on devolved on Sheikh Ahmad. But the austere Saint did not participate in *Sama* practised by this sect. He was all-in-all for the strict enforcement of Islamic Shariat. As regards mysticism, he strongly repudiated, *Wahdat-ul-Wajud* (the unity of existence), the doctrine of mystical unity advanced by Ibn-al-Arabi, the celebrated mystic of Spain.

This doctrine propounded by Ibn al-Arabi was extremely popular among mystics, but it failed to win the approval of orthodox religious teachers as it conflicted with the *Shariat* of Islam. Being an orthodox Muslim, Sheikh Ahmad was against the doctrine of *Wahdat-ul-Wajud* and was in search of a preceptor who could guide him in the matter. This he got in the person of Hazrat Khwaja Baqi Billah, a Naqshbandi Saint of Delhi. Sheikh Ahmad acquired highest spiritual teaching and experience from Hazrat Baqi Billah. Sheikh Ahmad discarded the doctrine of *Wahdat-ul-Wajud* and instead adopted the doctrine of *Wahdat us Shuhud* and developed it with exceptional thoroughness and daring. "According to Sheikh Ahmad", says Dr. Iqbal, "the Alam-i-Amr or the world of directive energy, must be passed through before one reaches that unique experience which symbolises the purely objective".

Imam Rabbani Hazrat Sheikh Ahmad Sirhindi, strove throughout his life to restore Islamic *Shariat* in all its purity among the Indian Muslims who were led astray in the anti-Islamic regime of Akbar and Jahangir. His new doctrine stirred the Muslim masses and narrowed down the gulf between the Ulema and the Sufis (mystics). He boldly practised what he preached and lived up to his convictions when he refused to kiss the ground before the Mughal Emperor Jahangir.

Sheikh Ahmad was a zealous missionary and a revolutionary religious reformer. He wrote epistles to Muslim nobles exhorting them to undo the evil effects of anti-Islamic activities carried on during the regime of Akbar. He campaigned for the full-blooded enforcement of *Shariat* Laws through epistles to nobles, lectures and discourses to the common man. His epistles exist in three volumes, namely (1) *Durul Maarifat* (containing 313 epistles), (2) *Durul Khalaiq* (containing 97 lengthy epistles, and (3) *Maarifat ul Haqaiq* (containing 124 epistles).

The first volume consists of epistles addressed to his teacher Hazrat Baqi Billah and Muslim nobles containing dissertations on religious and intellectual subjects. The second volume contains epistles dealing with tenets of Islam and mysticism. The third volume, compiled after his death contains an epistle addressed to Mughal Emperor Jahangir. His epistles fully bring out not only his spiritual and intellectual abilities but also his courageous stand against a despotic power countenancing irreligious activities. His epistles *(Maktubaat)* fully expose the irreligiosity of the majority of Ulema and their adherence to un-Islamic practices.

In one of his epistles he writes: "In the days gone by, the infidels being in power dominated the Muslims and openly ordered them to observe Hindu customs and injunctions. The Muslims could not practise their faith and if they attempted to do so, they had to pay with their lives. What a pity ! Woe betide the followers of the Prophet, the chosen and most favoured of God, are these days humiliated while the disbelievers are honoured and exalted. Not only this but also the infidels jeer at them, adding insult to injury".

In another epistle he writes: "The infidels are demolishing mosques and converting them into temples and godowns. At Thanesar, a mosque and the shrine of a Muslim saint have been razed to the ground. A large temple has replaced both. The infidels enjoy complete freedom in the observance of their religious rites; the Muslims are inhibited and helpless in the same measure". Such was the state of affairs in the reign of Akbar the Great, who, in the lust for Hindu women, had forsaken all morality, decency and propriety. Jahangir, in his later days, changed his mind, and under the influence of Sheikh Ahmad enforced *Shariat* Law throughout his vast Empire. He came to cherish great regard for the pious Sheikh, who, in one of his epistles, pays tribute to his love for Islam.

Sheikh Ahmad continued to wield great influence long after his death. His teachings as well as his courageous stand against the Mughal power continues to inspire the freedom fighters and his *Urs* (death anniversary) is celebrated with great pomp at Sirhind. Every year the pilgrims flock from all parts of the subcontinent to his shrine at Sirhind to pay homage to one who stood like a rock in the most critical period of the history of Muslim India.

His descendants continued his noble mission. Emperor Aurangzeb is said to have become a disciple of his son, Khwaja Muhammad Masoom.

The great Saint was the founder of Mujaddidiya sub-order which has made invaluable contribution to the enforcement of Shariat (Islamic Law). In his *Kalemaat-e-Tayyaba;* 'Imamul Hind Shah Waliullah of Delhi pays him high tributes, as the leveller of inequalities in Islamic thought, a paragon of spiritual guidance and a revealer of many special realities.'

Allama Iqbal, the greatest Poet-Philosopher of Islam, pays appropriate tributes to the Saint of Sirhind when he says :

"Gardan na jhuki jiski Jahangir ke aage,
Jis ke nafas-i-garm se hai garmi-e-Ahrar
Woh Hind men sarmaya-e-millat ka nigahban
Allah ne bar waqt kia jis ko khabardar."

(Whose neck did not bend before Jahangir and whose breath warms the hearts of fighters for freedom. He was the protector of Islamic faith in India and one who was alarmed by God at the right moment.)

# SHAH WALIULLAH

Dr. Iqbal, the poet of the East, has characterized the celebrated Mughal Emperor Aurangzeb as **"ترکش ما، خدنگ آخریں "** (the last arrow in the quiver of Muslim power in India). The anti-Islamic forces which had raised their head during the reign of the irreligious Emperor Akbar and later found their champions in Jahangir and Dara Shikoh were, to a great extent, checked by Aurangzeb, the most honest, conscientious and able Muslim monarch that ascended the throne of Delhi.

With his passing away in 1707 A.C. started the political chaos which later culminated in the disintegration of the Muslim power in the subcontinent. This political disintegration which was the result of spiritual confusion encompassed the socio-economic spheres also. Aurangzeb's successors were too weak and incapable of facing the rebellious forces emerging on all hands. At such a critical period of Muslim history was born Shah Waliullah, the greatest religious thinker produced by Muslim India who has contributed immensely to the reintegration of the structure of Islam.

Shah Waliullah was born in 1703 A.C. four years before the death of Aurangzeb. His grandfather, Sheikh Wajihuddin, was an important officer in the army of Shah Jahan who supported Prince Aurangzeb in the war of succession. His father, Shah Abdur Rahim, a sufi and an eminent scholar assisted in the compilation of *Fatwa-i-Alamgiri*—the voluminous code of Islamic law. He, however, refused an invitation to visit the Emperor and devoted his energies to the organisation and teaching at 'Madrassa Rahimia—a Theological College which he had established and which, later, played an important part in the religious emancipation of Muslim India and became the breeding ground of religious reformers and *'Mujahids'* like Shah Waliullah, Shah Abdul Aziz, Syed Ahmad of Bareli, Maulvi Abdul Haiy and Shah Ismail Shaheed. Writing about the teachings of Shah Abdur Rahim and his brother, Maulana Ubaidullah Sindhi observes:

"The essence of the teaching of the two brothers was the effort to discover a path which could be traversed together by the Muslim philosophers (the *Sufis* and the *Mutakallim*) and the Muslim Jurists *(Faqih)*".

Shah Waliullah received his early education from his illustrious father, who was his teacher as well as his spiritual guide. Being a precocious child with a retentive memory he committed the Holy Quran to memory at an early age of 7 years. On the death of his father in 1131 A.H. when he was hardly 17 years old he started teaching in his father's Madrassa Rahimiya and carried on the work for 12 years when he left for Arabia for higher studies. He was a brilliant scholar; during fourteen months' stay in Makkah and Madina he came into contact with the outstanding teachers of Hejaz. His favourite teacher was Sheikh Abu Tahir bin Ibrahim of Madina, from whom he obtained his *Sanad* (Degree) in *Hadis* (Tradition). The Sheikh was an erudite scholar, possessing encyclopaedic knowledge; Shah Waliullah benefited much from him too and speaks highly of his piety, independence of judgement and scholarly talents.

During his stay at Makkah, Shah Waliullah had a dream in which the Holy Prophet commanded him to work for the organisation and emancipation of the Muslim community in the subcontinent. He, therefore, returned to Delhi on July 9, 1732 and started his work in real earnest. His was an uphill task in a period when Muslim India was passing through the most critical phase of its history and its entire social, political, economic and spiritual fabric was torn to pieces. On his arrival in Delhi, he started training pupils in diverse branches of Islamic learning and entrusted them with the missionary work of enlightening people with the true nature of Islam. He embarked upon the task of producing standard works on Islamic learning and, before his death in 1762, completed a large number of outstanding works on Islam.

He rose to be a great scholar of Islamic studies, endowed with saintly qualities. So great was his dedication to work that, according to his talented son Shah Abdul Aziz, "he was rarely ill and once he sat down to work after *'Ishraq'* (post-sunrise prayers) he would not change his posture, till midday". He was a real genius, an intellectual giant who set himself to the mission of educating the misguided Muslim masses with the true spirit of Islam. His was the task of the revival of Islam in the subcontinent which had been clouded with mystic philosophy and to bring it out in its pristine glory. He was a humble devotee to his cause, who resisted all temptations of personal glory.

His activities were not confined to spiritual and intellectual spheres only. He lived in troubled times and witnessed during his lifetime about a dozen rulers occupying the throne of Delhi. Endowed with a keen political insight, he observed with deep anguish the breaking up of Muslim power in the subcontinent and wrote to leading political dignitaries like Ahmad Shah Abdali, Nizam ul Mulk and Najibuddaula to stop the rot which had set in the political life of Muslim India. It was on account of his call that Ahmad Shah Abdali appeared on the field of Panipat in 1761 and put an end to the Marhatta dream of dominating the subcontinent.

Shah Waliullah was a prolific writer. It is in the realm of Islamic learning that he made a lasting contribution and within a period of 30 years produced more than 50 works of outstanding merit, both in Arabic and Persian languages. Some of these are still unsurpassed in the whole domain of Islamic literature.

His most valuable service to the cause of Islamic learning was that he codified the vast store of Islamic teachings under separate heads. Both in thought and prediction, his works occupy an outstanding place. As a reformer and as a propounder of theories dealing with socialism, he may be considered as the forerunner of Karl Marx.

His works may be classified into six categories. The first deals with the Holy Quran. It includes his translation of the Holy Book into Persian, the literary languages of the subcontinent of those times. According to him, the object of studying the Holy Book is "to reform human nature and correct the wrong beliefs. and injurious actions". The second category deals with *Hadis* (Traditions) in which he has left behind several works including an Arabic and Persian Commentaries on *Muwatta,* the well-known collection of the Traditions of the Holy Prophet compiled by Imam Malik. He attached great importance to this collection of Traditions by Imam Malik, even greater than those of Imam Bukhari and Imam Muslim. He is an outstanding *Muhaddis* (Traditionist) and links of all modern scholars of *Hadis* in the subcontinent may be traced to him. Foremost among these modern Traditionalists were his son and successor Shah Abdul Aziz and Syed Murtaza Bilgrami. Shah Waliullah wrote a number of books and pamphlets dealing with *Hadis.* The third category deals with '*Fiqh*' or Islamic Jurisprudence, which includes *Insaf-fi-bayan-i-Sahab-al-Ikhtilaf* which is brief but a very interesting and informative history of the Islamic Jurisprudence of the last five centuries. The fourth category deals with his works based on mysticism. The fifth category pertains to his works on Muslim philosophy and *Ilm-al-Kalam.* He also wrote a pamphlet on the principles of '*ijtihad*' (independent interpretation) and *taqlid* (conformity). In his principles of *ijtihad* he clarifies whether it is obligatory for a Muslim to adhere to one of the four recognised schools of Islamic Jurisprudence or whether he can exercise his own judgement. In the opinion of Shah Waliullah, a layman should rigidly follow his own *Imam* but a person well versed in Islamic law can exercise his own judgement which should be in conformity with the practice of the Holy Prophet. But the most outstanding of all his works is *Hujjat-Ullah-il-Balighah* which deals with such aspects of Islam that are common among all Muslim countries. In its introduction he observes : "Some people think that there is no usefulness involved in the injunctions of Islamic law and that in actions and rewards as prescribed by God there is no beneficial purpose. They think that the commandments of Islamic law are similar to a master ordering his servant to lift a stone or touch a tree in order to test his obedience and that in this there is no purpose except to impose a test so that if the servant obeys, he is rewarded, and if he disobeys, he is punished. This view is completely incorrect. The Traditions of the Holy Prophet and the consensus of opinion of those ages, contradict this view".

The sixth category deals with his works on Shia—Sunni problem which had become somewhat acute in those days. His writings on this subject have done a great deal in simplifying this problem. His theories pertaining to economics and socialism are of revolutionary nature and he may be considered as the precurser of Karl Marx. Writing about his works in the *History of the Freedom*

*Movement,* Sheikh Muhammad Ikram states: "Shah Waliullah wrote learned works and initiated powerful and beneficial movements, but perhaps no less important are the invisible qualities of approach and outlook, which he bequeathed to Muslim religious thought in the Indo—Pakistan subcontinent. His work is characterized by knowledge, insight, moderation and tolerance, but the quality on which he laid the greatest emphasis, in theory and in practice, was *Adl* or *Adalat* (justice, fairness, balance). His works and views bear ample testimony to the ways he observed this principle in practice and he lost few opportunities of emphasising in theory its role in maintaining the social fabric".

Shah Waliullah introduced several reforms in religious and economic spheres. He was first to translate the Holy Quran in a popular language, a practice which was later usefully followed by others. His own son, Shah Abdul Aziz, translated the Holy Book into Urdu, the language of Muslim masses in India. There had been a conflict between orthodox Islam revived under Mujaddid-Alif-Sani, championed by Aurangzeb and heterodoxy introduced by Akbar and championed by Dara Shikoh. The reign of orthodox Aurangzeb had created aversion to Sufism and had led to the advent of extreme puritanism. Shah Waliullah struck a mean between the two extremes and retained the virtues of both.

He was born in an atmosphere deeply imbued with the spirit of Sufism. His father was a well-known Sufi. In his early age, he came under the influence of Ibn Taimiya, a great religious reformer. During his stay in Hejaz, he came into contact with scholars who were influenced by Wahabism. This provided a check to his blind following of Sufism. But unlike Wahabis, he did not totally discard Sufism. He was aware of the services rendered by Sufis in popularising Islam in the subcontinent and the spiritual self developed by the truly Islamic from of Sufism. But he was highly critical of the decadent and traditional form of Sufism which borders on the verge of asceticism and is, therefore, averse to true Islam. In his *Wasiyat Nama* (Will) he observes: "And the next advice *(Wasiyat)* is that one should not entrust one's affairs to and become a disciple of the Saints of this period who are given to a number of irregularities". Shah Saheb had urged for the reform and discipline of Sufism and not its rejection. He wrote several pamphlets on this subject in which he analysed the evils and virtues of Sufism. "With these books", writes Maulana Manazir Ahsan, "the disputes between the Sufis and the Ulema, provided one is just, come to an end. By giving an Islamic interpretation to the Sufi doctrines, Shah Waliullah removed the distaste which the Ulema had felt for Sufism and the Sufis". Shah Waliullah had, therefore, not only bridged the gulf between the Sufis and Ulema but also harmonised the differences prevalent among different sects of Sufis. His principles on the subject were put into practice in the great Theological College of Deoband, which had among its patrons such well-known Sufis like Maulana Rashid Ahmad Gangohi and Maulana Ashraf Ali Thanvi.

Shah Waliullah set upon the mission of reforming the social and political order of his day. Being a realist, he diagonised the ills which had entered into the body politic of Muslim society and suggested remedies. He criticised the un-Islamic customs which had crept into Muslim society due to its contact with Hinduism. He was particularly against excessive extravagance in marriages, festivals and other ceremonies. He advocated the remarriage of widows. He carefully analysed the factors responsible for the economic degeneration of Muslim society during his time and proposed radical changes in the economy of Muslim society. He advocated wider distribution of wealth on socialistic lines and in this way became the forerunner of Karl Marx. In an illuminating chapter of *Hujjat-Ullah-il-Baligah,* he outlined the evils of capitalism which brought about the fall of the Roman and Sassanid Empires. He is highly critical of the economic exploitation of the poor, which, in the past, had brought about many revolutions and is the root cause of all troubles and unrest in the world. He even criticised the Mughal rulers and nobility for their indolence and luxury. Addressing the rapacious nobility of his time he observes: "Oh *Amirs!* Do you not fear God? (How is it that) you have so completely thrown yourself into the pursuit of momentary pleasures and have neglected those people who have been committed to your care! The result is that the strong are devouring the (weak) people. . . . . All your mental faculties are directed towards providing yourself with sumptuous food and soft-skinned women for enjoyment and pleasure. You do not turn your attention to anything except good clothes and magnificent palaces".

Shah Waliullah was of the opinion that intellectual revolution should precede political change. He did not contemplate a change with political or social set-up through a bloody revolution, He wanted to bring revolutionary change in the society through peaceful means. In his well-known book, *Izalat-al-Khifa,* he discusses the ideology of political revolution which he envisaged.

No scholar of Mediaeval India had understood the various aspects of civics as had been done by Shah Waliullah. He considered "selfconsciousness" as a prerequisite of "political consciousness". He has dealt in detail the factors which contribute towards the growth of civil consciousness in his immortal work *Hujjat-Ullah-il-Baligah.*

Shah Waliullah was, perhaps, the only Muslim scholar of Mediaeval India who realised the importance of economics in a social and political set-up. He advocated the maintenance of economic equilibrium in the society and strongly criticised the accumulation of wealth which leads to all sorts of evils in the world. He had visualised a social order based on economic equality, fraternity and brotherhood which are the principles governing Islamic socialistic practices during the time of the pious Caliphs.

Born in an age of decadence and chaos, Shah Waliullah strove for a world of peace and prosperity. He has made a singular contribution to the socio-economic thought of Mediaevel India and visualised a Muslim society in which the individual enjoyed the fullest freedom, consistent with the maximum good of all. In such an ideal Islamic state, the ruler was to be governed by the Holy Quran and *Sunnah.* No economic exploitation was to be tolerated in such a state and the individual was free to earn his living by fair means.

His seminary, Madrassa Rahimiya became the centre of Islamic Renaissance in the subcontinent, where scholars flocked from the four corners of the country and after being trained, became the torch bearers of freedom movement in the subcontinent. The "Madrasa" in fact, had become the nucleus of the revolutionary movement for the reconstruction of religious thought in Islam. It produced many zealous workers who carried on their preacher's mission with a missionary zeal. Among these were Maulana Muhammad Ashiq of Phulat, Maulana Noorullah of Budhana, Maulana Amin Kashmiri, Shah Abu Saeed of Rai Bareli and his own son, Shah Abdul Aziz who was initiated into the religious and political philosophy of his father.

Shah Waliullah played a vital role in the Indian politics of his times. He was greatly instrumental in forging a united Muslim front against the rising Marhatta power which was threatening the last vestige of the Muslim power in northern India. It was he who wrote to Najibuddaula, and Nizam ul-Mulk and finally invited Ahmad Shah Abdali who inflicted a crushing defeat on the Marhattas in the Third Battle of Panipat in 1761. His letter to Ahmad Shah Abdali inviting him to take up arms against the menacing Marhatta power in India is one of the most important historical documents of the 18th century. It surveys the political situation in the subcontinent and the dangers which Muslim India faced from different quarters. He had chosen the most vivid, capable and disciplined Muslim leaders of his time for combating the Marhattas. Among these were Najibuddaula, the leader of the redoubtable Rohilas and Ahmad Shah Abdali, the ruler of the brave Pathans. His efforts towards forging a united front against the Marhattas were successful and the defeat of Marhattas in the Third Battle of Panipat in 1761 provided a turning point in the history of the subcontinent.

Shah Waliullah visualised an ideal State of the days of Pious Caliphs and strove to revive it. Analysing his political thought, Iqbal states:

"The prophetic method of teaching, according to Shah Waliullah, is that, generally speaking, the law revealed by a prophet takes especial notice of the habits, ways and peculiarities of the people to whom he is specifically sent. The Prophet who aims at all-embracing principles, however, can neither reveal different peoples nor leave them to work out their own rules of conduct. His method is to train one particular people and to use it as a nucleus for the build up of a universal *'Shariat'*. In doing so he accentuates the principles underlying the social life of all mankind and applies them to concrete cases in the light of the specific habits of the people immediately before him". *(Reconstruction of Religious Thought in Islam).*

The movement of political as well as spiritual regeneration of Muslim India did not die with Shah Waliullah. His talented son, Shah Abdul Aziz, and his worthy disciples and successors, strove for the realisation of his mission. The torch of Islamic revival kindled by Shah Waliullah was kept aloft by his worthy successors. The echo of the Third Battle of Panipat was heard in the Battle of

Balakot. Both form the landmarks of the same struggle. His followers and successors carried on the mission of their master with missionary zeal, both in political and intellectual spheres.

Shah Waliullah possessed a many-sided and versatile personality. His real greatness lies in the cumulative effect produced by his writings, by the contribution of persons trained by him and by the achievements of the school of thought founded by him. In religious matters he struck a mean between extremes, in social affairs he strove to introduce in the Muslim society the simplicity and purity of early Islam; in the sphere of economics he advocated the revolutionary Islamic socialism and in the political field he forged a united Muslim front against the non-Muslim forces which were threatening to storm Muslim India.

# SHEIKH ABD AL-WAHHAB

The passing away of the Khilafat-e-Rashida (the Caliphate of Pious Caliphs), the glorious democratic rule in the history of Islam, provided a serious setback to the spiritual growth of Islam. The material advancement, no doubt, continued and boundaries of the Muslim states expanded on all directions bringing new realms within their fold, but the spirit which guided the actions of Pious Caliphs was gone. The spiritual glory was replaced by material progress.

The advent of Omayyads, provided a death blow to the spiritual democratic rule witnessed during Khilafat-e-Rashida. Instead, a hereditary despotic monarchy in the name of Khilafat-e-Banu Umayya was introduced by the Umayyads in which *Baitul-Mal* (Public Treasury) was at the mercy of the rulers who used it as they wanted in furthering their nefarious ends and in maintaining their pomp and show. The nobility of Islam perished in their encounters with Umayyads, like Yezid ibn Ziyad and above all Hajjaj bin Yusuf, one of the greatest tyrants of all ages, on whose death the Saint of Basra, Hasan Basri, thanked God for relieving Muslims of such a 'Scourge'.

The Abbasides who succeeded Omayyads attained an unprecedented standard of pomp and glory. They were, no doubt, responsible for an unparalleled advancement of learning and culture, science and arts during the Mediaeval Ages, but they were much influenced by the Persian culture which had crept into the diverse walks of life of the Abbaside Metropolis, Baghdad. The introduction of Persian culture among the Arabs gave birth to many evils, including the advancement of mysticism of the Platonic type, which popularised the worshipping of Saints and their graves by the Muslims. The dynamic worldly life led side by side with the spiritual devotion as preached and practised by the Holy Prophet of Islam and his worthy Companions was replaced by the pessimism and negative spiritualism of Mystics who laid all emphasis on the world hereafter.

This pollution of Islamic spirit and thought reached a high pitch in a number of Muslim states, including India, where all sorts of irreligious and superstitious Hindu practices were adopted by the Muslims. The illiterate Mughal Emperor Akbar, who has been acclaimed as "Akbar, the Great" by the non-Muslim historians, had adopted many Hindu rituals and practices in his State and had introduced a new religion, 'Deen-e-Elahi', which could hardly fetch more than a few followers, including the Faizi brothers, and met its natural death on the passing away of its sponsor.

Arabia, the birth place of Islam, was languishing in a neglected state since the downfall of the Abbasides. The Arabs, torn by strife and tribal rivalries, had lost their spiritual as well as material progress. In such a gloomy atmosphere was born in 1703 A.C. in Najd, a great Muslim visionary and reformer, Sheikh Muhammad Abd al-Wahhab, who later became the pioneer of Muslim puritan movement, aimed at restoring Islam to its pristine glory. The Wahhabi Movement aimed at purifying Islam of the unhealthy and superstitious practices which had crept into it due to its contacts with non-Islamic influences.

Abd al-Wahhab, belonging to Banu Sinan, a branch of Tamim was born in 1703 A.C. at Uyaina, a place now in ruins. He studied at Madina under Sulaiman al-Kurdi and Muhammad Hayat al-Sindi, both of whom detected in this promising young man, the signs of *'Iitihad'*. Later, he spent many years in travels, four years in Basra and five years in Baghdad, one year in Kurdistan, two years in Hamdan and four years in Isfahan, where he studied the Mystic and Ishrakiya philosophy. Returning to Uyaina, he spent about a year in speculation. Thereafter, he publicly preached his doctrines as set forth in his *Kitab al-Tauhid*. Initially, he met with some success but much opposition, mostly from his own relations, including his brother, Sulaiman, and his cousin Abdullah bin Husain. His views attracted attention outside Uyaina. He left alongwith his family his ancestral place and was received at Dariya, where the Chieftain Muhammad bin Saud accepted his doctrine and undertook its propagation.

Within a year of his arrival at Dariya, Abd al-Wahhab won the assent of almost all the inhabitants of the town. He built a simple mosque there with a floor of uncarpeted gravel. His doctrine won more and more of adherents. His patron, the Saud family, was involved in a war with other chieftains lasting for 28 years. During this period Ibn Saud and his son Abd al-Aziz, a capable General, were steadily winning ground. In 1765, Ibn Saud died and was succeeded by his son, Abd al-Aziz, who retained Abd al-Wahhab as his spiritual guide.

The Wahhabi Theology is mainly based on the teachings of Ibn Taimiya and its jurisprudence on the Hanbali *Fiqh*. Its fundamental principles are: (1) Absolute Oneness of God, hence its followers call themselves *Mowahhidin;* (2) Return to the original teachings of Islam as incorporated in Holy Quran and Traditions; (3) Inseparability of faith from action like prayers, alms-giving; (4) Belief that Quran was uncreated; (5) Literal belief in Quran and Traditions; (6) Belief in predestination; (7) Condemnation of all non-orthodox views and act; and (8) Establishment of the Muslim State on Islamic Law exclusively.

The Wahhabis are distinguished from all other Muslims by their emphasis on oneness of God and their practice of admonishing Muslims to do good and avoid evil.

The name of Wahhabi was given to this community by its opponents which was later used by Europeans. In fact, they call themselves *Mowahhidin,* or unitarians and their system as "Tarika Muhammadi". Their theology was based on the teachings of Ibn Taimiya who criticised the cult of saints and condemned the visits to tombs. The aim of Abd al-Wahhab was to do away with all the innovations *(Bida)* that were adopted by Muslims later than the Third century A.H. This community acknowledges the authority of four *Sunni* Schools of *Fiqh* and the six books of Traditions. The Wahhabis are against the cult of saints as exhibited in the building of mausoleums, their use as mosques and their visitations. They believe that all the objects of worship other than that of Allah are false. According to them, it is polytheism to seek intercession from any person except Allah. The Wahhabis mosques were built with great simplicity without ornamentation. They destroyed tombs and graves, even at Jannat ul-Baqi, lest these may be worshipped by the non-orthodox and ignorant Muslims.

The *Mowahhidin* (Wahhabi) movement soon spread to other parts of Islamic world, where it had won many adherents. The House of Ibn Saud, exponent of Wahhabi movement, soon conquered almost the entire Arabian peninsula, including the Holy cities of Makkah and Madina. The movement started by Sheikh Abd al-Wahhab found its great champion in the Saudi ruling family and his disciple Sheikh Muhammad Abduh of Egypt rose to be one of the leading intellectuals of the Islamic world. It created a stir throughout the world and was greatly instrumental in uniting the striferidden Arabia under the ruling Saudi family.

In India, the doctrine was introduced by Syed Ahmed Barelvi, who had adopted its puritan views during his pilgrimage to Holy cities in 1822. He established a centre at Patna and acquired a large following. He undertook *Jihad* (Holy war) against the tyranny of Sikhs on the Muslims in the Frontier provinces and liberated most of the province from the Sikh Yoke but ultimately he was killed through a conspiracy of his own men who led the Sikh army through a secret route behind the Muslim lines at Balakot in 1831. His disciple Titoo Mir, started the *Mowahhid* movement in lower Bengal.

The *Mowahhid* movement had been a threat to British rule in the Frontier and Western Punjab till 1871, when the British Government conspired to get *Fatwa* of the Barelvi Ulema to treat Wahhabis as infidels *(kafir)*. A work of Muhammad Ismail known as *Sirat al-Mustaqim* is said to be the Quran of Wahhabis in India.

In India, the well-known Madrassa of Islamic Learning at Deoband, became the centre of *Mowahhid* (Wahhabi) movement in the subcontinent, which produced some of the leading religious scholars of the present century in the subcontinent. The great Muslim visionary Sheikh Abd al-Wahhab died in 1787 A.C. and was buried at Dariya. His mission was carried on by his disciples, which became a powerful Muslim reformist movement during 18–20 century A.C.

# SYED AHMAD BARELVI

The 18th century was a period of extreme decadence of Muslim power in India. On the death of the great Mughal Emperor Aurangzeb in 1707, had started the disintegration of his vast dominions embracing the whole of the Indian subcontinent. His successors were too weak to arrest the process of decadence and disruption besetting it. Not only the Muslim political power had rapidly declined and was soon at its lowest ebb but also their economic, religious and cultural life showed signs of extreme degeneration. The central power which held together the opposing groups and shielded their weakness was itself breaking up. The social contacts with the Hindus gave vogue to many whimsical and un-Islamic customs which struck at the root of the fundamentals of Islam and slowly weakened its hold in India. In such a disruptive and gloomy atmosphere was born Shah Waliullah, a great intellectual reformer, whose teachings paved the way for the renaissance of Islam in India, both in religious and political spheres. Shah Waliullah was followed in his noble mission by his son Shah Abdul Aziz of Delhi and his disciple Syed Ahmad Barelvi, assisted by his associates.

Syed Ahmad was born in a famous Syed family of Rai Bareli, known for its learning and saintlihood. His great grandfather, Maulvi Ilmullah Saheb was highly respected for his deep erudition, purity of life and devotion to God and His last Prophet. He refused to accept any gift even from a puritan like Emperor Aurangzeb and preferred a life of poverty and abstinence. He was very particular about following the *Sunnah* of the Holy Prophet of Islam.

Syed Ahmad, who was born on the 1st of Muharram 1201 A.H. (October 24, 1786), had little inclination towards education during his childhood. He was, however, very fond of manly exercises and passed his time in learning and practising the use of arms.

When fully grown up, Syed Ahmad, along with six companions, proceeded to Lucknow in search of employment. Lucknow, in those days, was the Capital of the Kingdom of Oudh and a great centre of learning and culture in Northern India. But, he did not stay there for long and set out on foot to Delhi in quest of knowledge. After a strenuous journey, he called on Shah Abdul Aziz, a well-known divine of Delhi, who, on being informed of family connections, entrusted him to the care of his brother Shah Abdul Qadir. Syed Ahmad stayed at the

Akbarabadi Mosque of Delhi and studied Quran and Tradition. His spiritual guide Shah Abdul Aziz, initiated him into the *Chistiya, Qadirya* and *Naqshbandiya* orders of Sufism.

After two years' stay at Delhi, which proved a turning point in his life, Syed Ahmad returned home, Rai Bareli, where he was hailed by the people as a divine, known for his exemplary character and simple, pious life.

His stay at Rai Bareli lasted hardly two years, when, at the age of 24, he set out for Tonk to enter the service of Amir Khan. Then followed several years of hazardous life and his participation in several campaigns fought by the Amir, prepared him for his ultimate struggle for the faith which he was destined to lead. His exemplary life and spiritual gifts brought about a transformation among the soldiers of Amir Khan. He was respected by all and had become a trusted Counseller of Amir Khan. When the latter became subservient to the British by accepting the state of Tonk, Syed Ahmad left for Delhi. His freedom-loving spirit could not reconcile itself to the service of a Ruler who was subordinate to an alien power.

In 1815, he again arrived at Delhi. His period of preparation was over. Now he was a matured man of experience possessing rare spiritual gifts. The two outstanding luminaries of Shah Abdul Aziz's family—Shah Ismail, his nephew, and Maulana Abdul Haiy, his son-in-law,—accepted Syed Ahmad as their spiritual guide. His enrolment as a spiritual disciple of these luminaries of the House of Shah Waliullah, enhanced Syed Ahmad's prestige, with the result that people began to flock around him in large numbers for spiritual guidance. His proclaimed objective was to restore Islam to its pristine purity and to cleanse it of all oriental and Hindu influences.

Syed Ahmad did not confine his beneficial activities to Delhi alone. He visited a number of places in Northern India, including Saharanpur, Muzaffarnagar, Deoband, Rampur, Bareli and Shahjahanpur. His two principal lieutenants, Shah Ismail Shaheed and Maulvi Abdul Haiy, known for their eloquence and learning, popularised his mission with exceptional success. The reform movement was in full swing. The tongue of Shah Ismail, the pen of Maulvi Abdul Haiy and the magnetic personality of Syed Ahmad, created a stir throughout Northern India. Their righteous life and spiritual stature and noble mission brought many adherents within its fold. Syed Ahmad, now headed a country-wide organization. Many evils which had crept into the Muslim society were eradicated. Syed Ahmad himself married a widow, which was considered a very obnoxious act, not only by Muslims in general but also by his own family.

During his stay in Rampur, Syed Ahmad came into contact with certain Afghans coming from Kabul, who related to him stories of Sikh atrocities committed on Muslims of North-Western India. The Sikhs had extinguished the religious freedom of Muslims inhabiting that region. They were prohibited from calling '*Azan*' and offering prayers in congregation. Enraged at the brutalities of Sikhs, he resolved to wage *Jihad* against them after his return from the holy pilgrimage to Makkah, whither he proceeded in 1821, accompanied by a large party.

His journey through Allahabad, Benares, Ghazipur, Azimabad (Patna), Monghyr, Bhagalpur, Murshidabad, terminating at Calcutta, was marked with unprecedented enthusiasm and reception. People came in large numbers to have a glimpse of the great Reformer and many became his devoted followers.

From Calcutta, Syed Ahmad and his entourage proceeded to Jedda by sea. His stay in the Holy land lasted for more than one and half years. During this period he came into contact with many renowned Muslim scholars and learnt about many reformatory and revivalist movements in the world of Islam, including Wahhabism.

On his return from the holy pilgrimage, he started preparations for the most important task of his life, *Jihad*, which ultimately ended in his martyrdom at Balakot in 1831. He sent Shah Ismail and Maulvi Abdul Haiy to different parts of the country to inform the people of his intentions to wage a holy war against the Sikhs, in whose territories the life, honour and religion of Muslims, had been gravely threatened. His appeal received an overwhelming response and a large number of persons volunteered themselves for the holy war. Finally, on January 16, 1826, he left home on an arduous journey, never to return. He was accompanied by five to six thousand companions, all prepared to die for delivering their brethren from the tyrannical Sikh rule. The party left for North-Western India by a circuitous route and arrived at their destination at Naushehra after passing through Tonk, Rajputana, Sind, Baluchistan, Qandhar, Kabul, Khyber Pass and Peshawar. This long arduous journey and the hardships of the way—the oppressive heat of Rajputana and Sind, the hazards of brigands and the difficult climbs of the barren hills of Baluchistan, did not diminish their crusading spirit. Wherever they went, they were given thundering ovation by the people, but the Muslim rulers of these areas were hesitant in giving him active support and thus antagonising the Sikhs who formed the most powerful state in Western India.

Syed Ahmad arrived in Naushehra and made it his headquarters in December, 1826.

The stage was now set for the *Jihad*. According to Islamic practice, a proclamation was addressed to the Sikh Ruler, Maharaja Ranjit Singh, who did not pay any heed to it. The Syed, now got ready for an attack on the Sikh forces stationed at Akora and led by Budh Singh, a cousin of Ranjit Singh. The assault took place on December 21, 1826, in which the Sikhs, despite their numerical superiority in men and arms, were completely routed. They retired leaving 700 dead on the battlefield.

But jealousy and rivalry among the tribal chieftains and their irresistible lust for loot hindered Syed Ahmad from accomplishing his mission. Despite the overwhelming superiority of the Sikh army which was disciplined and led by experienced foreign soliders and was equipped with the latest weapons of war, the *'mujahideen'* inflicted on them defeats in several encounters. At one stage Ranjit Singh even sued for peace, but his terms were not acceptable to Syed Ahmad. He, therefore, adopted other tactics. He sowed dissensions among the Pathan supporters of the Syed through bribery and intrigue. He made secret approaches to some of the influential tribal chiefs supporting the Syed, including Yar Muhammad, the Chief of Peshawar, asking them to withdraw their support on promise of concessions. He even warned them that the Syed's victory in the area would mean the domination of the Indian Muslims over the Pathans. Thus, a task which could not be achieved by Sikh arms, was accomplished through the treachery of Muslims themselves.

On the eve of the fateful battle at Saidu Sharif, fought in March 1827, the virtuous Syed was poisoned by the servants of Yar Muhammad. But, the Syed ordered his men to take him to the battlefied. Accordingly, the next morning he was carried to the battlefied in a subconscious state. The battle went on for four days, and despite the enemy's superiority in manpower and equipment, the *Mujahideen* were in a commanding position At a time when victory was in sight, Yar Muhammad, along with his men, deserted the Muslim ranks. This caused a great confusion and consternation among the Muslims. Their victory turned into a rout in which several thousand Muslims lost their lives.

This revealed the organisational weaknesses among the *Mujahideen.* The top leaders of the force resolved to enforce more rigid discipline among the rank and file, who were to be controlled by a central authority responsible for enforcing the *Shariat* rule among them. Syed Ahmad was selected as *Ameer-ul-Momineen.* The treacheries and hostilities of some of the tribal chiefs led to several skirmishes with the *Mujahideen,* in which Yar Muhammad Khan, the Chief of Peshawar, and Khadi Khan, the Chief of Hund, were killed. The *Mujahideen* occupied Peshawar in 1830. But, instead of removing Sultan Khan, brother of the treacherous Yar Muhammad Khan, the Syed retained him as the Governor of the city. He enforced the *Shariat* law throughout the conquered territory. Maulvi Syed Mazhar Ali of Azimabad was appointed as Qazi of Peshawar.

Sultan Khan, Governor of Peshawar, who had been pardoned, was secretly planning to avenge the death of his brother, Yar Muhammad Khan. He organised the mass killing of *Mujahideen.* One night, when the latter were offering their prayers, they were killed by hired assassins. The flower of Muslim chivalry and learning in the subcontinent perished in one night by the conspiracy of a brother Muslim and by the hands of Muslims themselves. This caused great dismay and grief in the Syed's camp. All that had been won was lost in a single night.

Syed Ahmad and his followers, being greatly disappointed with the treachery and hostility of the people inhabiting the Peshawar area, decided to go northward and concentrate their efforts against the Sikhs in Hazara and Kashmir. Arriving at Balakot, a small town in the Kaghan valley, surrounded on three sides by high mountains, he set up his Headquarters there, considering it safe for the *Mujahideen.*

Here, too, the local Muslims spied for the Sikhs and led them through a secret route in close proximity of the *Mujahideens'* camps. Here was fought the last decisive battle in the beginning of May, 1831. The Sikh army far superior in numbers and arms won the day. More than six thousand Muslims perished in the battlefield. The leader of the movement, Syed Ahmad, along with his chief lieutenant, Shah Ismail, died fighting till the end.

Syed Ahmad Shaheed was a great reformer, subscribing to the Shah Wali-ullah School. He kept aloft the candle of religious reformation lit by Shah Waliullah. Though he was not an accomplished scholar like his spiritual teacher Shah Abdul Aziz and his spiritual disciples Shah Ismail Shaheed and Maulvi Abdul Haiy, yet he was a man of action and his simple life and purity of heart inspired awe and respect among his followers. Whoever came into contact with him, was greatly influenced by his magnetic personality. He showed great zeal in denouncing all innovations in Islam, of which the most hated were those associated with the name and Divinity of Almighty God. In his *Sirat-ul-Mushtaqim* he classified such innovations into three categories: those which have sprung through association with corrupt Sufis, those of heretical origin and those which have come through Hindu influences. He exhorted the Muslims not to follow anyone except the Quran and the *Hadis.*

The marriage of widows had begun to be considered obnoxious among Muslims like those of Hindus. Syed Ahmad himself married a widow quite contrary to his family traditions. Lavish expenditures on the occasion of marriage, birth and death, was condemned by him. He denounced tomb-worship, a practice which was a negation of the Islamic doctrine of monotheism. He did not like the Sufis, who led a life of meditation and abhorred social contacts. Instead of making life worth living, such Sufis had preferred to withdraw from it.

Syed Ahmad was himself a Sufi, but not in conformity with its common concept. Instead of passing a life of renunciation, he passed a life of action. His insistence on *Jihad* distinguished him from an average Sufi, who usually believes in a life of meditation and inactivity. He laid greater emphasis on the importance of following the *Sunnah* of the Holy Prophet. According to him, one cannot attain a high spiritual status without strictly following the *Shariat.* He, therefore, accepted the teaching of 'Mujaddid-Alif Sani' in preference to those of Muhiyuddin Ibn-i-Arabi.

Syed Ahmad Shaheed was an idealist, a dreamer of dreams. With his simple straightforward manners, he raised a group of fanatical devouts who were ready to sacrifice their lives for Islam. Among his notable disciples were Shah Ismail

Shaheed, Maulvi Abdul Haiy, Maulvi Wilyat Ali Azimabadi and Maulvi Karamat Ali Jaunpuri. The last named had the distinction of being the greatest Muslim reformer and missionary in Bengal.

Syed Ahmad Shaheed possessed a magnetic personality. Whoever came into contact with him, became his devoted follower. He was the spiritual guide of more than four million followers, among whom were some of the well-known scholars, religious leaders and Sufis of the time.

He was the first popular political leader of the subcontinent, who created a political organisation for furthering his noble mission.

# JAMALUDDIN AFGHANI

During the last thirteen centuries whenever the world of Islam was plunged in the darkness of decadence, an outstanding personality emerged out of it, who, by his illuminating achievements, dispelled the gloom encompassing it. One such personality was Jamaluddin Afghani, the harbinger of Muslim Renaissance in the 19th century A.C. Being a wandering missionary, a versatile genius, an intellectual and orator of the highest calibre, he brought about a universal awakening throughout the world of Islam. He moved about in the capitals of Muslim countries—lecturing, discussing and writing about his mission to bring about the unity of Muslims, leaving behind him a band of zealous workers, who continued his work even after his death. Several movements of religious revival and social reform owe their origin to Afghani and were started by his disciples who were deeply influenced by him. In fact, no other person has influenced the 19th century Islam more profoundly than he. Another great thinker of the East, Dr. Iqbal, pays glowing tributes to Jamaluddin Afghani when he says :

"A pefect master of nearly all the Muslim languages of the world and endowed with the most winning eloquence, his restless soul migrated from one Muslim country to another, influencing some of the most prominent men in Iran, Egypt and Turkey. Some of the greatest theologians of our time, such as Mufti Muhammad Abduh of Egypt, were his disciples. He wrote little, spoke much and thereby transformed into miniature Jamal-uddins all those who came into contact with him"

"He never claimed to be a prophet or a renewer; yet no man in our time has stirred the soul of Islam more deeply than he. His spirit is still working in the world of Islam and no one knows where it will end"

Syed Jamaluddin was born in 1838 at Asadabad (Afghanistan). His father Syed Safdar, a descendent of Syed Ali Al-Tirmizi, later migrated and settled in Kabul. Even at the early age of eight years, Jamaluddin exhibited extraordinary intelligence. Before he was 18, he was well versed in almost all the branches of Islamic learning, including philosophy, jurisprudence, history, metaphysics, mathematics, medicine, sciences, mysticism, astronomy and astrology. His learning was encyclopaedic and his genius was versatile.

Having equipped himself thoroughly in diverse branches of Western and

oriental learning, he set out on his sacred mission of bringing about an awakening in the decaying world of Islam. He entered India, when he was hardly 18 and
roamed about in this country for more than a year, influencing those who came
into contact with him. At this time, India was passing through a critical period
of its history. It was a lull before the storm. The fire of native hatred against
the tyrannical alien rule which had installed itsef as the supreme power in the
country through intrigues and conspiracies, was smouldering slowly and at last
burst forth in May, 1857, in the form of the First War of Independence, in
which the Indians made a united effort to throw off the alien yoke. At this time
when the storm of revolt had engulfed northern India, Jamaluddin Afghani was
in Makkah, where he had gone for pilgrimage.

After performing Hajj (Pilgrimage in Makkah), he went to Kabul. Here
he was welcomed by the Afghan Ruler, Dost Muhammad, who bestowed upon
him an exalted position in his Government. He wielded much influence both
among the Afghan intelligentsia and the masses. On the death of his patron,
the throne of Kabul was occupied by Sher Ali who did not like the progressive
ideas of Jamaluddin. He was, therefore, obliged to leave Kabul.

Leaving Kabul, he proceeded again to Hejaz to perform the Holy Pilgrimage.
He was not allowed to take overland route *via* Persia. He had to travel through
India. In 1869, when he entered India for the second time, he was honourably
received by its Government. But he was not allowed to meet the Indian leaders,
except under the strict eyes of the Government of India. The alien Government
which had a bitter taste of the national upheaval in 1857 was afraid of his
revolutionary progressive ideas, and soon he was despatched in a Government
ship to Suez. He arrived in Cairo. Here he came into contact with the professors
and students of Al-Azhar, who were much impressed by his deep erudition and
high scholarship. He left an abiding impression of his progressive ideas on the
intelligentsia of Egypt which, later appeared in the person of Muhammad Abduh.
Instead of proceeding to Makkah he went to Constantinople (Istanbul), the
Capital of the Ottoman Empire. His learned discourses soon made him extremely
popular among the Turkish intelligentsia. During one of his lectures at the
Constantinople University, the Sheikhul Islam, who had become jealous of his
popularity raised a storm of objections against certain parts of his speech. This
inspired agitation gained momentum and the Ottoman Government had to order
him to leave the Capital for sometime. He, therefore, proceeded to Cairo,
where he arrived for the second time in March, 1871.

During his stay in the Egyptian Capital, Jamaluddin Afghani soon
commanded great popularity and respect among the educated class. His learned
discourses on Muslim philosophy, jurisprudence, religion and sciences couched
in an impressive language and bearing a progressive outlook were listened to with
rapt attention by his ever-increasing audience. His contacts and discourses fired
and a number of young progressive writers and scholars in Egypt with a
missionary zeal.

In the increasing popularity of his progressive ideas aimed at the unity of the Muslim world, the British, who happened to wield much political influence in Egypt at that time, smelled a danger for their divide and rule policy. Their interest lay in the division of the Muslim world and not in its unity—in the narrow-minded nationalism rather than in the pan-Islamism preached by Afghani. The British saw a danger to their evil game. They instigated the orthodox and out-of-date theologians, who raised a storm of agitation against him. This furnished an excuse to the British Governor-General who, it is learnt, advised the Egyptian Government to order the expulsion of Syed Jamaluddin from Egypt.

After a stay of about eight years in Egypt, Jamaluddin Afghani left Cairo in March, 1879, and arrived in Hyderabad Deccan (India). Here he wrote his famous treatise, *Refutation of the Materialists,* which created a stir in the materialistic world.

During this period a nationalist revolt broke out in Egypt in 1882 and the Syed was suspected to have a hand in it. He was summoned to Calcutta by the Government of India and interned there. He was, however, released when the nationalist struggle subsided in Egypt.

He left India and arrived in London, where after staying for a few days only he proceeded to Paris. There he met his life-long associate and disciple, Mufti Muhammad Abduh, who was exiled from Egypt.

The two outstanding celebrities of the Muslim World started their famous Arabic Journal *Al Urwat-ul-Wuthqa,* from Paris. It was an anti-British organ, whose scathing criticisms and fiery articles created a furore in the Imperialist circles and its entry was banned in India. Its expositions of the Imperialist designs in the Muslim East terrified the Western Imperialists who viewed with alarm its growing popularity in the Arabic speaking world.

His activities were not confined to Paris only. He moved about in the continent, contacting important personalities and impressing them with the progressive outlook of Islam. He even went to London and had prolonged discussion on international relations with Lord Salisbury, a high dignitary of Britain. Wherever he went and whomsoever he met, he left a deep impression of his magnetic personality and winning eloquence.

Leaving London, he proceeded to Russia, visited Moscow and St. Petersburg and remained in that country for about four years. He wielded much influence in the intellectual circles of Czarist Russia and enjoyed the confidence of the Czar.

It was through his influence that the Muslims in Russia were permitted to print the Holy Quran and other religious books, whose publications were earlier banned in Czarist Russia. Here, in St. Petersburg, he met Shah Nasiruddin

Qachar, the ruler of Persia. A little later, the Shah met Syed Jamaluddin in Munich, Germany, for the second time. He was so much impressed with his dynamic personality that he offered him the exalted position of Prime Minister-ship of Persia. The Syed hesitated, but yielded due to the extreme persuasion of the Shah.

He arrived in Persia along with the Shah. Soon he began to enjoy great esteem of the Persian masses. His growing popularity among the intelligentsia created apprehension in the mind of the Ruler. The Syed, being an extremely sensitive person, smelled this apprehension and souoht permission to leave the country. But he was not allowed to do so.

Now there was hardly any course left to him. He openly criticised Shah Nasiruddin Qachar and his reign of terror. His vehement denunciation of the autocratic rule in Persia won around him many disciples. He was arrested and deported from Persia. But the fire which he had kindled in Persia could not be put out and culminated in the assassination of Shah Qachar on May 1, 1895.

Syed Jamaluddin Afghani roamed about in Europe, until he arrived in London in 1891. In 1892, he proceeded to Constantinople where he was warmly received by the Ottoman Caliph. He was granted a monthly pension of £ 775 and a free furnished residence. He continued to expose the tyrannical rule in Persia through the press and the platform until the Persian Government appealed to the Ottoman ruler to put a stop to this ceaseless venomous propaganda. The Syed discontinued his scathing criticism of the Persian monarchy on a personal request of the Ottoman Caliph. But the words of Jamaluddin Afghani had done their work and, as stated earlier, the autocratic Ruler of Persian was assassinated on May 1, 1895. The Persian Government demanded four persons from the Ottoman Government, whom they suspected of the conspiracy leading to the assassination of the Ruler. One of them was Jamaluddin Afghani. The Ottoman Government surrendered the remaining three, but refused to surrender the Syed.

But Jamaluddin Afghani was not destined to live long. He had an attack of cancer of the jaw in 1896 and died on March 9, 1897. He was buried with great honour in the Sheikh's cemetry near Nishan Tash.

Thus ended one of the most dynamic personalities of the age—one who made the kings tremble.

Jamaluddin Afghani was a great Muslim revolutionary and reformer who aimed at the unity of Muslim people all over the world. He wanted to make Islam a great force in the world. The imperialists, whose interest lay in the division of the world of Islam, were always conspiring against him and did not allow him the peaceful propagation of his mission. But the magnetic personality of Jamaluddin Afghani, his versatile genius, his sincerity and eloquence, deeply stirred those who came into contact with him and gave birth to nationalist and progressive movements in several Muslim countries.

Jamaluddin Afghani was a linguist. He knew Arabic, Persian, Turkish, Pushto, French, English and Russian. His extremely busy and turbulent life did not give him respite to settle down to the writing of books. But he wrote a number of pamphlets on diverse subjects in different languages. In fact, he stirred the spirit of Muslim intelligentsia all over the world and directed their hitherto dormant energies towards constructive channels. The East has much profited from the writings of his disciples.

As a man, Jamaluddin was humble, courteous, laborious and amicable. He slept little, working for more than 18 hours a day. "He received those who came to visit him with great courtesy", writes Edward G. Browne, author of the well-known work, *"A Literary History of Persia"*, "the humblest as much as the most distinguished, but was very chary of paying visits, especially to persons of high ranks. In speech he was eloquent, always expressing himself in choice language, and avoiding colloquial and vulgar idioms, but carefully adopting his words to the capacity of his hearers. As a public speaker he had hardly a rival in the East".

Regarding his other qualities Browne states :

"He was abstemious in his life, caring little for the things of this world, bold and fearless in face of danger, frank and genial but hot tempered, affable towards all but independent in his dealings with the great. His intellectual powers and his quick insight and discernment were equally remarkable, so that he seemed able to read men's thought before they had spoken."

About his versatility Browne writes :

"His knowledge was extensive, and he was specially versed in ancient philosophy, the philosophy of history, the history and civilization of Islam, and learned French in three months without a master, sufficiently well to read and translate".

"He knew the Arabic, Turkish, Persian and Afghan languages together with a little English and Russian. He was a voracious reader of Arabic and Persian books. He appears never to have married, and was indifferent to female charms."

His influence throughout the East and specially in the world of Islam was indeed overwhelming. He was, to a great extent, responsible for the awakening of Muslims during the 19th century.

The contemporary high personalities of the East and the West vied with each other to win his favour. He was loved and respected by Muslim intelligentsia all over the world, but feared by the Imperialist powers, who were afraid of his mission and growing influence. "He raised up a living spirit in the hearts of his friends and disciples which stirred their energies and sharpened their pens, and the East has profited and will profit by their labours".

He was responsible directly or indirectly for the organisation of several progressive and reformist movements all over the Islamic world, including the nationalist and modernist movement in Egypt, movement of Union and Progress in Turkey, reform movement in Persia, Modernist and Khilafat movements of Muslim India. "It was really wonderful", writes Browne,

"that a wandering scholar, with no material resources save only an eloquent tongue and a pen, literally made kings tremble on their thrones and defeated the well-laid plans of statesmen by setting in motion forces which he knew how to evoke and with which secular politicians, both European and Asiatic, had utterly failed to reckon."

# SYED AHMAD KHAN

A revolt had broken out against the alien rulers of India in 1857. A wave of resentment swept through some of the principal towns of northern India against them. It was the first major uprising against European domination in India. The fire which had broken out in Delhi and Lucknow, and had swallowed up some innocent members of the ruling family, soon spread to the neighbouring districts. The rebels of Delhi reached Bijnore, where Syed Ahmad Khan was posted as a Sub-Judge. The local Europeans were naturally perturbed over the happenings and took refuge in the Collector's bungalow. Soon after a big mob, headed by Nawab Mahmud Khan, collected round the Collector's bungalow and threatened the Europeans. The situation had grown extremely grim. Syed Ahmad Khan risked his life, faced the unruly mob and persuaded their leader to spare the innocent Europeans, who were ultimately evacuated from the dangerous area and safely escorted to Meerut in the dead of night.

The British Government, soon re-established itself in northern India. The services rendered by Syed Ahmad Khan in the stormy days of 1857 were acknowledged and a big confiscated landed property of a Muslim landlord was offered to him but he refused to accept this award.

Born in 1817, Syed Ahmad Khan was destined to fill the big void created in the Muslim community with the disappearance of the Muslim Rule in India and provided the necessary link between the mediaeval and the modern Islam in India. He played a vital role in the awakening of Indian Muslims and introduced them to Western liberal ideas, thus shaping their destinies in a modern world.

Syed Ahmad's forefathers came from Persia and some of his ancestors known for their chivalry had won laurels on the battlefield. His grandfather held a military command and his father, Mir Muttaqi, a religious recluse wielded considerable spiritual influence in the Court of the Mughal Emperor, Akbar Shah II. Declining the service of the Mughal Emperor, Mir Muttaqi passed much of his time in the company of Shah Ghulam Ali, a Mujaddidi saint of his time. The young Syed Ahmad owes his deep devotion to Islam, to the teaching of Shah Ghulam Ali. He was trained in statecraft and introduced to Western civilization by his maternal grandfather, Khwaja Fariduddin, who, for eight years, had served as Prime Minister of Mughal Emperor Akbar II.

His wise mother was mainly responsible for his grounding in education and also for his love of learning he developed in his early life which, in his later years, enabled him to become the political, social and intellectual leader of his people.

His father died in 1836 and early next year he joined the British service as a *Serishtedar* (Reader) in the Court. Bahadur Shah, the last titular Mughal Emperor, conferred on him the titles of his grandfather and would have also given him some position in his Court, but forestalling the doom of the Mughals, Syed preferred the British service. His good work soon won recognition and after four years' service he was appointed as *Munsif*, a judicial officer, in 1841 and was posted at the historic town of Fatehpur Sikri.

In 1846, when his elder brother died and there was none to look after his family, he got himself transferred to Delhi, the great Metropolis of the dwindling Mughal Empire and the centre of Muslim education and culture. Delhi still possessed some of the greatest intellectual luminaries, including poets like Ghalib, Momin and Zauq; administrators like Nawab Ahmad Bakhsh and Nawab Aminuddin of Loharu and philanthropists like Hakim Mahmud Khan and Nawab Mustafa Khan.

Syed Ahmad Khan was a distinguished member of the talented society of Delhi patronised by Bahadur Shah, Syed Ahmad devoted his leisure time to private study and research and in 1847 his Research bore fruit in the publication of *'Asar-ul-Sanadid'* or 'the Traces of the Great'. This book gives an interesting account of the ruins of old Delhi and some of the outstanding literary and saintly personalities of his time. This book became very popular and has gone through several editions. It was translated into Franch by M. Garcin de Tassy in 1861. It also attracted much notice outside India with the result that Syed Ahmad was elected an Honorary Fellow of the Royal Asiatic Society in 1864.

He was transferred to Bijnore in 1855. Here too, he continued his literary activities and edited the well-known *Ain-i-Akbari* of Abul Fazal. He also edited the *Memoirs* of Jahangir and the famous history of Ziauddin Barni.

His long life, lasting for about 80 years may be divided into four equal periods. The first twenty years were devoted to education. The next twenty years (1837—57) were marked for his success as Judicial Officer in the United Provinces. It was during this period that the uprising of 1857 broke out and he saved the lives of a number of Englishmen and women. The next twenty years (1857—77) were noted for his interest in public welfare activities, specially the education of Muslim community. He also made a trip to England in order to have first hand knowledge of Western education and the working of British educational institutions. The fourth period (1877—98) was the most important period of his life in which he established his reputation as the greatest political leader and educationist of Muslim India during the 19th century. He made a lasting contribution to the educational progress of his country by founding the Anglo-Mohammadan Oriental College, Aligarh, the Scientific Society and the All-India Muslim Educational Conference.

During the uprising of 1857, Syed Ahmad was posted at Bijnore. He was then 40 and had acquired a high reputation as a just, competent and diligent Judicial Officer. During these troubled days he saved the lives of local Europeans of Bijnore and safely transported them to Meerut. After the re-occupation of Delhi by the British, Syed Ahmad visited his own home there and found a number of his family members slain and his own mother in a miserable plight. The awful scenes of torture and persecution, plunder and arson at the hands of British conquerors witnessed by him in Delhi, left a deep impression on his mind and considerably influenced his outlook towards life. The celebrities of Delhi, the flower of Muslim society, described in his *Aasar-ul-Sanadid,* were either killed or had gone underground. The best part of the city extending from the Red Fort to Shah Jahan Mosque, was razed to the ground and ploughed up. The mosque itself was occupied by British troops. The sufferings of his mother at Delhi undermined her health and she died soon after reaching Meerut. Being a painful witness of the ghastly tragedy of 1857, he wrote a book entitled *Asbab-i-Baghawat-i-Hind* (Causes of the Indian Revolt), which was translated into English by Sir Auckland Colin, with the assistance of Col. Graham, an admirer of Syed Ahmad Khan. According to his analysis, the Britishers were themselves responsible for the so-called Indian Mutiny. The main causes of the Mutiny as given in the book were: (1) Absence of Indian representation in the administration of the country. (2) Official interference in religion. (3) Social segregation between the ruler and the ruled. In this book, which is considered as the Charter of Indian freedom, Syed Ahmad had very boldly and fearlessly criticized the attitude of the Britishers towards the mutineers and patriotic Indians. The book laid the foundation of future reforms in India and led to the reorientation of British policy towards Indian administration. Allan Octavian Hume, the founder of the Indian National Congress once told Sahibzada Aftab Khan: 'It was after reading this book on the causes of the Mutiny that I first felt the need of having a forum of public opinion in India, and eventually the Indian National Congress came into existence". Syed Ahmad Khan strongly criticised British policy in India at a time when the major part of the country was under martial law, the Anglo-Indian Press was advocating a firm line and public opinion in England was stirred up and advocated stronger measures against mutineers and their supporters. He wrote: "In the pre-Mutiny period, Government could never know the inadvisibility of the laws and regulations which it passed. It could never hear, as it ought to have heard, the voice of the people on such a subject. The people had no means of protesting against what they might feel to be a foolish measure, or of giving public expression to their own wishes . . . . Now the English Government has been in existence upwards by a century, and up to the present hour it has not secured the affections of the people" (Quoted in Graham's *Life of Syed Ahmad Khan).*

In 1862, Syed Ahmad Khan was transferred to Ghazipur, where his associations with his later biographer Colonel Graham, led to the establishment of a Scientific Society for translating Western books on sciences and arts into the Urdu language. In an informal meeting convened for the purpose, Syed Ahmad Khan, in an eloquent speech, stressed the need of acquainting the Indians with the scientific development of the West. This society received further impetus when Syed Ahmad Khan was transferred to Aligarh, a city which became the centre of his reformatory and educational activities and later developed to be the highest seat of Muslim Education in the subcontinent. Here, his associations with cultured aristocracy, who sympathised with his reformatory ideas procured the most congenial atmosphere for the growth of the new movement, which was meeting a stiff opposition from the conservative Muslim quarters all over India. Syed Ahmad was even denounced as a *'Kafir'* (infidel) and *'nachuri'* by religious heads in the country. Any other person would have succumbed to the wave of resentment which swept over the country against this group, but Syed Ahmad Khan, a man of indomitable withstood like a rock and carried on his beneficial activities despite severe opposition. He, along with hs capable associates, relentlessly worked for reorientating Muslim outlook towards the West which earned him the title of Maker of Modern Muslim India. His efforts were at last crowned with success and led to the establishment of Muhammadan–Anglo Oriental College, Aligarh, which later became the famous Muslim University of Aligarh.

In 1876, Syed Ahmad retired from government service and settled down at Aligarh. Here he started his work with his characteristic energy and devotion. On January 8, 1877, the foundation stone of the Muhammadan–Anglo Oriental College, Aligarh, was laid by Lord Lytton, the Viceroy of India.

His associations with Western writers and thinkers as well as his trip to England where he visited universities of Oxford and Cambridge gave him an insight into the working of western educational institutions, which he ultimately introduced into his college at Aligarh.

One of the secrets of Syed Ahmad's success was that he gathered around him a galaxy of well-known writers and administrators who carried on his mission with unabated zeal. He was a born leader of men, who held sway over the destiny of Muslim India for over two decades and influenced as well as brought to the forefront a greater number of capable men, than has been done by any Muslim leader in modern India. Among these men were Hali, the originator of Modern Urdu Poetry; Shibli, a versatile literary genius; Nazir Ahmad, the celebrated Urdu novelist, humourist and stylist; Nawab Mohsinul Mulk, the well-known orator and administrator and Maulvi Chiragh Ali, a versatile writer and organiser. For his Muhammadan–Anglo Oriental College at Aligarh he was fortunate to have secured the services of three well-known literary figures and educationists of England, namely Theodore Beck, Morison and Arnold, who were greatly instrumental in making the Aligarh College a model institution in the East, in which Western Sciences were taught side by side with oriental learning. Arnold learned Arabic and wrote an outstanding book.

Syed Ahmad was a great patriot and a fearless advocate of the Indian cause in the Viceroy's Council to which he was nominated in 1878 by Lord Lytton and renominated in 1880 for two years by Lord Ripon. In this respect he was the forerunner of the great Indian leaders who came after him. He was the first powerful advocate of the Indian rights, who paved the way for the later struggle for Indian freedom.

Like Maulana Muhammad Ali, Maulana Hasrat Mohani and Mr. Muhammad Ali Jinnah, Syed Ahmad too started his political career as an Indian patriot who fearlessly, though with some moderation, championed the Indian cause through the press and the platform. But, the later political developments in the country, specially the rival Hindi movement started at Banares, obliged him to change his views. The stark realities of the political front disillusioned him and, being a realist, he could prophesy that Hindus and Muslims, having different cultures could not unite together. Thus, he may be called a forerunner of the Pakistan Movement. Hali, his celebrated biographer writes: "In 1867, some Hindu leaders of Banares resolved that, as far as possible, the use of Urdu language, written in Persian script, should be discontinued in Government courts and should be replaced by Hindi language, written in Devanagri script. Sir Syed used to say that this was the first occasion, when he felt that it was now impossible for the Hindus and Muslims to progress as a single nation and for anyone to work for both of them simultaneousy. His words were :

"During these days, when Hindi—Urdu controversy was going on in Banares, one day I met Mr. Shakespeare who was posted there as Divisional Commissioner. I was saying something about the education of the Muslims,. and Mr. Shakespeare was listening with an expression of amazement, when at length, he said, 'This is the first occasion, when I have heard you speak about the progress of the Muslims alone. Before this you were always keen about the welfare of your countrymen in general'. I said: 'Now I am convinced that both these communities will not join whole-heartedly in anything. At present, there is no open hostility between the two communities, but on account of the so-called educated people, it will increase immensely in future. He who lives, will see. Mr. Shakespeare thereupon, said, 'I would be sorry if your prophecies were to be true'. I said, 'I am also extremely sorry, but I am confident about the accuracy of this prophecy."

Maulana Muhammad Ali, a great Indian patriot, said from the Presidential chair of the Indian National Congress :

"Reviewing the actions of a bygone generation, today, when it is easier to be wise after the event, I still think that the attitude of Syed Ahmad Khan was eminently wise, and much as I wish that something which he had said should have been left unsaid, I am constrained to admit that no well-wisher of Mussalmans, nor of India, as a whole, could have followed a different course in leading the Mussalmans."

Syed Ahmad occupies an eminent place among the Indian reformers. After retirement from Government service he devoted all his time and energy to social and educational work. He originated the movement of independent religious thought among Indian Muslims, and introduced rationalism in religious thinking. He analysed the causes of the decline of Muslims and found it due to their apathy towards Western education. His magnetic personality and his inexhaustible energy, his indomitable will and his keen insight, enabled him to surmount all obstacles and finally succeed in his difficult mission.

As a writer of Urdu, Syed Ahmad occupies a high place. He was a versatile and prolific writer, who has left behind no less than 25 valuable works both in Urdu and Persian, on history, archeology, politics, religion and philosophy. He edited Abdul Fazal's, *Ain-i-Akbari* and *Tozak-e-Jahangiri,* the autobiography of Mughal Emperor Jahangir. His *Asbab-e-Baghawat-e-Hind* (Causes of Indian Revolt), translated into English by Sir Auckland Colin was the first outspoken book on the subject. His *Aasar-ul-Sanadid* or the Antiquities of Delhi, translated into French by M. Garcin de Tassy in 1861, won him the fellowship of the Royal Asiatic Society of London. After returning from London, he started his *Tahzib-ul-Akhlaq,* an Urdu Journal in 1870. Through this journal he propagated his reformative doctrines regarding society and religion, which offended the religious hierarchy who denounced him as a *'Kafir'* (Infidal). During his stay in London he arranged the publication of his voluminous Essays on Muhammad, in which he met a number of objections on the life of the Prophet raised by Western writers. He also wrote a *Tafsir* (Commentary on the Quran) in 7 volumes, in which he tried to give a rational explanation of religious doctrines embodied in the Quran.

Syed Ahmad is universally acknowledged as one of the pioneers of Urdu Prose. Like Ghalib, he possesses a simple and lucid style in Urdu prose, devoid of all decorative ornamentations. He preferred matter over form. He was the first to write business-like Urdu prose, which was later adopted by all the succeeding writers like Hali, Shibli, Nazir Ahmad, Sharar, Sarshar and Maulvi Zakaullah. In this way he is correctly called as the 'Father of Modern Urdu Prose.'

The greatest contribution of Syed Ahmad was in the educational sphere. His greatest achievements were the establishment of Muhammadan Anglo-Oriental College, Aligarh, and the Scientific Society of Aligarh. He was undoubtedly the Father of Muslim Education in Modern India. He had realised that Muslims could not progress without modern education, hence he established English Schools, first at Muradabad, then at Ghazipur and finally an Oriental College at Aligarh. Had he not taken the initiative, the social and educational development of Muslim India would have receded into background. Graham, his biographer writes: "Syed Ahmad's Motto was "Educate, Educate, Educate". 'All the socio-economic ills in India, he once said to me, may be cured with this treatment'. Cure the root and the tree will flourish". The Scientific Society, which, in reality, was an organisation for translating scientific and other useful literature from the Western languages into Urdu was established by Syed Ahmad at Ghazipur in January, 1864. It was managed by his life long friend, Raja Jai Kishan Das.

It was later shifted to Aligarh, where it developed into a great organisation, which with its organ, the *Aligarh Institute Gazette,* did very useful work in popularising Western learning among the Muslims. He founded in 1886, the Mohammadan Educational Conference, which held meetings in all Indian major cities and spread the message of Aligarh to all parts of the country.

Syed Ahmad lived a long life of more than 80 years. Of these, he spent 60 years in hardwork in diverse spheres of life. During his last days, when he needed rest he worked 18 hours a day. At last he died on March 27 1898, at a ripe age of 81. His death was deeply mourned throughout the country.

Syed Ahmad was undoubtedly the greatest figure in the transitional period of Indian history. His was a many-sided personality. His greatness lay in the fact that he was a true leader of men, who had attracted around him some of the ablest intellects of his age and provided an enlightened leadership at a crucial period of Indian history.

# MUSTAFA KAMAL

The Sultan of Turkey on whom the West had conferred the sobriquet "Sickman of Europe", was in an extremely difficult position. Turkish armies in Iraq and Syria were gravely threatened during the First Great War of 1914—18. Her principal ally Germany was not in a position to help her.

Meanwhile, the Allies had opened another front in Turkey. They wanted to capture Constantinople, the Turkish Capital, by forcing the Dardanelles. A crack army of Anzacs (Australians and Newzealanders) was landed on the Gallipoli peninsula on April 25, 1915. The German Supreme Commander of the Turkish forces, General Von Sanders, saw no immediate threat in the small force brought by the enemy. But the young Mustafa Kamal, serving as one of his Commanders, rightly took it as the spearhead of the formidable Allied attack. Ignoring General Von Sanders's orders, he launched, a counter attack. for about four months wave after wave of Allied forces comprising Newzealander, Australian, British and Indian soldiers, tried to capture the ridge on the beach, but each time they were repulsed by a withering fire. The Turks under Mustafa Kamal were determined not to give way, though pressed by a force much superior in arms and numbers. At last, after a fruitless campaign lasting for months, the British were forced to withdraw, losing thousands of men and much equipment. Late in August 1915, the furious charge of Kamal at Suvla won back the key position of Chunuk Bay, pinned the Allies to the beach and eventually forced them to abandon the Gallipoli Expedition as an utter failure.

Mustafa Kamal had won the most glorious victory of the First Great War and the British had undoubtedly suffered one of the worst defeats in their long history. Kamal was hailed in Constantinople as the Saviour of Dardanelles and Turkey.

Born at Salonika in 1881 A.C., Mustafa Kamal came of a hardy peasant family of Macedonian highlands—the abode of fiery revolutionaries in Europe. His father, Ali Raza, was a timber merchant, who died when Mustafa was young, leaving him to the care of his talented mother Zubaida Khanum. Mustafa, a very energetic and talented boy, had a natural aptitude for military education. After completing his primary education, he joined the Rushtiye Military School. His proficiency in mathematics won for him the nickname of Kamal and henceforward he was called Mustafa Kamal.

Mustafa Kamal was exceptionally brilliant among his class-fellows. At 17, he left Salonika for the military school at Monastir. After two years at Monastir, he was gazetted as a sub-lieutenant and sent to the Imperial Staff College at Constantinople. Here he had an early taste of political life.

Turkey at the time was passing through the worst period of her history. Her economic and political life was paralysed and the brave Turkish nation was groaning under the despotic rule of Sultan Abdul Hamid. Her Capital had become a hot bed of foreign intrigues and the loosening grip of the despotic Sultan over his vast territories and in the international field had earned her the nickname of "Sickman of Europe".

A group of young officers of the Imperial Staff College of Constantinople formed a secret revolutionary society known as *'Vatan'* (Motherland), with a view to ridding Turkey of the Despotic and corrupt rule of Sultan Abdul Hamid. Young Kamal became its leader.

The secret Turkish Police discovered the plot against the Sultan. One night, when the meeting was in progress, it forced its entry and hustled away the conspirators to the Red Prison.

It was a sultry evening of 1905. Death by the strangler's noose was the fate expected by a young cadet, who paced restlessly in the dark dungeon of Constantinople. He was Mustafa Kamal.

But the Sultan hesitated. His co-prisoners were the future Generals and military leaders of his country. Their execution might cause a revolt in the country. The Director-General of the Military Academy was, therefore, ordered to keep a watch over their movements and suppress any attempt at revival of the *'Vatan.'* Thereafter, the prisoners were set free.

Mustafa Kamal was particularly warned not to take part in such activities. He was posted in a cavalry regiment, south of Damascus. Here, in collaboration with his colleagues he formed a party called *"Vatan wa Hurriyat"*.

He had been receiving information of a new revolutionary society called the "Committee of Union and Progress" formed under the leadership of Enver Pasha, a military genius among the Turks. Mustafa had realised that Salonika was going to be the place for the uprising against Sultan Abdul Hamid and yearned to join the patriots, who were plotting to overthrow the corrupt despotic rule in Turkey.

At last, his efforts succeeded and in 1908 he was transferred to Salonika and appointed on the Staff of the 3rd Army Corps. Mustafa, too, joined the Committee of the Union and Progress and he, being a grim and sardonic realist, procured a pleasant contrast to the extremely impetuous, virile and idealist Enver, but both being military geniuses, played a vital role in saving Turkey from total extinction during this century.

In 1908, Niazi, with a few hundred men defied the Turkish Government in the mountains of macedonia. The country groaning under poverty and tyrannical rule joined the rebels. Enver, at the head of a large mob was about to march on Constantinople, when the clever Sultan announced a constitution accepting most of the demands of the revolutionaries.

The history of the brave Turks is full of innumerable campaigns. Being one of the most virile and fighting nations in the world, there had hardly been a period exceeding 10 years in their long history in which they had not to fight a major battle.

In 1911, the Italian troops invaded Tripoli and massacred a large number of local inhabitants. Mustafa Kamal was at once despatched to this North African theatre of War and fought bravely at Tobruk and Derni.

While he was in North Africa, the Balkan Wars broke out in 1912 and the Turkish satellite states declared their independence and attacked Turkey. The Bulgarians had captured Adrianople and were marching on the Turkish Capital.

The conspiracy of the Christian States to wipe Turkey out of Europe would have succeeded, had the daring Enver not come to her rescue. He forced his entry into the Cabinet meeting debating surrender, shot down the War Minister and rallied the Government to a successful defence. His recapture of Adrianople, the last Turkish stronghold in Europe, against heavy odds from the Bulgarians, is a lasting testimony to his military genius. Enver was hailed as the saviour of Adrianople and the idol of Turkish people.

Meanwhile Mustafa Kamal had returned to Turkey and was posted by Enver, Minister of War, as the Turkish Military Attache in Sofia.

In 1914, the declaration of the First Great War found Turkey on the side of Germany. Enver was dreaming of regaining the lost Turkish glory, by creating a vast Turkish Empire. He appointed General Liman Von Sanders as the Supreme Commander of the Turkish forces. In August 1915, Kamal won one of the sensational victories of the war at Gallipoli. He was hailed as the Saviour of Turkey and recognised as one of the world's greatest Generals.

The defeat of Germany by the Allies in the First Great War turned the tables on Turkey too. The Allied armies were in control of Constantinople. Wahiduddin, had become Sultan on the death of his father. The Allies used the Sultan of Turkey as a tool in their hand, to further their ends of almost finshing Turkey for ever. The Sultan and his Government thought it in their own interest to collaborate with the Allies and sign the humiliating Treaty of Sevres. But the spirit of the brave Turks was not broken and the entire nation protested, refusing to accept the humiliating terms of the Treaty. According to Mustafa Kamal,

"The essential thing for the Turkish people was to live with dignity and honour. This was only possible if they enjoyed complete freedom. However, prosperous or rich a nation may be, if it is deprived of its independence, it does not merit a place higher than that of a slave in civilised humanity. For any nation like the Turkish, it would be better to cease to exist than to live in slavery. Consequently, either independence or death".

The Sultan of Turkey, being a tool in the hands of Allies, Mustafa Kamal escaped to Anatolia to keep alive the people's struggle against the enemy. For this purpose he convened a National Congress at Sivas, composed of the representatives of the provinces.

The conference was a great success and the valiant Turks swore to carry on their resistance till complete freedom was achieved. After ceaseless warfare lasting for more than 10 years, they were totally exhausted and their resources were paralysed, but their spirit was not broken. Mustafa Kamal took advantage of this spirit, mobilised their shattered strength and performed a military feat which would go down as a miracle in the history of military warfare.

The activities of Mustafa Kamal caused an alarm in the Allied Camp in Constantinople. The Sultan, a stooage of the Allies, was made to sign the death warrant of Kamal and announced a high price on his head. He was denounced as a *'Kafir'* (Infidel) by the hired *Ulema*—one who had rebelled against the Caliph of Islam. But, undaunted by all these happenings, Kamal continued his mission.

Meanwhile the well-equipped Greek army invaded Anatolia and occupied Smyrna (Izmir). The ambitious Greek Premier was dreaming of carving out a Greek Empire out of Turkish Empire. Backed by the moral and material support of the Allies, he had assembled a large invading force equipped with most modern weapons of war. He had offered to smash the Kamalists in Anatolia, who were irregular troops with no artillery. His offer was accepted.

The beginning of 1921 was a very critical period for the new People's Government formed under Mustafa Kamal. Despite the two victories of Turks at Inonu on January 14 and April 1, the Greek army advanced as far as Sakarya and threatened Angora (Ankara). They were sure to wipe out the irregular Kamalists.

The Greek army advanced towards Eska Shehir and Afion, the former being key to Angora and was held by Ismet Pasha, the ablest lieutenant of Kamal.

"In a stone house 'n the village of Chan Kaya', writes a well-known European writer, "a few miles from Angora, Mustafa Kamal pored over maps and plans, and awaited the Greek onslaught. He had reached the biggest crisis of his life. If he failed to withstand the Greeks, both he and Turkey were doomed. He had only a few regular troops; the rest of his army consisted of roving bands of tribesmen. Food and equipment were scarce; he had neither artillery nor transport. And facing him was an enemy far superior in numbers, well conditioned, and trained and equipped to a high degree of efficiency.

"In the first week of July, 1921, the Greeks swept forward, took Afion and menaced Eska Shehir. The Kamalists were suffering heavy losses in a hard fought battle. Kamal decided to fall back two hundred miles to the last natural line of defence before Angora—the Sakarya river".

"And here, on August 24, began one of the bloodiest and most decisive battles of modern history. After a heavy artillery bombardment by the Greeks, the two armies came to death-grips. Centuries of hatred between the Greeks and the Turks, Christians and Infidels, fused into the white-hot fury of fourteen days indescribable carnage."

"When at last the Greeks were driven back from a battlefield that had become a shambles, and retreated to Eska Shehir, the Turks were too shattered by the victory to pursue them."

"Nations all over the world swelled the chorus of praise that met Kamal on his return to Angora. But the *Ghazi* (Victorious) knew that his task had only begun. He must drive the Greeks back to the sea."

He exclaimed: "we shall completely vanquish the enemy". He had won one of the most memorable victories of living history which had astounded friends and foes alike.

At dawn on August 26, before the Greek position at Afion he ordered his troops: "Forward! your goal is the Mediterranean".

Amids terrible Greek artillery barrage the Turkish soldiers marched forward and cut the Greek army into two. The Greeks broke and fled in disorder leaving much military stores for the Turks. They were panicstricken and made a dash to the sea to save their lives. Kamal had no ships to pursue them on sea.

Allied forces occupying Constantinople and Dardenelles were now in a precarious position. The great military victories of Kamal forced them to revise their stand and the Treaty of Lausanne signed on July 23, 1923 recognised the Independence of the Turksh People.

The terrified Sultan Wahiduddin of Turkey escaped on an Allied Warship and in his place his nephew Abdul Majid was crowned. But, he too, was dethroned a few months later when Turkey was declared a Republic.

The Independence of Turkey was secured. Having accomplished this difficult task, Mustafa Kamal embarked upon a more difficult task of building

Turkey into a modern state. His achievement in this sector, too, was marvellous and projected him a remarkable man of the Twentieth Century—great both in war and peace.

In order to secure an honourable place for Turkey among the comity of civilized nations, Mustafa Kamal had to institute far-reaching reforms in the political, social, judicial, economic and cultural fields. He adopted revolutionary methods in introducing these reforms and the short-lived conservative opposition was put down with an iron hand.

Being a sincere well-wisher of his country—one who had saved Turkey from total extinction at the most critical period of her history, the saner elements among his people rallied round him even at the time of his seemingly unpopular reforms. The advantages of his revolutionary reforms were soon apparent, which changed the entire complexion of Turkey and made her a powerful modern state in Europe.

He formed his powerful political party and with the support of a United Chamber of Deputies, he proclaimed the Turkish Republic on October 29, 1923, and abolished the Caliphate on March 3, 1924. He was unanimously elected as the First President of the Turkish Republic.

In 1928, the Clause of the Secularity of the State was included into her constitution. This put an end to the age long tradition which had existed in the country.

Mustafa Kamal was now an absolute ruler of Turkey. He was not only their Saviour and nation builder but, in fact, the father of their people, known as Ataturk. He was loved, respected and feared. His aim was to transform the life of his people from oriental to modern—'a colossal task of centuries which he was determined to accomplish in a few short years'.

He introduced a number of revolutionary reforms in the social, political and cultural fields of Turkish life. He banned Fez, adopted European dress and introduced Latin script in place of Arabic. Latin script was prevalent in the modern world and in bringing Turkey in line with the modern world, this reform proved very beneficial. It was the most difficult task to make his people write their language in the Latin script. Kamal went through the streets himself with blackboard and chalk, teaching the Latin script to the crowds.

His other reforms included the abolition of veil, worn by the Turkish women and the introduction of co-education in educational institutions. During the Ottoman times, the rights of Turkish women were circumscribed. Mustafa Kamal gave greater freedom and rights to Turkish women, which brought them at par with men.

He cleansed the civil service which for over 100 years was the most corrupt in Europe. He made bribery a heavily punishable offence and established a "Code of Honour" for all State Departments.

He reorganised the Turkish army on modern lines and made it one of the most efficient and well-equipped armies in the world.

Kamal also introduced several agricultural and industrial reforms. He rapidly industrialised his country, set up a large number of modern factories and carried out a good many national enterprises, including the building of modern Turkish Capital, Ankara.

The far-reaching reforms of Kamal brought about a great change in Turkey and immensely added to her economic prosperity and political stability.

Mustafa Kamal, the hero of hundred's battles, the maker of Modern Turkey, died in November, 1938, He was undoubtedly the greatest figure of his time—a military genius, an outstanding statesman, a courageous revolutionary and a hero who saved his shattered country from total extinction and rebuilt it on a new and enduring foundation. Modern Turkey is his living monument.

# MAULANA MUHAMMAD ALI

Addressing the plenary session of the First Round Table Conference in London in 1930, Maulana Muhammad Ali said, "I want to go back to my country as a freeman. If you cannot accept it, then you will have to give me a piece of land for my grave". His prophetic words proved to be true, and he died in London a few weeks later.

Maulana Muhammad Ali, the renowned Indian Muslim leader, was a prince among the patriots. Possessing a dynamic personality, he towered high above his contemporary Indian politicians and instilled courage and confidence in the hearts of the ignorant masses which awakened them from their deep slumber. His fearless leadership and selfless devotion to his mission were greatly instrumental in dispelling the inferiority complex, which, the alien rulers had enshrined in the hearts of the teeming millions inhabiting this vast subcontinent and enabled them to brave the onslaughts of the foreign rule with courage and conviction. The policy of co-operation with the British Government, followed by Sir Syed Ahmad Khan and his associates, at last gave place to the revolutionary politics of Maulana Muhammad Ali and Abul Kalaam Azad in which the attention of the Indian Muslims was diverted towards the rival of the Pan-Islamic Movement and the restoration of the *Khilafat.*

Born in an aristocratic family of Rampur State (U.P.) in 1878, Muhammad Ali was destined to play a glorious role in the Indian politics. His father, Abdul Ali Khan, died when he was 2 years old, leaving behind three sons, Zulfiqar, Shaukat and Muhammad. His mother, Abadi Bano being an enlightened lady, sent his sons to Bareilly and afterwards to Aligarh to receive the best education available in the country. At Aligarh University, where Shaukat Ali was the idol of cricket fans, Muhammad Ali became the favourite of the literary circles. During his stay at the University, he took active interest in its extra-curricular activities and earned a high reputation as a student, poet, orator and writer. In 1896, at the age of 18, he topped the list of successful B.A. students from the Allahabad University, which conducted the degree examinations for the whole of the United Provinces. Muhammad Ali exposed the high-handedness of the European staff, who dominated the Aligarh University of those days. According to Sajjad Haider Yaldaram, who was his associate, the European Principal heaved a sigh of relief when Muhammad Ali left the University for U.K., as he was very outspoken in his criticism of the European staff. His free expression of views in the college debates on various national and international issues, caused great embarrassment to the European professors. In England, he remained for 4 years at the Lincoln College and obtained his B.A. (Hons.) in Modern History. He had the distinction of being the first President of the Indian Majlis in the Cambridge University. He, however, was fortunate in not being selected for Indian Civil Service, which in those days was reserved for a privileged few, otherwise India would have been deprived of the most colourful and dynamic personality of her modern history.

On his return from U.K., Muhammad Ali was appointed as Chief Education Officer of the Rampur State. But, due to the educational reforms which he wanted to enforce in the State, he had differences with the higher authorities.

He resigned his job and joined the Baroda Civil Service. He served the Baroda State for 7 years and his reforms in the State are still remembered with gratitude. During his stay in Baroda, he frequently contributed articles to the *Times of India,* and his article *"Thoughts on the Present Discontent",* was highly appreciated. His high intellect and his restless soul could not cope with the restrictions of the Civil Service. He was meant for something higher. Nature had endowed him with extraordinary abilities of head and heart which should have been devoted to better and higher purposes. The extreme poverty and sufferings to which the Indian masses were reduced under the alien yoke, only added fuel to his fiery temperament. He left the job and hurried to Calcutta to start his *Weekly Comrade* on January 1, 1911. An interesting story is related in this connection, which throws light on his determination to fight for the cause of the people through the Press. He was offered the Chief Ministership of an Indian State but he did not open the letter of appointment until the first issue of his paper was out. Maulana Muhammad Ali was an ideal journalist, and the high standard of professional integrity set by him will serve as a beacon light for the coming generations. His paper formed the vanguard of the struggle against exploitation and oppression of the alien Government. He was the first to raise his voice against the despotic Press laws. He had joined the fourth estate for pleading the cause of the downtrodden humanity inhabiting this subcontinent. His *Comrade* had set an example of independent journalism and was a class by itself. It played a vital role in moulding the political outlook of Modern India. Due to its frank views and flawless English, *Comrade* was very popular in official circles too. An *ex*-British Finance Member of the Government of India took its bound copies with him to England. Writing in the first editorial of *Comrade* on January 1, 1911, he gave out the policy of his paper: "We are all partisans of none, comrades of all. We deeply feel the many hazards of increasing controversy between races and races; creeds and creeds, and earnestly desire a better understanding between the contending elements of the body politic of India". As the time passed, the national and international developments obliged him to be more anti-imperialist in his outlook and more outspoken in his criticism against the British Government. In 1914 when Turkey was involved in the Great War, Maulana Muhammad Ali after a continuous sitting of 36 hours wrote his memorable editorial, *'The Choice of the Turks'* a befitting reply to the insulting article of the *London Times* under the same caption. The Indian Government forfeited its security. He was marked as a dangerous man by the authorities and his paper forfeited its security several times.

The *Comrade* was transferred to Delhi in 1912, when the Indian Capital was shifted from Calcutta to Delhi in 1911. It played a great part along with *Al-Hilal* of Azad and *Zamindar* of Lahore in the awakening of the Muslim masses and in forming their political outlook. Muhammad Ali started *Hamdard,* an Urdu Daily, from Delhi in 1913. He wrote his autobiography 'My Life a Fragment' the only work he has left behind for the future generations. Writing in his autobiography he mentions the reasons which impelled him to take up the career of journalism, "The reasons which so irresistibly impelled me to take up journalism was, that the affairs of my community at the juncture made it the only avenue, through which I could prove of any appreciable use—I felt, I should now assist my community in taking proper share in the political affairs of the country".

Maulana Muhammad Ali played a vital part in preparing the Muslims in particular and Indians in general for the final struggle of freedom. Thus to a great extent he was responsible for shaping their political destiny. Under his dynamic leadership, Muslims grew into a virile and self-assertive nation. His heart which surged with the love of his countrymen awakened their self-respect. Being an ardent anti-imperialist, he virtually dominated the national stage for the first quarter of the present century. Along with Mohsinul Mulk and Wiqar-ul-Mulk, he was present in Dacca when the Muslim League was founded in 1906. On their suggestion, he wrote in his immaculate style an account of this historic session in the form of a pamphlet called, *"Green Book".* He may be counted as one of the founders of All-India Muslim League along with Mohsinul Mulk, Wiqarul Mulk, Nawab Samiullah of Dacca and Agha Khan.

The Balkan War was declared in 1912. The machinations of the European powers against Turkey brought him in the arena of active politics. He appealed for funds in aid of Turkish victims. A medical mission was despatched to Turkey under the leadership of Dr. M. A. Ansari, which included Messrs A. R. Siddiqi and Shoaib Qureshi as well. This was the first embassy of practical goodwill sent by Muslim India to a foreign country. The mission performed valuable service, which is still acknowledged by the Turks with gratitude. The agitation launched by him for the assistance of Turks, revived the Pan-Islamic Movement in India. He wrote in *Comrade:* "Pan-Islamism when we consider its etymology is a meaningless issue of passion and prejudice. If it means anything, it refers to a community of sentiment and aspiration among the Mussalmans of the world, as brought into existence by their religion. In that case Islam bears exactly the same connotation, being the name of a set of beliefs and ideals common to the entire Muslim races. Interpreting the world in this sense no Muslim need be ashamed of its application. The sympathies of a Muslim are co-extensive with his religion, a race and a country has never captured him to the extent of the utter immersion in a narrow patriotism of the ideals which the acceptance of Islam had made obligatory. Territorial patriotism is not at all compatible with the spiritual catholicity of a religion that has declared in a set of common ideals the brotherhood of man".

The brutal firing of Machhli Bazaa., Cawnpore, in 1913, sent a wave of resentment throughout the length and breadth of the subcontinent. It was too painful an incident for the sensitive Muhammad Ali. It shook his heart and made him an active agitator from an armchair politician. He led a deputation to England accompanied by Syed Wazir Hasan, Secretary of the Muslim League. He canvassed there day and night, lecturing, writing in papers and interviewing the high British authorities, for securing an honourable settlement of the Cawnpore episode, but all in vain. He came back to India to find that Great War was declared in Europe in 1914, a few months after his return. Turkey was an ally of Germany and Muhammad Ali wanted that the British Government should take into consideration the feelings of Muslim India.

His bold and inspiring criticism of the imperialist powers, could not be tolerated by the British Government during the war and he was interned for a period of about 5 years, ranging from November 23, 1915 to 1919. When he was released in 1919, the international scene was totally changed. The Great War had come to an end. The Turks were badly pressed in the Treaty of Versailles and their very existence was at stake. Turkey was in danger of total extinction and Llyod George was contemplating to obliterate her from the map of Europe. Political storms were raging on the Indian horizon too. The Indian political atmosphere was tense and explosive. Martial Law had been proclaimed in the Punjab following the great tragedy of Jallianwala Bagh in 1919. These political developments only served as an incentive for the fiery Muhammad Ali. It was the most tumultuous period of his life. He rushed to Amritsar where all Indian political parties were holding their sessions. He started the Khilafat Movement and joined hands with the Congress in 1919. His association with the Congress changed its entire complexion. This stormy patriot of Indian politics transformed the Indian National Congress from a constitutional body into a revolutionary mass organisation. His appeal for Turkish aid fund met with a wonderful response. The Muslim ladies parted with their valuables for helping their Turkish brethren. The Maulana led a deputation to Europe to muster public support for the dwindling Khilafat, but returned disappointed. His joining hands with Mr. Gandhi to force the British to change their attitude towards the Turks resulted in the ideal Hindu—Muslim Unity during 1920—22. The massacre of Jallianwala Bagh and non-restoration of Khilafat led to the adoption of Non-Co-operation Resolution at the Nagpur Congress in 1921. Muhammad Ali is mainly credited with winning over the influential C. R. Dass Group in the Congress to support the move, thus paving the way for the adoption of the Resolution, which implied surrender of titles, resignation from government services and boycott of educational institutions and courts. He was so sincere in the application of the Resolution that when Dr. Ziauddin refused to close the Aligarh Muslim University, he founded Jamia Millia, a parallel institution at Aligarh with the help of Dr. M. A. Ansari, Hakim Ajmal Khan and Dr. Zakir Husain. The Institution was opened by Maulana Mahmood Hasan of Deoband. The teachers and the taught passed a truly Islamic life in this institution, being the very embodiment of simple living and high thinking.

He made extensive tours of the subcontinent during the period extending from October, 1920 up to his arrest for Karachi trial on September 1, 1921. This period was spent virtually in the Railway compartment. He roused the Indian masses from their torpor and infused in them a new political consciousness. He never aspired for any position or privilege for himself. The Indian political consciousness was the result of his 8 years' untiring efforts—a remarkably short period for such a gigantic work. India was echoing with this song:—

> *"Bolin Amman Muhammad Ali Ki*
> *Jan Beta Khilafat Pai Dedo"*

(So spoke the mother of Muhammad Ali. My son, lay down your life for the sake of Khilafat).

A resolution was adopted at the Khilafat Conference held at Karachi in 1921, according to which, it was considered an irreligious act for the Muslims to enroll in the British army. This resulted in the Karachi trial which commenced in October, 1921 in which Maulanas Muhammad Ali, Shaukat Ali, Husain Ahmad Madni, and three others were awarded two years' rigorous imprisonment. His imprisonment evoked a country-wide protest. The Resolution for which he was prosecuted was adopted and published throughout India. The statement given by Muhammad Ali before the court brings out his truly Islamic spirit. He acknowledges the supremacy of the Divine Law over the man-made legislations. The boldness and daring exhibited by him before the court was amazing. He was still in prison when Mustafa Kamal abolished the Khilafat, hence the movement in India for its revival also crumbled down.

Muhammad Ali, when released from jail in 1923, was elected President of the Indian National Congress and he delivered his memorable Presidential address in the momentous session at Cocanada in 1923. Pandit Nehru was his Secretary and he has devoted one full chapter on this session in his autobiography "Nehru". Both in thought and diction, this Address is matchless in the long history of A.I.C.C.

In 1923-24, Pandit Madan Mohan Malviya who was behind the bars was suddenly released following a secret meeting with the Viceroy. He, along with Swami Shardhanand, started the Shuddhi—Sanghatan Movement which led to communal riots throughout India. It destroyed the strong edifice of Hindu—Muslim unity built by the gigantic efforts of the Ali brothers. Mr. Gandhi, too, was carried away by the communal cries of Malviya and his henchmen. Muhammad Ali struggled hard to stop the riot and arrest the disruptive tendencies. He was, however, immensely shocked at the transformation of Gandhi.

The Maulana possessed a restless soul, an undaunted courage and an indomitable will. He had the courage to practise what he preached. Being a valiant fighter of the hundreds of political battles, he magnificently withstood all the trials and temptations that beset his path. He was a true Muslim who had implicit faith in his mission and had always lived up to his convictions. In 1926, he attended the World Muslim Conference *(Motamar Alam-i-Islam)* called by Sultan ibn Saud at Makkah, in which he boldly laid down his views, when other delegates hesitated to speak the bitter truth before the despotic monarch.

Maulana Muhammad Ali organised several Hindu–Muslim unity conferences, but without success. He was instrumental along with Quaid-i-Azam Muhammad Ali Jinnah, in formulating the Delhi Proposals which demanded among other things, the separation of Sind from Bombay Province and the Reforms in N.-W.F.P. But, the publication of Nehru Report in 1928, sealed the fate of Hindu–Muslim unity for ever, and exposed the Congress as well as the Hindu Nationalists in all their nakedness. It proved to be a bitter pill which neither the Quaid-i-Azam nor Maulana Muhammad Ali could swallow. They tried to modify the Report at the Calcutta All Parties Conference held in December 1928, but failed due to want of Hindu support. Later, Quaid-i-Azam and Maulana Muhammad Ali participated in an All Parties Conference held under the Presidentship of Agha Khan in Delhi. Maulana Muhammad Ali, at last had to change his course after 16 years' ceaseless efforts for the cause of Indian freedom. He had given his best for the sake of Hindu–Muslim unity, but to no purpose. He was not destined to live long. His health was shattered, his heart broken and he was only a shadow of his former self.

He started on the final phase of his life journey. Against all medical advice, he decided to participate in the Round Table Conference in London and was carried on a stretcher. Addressing the plenary session of the first R.T.C., he delivered his memorable speech quoted at the top which thrilled his countrymen. He breathed his last on January 4, 1931, and was buried near the sacred Aqsa Mosque in Jerusalem and thus joined the few immortals. His death cast a gloom all over the East and he was mourned by friends and foes alike. He was paid eloquent tributes by the great men of the world. Dr. Iqbal, the poet of the East, said:

*"Soo-e-gardun raft zan rahe ki paighambar guzasht".*

(He proceeded to the Heaven by the same route which was taken by the Prophet of Islam).

H. G. Wells, the celebrated English novelist proclaimed: "Muhammad Ali possessed the pen of Macaulay, the tongue of Burke and the heart of Napolean".

Such was Maulana Muhammad Ali, a person gifted with extraordinary qualities—a dynamic leader, a born poet, an eloquent orator, a forceful writer and above all a true Muslim.

# MAULANA HASRAT MOHANI

It was in May 1951, when Muslim India lost one of its greatest and most illustrious sons in Maulana Fazlul Hasan Hasrat Mohani who was the living symbol of Iqbal's conception of *Momin* (True Muslim).

Hasrat was born at Mohan, District Unnao (U.P.) in 1875. He topped the list of successful candidates in Urdu Middle Examination of U.P., was admitted to Government High School, Fatehpur, and passed High School Examination with distinction, obtaining a scholarship. He graduated from Anglo-Muhammadan College, Aligarh, in 1903 with distinction. He professed progressive and independent views during his college days and openly opposed British domination over India.

He started his celebrated journal *'Urdu-e-Moalla"* from Aligarh in 1904 which was the best literary and political magazine in Urdu of its time in India. Prominent literary and political figures of the country, including Maulana himself, used to contribute to it. An article entitled: "British Policy in Egypt", published in it was legally regarded seditious by the Indian Government. The Maulana was asked to disclose the name of the author, but he declined to do so and preferred to undergo one year's rigorous imprisonment *plus* Rs. 500 as fine. He raised his solitary voice in favour of freedom of the Press, when people shuddered even to utter a word against the Government, and the Congress leaders used to pass resolutions in support of British rule in India.

Maulana Hasrat published *'Urdu-e-Moalla'* firstly from Aligarh and later on from Cawnpore where he had migrated and settled down for the rest of his life. He greatly contributed to popularising 'Ghalib' by publishing an authentic but cheap key of Ghalib's Urdu *Diwan*. Formerly, reference books on Ghalib like Hali's *Memoirs of Ghalib* and the key written by Taba Tabai, were too voluminous and limited to higher circles only. The key written by Maulana became very popular. He wrote on the principles of criticism and the art of poetry in his magazine *"Nukat-i-Sukhan"* (Secrets of Verse). He showed the correct attitude to budding poets and writers by his enlightened criticism of literature. He also brought out the forgotten poets out of their obscurity, by publishing their works in this journal. He created a good taste for poetry among the people by publishing the selected works of Urdu poets. In this respect he may be termed as a prototype of Maulvi Abdul Haq.

The Maulana was perhaps the first political prisoner in British India convicted under the Press Laws. He had to undergo rigorous imprisonment and was not treated as luxurious "A" Class Prisoner, but like ordinary criminal convicts. He was given the following garments for his use in the jail, namely a knicker, a shirt, a cap, a piece of jute cloth and a rough dirty blanket for his bedding. A big iron cup was supplied for eating and for other necessities. In order to realise the fine, the Magistrate confiscated the valuable books and rare manuscripts of his library and auctioned them for a paltry sum. These books were his only earthly possessions. He was kept in solitary confinement and had to grind one maund of wheat per day which is not an easy task and requires much physical labour to which the Maulana was totally unaccustomed. He was, whipped for any loss of wheat which was sometimes deliberately stolen by his wards. His body bore the marks of whipping inflicted in jail. The Maulana wrote in his 'Urdu-e-Moalla' that in the beginning he really felt the rigour of jail life and was much distressed by his meagre clothing and lack of proper arrangement for ablution which served as great obstacles in offering his prayers. After some-times, he was habituated to this sort of life and he realised that bliss lies not in multiplicity of wants but in their negation and was thankful to God for all his trials and tribulations. He was trained to lead a simple life, free of wants, which steeled his character and gave him courage to live up to his convictions and raised his voice in support of truth. It was the first trial of Maulana. His very life was a struggle against the forces of evil. He propagated the boycott of Italian goods during the Tripoli War whereupon his poor (small) press was called upon to submit a security of Rs. 3,000/- by the Government of Sir James Meston. He had to close his magazine and start another one named *"Tazkira-i-Shoara"* (History of Poets). In 1916 he was again sent to jail for two years under the Safety Act. He was put to greatest hardships during this term. His pair of spectacles was confiscated, none was allowed to see him and he had to grind wheat throughout the holy month of Ramazan. During his imprisonment he was unnecessarily transferred to dozens of places and at one place he was given very dirty clothes to wear. He was taken in chains from one place to another and during his journey once he was not paid even one anna per day which was given to ordinary convicts on such occasions and he had to content with a handful of rotten gram for the whole day.

Such hardships tended to steel the Maulana's character and taught him to lead an abstemious life, caring for and fearing none except God. These were the stimulants which brought out the nobler traits of his character and taught him to live up to his convictions, leading a life which would serve as beacon light to the strugglers for truth and freedom of future generations. His dynamic personality awakened the dormant qualities of Indian people and harnessed them for purposes of achieving their destiny.

In the historical session of the All India National Congress at Ahmadabad in 1921, he submitted the Resolution of complete independence for India, but it was opposed by no less a person than Mr. Gandhi himself who pleaded for Dominion Status within the British Commonwealth. No doubt, the Maulana, to some extent, justified the saying that 'genius is eccentric'', and he entertained no some extent, justified the saying that 'genius is eccentric", and he entertained no compromise on his convictions. In his character and composition his opponents could only see disabilities for the task undertaken by him and no end of logic was spared to prove the futility and impossibility of his undertaking. He was in the vanguard of freedom movement of India and took a leading part in the Non-cooperation Movement launched by the combined efforts of the Congress and the Khilafat Movement in 1922-23 and was sent to jail in 1924. He dedicated his life to the service of humanity and truth. He was disillusioned on the publication of the Nehru Report in 1929 and along with some of the great Muslims of those times severed his connection with the Congress. The Nehru Report had totally exposed the political aspirations and ambitions of the majority community to dominate the minorities in India.

The Maulana took a leading part along with Quaid-e-Azam and Ali Brothers in the welfare and political awakening of the Muslim community in India. He presided over the annual session of the All India Khilafat Committee in 1923 and was elected President of the All India Muslim League in 1923. He was a zealous worker of Muslim League and took a prominent part in its reorganisation since 1936 and actively participated in the movement started by Quaid-e-Azam to achieve the political emancipation of Indian Muslims and secure an honourable place for them in the socio-economic structure of India. He was a loyal soldier in the army of Muslim League led by Quaid-e-Azam which ultimately won Pakistan. After the birth of Pakistan, he stayed behind in India to face the aftermath and to safeguard the interests of Muslims left in India. It was he alone who had the courage to face the fanaticism of the Hindu community drunk with power. His memorable words challenging Sardar Patel, the iron man of India in the Constituent Assembly, will long ring in the memory of future generations:

"You should not think that Muslims are orphans today. I am here to defend their rights against all odds and will fight for them till death".

He actually lived up to his convictions and professions. A person who had withstood the combined onslaught of British Imperialism and Hindu fanaticism in the early twenties of the present century did not give serious consideration to the threats, intimidations and insinuations of post-partition Bharti leaders. He stood like a rock against the storm of Hindu communalism which was let loose on helpless Muslims after the division of India. The Maulana who had defied the authority of British aristocrats and had worked side by side with such Indian political giants like Quaid-e-Azam, Ali Brothers, Gandhi, Tilak and C. R. Dass, never bothered about the petty challenges of lesser leaders like Nehru, Patel and Rajaji. He was conscious of the dangers to Muslims inherent in the Indian society after the blood bath of August 1947, but like a true Muslim he stuck to his post and resolved to face the calamities with courage and perseverance. He was confronted with a dangerous task, but a person like him who had weathered great storms that shook the country during the present century, did not shirk to face them again.

The exceptional qualities of sincerity, forbearance, fearlessness, perseverance, patience and contentment which the jail life had developed in his character, are profoundly reflected in his poetry. His career as a poet begins from 1894, when he was a student of Government High School, Fatehpur. He has left behind him ten volumes of poetical works. His individuality as a poet is reflected in his poems throughout his career, but the best part of his contribution to Urdu Poetry was composed in jail, wherefrom each time when he was released, he used to bring out a volume of Urdu poems. Though he was not supplied with paper and ink in the jail, he memorised his couplets and released them to the press on the expiry of his term of imprisonment.

He was the founder of the Modern Urdu Lyrics. He revived the lyrics in Urdu which had lost its soul and had much degenerated into the hands of the Lucknow School of Urdu Poets, namely, Rind, Wazir, Amanat, etc., who laid more emphasis on the pun of words rather than on depth of feelings and sincerity of thought, with the result that Urdu lyric had become a mixture of unnatural and artificial picture of human life. The Maulana had, on one hand, such predecessors as Amanat and Wazir who believed in the jugglery of words, while, on the other, he came into contact with contemporaries like Juraat and Dagh who depicted the vulgar and base sentiments of love. Hali had already advanced his weighty arguments against Urdu lyrics in his famous book *An Introduction to Poetry* and had propagated either its abolition or reformation. The Maulana knew that the lyric was very deep rooted and was the very soul of Urdu poetry. So he steered a midway between the two extremes, and brought about the renaissance of Urdu lyric. He concentrated mainly on the sincerity of thought and simplicity of diction, hence his poems paint the true but dignified sentiments of love and portray the multifarious phases of human passions. In this way, though Hasrat may be termed as a conservative lyrist, yet he infused a new life in its fast decaying body and after Mir may be classed as the best Urdu lyrist. Had there been no Hasrat, Urdu lyric would have had a very dark future. All the later lyrists like Asghar, Jigar, Fani and even Iqbal, took inspiration from the Maulana's poetry. He has an individuality of his own and was the pupil of Taslim in the realm of poetry. He comes in line Momin and Naseem Dehlavi in respect of the type of his verses, but he carved out an independent course for giving vent to his true sentiments. His main attributes are the purity of thought, sublimity of sentiments and simplicity of diction. Like Mir, Hasrat, too, passed a life of despair and anxieties, hence there is a spiritual connection between the two and the works of both reflect deep pathos. But, in Hasrat, the pathos is neither so deep like that of Mir nor so philosophical like that of Ghalib or Fani. His poetry, according to Arnold, is the mirror of his life, hence it has been much affected by his environments and portrays much variety of subjective phases of his many-sided personality. His poetry is mainly subjective and he has tried to avoid the objective colour which had crept into the works of Urdu lyrists of Lucknow. He has depicted numerous pictures of those turbulent times, giving a realistic touch to his poems.

Hasrat is a lover of Nature. Like Wordsworth, he learns sermons from stones and books from running brooks. He founded a new School of Urdu Lyrics whose aim is to depict true human sentiments and reactions to his environments. He is the true product of his time. According to Mathew Arnold, "Literature is the mirror of life", and like the celebrated English poet Lord Tennyson, Hasrat too has been much affected by his environments. His verses are full of revolutionary thought, reactions and national aspirations of a person whose life was so stormy and turbulent. In this respect he comes very close to Chakbast, the national poet of Urdu, but Chakbast is out and out a national poet, while Hasrat simply makes a passing remark on such matters in his lyrics. His lyric composed in the Faizabad jail, carrying the following couplet, is a typical instance in point :

ہے مشقِ سخن جاری، چکی کی مشقت بھی<br>
کیا طُرفہ تماشا ہے، حسرت کی طبیعت بھی

(Hasrat is continuing his hobby of composing verses side by side with the grinding of wheat. What a peculiar nature does Hasrat possess!) Hasrat also composed a poem on Tilak which is very sentimental. Taken together, Hasrat as a poet is very close to Robert Burns, the celebrated poet of Scotland, hence he may be called the 'Robert Burns of Urdu'.

Hasrat was a true Muslim. His greatest virtue was that he was a gentleman in the real sense of the word. As a man, his chief attributes were simplicity, sincerity, truth, fearlessness, straightforwardness, forbearance and contentment. Amongst the politicians and poets of our times, he had the rare distinction of living up to his convictions. Sardar Abdur Rab Nishtar, who had been a distinguished colleague of Maulana since the Khilafat days, paid rich tributes to Hasrat at the time of his death. He said, "Hasrat was a great poet, a great politician, a great litterateur but above all he was a great man".

The Maulana led a life of simplicity and austerity. He was a man who was free from worldly desires and wants. He was a selfless but fearless person who was afraid of none except God. He passed a saintly life and himself did all his household work. Even he brought buckets of water from the water tap and always gently refused offers to share his household duties with others. He used very cheap and tattered clothes and wore a typical Turkish cap. He always travelled in a third class compartment and made several pilgrimages to Makkah declining the comforts of the first class journey offered to him by shipping companies. He even declined the luxurious hospitality of the King of Arabia. His total luggage on such long and hazardous pilgrimages was a small bundle comprising his bedding and some necessary clothes. Being a true Muslim he was never attracted by worldly pleasures or wealth. Whenever he received some monetary return for his publications, he distributed it among the needy. For days his family suffered starvation for want of food, but he bore all these trials with a smiling countenance. He possessed the rare qualities of sincerity, piety, straightforwardness, fearlessness and above all the spirit of contentment and sacrifice. Whenever he ascended the high pedestal of the Presidentship of All-India

Muslim League or All-India Khilafat Committee, he performed his duties like the early Caliphs treading on the footprints of the Holy Prophet. It may be said without fear of contradiction that Maulana Hasrat Mohani belonged to the illustrious tribe of great Muslim heroes of early Islam.

As a whole he was a versatlle genius. He possessed a many-sided personality who acquired greatness in contradictory traits of character and spheres of life-like poetry and politics; literature and religion, which is rather unparalleled in the history of Indo—Pak subcontinent. He was the very embodiment of truth and sincerity, who in his person, translated into reality the following immortal couplet of Iqbal—the Poet of the East:

هزار خوف ہو پر دل رہے زباں کا رفیق

یہی رہا ہے ازل سے قلندروں کا طریق

# MUHAMMAD ALI JINNAH

Pakistan, one of the biggest Muslim States in the world, is a living monument of Quaid-e-Azam Muhammad Ali Jinnah, who, with his untiring efforts, indomitable will and dauntless courage, united the Indian Muslims under the Muslim League banner, and carved out a homeland for them despite stiff opposition from the Hindu Congress and the British Government.

The late Agha Khan acknowledges Mr. Muhammad Ali Jinnah as the greatest man of this century, when he states: "Of all the statesmen that I have known in my life—Clemenceau, Lloyd George, Churchill, Curzon, Mussolini, Mahatma Gandhi— Jinnah is the most remarkable. None of these men in my view outshone him in strength of character and in almost uncanny combination of prescience and resolution which is statecraft. It may be argued that he was luckier than some—far luckier for example, than Mussolini, who perished miserably in utter failure and misery".

Maulana Muhammad Ali Jauhar, the celebrated Muslim patriot of India, is reported to have said, "I learned Islam from Abul Kalam Azad and Iqbal— one pulls me in one direction and the other points to the opposite way". But certainly during the last days of his life he was drawn to the viewpoint of the poet (Iqbal) and considered Muhammad Ali Jinnah as the most promising leader of Muslim India. Muhammad Ali Jinnah, the one time 'Ambassador of Hindu— Muslim Unity' was destined to give a practical shape to the dream of Pakistan, visualized by the poet Iqbal in 1930.

Muhammad Ali Jinnah was born at Karachi on December 25, 1876. His father belonged to a prosperous business community of Kathiawar, which had settled in Karachi. Reared up in careless affluence, Muhammad Ali Jinnah might have easily grown into indolent and ignorant boyhood. But fortunately for Indian Muslims, his father decided for his son a career different from the traditions of his community. He received his early education at the Sind Madrassa and later at the Mission School, Karachi. In 1892, on the advice of an English friend of the family, he was sent to England for higher studies at the tender age of 16. It was in England that Muhammad Ali Jinnah first met Dadabhai Naoroji, who was much impressed by the young Jinnah and who, later played an important role in shaping his early political career. He returned from England in 1896 after qualifying himself for the Bar, and was called to the Bar in 1897.

On his arrival in India from England young Jinnah had to undergo great financial hardships as his father had a run of bad luck in his business. Suddenly he had to face unexpected poverty, but instead of losing heart, he set himself earnestly to carve out a successful independent career for himself. He started his legal practice in Bombay in 1897 and soon earned a respectable place in the Bombay Bar. The first three years of his legal career were of severe hardship, but shortly afterwards his career became just one continuous record of successive triumphs, and he rose to be one of the greatest lawyers and parliamentarians that India has produced. His advocacy, legal acumen and impressive way of speaking contributed immensely to his building up a roaring legal practice in Bombay. He was universally recognised as one of the greatest legal brains of his time and one amongst Motilal Nehru, Ali Imam, C. R. Dass, Shah Muhammad Sulaiman, Bhulabhai Desai and Sir Tej Bahadur Sapru.

Muhammad Ali Jinnah started his political career in 1906 when he attended the Calcutta session of the All India National Congress as the Private Secretary of the President, Dada Bhai Naoroji. During his early political career he was closely associated with Dada Bhai Naoroji and S. N. Banerji and was much influenced by Gopal Krishna Gokhale and, according to his own admissions, he aspired to become "Muslim Gokhale". G. K. Gokhale was also much impressed by the earnestness and abilities of his political disciple and once predicted: "He has true stuff in him and that freedom from all sectarian prejudice which will make him the best Ambassador of Hindu—Muslim Unity" (Mrs. Naidu's article— *Pakistan Standard*, 25-12-54).

Muhammad Ali Jinnah combined in himself the rare gifts of a sincere heart and a high intellect. Being an Ambassador of Hindu—Muslim unity, he tried to bring Muslim League and Congress closer to one another. His efforts in this respect were crowned with success. The session of the All India Muslim League held at Bombay in 1915, under the Presidentship of Mr. Mazharul Haq, well-known for his pro-Congress views, was the first step towards League—Congress rapproachment. A resolution was moved by Muhammad Ali Jinnah in this session to appoint a Committee which would negotiate with the major parties of India. The resolution was adopted. In 1917, the annual sessions of both the Congress and the League were held at Lucknow. The League session, which was presided over by Muhammad Ali Jinnah marked the culmination of his efforts towards the achievement of Hindu— Muslim unity. A joint scheme for Reforms was evolved by the Negotiating Committee which was adopted both by the League and the Congress. This is known as the famous Lucknow Pact, which marks the greatest measure of agreement achieved between the two major parties of India.

Muhammad Ali Jinnah, by this time, had become one of the most important National Leaders of India. He presided over a function in Bombay at which an address was presented to Mr. M. K. Gandhi on his arrival from South Africa. He was elected as the Chairman of the Bombay Branch of Home League. Mr. Montague, the then Secretary of State for India who saw Mr. Muhammad Ali

Jinnah in 1917, records in his diary: "They were followed by Muhammad Ali Jinnah, young, perfectly mannered, impressive looking, armed to the teeth with dialectics and insistent upon the whole of his scheme" (The Makers of Pakistan— Al-Beruni). Lord Chelmsford has also acknowledged on one occasion that "Jinnah is a very clever man, and it is of course an outrage that such a man should have no chance of running the affairs of his own country". (The Makers of Pakistan). In 1918 he led a powerful agitation against presenting a farewell address to Lord Willingdon, the retiring Bombay Governor. It was in reality an effective protest against the autocratic regime of Lord Willingdon as the Governor of Bombay and marked the beginning of the post-war agitation. Mr. M. Syed in his book, *'Muhammad Ali Jinnah'*, writes that after this incident Jinnah, "was at once a hero". Public addresses were presented to him, and garden parties were given in his honour. "For the first time in his lonely career, Jinnah was a popular figure—a leader of the people. His admirers contributed thirty thousand rupees to build a Memorial Hall in his honour and in spite of the ravages of partition, it is still called the Jinnah Hall. On the wall is a marble plaque recalling the historic triumph of the citizens of Bombay, under the brave and brilliant leadership of Muhammad Ali Jinnah" *(Hector Bolitho's Jinnah)*.

In 1919, Mr. Jinnah resigned his membership of the Imperial Legislative Council as a protest against the adoption of "Rowlatt Act". He vehemently criticised the Act during the Calcutta session of All India Muslim League in September 1920. He had also developed differences with Mr. Gandhi and did not approve of the Gandhian methods of handling the situation. Moreover, Mr. Gandhi had also captured the Presidentship of Home Rule League, changed its constitution and named it as Swaraj Sabha. This caused his open opposition to Gandhian policies. These differences cluminated in his break with the Congress when in the Annual Session of the All India Congress held at Nagpur in 1920, a resolution of nonco-operation with the Government was adopted by an over-whelming majority. Mr. Jinnah, who opposed such a move, had no option but to resign from the All India National Congress. Mr. Kanji Dwarkadass, one of his colleagues in the Home League describes this incident. "Once again Jinnah put up a bold fight against Gandhi at the Nagpur Session of the Congress during the Christmas week in 1920. In the meantime Umar Subhani and Shankarlal Banker had left the Home Rule League to join Gandhi and K. M. Munshi later Governor of U.P. and I worked as Honorary Secretaries with Jinnah as the President. Gandhi not satisfied with having got the control of the Congress, started poaching on other political organisations and captured the Home Rule League and changed its Constitution. Jinnah and 20 of us resigned our memberships. I have the most pleasant recollections of my work with Jinnah during those and subsequent years. I found extremely amiable, fairminded and tolerant. He was a judicial minded chairman and he never took sides when he was in the Chair" (Article— *"Jinnah—A Great Political Leader and Great Fighter"*).

Muhammad Ali Jinnah continued his efforts to bring the two major communities of India closer, but he was greatly handicapped by the 'Shuddhi Sangathan' Movement started by Pt. Madan Mohan Malaviya and his associates

which had begun to exercise greater hold over the policies of the All India
National Congress and to some extent changed the outlook of even the great
'Mahatma'. This resulted in a wave of communal riots which swept over the
entire country, undoing all work of Hindu–Muslim unity. In 1924, Jinnah called
a general meeting of the Muslim League at Lahore and tried to repeat his
performance of the Lucknow Pact. He had a great hand in formulating the Delhi
proposals which were opposed by the Punjab Muslim League but endorsed by
the All India Muslim League. His efforts for bringing the two major communities
closer did not receive the support it deserved as the two communities had a
bitter experience of Hindu–Muslim riots all over India.

The issue of the boycott of the Simon Commission caused a split in the
ranks of Muslim League–Sir Muhammad Shafi and his Punjab followers
cooperated with the Commission, while Muhammad Ali Jinnah and Maulana
Muhammad Ali with rest of the Muslim League members, co-operated with the
Congress in the boycott of the Simon Commission. Shortly after, Muhammad
Ali Jinnah went to England and during his absence the Nehru Report was
published which was severely criticised by all sections of Muslim opinion except
the Nationalists. This further widened the branch between the two major Indian
communities and one last effort to narrow down the differences was made when
a National Convention was called at Calcutta in December 1928 to consider the
Report. The Convention turned down the amendment moved by Muhammad Ali
Jinnah both in the subject committee and the open session. The so-called
Congress Nationalists exhibited no desire for a compromise and Jinnah left a
sadder but a wiser man. According to Kanji Dwarakadass, "The resolution on
adult franchise and joint electorate and weightage was about to be passed when
Jayaker sprang a surprise, made a strong anti-Muslim speech and the resolution
could not be passed. It is essential that I should say this because it was not
Jinnah who took up an impossible and obstinate communal attitude to prevent
the settlement of Hindu–Muslim problem". (Article–*'Jinnah–A Great Political
Leader and a Great Fighter')*. This impossible and extremely communal attitude
of the Hindu leaders of the Congress caused him disillusionment that the Muslims
could not expect a fair deal at the hands of Hindus in united India. This brought
about his final parting of ways with the Congress and other Hindu organisations.
Being a realist, he found no reason in running after a futile and impractical ideal
of one and a united nationality for India.

As a parliamentarian and debater, Mr. Jinnah outshone all his contemporaries in India. During his long record as the member of the Central Legislative
Assembly of India, starting as early as 1910 and lasting up to 1947, there was
hardly any important enactment of the Legislature in the shaping of which he
had not a share.

Mr. Jinnah was more of a debater than an orator. His great power as a
debater earned for him the nickname of Parliamentary Juggler . According to
Mr. O. N. Nambiyar, "it is in debates that Mr. Jinnah creates a great impression.
Ask him to reply on or to take part in a debate on a highly controversial question:

he likes it and he does it better than any member of any Legislature in India today. Mr. Jinnah is one of those few speakers whom an audience is not tired of hearing; in fact, Mr. Jinnah's audience is never tired because he does not tire them". His success as a powerful parliamentary debater lay in his magnetic personality, an impressive delivery, his clear cut persuasive arguments and a voice which while lacking in volume had an arresting timber. "But though occasionally", writes Mrs. S. Naidu, "he has attained a moment of wholly unconscious and stirring eloquence, he has the cogent force of a brilliant advocate rather than the glowing fervour of a brilliant orator. And it is not 'public platform, but at a Round Table Conference that he finds full scope of his unusual powers of persuasion, luminous exposition, searching argument and impeccable judgement".

Muhammad Ali Jinnah was first elected to the Supreme Legislative Council of India in 1910 from the Muslim Constituency of Bombay Presidency. In the Legislature he supported all liberal measures involving larger national issues. He lent his support to all labour, and social reform legislations that came up before the Council. "His attitude towards all problems of India was one of progress and reform", writes Kanji Dwarkadass. "He was never a reactionary in politics". He supported Gokhale's Elementary Education Bill and Mr. Basu's Special Marriage Bill, which had created a violent opposition from conservative India. But it was in his successful piloting of Waqf Validating Bill that he rendered a singular service to Muslims and earned their gratitude. For sometime "Muslim opinion had been clamouring for a measure to counteract the effect of certain Privy Council decisions based on an interpretation of Muhammadan Law considered to be wrong and injurious. The opinion finally crystallised into the Waqf Validating Bill of 1913 to introduce which Jinnah was specially nominated for an extra term by the Viceroy Lord Hardinge". *(Great Men of India)*. He showed great skill in piloting through such a intricate and controversial measure. The passing of this Bill into law earned him the appreciation of his colleagues as well as the first recognition of his co-religionists all over India, who now began to look to him for political guidance.

After this, there was a short break of three years in his work as a legislator, when he proceeded to Europe on a long holiday. In 1916 he was again elected to the Imperial Legislative Council from the Bombay Presidency. Till 1947 he continued to be a member of the Central Legislature of India. His association with it all these long years was so intimate that there was hardly any important legislative enactment in which he had not taken major share. He wielded great influence and respect in the Central Legislature due to his honesty and integrity, parliamentary abilities and independent outlook. He never placed himself under the slightest obligation to the Government Benches and in all liberal issues sided with the Opposition. He played an important part in sending the Shariat Bill to the Statute Book.

Mr. Muhammad Ali Jinnah was the leader of the Independent Party in the Second and Third Central Assemblies of India. He severely criticised the Treasury

Benches and during the Annual Budget Session, his party occasionally moved a
cut motion and had it carried to censure the Government. But, as the leader of
the Independent Party in the Fifth Central Assembly, he did not support the
nefarious tactics of the Congress benches which by this time were totally exposed
in their anti-Muslim activities. He openly accused the Congress of its designs to
exploit and terrorise the Indian Muslims for strengthening the Congress. A
Muslim League Party was formed in the Central Legislative Assembly with Mr.
Jinnah as its leader. This party challenged the claim of the Congress to represent
all communities in India. Never before Muslim members of the Assembly had
worked better as a team. With their capable as well as experienced leader they
gave a tough fight to the Congress party in the Central Assembly debates. In
1945, when fresh elections to the Central Assembly of India were held, the
Muslim League captured all Muslim seats and thus formed a powerful Muslim
Bloc under the leadership of Mr. Muhammad Ali Jinnah. It was this party,
which, under his able guidance, fought inside the Central Legislature a two front
battle for the achievement of Pakistan. Writing about it, Mr. O. N. Nambiyar
stated: "Mr. Jinnah today is certainly the most prominent member of the
Assembly. The Government knows that the Congress has no right. Every member
of the League Party is proud of its leader: a leader who knows how to lead . . . .
The part played by Mr. Jinnah is a part which every Indian Muslim may be
proud of".

The Gandhian policies which dominated the Congress since 1920 and the
Shuddhi Sanghatan Movement backed by an influential section of the Congress
culminating in countrywide communal riots, widened the gulf between the two
major Indian communities and drove Muhammad Ali Jinnah farther and farther
away from the Congress. The Nehru Report which exposed the Hindu nationalists
in all their nakedness brought about the final break. Some of the staunch Muslim
nationalists like Maulana Muhammad Ali, and Maulana Hasrat Mohani resigned
from the Congress. Muhammad Ali Jinnah who had resigned from the Congress
during the Nagpur Session in 1920, continued his unabated efforts for Hindu—
Muslim unity, but after the publication of the Nehru Report he considered all
such attempts to be utterly futile. To counter the Nehru Report, Mr. Jinnah
evolved his famous Fourteen Points some of which related to (1) Effective
Representation of Minorities in the Provinces; (2) Separate Electorate; (3) No
Disturbance of the Muslim Majority in the Punjab, Bengal and N.-W.F.P.;
(4) Religious Liberty, etc.; (5) Machinery for Enforcing Religious Liberty.

In 1929 he attended the All Parties Conference for evolving a united stand
of Muslim political parties held under the presidentship of H. R. H. Agha Khan
at Delhi. Next year, Muhammad Ali Jinnah sailed to England to attend the First
Round Table Conference. Dewan Chaman Lal, a Congress leader of Punjab who
was a fellow traveller wrote: "Jinnah is frankly in a despondent mood. He is one
of the few men who have no personal motives to nurse or personal aims to advance.
His integrity is beyond question. And he is the loneliest man". Muhammad Ali
Jinnah tried to evolve a Hindu—Muslim formulae in the First Round Table
Conference, but it was vetoed by Dr. Jayaker. Later, Agha Khan tried to come

to an understanding with Gandhi on the Hindu–Muslim question which was accepted by all other communities of India except caste Hindus. This enabled the British Premier to give the Communal Award to the Indian minorities. Jinnah opposed a strong Centre, which, in his opinion, would reduce Provincial autonomy to a mere farce.

Even at the Round Table Conference, Muḥammad Ali Jinnah supported the broader national interest. According to Kanji Dwarkadass, "At the first Round Table Conference Jinnah and C. Y. Chintamani were the only two leaders who opposed the commercial safeguards which the Britishers wanted for their own countrymen in India. A small incident may be mentioned. The late Prime Minister, Ramsay Macdonald sent for Jinnah and told him that in the new order of things that would come in India, the British Prime Minister would have to look for prominent Indian to take up the Governorship of the Provinces, suggesting without saying so that Jinnah would have excellent chance if he proved to be a good boy. Jinnah asked Macdonald if this was an attempt to bribe him to get his support on the British Government's compromise suggestions". Iqbal, who was also a Muslim delegate in the Round Table Conference, convinced Muhammad Ali Jinnah the desirability of creating a North–Western State for Muslims in India. This scheme did not find favour, but in the 1935 Act, Sind and N.-W.F.P. were made separate Provinces–a measure which proved to be very useful for Muslims.

The years 1928–35 may be considered as a period of his political wilderness. Being disgusted with the disappointing Indian politics, Mr. Jinnah had settled in England and had started practice in the Privy Council. But, with the passing away of the magnetic personality of Maulana Muhammad Ali, Indian Muslims were left without effective leadership, and Mr. Jinnah was induced to come back to India in October 1935. He reorganised the Muslim League and made it more democratic. A Central Election Board was set up to fight the Provincial Assembly Elections held under the 1935 Act. The Jamiat-al-Ulema-i-Hind supported the League. Mr. Jinnah made a countrywide tour and his efforts met with some success specially in the Muslim minority provinces.

The 1937, Provincial Assembly elections produced many surprises. The Congress secured absolute majority in seven out of the eleven Provinces. This unexpected success of the Congress made their leaders still more cold towards non-nationalist Muslim organisations. Its haughty President, Pt. Nehru, proudly declared that there were only two parties in India–Congress and the British Government. Jinnah accepted this challenge and declared that there was a third party, too, and that was the Muslim League. The Congress President Pt. Nehru, with the help of Nationalist Muslims and Jamiat-al-Ulema leaders (who had now allied themselves with the Congress) started the Muslim mass contact movement which proved to be an utter failur. Several bye-elections of Muslim seats in the United Provinces, the centre of Congress, ended in crushing defeats to the Congress candidates and established the claim of Mr. Jinnah about the existence of a Third Party. In 1938, Congress Ministries were formed in eight out of eleven Indian Provinces, and their professions, when put to practice, fell miserably short of public expectations, specially of the Muslims. The utterly communal policies practised by the Congress high ups like Patel, Tandon, Shukla, Misra and Sanpurnanand, coupled with the narrowminded communal outlook of the Hindu masses, exposed the Congress in all its nakedness. Their practice procured a strange contrast to their professions which created a stir throughout Muslim India and immensely added to the Muslim distrust towards the Congress, resulting in rallying of the Muslim masses under the Muslim League banner. The anti-Muslim policies of the Congress Ministries had greatly contributed to the popularity of the Muslim League in the Muslim minority provinces. A series of Hindu–Muslim riots broke out in the Congress administered provinces which knew no ending. When the Provincial Ministries resigned in 1939, the Muslims and the untouchables celebrated the "Deliverance Day' throughout India. A Muslim League Committee was set up earlier to enquire into the atrocities of the Congress Regimes in the provinces, and the Pirpur Report was published detailing the persecution of Muslims under the Congress Ministries.

The Muslim League had acquired great popularity among the Muslims due to the wise statesmanship of its leader, Mr. Jinnah, and the short-sighted and unrealistic policies of the Congress leadership. He secured another victory when, in 1937, the Muslim members of Punjab, Bengal and Sind Provincial Assemblies came to terms with Mr. Jinnah and agreed to abide by the policy and programmes of the All India Muslim League in all-India matters. Muslim India had rallied round the Muslim League and Mr. Muhammad Ali Jinnah. The Annual Session of the Muslim League at Lucknow in 1937 provided a turning point in the history of Muslim India.

The atrocities perpetrated by the Congress Provincial Ministries over the Muslims had greatly alienated them from the Congress. This treatment was taken as a challenge by Muslim India. This unstatesman-like attitude of the Congress leadership was criticised by some of the far-sighted non-Muslims including Mr. Tairsee, Sardar Sardul Singh Caveesher and Sir Chaman Lal Sitalvad.

Mr. Jinnah took full advantage of the situation created by the Congress leadership. He had now become the sole leader of Muslim India. Except a handful of nationalist Muslims, the Muslims recognised him as their Quaid-e-Azam (Great Leader). The Congress also realised this but it was unwilling to recognise the representative character of the Muslim League. Hence all unity talks between Jinnah and Gandhi representing the Muslim League and the Congress, respectively broke down on this vital issue. The unrealistic attitude of Mr. Gandhi, who insisted that Congress, too, represented the Muslims, marred any solution of the Hindu–Muslim problem in India and Mr. Jinnah was by now convinced that Indian Muslims should not expect justice from the Congress.

In the session of All India Muslim League held at Karachi in 1938, it was resolved that the entire question of the future Constitution of India should be reviewed in a manner of finding out a way for securing an honourable status for

Muslims in India. The matter was entrusted to a sub-committee, which suggested the creation of a separate Muslim state as a safeguard against Hindu domination. The Report of the sub-committee was published, but it was ignored by the hot-headed Congress High Command. At last the recommendations of the sub-committee came out in the form of the famous Pakistan Resolution adopted by the All India Muslim League in its historic session at Lahore in March 1940, according to which, "the areas, in which the Muslims are numerically in majority, as in the North-Western and Eastern zones of India, should be grouped to constitute independent states". The Lahore Resolution demanding a separate independent State for Indian Muslims, created a stir throughout non-Muslim India and a wave of opposition started from the interested quarters, and backed by the powerful Congress and allied press, swept through India. But, according to the author of the *"Makers of Pakistan"*, "Little did those who sponsored the Delhi Proposals in 1928 or those, who in 1937, treated the Muslims in a rigid, dictatorial manner, realise that they were sowing the wind and would reap the whirlwind".

The course for Mr. Jinnah was now clear. The Muslim League had adopted Pakistan as its goal and now it was for its supreme leader to direct all his efforts towards its realisation. The goal for Indian Muslims dreamt by Iqbal as back as 1930 at Allahabad, had begun to take concrete shape and it was finally realised on August 14, 1947.

The critical war situation in South East Asia compelled the British Government to strive for a settlement with the principal political parties in India. Sir Stafford Cripps arrived in India, talked to the leaders of the principal political parties and was prepared to concede the right of self-determination to the provinces. But his proposals were ultimately rejected both by the Muslim League and the Congress for different reasons.

Shortly after the departure of the Cripps Mission, the Congress started the "Quit India" Movement in 1942 and the prominent leaders of the Congress, including Mr. Gandhi were put behind the bars. This caused a short lull on the political front of India.

Lord Wavell, the new Viceroy, made a fresh effort to solve the constitu·tional problem of India through the representatives of different communities on the proposed Executive Council of India. A conference of prominent Indian leaders was called at Simla in June 1945, which failed to produce any results.

Meanwhile, with the termination of war in Europe and with the election of the Labour Party to power in U. K. the political situation also changed in India. The British Labour Party had greater sympathy with the political aspirations of the inhabitants of India. Hence the prospects of the Indian independence brightened. The British Labour Party sent a Cabinet Mission to resolve the constitutional tangle in India. The Congress still insisted upon its claim that it represented the entire population of India, including the Muslims, though the results of the recent elections of the Central as well as Provincial Legislatures in which the Muslim League had captured almost all Muslim seats, had belied the Congress claim. The Cabinet Mission after considerable deliberations and negotiations with the Indian leaders, came out with a plan, which divided India in three zones with Foreign Affairs, Defence and Communications as Central subjects. The plan was originally accepted by both the Congress and the League. But the Congress leaders started their own interpretations of the Plan which envisaged a strong Centre. This interpretation completely changed the entire Plan, hence the Muslim League rejected it in its session at Bombay.

The Labour Government made one more effort to resolve the deadlock. In December 1946, four Indian leaders representing the two principal Indian parties, including Mr. Jinnah were invited to London to straighten out the issue. This effort also failed. The British Premier made a declaration in the House of Commons on February 20, 1947 that the British Government would quit India by June 1948 and would hand over power to one or more Central Governments. This statement alarmed the Congress leadership, which instigated violent communal riots in Punjab, Bihar and Western U.P. Having failed in their conspiracy to suppress Muslims in Punjab through political intrigues and violence, the Congress now demanded the partition of Punjab and Bengal—a strange demand from a party which, till lately, had opposed the partition of India. Hence the Mountbatten Plan of the Partition of India was announced on June 3, 1947 and Pakistan was established on August 14, 1947 with Mr. Jinnah as its first Governor-General.

The establishment of Pakistan brought greatest responsibilities on the shoulders of Mr. Jinnah, who being the beloved leader as well as the Head of Pakistan Government had to build the newly-born State, starting from scratch. The holocust in the East Punjab, Delhi, Rajputana State and Western U.P. as well as the harassment of Muslims all over the Indian State, drove more than eight million Muslims across the border and created an unprecedented refugee problem for the newly-born State of Pakistan. In the meantime, the Indian forces invaded and occupied the Muslim populated State of Kahmir, whose Hindu Maharaja had entered into a secret understanding with the Indian Government against the wishes of his people. The Indian Government also withheld the Pakistani share of the divided assets. But the indomitable will of the Quaid-e-Azam and the administrative ability of his trusted lieutenant Mr. Liaquat Ali Khan, the Prime Minister of Pakistan, enabled the new State to tide over its initial difficulties. Within a short span of one year, Pakistan had displayed to the astonished world its financial as well as administrative stability and was marching forward on road to progress. The Quaid-e-Azam laid greatest stress on the financial stability of Pakistan. He worked out a sound economic policy, established an independent currency and a State Bank for Pakistan. He made Karachi, the Federal Capital. His decisions were final as he was the undisputed leader of Pakistan, who was respected as well as loved by his people.

The Quaid-e-Azam was a selfless leader who was the real benefactor of his people. He had realised that provincialism was the greatest threat to the solidarity of his country. He warned his people: "Have you forgotten the lesson that was taught to us thirteen hundred years ago. . . . . so what is the use of saying, 'we are Bengalis or Sindhis or Pathans or Punjabis.' No, we are Muslims . . . You belong to a nation; you have carved out a territory, vast territory: it is all yours; it does not belong to a Punjabi or a Sindhi or a Pathan or a Bengali, it is yours". The Quaid was equally uncompromising in favour of making Urdu as the only State language of Pakistan. He was on his sick bed, when he learnt that an agitation against Urdu was started by interested persons at Dacca. Disregarding medical advice, he went all the way to Dacca in March 1948 and advised the East Pakistani brethren: "Let us make it very clear to you that the State language of Pakistan is going to be Urdu and no other language . . . . . . . . Therefore so far as the State language is concerned, Pakistan's language shall be Urdu. And anyone who disrupts this unity and misleads you is really the enemy of Pakistan . . . . . . I must warn you to beware of the fifth columnists . . . . . For official use in this Province, the people may choose any language they wish. There can, however, be only one *Lingua Franca*—and that language should be Urdu and cannot be any other . . . . .The State language, therefore, must obviously be Urdu, a language that has been nurtured by a hundred million Muslims of this subcontinent, a language which is understood throughout the length and breadth of Pakistan and, above all, a language which, more than any provincial language, embodies the best what is in Islamic culture and Muslim traditions and is nearest to the language used in other Islamic countries. It is not without significance that Urdu has been driven out of the Indian Union and that the official script of Urdu has been disallowed". The Founder of Pakistan had given his final verdict on the controversy of the State language of Pakistan but also he did not live to see that his followers had forgotten his valuable advice soon after his death.

The Quaid-e-Azam was a great champion of minorities. He guaranteed full freedom and equal partnership for the minorities in Pakistan. Addressing the Pakistan Constituent Assembly once he said: "You are free; you are free to go to your temples, you are free to go to your mosques or to any place of worship in this State of Pakistan. You may belong to any religion or caste or creed—that has nothing to do with the fundamental principles, that we are all citizens and equal citizens of One State".

The Quaid-e-Azam did not live long to witness the progress of the State which he had founded. His excessive work soon confined him to bed. Disregarding medical advice, he devoted much time to his official work which impaired his health and after a protracted illness he died on September 11, 1948 at Karachi. The entire Nation was plunged into grief on his passing away at a time when he was needed most.

It would not be out of place to give a portrait of Mr. Jinnah, given by Mrs. Naidu, the celebrated Congress leader: "Few figures of the Indian renaissance are so striking and so significant to a student of psychology, more singularly attractive by the paradox of a rare and complex temperament, of strange limitations and subtle possibilities that hides the secret of its own greatness like a pearl within a shell. Never was there a nature whose outer qualities provided so complete an antithesis of its inner worth".

# RULERS, STATESMEN AND ADMINISTRATORS

# WALEED—THE UMAYYAD CALIPH

On the death of the Umayyad Caliph, Abdul Malik, known as the Charlemagne of the Arabs, in 705 A.C., his highly talented son, Waleed, succeeded him. In Waleed's reign the Arab rule was extended to its farthest limits which included Spain and Southern France in the West, Sind, Baluchistan and Southern Punjab in the East and Transoxiana and Turkistan in the North. Three of the greatest Muslim conquerors, namely, Tariq, Qasim and Qutaiba, swept away all resistence encountered in these lands.

Waleed was born in 651 A.C. He was brought up amidst the growing luxury and aristocracy of the House of Umayyad. He had developed an artistic taste from his childhood which led him to become the greatest builder of the Umayyad dynasty that ruled in Damascus.

Hardly 54 at the time, he brought to his high office the aristocratic outlook and religious fervour scarcely known among his predecessors.

Waleed's reign is known as the golden period of the Umayyad Caliphate distinguished for its all round progress. He embarked upon an unprecedented career of conquest in three directions which extended the Arab rule to its widest limits. He established a wise and firm administration which enabled him to devote himself to social and public welfare works.

Waleed appointed his saintly cousin Umar bin Abdul Aziz, as Governor of Hejaz. The new Governor set up a council of jurists and notables of Madina, which was consulted on all administrative matters. He beautified Makkah and Madina, rebuilt the Mosque of the Prophet, improved roads and tried to erase signs of ravages committed in the Holy cities during the time of earlier Umayyad rulers. His just and generous administration in the Holy cities attracted many people who were groaning under the tyrannical rule of Hajjaj bin Yusuf, the Umayyad Viceroy of Iraq. The despot Hajjaj, who has become a legend of tyranny in the history of Islam, was an exceptionally capable Administrator who established firmly the Umayyad rule among the fickle-minded Iraqis. He was annoyed by the migration of a large number of Iraqis to Hejaz. At the instance of Hajjaj, Waleed removed Umar bin Abdul Aziz from his post amidst universal mourning.

Waleed's fame rests on the marvellous Muslim victories which extended the boundaries of the Umayyad Empire from the mountains of Pyrenees in the West to the walls of China in the East and from Kashgar in the North to the source of the Nile in the South.

The Modharite Chief Qutaiba bin Muslim Baheli who had been appointed as the Deputy Governor of Khurasan was an able strategist and General. He conquered Transoxiana and subjugated the whole of Central Asia up to the confines of Kashgar. He captured the important cities of Bukhara, Samarkand and Farghana.

The territories of Baluchistan, Sind and Southern Punjab were annexed by the youngest General in history, Muhammad bin Qasim, who through a glorious military campaign defeated the mightiest Indian ruler of the time, Raja Dahir of Debal. Through a lightning march along the Indus river valley he swept away all resistance encountered in the way and in less than two years conquered the entire lower Indus valley up to Multan. Muhammad bin Qasim annexed a major portion of Southern Punjab and penetrated as far as the Beas. He set up a wise and benevolent Administration in the conquered territory which endeared him equally to Muslim and non-Muslim subjects.

Waleed's brother, Maslamah who was the Captain-General of Muslim forces in Asia Minor, captured many important cities and annexed a large part of Asia Minor.

But the greatest military campaign in Waleed's time was launched in North-Western Africa and Spain—under the able leadership of Musa bin Nusair, a Yemeni, and his able lieutenant Tariq bin Ziyad. Musa, son of Nusair, was the Umayyad Viceroy of Africa. He put down the Berber rebellion with a strong hand and pacified the entire North African territory. The Muslim settlements were harassed by the Byzantines from the Mediterranean. Musa, therefore, sent out expeditions, which captured the islands of Majorca, Minorca and Ivica, which soon came to flourish under the Muslim rule.

Whilst Africa was enjoying peace and prosperity under the benevolent Muslim rule, Spain was groaning under the iron heels of the Goths. The Gothic King, Roderick, a debauchee, had dishonoured his Governor Julian's daughter, Florinda. The Governor invited Musa to liberate Spain from Roderick. Musa despatched his lieutenant, Tariq, with a small force for the purpose.

Tariq, son of Ziyad, an able lieutenant of Musa, landed on April 30, 711 A.C. with his small force at the Rock which now bears his name. He ordered his men to burn their boats and thus ended all hopes of their return. A fierce battle was fought in September 711 A.C., on the banks of the Guadalquivir, in which Roderick's heavy forces were routed by the small Muslim force led by Tariq. Roderick was drowned in the Guadalquivir.

The moral effect of this memorable victory was immense. City after city of Gothic Spain threw open its gates to the Muslim Conqueror. Tariq divided his small army into four divisions which advanced in Spain in four directions. In June 712 A.C., Tariq was joined by Musa and the two Muslim conquerors reached as far as the Pyrenees. Leaving Tariq in Spain, Musa crossed into France and soon annexed a sizeable portion of Southern France. Standing on the Pyrenees, the dauntless Viceroy conceived the conquest of whole of Europe and in all human probability he would have done so, had he not been recalled by Waleed. The West completely lay at his feet. The cautious and hesitant policy of the Umayyads deprived the Muslims of the glorious opportunity of conquering Europe. As a result, Europe remained enveloped in darkness for the next seven or eight centuries.

The recall of the two Muslim conquerors, Musa and Tariq, by Waleed, was, no doubt, most disastrous to the cause of Islam in the West.

The conquest of Spain by Muslims ushered there an era of unprecedented peace and prosperity which, in later years, gave birth to a glorious Muslim civilization that ultimately dispelled the darkness that had enveloped Mediaeval Europe.

Waleed is known as the greatest builder in Umayyad dynasty. He built the Grand Mosque of Damascus, enlarged and beautified those of Madina and Jerusalem. Under his direction mosques were built in every city. He beautified the Capital city of Damascus with magnificent buildings, luxuriant gardens and refreshing fountains. The city bore broad roads lined with shady trees and aqueducts. He erected fortresses for the protection of frontiers and constructed roads and sank wells throughout the Empire. He established schools and hospitals, built orphanages and houses for the poor. He stopped promiscuous charity by granting allowances to the infirm and the poor from the State Treasury. He created asylums for the blind, the crippled and the insane where they were lodged and looked after by attendants appointed by the State. He himself visited the markets and noted the fluctuation in prices.

He was a great patron of art and learning; he granted pensions to poets and savants, legists and Sufis. He was known for his generosity and benevolence.

His reign is known for its peace and prosperity. He is distinguished for giving the Arabian pattern to his Administration. He enjoyed undisputed popularity throughout the world of Islam, especially in Syria.

Waleed breathed his last on February 23, 715 A.C. at the age of 64 after a glorious reign of nine years and seven months.

# HAROON AR-RASHID

Haroon ar-Rashid, the celebrated Abbaside Caliph of Baghdad, is universally recognised as one of the greatest rulers of the world, whose reign ushered in the most brilliant period of Saracenic rule in Asia. "The stories of *Arabian Nights*", says Ameer Ali, "have lent a fascination to the name of the remarkable Caliph who was wont to roam the streets of Baghdad by night to remedy injustice and to relieve the oppressed and the destitute. Faithful in the observation of his religious duties, abstemious in his life, unostentatiously pious and charitable and yet fond of surrounding himself with the pomp and insignia of grandeur, he impressed his personality or popular imagination and exercised a great influence by his character on society".

Haroon ar-Rashid, son of the Abbaside Caliph Mehdi, was born at Rayy in February 763 A.C. He was given a thorough education by the talented Barmakide Yahya bin Khalid and succeeded his brother Hadi, as the Abbaside Caliph in September 786 A.C. He was only 23 at that time.

Soon after his accession, Haroon ar-Rashid appointed Yahya Barmaki as his Prime Minister and for the next 17 years, Yahya and his four sons, particularly Jafar and Fazal, virtually ruled the state and assumed unlimited power in the Abbaside Caliphate.

Haroon's reign forms the golden period of Abbaside Caliphate in which all round progress was made and Baghdad reached the heights of its glory as the dream city of the *Arabian Nights,* unrivalled in the Mediaeval world.

Haroon was great both in war and peace. The Abbaside dominions of northern Africa, then known as "Ifrika" were made an autonomous Province under Ibrahim, son of Aghlob. In Asia, the Government was conducted with vigour and foresight. In 171 A.H., the whole of Kabul and Hansar were annexed to the Abbaside Empire which now extended up to the Hindu Kush in the East. Rashid also separated the Marches in Asia Minor from the ordinary Governorship and placed it under the control of a military Governor. Tarsus in Clicia was converted into a strong military base.

Rashid's most important military campaigns were launched against the treacherous Byzantine rulers who broke their pledges soon after the Abbaside

Caliph turned his back upon them. But there is hardly any other example of the generosity shown by the Abbaside Caliph who pardoned the Byzantine Emperor's breach of pledge more than half a dozen times only to be repeated again. In 791 A.C. the Byzantines broke the treaty concluded in Caliph Mehdi's time by invading the Muslim territories only to be repulsed with heavy losses. The cities of Matarah and Ancyra were captured, Cyprus was re-conquered and Crete was overrun. The Byzantines begged for peace which was granted on promise of the regular payment of tribute fixed in the former treaty.

A few years later, when Nicephorus seized the Byzantine throne, he broke the treaty and sent an insulting letter to the Abbaside Caliph, Haroon ar-Rashid: "From Nicephorus, the Roman Emperor, to Haroon, Sovereign of the Arabs: Verily, the Empress who preceded me gave thee the rank of a rook and put herself in that of a pawn, and conveyed to thee many loads of her wealth, and this through the weakness of women and their folly. Now when thou hast read this letter of mine, return what thou hast received of substance, otherwise the sword shall decide between me and thee". When Rashid read this letter, "he was so inflamed with anger that no one could dare to look at his face". Then he wrote on the back of Byzantine Ruler's letter: "From Haroon, the Commander of the Faithful, to Nicephorus, the Roman dog: Verily I have read thy letter; the answer thou shall behold, not hear. And he was true to his word. The same day he started on a nonstop march to Heraclea, a Byzantine stronghold. The boastful Byzantine Emperor suffered a humiliating defeat at this place. "The warlike celerity of the Arabs could only be checked by the arts of deceit and a show of repentence". The Byzantine Emperor, Nicephorus begged for peace from the kind-hearted Abbaside Caliph which was granted on promise of regular payment of increased tribute by the Byzantine Emperor. But Rashid had hardly reached his Headquarters when the Byzantine Emperor broke his pledge, thinking that the Abbaside Caliph would not take to field in severe winter. But he had mistaken his adversary. When Rashid came to know of this breach of pledge, he retraced his steps. "Nicephorus was astonished by the bold and rapid marches of the Commander of the Faithful, who repassed, in the depth of winter, the snows of Mount Taurus; his stratagems of policy and war were exhausted and the perfidious Greek escaped with three wounds from the field of battle overspread with forty thousand of his subjects". (Gibbon). The Byzantine Emperor again implored for peace, which was granted. But "over and again when Haroon was engaged elsewhere, Nicephorus broke his treaty, and as often was beaten" (Muir). In 189 A.H., the Abbaside Caliph proceeded to Rayy to suppress the rebellion of the Governor. This was too good an opportunity for the Byzantine Emperor to miss. Leaving aside all his promises and solemn pledges he burst into the Abbaside dominions, where he caused widespread devastation and havoc. Leaving his son, Mamoon at Rakka, with absolute control of the Government, Haroon hurried to meet the Byzantines. The Abbaside army swept over the whole of Asia Minor as far as Bithynia on the north and Mysia on the west. City after city opened its gates to the Abbaside armies. A large force sent by Nicephorus was routed with fearful losses. Heraclea was stormed. The Byzantine Emperor again begged for pardon and the kind-hearted Abbaside Caliph with "shortsighted indulgence acceded to his prayer". The whole of Byzantine Empire, including its formidable Capital, Constantinople, lay at his feet. It would have been far better for the peace of the area, if Haroon Rashid had taken Constantinople at that time. The world would have been spared much bloodshed in future and the horrors of the Crusades, the bloodiest and longest war in human history.

The real greatness of Haroon ar-Rashid lies in his efforts for peace— in his wise and able administration, his intellectual pursuits and his promotion of the well-being and unprecedented prosperity of his people which won him a high place among the few greatest rulers of the world. He had surrounded himself with wise and capable men whom he had entrusted the Government of his vast Empire. His Prime Minister, Yahya Barmaki, whom he affectionately called "father", and his four sons, particularly Jafar and Fazal were greatly instrumental in making his reign as one of the most glorious epochs in human history. Their patronage of art and learning attracted around them some of the greatest intellects of the age, which made Baghdad the highest seat of art and learning in the world. But their unbounded generosity and unlimited power aroused suspicion in the mind of the Caliph which was responsible for their ultimate doom.

The welfare of his people was dearest to his heart. He used to roam about the streets of Baghdad accompanied by Masroor to render justice and relieve the people of their distress. "A soldier by instinct and training", writes Ameer Ali, in his well-known work, *History of the Saracens*, "he repeatedly took the field himself; he frequently traversed his dominions in every direction to repress lawlessness and to acquaint himself with the condition of his subjects, personally inspected the frontiers and passes, and never spared himself the trouble or labour in the work of Government. The perfect immunity from danger with which traders, merchants, scholars and pilgrims journeyed through the vast Empire testify to the excellence and vigour of his administration. The mosques, colleges and schools, the hospitals, dispensaries, caravan, serais, roads, bridges and canals with which he covered the countries under his sway, speak of his lively interest in the welfare of his people. As a patron of arts and literature, Rashid was surpassed by his equally brilliant and gifted son; but in the strength of character and grandeur of intellect he had no superior. And although his reign, unlike Mamoon's, was not altogether free from the evils which often spring from the possession by one individual of unlimited and irresponsible power, the general prosperity of the people, and the unprecedented progress made in his reign in arts and civilization, make amends for many of the sins of despotism".

Rashid's mother Khaizuran and his favourite wife, Zubaida, took lively interest in the welfare of the state and people. Empress Zubaida's notable visit to the Holy cities of Makkah and Madina, and her munificence have been described by the historians. In view of the acute scarcity of water from which the inhabitants of Makkah suffered deep agonies, she built from her private purse, the famous aqueduct, which is known as "Zubaida Canal" and has since then proved a blessing to the inhabitants of the Holy city.

Rashid gave a thorough education and training to his two sons, Ameen and Mamoon, who were well versed in the arts of peace and war. In 186 A.H., the Caliph made a pilgrimage to Makkah and deposited in the Kaaba two documents executed by his two sons, binding them in solemn terms to abide by the succession arrangements made by him.

The munificence of Haroon ar-Rashid, his talented Ministers and Courtiers, especially the Barmakides, who vied with each other in the patronage of sciences and arts, attracted around them in Baghdad a galaxy of intellects from all over the known world. This enabled Baghdad to become in a short time the greatest metropolis and the highest seat of learning in the world. Rashid expanded the Department of Translation and Scientific Studies founded by his grandfather Mansoor. It reached its zenith during the reign of his son, Mamoon ar-Rashid. Eminent scholars and artists who flourished during the time included the grammarian Asmai; legists and theologians, Imam Yusuf, Imam Shafi, Abdullah bin Idrees, Isa bin Yunus and Sufian Suri; musician Ibrahim Mosuli and physician Gabriel. "Rashid", says Ibn Khaldun, "followed in the footsteps of his grandfather except in parsimony for no Caliph exceeded him in liberality and munificence".

Rashid established diplomatic relations with a number of countries in the West and the East. He was the first to receive at his Court embassies from the Emperor of China and the Ruler of France, Charlemagne. He presented him a clock which was an object of wonder for the people of the West.

While on his way to put down disorders which had broken out in Khorasan, Haroon's illness from which he was suffering took a serious turn at a village named Sanabad near Toos. Feeling his end near, he assembled all his family members and said: "All those who are young will get old, all who have come into the world will die. I give you three directions: observe faithfully your engagements, be faithful to your Imams (Caliphs), and be united amongst yourselves". He then distributed large sums of money among his attendants and troops. He breathed his last two days later, on the 4th of Jamadi-us-Sani, 193 A.H. (809 A.C.), after a glorious reign of 23 years and six months.

Ameer Ali pays eloquent tributes to Rashid's brilliant rule in the following terms; "Weigh him as carefully as you like in the scale of historical criticism, Haroon ar-Rashid will always take rank with the greatest sovereigns and rulers of the world. It is a mistake to compare the present with the past, the humanities and culture of the nineteenth century and its accumulated legacy of civilization, the gifts of ages of growth and development, with the harshness and vigour of a thousand years ago. The defects in Rashid's character, his occasional outbursts of suspicion or temper were the natural outcome of despotism. That he should with the unbounded power he possessed, be so self-restrained, so devoted to the advancement of public prosperity, so careful of the interests of his subjects, is a credit to his genius. He never allowed himself the smallest respite in the discharge of his duties; he repeatedly travelled over his Empire from the East to the West to remedy evils, to redress wrongs, and to acquaint himself personally with the condition of his people. Nine times he himself led the caravan of pilgrims to the Holy Cities, and this brought the nations under his sway to recognise and appreciate his personality, and to value the advantages of Islamic solidarity. His Court was the most brilliant of the time, to it came the learned and wise from all parts of the world, who were always entertained with munificent liberality. Unstinted patronage was extended to arts and science, and every branch of mental study. He was the first to elevate music into a nobel profession, establishing degrees and honours, as in science and literature".

"Haroon took great interest in art and science", observe Encyclopaedia of Islam, "a..d his brilliant Court was a centre of all branches of scholarship. In legend and tradition he has always been looked upon as the personification of oriental power and splendour and his fame spread throughout the East and the West by the *Arabian Nights*".

# YAHYA BARMAKI

The Barmakides have been one of the most talented and versatile families that have lived in the world of Islam. They have been, to a great extent, responsible for the glorious reign of the Abbaside Caliph, Haroon ar-Rashid, which has been immortalised by the famous *Arabian Nights*. The glory that was Baghdad, its cultural and literary life, was due to the Barmakides' munificence and patronage, which has few parallels in living history.

Yahya bin Khalid Barmaki came into prominence during the reign of the Abbaside Caliph, Mansoor, who appointed him in 744—75 A.C., Governor of Azerbaijan. Three years later, he was appointed the tutor of young Haroon who later became the Viceroy of the Western half of the Empire, lying West of the Euphrates. Yahya was placed at the head of his Chancery.

After the death of Mehdi in August 785, Yahya gave his protege Haroon the wise advice to retire voluntarily in favour of his elder brother, whereupon Musa was acknowledged as Caliph with the title of Al Hadi. But relations between Yahya and the new Caliph who was extremely fickle -minded were strained. He suspected Yahya of supporting Haroon against his teen-aged son, Jafar, whom he wanted to make his successor against the will of his deceased father. Yahya refused to support this injustice to the highly talented Haroon as this was also against the interest of the Abbaside Caliphate. He was, therefore, put behind the bars and the night on which he was to be executed under the orders of the Caliph, Al Hadi died suddenly in September 786 A.C.

When Haroon ascended the throne of Baghdad in 786 A.C., Yahya Barmaki was appointed the Vizier and was entrusted with absolute power. He also associated his two sons Fazal and Jafar with the Government Administration. The glory of Haroon ar-Rashid's Administration was mostly due to the Barmakide family who governed the State with undiminished glory for 17 years—786 to 803 A.C. The official seal initially withheld from him was soon placed under his control.

Yahya's two sons Fazal and Jafar held important positions in the Government. Jafar was later appointed Vizier of the Caliph. Fazal was the foster brother of Haroon ar-Rashid who called Yahya "Father" as a mark of affection and regard for him.

Yahya's Administration was wise, firm and benevolent. He neglected no details and considered the well-being of the people as his primary duty.

His four sons, Fazal, Jafar, Musa and Muhammad, possessed administrative capacity of the highest order. Fazal held the post of Governor of Khurasan and Egypt and brought about the submission of Yahya bin Abdullah who had proclaimed himself the sovereign of Deilem. Jafar also held the post of Governor of several Provinces and was instrumental in bringing about peace between the rival tribes of Modhar and Himyar in Syria. Later on, when Yahya resigned due to old age, Jafar took his place.

Fazal was first to forfeit the favour of the Caliph whom he displeased and was deprived of all offices except his appointment as the tutor of Prince Ameen, the Heir Apparent. Jafar who was eloquent and legal minded was the tutor of Prince Mamoon, who later on succeeded Haroon ar-Rashid.

The Barmakides who served Haroon ar-Rashid with unswerving fidelity and extraordinary ability for 17 years fell from grace in 803 A.C. Their grandeur and magnificence, as also their benevolence and lavish charity which had made them the idol of the masses, created a host of enemies who were continuously plotting for their fall. A number of causes have been assigned to their sudden fall, including the romance between Jafar and the Caliph's sister, Abbasa, which is a mere fib disproved by later historical research. The celebrated Muslim historian Ibn Khaldun says that the true cause of the fall of Barmakides is to be found in "the manner in which they seized upon all authority, and assumed absolute control over public revenue, so much so, that Rashid was often forced to the necessity of asking for and not obtaining from the Chancellor small sums of money. Their influence was unlimited, and their renown had spread in every direction. All the high offices of the State, civil as well as military, were held by functionaries chosen from their family, or from among their partisans. All faces were turned towards them; all heads inclined in their presence; on them alone rested the hopes of applicants and candidates; they showered their bounties on all sides, in every province of the Empire, in the cities as well as in the villages; their praises were sung by all, and they were far more popular than their master". All this earned them the hatred and jealousy of their Arab colleagues and ultimately aroused the suspicion of the Caliph. Their most sworn enemy was Fazal bin-Rabi, the Arab Chamberlain of Rashid's Court who ultimately succeeded Jafar after his fall. Fazal first incurred the displeasure of the Caliph for his pro-Allied Policy and was removed from power in 799. Jafar, too, was reproached at occasions for abusing his power.

Haroon ar-Rashid, while returning from his pilgrimage in 802 A.C., suddenly decided to put an end to the Barmakide domination. In the night of January 28/29, 803, A.C., Jafar was executed. His brothers were incarcerated and their aged father, Yahya, was put under surveillance. Their property was confiscated. The aged Yahya died in prison in November 805. He was 70. His able son, Fazal, followed him to the grave, some years later.

Thus ended the career of Yahya Barmaki and his two illustrious sons who were greatly instrumental in adding a golden chapter to the history of Islam. Their proverbial generosity and patronage of art and learning had made Baghdad the Makkah of learned and talented persons who flocked there from all corners of the world. "They seem primarily to have served", writes a Western writer, "the Caliphate effectively and loyally, pacifying Eastern Iran, repressing the risings in Syria and even Ifrikiya, obtaining the submission of rebels, even Alids, directing the Administration in an orderly fashion, guaranteeing to the State important resources, undertaking works of public interest (Canals of Katul and Sihan), setting wrong aright with equity and in accordance with the requirements of Islamic law and reinforcing the judicial institution of the office of the Great Qazi".

The Barmakides' activity was not confined merely to political and administrative spheres only. They were great patrons of art and culture science and learning. Their munificence to the persons possessing talents, including poets and writers, artists and musicians, scholars and theologians, philosophers and scientists, was unbounded. Their assemblies were distinguished for the attendance of the most talented men of Baghdad who wrote and sung their praises long after their fall. The *Arabian Nights* has immortalised the figure of Jafar the Vizier and intimate companion of Haroon ar-Rashid.

# MAMOON AR-RASHID

It was a fateful night of 170 A.H. (786 A.C.) when the ruling Caliph Hadi departed from this world, a second Caliph, Haroon succeeded him and a third Caliph Mamoon was born.

Mamoon was hardly 5 years old, when his elementary religious education was entrusted to two eminent scholars, Kasai Nahvi and Yazidi. Mamoon was a born genius, precodious and exceptionally intelligent. He used to recite the Quran in the presence of his teacher Kasai. The latter would raise his downcast head only when the boy committed some mistake. Mamoon would at once realize his mistake and correct it.

One day while Mamoon was reciting the lines from the Quran, meaning: "O' faithful! why do you promise that which you do not wish to do", suddenly Kasai, his teacher, raised his head and gazed at him. There was a meaning in his looks which the little intelligent boy understood.

The same evening when he met his father Haroon ar-Rashid, he enquired of him if he had promised anything to Kasai. Haroon replied: "Yes, I had promised him some allowance. But how did you come to know of it my son? Did he hint it to you about it?" "No Sir", replied Mamoon, and he related the story to his father.

The great Caliph was highly struck by the extraordinary intelligence of his little son and fulfilled his promise immediately.

Mamoon ar-Rashid, the greatest Abbaside Caliph, who ruled over an Empire extending from the shores of the Atlantic in the West to the Great Wall of China in the East, was one of the most talented, enlightened and learned rulers that the world has ever produced. Endowed with extraordinary intelligence, magnanimity, administrative ability, political acumen and versatile taste, he rallied around him a galaxy of talented scholars, professing different faiths and hailing from distant parts of the world.

Mamoon was born on 15th Rabiul Awwal, 170 A.H. (786 A.C.). His mother, a Persian lady, survived only a few days after his birth. He was given the best possible education and training. It was customary with the Abbaside Caliphs to entrust their children to the care of talented scholars, hence Mamoon was entrusted to the care of Yazidi. Young Mamoon was brought up under the able guardianship of the Grand Vizier, Jafar Barmaki.

The Caliph, Haroon ar-Rashid invited the celebrated traditionist Imam Malik to Baghdad to teach *Muwatta* (a well-known book of Traditions written by Imam Malik) to his sons Mamoon and Ameen but the learned Imam declined to leave Madina, the city of the Prophet saying: "People go in search of learning and learning does not go in search of people". The wise Caliph took his two sons to Madina and attended the lectures delivered by the learned Imam. Thus Mamoon's receptive mind imbibed and assimilated knowledge that was imparted to him and he soon became well-versed in rhetoric, literature, jurisprudence, traditions, philosophy, astronomy and other sciences. He knew Quran by rote and excelled in its interpretation.

After mastering almost all branches of learning, he was given training in statecraft. His high attainments enabled him to preside over literary meetings attended by scholars of diverse branches of learning during his Caliphate, and infused in him a life-long interest in literary activities which marked out his regime as the golden period of Islamic learning.

His father Haroon ar-Rashid, had twelve sons, of whom three were contestants for his succession. Ameen, by his favourite Empress Zubaida though well educated, possessed volatile and pleasure-loving character; Mutasim was courageous, robust but uneducated; Mamoon was much more accomplished and suitable than the former two but lacked official support. Haroon did realise the suitability of Mamoon for the high office, but he could not displease his favourite Queen. Hence an administration of North Eastern Provinces was entrusted to Mamoon with his Headquarters at Merv, while Ameen was to administer the Imperial Capital and South Western Provinces.

On the death of Haroon ar-Rashid in 809 A.C., there started a war of succession which ultimately resulted in the success of his ablest son, Mamoon ar-Rashid who made a triumphal entry into Baghdad in 819 A.C.

On reaching Baghdad, he was confronted with a number of problems ranging from the internal conspiracies of the Abbasides and the Fatimides, to external disorders in Yemen and Syria. Mamoon faced the critical situation which existed in his vast Empire with courage and statesmanship. His vast Empire was in a state of turmoil.

The rebellions in Yemen and Khorasan were quelled and the insurgents were treated with exceptional leniency. Babak, the nihilist, who had established himself in one of the most inaccessible defiles of Mazendran, defied the Imperial authority and had become a menace in the early reign of Mamoon. Being hard pressed by the Imperial troops, he entered into relations with the Byzantine Emperor Theophilus.

The Byzantine Emperor attacked the Abbaside dominions and massacred a large number of Muslims. The news of this treacherous and unprovoked attack of the Greek Emperor highly enraged Mamoon who took the field in person and after successive campaigns inflicted a crushing defeat on the Greeks who were obliged to sue for peace. To guard against the future Greek raids, Mamoon ordered the building of strong fortifications at Tyana, situated about 70 miles north of Tarsus. After defeating the Greek Emperor, Mamoon proceeded to Egypt where his celebrated Turkish General Afshin had captured Al Ferma, the farthest part of upper Egypt.

This period of Abbaside Caliphate is known for its conquests by the sword and the pen. The territorial expansion as well as literary pursuits continued with unabated zeal. Despite Mamoon's literary preoccupations and internal disorders in the State, territorial conquests continued as before and the boundary of the Abbaside Caliphate was extended to its farthest limits during his regime. Afghanistan was annexed to the Abbaside Caliphate and thus formed a permanent part of this great Empire. Kashmir and Tibet were invaded by the Imperial forces, which conquered a major part of Turkistan including Karab, Shagar and Farghana. Mamoon in person took the field against the Byzantine Empire which was beaten with heavy losses in several combats. His valiant son, Ishaq captured thirty Byzantine forts.

In Europe, too, the Imperial forces met with spectacular success. A military expedition under the leadership of Zaidatullah Aghlab brought the island of Sicily under the sway of the Caliph. Two years later a few hundred Muslim enterprisers effected a landing on the island of Crete and captured it without much difficulty.

Mamoon was a great Administrator who was known for his sagacity and forbearance. He applied himself vigorously to the task of reorganising the Administration which had very much deteriorated during the regime of Ameen. He made secret rounds in the city accompanied by his Chamberlain, Ahmad ibn Abu Khalid. He appointed capable Administrators as Governors of his Provinces and kept a constant watch over their actions.

Mamoon had established a regular Council of State, composed of representatives from all communities found in his Empire. He recognised no distinction of caste and creed, and his public services were open to all. The representatives of the people enjoyed complete freedom of expression and had free discussions in the presence of the Caliph.

He had established an efficient intelligence service throughout his vast Empire. It kept him fully informed of even the minor incidents occurring in the remotest corner of the Empire. The secret agents and spies of the Caliph were working in the alien countries also, especially in the Byzantine dominions. Thus Mamoon had established the most elaborate intelligence services of his time. More than 1,700 women were employed for intelligence service in Baghdad alone. According to the celebrated historian Ibn Khalikan, every branch of Central and Provincial Administration had its secret reports and chronicler. Once, in a distant part of the Empire, a soldier took forced labour from an ordinary subject. The man cried out: "Alas! Umar where are you?" The matter was reported to the Caliph who summoned the oppressed person and asked. "Had you cried for Caliph Umar?". "Yes", replied the man. Thereupon the Caliph said, "By God, had my people been as good as those of Umar, I would have been more just than him", and rewarded the man and suspended the soldier.

Tahir wielded great influence in the Caliphate and was the Viceroy of the East. He had acquired so much power that he had become a danger for the State. His movements were strictly watched and reported to the Caliph by the intelligence staff. One day, he did not mention the name of Mamoon in the Friday oration from the pulpit. This was a clear sign of revolt. The same night Tahir had an attack of violent fever and died the next day. It is said that he was poisoned at the behest of Mamoon.

Mamoon was free from sectarian feelings which characterised most of the Umayyad and Abbaside rulers. He had great regard for the Fatimides despite their secret machinations and open revolts against the State. He had appointed a number of Fatimides on high posts and said that with these appointments he was returning the gratitude which the Abbasides owed to Caliph Hazrat Ali, who had appointed a large number of Abbasides on important posts.

In 816 A.C. he declared Fatimide Imam ar-Riza as his Heir Apparent and the oath of fealty was taken to him as the Heir Apparent to the Caliphate on the second of Ramzan, 201 A.H. Mamoon openly declared that Imam Ali ar-Riza was his most suitable heir and he found no better person among the Abbasides. But the virtuous Imam did not survive to occupy this high office and died at Tus before the triumphant entry of the Caliph in the Capital.

The Abbasides are particularly known for their pomp and pageantry. The Arabs under the Abbasides in Iraq, and the Umayyads in Spain had built a splendid civilization whose glory dazzled mediaeval travellers.

Baghdad and Cordova, with their grand palaces, broad highways, shady canals, green parks and gardens, busy business centres and magnificent universities, colleges and hospitals, were considered as the glory of Mediaeval civilization. Mamoon ar-Rashid, the greatest of the Abbaside Caliphs, though inclined towards literary pursuits and patronage of the learned, was responsible for some of the most striking events of splendour recorded in living history.

One of them is his marriage with Buran, daughter of Hasan ibn Sahl, an event which has become classical. A modern historian has recorded thus! "The marriage was celebrated with great festivals and rejoicings at a place called Fam-us-Salh, where Hasan resided at that time. The Vizier entertained the whole company for seventeen days on a lavish and gorgeous scale. Zubaida and her daughter, with other ladies of the Imperial household, were present at this wedding; their surpassing beauty and the magnificence of their attire were sung by the poets invited on the occasion. But the most beauteous of them all was the bride herself. At the ceremony, her grandmother showered upon the Caliph and his bride from a tray of gold a thousand pearls of unique size and splendour; they were collected under his orders, made into a necklace and given to the young Queen.

The hymeneal apartment was lighted by a candle of ambergris, weighing eighty pounds, fixed in a candle stick of gold. When the imperial party was departing the Vizier presented the chief officers of the State with robes of honour, and showered balls of musk upon the princes and chiefs who accompanies the Caliph. Each of these balls contained ticket on which was inscribed the name of an estate, or a slave or a team of horses, or some such gifts; the recipient took it to an agent who delivered to him the property which had fallen to his lot. Among the common people he scattered gold and silver coins, balls of musk and eggs of amber".

According to historical records, Baghdad, the Imperial Capital, housed more than thirty thousand mosques and ten thousand public baths. The celebrated historian Gibbon states that Baghdad of those times had 860 medical practitioners.

The dominions of Mamoon extended from the shores of the Atlantic in the West to the walls of China in the East. On several occasions the Byzantine Emperor was obliged to pay tribute to Mamoon. His annual revenues exceeded 32 crores. This did not include other taxes which were deposited in the *Baitul Mal* (Public Exchequer).

His armed forces comprised about a quarter million soldiers. Each cavalier was paid Rs. 25/- p.m. and infantry man Rs. 10/- per month. Till lately the pay of an Indian soldier of the British army was Rs. 16/- per month. His high officials were paid fat salaries and lived like princes. His Prime Minister, Fazl bin Sahl was drawing three million Dirhams a month.

The regime of Mamoon was a period of prosperity and plenty. The standard of living was high and the common man passed a life free from anxieties for the necessities of life. According to a well-known historian, on the occasion of his visit to Egypt, Mamoon toured village after village. In each village he was the guest of some villager. In one village he was the guest of a poor old woman. While departing he was presented ten bags full of gold coins by the old woman. Mamoon hesitated to accept this valuable gift, whereupon the old woman said: "Gold is produced by our soil. I have plenty of it and I have presented only a part of it to Caliph". This shows the state of prosperity in Mamoon's dominions. Commerce was free and enormous. New cities sprang up and each village in Iraq was provided with canals and fountains which added to the agricultural and industrial prosperity of the country. Asylums and poor houses were built all over the vast Empire for widows, orphans and destitutes who were looked after by the State. It was the duty of the State to provide employment for the people or to pay the unemployed. This was one of the important laws of the Caliphate which was scrupulously followed.

Mamoon ar-Rashid is particularly known as one of the greatest benefactors and promoters of learning in recorded history. So far as patronage of letters and litterateurs is concerned, he stands unrivalled among Eastern as well as Western monarchs. He himself being a well-known scholar attracted around him a galaxy of intellectual luminaries, with whom he held weekly discourses on sciences and arts. He is reputed to be the founder of Darul Hukama (House of the Wise), which housed a big Translation Department, a Research Section and an Astronomical Observatory. His Caliphate constitutes the most glorious epoch of Muslim history and has rightly been characterised as the Augustan age of Islam.

His twenty years reign recorded an unprecedented intellectual development embracing all branches of knowledge, including astronomy, mathematics, medicine, philosophy, fine arts, tradition and literature.

The interest shown by the Caliph in the promotion of learning created a love for knowledge among his subjects, who vied with one another in furthering learning.

It was for such a period, more than anything else that Robert Briffault writes: "The incorruptible treasures and delights of intellectual culture were accounted by the princes of Baghdad, Shiraz and Cordova, the truest and proudest pomps of their Courts. But it was not a mere appendage of princely vanity that the wonderful growth of Islamic science and learning was fostered by their patrons. They pursued culture with the personal ardour of overmastering craving. Never before and never since, on such a scale, has the spectacle been witnessed of the ruling classes throughout the length and breadth of a vast Empire given over entirely to a frenzied passion for acquirement of knowledge. Learning seemed to have become with them the chief business of life. Khalifs and Amirs hurled from their Diwans to closet themselves in thier libraries and observatories. They neglected their affairs of the state to attend lectures and converse on mathematical problems with men of science" *(Making of Humanity).*

Writing about Mamoon another Western writer Oelsner states: "We see for the first time perhaps in the history of the world a religious and despotic government allied to philosophy, preparing and partaking in its triumphs".

The interest exhibited by the talented Caliph in the pursuits of learning was responsible for the establishment of a large number of educational institutions all over his vast Empire.

The Caliph collected invaluable books on sciences and arts from distant parts of the world. He had requested the Byzantine Emperor to send him rare manuscripts of Greek philosophy and science which were locked in a dark-room of an unknown monastery. His Translation Department employing competent translators on high salaries, rendered the works from Greek, Syraic, Chaldaic, Persian and Sanskrit into Arabic under the supervision of Costa bin Luqa: from Persian under Yahya bin Haroon and from Sanskrit under Duban, the Brahmin. As many as 60 translators worked under Costa bin Luqa. In fact, the translation of invaluable works from other languages into Arabic paved the way for later original researches and provided the firm ground on which the stately edifice of Islamic learning was built.

The study of astronomy received great impetus during the reign of Mamoon. Astronomical observations and research were made in the observatory at Shamassia and the observations regarding equinoxes, eclipses and other celestial phenomena are worth mentioning. The measurement of a degree on the Red Sea enabled the calculation of the size of earth. Abdul Hasan invented Telescope during this period which immensely facilitated the carrying out of astronomical observations. A large number of high class works were produced during the Caliphate of Mamoon in medicine, mathematics, optics, philosophy, astronomy, meteorology, mechanics, ethics and literature.

"Mamoon's reign", writes Ameer Ali, "was unquestionably the most brilliant and glorious of all in the history of Islam. The study and cultivation of humanitarian science is the best index to a nation's development. Mamoon's Court was crowded with men of science and letters; with poets, physicians and philosophers from every part of the civilized world and of diverse creeds and nationalities".

Mamoon extended his patronage to scholars irrespective of their castes and creeds. Tuesdays were reserved for literary and philosophical discussions. Scholars of diverse castes and creeds assembled at the place in the afternoon. They were entertained there and had free discussions on all sorts of subjects till late in the night. Such literary meetings were presided over by the Caliph himself who freely took part in such discussions.

The two greatest scholars of his time were Yaqub bin Ishaq Kindi and Abu Musa Khwarizmi. Kindi, a talented translator, is known as the philosopher of the Arabs who has been recognised as one of the 12 subtlest minds of the world by Cardon and who has left behind him 282 invaluable works on philosophy, logic, medicine, mathematics, music, physics and astronomy. Abu Musa Khwarizmi, the founder of Algebra who is recognised as one of the highest intellects of Islam, greatly contributed to the study of mathematics, astronomy, geography and other sciences. His book on Algebra was translated into several oriental and Western languages.

Mamoon was so fond of philosophy that he requested the Byzantine Emperor to lend a certain Greek philosopher for teaching philosophy and in return promised him lasting friendship as well as payment of five tons of gold. Hardly anyone would have paid such a high price for learning.

Mamoon was an able Administrator and a wise statesman. During his twenty years of reign he established an administration throughout his vast Empire which maintained a high standard of justice, thus adding to the peace and prosperity of his people. Sundays were meant for his public audience. From early morning till afternoon, everyone was at liberty to present to the Caliph in person his or her complaint which was instantly attended to. One day a poor old woman complained to the Caliph that a certain cruel person had usurped her property.

"Who is that person?" asked the Caliph.

"He is sitting beside you", replied the old woman and pointed out to the Caliph's favourite son, Abbas, who was sitting next to the Caliph.

The Prince defended his action in a halting tone while the old woman was getting louder and louder in her arguments. The Caliph stated that honesty of her case had made her bold and decided the case in her favour.

Once a certain person filed a suit in the Court of the Grand Qazi, claiming thirty thousand dirhams from Mamoon. The Caliph was summoned to the Court. On his arrival, his attendants wanted to spread a carpet for him. The Grand Qazi sternly rebuked them, saying that in a court the Caliph and an ordinary man were equal. The Caliph was immensely pleased with the remark of his judge and increased his salary.

Mamoon was a very kind-hearted ruler, reputed for his forbearance and humanitarianism. He used to say that if people could know of his kind nature, they would commit more crimes. He would often say that he got greater pleasure in forgiveness than in awarding punishment. His treatment of the sons and the mother of his rival brother Ameen, was exemplary. He brought them up like his own sons and married them with his daughters.

On several occasions he granted pardon to rebels and conspirators. He quelled the rebellions in Yemen and Khorasan and treated the rebels with exceptional leniency. His uncle Ibrahim who had proclaimed himself as the Caliph in Baghdad when Mamoon was in Merv, was hiding himself here and there. At last he was caught and brought in the presence of the Caliph. Ibrahim was expecting nothing less than a death sentence, but the humane Caliph pardoned him and restored him his former position.

A dangerous conspiracy against his life was unearthed in 824 A.C., the conspirators who were Abbasides were arrested and treated with extraordinary leniency.

Mamoon used to say that on the Day of Judgement he would not expect God's blessings for his forbearance as he derived much pleasure out of it.

There was complete freedom of expression in his Caliphate. Once when his uncle Ibrahim drew his attention to a certain poet Dabal's disgraceful satire on him and the members of the Royal Family, he pardoned the poet.

His treatment of non-Muslims was exemplary. His non-Muslim subjects enjoyed complete freedom of speech, worship and liberty of conscience. They were allowed all sorts of privileges enjoyed by the Muslims. He had established a regular Council of State, on which members of different communities, including Muslims, Christians, Jews and Zoroastrians inhabiting his vast Empire, were duly represented. Several non-Muslims occupied high posts in the Government. One of them, Gabrail bin Bakhtushu, a Christian scholar, had attained a high position in the Caliphate. All new employees, high or low, reported to him before their postings.

Mamoon's liberal policy towards non-Muslims had added to their peace and prosperity. There were more than eleven thousand churches in his State, in addition to numerous synagogues and Zoroastrian temples. The administrators of churches and other non-Muslim shrines enjoyed the same privileges extended to them under the rulers of their own faith.

His behaviour towards his servants and slaves was extremely humane. He was always tolerant to their criticism and never objected to their freedom of expression.

One night, Qazi Yahya who was his guest felt extremely thirsty at midnight. The Caliph woke up and himself brought for him a goblet of water from the adjacent room. The Qazi felt somewhat embarrassed at this act of the Caliph and said that it would have been better if he had asked his servants to do so. The kind-hearted Caliph replied that in accordance with the traditions of the Prophet of Islam, he refrained from troubling his servants during the dead of night.

Mamoon died when he was 48 years old. He had marched at the head of a huge army to stop the incursions of the Greeks in Asia Minor. The Greeks were defeated with heavy losses and were obliged to sue for peace. Mamoon ordered the building of fortifications at Tyana, to provide a permanent check to the Greek incursion. Encamped near Tarsus, Mamoon, along with his brother Mutasim, was sitting on the bank of the river, washing their feet in its icy cold water. The same night, they had an attack of violent fever from which Mutasim recovered but Mamoon died on 9th August 833 A.C.

Mamoon ar-Rashid was undoubtedly one of the greatest monarchs that the world has produced. As an enlightened, talented, humane, magnanimous and sagacious ruler, he would always rank amongst the greatest in history. "He was the most distinguished of the House of Abbas", says one of the annalists, "for his prudence, his determination, his clemency and judgement, his sagacity and awe-inspiring respect, his intrepidity, majesty and liberality. He had many eminent qualities, and a long series of memorable actions are recorded of him. Of the House of Abbas none wiser than he ever ruled the Caliphate".

# ABDUR RAHMAN AL-NASIR

Muslim Spain has added a golden chapter to the history of Saracens. The light of knowledge which illumined Moorish Spain was greatly instrumental in dispelling ignorance that had enveloped Mediaeval Europe since the fall of the Roman Empire. "It was under the influence of Arabian and Moorish revival of culture", writes Robert Briffault, "and not in the 15th century, that the real renaissance took place. Spain and not Italy, was the cradle of the rebirth of Europe". Another well-known orientalist, Phillip K. Hitti, acknowledges that "Moslem Spain wrote one of the brightest chapters in the intellectual history of Mediaeval Europe. Between the middle of the 8th and the beginning of the 13th centuries, as we have noted before, the Arabic speaking people were the main bearers of the torch of culture and civilization throughout the world. Moreover, they were the medium through which ancient science and philosophy were recovered, supplemented and transmitted in such a way as to make possible the renaissance of Europe. In all this, Arabic Spain has a large share".

The ablest and the most gifted of all the rulers of Muslim Spain was Abdur Rahman al-Nasir who established an era of unparalleled peace and prosperity in that country which led to the cultivation and development of sciences and arts, commerce and industry, education and culture on an unprecedented scale.

Abdur Rahman succeeded his grandfather Abdullah at the age of 22. His father was sentenced to death for some capital offence under the orders of his grandfather, King Abdullah. The child Abdur Rahman was then barely three years old. He was brought up most tenderly by his grandfather who wanted to make amends for the severity shown to his father.

The accession of young Abdur Rahman in 912 A.C. was hailed by his kith and kin as well as by the general public and was considered a happy augury for the State. They all perceived in him the signs of greatness and accepted him as the saviour of the distracted Empire of the Umayyads.

His was an uphill task of pacifying the strife-ridden country as well as dealing with the external enemies—the neighbouring Christian states who were always conspiring to strike at the rising Muslim power in Europe. Abdur Rahman dealt with this twin danger with determination and foresight. He abandoned the tortuous and temporising policy of his grandfather and pursued against the rebels a course which was at once bold and straightforward. Disdaining the middle course, he warned the rebels that he wanted their complete surrender. If they submitted, they would be given a free pardon, otherwise they would be dealt with severely. Most of the principal cities submitted spontaneously.

Abdur Rahman's frank and chivalrous manners and his desire to share with his soldiers not only their glory but also their perils, evoked an exceptional enthusiasm in the army and enhanced its morale.

In less than three months, the provinces of Elvira and Jaen were subjugated, the strongest castles were captured and even the inaccessible heights of Sierra Nevada were cleared of the brigands. The bandits who were harassing the country either submitted or were put to death, in less than a year, a major part of the country had been pacified. Even the Christian Spaniards, convinced of the generosity and firmness of the young King, began to lay down their arms. Dozy, a Christian historian says: "The government, be it said to its honour, conducted itself with the greatest justice towards the Christians who capitulated".

In 928 A.C. Bobastro was captured and Serrania was finally pacified. Abdur Rahman next turned his attention to the North. Badajoz and Toledo capitulated after a long-drawn siege and despite the Christian instigation. Thus, Abdur Rahman became the undisputed monarch of the land of his ancestors.

But, he had still to face two formidable enemies, who cast their longing eyes on the fertile lands of Andalusia—the Christian tribes of the North and Fatimides of Africa. A terrible famine in Spain obliged the Arab settlers in the north to migrate to Africa. This provided a golden opportunity to the Galicians to rise in insurrection. They massacred a large number of Muslims and elected Alfonso as their King.

The Muslims had experienced the cruelty of the Christians in the previous century. "Fanatical, cruel and pitiless", says Dozy, "they rarely gave quarter; when they took a city they indulged in promiscuous slaughter, sparing neither age nor sex". They were wholly unaware of the tolerance shown by the Muslims to the Christians. The young King was faced with saving not only his kingdom but also the glorious civilization existing there which was hated by the fanatical Christians.

The treacherous Christians of the North were a constant menace to Spain. King Abdur Rahman fully realised that lasting peace could not be established in his dominions without permanently stamping out this evil. Hence he resolved to crush them with a strong hand.

In 914 A.C., the Leonese, under their chief Ordono II, burst into the Province of Merida, ravaged the country with fire and sword, and massacred a large number of Muslims. Abdur Rahman who was engaged at this time with the Fatimides in Africa sent a punitive expedition. It failed to achieve the object.

In 918, he despatched another army under Hajib Badr and in 920 he himself took the field in person. Ordono was beaten and was pursued into the mountains. Osma, San Estevan, Clunia and several other important cities were captured. The King next turned his attention to Naverre. Muhammad bin Lope, Governor of Tudela, inflicted a humiliating defeat on Sancho, the Navarrean chief. He was pursued by the Muslims in the narrow Pyrenees defiles. The Christians hurled rocks on the pursuing Muslims from the mountain tops. Abdur Rahman saw the danger and halted his troops in a small valley surrounded by mountains. "The Christians now committed a mistake", observes Dozy; "Instead of remaining on the mountains, they descended into the plains, and audaciously accepted the battle the Mussulmans offered. They paid for their temerity by a terrible defeat. The Mussulmans pursued them until they were concealed from sight by the darkness of night, and many of their chiefs fell into the hands of the victors, among them two bishops, who were fighting clad in mail". Navarre was overrun by Abdur Rahman who razed to ground all their towers and fortifications. He returned triumphant to his Capital on September 24, 918.

In 921 A.C., Ordono and Sancho again rose in revolt and came down up to Viquera. The Christian chief put to sword a large number of Muslim families, including some of the most illustrious Arabs. Abdur Rahman hastened to meet the insurgents and on July 10 he entered Navarre. The enemy chief fled from this country on his approach, leaving behind his fortresses undefended. Sancho tried to bar the way of Abdur Rahman, but was badly beaten. He entered Sancho's Capital, Pampeluna without any resistance and razed to the ground Sancho's citadel palace and other important buildings.

The chiefs of Basques and Leon were completely subdued. In 925, a civil war broke out between the sons of Ordono. Abdur Rahman applied himself more vigorously to crush the insurrections and by 929 A.C., complete order was restored in his vast country.

At this period, when the Abbaside Caliphate had declined to its lowest ebb and could hardly keep its control over the Muslim world, especially on the Holy cities, Abdur Rahman Al-Nasir assumed the title of *Ameer-ul-Momineen* (Commander of the Faithful). In a large gathering of his subjects, he was invested with the Caliphate under the title of "Al-Nasir il Din Illah".

In 933 A.C., Ramire II seized the chieftaincy of Leon and started raiding and ravaging the Muslim country. Abdul Rahman once again marched against him when Ramire hesitated to give battle. The Caliph advanced towards the North and swept through Castile and Alva, razing to the ground towns and fortresses of the Galicians. Saragossa, in the extreme North, capitulated. Ramire who was severely beaten in several engagements, at last retired to the hills. The whole of Spain now lay at the feet of Caliph Abdur Rahman.

Abdur Rahman who disliked the Arab aristocracy and their factions and turbulent spirit, formed a new corps called Slavs, comprising European converts to Islam and appointed them into important positions. This aroused the Arab jealousy and alienated them from him.

In 939 A.C., when the Galicians and Basques again rose in revolt, the Caliph despatched a force under a Slav General named Najd. The Arabs refused to fight under a Slav General which led to the disaster of the Muslim force in the battle of Khandak. The Slavs fought with great determination, but were almost annihilated.

This did not damp the Caliph's determination to put down the insurrection with a strong hand. He despatched another force which severely punished the Galicians and the Basques. In 940, his Governor of Badajoz inflicted a crushing defeat on Ramire and laid waste his country.

The Chiefs of Navarre and Leon, at last sued for peace and agreed to pay annual tribute to the Caliph. The boundary of Muslim Spain was withdrawn to the River Ebro, which formed a natural barrier.

After peace with Ordono III, the Caliph paid his entire attention to Africa, where the Fatimides were creating trouble and were jeopardising his interest. But on the death of Ordono, the chieftaincy of Galicia and Leon fell upon Sancho, who refused to abide by the treaty concluded by his brother. The Caliph was thus obliged to apply force and his able General Ahmad bin Ila, who was Governor of Toledo, won a memorable victory against the Galicians and Leonese. Sancho was expelled from his dominions and Leon, Castile, Galicia and Navarre practically became the dependencies of the Umayyad Caliphate.

The great Caliph could not enjoy his triumph for long and died on October 16, 961 A.C., at the age of 73 amidst universal mourning, after a glorious reign of over half a century. Abdur Rahman al-Nasir was undoubtedly the greatest and ablest ruler of Muslim Spain. "He had found the kingdom", says Ameer Ali, "in chaos, torn by factions, and parcelled among a number of feudal chieftains belonging to different races; a prey to anarchy and civil war, and exposed to continued raids on the part of Christian tribes of the north. In spite of the immovable difficulties he saved Andalusia, and made it greater and stronger than it ever was before". Muslim Spain enjoyed an unprecedented peace and prosperity. Order was restored throughout the Empire and safety of the road was established as never before which led to the thriving of commerce and industry throughout his vast dominions.

The prices of consumer goods considerably fell down and the people's living standards considerably enhanced which testified to their great prosperity. The splendid hydraulic works and the scientific system of irrigation gave a wonderful impetus to agriculture and horticulture. The smiling fields and the luxuriant gardens spoke of the great agricultural development in the country. A large number of industries sprang up throughout Spain. Cordova, Seville and

Almeria were important industrial centres. All this greatly added to the wealth of the State and the prosperity of her people. The custom dues alone supplied considerable portion of State revenue and amounted to over 12 million dinars.

Science and literature, art and culture were cultivated with unabated zeal during his time. Muslim Spain became the greatest educational and cultural centre in the world, where students flocked from all parts of the world. Its great educational institutions became the training ground for the future leaders of European renaissance.

Al-Nasir possessed a formidable army and a strong navy which disputed the Fatimide supremacy over the Mediterranean. A well disciplined army, "perhaps the best in the world", says Dozy, "gave him a superiority over the Christian Chiefs of the North".

The great rulers of Europe, including the Byzantine Emperor of Constantinople and the Kings of Germany, France and Italy, sought his favour and exchanged their Ambassadors with him. "But what excites the admiration and wonderment of the student of this glorious reign", observes Dozy, "is less the work than the workman". Even the minutest details could not escape his attention. "This sagacious man", continues Dozy, "who centralised, who founded the unity of the nation and that of the monarchical power, who by his alliances established a kind of political equilibrium who, in his large tolerance, called to his counsel men of every religion, is especially a King of modern times than ruler of the Middle Ages".

# NIZAMUL MULK TOOSI

Abu Ali Hasan ibn Ali ibn Ishaq, better known as Nizamul Mulk Toosi, was the celebrated Grand Vizier of the Saljuk ruler, Malik Shah. Being one of the ablest and most talented Prime Ministers that the Muslim world has produced, Nizamul Mulk ranks high among the greatest administrators and statesmen of the world. The celebrated historian Phillip K. Hitti calls him as "one of the ornaments of the political history of Islam", and another well-known orientalist, Ameer Ali says: "Nizamul Mulk was probably, after Yahya Barmaki, the ablest Minister and Administrator Asia has ever produced".

Nizamul Mulk was born on April 10, 1018 A. C. at Radkhan, a village near Toos. His father was a revenue agent on behalf of the Ghaznavide King. He got proficiency in almost all sciences and arts at an early age. In 1054 he joined the service of Alp Arsalan, the Saljuk Prince. Later, when Alp Arsalan ascended the throne, Nizamul Mulk was made his Grand Vizier. Nizamul Mulk Toosi continued in office under two succeeding Saljuk Rulers. He held great sway over Alp Arsalan and accompanied him on all his campaigns and journeys. He was present at the famous battle of Manazgrid. He also undertook military operations on his own and was responsible for the capture of Istakhr citadel in 1076 A.C. For more than 20 years during the reign of Saljuk Monarch, Malik Shah, Nizamul Mulk was the real ruler of the Saljuk Empire, the entire authority vested in his capable hands.

Nizamul Mulk was the man behind the glorious reign of Malik Shah Saljuki. His wise Administration and the prestige of Saljuk arms had established such peace and prosperity in the vast Saljuk Empire that none dared to rebel against the State. "Nizamul Mulk was in all but name a Monarch", adds the *Encyclopaedia of Islam* "and ruled his Empire with striking success". He was kind and merciful in nature but firm and decisive in action.

His work on Administration and Government form enduring monuments of his genius and capacity. Peace reigned in his vast Empire. For twelve times he traversed his wide dominions and personally examined the conditions and requirements of each Province.

Nizamul Mulk paid much attention to the welfare of his people. Life became happy, safe, peaceful and cheap, resulting in the unwonted security of road and low cost of living in his dominions. He set up a network of colleges, *madrassas,* hospitals, mosques and palaces in the cities of Western Asia. He established resting places and guard houses along the trade and pilgrim routes for protection of merchants and travellers. In peace and prosperity, good administration and pursuits of learning, the Saljuk Empire administrated by Nizamul Mulk rivalled the best Arab and Roman rule. He made the road leading to Makkah from Iraq safer and more comfortable for pilgrims.

Nizamul Mulk was one of the greatest patrons of learning that the world has seen. His Court was the meeting place of scholars, statesmen and poets, who flocked around him from all parts of the world. Being one of the greatest sponsors of Islamic learning in history, he founded a chain of great educational institutions all over his vast dominions. He founded the Nizamiya types of higher educational institutions at Neshapur, Baghdad, Khurasan, Iraq and Syria. The first great institution founded by him in 1066 A.C. was the Nizamiya University of Neshapur, which, in fact was the first university of the Islamic world. According to Allama Ibn Khalikan, Nizamul Mulk Toosi was the first in Islamic history to lay the foundation of a regular educational institution.

The State Exchequer was enriched by the munificence of Nizamul Mulk Toosi for purposes of advancement of education. The Saljuk Sultan Malik Shah once called him and said: "Dear father, you can organise a big army with so much money". The wise Minister replied: "My son, I have grown old, but you are young. If you are auctioned in a Bazaar, I doubt if you will fetch more than 30 dinars. In spite of this, God has made you the Monarch of such a vast Empire. Should you not be grateful to Him for the same? The arrows thrown by your archers will not have a range of more than 30 yards, but even the vast shield of the sky cannot check the arrow of prayers flung by the army which I have undertaken to produce". Malik Shah was struck with the reply of his talented Vizier and cried out: "Excellent father, we must produce such an army without the least delay".

Institutions of higher education sprang up all over the Saljuk Empire. The big cities of Khorasan, namely, Merv, Neshapur, Herat, Balkh and Isphahan had a chain of Nizamiya Institutions of higher education. But the greatest of these was the Nizamiya University of Baghdad set up in 1066 A.C. which stands as a landmark in the educational advancement of Muslims during the Mediaeval times. It was a model institution in the whole world of Islam, known for the high standard of teaching and great scholarship of its teachers, attracting students from all over the world. It was, in fact, the first Academy of Islam. Imam Ghazali, the well-known thinker of Islam, had been its Principal and the celebrated Persian poet, Sheikh Muslehuddin Sa'adi, a student of this institution.

Nizamul Mulk spent 1/10 of the State income on education, spending three million rupees on building of higher educational institutions and one million on the Nizamiya University of Baghdad.

Nizamul Mulk was instrumental in the inauguration of *Jalali* Calendar, a much improved one, formulated by a body of astronomers headed by Umar Khayyam.

Nizamul Mulk wrote in 1091 A.C. for the guidance of Malik Shah, his monumental political treatise, *Siyasat Nama,* which stands as a landmark in the annal of political treatises, written during the Mediaeval times. He added 11 chapters to the book, the following year. It is a book on the Art of Administration for the benefit of Rulers. Being an able Administrator, he incorporated his personal experiences in this book, which can serve as *Magna Charta* for an ideal state. It deals with topics of kingship, judiciary, espionage, ambassadorship, the qualifications and functions of all classes of officers. He complained that a sound intelligence service was not being maintained in Mediaeval states whereby corruption may be revealed and rebellion forestalled. The book was written in Persian, containing 50 chapters of advice, illustrated by historical anecdotes. The last 11 chapters added to the book in 1092 A.C. deal with dangers which threatened the Empire, specially from the Ismailis.

In *Siyasat Nama,* he insisted on limiting the rights of fief holders to the collection of fixed dues.

His Administration greatly resembled the Buyid Administration of the golden days of the Abbasides. He had very successfully accomplished the maintenance of a large tribal army by abandoning partially the traditional tax framing system of revenue collection for that of the fief, whereby the Military Generals supported themselves and the army under their command, through the land allotted to them by the State for the purpose. Nizamul Mulk elaborately systematised it.

In the absence of regular intelligence service, he managed to intimidate the rebels through a judicious display of Saljukide might. He was a follower and champion of Shafii sect and had gained the support of famous and powerful Ulema. Among these were a Al-Ishaq, Al-Shirazi and Al-Ghazali.

In 1091 the first challenge to his authority was made when Basra was captured by Carmatians and the citadel of Almut by Hasan bin Sabah.

Nizamul Mulk Toosi was assassinated by a follower of Hasan bin Sabah on October 4, 1092 near Sihna while on his way to Baghdad. The assassin had disguised himself as a Sufi. Thus died one of the greatest administrators and benefactos of the world of Islam.

# SULTAN MAHMOOD
# OF GHAZNI

A formidable force of Hindu warriors drawn from different parts of India had arrayed themselves on the plains of Kathiawar against a small Muslim army led by Mahmood of Ghazni. The large Hindu army led by hundreds of war elephants was characterised by massive pomp and pageantry. On the other hand, Mahmood's troops hardly one-tenth of the opposing force, who treked through a trackless desert, were too tired and, therefore, hesitated to meet such a powerful enemy. But Mahmood was too steadfast and valiant to lose heart. He prayed for Divine assistance against the infidels who, in the past, had broken many pledges and treaties made with the Muslims and he had come to punish them for their treachery. He made a memorable speech before his weary soldiers which steeled their determination to crush the enemy. A loud cry of *Allah-o-Akbar* (God is Great) rent the air, and the Muslims, led by Mahmood, made a desperate charge on the serried ranks of the perfidious infidels. They fought like heroes in a sea of men, which swarmed and closed in upon them from all sides to devour them. The occasional cries of *Allah-o-Akbar* raised by them above the din of the battle proclaimed their existence.

At last, an irresistible charge by Mahmood won him the day; the Hindus were routed with terrible losses. They fled, leaving behind a large number of dead on the battlefield. They had to pay a heavy price for their treachery and broken pledges.

The famous temple of Somnath lay before the Conqueror from Ghazni. The inmates of the temple offered an extremely high price to save their idols but Mahmood declined their offer, saying: "I want to be known in history as the destroyer of idols and not a idol seller". He struck the biggest idol with his staff. Its interior was found filled with invaluable precious stones which gushed forth and strewed the floor.

Sultan Mahmood was a great conqueror, builder and patron of art and literature. According to the noted chronicler, Farishta, he "was endowed with all the qualities of a great prince". "The real source of his glory", says Elphinstone, "lay in his combining the qualities of a warrior and a conqueror with a zeal for the encouragement of literature and arts, which was rare in his time, and has not yet been surpassed".

Mahmood, the eldest son of Subuktagin, was born in 969 A.C. His father, posted as Governor of Khorasan by King Nuh II of Bukhara, appointed Mahmood as his Deputy. He took Neshapur from the Ismails and made it his Capital. On the death of his father in 997 A.C. Mahmood seized Ghazni from his brother and ascended its throne in 999 A.C.

Sultan Mahmood proved himself a capable and enlightened ruler, who was great both in war and peace. He was an invincible conqueror, a successful administrator, and a great builder. The Abbaside Caliph of Baghdad, Al-Kadir Billah, recognised Mahmood as the ruler of Ghazni and Khorasan and conferred on him the title of "Amir-al-Millat" and later "Yameen-ud-Dawala".

During the last 30 years of his life, he made 17 invasions of India. In 1001, he defeated and captured Raja Jaipal I of Punjab. He was later released on promise of paying tribute. But he soon broke it and was later punished by the Sultan. Mahmood invaded Multan and besieged its ruler Dawood who had adopted the Carmathian creed. Later he captured Ghur.

The Princes of India made a confederacy against Mahmood. A number of Rajas who had promised to pay tribute to him also joined them. When he crossed the Indus in 1008 he was met at Und by a great Hindu army composed of the troops of Anand Pal and the Rajas of Ujjain, Gwalior, Kalanjar, Kanauj, Delhi and Ajmer. The Sultan routed the Hindus after a hotly contested battle. The Hindus fled from the battlefield littered with their dead bodies. The Rajas later lost faith in each other and the confederacy was dissovled. Mahmood pressed on and the fortress of Bhavan and the temple of Kangra fell to him.

In 1009, the Sultan again invaded Punjab to punish Anand Pal who had broken his pledge to pay tribute. In 1011, he captured the temple of Thanesar. In 1014 Mahmood defeated the Hindu Princes in the Mangla Pass, captured the fortress of Naudana and pursued them into Kashmir.

In 1018 the Sultan set out on an expedition to punish the treacherous Hindu Rajas who had broken their pledges and taken up arms against him. He crossed the Jamuna, received submission of the Raja of Basan, defeated Raja Kulchand of Mahaban and captured Mathura and Bindraban. He marched with his picked force on Kanauj, guarded by seven forts built on the Ganges. The Raja of Kanauj fled, leaving behind his Capital city to Mahmood.

The Rajas of Kalanjar and Gwalior murdered the Raja of Kanauj for his cowardice and formed a confederacy against the Sultan who broke it by inflicting a crushing defeat on them in 1022. The Rajas promised to pay him an annual tribute.

In 1023, the Sultan invaded Transoxiana to establish his authority there. In 1025, he set out on his expedition against Somnath and there in January 1026, he defeated and routed a combined force of Hindu Rajas.

In 1027, the Sultan launched his last expedition to India to punish the rebellious and treacherous *Jats*. He collected a flotilla of boats at Multan and defeated them in a bloody naval battle fought on river Indus.

In the remaining period of his life he devoted his attention to consolidating the Western provinces of his vast Empire. He wrested Iraq, Rayy and Isfahan from the Buwayhids and invested his son Masood with the Government of the newly conquered territories.

Great in war, Mahmood was greater in peace. Whenever he got respite from his long-drawn-out campaigns, he devoted himself to the peace and prosperity of his people.

He built Ghazni into a magnificent Capital, the Queen of the East. The Grant Mosque of Ghazni, known as the "Bride of Heaven", built by him, was a wonder of the East in those times. Besides this, Mahmood adorned his Capital with a museum, a library, and a university as well as beautiful mosques, porches, fountains, reservoirs, aqueducts and cisterns.

The Sultan also constructed many dykes and aqueducts for his subjects which gave an unprecedented impetus to agriculture. His far-flung dominions were connected with good roads, dotted with caravansarais and protected under a strict Administration which ensured a flourishing trade in his Empire. Among his great public works, the Sultan's dyke is still extant and is used even up to the present day. The dyke was constructed at the mouth of a pass, 18 miles from Ghazni, 25 feet above the water level of the Nawar. It is 200 yards long.

Historians are all praise for Mahmood's Capital, Ghazni. "The civilization and grandeur possessed by the Samanids of North-Western Persia", says Sir John Marshal, "were handed down to Ghaznavids, as if by right of inheritance . . . . . Under Mahmood the Great, and his immediate successor, Ghazni became famous among all the cities of the Caliphate for the splendour of its architecture *(Cambridge History of India*. "The splendour of its courtiers' palaces", writes Lane Poole in his *Mediaeval India* "vying with his own, testified to the liberal encouragement of the arts which raised Ghazni—from a barrack of outlaws to the first rank among the many stately cities of the Caliphate". Another historian, Marshman has described it as "the grandest in Asia" *(Cambridge History of India)*.

Sultan Mahmood was one of the greatest patrons of art and learning that the world has seen. He gathered around him in his Court a galaxy of intellectual luminaries hardly ever seen in a Royal court of the Medieval times. The Sultan loved the society of learned men. "This restless adventurer", says Lane Polle, "after sweeping like a pestilence for hundreds of miles across India, or pouncing like a hawk coursing south to Hamadan almost within call of Baghdad itself, would settle down to listen to the songs of poets and the wise conversation of divines".

The Sultan stands unrivalled even up to the present times in his munificence and expenditure to the cause of education and learning. He founded a university equipped with a vast collection of books on different subjects and in different languages. A museum of natural curiosities was attached to the university.

"He showed so much munificence to individuals of eminence", says Elphinstone, "that his Court exhibited a greater assemblage of literary geniuses than any other monarch in Asia has ever been able to produce". *(Cambridge History of India)*. The number of poets alone attached to his Court was more than 400.

The Sultan, himself being a poet and scholar of repute, enjoyed the Company of intellectual luminaries who adorned his Court. Iran immensely benefited from Mahmood's patronage of learning. "It is to Sultan Mahmood" writes Elphinstone, "that the (Iran) is indebted for the full expansion of her national literature". According to Professor M. Habib "among the patrons of Persian renaissance, he (Mahmood) is the most remarkable".

Amongst the brightest intellectual luminaries which illuminated the Court of the Sultan was the encyclopaedist Abu Rehan Biruni, the philosopher—musical theorist Farabi, the philosopher—linguist Ansari, the witty poet Manuchehri, the celebrated poet Asjadi and the great epic poet Firdausi, whose *Shahnama* ranks amongst the greatest epic poems of the world.

The Sultan's boundless generosity to these men of letters has been recorded in history. The story of his paying sixty thousand silver coins instead of the gold ones to Firdausi as settled with him is a fiction that has been contradicted by modern historical research.

The great Sultan breathed his last at Ghazni on April 30, 1030 A.C. at the age of 63, being worn out by the labours of 40 years' rule.

# ZAHIRUDDIN BABUR

Babur, the founder of the great Mughal Empire in India, was a direct descendant of the two greatest conquerors of the world: Timur and Chengiz Khan—from the former from father's side and from the latter from mother's side.

Born in 1482 at Farghana, a small town situated in a charming country of vales and mountains, enclosed by the Amu Darya and Syr Darya, abounding in roses, melons and pomegranates, and reputed for all sorts of games and sports, Zahiruddin Muhammad, surnamed Babur "the Tiger" was a Chaghtai Turk by race.

His father, Sheikh Umar, was a pleasant brave man whose generosity was large and who possessed great humour and eloquence. Babur's uncle, a great soldier, was the King of Samarkand.

Babur himself, a true child of the race, was handsome, affable and fearless, an expert polo player and a deadly shot with the bow. He could swim across mighty rivers and could climb mountains with two men under his arms.

In 1494 A.C. Sheikh Umar died in an accident. Immediately anarchy broke out in Samarkand and Babur had to flee for his life. Three years later, he captured Samarkand. But his stay there was shortlived. His enemy seized it again when he was out on an expedition. Being driven once more into exile, he wandered for three years and in 1500 A.C. he swooped down on Samarkand with a handful of men and recaptured it. The boy King was seated on the throne of his world famous ancestor—Timur—in Samarkand, the glorious city of orchards and pleasure gardens, adorned with a magnificent Friday Mosque, Colleges, Observatory and the Famous Palace of the Forty Pillars.

Babur was not destined to stay there for long. The following year, Shahi Beg, the great Khan of the Uzbeg expelled him from Samarkand. Young Babur once again found himself a fugitive. He wandered for four years and turned towards the south to Kabul which was ruled by one of his uncles.

His uncle died, leaving the state of Kabul in disorder, Babur occupied Kabul in October 1504 and henceforth he embarked upon a meteoric career.

He liked Kabul and the country surrounding it, known for variegated luscious flowers and fruits. In 1512 A.C., he again got a chance of capturing Samarkand but his triumph was shortlived, lasting for eight months only.

Finally returning to Kabul, he thought out a plan of conquering India, a land of gold, watered by the mighty Indus and Ganges.

On Friday, November 17, 1525 A.C., Babur set out for India with a force of 12,000 men. The Lodhi Governor of Lahore, Daulat Khan, promised to help him against his master Ibrahim Lodhi, King of Delhi. When Babur reached Lahore the treacherous Daulat Khan changed his mind, but was easily defeated.

Babur marched upon Delhi, Capital of the Afghan Empire, ruled over by Ibrahim Lodhi.

The two armies met on April 21, 1526 on the historic plain of Panipat Babur's force was hardly a tenth of his enemy's but it was better disciplined and equipped with a number of firearms unknown in the East.

Babur followed the traditional Mongol manoeuvre to camouflage the bound waggons, and while the enemy was attacking them, to counter attack simultaneously on both flanks with swift masses of cavalry.

The unskilful young Ibrahim Lodhi was tempted to make a frontal attack led by his war elephants. This was what Babur desired. Withholding his fire till the elephants came at point blank range, he suddenly opened fire. The savage brutes stampeded and turned round on their own men. Babur, thereafter, made fierce cavalry charge which totally routed the enemy.

By midday the battle was over, Sultan Ibrahim Lodhi was killed and lost 20,000 men. Immense spoils including the famous Koh-i-Noor diamond fell into the hands of Babur's men. Babur marched on Delhi, which capitulated without any resistance. He was proclaimed as the Emperor of Hindustan from the pulpit of the Friday Mosque in Delhi.

Babur settled down to rule over India. He had a very poor opinion of India and its inhabitants. He set to work to make India more tolerable for himself and for that purpose he laid out gardens and orchards containing fruit trees and flower plants of his choice. He built palaces of his choice dotted with fountains and aqueducts.

But a vital danger still loomed large over the horizon. He had to face a greater challenge thrown by the veteran Rajput Ruler, Rana Sangram Singh, the "Sun of Mewar", better known as Rana Sanga. The Rajput army, comprising 80,000 horse and 500 elephants and commanded by 120 Chieftains of ancient lineage, were the flower of Hindu chivalry. The Rana himself, a mere "fragment of a man", who had lost an arm and an eye on the battlefield had fought 18 pitched battles against the Afghans.

Babur advanced from Agra to a place called Kanua, where he awaited the approach of Rajput forces. He adopted the Mongol tactics. "His waggons were bound together with iron chains, with the cannons at intervals, and, in addition, he had mounted his matchlocks on wheeled tripods which could be moved quickly to the threatened point. His flanks were protected by deep ditches and entanglements".

The Mughal army became somewhat nervous at the arrival of the mighty Rajput force. But their leader was not a man to lose heart. He took a vow that if God gave him victory he would never taste wine again. He made a memorable speech before his men :

"Noblemen and soldiers! Everyman who comes into the world is subjected to death. When we pass away and are gone, God only survives, unchangeable. Whoever comes to the feast of life must, before it is over, drink from the cup of death. He who arrives in the inn of mortality must one day inevitably take his departure from this house of sorrow, the world. How much better it is to die with honour than to live with infamy!"

"The Most High God has been propitious to us, and has now placed us in such a crisis, that if we fall in the field we die the death of martyrs; if we survive, we rise victorious, the avengers of the cause of God. Let us then, with one accord, swear on God's Holy Word that none of us will even think of turning his face from this warfare, nor desert from the battle and slaughter that ensues, till his soul is separated from his body."

The army electrified by these noble words swore to fight till death. On March 16, 1527 the Rajput army appeared on the scene. Babur divided his army into three portions, with a strong reserve. The attack started soon. Wave after wave of Rajputs threw themselves against the gallant Mughals and Babur's artillery did a terrible slaughter. When the Rajputs were exhausted, Babur ordered a simultaneous attack on the centre and on either flank. The Rajputs were routed with terrible losses and were pursued relentlessly to their camp. A minaret of Rajput heads was erected on the battlefield. Babur, with his small force, hardly one-ninth of the mighty Rajput force, had smashed the Hindu power in India for ever.

The next year Babur captured the stronghold of Chanderi. The same year his forces overthrew the Afghan kingdom of Bihar and Bengal and he became the undisputed Emperor of India, and the foundations of the great Mughal Empire were laid firmly on the Indian soil.

But Babur was not destined to live long to enjoy the fruits of his labour and administer his vast Empire. He undertook the task of beautifying his new Capital, Agra, with gardens, palaces and buildings. In December 1529, he held a grand Durbar, attended by ambassadors from Persia, Herat and Bengal.

In December 1530, his most beloved son, Humayun fell seriously ill. All medical treatment proved ineffectual. Some wise men suggested the life of the Crown Prince could be saved only if the Emperor sacrificed his most precious thing. He at once offered to sacrifice his most precious thing, life, to save Humayun. Walking thrice round the sick Prince's bed, he prayed, "On me be the sickness". Then he cried out ecstatically, "I have succeeded! I have taken it". From that moment Humayun gradually recovered and Babur sickened and died on December 26, 1530 A.C.

He was buried in a beautiful garden on the hillside of Kabul, where he once delighted to sit and gaze on the beautiful and panoramic world around.

Babur, a great warrior General, was a litterateur of repute. He was well versed in Persian and Turkish languages. Besides being an accomplished poet, he was a well-known writer of Persian prose and his *"Memoirs"* bear an immortal testimony to it.

# SHER SHAH SURI

Some are born great, some acquire greatness and some have greatness thrust upon them. Sher Shah Suri belongs to the second category of great men. From the position of an ordinary soldier he rose to be the monarch of a mighty Empire stretching from the vale of Brahamputra in the East to the borders of Afghanistan in the West. He was undoubtedly a great genius, endowed with varied talents. With his sagacity and chivalry, indomitable will and undaunted courage, he founded a vast Afghan Empire. Because of his dynamic and enlightened administration he carved for himself a unique place in the history of Muslim India. During his short reign he introduced laudable reforms and organised public works on an unprecedented scale which added to the peace and prosperity of his people. "No Government", says Keene, "not even the British, has shown so much wisdom in the administration of the country as this Pathan".

Farid Khan, son of Hasan Khan was a member of the Afghan tribe of Sur, who claimed themselves as descendants of the princes of Ghor. His grandfather, Ibrahim Khan, was first in the family to enter the Imperial service, when Bahlul Lodhi was the Emperor of Delhi. When Bahlul Lodhi was succeeded by Sikandar Lodhi, Hasan Khan, the son of Ibrahim and the father of Farid (Sher Shah), joined the service of Jamal Khan, Governor of Jaunpur, who conferred on him the Jagir comprising the districts of Sasaram and Tanda in Bihar for the maintenance of his five hundred horses.

Farid Khan was one of the eight sons of Hasan Khan. His father neglected the mother of Farid, who was an Afghan woman. Hence, when Farid grew up, he left his home and enlisted himself as a private soldier in the army of Jamal Khan, Governor of Jaunpur. Farid Khan had his education and proficiency in other sciences at Jaunpur, a well-known educational and cultural centre of those times. But for years later, when his father visited Jaunpur, the differences between the father and the son were composed and Hasan Khan appointed his son Farid as Manager of his Sasaram estate, while he himself settled down at Jaunpur.

The meteoric rise of Farid Khan, an ordinary soldier, to the highest position of the Emperor of Delhi added a glorious chapter to the history of India. His ascendancy to power is a story full of ambition and brilliance.

Farid, who was made the Manager of the Sasaram estate by his father, Hasan Khan, once again fell a prey to his family intrigues. His step-mother was constantly forcing his father to appoint his step-brother in his place as the Manager of the estate. In order to avoid domestic unpleasantness Farid voluntarily vacated the place in favour of his step-brother and left for Agra, where he entered the service of Daulat Khan Lodhi. He was still at Agra, when his father Hasan Khan died and through the influence of Daulat Khan, Farid obtained the Sasaram estate.

Meanwhile the throne of Delhi changed hands, Babur invaded India in 1526 A.C., and defeated Ibrahim Lodhi in the first battle of Panipat. Ibrahim Lodhi was killed at the battlefield and Babur was crowned as Emperor of India. Farid joined one Bahar or Bahadur Khan Lohani, who had proclaimed himself King of Bihar under the title of Muhammad Shah. It was during this period that Farid Khan changed his name to Sher Khan. His master, who was out on hunting, was charged by a tiger. He was in mortal danger. Suddenly Farid Khan leapt forward and killed the tiger with a timely blow of his sword. Muhammad Shah conferred on young Farid the title of Sher Khan for this exceptional act of bravery. This title he afterwards used as his name. But despite his extreme loyalty, his ungrateful master Muhammad Shah, withdrew his favour from him and forced him to surrender his estate to his step-brother Sulaiman. Sher Khan was obliged to take refuge with Sultan Junaid, Mughal Governor of Karra Manikpur. Later, obtaining military assistance from Shah Junaid, he defeated Shah Mahmood and not only recovered his lost estate but also occupied vast areas in Bihar. He deputised Emperor Babur in the new territories and through the recommendations of Shah Junaid, the Mughal Emperor confirmed Sher Khan in his holdings and gave him the military command of Bihar.

But this favour of the Mughal Emperor did not last long. He came to know of the secret ambitions of young Sher Khan, who clandestinely left Agra and joined hands with Mahmood Shah Lodhi, son of ex-king Sikandar Lodhi. Mahmood Shah Lodhi conquered Bihar, but soon after Babur recovered Bihar from him, by defeating him and his Rajput allies. Sher Khan, later joined the service of Muhammad Shah Lohani, who occupied Bihar. His patron died soon afterwards, leaving behind him his widow and a minor son Jalal Khan. Sher Khan was now the virtual Administrator of Bihar. Jalal Khan was forced to seek military assistance from Mahmood Shah Purbia, the King of Bengal. An army under the command of Ibrahim Khan was despatched by the King of Bengal which was routed by the numerically inferior forces of Sher Khan. He now became the undisputed monarch of Bihar. Meanwhile, with his marriage to one Lado Malika, the widow of Taj Khan, Commandant of Chunar, he got possession of the famous Chunar fortress as well as vast treasures. It is said that "Sher Khan took from the Bibi (Lado Malika) 300 maunds of gold to equip his army and gave her two parganas for her support besides leaving her some ready money for her immediate expenses". *(Great Men of India).*

Babur was succeeded by his son Humayun in December 1530 A.C.

Humayun, as Mughal Emperor of India, was far less talented and fortunate than his illustrious father. He had to face a formidable and valiant foe in the person of Sher Khan who had begun to threaten as his serious rival for the throne of Delhi. The first nine years of Humayun's reign were occupied with internal rebellions of his intriguing brothers and it was in 1539 that he resolved to check the rising power of Sher Khan. In the meantime, Sher Khan had invaded Gaur, the Capital of Bengal. Mahmood Shah Purbia, was defeated and was forced to flee, thus leaving the fertile kingdom of Bengal for the Afghan invader. Humayun thought it an opportune moment to deliver a blow to Sher Khan from behind, but his military advisers urged him to capture Chunar, a stronghold of Sher Khan near Mirzapur, before proceeding ahead. The fortress held out for long and by the time Chunar had fallen to Humayun, Gaur had also surrendered to Sher Khan, who was now free to meet the Mughal forces.

The army led by Sher Khan, both numerically and militarily, was too weak to face the Mughal Imperial army. In order to deposit the captured treasures of the King of Bengal at a safe place, he captured the strong fortress of Rohtas through a strategic military device. Humayun by this time occupied Gaur without difficulty, but Monsoon overtook him and he rested for three months in Gaur. At last he moved westward on hearing the disaster which had befallen his lieutenant Khan-i-Khan Lodhi at Mungher. He reached Chounsa in Bihar, where he met Sher Khan, the valiant Afghan who had made a lightning march in order to prevent the Mughal Emperor and his army from crossing the river Ganges. The two armies, encamped on the opposite banks of the river, watched each other for over two months. At last Humayun collected boats and tried to make a bridge on the river. Now it was the time for the enterprising Afghan to act. Leaving his tents intact and a party of his army occupying it, through a camouflage movement, he made a secret crossing of the river in June 1539, and suddenly fell on the Imperial army. The Mughal Emperor and his army was taken by surprise and was completely routed. Humayun, himself plunged his horse into the river and saved his life with great difficulty with the help of a watercarrier named Nizam. The Mughal Empress, Bega Begum, who had fallen into the hands of Sher Khan, was treated with utmost respect and was sent with all honours to a place of safety. Humayun fled towards Agra pursued by Sher Khan. Thus the brilliant victory of Sher Khan over the Mughal forces at Chounsa opened for him the Empire of India. He occupied the Mughal strongholds of Chunar and Jaunpur and proclaimed himself as Sher Shah, King of Bengal, Bihar and Jaunpur. As usual, the proclamation of Sher Shah as the King of the Eastern Provinces was accompanied by customary rejoicings. According to Abbas Sarwani, "For seven days drums were beaten in token of rejoicings. Troups of Afghan youths came from every tribe and danced according to their specific custom. Gifts were made to the musicians and the servants of Sher Shah sprinkled saffron and musk, mixed with rose water and ambergris of various colours, upon the heads of dancing youths. Delicious dishes emitted sweet scents that suggested the perennial flavour of the dinner table of heaven, and drinks which suggested the sweetness of Divine Love, were distributed among the revellers" (quoted by Kali Karanjan Qanungo in his *Sher Shah*).

Humayun once again tried to face the Afghan ruler and on May 17, 1540, the two forces met at Bilgram. Sher Shah led a force of 15,000 soldiers, while the Mughal army numbered more than 40,000. The Mughal army could not stand before the disciplined Afghan soldiers and broke up without giving any serious battle. Sher Shah made a hot pursuit of the defeated Mughal Emperor. Passing through Lahore, where he was joined by his brother Kamran, he made a vain effort to establish himself in Sind, but it was destined otherwise. At last he took refuge in Kandhar in 1543 A.C., leaving his vast Indian Empire to Sher Shah.

Sher Shah, now ascended the throne of Delhi as the most powerful ruler of India. But, he had to reduce a number of pockets in Rajputana and Central India before considering himself as the undisputed and supreme monarch of India. In January 1543, he dispatched a force to Malwa under the command of his son, Jalal Khan, to meet Puran Mal, a Rajput Chieftain who was extremely intolerant towards Muslims. Puran Mal capitulated after stiff resistance. From Central India, Sher Shah marched against the ruler of Jodhpur (Rajputana), who was a great stumbling block in the way of his attaining supreme power in India. He defeated the forces of Jodhpur through a rare strategic move, which provide ample proof of his military skill and intelligence. Thereafter, he overran the whole of Rajputana and Mewar which offered no resistance. Returning to Central India, he laid siege to Kalinjar in November 1544 A.C. The siege lasted long. In the words of the author of *Tarikh-i-Daudi,* "Sher Shah encircled Kalinjar and began to construct mines and a lofty tower for mounting a battery and covered approaches. The latter negotiated the fort and the tower was built so high that the land within the fort could be overlooked from its top. For the space of seven months, the soldiers and camp followers laboured day and night", (quoted by K. K. Qanungo in his *Sher Shah).*

A general assault on the fortress of Kalinjar was ordered on May 22, 1545 but it was rolled back by the defenders. A second assault with hand grenades directed by the Afghan Emperor himself resulted in a mortal blow to his person. A bomb rebounding against the fort wall fell into the powder mine which blew up, thus mortally wounding Sher Shah. But despite extremely serious injury, he continued directing the assault and when the fortress was finally carried, he exclaimed, "Thank God", and expired.

Thus closed in 1545 A.C. the career of one of the most chivalrous, enterprising and brilliant personalities that lived in India who, through his sagacity, chivalry, strategy and administrative ability, wrote the brightest chapter in the history of the subcontinent.

A great warrior and a skilful commander, Sher Shah was averse to bloodshed and savagery. He was humane and kind-hearted and a real benefactor of his people. He was stern to the unruly but kind to the weak. According to Professor Qanungo, "he was one of the most humane conquerors of the world", He was immensely loved and respected by his men and admired by his enemies for his humanity and forbearance. "No General was more beloved of his soldiers than Sher Shah", says Prof. Qanungo. He inspired love from his own men including soldiers and respect from his foes. His men volunteered themselves to perform the most difficult tasks for him, which crowned his moves with success and enabled him to build for himself, the most enterprising career in Indian history. Sher Shah is known for his love of justice in the history of India.

During his short reign, occupied with incessant warfare, his successful administration is based on his attachment to justice. It is said that once a Hindu complained to Sher Shah that his (Sher Shah's) son had thrown a betel in front of his wife, while she was passing by his house. The matter was immediately enquired into the open court and the prince found guilty, Sher Shah ordered that the Hindu should also throw betel in front of his son's wife in the same manner. Charles Kincaid, in the *"Great Men of India"* writes: "Farid (Sher Shah) when accepting the post of (Manager, Sasaram Estate) is reported to have said: "That the stability of every administration depended on justice and that it would be his greatest care not to violate it, whether by oppressing the weak or by permitting the strong to infringe the laws with impunity. This promise which sounded like a pompous platitude, Farid (Sher Shah) kept alike as Manager of his father's *jagir,* as King of Bengal and as Emperor of Delhi". *(Great Men of India).* He never favoured the oppressor and always sided with the oppressed. Even his dear ones were not immune from law and were treated like ordinary criminal if found guilty. According to Abbas Khan, a historian of his time, Sher Shah was also adorned with the "Jewel of Justice". Nizamuddin, a well-known historian of Mughal times pays glowing tribute to his wise and able administration, whose exceptional success greatly depended on his adherence to justice. He says: "Such was the state of safety of the highways that if anyone carried a purse of gold *mohars* with him and slept in the desert for nights, there was no need of keeping watch".

Another trait of his which greatly contributed to his success in life was his capacity for incessant hard labour. It was against his nature to sit idle or to complain of weariness. He never frittered his time in idle pursuits and spent the major part of the day over the affairs of the State. Once he said to his nobles: "It behoves the great to be always active". Even the minutest details of the State administration did not escape his vigilant eyes.

Sher Shah was not only a great General but also a wise and capable Administrator as well an outstanding reformer. His short reign occupied with incessant warfare is punctuated with useful reforms and public welfare activities which has earned for him an outstanding place among the great conquerors and administrators of the world. His most laudable reform, universally recognised as a great achievement of his administrative genius was the revenue system he introduced in the country. This immensely added to the prosperity of the peasantry, and contributed to the peace and tranquillity of his State. His experience as Manager of Sasaram estate of the plight of his peasants enabled him to plan his revenue system on a realistic and humane basis, when he became the Emperor of Delhi. Knowing that peace and tranquillity of the State depended greatly on the prosperity and well-being of the peasants, he consistently strove to improve the lot of the cultivators. He abolished the *Jagirdari* system and brought the land direct under State control. The holdings of each cultivator were separately measured and it was made obligatory for him to deposit one-fourth of his produce with the Government either in cash or kind.

Sher Shah divided his kingdom into forty-seven units, which were called *Sarkars.* Each *Sarkar* was further divided into parganas or districts. Each pargana was administered by a *Siqdar* and *Munsif* who were assisted by subordinate officials. The *Siqdar* was entrusted with police and civil administration, while the *Munsif* was mainly concerned with the collection of revenue through *Amils,* *Muqaddums* and *Qanungos.* Government officers and functionaries used to be transferred from place to place after every two or three years in order to avoid the possibilities of corruption and favouritism.

The revenue system introduced by Sher Shah in his vast kingdom, better known in the Indian history as Sher Shahi Bandobast, was adopted and practised during the Mughal Rule in India. Its salient features were also retained in the most applauded Ryotwari Settlement, introduced during the British rule in India.

Sher Shah was the true benefactor of the peasantry and the common man. Any wrong done to the peasants was promptly enquired into and the offender was severely dealt with. Even during his military marches he avoided, as far as possible, to trespass any field. The cultivators whose crops were damaged in his military marches were promptly compensated. Once he said to his officers: "If a little favour is shown to the cultivator, the ruler benefits by it".

Sher Shah took keen interest in public welfare activities. Being a true well wisher of his people, his foremost thought was the prosperity and well-being of the common man. He built the famous Grand Trunk Road, which starting from Bengal in the East and passing through the principal towns of Bihar, United Provinces and Punjab, terminated at Peshawar in the West. This important thoroughfare, which is still recognised as the most important road in the Indo—Pakistan subcontinent, was dotted with wells, bazaars, caravansarais and rest-houses at short stages. Writing in the *"Great Men of India",* Charles Kincaid states: "A most skilful and active General, yet he found time to bring order in his territories and he constantly sought to improve the civil Government. He made roads with rest-houses at every stage and he dug wells at intervals of a mile or two miles. By roadside he planted innumerable trees and compelled the owners of the land through which the roads passed to suppress brigandage and to see to it that travellers could journey in safety. His early death was a heavy loss to India". *(Sher Shah in Great Men of India).*

Such was Sher Shah Suri—great both in war and peace, whose short reign full of activity in the fields of war as well as in peace, contributed immensely to the peace and prosperity of his vast Empire.

# SULAIMAN, THE MAGNIFICENT

The great Ottoman Empire, spread over three continents—Europe, Asia and Africa—was like a tongue, surrounded by 32 teeth—the Christian European States—which were continuously plotting against it. It was headed by a succession of six brilliant rulers, who, side by side with braving the onslaughts of Christian monarchs, extended the boundary of the Turkish Empire up to the gates of Vienna. The greatest of all Ottoman Emperors was Sulaiman I, better known in history as Sulaiman, the "Magnificent", or Sulaiman, the "Lawgiver".

Sulaiman, son of the Ottoman Emperor Salim and Aisha Sultan, was born in 1494-95 A.C. He was given a thorough education, both in the arts of war and peace, by his illustrious father. Later, he was appointed the Governor of Maghnisa, and ascended the throne on September 20, 1520 A.C., eight days after his father's death.

Thereafter, started a career, which was brilliant both in war as well as in peace and won for Sulaiman an honoured place amongst the greatest rulers of the world. A man of indomitable will and untiring energy, as he was, he proved his greatness on the battlefield and at the conference table alike. He was essentially a man of peace who ceaselessly strove for the peace and prosperity of his people, but when the call for war came, he was never found wanting and always took the field in person.

Sulaiman took part in 13 major campaigns—ten in Europe and three in Asia. The first campaign against Belgrade was provoked by the illtreatment by the King of Hungary of the Turkish Envoy who had gone to collect annual tribute from him. The Ottoman army advanced under the Grand Vizier Piri Pasha and captured Belgrade on August 29, 1521. This was preceded by the fall of Sabacz, Danubian town, to the Ottoman forces. Sulaiman, the Magnificent, entered Belgrade on August 30 and stationed a Brigade there.

The following year he captured Rhodes, a strategic island, from the knights of St. John who had been for long a "menace to the Ottoman power because they supported the Christian Corsairs".

The Grand Vizier Piri Pasha was replaced by Ibrahim Pasha who remained a faithful companion of the Sultan till his sudden execution in 1536.

In 1524 Sulaiman set out with the Grand Vizier, arrived in Belgrade on July 15, took Peterwarden and crossed the Drave at Eszed. Here in August 1524, was fought a bloody battle against the Hungarian army which was routed with terrible losses. The Hungarian resistance was completely crushed. The Sultan advanced further and occupied Hungarian Capital, Budapest, on September 11. The Capital was in flames despite Sultan's orders to the contrary.

The victorious Sultan returned to Constantinople in November to deal with trouble in Asia Minor. Meanwhile war continued in Bosnia, Dalmatia and Slavonia.

Disturbed conditions in Hungary, obliged the energetic Sultan to set out in May 1529 for his new expedition, known as the Vienna campaign. Budapest capitulated on September 8 and the Sultan installed Zapolya as King of Hungary. The Turks reached the gates of Vienna and laid siege to the famous city on September 27 which was raised on October 15. In the following two years, war with Austria continued.

In 1532, Sulaiman undertook a campaign against Charles V, King of Spain, and captured Guns after a long-drawn siege. The Sultan remained in Syria for the next few months and the Spanish King did not dare to face him.

The Sultan's return to Constantinople was soon followed by an armistic with Austria signed on January 14, 1533.

His sixth campaign was directed against Persia, which was caused by Ottoman claims to Bitles and Baghdad. The Grand Vizier, Ibrahim Pasha, occupied Tabriz in July 1534. The Ottoman army marched towards Baghdad *via* Hamadan without meeting any resistance. The Sultan made a ceremonial entry into Baghdad on November 30, 1534. During his four months stay in the historic city he built the mausoleum of Imam Abu Hanifa and meanwhile visited a number of historic cities including Kufa, Najef and Karbala.

The next two campaigns in 1541 and 1543 took him again to Hungary, where the death of Zapolya in 1540 had put that country into commotion. The Sultan entered Budapest in August 1541 and placed the country under the direct Ottoman Administration. In 1543, he captured a number of towns including Valpo, Siklos, Funfkirchen, Gran and Stunl-weissenberg.

His relations with Persia had become more strained, while the Hungarian war had come to an end through a seven-year truce with Ferdinand of Austria who undertook to pay an annual tribute of 30,000 ducats. The Persian campaign of 1548-49, provoked by the Shah of Persia's brother Elkas Mirza ended following the latter taking refuge in the Ottoman Court. Sulaiman entered Tabriz, spent his winter in Aleppo, while his Vizier had made some conquests in Georgia.

The Sultan's outstanding campaign was directed against Austria on account of the Ottoman claim over Szigeth which was besieged in August 1565. The city capitulated on September 8, 1565 while the Sultan died on September 5/6 and did not live to witness it.

The last few years of the Sultan were darkened by the death of his son Khurram and the conflict between his sons Salim and Bayazid, which ended with the execution of the latter. Hence the Sultan's death was kept a secret for three weeks in order to prevent trouble in the army and to enable Salim II to ascend the throne. The Sultan was buried in the Sulaimaniya Mosque at Constantinople.

Sulaiman made the Ottomans the most invincible power in the world, both on land and sea. In the battles fought on land, the Ottoman forces were mostly led by Sulaiman himself, while on sea, his able Admiral Khairuddin Barbarossa had become a terror for the Spanish, Genoese and Valentine fleets and had established Ottoman supremacy over the Mediterranean. He captured a number of islands in the Mediterranean and almost all important north African ports, including Tunis. He was responsible for the great naval victory of the Ottoman Fleet in the Mediterranean against the Spanish Fleet commanded by Admiral Andreas Doria and successive Ottoman victories on the African, Italian and Dalmatian coasts.

The enormous expansion of the Ottoman Empire under Sulaiman was the result of his untiring energy and exceptional military skill as well as the military system he had evolved. His great victories brought fundamental changes in the position of the Empire in international affairs. The Christians who lost all hopes of driving the Turks out of Europe, concluded the famous alliance with Turkey through Francis I of France.

"He was a born ruler of remarkable dignity", writes a Chronicler; "a striking figure in the midst of a brilliant Court". He made the Ottoman Empire an undisputeely supreme power in the world—both among Christians and Muslims. He was fortunate to secure the services of brilliant men for Turkey, including Admiral Khairuddin Barbarossa, Mufti Kamal Pasha and Architect Sinan. Each one played his brilliant role in making Turkey the most powerful State in the world.

Sulaiman's contribution to the peace and prosperity of his people, to the cultural achievements and legislative reforms of his country, were as great as his territorial conquests. It was a period of intense literary and artistic creation in which the Ottoman civilization expressed its personality to the full. Constantinople became the centre of Islamic civilization and culture as well as the centre of its political power.

Sulaiman has been recognised as a great patron of art and literature. The Ottoman civilization gained its own special character in the fields of literature and art under him. A poet himself, Sulaiman recognised and encouraged talents in others, among them were the Turkish poets Baki and Fazuli whose works have become classics. Sulaiman himself composed several *ghazals* and *diwans*. In this way, his glorious reign developed art, poetry, literature and architecture as never before.

Sulaiman is recognised as a great builder. The development of architecture owes much to his initiative and the famous Turkish architect Sinan raised some of the greatest Turkish architectures under his patronage. These included the mosques in Constantinople, namely the famous Sulaimaniya, built in 1550—56 where Sulaiman, the Magnificent, Sulaiman II and Ahmad II lie buried; Salimiya built in 1522 in memory of Salim I; Shahzadi Jami, built in 1547-48, in memory of Prince Muhammad and containing the mortal remains of Prince Jahangir; the Kassaki Jami, built in 1539, in memory of Khurram Sultan. Two more mosques were built in Stanbool and Skutari, in memory of Princess Mehr-o-Mah, wife of the Grand Vizier Rustam Pasha. All these mosques, except the Salimiya, are the works of architect Sinan. The Amirs and dignitaries of the Ottoman Empire vied with one another in building a large number of mosques and works of Sinan included the aqueducts of Constantinople and the Sultan's Palace at Skutari.

The Sultan did not confine his architectural works to Turkey alone. He built the mausoleum of Imam Abu Hanifa at Baghdad and the tomb of Maulana Jalaluddin Roomi at Konia. He built aqueducts at Makkah and was responsible for the restoration of the walls of Jerusalem, and beautification of the Kaaba. Throughout Turkey today, fountains, aqueducts, schools and other monuments of public interest, bear the stamp of Sinan and his school.

As a Legislator, he gave Turkey stable institutions and a legal system that remained unchanged for centuries thereafter. This earned him the title of Sulaiman, the "Law Giver" *(Qanuni)*. His legislative system promulgated throughout the Empire, dealt mainly with the laws relating to the reorganisation of the armed forces, military, feudality, landed property, the police and the feudal code. Thus, by his enactments, he brought together a system of laws and reformed the administration of the army, the land tenure system, and the collection of taxes. He opposed the inheritance of high positions, hitherto followed in the Ottoman Empire and thus prevented the establishment of separate fiefs within the State.

His treatment of his Christian subjects was generous; he conferred on them some of the highest positions in the State.

Sulaiman was a pious and religious-minded ruler. The short and fervid prayer uttered by him before the battle of Mohacs and the humility with which he assisted the bearers of the bier of Gul Baba after the occupation of Budapest in 1529, are ample testimony to this fact. He had copied eighth volumes of the Quran which are preserved in the Sulaimaniya Mosque. He strictly followed the tenets of Islam. He was undoubtedly the greatest of Ottoman Sultans who ranks amongst the greatest rulers of the world. He was just and generous, capable and energetic, wise and prudent and a real leader of his people in war and peace alike. With him ended the line of the great Turkish Sultans.

# AURANGZEB ALAMGIR

The Mughals, led by Prince Aurangzeb were engaged in a fierce battle against the tough Uzbek horsemen, led by Abdul Aziz. The battle which was fought near Balkh in 1647 reged all day long and the Mughals made repeated charges which were successfully repelled by the gallant Uzbeks. Aurangzeb who was leading the attack suddenly dismounted from his horse at sunset to offer his obligatory prayer. The Uzbeks who were stunned by the cool courage of the Mughal Prince stayed their hands. Their Commander cried out: "He is a Saint. We cannot fight against such a brave and pious man", and withdrew from the battlefield.

The Mughal Emperor Aurangzeb was the greatest of the Mughals who ruled over the subcontinent for about 5 decades. He fought all his life to correct the wrongs done by his lust-ridden apostate great grandfather, Akbar, and his epicurean grandfather, Jahangir.

The illiterate Akbar who was merely a slave of his lust for Rajput women had the audacity to invent a new religion, "Deen-e-Elahi", which could not fetch even a few adherents during his lifetime and did not survive after his death. His long rule dealt a deadly blow to the cause of Islam in the subcontinent. He alienated the Muslims and pampered the Hindus who, becoming strong, raised their heads during the time of Aurangzeb and were, at last, responsible for the downfall of the Mughal Empire. Later his son, Jahangir, who was a voluptuary entrusted the affairs of his Empire to his Queen, Noor Jahan. Shah Jahan, Aurangzeb's father, no doubt, tried to give Islamic pattern to his Adminstration and the national institutions, but he was more interested in setting up magnificent buildings like the Taj Mahal, the Pearl Mosque, the Juma Mosque and the Red Fort at Delhi. He is known as one of the greatest builders of mangificent buildings in history.

The task of establishing true Islamic rule fell upon the sturdy shoulders of Aurangzeb, who discharged his duties as a monarch with exceptional courage and firmness. His was an uphill task to suppress the evil forces which the short-sighted policies of Akbar and Jahangir had tended to strengthen. When he died, the Mughal Empire had been extended to its farthest limits. He had established it on a sounder footing. But for his weak and incompetent successors, the history of the Muslim rule over the subcontinent would have been totally different.

Muhammad Mohiuddin Aurangzeb, the third son of the Mughal Emperor Shah Jahan, was born at Dhud on November 4, 1618. In young Aurangzeb there was something of a saint which created a feeling of revulsion in his heart against the effeminate and voluptuous trends of his grandfather Jahangir with whom he had spent two years.

He was given a thorough education which included religious and secular learning, state-craft and military training. At an early age he proved himself the most competent and promising Prince for the Mughal throne.

He was quite young, when along with his father, Emperor Shah Jahan, brothers and other dignitaries of the State, he was one day witnessing an elephant fight in the Fort. One of the elephants lost his temper and rushed towards the audience. The Emperor, the Princes and the dignitaries all ran off for their lives. But Prince Aurangzeb, despite repeated pleadings stood at his place. The elephant attacked the lonely Prince and tried to lift him with its trunk. Aurangzeb, by his time, had taken out his sword and dealt a severe blow at its trunk which sent back the elephant trumpeting.

Shah Jahan was immensely pleased at Aurangzeb's exceptional courage and weighed him in gold which was distributed among the poor.

Hardly 18, Aurangzeb was appointed Viceroy of the important and turbulent Province of Deccan, which included Khandesh, Berar, Telangana and Daulatabad, and was dotted with sixty-four forts. He administered it with great ability and courage. He subdued the Mahratta leader Shahji Bhonsla who surrendered to him in 1636.

Later, the young Prince was appointed Governor of Gujrat where he suppressed lawlessness and robbery by his vigorous rule lasting two years. His able administration won him the admiration of Emperor Shah Jahan.

Aurangzeb's success as an administrator and general received so much recognition from the Emperor that he was assigned to lead difficult military expeditions in Balkh and Badakhshan in 1647. In appreciation of his successful conduct of the campaigns in the midst of extreme dangers, he was appointed Governor of Multan in March 1648.

He was again given the most difficult assignment in the Empire when he was appointed the Viceroy of Deccan for the second time in January 1653. The condition of this largest Province of the Empire was pitiable due to the neglect of the governors and administrators who were making hay after the departure of Aurangzeb when he was transferred to Gujrat in 1645. The condition of the people became miserable. Large tracts of land remained uncultivated, jungles unreclaimed; villages in many places were abandoned and collection of revenue was much below the estimates.

The young Prince devoted himself to the task of improving the administration of the Province. Land was resurveyed and classified according to its
fertility. Efficient management increased its productivity.

The Prince wanted to annex the neighbouring state of Golkanda which
was highly mismanaged. A large number of its Hindu employees conspired with
the Mahratta plunderers against the Mughal rule. But he was dissuaded from this
course by Emperor Shah Jahan who had been systematically poisoned against
him by his eldest son, Dara, and his ill-advisers.

The same thing happened when he attacked the Kingdom of Bijapur
whose Ruler was a friend of Prince Dara. Meanwhile, Aurangzeb had occupied
Bidar and Kalyani. Further progress was, however, stopped by Shah Jahan at
the instance of Dara.

The news about the serious illness of Emperor Shah Jahan in September
1658 led to a bloody war of succession among his four sons. Each of the four
brothers cherished the ambition of succeeding to the throne.

Dara, the eldest son, being at the Court exercised some of the Imperial
prerogatives. He was a true disciple of his great grandfather Akbar and was
inclined towards Hinduism much to the disgust of Muslims. Shah Jahan who
was more interested in erecting magnificent buildings than anything else, was
under Dara's evil influence. Shuja, the second son, who was the Governor of
Bengal, believed in the epicurean philosophy of his grandfather Jahangir. Murad,
the fourth son, who was the Governor of Gujrat, was no better. Both Shuja
and Murad declared their independence and also had their names read in Khutba
and struck on the coins in their respective Provinces.

Aurangzeb, the third and the ablest son, preferred to sit on the fence,
watching developments. All the three sons marched upon Agra. Aurangzeb
joined hands with Murad and routed the Imperial army led by the Rajput
General Jaswant Singh, in the battle of Dharamatpur in April 1658 A.C. The
Rajput General escaped with barely 500 troops.

Aurangzeb and Murad marched upon Agra. Dara, proud of his military
power, came out of Agra with one lakh horsemen and 20,000 infantry, to bar
the way of his two brothers. A fierce battle was fought at Samugarh on June 5,
1658 in which the Imperial forces led by Dara were defeated with terrible losses
and Dara fled from the battlefield for his life. He wandered from place to place
pursued by Aurangzeb's men, visiting Muthra, Punjab, Multan, Sind and Gujrat.
He sought the help of General Raja Jaswant Singh who betrayed him. Earlier,
his son Sulaiman Shikoh, was betrayed by Raja Jai Singh, another Rajput
General of the Mughal Empire. Dara was at last captured at Lahore and beheaded
at the behest of religious leaders who condemned him to death for his irreligious
beliefs.

Shuja was met by Aurangzeb's famous General Mir Jumla, at Khajua near Fatehpur. He was defeated and was pursued up to the Eastern Frontiers of Bengal. He disappeared in the Arakan Hills, never to return. Here, too, Jaswant Singh repeated his treachereous role. While fighting on the side of Shuja, he slipped away along with his men in the thick of the battle.

Murad was imprisoned in the Gwalior for his addiction to liquor.

Shah Jahan, biased towards Dara and too dangerous to be kept free, was confined by Aurangzeb in the Agra Fort, receiving all considerations and comforts befitting his dignity.

Aurangzeb ascended the Mughal throne in June 1659. He held his Court in Delhi. His path was beset with insuperable difficulties. The erstwhile trouble makers, especially the Mahrattas, the Rajputs, the Jats and the Sikhs, who were not pleased with a stern Muslim like Aurangzeb coming to power, started conspiring against the Mughal rule. The Pathans, too, wanted to take advantage of the war of succession among the Mughal Princes. The mounting discontentment in the Northern Frontier areas, obliged Aurangzeb to make Hasan Abdal his headquarters where he remained from June 1674 to December 1675.

Next year he marched to the South where he remained all his life, engaged in suppressing the revolts of Mahrattas and the conspiracies of Rajputs and Jats.

His able General Mir Jumla effectively put down all turbulent elements in far flung Bengal and conquered Assam and Cooch Bihar. This redoubtable General died in 1663 and in his death Aurangzeb lost his ablest General. The lower Bengal, including the Chittagong hill tracts and the island of Sandwip were conquered by Aurangzeb's uncle Shaista Khan.

The Hindu revolt which was brewing against the strict Muslim rule of Aurangzeb had its first demonstration near Agra where the Jats led by Gokla, the Zamindar of Tipat, revolted against the Mughal authority in 1669 A.C. This rebellion was suppressed without much difficulty.

The Santamis, a Hindu Sect, which practised witchery, rose in revolt, being assisted by Rajputs. They were routed with terrible losses by the Mughal army.

The treacherous Rajput General Raja Jaswant Singh who was pardoned by Aurangzeb on three occasions for his teachery, died in 1678, leaving behind no son to succeed him. Jaswant Singh's Rani gave birth to a posthumous son, afterwards named Ajit Singh, who was not recognised by the Mughal Emperor as the heir to Jaswant's estate. This led to a revolt by the Rathors. In a pitched battle near the lake Puskar in which the Emperor himself took part, the Rathor Rajputs were defeated.

Another troubled spot was in the south where the Mahratta plunderers under Shivaji, the "Mountain Rat", as Aurangzeb called him, had raised their head. He had to deal with a strong hand the Hindu agitators, pampered and spoilt by Akbar and Jahangir's too much liberalism.

Shivaji, the leader of a band of Mahratta plunderers, had accumulated much wealth and had become a menace to the neighbouring Muslim states of Golkanda and Bijapur. After a quick surprise attack he would disappear in his mountain defiles on the approach of the Bijapur or Mughal armies. He seldom dared to face them in the open and whenever he did so, he was beaten back with heavy losses. Like all brigands and robbers he believed in shock tactics and preferred to attack from the rear. He invited the Bijapura General Afzal Khan to negotiate peace, on the condition that both will be unarmed. When the brave Khan, unsuspecting any mischief, went to meet him, Shivaji treacherously thrust a tiger's claw in Afzal Khan's stomach during the conversation.

Aurangzeb appointed his uncle Shaista Khan to crush the Mahrattas. The Mughal forces soon captured Chakan and Poona, but they found it difficult to deal with the guerilla bands who disappeared with great ability into mountains and jungles on the approach of the former. Shivaji made a night attack on the Mughal camp in Poona, entering the city under the disguise of a marriage party. He along with his band of marauders, sacked the wealthy city of Surat for four days in January 1669 and plundered enormous wealth. A strong offensive launched against the Mahrattas under the command of Diler Khan in 1665 brought Shivaji and his brigands to their senses and the treaty of Purandar was signed on June 11, 1665 by which Shivaji had to surrender his 23 forts yielding a revenue of 4 lakh Huns. He was allowed to retain 12 forts.

Shivaji, henceforward, became a vassal of the Mughal Emperor and assisted him in his Bijapur war. He also visited the Mughal Court at Agra on May 12, 1666 and was put under house arrest for his insolence there. He, however, escaped with the connivance of Raja Ram Singh, a State Dignitary.

Shivaji died in 1680 and his successor Sambhuji, an insolent sensualist could not face the Mughal power for long. A Hindu historian describes the Mahratta method of warfare thus: "As soon as the enemy's back was turned, Shivaji's son Sambhuji swiftly led his active battle horsemen behind their flank, and crossing over to Khandesh burned Burhanpur and set the whole countryside ablaze. Before the Mughals could get at them; they were safe again in their fastness in the Ghats. This was a typical method of their warfare. They never risked an engagement in the open field unless their numbers made victory a certainty". *(Mediaeval India*—by U. N. Ball).

The Mughal General Tukkarrib Khan took Sambhuji by surprise at Sangameswar and forced him to take to the field. In a fierce engagement in which about 10 thousand Mahrattas perished, Sambhuji and his Minister were captured. They were brought before the Mughal Emperor who wanted to pardon the Mahratta leader, but the insolent reply of Sambhuji cost him his life. He was beheaded on March 11, 1689 and was succeeded by his son Shivaji II.

The Imperial army now launched a massive attack on the Mahrattas. The Mughal General, Ittiqad Khan, who captured Raigarh, the Mahratta Capital, in November 1689 carried the child king with his mother to the Imperial camp. A number of Mahratta forts in Konkon also fell into his hands. Raja Ram, the Mahratta Commander, retreated to Jinji. Trichinopoly and Tanjore were captured in 1694. At Jinji, the Mahrattas surrendered on 1697 while Satara and Parli fell to Mughal arms in 1700. "In the next four years he (Aurangzeb) conquered almost all the important forts . . . . . He occupied Panbola, Vishalgarh Raigarh and Torna" *(Mediaeval India—by* U. N. Ball).

Now Aurangzeb was at the zenith of his power. He had crushed the Mahrattas and had occupied their territories and forts. He had fulfilled his ambition. But he had grown too old. He breathed his last on February 20, 1707 and was buried in an ordinary tomb in Aurangabad. "The tomb of the last great monarch of Hindustan is a very simple masonry work without any marble platform, grass grows on the top, and this is emblematic of the simplicity of his life".

Pious and Just, austere and energetic, Aurangzeb was a model of true Muslim monarch. His life was characterised by simplicity and unbounded energy. He was the most learned person among all the Mughal rulers.

He discarded the unIslamic custom of appearing before the public twice a day in a window, stopped distillation, sale and consumption of liquors and closed down the brothels. He introduced beneficial Islamic laws which added to the morality and prosperity of the people. His life provided a model to his people, inculcating plain living and a sense of Justice among them.

"He never indulged in frivolities", writes Ball, "and was always dignified in his conduct. He never put on clothes prohibited by religion, nor did he ever used vessels of silver or gold. In his Court no improper conversation, no word of backbiting or falsehood was allowed".

About his energy and sense of justice, Mr. U. N. Ball writes: "Aurangzeb took up his task as a ruler very seriously. He possessed a keen sense of justice, unflinching courage, and indomitable power of endurance. He guided the military operations personally even at the age of 88. He maintained his energy till his last campaign". *(Mediaeval India—by* U. N. Ball).

We might refer here to a few incidents in the life of Emperor Aurangzeb that shed light on his bravery, strength of character and devoutness that have elicited praise even from non-Muslim historians.

It is said that one day as he was about to offer his prayers in a jungle in Hyderabad Deccan, he saw a tiger stealthily emerging out of the thickets and heading towards him. The moment it was about to pounce upon him he gave no opportunity to his bodyguards to kill it, but killed it himself with his sword he was carrying at the time. He resumed his prayers soon after killing the tiger.

There is an inspiring story relating to the foundation laying of the Shahi Mosque at Lahore. On getting timely information that his brother Murad was going to build a pleasure-house in front of the Fort, he hastily came back from Deccan and ordered the construction of a massive mosque on the site. He issued a Royal Proclamation to the effect that the foundation stone of the mosque would be laid by himself in his capacity as Emperor and as one who had been regularly saying his prayers ever since it became obligatory for him to pray five times a day.

The Great Mughal Empire reached its zenith before his death and was extended to its farthest and widest limits. He fulfilled his mission with unparalleled courage, ability and energy. But his successors proved too weak and incompetent to hold together such a vast Empire.

# TIPU SULTAN

Seringapattam, the Capital of Mysore, was surrounded on all sides by the formidable invading forces, comprising the British, the Marhattas and the Nizam. This Triple Alliance strengthened by the subversive activities of the State traitors had compelled the "Lion of Mysore", as he was called, to make a strategic retreat and fall back to defend his Capital. The alien Generals had conspired with some of the highest dignitaries of the State to storm the Capital on an appointed day when, as pre-planned, one of the principal traitors, Mir Sadiq, started distributing pay to the State soldiers. Just at that moment the alien forces stormed the opening in the front wall guarded by zealous soldiers, many of whom had been summoned to receive their pay, and entered the fort without much resistance.

Iqbal refers to this treachery on the part of Mir Sadiq in the following couplet :

جعفرے از بنگال و صادق از دکن
ننگِ آدم، ننگِ دیں، ننگِ وطن

Jafar from Bengal and Sadiq from Deccan—
Are a shame on humanity,
Shame on religion and shame on country.

The Sultan was taking his lunch, when he was informed of the treachery of his trusted officers and the entry of alien forces. Leaving his meals and with sword in hand, he rushed forth towards the danger spot. Here he gallantly fought a hand to hand fight. Just in the heat of the battle, he was advised to accept the British offer of Subsidiary Alliance. But the reply which the lion-hearted Tipu gave will go down as the most chivalrous recorded in history. He said: "One days's life of a lion is preferable to hundred years' existence of a jackal", With these words he fought heroically to the last drop of his blood and became a martyr to the cause of national freedom.

Tipu Sultan, one of the most talented, valiant and enlightened monarchs that India has produced, was destined to struggle against heavy odds at a time when the British power had, to a great extent, established its supremacy over the major part of the subcontinent and had successfully conspired with the

Marhattas and the Nizam to overcome the only formidable hurdle in the South—the Muslim State of Mysore. Tipu Sultan put up a gallant fight against much superior forces. But, for the treachery of his own men, the history of the subcontinent would have been different from what it has been during the last 150 years.

Sultan Fateh Ali Khan Padshah, popularly known as Tipe Sultan, was born on November 21, 1750 at Devanhali, a small town near Bangalore. He was the eldest son of Haider Ali, the ruler of Mysore. He was named Tipu after the name of Tipu Mastan, a saint of Arcot, whose tomb Haider Ali and his wife had visited a few months before Tipu's birth and prayed for the birth of a son.

Young Tipu was given the best possible education by his father, who employed competent teachers for the purpose. He soon became well versed in different branches of learning and could speak Urdu, Persian and Arabic very fluently. He received excellent coaching in the art of war. from Ghazi Khan, an experienced warrior. Even in his young age, the Prince used to attend military parades and reviews along with his father.

Tipu Sultan married three wives one after another. After the death in 1797 of his last and favourite wife Khadija Zamani Begum, a lady of great culture and scholarship, he remained a widower for the rest of his life. Unlike other oriental monarchs, Tipu Sultan never kept concubines. He was an affectionate father and an obedient son of his mother, who exercised tremendous influence over him.

Tipu, during the time when he was a Prince, made no mean contribution to the victories of his father, Haider Ali, over the British and the Marhattas on several occasions. In fact, he was the right hand man of his father in almost all the campaigns which he fought during his last days. The swift movements of Tipu Sultan surprised the enemy in several sectors and led to his victories. He was a terror for the English army. English mothers used to silence their naughty children by terrorising them : "Tipu has come. Be silent".

Even during his teens, Tipu Sultan exhibited dauntless courage and great military skill in wars waged by his father, who was proud of him and conferred on him the command of 200 horses, later increased to 500, and also gave him several districts as *'Jagir'.*

On June 19, 1767, Tipu Sultan was given his first military assignment. He joined his father, who was in a precarious position. By his swift movements, he dodged the British Generals who tried their best to intercept him. This resulted in the conquest of the forts of Tirppatur and Vaniyambadi.

Later he was ordered to rush to the help of Lutf Ali Beg, fighting against the British forces on the Malabar Coast. The Prince captured Mangalore fort from the English who retreated towards Madras, in great panic.

During Haider Ali's campaigns against the Mahrattas (1769–78), Tipu played a heroic role in harassing, defeating and recapturing a ceded property from the enemy. In July 1780, when Haider Ali with his 80,000 men came down "like an avalanche" on the plains of Carnatic, Tipu Sultan was deputed to intercept Colonel Baillie's forces, that had made a bold bid to join the main British forces engaged with Haider Ali. Through a clever move, Tipu intercepted Baillie's forces and inflicted on them a crushing defeat. Colonel Baillie, along with 150 soldiers, was taken prisoner. Sir Thomas Munro described the disaster of Colonel Baillie's army as "the severest blow that the English ever sustained in India". "Had Haider Ali followed up his success at that time to the gates of Madras", writes Sir Eyre Coote, "he would have been in possession of the most important fortress", and the history of Southern India would have taken a different turn. But, instead of attacking demoralised Munro, he hurried to capture Arcot and, thus, let slip from his hands the prospects of dominating Southern India.

Another notable achievement of Prince Tipu Sultan was his victory over the British Commander, Colonel Braithwaite, on February 18, 1782, at Tanjore which seriously foiled British designs in this area. Tipu Sultan was engaged in the siege of Ponnani, when he received the news of his father's death. He hurried to Chittoor, the place where his father, Haider Ali, had died and reached there on December 26, 1782. There, at the age of 32, he ascended the throne and succeeded to a large principality bordered by river Krishna in the North, by the Arabian Sea in the West, by the Eastern Ghats in the East and by the State of Travancore in the South.

Tipu's life mission was to save his country from the machinations and political domination of a foreign power, which, with its political intrigues, had established its supremacy over the major part of India was now threatening his own State of Mysore. His whole life, his entire efforts, were directed towards the fulfilment of this mission of saving his motherland from being dominated by a foreign power. He had seen with his own eyes, how, this foreign power, had, step by step established its power over different states of India by entangling them into a Subsidiary System. Tipu Sultan was made of a different metal. He was a farsighted ruler, who could foresee the danger ahead and like a true patriot he waged war against the evil forces which had conspired against the freedom of his country and even sacrificed his life at last. He implored other Indian states, the Mahrattas and the Nizam to sink their differences and unitedly face the common danger against their country. He even sought the help of foreign powers like Turkey and France for driving out the British from India, as he rightly considered them the greatest Imperialist Power in the world which later, proved to be the greatest threat to the unity and glory of Islam in the world.

Practically the whole life of Tipu Sultan was spent in warfare. He was a real *"mujahid"* and a true patriot, who relentlessly fought against the enemies of his state and his country. Despite his troubled life, the extent of reforms introduced by him into different departments of his Government and the social life of his people, is simply amazing which places him at par with the most enlightened and progressive monarchs of the world. Despite the heavy drain on the national exchequer due to his incessant warfare, his people passed a happy and prosperous life. Being a true Muslim, he was not only just but generous towards minorities. His subjects, both Muslims and non-Muslims were happy and contented.

Tipu Sultan was a great warrior and an outstanding General. He was a hero of hundreds of battles in which he had inflicted crushing defeats on his enemies. The British forces had suffered some of their worst military disasters in India at his hands. He repeatedly successfully adopted the military strategy of swift movement and sudden surprise blitzkrieg against his enemies who would either surrender or retreat in panic.

On his accession, Tipu Sultan found formidable forces arrayed against him. The Mahrattas, tied up with the British by Subsidiary Alliance, were jealous of the foreigners' machinations. The Nizam, on the other hand, was won over by the clever Lord Cornwallis on the promise of being granted the conquered territory of Tipu Sultan.

Thus the Triple Alliance of the Mahrattas, the Nizam and the British formed against the rising power of Mysore, was, in reality, aimed at achieving British supremacy in India, which the two shortsighted Indian partners could not foresee. Among the Indian Chiefs, Tipu Sultan alone had the vision to foresee the danger of foreign domination and he staked his all to expel it from India.

Earlier, British Governor-General Warren Hastings had concluded treaties with the Mahratta chief and the Treaty of Salbai in May 1782, brought to an end the Anglo-Mahratta hostilities. Then his entire diplomacy was directed against the rising Muslim power of Mysore, which led to the second Anglo-Mysore war.

Soon after his accession, Tipu's terriories on the Malabar coast were threatened by British forces under the command of General Matthews. The treachery of the Mysore Governor Ayaz led to the surrender of Badnur on January 28, 1783. Lutf Ali Beg, who was sent by Tipu Sultan for the defence of Badnur reached there too late. Before he could reach Mangalore, he heard of the sack of this port by tne British forces on March 9, 1783 in which even women, children and old men were not spared. According to Mill, "Orders were given to shed blood of everyman who was taken under arms: and some of the officers were reprimanded for not seeing those orders rigidly executed" (Mill, *History of British India).*

The Sultan was much distressed by the atrocities committed by the British soldiers on helpless citizens. He hurried to Badnur and after making a dangerous thrust in the enemy ranks defeated General Matthews who retreated into the fort. The British forces shut up into the fort were besieged by the Sultan's army.

At last the British General was forced to capitulate on terms dictated by the Sultan. But on search, the British soldiers were found in possession of about 40,000 pagodas, which being a clear violation of surrender terms the British General and his men were placed under arrest. The Sultan arrived at Mangalore on May 20, 1783 and in the very first engagement, the British army was defeated with heavy losses. The remaining British forces shut themselves in the fort which was besieged by Tipu Sultan himself. Their Commander Campbell disheartened by the hardships which he had endured for several months, capitualated on January 29, 1784. He delivered the fort to Tipu Sultan, "under articles", says Campbell, "the most beneficial I could ask for the garrison, and which the Nawab has most honourably and strictly adhered to". *Military Consultations,* Madras Records).

His primary aim was the expulsion of the British from India and for this purpose he sought assistance wherever he could. But the two other important powers of Southern India, namely, the Mahrattas and the Nizam, had shut their eyes to the impending danger of foreign domination and the British used them as tools to achieve their objects.

The British were not happy with the Treaty of Mangalore concluded with Tipu Sultan. Ever since then they were planning against him. The British Governor-General, Lord Cornwallis, started preparations against Mysore which was the greatest stumbling block in the realisation of his dream of dominating India. After organising the East India Company's army and finances on a sound basis he started negotiations for an alliance with the Mahrattas and the Nizam directed against Tipu Sultan. He promised them the distribution of the conquered territories of Tipu Sultan. Having achieved this Triple Alliance, Lord Cornwallis sought some excuse of waging war against Mysore. This was soon forthcoming Tipu Sultan wanted to punish the Raja of Travancore for his misdeeds. The British decided to intervene as, according to the text of the letter by Cornwallis to the Governor of Mardras, they had every prospect of aid from the country powers, whilst he (Tipu Sultan) could expect no assistance from France. The British Governor-General was not content with the Triple Alliance. He even tried to win the support of the tributaries and refractory subjects of Tipu Sultan. He also bribed and conspired with the State dignitaries to work against their own ruler.

Having achieved all this, he started the Third Mysore War through an assault made by General Meadows on May 26, 1790. He advanced towards Coimbatore and occupied it on July 21. The first encounter of Tipu Sultan against the British army took place at Satyamangalam in which the Sultan was victorious. This was followed by rapid blows inflicted on the British forces by him in different sectors. The swift movements of Tipu Sultan was a problem for the enemy forces. The Sultan was preparing for a final attack on the main British forces when the treachery of Krishna Rao foiled his designs. His treachery led to the fall of Bangalore into the hands of Lord Cornwallis who was commanding the British forces. The Sultan was shocked at the fall of Bangalore. The allied forces made a final assault on Seringapattam, the Capital of Mysore, but they were badly beaten by Tipu Sultan and, therefore, retired to Bangalore. The assault was put off for the next year.

The war was renewed next year and a treaty was signed in which Tipu Sultan lost much of his territory. But the gallant Sultan, though hard hit by this treaty, did not lose his heart. He had fought against overwhelming odds. His continuous warfare had been a heavy drain on his finances. But he was not a man who could be unnerved or disheartened by misfortunes. He reorganised his finances and army, improved his agriculture and industry to a great extent and regained his past glory. He again rose to be a formidable power which could meet the challenge from any quarter.

Lord Wellesley who had become the Governor-General of British India reached Madras in January 1799. Here he conspired with the Mahrattas, the Nizam and the highest dignitaries of Mysore state to wipe out Tipu Sultan, the only serious obstacle in his way of domination over India. In utter disregard of the Treaty concluded after the Third Mysore War, Lord Wellesley made an unprovoked attack on Mysore. On February 3, 1799 General Harris marched from Vellore and General Stuart from Cannanore. The Mahrattas and the Nizam too moved their forces into Mysore territory. Arthur Wellesley was in command of an army from Hyderabad. Tipu Sultan, who was surprised by this unexpected as well as unprovoked attack, fought valiantly, displaying brilliant strategy. But the treachery of his own Generals foiled his efforts and the allied forces appeared before Seringapattam on April 17, 1799.

A siege was laid to the Capital of Mysore. High dignitaries of the Mysore Government, including Dewan Purnia, Prime Minister Mir Sadiq, and Mir Ghulam Ali, were in secret league with the British. The final assault on the city was fixed for May 4. On that day, according to the plan, Mir Sadiq started distributing salary to the army. The soldiers left their posts and hurried to receive their pay. At this moment, the British troops in conjunction with the treacherous elements in the fort, crossed the Kaveri, stormed the opening guarded by Syed Abdul Ghaffar together with his few gallant soldiers, and entered the fort. Syed Abdul Ghaffar was killed in action. Sultan was taking his meals and when informed of this disaster, he hurried to the spot and gallantly fighting a hand to hand battle fell a martyr to the cause of national freedom. Thus perished on May 4, 1799 A.C., Tipu Sultan, one of the most chivalrous and enlightened monarchs that India has produced. He preferred an honourable death to a life of humiliation and subjugation to a foreign power.

Tipu Sultan was an embodiment of nobility, chivalry and magnanimity.

His life was a constant struggle for a noble cause against heavy odds. He sacrificed his life for the realisation of his ideal of freeing his country from foreign domination and thus set an example for future generations. He was a true patriot, and a true Muslim who practised what he preached. He was a far-sighted ruler who foresaw the danger which loomed on the Indian horizon and staked his all to remove it.

Tipu Sultan was an outstanding administrator and a great reformer, endowed with great vision and calibre. Despite his troubled life, he introduced great reforms in almost all departments of the State Administration which brought unprecedented peace and prosperity to his people. He highly developed agriculture and industry in his dominion and initiated progressive agricultural reforms beneficial to the peasantry. Mill, the celebrated English historian, considers his territories to be "the best and its population the most flourishing in India" and Tipu Sultan, a ruler who "sustains an advantageous comparison with the greatest princes of the East" *(History of India,* London 1848). He kept a watch over his people and received reports about the economic condition through the *"Amils"* who were instructed to make annual tours of their districts for this purpose. The "patels" could not subject the poor cultivators to do forced labour.

The Sultan took effective steps towards the promotion of trade and industry in his country. He established several factories and built an Armada to protect his marine commerce from pirates. This led to the development of international trade with several countries, specially of the East. He set up trading agencies in several coastal towns and established large factories for manufacturing watches, ammunition, cutlery and paper. Cottage industries also thrived. His State was surplus in foodgrains, sugar, glassware, paper, silk and cotton cloth. Buchanan who visited his State acknowledges that "Tipu was born with a commercial mind".

He set up his military machine on a sound footing and divided the army administration into eleven different departments. He adopted modern weapons of war and divided his dominion into 22 military districts. His reforms, both in civil and military spheres, were far in advance of those of his predecessors and contemporaries. He was a well-wisher of his people and considered them as a "unique trust held for God, the real Master". (Quoted from Records in the National Archives of India, by Muhibbul Hassan Khan in his *"History of Tipu Sultan"*). He was generous towards his non-Muslim subjects and bequeathed to them rich grants for the maintenance of their sacred places. He held the Swami of Sringari Temple in high esteem and protected him when the temple was raided by Mahrattas. In a letter to the Swami he stated: "People who have sinned against such a holy place are sure to suffer the consequences of their misdeeds".

Being himself a very learned man, well versed in Persian, Arabic and Urdu, he immensely promoted learning. During his short troubled reign he popularised education. The Imperial Library of Seringapattam was finest of its kind in the East. He was also a writer of repute. He wrote *Fateh-al-Mujahidin,* an Army Manual and *Muaiyyad al Mujahidin,* the Collection of his Friday Sermons.

The enlightened and good administration of Tipu Sultan made Mysore the most prosperous State of the East and him as "unquestionably the most powerful of all native princes of Hindoostan" (Rennel, *Memoirs*). He was rightly considered as the greatest stumbling block in the way of foreign domination over the subcontinent.

The real greatness of Tipu Sultan, therefore, lies in his struggle against heavy odds and ultimately laying down his life for a noble cause. This has earned for him an immortal place among the great men of the world.

# MALIK ABD AL-AZIZ
# IBN SAUD

Arabia, the birth place of Islam, which had witnessed its golden era during the lifetime of Prophet Muhammad (peace be upon him) and the thirty years of unprecedented glorious rule of the four Pious Caliphs, better known as "Khilafat-e-Rashida", later degenerated into a regrettable state of disintegration and discord, lasting for about a thousand years.

With the decline of the Abbaside Caliphate, the Arabian peninsula was left to its fate, culminating into tribal rivalries and discord which led to its degeneration. The Ottomans, no doubt, did take interest in the building of Holy Shrines in the cities of Makkah and Madina, but they paid little interest to the welfare of the Arabs, who were groaning under poverty and tribal strife. They acted on the well-known maxim of divide and rule by setting one tribe against the other. The Western powers, too, had shown their interest in Arab affairs, particularly in the Gulf States by the end of 18th Century A.C. The British people, who entered Arabia as peace makers, later proved to be exploiters of Arab interests and were responsible for installing Sharif Hussain as King of Hejaz and his two sons as Rulers of their protectorates in Iraq and Trans-Jordon. They had, under Balfour Declaration, planned setting up a Jewish State in the heart of the Arab World (Palestine) which proved to be a trouble spot in the Middle East and continues to be a threat to the world peace.

There was born in 1703 A.C. in Najd a great Muslim visionary, Muhammad Abd al-Wahab, who later started a Muslim puritan movement in Najd which aimed at bringing Islam to its pristine glory. This interpretation of Islam was later adopted by the Saudi Ruling family in 1744 A.C. The Wahabi movement was aimed at purifying Islam of the superficial and superstitious practices which had crept into it due to non-Islamic influences.

The *Mowahhid* (Wahabi) movement started by Muhammad Abd al-Wahab found its great exponent in the Ruling Saudi family, and his great disciple Sheikh Muhammad Abduh later became one of the leading intellectuals of the Islamic world.

Abd al-Aziz ibn Abd al-Rehman ibn Faisal al-Saud, the Founder in 1932 of the Kingdom of Saudi Arabia was born in 1880 A.C., at the Saudi Capital of

Riyadh in Najd. In the turbulent society of Arabia, occasional tribal leaders have influenced the world scene. Such a leader was Abd al-Aziz. He ranks among the foremost figures of his age—a person who has left ineffaceable prints on the pages of world history. Not since the Arabian Prophet and his Four Companions (Pious Caliphs) called a nation into being, had so much of the Arabian Peninsula been assembled under one man. He was greatly instrumental in bringing about the unity and solidarity of the Arabs, inhabiting the vast Arabian Peninsula, and has earned for them an honourable place in the comity of nations. The House of Saud, later on, had a chequered career, witnessing occasional rise and fall until the emergence of Abd al-Aziz to power, who founded the Kingdom of Saudi Arabia in 1932.

By the beginning of the 20th century A.C., the youthful Abd al-Aziz, better known as Ibn Saud, with 200 comrades-in-arms undertook the reconquest of his Saudi patrimony. On 15th January 1902, Abd al-Aziz, with 15 warriors, captured Riyadh in a dramatic surprise attack. His parting words to his father were : "You will see me victorious or will never see me again". But his father did see him victorious. This exceptionally courageous feat of young Abd al-Aziz which will go down as one of the most daring exploits recorded in history makes the starting point in the history of the Kingdom of Saudi Arabia. During the next decade, he proceeded to reconquer Najd and other cities and provinces from Rashidis.

Before he could settle down, Abd al-Aziz had to solve three outstanding problems: (1) Hostility of neighbouring Arab States; (2) Ottoman opposition supported by Rashidis and Sharif Hussain, appointed Amir of Makkah in 1908 : and (3) British policy of keeping *status quo* in the Persian Gulf. He was successful in tackling all the three problems.

His first move was to strengthen ties between his dynasty and descendents of Wahabis. He founded a military religious organisation of *Ikhwan* (Brethren). The *Ikhwan* in their first major operation expelled Turks from Al-Hasa in 1913, thus giving Abd al-Aziz direct access to Persian Gulf. During 1921-22 Abd al-Aziz conquered Hai'l, and all Rashidi territories and assumed the title of Sultan of Najd and its dependencies.

Meanwhile, his relations with Sharif Hussain of Makkah who, during the Great War I, had become the King of Hejaz and self proclaimed Caliph in 1924, had rapidly deteriorated. This unwise step by Sharif Hussain was much resented by the Arabs and the Muslim world. This necessitated military action by Abd al-Aziz, who captured Jeddah in December 1925. Sharif Hussain abdicated and his son Ali surrendered on January 8, 1926. Abd al-Aziz ruled the Holy Land as a Trust till the inhabitants themselves chose him as their King. He was proclaimed as the King of Hejaz in the Great Mosque of Makkah. In September 1932, he unified the kingdoms of Najd and Hejaz, under the title of the Kingdom of Saudi Arabia.

In 1930, he added one more province to his Kingdom, when he incorporated the northern half of the Red Sea principality of Asir, over which he had recently established a protectorate.

Repeated Yemini aggression against Saudi Arabia, resulted in a seven week war between the two countries in 1934 in which his two sons, Saud and Faisal won a brilliant victory.

The development of Saudi Arabia has few parallels in history. The fact that a single person, namely Abd al-Aziz welded four separate provinces, inhabited by scores of independent tribes into one Nation is a marvellous achievement. The rapid transition of a poor country with almost unknown areas of the desert, torn by tribal conflicts to the position of a respected member of the United Nations is great achievement.

Abd al-Aziz consolidated his State, by dividing it into four divisions of (1) Najd, (2) Hejaz, (3) Hasa and (4) Asir, each headed by one Ameer. Each Ameer of the division commanded over considerable military force which served as Escort, Police and Reserve.

Immediately after becoming King of Hejaz, Abd al-Aziz convened an Islamic Congress at Makkah in 1926, to conciliate adverse sectarian opinion and gave guarantee for the welfare of Muslim pilgrims, visiting Holy cities. His generous settlement with Imam Yahya of Yeman, despite latter's aggression and ultimate defeat in 1934, is a testimony of his magnanimity and Islamic brotherhood.

His wise administration was acclaimed throughout the world, and between 1926—31, Saudi Arabia was accorded diplomatic recognition by all major European countries, including Russia, and also by U.S.A. This was a diplomatic triumph of King Abd al-Aziz who had won an honourable place for his country in the comity of nations.

His neutrality during World War II, despite pressure from His Majesty's Council to side with the Germans speaks volumes on his farsighted policy which was vindicated in the end.

After the unification of the two Kingdoms of Najd and Hejaz under the name of Saudi Arabia in 1932, King Abd al-Aziz embarked upon an unprecedented development work which immensely added to the peace and prosperity of his great country. Earlier, he settled Bedouins as agriculturists in suitable oasis and welded them into a nationally conscious community. The first *Ikhwan* colony, Artawiya, established in 1912, became prototype of nearly 100 agricultural settlements.

In 1933, he took a momentous step by granting oil concessions to an American Oil Company, later known as ARAMCO after January, 1944. This, and a subsequent concession, of 1939, allocated 440,000 sq. miles of Saudi territory for oil exploration. This added immensely to the revenue of Saudi State through increasing royalities from oil.

Before his death, King Abd al-Aziz had launched his first medical, irrigation and flood control projects. He built new ports, good roads, 300 miles long DAMMAN Riyadh railway and initiated the first elaborate School programme, radio communication network and an Air Force Training Centre. This amounted to a veritable social and economic revolution which was inaugurated in Saudi Arabia by the King.

King Abd al-Aziz was a great exponent of unity of the Arabs and the Islamic world at large. His magnanimous and chivalrous peace with the defeated Yeman inaugurated a good neighbourly policy. He opened an era of constructive statesmanship of reapproachment with neighbouring Arab States of Kuwait, Bahrain, Iraq and Trans-Jordon, the last two ruled by the sons of his erstwhile opponent Sharif Hussain of Makkah. The famous Treaty of Arab Brotherhood and Alliance made in 1936, was later adhered to by Yeman. He mediated in Palestine Arab national strike of 1936, jointly with the Rulers of Iraq, Trans-Jordon and Yeman. In 1936, the Saudi King negotiated a treaty with Egypt.

The active role played by King Abd al-Aziz in uniting the Arabs and working for the Arab cause made him an international figure and the Leader of the Arab World.

# MALIK FAISAL
# IBN ABD AL-AZIZ


About 50 years ago, in 1926, when my mother, grandmother and father had gone for pilgrimage to the Holy cities of Makkah and Madina, they tredded on camel back in July Sun, reaching Madina, about 475 kilometers from Makkah in more than a fortnight. Today, this distance is covered in 3½ to 5 hours by a first class car, running at a speed of 120 K. M. per hour on a first class metalled road.

Saudi Arabia is totally a changed country today. Its rise has been meteoric and its transformation so wonderful as if accomplished through the legendary Aladin's Lamp of the famous *Arabian Nights*.

The factors responsible for this dramatic change have been the discovery of enormous quantity of fluid gold beneath its arid surface which has made Saudi Arabia the greatest oil exporter in the world and the wise statemanship of its dynamic and beloved ruler, Faisal bin Abd al-Aziz who united the oil producing Middle East countries as never before and used this as a weapon against the Western Oil Exploiters.

Malik Faisal, born in 1906, was the third and the most talented, dynamic and virtuous son of King Abd al-Aziz, Founder of the Kingdom of Saudi Arabia. Abd al-Aziz, better known as Ibn Saud, had gradually regained the Kingdom of Saudi Arabia in rolling battles that involved shifting tribal loyalties and finally British intrigue. He had roared out of Kuwait in 1902 accompanied by a handful of compatriots to capture Riyadh.

His favourite son, Malik Faisal, though not his Crown Prince, later served as the Commander-in-Chief of Saudi Forces and was greatly responsible for the capture of Makkah in 1925 and defeat of Yeman in 1934. Later, he was appointed the Foreign Minister of the Kingdom and his wise Foreign Policy was greatly instrumental in winning the friendship and recognition of progressive nations of the world.

On the death of his father, King Abd al-Aziz in 1953, the Crown Prince Saud ascended the throne of Saudi Arabia and Faisal became his Prime Minister. As against Faisal, Saud led an extremely luxurious and extravagant life. He had dozens of wives and more than 100 children. His extravagance had made Saudi Arabia, virtually a bankrupt state. Fortunately he abdicated in favour of Faisal in 1964 due to ill health. Thus Faisal started with a deficit finance.

The Organisation of Petroleum Exporting Companies, under the able leadership of King Faisal, realised the importance of oil in the modern world, whose major profit was gulped by the Western Oil Companies. The OPEC, therefore, raised the price of oil from $ 1 per barrel in 1944 to $ 10 by the end of 1974. "This", according to *Time Magazine,* "resulted in the greatest and swiftest transfer of wealth in all history; the 13 OPEC countries earned $ 112 Billion from the rest of the world last year (1974). This sudden shift of money shook the whole fragile structure of the international financial system, severely weakened the already troubled economies of the oil importing nations and gave new political strength to the exporters. . . . .The new financial giant of the world, Saudi Arabia, in 1974 stood to accumulate a surplus of about $ 23 billion a potentially unsettling force in the Global finance".

On the termination of the Arab—Israel War in 1973, when the Arab oil exporters, under the inspiring leadership of King Faisal of Saudi Arabia decided to enforce oil embargo against the advanced oil importing countries, which had economic, financial and political relations with Israel, it looked doubtful if such an embargo would be effective and last long. The oil importing countries of the West and Japan led by U.S.A., tried to forge a united stand against the Arab oil exporters and attempted to divide the Arabs, but they miserably failed in this respect. The wise statemanship of King Faisal, the greatest and most sagacious Muslim ruler of the present century, united the OPEC countries as never before, which resulted in the division in the ranks of the oil importing countries, culminating in the formation of a very liberal Policy towards the Arabs and hardening of their attitude towards Israel by three major industrial powers, namely Japan, France and West Germany. As opposed to U.S.A., they lined up behind the Arabs in condemnation of Israel, asking for her total withdrawal from the occupied Arab territories. In this way, the Western countries led by U.S.A. which had tried to divide the Arabs, ultimately faced a division in their own ranks. This unexpected development which alarmed the U.S.A., resulted in paralysing the economy of the advanced countries and shifting the monetary balance in favour of the Arab oil exporters, especially Saudi Arabia. The emergence of Saudi Arabia under King Faisal, as the political as well as the spiritual leader of the Arab world, nay of the entire Muslim world, was a blessing to the Third World in general and Muslims in particular. Sincere and austere, unassuming and farsighted, courageous and virtuous, Faisal who was much respected by friends and foes alike throughout the world played a dominant role in the international politics. His courageous and unbending stand against Israel emboldened the Arab world to stake their all for the liberation of the Holy city of Jerusalem from the hands of Israel and lined up the Third World behind the Arab demand for the evacuation of occupied Arab territories by Israel. The show of hands in favour of the Arab demand in the United Nations General Assembly during 1974 had alarmed the U.S.A., the principal supporter of Israel in the world today. The General Assembly Session had voted with an overwhelming majority for recognising Palestine Liberation Organisation (PLO) as a party to the Palestine Dispute.

Saudi Arabia, a sparsely populated country is the greatest seller of oil in the world today. Ruled by Faisal, a "dour, ascetic and shrewd man", according to *Time Magazine,* he had been mainly responsible for raising the oil prices in the world, much to the benefit of the oil producing countries. He nationalised ARAMCO, the US oil producing company in Saudi Arabia, thus bringing to an end an era in which the Western oil companies dominated and exploited the oil resources of Persian Gulf States, including Saudi Arabia, leaving only a nominal benefit to the oil producing countries of the Middle East.

King Faisal was not only the richest of the OPEC leaders, he was one of the most respected persons in the world and being the Custodian of the Holy cities of Makkah and Madina, he was the spiritual leader of world's 600 million Muslims. He had warned U.S.A. that peace could not be established in the Middle East without the liberation of Jerusalem from Israel and unless he could pray freely in the Aqsa Mosque, without setting his foot on the Jewish territory. According to the *ex*-US-Secretary of the State, Mr. Henry Kissinger, "The King is a sort of moral conscience for many Arab leaders. By having great religious stature, he can act as a King of pure representative of Arab nationalism. He has been able to manoeuvre Saudi Arabia from being a conservative state into a political bellwether".

The West had under-estimated the power and sagacity of King Faisal, who united the oil producing countries to teach a lesson to the friends of Israel. This enormously added to the prosperity and prestige of the Arab countries and paralysed the Western economy. This new success gave new pride and political power to the Arabs and brought King Faisal widespread respect in the Arab World. His emphasis on the unity of the Islamic world instead of the narrow Arab nationalism earlier preached by late President Nasser of Egypt, endeared him to the Muslims throughout the world. He was reorganised as the greatest Champion of Muslims cause in the world. His heart bled on the miseries and misfortunes of Muslims and his eyes glittered with joy on their success in any part of the world. He was rightly acclaimed by the Muslims all over the world as their greatest spiritual and political leader.

Malik Faisal was a true Muslim. Like the Pious Caliphs of early Islam, he believed in simplicity, piety and service to mankind. He never compromised on principles and his life was free from all sorts of human weaknesses. He was a quiet sort of person. Once questioned that he seldom spoke even in the meetings of Arab Heads of States, Faisal replied: "God has given us two ears and one tongue, meaning that we should listen twice as much as we talk". Although the richest ruler of his time, he disliked gorgeous dress, pomp and show, ate coarse food, neither drank nor smoked. He disliked obeisance which, according to him, was meant for Almighty God. His personal life was more simple than that of most of his subjects. He usually shared the seat with his driver while going out in his old car, when many of the Princes in Riyadh drive in gold plated cadillacs. He disliked opulence. Succeeding King Saud, he declared that his brother's Alhamra Palace in Jeddah was "too ornate for me", and decreed it to be used for visiting foreign dignitaries. He disliked kissing of hand and preferred to be addressed as Malik Faisal or Brother Faisal, instead of Your Majesty or Jalalat-ul-Malik, which he said were attributes meant for God only.

Faisal, according to the celebrated Maulana Maududi, had been the most versatile, virtuous and universally respected Muslim Ruler since the time of Sultan Salahuddin Ayyubi. He was greatly responsible for modernising and industrialising his Kingdom in a short period of 11 years of his regime. He established a network of good roads, magnificent buildings, schools, colleges, universities, libraries, hospitals and modern factories; enlarged and renovated the Holy Shrines at Makkah and Madina; popularised female education and abolished slavery in his State which unfortunately have enormously increased in many of our advanced and developing countries today.

This benevolent, virtuous and sagacious Muslim Ruler was, alas assassinated on March 26, 1975 by one of his nephews. The entire Muslim world was stunned with grief on the assassination of the greatest Muslim leader of his time and the world mourned the loss of such a noble and farsighted ruler.

# SOLDIERS, GENERALS
# AND
# CONQUERORS

# SA'AD IBN WAKKAS

Hazrat Sa'ad ibn Wakkas, one of the oldest and most trusted companions of the Prophet of Islam, was the conqueror of Iraq and Persia. He was a great Arab General, who embraced Islam at the early age of 17. He was one of the ten Companions of the Prophet who were promised Paradise during their lifetime.

Hazrat Sa'ad was a famous warrior and General who took leading part in the battles of Badr and Uhd and also in the campaigns that followed. When Muthanna who assumed command of Muslim forces at Al Hira (Iraq) after the departure of Khalid bin Waleed to Syria, asked for reinforcements in order to meet the threat of the ever-increasing Persian hordes, the Second Caliph of Islam himself wanted to assume the command. A large force gathered at Madina and Umar wanted to march at their head. Great enthusiasm prevailed there. But he was dissuaded by his Companions, who insisted that the central authority should remain in the Capital. At last Sa'ad ibn Wakkas was selected to assume the Chief command. The entire campaign in Iraq was planned by the Caliph himself, who was daily informed of the developments in the military situation.

Sa'ad ibn Wakkas, the trusted Companion of the Prophet and highly respected by Muslims, advanced with a force of 20 thousand Muslims. His army contained about 400 Companions of the Prophet and their 700 sons. Sa'ad advanced towards Kadessia, where the formidable Persian forces under their famous General Rustam were encamped and were harassing the neighbouring Muslim dominions. Here, in the Summer of 637 A.C., a memorable battle was fought, which was hotly contested lasting for several days. The Muslim soldiers fought like real heroes, and displayed great feats of bravery which unnerved and discomfited the enemy. Illness prevented Sa'ad from taking part in the battle personally, but a shrewd and skilful soldier as he was, very ably he directed the whole operations from a house top, situated by the side of the battle-field.

The Muslims, for the first time, encountered an array of elephant and the Arab horses could hardly be controlled while facing these black giants. The Muslim army had been suffering heavily. Seeing this, Sa'ad ordered a charge with lances on the elephants. Accordingly, the Arabs made a fierce charge on the elephants with pointed lances and pushed them back and made them flee from the battle-field in panic.

Kaaka, a renowned Arab warrior, who joined the Muslim forces in the thick of the battle, challenged two renowned Persian warriors to personal combat and killed both of them. A number of famous Persian warriors were slain.

The battle of Kadessia, which lasted several days, was at its highest pitch. Abu Mahjan, the celebrated Arab warrior and poet, was at the time in chains due to drinking wine. He was extremely impatient to take part in the battle. He implored the Commander's wife to let him participate in the battle on the undertaking that if he survived, he would willingly come back to their custody. The Commander's wife agreed and gave him Sa'ad's horse. All of a sudden an unknown warrior made a fierce charge on the Persian ranks who were at the moment routing the Muslims at certain points of the theatre of war. With his swift lightning charge Abu Mahjan paralysed the entire Persian defence, and when in the evening, he returned to Sa'ad's custody he was pardoned by the Commander. In return the poet swore not to taste wine again.

On the last day of the battle, Kaaka made an attack on the leading white elephant and drove his lance into his eyes. With his sword he cut down his trunk. Bleeding profusely and trumpeting frantically the white elephant turned back and with him other elephants, too, fled in panic. Thereupon, the Muslims made a fierce charge and pushed back the Persian forces. Their great General Rustam fled in panic and was killed while swimming across a canal.

Defeated with terrible loss, their General killed, the Persians fled towards the North. The battle of Kadessia practically decided the fate of Persia. Sa'ad was now the master of the whole.of Iraq.

Hazrat Umar, the Second Caliph of Islam, was extremely anxious about the outcome of the battle of Kadessia. He used to wait outside Madina for the messenger who regularly brought him reports about the war situation. At last, one day, he met the camel driver bringing the news of victory. The Caliph did not disclose his identity and quickly followed him enquiring about the news. He broke the news to the people assembled in the Mosque of the Prophet.

After receiving the submission of neighbouring towns, Sa'ad now advanced towards Babylon. Here some of the famous Persian warriors including Firuzan, Hurmuzan and Mihran, had reassembled the scattered Persian forces. But they could not withstand the initial charge of Sa'ad and fled in panic. Mihran escaped to Madain, Hurmuzan fled to Ahwaz and Firuzan to Nehawand. It was difficult to hold Chaldea. The fall of Madain, the Capital of the young Persian King Yezdjard was now imminent where Mihran was encamped with a strong Persian force.

Madain was situated on the Tigris. This river lay between the Muslim and Persian forces. On approaching the bank of river, Sa'ad observed that the Persians had blown up the bridge. He plunged his horse into the river which was in flood.

His army followed him and in a few moments crossed the river without breaking their lines. The Persians watching this seemingly impossible feat cried out. "The Demons have come", and fled in panic. The Persian Emperor, too, hurriedly fell back leaving behind his luxurious palaces and countless booty into Sa'ad's hands.

The fall of Madain led to the submission of the entire country lying west of the Tigris to Muslims. A service of thanks giving, led by Sa'ad, was held in the Palace of Chosroes.

Sa'ad, the civil and military Governor of Iraq, made Madain his Head-quarters. He administered the conquered country very ably. The Persian King made one more effort to recapture Madain. He sent a large force which was defeated with terrible losses. According to Tabari, more than one lakh Persians perished in this battle and the Arabs captured vast booty. Seeing the rich spoils of Jalula, the Caliph wept bitterly. Asked for its reason, he replied that he saw in that wealth the ruin of his people.

During the Governship of Sa'ad, the foundation of the Arab settlement of Kufa was laid, which soon grew to be an important, prosperous city, military and literary centre.

Sa'ad was nominated by the Second Caliph of Islam, on his death bed as one of the six trusted Companions of the Prophet of Islam to choose the next Caliph. Hazrat Usman, the Third Caliph of Islam, reappointed him as the Governor of Kufa.

Sa'ad ibn Wakkas retired to Akik during the Caliphate of Hazrat Ali and passed a retired and peaceful life till his death in 50 A.H. (670 A.C.) at a ripe age of 70. He was buried at Madina.

# KHALID BIN WALEED

The ill-equipped and untrained Arab armies had fought on two fronts at the same time during the early regime of the Second Caliph. On the Iraqi front they engaged the large armies of Chosroes, the mighty Persian Emperor and on the Syrian front they were arrayed against the formidable forces of the Byzantine Emperor.

The Arabs fought a battle all day long against the formidable Roman forces in Syria. The issue hung in balance. The Arab warriors assembled in their camp to review their day's progress. At last a gallant soldier stood up and addressed them in a resolute voice :

"Brothers! God is with us. We are fighting for the noble cause of establishing a regime based on equality, fraternity and justice. Tomorrow I want to teach a lesson to these Roman hordes."

"What?" enquired a voice.

"I propose to face the sixty thousand sturdy soldiers of Jabla, leader of Ghassans, with 30 Muslims only."

"Are you serious, Abu Sulaiman?" enquired the aged Abu Sufian.

"Yes", replied Khalid bin Waleed whose nickname was Abu Sulaiman.

"I think you have overestimated your strength. In this way you would be playing with the valuable lives of Muslims", retorted Abu Sufian.

"No, not at all. In reality I want to save the valuable lives of Muslims. In this way I want to overawe the enemy who are proud of their superior strength and military equipment", replied Khalid bin Waleed.

At last Abu Ubaidah, Commander of the Arab forces, intervened and it was compromised that the lion-hearted Khalid bin Waleed would face the sixty thousand well equipped sturdy soldiers of Jablah bin Ghassan with sixty Muslims instead of thirty. The next day Khalid bin Waleed with 59 companions fought a memorable battle unparalleled in the history of military warfare against

60 thousand Christians. The battle raged all the day long and the sixty Arabs were lost in a sea of armed men, and fought like lions against the surging waves of enemy forces bent upon sweeping them off their feet. The occasional cry of *Allah-o-Akbar* (God is Great) raised above the din of the battle proclaimed their existence to their fellow fighters who were watching the progress of the battle with great anxiety. At last with one last effort Khalid bin Waleed who was fighting like a hero, won the day and the Christians were routed with heavy losses. The invincible Khalid won a memorable battle unheard of in the history of warfare. This victory established Arab's superiority over the Romans despite their exceptional inferiority in numbers and equipments.

Abu Sulaiman, Khalid bin Waleed al-Qarshi belonged to the most respectable Quraish clan. His father Abd Shams al-Waleed bin al-Mughaira was considered among the wisest men of Quraish who was known for his oratory and bravery throughout Arabia. Khalid who was hardly 17 years old at the birth of Islam, evinced keen interest in the science of warfare, including riding, lancing and archery, in which he soon earned a high reputation. His memorable charge in the battle of Uhad against the Muslims from the rear was repulsed after hard fighting. Khalid bin Waleed accepted Islam in the 8th A.H. along with Amr bin Aas, another well-known figure in early Islam. His first appearance as a soldier of Islam was in the battle of Mauta, fought in the 8th A.H. in which he exhibited exceptional bravery and military skill. The Muslims, with barely 3,000 men faced a Roman army of 150 thousand well trained soliders. The earlier Muslim commanders were killed fighting in the battle-field when the command of the Muslims was entrusted to Khalid bin Waleed who fought like a lion and broke eight swords in a single battle. Fighting a tough rear guard action, Khalid bin Waleed exhibited a rare military skill and got his men safely out of the thick of the battle.

The breach of agreement by the Quraish of Makkah led to the invasion of the Holy city in which Khalid was entrusted with the command of the right flank of Muslim army. The Muslims entered the Holy city without any resistance and the insurgents were granted free pardon by the kind-hearted Prophet of Islam. "The people themselves (i.e. of Makkah) however, were treated with special magnanimity", writes Phillip K. Hitti, "Hardly a triumphal entry in ancient annals is comparable to this". The other campaigns in which Khalid took active part during the lifetime of the Prophet are the battles of Hunain, Najran and the seize of Taif.

The death of the Prophet caused gloom over the Muslims. With the disappearance of Central authority, the Arabian tribes rose in revolt against their new faith. Hazrat Abu Bakr who was elected as the First Caliph of Islam was adamant in his insistence on unconditional surrender by the seceders or war unto destruction. Khalid bin Waleed was the hero of these wars. "Within some six months of his Generalship he had reduced the tribes of Central Arabia to submission" (Hitti). Before his death, the Prophet had assigned to Usama the command of a campaign against the Romans. Hazrat Abu Bakr, on his election as the Caliph, was advised by his most trusted lieutenants not to despatch Muslim force outside the Capital which was threatened from all sides. But the pious Caliph declined to set aside the order of his deceased master and despatched the force under Usama which had a sobering effect on the recalcitrant Arab tribes and contributed immensely to establish the dwindling military prestige of Islam.

Khalid bin Waleed, the Sword of God, as the Prophet once called him, was the hero of the successive campaigns against the seceding Arabian tribes. He played a leading role in the pacification of Arabia. Toleiha, Musailima, the impostor and Malik bin Nawera, were defeated one after the other after hard fighting. According to early historians of Islam, the campaign against the forty thousand sturdy soldiers, led by Musailima, was the hardest ever fought by the warriors of early Islam in which the extraordinary bravery and military skill of Khalid won the day and Musailima was killed in an adjoining garden. This victory established once more the military superiority of Islam all over Arabia.

The neighbouring Persian and Roman Empires, which, hitherto, scoffed at and underrated the Arabian military strength, now saw a threat to their interests in the rising power of Islam. The pacification of Northern Arabia brought Muslims in conflict with Persians who ruled over Arabian Iraq and were acknowledged as overlords by the Nomad Arabian tribes inhabiting the neighbouring areas. The Persians instigated these tribes to rise against Islam. Such machinations on the part of Persians against Islam, obliged the kind hearted virtuous Caliph, Abu Bakr, to despatch forces under the command of invincible Khalid bin Waleed to Iraq on the 12th of Muharram 12 A.H. The first to oppose them was Hormuz, a tyrant hated by his Arab subjects who ruled over the Delta Region. Khalid divided his troops in three portions, placing Muthanna in command of the advance column, Adi, son of Hatim over the second and himself bringing up the rear, advanced strategically on Al Hafir, the frontier military post of the Persian Empire. "Thereupon Hormuz challenged Khalid", writes Sir William Muir, "to single combat and though he treacherously posted an ambuscade, was in the encounter slain. The Muslims then rushed forward and great slaughter put the enemy to flight, pursuing them to the bank of the Euphrates", *(The Caliphate–Its Rise, Decline and Fall)*. The battle was called *"Dhat as-Salasil"* (Mistress of the Chains) due to a major portion of Persian army tried up with one another by chains to prevent their giving way.

In another campaign near the great Canal of Tigris in which a small flying column under the command of Al-Muthanna was in great peril. Khalid, who arrived just in time to relieve his lieutenant, defeated the reinforced Persian army with heavy losses, a large number of enemy soldiers being either killed or drowned.

The Persian Court was now alarmed at the unexpected victories of a handful of untrained and ill-equipped Muslims against their forces, much superior in numbers and organisation. The Persian Emperor raised a levy of the loyal Arab clans and hastily despatched a formidable force under the command of Bahman. a veteran Persian General. The two armies met at Al Walaja, near the confluence of the two rivers in April 633 A.C. Khalid who divided his army into three portions, marched forward his advanced columns to meet the enemy while he kept two columns in reserve and "surprised the exhausted enemy by ambuscade placed in the rear". Thus the superior tactics and the great military skill of Khalid won the day for the Muslims against the much superior Persian forces.

A bitter feeling was aroused among the bedouin Christian tribes, who appealed to Ardashir, the Persian Emperor, to avenge their defeat. A large combined force comprising bedouins and Persians was hurriedly despatched under a tried Persian General Japan to meet the Muslim forces at Ulles in May 633 A.C. Leaving a strong detachment at Al-Hafir, to guard his rear, Khalid hastily marched forward to meet the enemy. The battle was fiercely contested and for a long time the issue hung in balance. At last, after a fierce charge by Khalid, the Persians gave way and fled, leaving behind 70 thousand dead on the battle-field. In a single combat, Khalid had killed a Persian warrior, who was reputed to be equal to one thousand warriors.

By this time the Persians were thoroughly disillusioned and their spirit was broken. Nevertheless, the bedouin Christians insisted on expelling the invaders. Amghisiya, a prosperous town in the neighbourhood of Al Hira, was surprised by Khalid. The Caliph when apprised of these victories of the Muslim armies, cried out, "O, Ye Quraish, verily your lion, the lion of Islam, hath leapt upon the lion of Persia, and spoiled him of his prey. Women shall no more bear a second Khalid".

Khalid with a flying squadron hastened to the canal head to close the sluices to enable his grounded boats to ascend the canal. Al Hira was besieged by Muslims and capitulated shortly after. A treaty was signed with the residents of Hira in 633 A.C. which was later rectified by the Caliph of Islam. Hira was made the Headquarters of Islamic forces and from here Khalid started the consolidation of his gains. The beneficial reforms introduced by Khalid in consultation with the Caliph in favour of agriculturists and the common man inhabiting the conquered countries provided a striking contrast to the Persian feudalism hitherto prevailing in these regions. Hence Muslims were welcomed as benefactors replacing the tyrannical Persian overlords. For precautionary measures Muslim garrisons were quartered here and there and the troops were kept ready in movable columns.

The next to be besieged was the fortress of Anbar, situated on the Euphrates about 80 miles above Babylon. The deep fosse adjoining the fortress was crossed by casting the bodies of worn out slain camels and the city capitulated without much resistance. Ain at Taur, a green spot in the neighbourhood of Anbar, was also captured by the Muslims.

Khalid had now reached Al Firad, a place on Syrian Iraqi borders, which was divided by a river. The Syrian frontiers were guarded by a strong Byzantine garrison, which being alarmed at the success of Khalid, made a common cause with Persians and bedouin Christians in order to defeat the Muslim invaders. A long and severe conflict ensued, in which Muslims were victorious and the enemy lost more than one lakh soldiers.

The victories of Islam over Persians established the supremacy of Islamic arms and the invincibility of Khalid bin Waleed, the Sword of God. Khalid stayed in Iraq for about 14 months and during this period he fought and won 15 engagements against an enemy which was far superior in men and arms. The Arabs, who hitherto, considered themselves much inferior to the Persians in all walks of life and acknowledged them their overlords, now shed off their inferiority complex and regained their self-confidence. The lightning victories of Khalid in Iraq which paralysed the vast and resourceful Persian Empire in such a short space of time, may rank among the most glorious campaigns in the annals of military warfare and have placed him amongst the greatest Generals of all times. He had devised several new tactics which were hitherto unknown to the world, including the charge by the reserve force. He also proved to be a good administrator who consolidated his gains, stationed military garrison at suitable places to secure the rear, effected agrarian and other reforms advantageous to the common man which endeared the Muslims to the locals in contrast to their previous feudal Persian overlords. The Muslims with their democratic and socialistic leanings were preferable to Persian bureaucrats.

After the defeat of the combined forces at Firad in January 634 A.C. the season for Hajj pilgrimage having drawn close, Khalid made a secret rites. Sir William Muir in his well-known work *"The Caliphate—Its Rise, Decline and Fall"*, writes: "The season for the Makkah pilgrimage being now at hand. Khalid formed the singular resolve of performing it incognito unknown even to his Royal master. So, having recruited his army for ten days on the well fought field, he gave orders to march slowly and by easy stages back to Al Hira. Then making as though he remained behind, he set out secretly with a small escort on the pious errand. Without a guide he traversed the devious desert route with marvellous sagacity and speed. Having accomplished the rites of pilgrimage, he retraced his steps from Makkah with the like despatch, and re-entered Al Hira in early spring, just as the rearguard was marching in. So well had he kept his secret, that the army thought he had been all the while at Al Firad, and now was journeying slowly back. Even Abu Bakr, who himself presided at the pilgrimage, was unaware of the presence of his great General".

The attitude of the Byzantine armies on the frontiers bordering Syria was equally threatening since the time of the Prophet. The Byzantine armies had made frequent incursions into the Arab territories bordering Syria and carried away their cattle and other belongings. Khalid who was stationed on the Syrian frontiers, met with some success against the Byzantine armies. Caliph Abu Bakr, having realised the great danger looming large on the Syrian horizon, requested the Muslims to enroll themselves for active service on the Syrian front. More than a thousand Companions of the Prophet, including one hundred who had participated in the battle of Badr volunteered themselves. The Caliph in person went up to the plain of Jurf to bid farewell to each brigade bound for Syria and gave the following command;

> "Men, I have ten orders to give you, which you must observe loyally : Deceive none and steal from none; betray none and mutilate none; kill no child, nor woman, nor aged man; neither bark nor burn the date palms; cut not down fruit trees nor destroy crops; slaughter not flocks, cattle nor camels except for food. You will also meet with men living in cells; leave them alone in that to which they have devoted themselves" . . . . .
> "Instructions of a more general character were given to the leader—to promise good government to the invaded people, and to keep his promise; not to stay much at a time, and always to be straightforward; to respect ambassadors, but not to detain them long lest they become spies; to preserve secrecy where necessary, to make the round of sentinels by night and by day; and never to be slack." *(The Caliphate—Its Rise, Decline and Fall).*

Three Divisions comparising 5,000 soldiers each were despatched to the Syrian front under the command of Shurjil bin Hasana, Amr bin Aas, and Yazid bin Abu Sufian. Abu Obaidah, the would-be Supreme Commander on the Syrian front, was also entrusted with the command of a separate Division. But the Byzantines had mustered a force in the neighbourhood of Yermuk which was ten times stronger than that of Muslims. This necessitated the transfer of Khalid bin Waleed to the Syrian front. The wise Caliph Abu Bakr ordered Khalid to hurry up to the Syrian front with half of his forces, leaving the second half in Iraq under the command of Al-Muthanna. According to historians Tabari, Moqaddasi and Balladhuri, the Caliph had appointed Khalid as Supreme Commander of the Muslim forces on the Syrian front. The lighting march of Khalid and his men through a trackless, waterless and impassable desert lying between Iraq and Syria, is one of the most daring feats ever recorded in living history. He crossed the desert in five days and the eminence on which he stood still bears the name *'Thaniyat al Okab'* (the Pass of the Eagle).

The Muslim army in Syria was divided into four corps which were operating under the command of four Generals in different sectors. Abu Obaidah was in command of the division of Hems, with Headquarters at Jabia. Amr ibn Aas was in command of the Damascus Division and Sharjil ibn Hasana was in command of the Division operating in Jordon. On the advice of Umar, Caliph Abu Bakr ordered the concentration of the Entire Muslim force at Jaulan near Yermuk in April 634 A.C. in order to meet an enemy whose resources, wealth and supply of fighting material were unlimited. Khalid was summoned from Iraq to take command of the combined Muslim forces. The Romans, too, drew together all their corps, and the huge Roman army encamped in the semi-circular loop of Yermuk river, protected on three sides by the river which they considered to be an ideal camping ground. The Muslim army arrived later and occupied the bottle-neck. The Romans realised their mistake but it was too late. The two armies watched each other for two months when Khalid arrived on the scene. He was entrusted with the Supreme Command of the Muslim forces. According to all authentic historical sources, including that of Tabari, the army of Heraclius numbered 240,000 whilst the Muslims were only 40,000. The Roman army was commanded by some of their famous Generals and warriors, including Theodore the Sakkellarius, Bannes the Armenian and Jarja (George). Khalid ibn Waleed, realising the superiority of the Romans in numbers and arms, resorted to his usual tactics and divided his army into 38 equal corps, each commanded by tried warriors. On August 30, 634 A.C. the Romans, inspired by the priests, issued from their camp to encounter the Arabs. A terrible carnage ensued and the Romans were defeated with fearful slaughter. According to Tabari, more than 120 thousand Romans perished in the valley of Wakusa and were drowned in the river. With this memorable victory in the Battle of Yermuk, the whole of Syria lay at the feet of Muslims. In this memorable battle Khalid bin Waleed exhibited a super military skill, extraordinary chivalry and rare strategic moves. When the news of the disaster was conveyed to the Byzantine Emperor Heraclius at Antioch, he said, "Farewell Syria, my fair province. Thou art enemy's now"; and he quitted Antioch for Constantinople. Khalid declared "Syria sat as quiet as a camel". But before the decision of the battle of Yermuk, Caliph Abu Bakr died and was succeeded by Umar. Immediately after his election as Caliph, Umar issued orders for the deposition of Khalid from the Supreme Command. The letter delivered to Khalid in the heat of battle of Yermuk was kept a secret till the issue was decided. Khalid gladly bowed down to the orders of the Caliph and till his death fought as an ordinary soldier in the armies of Islam. He exhibited a sense of discipline scarcely shown by a General of his calibre. Disregarding all humiliations which this order might have caused him, he continued to serve with unflagging zeal as a faithful soldier of Islam in all campaigns fought in Syria thereafter.

During the Caliphate of Umar, Muslim forces won brilliant victories in Syria, Iraq, Persia and Egypt and the Islamic banner was carried to the western extremities of Egypt in the West and to the shores of the Caspian in the North. The siege of Damascus lasted for more than two months and one night when the birth of a child of the Lord Bishop was being celebrated in the city, Khalid along with his associates scaled the walls and opened the Eastern gate. The cry of *Allah-o-Akbar* rent the air, and the feasters having understood the critical situation capitulated to Abu Obaidah, the Muslim Commander guarding the Western gate. The two armies—one led by Khalid claimed to have captured the city and the other commanded by Abu Obaidah which had accepted capitulation of the city on certain terms, met in the heart of the city. At last the terms of the capitulation accepted by Abu Obaidah were held good for the entire city and it was ratified by Caliph Umar.

Khalid took part in several campaigns fought in Syria, including those of Hems and Kansarain. With the conquest of Kansarain, the last stronghold of the

Byzantines in Syria, the rule of Byzantines in Syria came to an end and the Emperor Heraclius retired to Constantinople never to return. The exceptional valour exhibited by Khalid in the campaign of Kansarain obliged Umar to change his view about him. He acknowledged openly : "God may bless Abu Bakr. He had greater sense for the right type of men than myself".

The respect shown by the Muslim conquerors towards the conquered races in Iraq and Syria was, to a great extent, responsible for establishing a stable Government and sound administration in these regions. Writing in *"Caliphate—Its Rise, Decline and Fall"*, Sir William Muir acknowledges, "Had the Muslims ill-treated the people of Syria or persecuted their religion, their position would have been desperate indeed; but their leniency towards the conquered and their justice and integrity presented a marked contrast to the tyranny and intolerance of the Romans . . . . The Syrian Christians enjoyed more civil and political liberty under their Arab invaders than they had done under the rule of Heraclius and they had no wish to return to their former state . . . . . . The Muslims, when they withdrew, returned the taxes which they had collected, since they were no longer able to fulfil their part of the bargain in guaranteeing security of life and property. A Nestorian Bishop writes about the year 15: The Talites (Arabs) to whom God had accorded in our days the dominion, have become our masters; but they do not combat the Christian religion; much rather they protect our faith, they respect our priests and our holymen, and make gifts to our churches and our convents". Thus, Muslims in Syria ruled both over the body and the heart of their subjects in Syria and Iraq.

The reason behind the deposition of Khalid was not malice on the part of the great Caliph Umar. He was too great a person to be associated with such acts. As Sir William Muir puts in: "The Military Chief had to give place to the civil functionary; sword to pen; Khalid to Abu Obaidah. There is no occasion to seek any ulterior motives which might have led Umar to replace Khalid by Abu Obaidah. Least of all can personal dislike have influenced him. Umar was too great for that" *(The Caliphate—Its Rise, Decline and Fall)*. Umar tried to remove the misunderstanding created among the people about the deposition of Khalid bin Waleed. He sent a rescript to the various provinces announcing that he had not deposed Khalid because of any fault on his part, but because people had begun to repose greater trust in Khalid than in God.

According to celebrated historians Tabari and Ibn Asakir, Khalid bin Waleed, the Sword of God, died in Hems in 21 A.H. (642 A.C.).

Thus passed way the hero of hundreds of battles with an unrealised wish for martyrdom on his dying lips. "Alas", he murmured, "I who fought hundreds of battles and have innumerable battle scars on my body, could not be blessed with martyrdom—the greatest ambition of all true Muslims". On hearing the news of his death, Caliph Umar exclaimed, "The death of Khalid has created a void in Islam which cannot be filled".

"The military campaigns of Khalid ibn al-Waleed and Amr ibn al-Aas", writes Phillip K. Hitti, in his monumental work, *'The History of the Arabs'*, "which ensued in al-Iraq, Persia, Syria and Egypt, are among the most brilliantly executed in the history of warfare and bear favourable comparison with those of Napoleon, Hannibal or Alexander".

# MUSA IBN NUSAIR

Of all the great nations of the world that have contributed to the building of human civilization, none perhaps have wielded the sword and pen with equal success than the nomadic Arabs. Issuing from their desert tents, they, in a remarkably short time, founded the mightiest Empire of the Mediaeval era, which stretched from the shores of the Atlantic in the West to the walls of China in the East. Their territorial conquests were not like those of Changiz, Hulaku, Atilla and Hannibal, culminating in the destruction of humanity and civilization. Instead, the Arab conquerors were the harbingers, protectors and patrons of civilizations and cultures. They proved to be the greatest administrators, and reformers. In this way, they had won the hearts of the conquered races and ruled not only on their bodies but also on their souls. Thus they brought about the greatest revolution in the history of mankind—a revolution which embraced all branches of human activity.

The outstanding Generals, during the Caliphate Rashida were Khalid bin Waleed, Saad ibn Al-Wakkas and Amr bin al-Aas and during the Umayyad Caliphate were Musa bin Nusair, Tariq bin Ziyad Qutaiba and Muhammad bin Qasim.

The Umayyad power reached its zenith during the reign of Waleed. The brilliant military achievements during his regime centre on the name of Muhammad bin Qasim in the East and Musa ibn Nusair in the West. "The conquests on the Western front", writes Phillip K. Hitti, in his outstanding work, *The History of the Arabs*, "Under Musa ibn Nusair and his lieutenants, were no less brilliant and spectacular than those on the East by al-Hajjaj and his Generals".

Musa ibn Nusair was born in 640 A.C. His father was the Police Chief of Amir Muawiya. His talents as an administrator and man of valour were early recognised and he was appointed by Caliph Abdul Malik as Collector of Revenue at Basra. Later, he was appointed as the Viceroy of Africa and governed over a vast territory extending from the borders of Egypt to the shores of the Atlantic. He administered his vast territories with a firm hand and introduced several reforms. The Berbers found in their new Viceroy an outstanding administrator as well as an extraordinary military genius. Musa and his troops then entered on a career of successful conquests which ended in the consolidation of Arab power in Africa and the conquest of the rest of North Africa and Spain.

By a series of daring and brilliant operations carried out by himself and his sons, Musa broke the Berber opposition, drove out the Greek conspirators and pacified the entire country. His wise administration and his conciliatory attitude endeared him to the Berbers and won him their confidence. He administered from Al-Qayrawan and was directly under the Caliph. The forbearance and equality, chivalry and fraternity justice and tolerance shown by the new conquerors towards the conquered races, won their hearts so much so that within a short time the entire Berber nation embraced Islam. They, in later years, became a formidable force, who carried the banner of Islam as far as the heart of France.

The Islamic countries of North Africa were harassed by the Byzantine Navy, stationed in the Mediterranean Islands. Musa, therefore, sent an expedition and the strategic Mediterranean islands of Majorca, Minorca and Ivica were captured and under the Islamic rule soon became extremely flourishing regions. "Musa's viceroyalty", write Amer Ali, "was now almost equal to that of Hajjaj in extent; but its importance in the demand for administrative ability and generalship, was far greater".

Musa, who had driven the Byzantines out of Africa for ever, had pushed his conquest up to the shores of the Atlantic, thus securing a point for the invasion of Europe. In 710 A.C., the first reconnaissance was made under the leadership of Tariq, an illustrious lieutenant of Musa. In the following year, Tariq ibn Ziyad landed in Spain with a small force of 7,000 men. A decisive battle was fought at the mouth of river Barbate between the tiny force of Tariq and the huge army of the Gothic King, Roderick, comprising one lakh soldiers in which the Christians were routed with terrible losses. Now, Tariq made a triumphal march into Spain, meeting little resistance. A year later, Musa too entered Spain with 10,000 Arabs and taking a different course captured Merida, Sidonia and Seville. Merida was taken by storm. Musa joined Tariq at Toledo and the two conquerors pushed on as far as the Pyrenees. In less than two years the whole of Spain was in Muslim hands. Portugal was conquered, a few years after, and was named al-Gharb. (The West). "In its swiftness of execution and completeness of success", writes Phillip K. Hitti, "This expedition into Spain holds a unique place in Mediaeval military annals". Leaving Tariq behind, Musa crossed into France and conquered a part of Southern France. "Standing on the Pyrenees", writes Ameer Ali, "the dauntless Viceroy conceived the project of conquering the whole of Europe; and in all human probablity had he been allowed to carry his plan into execution, he would have succeeded. The West lay completely at his feet. . . . . The cautious and hesitating policy of the Damascus Court lost the glorious opportunity, with the consequence that Europe remained enveloped in intellectual darkness for the next centuries".

Musa was engaged in reducing a few guerrilla bands in the defiles of the Pyrenees when orders were received from the Caliph, summoning him and Tariq to Damascus.

Musa made a triumphal march through Africa, but they were not well received by the new Umayyad Caliph Sulaiman. Musa died in Syria in 98 A.H. (716-17 A.C.).

Before leaving Spain, Musa made all necessary arrangements for the Government of the country. He made one of his sons as Viceroy of Spain with his Headquarters at Seville, and entrusted the charge of Africa to his son Abdullah, a great warrior and administrator.

The discipline shown by the Muslim conquerors is unique in the history of military conquests. Musa also withstood this test magnificently and when the whole of Europe lay at his feet and he was on his triumphal march, he preferred to cut short his career and obeyed the orders of the Caliph summoning him to Damascus.

Musa was a great warrior, an outstanding General, a wise Administrator and above all a great Disciplinarian. It was on account of such capable men that Islam established its supremacy and permanent footing on extensive territories of the world and that too in such a short time.

# TARIQ IBN ZIYAD

After landing on the coastal strip overlooking the rock which was later named as Jabal al-Tariq (Gibraltar), its conqueror Tariq ibn Ziyad, ordered the burning of the ships that had brought his Muslim troops from Africa in 711 A.C.

"Why are you doing this, Sir?" cried the astonished soldiers.
"How will we return?" enquired some.

Tariq remained unmoved by these appeals.

In reply, he uttered those historic words, which will always inspire people to embark on brave deeds. He said: "We have not come here to return. Either we shall conquer this country and establish ourselves here or we will perish".

Iqbal has versified as follows this inspiring historical incident in his Persian work *"Piyam-i-Mashriq"* :

طارق' چور کن ارۀ اندلس ،سفینہ سوخت
گفت ند کار تو بہ نگاہِ خرد خطاست
دوریم از سواد وطن باز چوں رسیم
ترک سبب ز رُوۓ شریعت کجا رواست
خندید و دستِ خویش بہ شمشیر برُد و گفت
ہر ملک ملکِ ماست کہ ملک خدائۓ ماست

"When Tariq burnt his boats on the shore of Andlusia (Spain), his soldiers said that his action was unwise. How could they return to their native country and the destruction of means was against the Islamic law. Thereupon Tariq placed his hand on his sword and declared that every country of our God is our country (Homeland)."

Emboldened by these words, Tariq and his soldiers routed one of the most formidable armies of the West and carried the banner of Islam even beyond the high walls of the Pyrenees.

Soon after the death of the Holy Prophet of Islam the Muslims were threatened from all sides. The mighty neighbouring Empires of the Romans and Persians were conspiring to uproot this new force. But the Arabs not only met this challenge but also crushed the two greatest Empires of the world, and in less than half a century their arms held sway over the three known continents.

The Islamic principles of equality and fraternity had enabled the conquered and newly converted races to take their share in the government along with the noblest of the Arabs. Islam recognised no distinction of caste and creed and readily patronised talent wherever found. This is why evey capable slaves have occupied highest positions in Islamic polity and many slave dynasties have magnificently ruled over Muslim subjects.

Tariq ibn Ziyad, a newly converted Berber slave was a lieutenant of Musa ibn Nusair, the Muslim Viceroy of Africa. This Berber slave was destined to be the conqueror of Spain, the biggest Muslim territory in Europe, which, for eight centuries under Muslims, kept aloft the torch of civilization and culture that at last dispelled the gloom that had enveloped the Mediaeval Europe.

At this time, when Africa was enjoying the blessings of toleration, justice and prosperity under the Muslims, neighbouring Spain was groaning under the tyranny and bigotry of Gothic ruler. The honour of women was not safe and the tillers of the soil were put to heavy taxation. The rulers and their henchmen revelled in luxury while the masses groaned in poverty. A large number of refugees from Spain both Christians and Jews who had suffered under the Gothic rule had taken refuge in Muslim Africa. One of them was Julian, the Governor of Ceuta, whose daughter, Florinda, had been dishonoured by Roderick, the Gothic King of Spain. They appealed to Musa to liberate their country from the tyrant's yoke.

In response to their prayer and with the sanction of the Caliph, Musa made a reconnaissance on the Southern Coast of Spain. The report was favourable and in May, 711, Tariq ibn Ziad with 7,000 Muslims crossed the Straits in ships in small contingents. As his troops landed in Europe, Tariq concentrated them on a hill, which took the name of Jabl al-Tariq (The Rock of Tariq) now called Gibraltar, and urged them either to conquer or perish. They had no intention to go back home.

Emboldened by these words, his army crushed all resistances which impeded their progress.

The Gothic King Roderick collected a huge army of more than one lakh soldiers. Tariq, too, was reinforced by 5,000 soldiers dispatched by Musa and now his army numbered 12,000. The two armies met at the mouth of river Barbate, on the shores of a lagoon of Janda and fought a decisive battle on July 19, 711, A.C. The two armies were unequally matched. The Christians were much superior, both in numbers and arms but the last charge by Tariq was irresistible and the Goths were completely routed with terrible losses. King Roderick was drowned in the river. This remarkable victory of Tariq broke the morale of the Spaniards and henceforward, they did not dare face the Muslim in the open.

Hereafter, the armies of Tariq met little resistance in the interior of Spain. His was a triumphal march from place to place in the Peninsula. Tariq had divided his small army into four divisions and directed one of his lieutenants towards Cordova, the other towards Malaga, the third towards Granada and himself at the head of the main body hurriedly marched upon Toledo, the Capital of Spain. All these cities capitulated without much resistance. The Goths were paralysed by the rapidity of Tariq's movement and the severity of his blows. The Gothic armies fled before him. "God", says an annalist, "filled the hearts of idolators with terror and alarm". The oppressed masses of Spain hailed the Muslims as their liberators. The exemplary treatment of Tariq and his men endeared him to the conquered races.

The fiercest battle of the entire campaign was fought at Ecija, which resulted in the victory of Tariq's forces. Toledo, the Capital of Spain also capitulated after little resistance. Here Tariq was joined by his Master Musa ibn Nusair, the Muslim Viceroy of Africa. Henceforward the two Generals moved side by side and in less than two years, the whole of Spain was in Muslim hands. Portugal was conquered, a few years after. "This constituted the last and the most sensational of the major Arab campaigns", writes Phillip K. Hitti, "and resulted in the addition to the Moslem world of the largest European territory ever held by them . . . . . In its swiftness of execution and completeness of success this expedition into Spain holds a unique place in the Mediaeval Military Annals".

Musa and Tariq would have easily conquered the whole of Europe which lay at their feet. There was none to stop their victorious advance, but Providence meant otherwise. When they were planning the conquest of Europe, they received sommons from the Caliph to present themselve at Damascus. They exhibited a rare discipline by obeying the orders of the Caliph, reaching Damascus at the earliest possible time Tariq died there afterwards.

The conquest of Spain by Muslims opened a new era for the Peninsula. It brought about a social revolution in which the freedom of religion was fully recognised. The intoleration and persecution of the Christians gave place to toleration and large-heartedness. The captured Christian cities received favourable terms which were faithfully observed. Individual acts of violence by the Muslim soldiers were severely punished. No properties or estates were confiscated. Instead, the Muslims introduced an intelligent system of taxation, which soon brought prosperity to the Peninsula and made it a model country in the West. The Christians had their own judges to settle their disputes. All communities had equal opportunities for entry into the public services.

This wise and generous administration of Muslim conquerors had its good effects. The Christians including their priests, who had first left their homes in terror came back and passed a happy and prosperous life. A well-known Christian writer says, "The Moors (Muslims) organised that wonderful kingdom of Cordova, which was the marvel of the Middle Ages, and which, when all Europe was plunged in barbaric ignorance and strife, alone held the torch of learning and civilisation bright and shining before the Western world".

# MUHAMMAD BIN QASIM

The military exploits of Muahmmad bin Qasim, a young lad of hardly 17 years of age against the most formidable forces that the subcontinent could assemble and his amazing success with a small army of six thousand, in less than two years, forms the golden chapter of the history of warfare during the Mediaeval times which, according to the well-known British historian Lane Poole, is a "fascinating romance of history".

Muhammad bin Qasim was born at a time when the Islamic arms held sway over the three known continents. In the West, Musa ibn Nusair had conquered the whole of North Africa. He and his able lieutenant, Tariq bin Ziyad, had occupied the Iberian Peninsula with a lightning speed.

In the East Kutaiba ibn Muslim had crushed the Tatar opposition and had brought Central Asia under the banner of Islam. In Sind, Muhammad bin Qasim appeared in 712 A.C. and in less than two years captured the entire Baluchistan, Sind and Bahawalpur up to Multan.

Sind at that time was ruled by Raja Dahir, son of Chach, a great statesman-administrator that the subcontinent has produced. The State ruled by Raja Dahir was the most powerful State of the subcontinent and comprised the whole of Sind, Baluchistan, Makran, Gujrat, Marwar and half of the Punjab. Its Capital was Debal, situated on the bank of river Indus near the sea coast.

Raja Dahir was a very arrogant ruler. He had given shelter to a number of rebels of the Caliph of Islam. Moreover, his men had looted the property of Muslim traders near Debal, who were on their way to Arabia from Ceylon.

The men of Raja Dahir had taken away not only the merchandise of Muslim merchants but also took into custody their children and women and the Raja refused to release them despite a complaint from the Caliph. This led to the invasion of Sind.

Hajjaj bin Yusuf, the Umayyad Viceroy of Iraq, who was the uncle and father-in-law of Muhammad bin Qasim organised the entire campaign and entrusted to young Qasim, the command of a well-equipped small army of six thousand men. The young General marched with lightning speed and laid siege to Debal.

He had brought two new weapons with him, a huge catapult and a fire ball. The former rained stones while the latter fired on the enemy. His force was small, which opposing him was a formidable force of more than hundred thousand men supported by war elephants and an array of excellent archers.

Raja Dahir was not alone. He had the support of his fellow Hindu rulers spread all over the subcontinent. His usual tactics was to exhaust and finish the enemy. He had shut himself inside the impregnable walls of Debal.

The Muslim victory at Debal is ascribed to the giant catapult named *"Uroos"*. A stone hurled by *"Uroos"* brought down the banner flying on the top of its biggest temple. The besieged, considering it an ill omen, came out in the open only to be defeated with terrible losses.

During a short span of two years, from 712 to 714 A.C., Muhammad bin Qasim fought and won eleven bloody battles against the formidable forces of Raja Dahir and his henchmen. Despite heavy odds and with a small force, he was never defeated.

After capturing Debal, he marched towards Nerwan which capitulated without any opposition. Then he marched on Bherah where he defeated Raja Vijay Ray. Next, he captured Sehwan, Forts of Sesam and Ashihah without much opposition. He had been moving on the western side of river Indus. Near Jhimpir he came across a strong force of Raja Dahir under the command of Jai Singh which was stationed on the eastern side of river Indus.

Muhammad bin Qasim made a unique plan to cross the broad stream of the river. He got boats tied in a length which was equal to the breadth of the river and manned each boat with five picked archers and the front boat with mangonel. He ordered the boats to move on the stream. The boats moved systematically and under the hail of arrows the formidable forces of the enemy commanding the other side of the river were pushed back. Soon the catapults were landed and the Muslim troops disembarked and fell upon the enemy and inflicted a defeat with terrible losses.

The Muslim forces captured Jhimpir and followed the forces of Raja Dahir who was in fort Rawar where was fought the memorable battle in which, despite much superior forces, the Hindus were defeated and Raja Dahir was killed. Another fierce battle was fought by Muhammad bin Qasim at Brahmanabad where Jai Singh faced him with forty thousand men. He was routed and fled to Kashmir.

Next, the Muslim forces captured Aror (Rohri) after a bloody campaign. The marching Muslim forces pushed ahead towards Sikka, which they captured after Herculean efforts. Lastly, they conquered Multan where they captured a vast treasure.

The success of the Muslim arms was due to the superior military tactics and personal valour and skill of its young commander, Muahmmad bin Qasim as well as to the valour and discipline of Muslim forces. He excelled both in laying siege and in open warfare. His secret plans and charge of the reserve forces often won him the day.

Muhammad bin Qasim was great both in war and peace. He proved himself an able administrator. His two years of wise and just rule, his agricultural reforms and liberal policies soon endeared him to his Muslim and non-Muslim subjects. When after the death of his patrons, Hajjaj bin Yousuf and Caliph Waleed, he was arrested and recalled by Caliph Sulaiman, the people of Sind bade him farewell with a heavy heart.

# SULTAN BAYAZID YILDIRIM

The combined force of Christian Europe numbering more than a quarter million strong, led by the brave chiefs of French, German and Hungarian states, had arrayed themselves in the vast plain of Danube near Nicopolis. They had mustered their strength in the last Crusade against the Muslim Turks who were knocking at the gates of the Hungarian Capital, Budapest. The Christians boasted that "If the sky were to fall they would hold it up by their spears".

The Turkish Sultan, Bayazid Yildirim, through his rare strategy and military skill, routed at Nicopolis in 1396, this formidable force of European countries. The Europeans were tricked to attack the Turkish centre, which drew back, pretending to be pressed hard. Thereafter, the Turkish flanks attacked and closed upon the advanced European army, totally encircling it. When completely encircled, the Europeans met a terrible slaughter at the hands of Turks.

Bayazid Yildirim, known as lightning was the son of Murad I. He was born in 761 A.H. and was given a thorough education which included different sciences and arts as well as military training. He was a born warrior and with his exceptional military skill, he soon earned the title of lightning.

Bayazid succeeded his father in 1391 A.C. His accession was enthusiastically welcomed by the Turkish army with which he was very popular.

The Turkish Sultan reduced the three small states in Anatolia (Asia Minor) which were a constant menace and were in league with the neighbouring Christian States of Eastern Europe.

After completing this task, the Turks now paid their attention to Eastern Europe. They overran the Balkans and the shores of the Black Sea.

Bayazid crushed the stalwart Serbians in the field of Kossova and thereafter penetrated into Hungary. Their cavalry, especially the *'Sipahis'* were good and their infantry, known as *'janissaries'*, was superb.

The Byzantine Emperor of Constantinople was only a shadow of his forefathers and was totally at the mercy of the Turkish Sultan. "He (Bayazid) was Lord of Constantinople in all but name", says a Chri tian writer, "his lands extended up to the city walls; his judges were installed in several of its courts and from two minarets in the city muezzins called the Turks to prayers. Manuel, the Emperor of Constantinople, paid him tribute for possession of the city, Venice and Genoa treated him (Turkish Sultan), as its future master".

Bayazid wanted to occupy the city and had actually besieged it when he was obliged to raise the siege and hurried to meet the combined force of Christian Europe that had started a Crusade against the Turks. Sigismund, the King of Hungary, being most menaced by the approach of "Lightning" was the sponsor of the Fourth Crusade and Phillip of Burgandy was its advocate.

The King of France lent his full support to the King of Hungary. From England and Netherland came volunteers. The formidable force of Crusaders included the Bastard of Savoy, the Master of the Prussian Knights, Frederick of Honenzollern, the Grand Master of Rhodes—Knights of St. John, electors, burgraves and palatines. The strongest force came from France. Among them were scions of houses of Bar and Artois, Burgandy and St. Paul.

The mighty force of Crusaders assembled in the plain of Danube near Nicopolis. The battle which was fought in 1396 has been described by Harold Lamb as follows :

"Some twenty thousand chevaliers, including their squires, and men-at-arms, rode to the west and joined the host of Sigismund, nearly a hundred thousand in all. They seemed to be well supplied with women and wine. So great was the multitude that the chevaliers boasted that if sky were to fall they would hold it up by their spears . . . . . . They encamped in a fair country to besiege Nicopolis, and here they heard that Bayazid with a formidable army was approaching rapidly."

"At first they were incredulous. But Sigismund convinced them of the truth. The battle line was drawn up and Sigismund—who knew the strength of the Turks—urged the chevaliers to form in the rear and let his sturdy infantry, the Hungarians, Wallachians and Croats, bear the shock of the Moslem attack."

This enraged the nobles and the dispute grew violent when Bayazid's skirmishers appeared. Philip of Artois, High Constable of France, cried out :

"The King of Hungary would have the honour of the day. Whoever agrees with him, I shall not. We have the advance guard and the first battle belongs to us." Whereupon he gave command to lift his banner Forward, in the name of God and Saint George !

"In a mass the other lords followed him, with their squadrons of mailed raiders—after first massacring their Turkish and Serbian prisoners. Streamers fluttering from their lance tips, shields erect, their barded chargers thundering into a gallop, the chivalry of Europe charged. Princes knights and men-at-arms, they scattered the skirmishers, forced their way up a long slope, cut to pieces the ranks of foot archers they found there, and reformed to assail the regiment of "Sipahis" who now appeared."

"They smashed through the Sipahis, the Turkish light cavalry, and broke them, and pressed on again. It was a very gallant charge and it lost the battle."

"These first three lines had been no more than Bayazid's advance. When they gained the next ridge, the wearied chevaliers found themselves confronted by the flower of the Turkish army, sixty thousand strong by the white turbans of the "janissaries" and the armoured regiments of cavalry drawn up in a halfcircle about them. Without wasting men in a counter charge, the Turks began to shoot down the horses of Christian knights with their arrows. Dismounted, hindered by their heavy armour, some of the Crusaders fought on grimly—others turned and fled before their horses went down."

"But with the forces of Turks closing up around them and their own allies outdistanced, most of the chevaliers threw down their arms."

"It is certain that the rout of chevaliers lost the battle beyond hope. The rush of exhausted and bloodied fugitives with the Turks at their heels shook the courage of the infantry. On the wings, the Wallachians drew away to save themselves. Sigismund's Hungarians and the Elector's Bavarians made a valiant stand, but Sigismund himself and his nobles were soon galloping down to the river to seek refuge on the Venetian galleys."

Bayazid massacred about ten thousand captive chevaliers as a reprisal against the earlier massacre of Turkish prisoners by the Crusaders. Only 24 Christian peers were released on payment of heavy ransom.

"Soon ended ingloriously", writes Harold Lamb, "the last Crusade, and the mourning of European Courts was equalled by the despair of Constantinople that had seen aid so near at hand and now believed itself doomed".

After his resounding victory in the battle of Nicopolis in 1396 against the combined force of Christian Europe, Bayazid now directed his forces to the conquest of Greece. The entire Morea was occupied. Bulgaria was also conquered and added to the fast expanding Turkish Empire. Serbia too was occupied.

The Christian states of Venice and Genoa vied with each other to win the favour of the Turkish Sultan.

The Abbaside Caliph, Mutawakkel-billah was much pleased with the exploits of the Turkish Sultan in Europe and being the Spiritual Head of the world of Islam, he accepted Bayazid as the ruler of the occupied territories. The Turkish Sultan respectfully kissed the Caliph's firman and in return sent him a large number of presents.

Sultan Bayazid again invaded the important city of Constantinople, which continued to be like a thorn surrounded by his vast territories. The Byzantine Emperor, Manuel grew heart sick and the men of Constantinople were extremely hard pressed due to the blockade of the city. The terms of the surrender of Constantinople were being drawn up, when the city was granted another respite.

The report of Timur's appearance in Anatolia (Asia Minor) obliged Bayazid to call off the siege of Constantinople. He hastened to Anatolia with a large army to meet the great Tatar conqueror, Timur.

Timur was much annoyed at the protection granted by the Turkish Sultan Bayazid to Sultan Ahmad of Baghdad, whom Timur wanted to punish for his treachery. Timur did not want to disturb Bayazid who was engaged in a holy war with the Christian West. But Bayazid's discourteous reply however, infuriated Timur and he decided to fight with the Turks.

In less than 13 months, Timur eliminated all Bayazid's allies one by one before he appeared on the scene of battle in Anatolia.

Early in 1402 A.C., the conqueror of Eastern Europe, Bayazid Yildirim mustered his strength to meet the conqueror of Asia, Timur. The Turkish Sultan had with him more than two lakh soldiers and was overconfident of his victory.

Timur, a seasoned warrior, studied the country West of Sivas and found it unsuitable for cavalry. He turned to South and marched along the valley of River Halys. He pushed forward, laying waste the country and thus compelling the Turks to follow him. The Turkish army being mostly infantry, was soon exhausted.

Bayazid left his base near Angora and followed Timur. After a week's rapid marches, the Turkish army was exhausted with hunger and thirst. Such marches, on the other hand, were daily routine of Tatar chevaliers. In the end, Bayazid found the Tatars occupying the Turkish base with plenty of water and provision. Water was found nowhere in the area except behind the Tatar lines.

Bayazid was, therefore, forced to take the offensive against the Tatars which he did not like. He launched his inferior cavalry against the tough Tatar horsemen. He was out-manoeuvred by Timur and the pride of Turkish army, the Janissaries (Infantry) could hardly be used even. Bayazid, with a thousand Janissaries drove the Tatar horsemen from a ridge and fought there grimly throughout the afternoon, holding an axe himself and standing with his men.

"As one battalion of Old Guard held its ground on the field of Waterloo", says Lamb, "when Napoleon's army had become a rout of fugitives these household soldiers of the Sultan died weapon in hand".

But Bayazid's pride was broken and he died a few months after on July 20, 1402.

Tears rolled down Timur's fiery eyes, when he came to know about the death of Bayazid. He was buried with all honours at Brusa, by the side of other Turkish Sultans.

Thus ended the ambitious career of one of the bravest Turkish rulers who was a vital threat to the Christian Europe. His dream of the conquest of France and feasting his horses at the altar of St. Peters, could not be realised as his career was cut short by his defeat at the hands of Timur, which served as the greatest blow to the cause of Islam in Europe.

# TIMUR, THE WORLD CONQUEROR

"Impossible is a word found in the dictionary of fools", said Napoleon, while climbing over the impassable Alps along with his formidable army. But he did not live up to his convictions and had to admit the existence of this word after his defeats at Leipzig and Waterloo.

This word was, however, disproved much earlier by Timur, the Great Asian conqueror, who, rising from a humble origin, defeated during his lifetime, the two mightiest rulers of his time—Toktamish, the Mongol and Bayazid, the Turk, and was held supreme both in Asia and Europe. He accomplished many impossible tasks through his indomitable will, matchless military skill and exceptional courage. His achievements were considered superhuman by his contemporaries.

The armies led by Napoleon and Hitler were exhausted in the vast Russian plains which proved to be the graveyard of some of the greatest armies in the world. Barring Changiz Khan, Timur was perhaps the only conqueror who overran the vast plains extending from the shores of the Pacific in the East to the banks of the Don in the West, and defeated the formidable forces led by the Mongol Emperor, a descendant of Changiz Khan. Even Changiz Khan had not to race and overcome such mighty forces as Timur had. His opposition in the Russian plains was feeble, while Timur faced a much superior force led by the mighty Mongol Emperor, Toktamish, the Master of the Golden Horde and totally routed them.

There were six ruling dynasties during his lifetime—the powerful Mongol Khan of Siberia, the mighty Ottoman Turks, the formidable Memluks of Egypt, the Great Khan of China, the Muslim rulers of Baghdad and Delhi. He defeated five of them and was on his way to meet the Great Khan of China when death overtook him, hence he could not accomplish his last ambition.

Conquerors like Caesar, Hannibal, Napoleon and Bismark pale into insignificance when compared with Timur. As a world conqueror, he ranks only with Alexander, the Great and Changiz Khan. But, in a way, he was superior to these two also. Alexander and Changiz had to face less formidable forces in their campaigns of conquest.

"Five hundred and fifty years ago a man tried to make himself master of the world", writes Harold Lamb in his well-known book, *Tamerlane—the Earth Shaker.* "In everything he undertook he was successful. We call him Tamerlane".

"In the beginning he was a gentleman of little consequence—master of some cattle and land in that breeding ground of conquerors, Central Asia. Not the son of a king as Alexander was, or the heir of a chieftain like Changiz Khan. The victorious Alexander had at the outset his people, the Macedonians and Changiz Khan had his Mongols. But Tamerlane gathered together a people.

Comparing Timur with other great conquerors of the world, Harold Lamb says :

"Timur, in common with Changiz Khan, had the strange genius of war that made them appear superhuman. Much as we admire the campaigns of Caesar, the exploits of Hannibal, or the inspired strategy of Napoleon, upon reflection, it is becoming clear, that these two conquerors from Asia are, with Alexander, the masters of war upon the stage of the world. Their feats of arms may have been duplicated by others in miniature, but never on the earth as a whole."

Of Timur, Sir Percy Skyes says : "No Asiatic conqueror in historical times has performed such feats of arms as these, and consequently none is entitled to fame of Tamerlane. His achievements seemed almost to border on the superhuman".

Timur was born into a poor family of the Green city. His father a chieftain of Barlas Tatars, spent most of his time in the company of holymen. "The world", Taragai, the father of Timur, told his son, "Is no better than a golden vase filled with scorpions and serpents". Timur was influenced by his father's Islamic teachings and gave up Polo and Chess.

A youth of few words, he had no love for foolery and in all his life he never appreciated a jest. He married a beautiful lady, Aljai Khatun Agha.

Timur, a valiant and wise youth, united the warring Tatar tribesmen. During his early career he captured the Green city by a trick. He scattered his small army all round. They cut branches which raised enormous dust and the Jat garrison thinking that a big army was invading them, surrendered. During the same period, against the formidable Jat General Bikijuk, Timur scattered his men during the night, asking them to light as many fires as they could around the hostile camp. The sight of these fires frightened the enemy who hurriedly left before dawn, with Timur charging from the rear. One of Timur's chroniclers said : "The Lord Timur, always fortunate in war, in this year defeated an army by fire and captured a city by dust".

Timur inflicted a crushing defeat upon the attacking Mongols, led by Ilias Khan, in the Battle of Rain in which horses were stuck up in knee deep mud.

Having established his superiority as a leader and warrior, Timur was elected as the Chief of the Tatars by Muslim theologians led by the spiritualist, Zainuddin, who coronated him by taking oath from chieftains to obey him.

Timur, destined to become one of the greatest conquerors that the world has produced, had no favourites and favoured only the most talented and chivalrous persons. He was convinced that the best defence against the menacing Jat and Mongol hordes was offence.

Soon after his election as the Chief of Tatars, Timur embarked upon a glorious career of conquests, unparalleled in the history of the world. He captured Herat, an important city, housing a quarter million people, several hundred educational institutions and more than 3,000 baths.

But the greatest menace to the Tatar lands were the Mongols known as Golden Horde, who were led by the descendants of Changiz Khan. The Horde was at the zenith of power and roamed about the vast Russo—Siberian plains bordered on the North by Tundras and occasionally descending into the Tatar dominions with ferocious speed. At this time, they were led by Toktamish, a Crimean Prince, who had once taken refuge with Timur, had now become the leader of the Horde on the death of Urus Khan, the Mongol Chief. But now Toktamish, the Master of the Golden Horde, was not Toktamish, the fugitive, who had taken refuge with Timur. He cast a longing eye over Timur's dominions and made repeated hurried incursions into Tatar lands.

Once, in a bitter winter, Toktamish came down with a strong force towards the river Syr. Timur's Amirs advised him to wait till his scattered armies were brought together. But Timur refused to wait, and heading his army divided his forces into small regiments. Then riding through rain and snow, with horses sunk into knee deep water and mud, Timur attacked the outposts of the Horde, filtering through their division. His masterly manoeuvring led the encircling of Toktamish forces which retreated hastily.

Timur, who believed in offensive rather than defensive war, resolved to meet the Golden Hordes in their own land and to finish, if possible, their striking power for ever.

Timur, then set out with a large force to meet the Golden Horde in their own lands. He wandered through a desolate and vast plain, called steppes, graveyard of many great armies. Timur penetrated into Russia. His information failed, his provisions whittled down and his army exhausted, when he saw the horned standard of the Golden Horde. Timur decided to risk everything to settle the menace of the Horde for ever. His scouts, at last camp up with the rear guard of Toktamish forces in the land of shadow—the cold forests. Timur's army was exhausted and was extremely short of supplies. Toktamish moved further north in the extremely cold forest, clearing all game to deprive Timur's hungry men of any food.

Timur knew that it was a struggle for life and death. His march of 1,800 miles covered in 18 weeks had ended. Both the armies camped facing each other. Timur ordered his exhausted army to cook food and take rest which surprised his opponent.

Next morning, Timur divided his army into seven divisions, commanded by his sons and seasoned Generals. He stood behind Centre with his war veterans and Generals. The first charge was led by grey haired Saifuddin. Timur ordered his Centre forward in support of his son Miran Shah. They smashed their way into Toktamish's flanks, which gave way under the impact of heavy cavalry. Toktamish fled and with his disappearance the great horned standard of the Horde also fell.

Timur pursued the defeated Horde, which scattered all round, leaving behind enough spoils for Timur's men. Toktamish fled to the cold Northern forest. His power was broken for ever. Timur stormed Serai and Astara Khan on the Volga, thus avenging Toktamish burning of Bukhara.

Timur marched along the river Don and reached near Moscow uninterrupted. The Russian Grand Prince took to field with little hope. "In procession", writes Harold Lamb, "the image of the Virgin was drawn back to Moscow, between lines of kneeling people who cried out as it passed : Mother of god saved Russia. And to this the Russians attribute their deliverance. No one knows why"? Timur turned back without capturing Moscow which lay at his feet. A number of historians persist that he took Moscow.

On his return, he stormed the rock nests of the warlike Georgians who disputed his path with their exceptional courage. Timur called upon his men to accomplish a task that seemed beyond human power. A mountain clan had withdrawn to a place which seemed to be impregnable, surrounded by high and steep mountain cliffs. Even arrows could not reach there. The Tatars managed to climb this "impassable place", through ropes and the Georgians had to surrender the insurmountable citadel of Takrit, built on a high rock, facing Tigris, which was taken.

Now Timur was the master of a vast dominion extending both in Europe and Asia. "For 2,200 miles, the great Khurasan road, ran through his lands".

Timur's next target was Persia. Here he came down in 1386 with a large army to settle the differences among his satellite ruling Muzaffar princes. One of these, Mansoor, had slain certain Tatar chieftains. This led to the sack of Isfahan by the Tatars. All the Muzaffar princes surrendered to Timur except Mansoor who fled to mountains. Shiraz also capitulated and here Timur had his memorable meeting with the famous Persian Poet, Hafiz of Shiraz, whom the conqueror loaded with presents.

During the Spring of 1399, Timur invaded India *via* Khyber Pass, where he got little resistance, and captured Delhi without much difficulty. He brought back with him elephants and 200 Masons for building the principal Samarkand Mosque.

Later, he captured the "White Castle", the inaccessible nest of Ismailis, which was considered impregnable since the time of Rustam. He also broke an alliance of Kurra Yusuf and Sultan Ahmad of Baghdad, and captured Baghdad by forced marches.

Thereafter, started three years of war, through which Timur emerged as the mightiest figure of his time. He wrote a letter to the Turkish Emperor, Bayazid Yildirim, requesting him not to give any aid to Kurra Yusuf and Sultan Ahmad of Baghdad who had played mischief with Timur. Bayazid, who was at the height of his power, sent a very arrogant and discourteous reply to the Tatar Conqueror, calling him a dog. Timur, who wanted to leave Bayazid alone, to deal with Christian Europe, got infuriated at this insulting reply. He was surrounded by enemies on all sides and he annihilated them one by one. He left the bulk of his army at Karabagh and sent separate divisions to deal with each of them. One of his divisions crushed the Georgians in their inaccessible defiles. His main divisions were on march in Asiatic Turkey and by the middle of 1400 had reached up to Sivas, the key city of Asiatic Turkey. By forced marches he captured Malayta and the Turkish Governor retreated in haste.

On his way to Syria he defeated the Turkomans. He defeated the Memluk Sultan of Egypt at Aleppo and marched on Damascus which capitulated without resistance. Timur's armies chased the Egyptians out of Palestine. One of his divisions marched on Baghdad and its Sultan fled from his Capital, leaving it to the Tatars. "Timur had marched from one end of the arc of his enemies to the other", writes a Western chronicler. "In fourteen months he had fought two major battles and any number of smaller engagements and had taken by assault nearly a dozen fortified cities. As a feat of arms, it was remarkable, and it eliminated all of Bayazid's allies before Timur appeared on the scene".

Early in 1402 A.C., the Conqueror of Eastern Europe, Bayazid Yildirim mustered his strength to meet the Conqueror of Asia, Timur. He had with him more than two lakh soldiers and was over confident of victory.

Timur studied the country West of Sivas and found it unsuitable for cavalry. Hence he turned off to south and marched along the valley of river Halys. There were two courses open to him. Either to wait and refresh his horses or to push forward, laying waste the country, compelling the Turks to follow him. The Turkish army being mostly infantry, was bound to be exhausted by swift marches. Timur, therefore, adopted the second course.

Bayazid followed Timur, marched rapidly for a week and was exhausted with thirst and hunger. In the end he found Timur having occupied Turkish base with enough provision and water. Water was found nowhere except behind the Tatar lines. Bayazid was, therefore, forced to take offensive, which he did not like, against the Tatars. He launched his inferior cavalry against the much superior Tatar cavalry. He was outmanoeuvred by Timur and the pride of his army, the Janissaries (Infantry) could not be used even. Timur did not mount his horse until the last moment. He directed the battle from a ridge, in the rear of his army commanded by his sons and Generals. "The splendid Othmanji infantry", writes Harold Lamb, "the Janissaries, had not struck a blow. They were predoomed, their situation hopeless, their Emperor helpless before the manoeuvring of the great chess player of Asia".

The Turkish Emperor, Bayazid Yildirim was defeated. He was brought before Timur. He received him with honour and seated him by his side as well as restored his favourite wife and robes. But Bayazid's pride was broken and he died a few months after.

Timur reached Smyrna, the gate of Europe. His rebel Kurra Yusuf and Sultan Ahmad of Baghdad fled to Arabia and Egypt respectively. The Memluk Sultan of Egypt hastened his submission to Timur, offering an annual tribute to him. The rulers of Europe vied with each other in paying their humble congratulations and submissions to the great conqueror. The Genoese even flew Timur's standard from the Towers of Pera.

The great conqueror, now wanted to realise his last ambition of conquering Cathay (China) and thus overcome the last power in the world which could oppose him. He summoned before him the council of Princes and Amirs. "We have conquered", he told them, "all of Asia except Cathay. We have overthrown such mighty kings that our deeds will be remembered always. You have been my companions in wars and never has victory failed you. To overthrow the pagans of Cathay, not much strength or power will be needed and thither you will march with me".

About a quarter million warriors, led by Timur, set out from Samarkand for Cathay. Soon, winter overtook them and they moved into a world white with snow. But Timur was not a man to turn back. They reached Ortar, on road to Cathay. Here Timur rested during the winter and planned to resume his march during March 1405 but death overtook him.

With the disappearance of the master-mind, there started a war of succession in Samarkand and the war veterans of Timur's army had to give up reluctantly the march to Cathay and, therefore, could not realise the last ambition of their great master.

Timur was not only one of the greatest conquerors of the world but he was also a great administrator as well as an outstanding patron of art and learning. He adorned his native city, Samarkand, with buildings, tombs, gardens, parks, and spacious roads. He built a grand mosque in Samarkand in three months. He made it a centre of art and learning during his lifetime, it became the Rome of the East. He brought to this city treasures of art and learning from all parts of the world which included artisans, artists, scholars and all types of talents.

He evolved a new type of architecture according to his fancy which was graceful as well as grand. His buildings were stark and magnificent. He built garden palaces.

As an administrator, Timur devoted himself equally to the building of his dominions. Road couriers and secret services were maintained in his dominions. "Timur's service of information" writes a Western historian, "was complete, probably swifter than anything of the kind until the days of rail roads". He framed wise laws for land, property and duties. Soldiers were paid from the Exchequer. They were neither allowed to levy tributes on the inhabitants nor allowed to enter a civilian's home without a cause. Farmers were not taxed for the first year.

Trade flourished through his dominions. Samarkand and Tabriz became great commercial centres in the East. For merchants, Timur's Government was a boon. They travelled his vast dominions under guard and paid one custom duty only. The westward march of Timur changed the political scene of things and affected the destinies of Europe. He opened again the trans-continental trade routes, which had been blocked for hundreds of years.

Peasants became prosperous under his land reforms and he freed them from the oppression of nobles.

Timur was intolerant of weakness. He forbade beggary and built poor houses for disabled and weak persons.

He cleared his dominions of thieves and robbers. Every magistrate in the town and every captain of the road guard was made responsible for the theft within his district. Any article stolen had to be replaced by him.

Timur was simple and straightforward. He abhorred pomp and pageantry and disliked lying and jesting. He looked for truth even if it was distasteful for him. He was not depressed by misfortunes and never lost heart.

He never took the title of Emperor and begin his documents with short phrase. "Lord Timur has given the Command", or "I, Timur, servant of God, says".

Timur knew no failures. He came from a humble origin and rose to be the most powerful man of his age and the greatest conqueror of all times. "To Europeans", says a Western Chronicler, "Timur's magnificence seemed unearthly and his power demoniac".

Acknowledging his greatness, Harold Lamb says: "No man since Timur has attempted to dominate the world. He accomplished all that Alexander was able to do—Alexander of Macedonia who followed on the heels of Cyrus, the great, as the Tatar conqueror followed Changiz Khan. And he was the last of the great conquerors. It is not likely that any human being will win such power with sword again. Throughout Asia today, if you go there, you will be told that three men conquered the world—Iskandar (Alexander), Changiz Khan and Timur".

# SULTAN SALAHUDDIN AYUBI

Sultan Salahuddin Ayubi, the hero of hundreds of battles, was the person who for twenty years braved the storm of Crusaders and ultimately pushed back the combined forces of Europe which had come to swarm the Holy Land. The world has hardly witnessed a more chivalrous and humane conqueror.

The Crusades represent the maddest and the longest war in the history of mankind, in which the storm of savage fanaticism of the Christian West burst in all its fury over Western Asia. "The Crusades, form", says a Western writer, "one of the maddest episodes in history. Christianity hurled itself against Muhammadanism in expedition after expedition for nearly three centuries, until failure brought lassitude, and superstition itself was undermined by its own labours. Europe was drained off men and money, and threatened with social bankruptcy, if not with annihilation. Millions perished in battle, hunger or disease and every atrocity the imagination can conceive disgraced the warriors of the Cross". The Christian West was excited to a mad religious frenzy by Peter the Hermit, and his followers to liberate the Holy Land from the hands of the Muslims. "Every means", says Hallam, "was used to excite an epidemical frenzy", During the time that a Crusader bore the Cross, he was under the protection of the Church and exempted from all taxes as well as was free to commit all sins.

Peter the Hermit himself led the second host of Crusaders comprising forty thousand people. "Arriving at Mallevile, they avenged their precursors by assaulting the town, slaying seven thousand of the inhabitants, and abandoning themselves to every species of grossness and liberalism". The savage hordes called Crusaders converted Hungary and Bulgaria into desolate regions. When they reached Asia Minor, they, according to Michaud, "committed crimes which made Nature shudder".

The third wave of Crusaders commanded by a German monk, according to Gibbon, "comprised of the most stupid and savage refuse of people. They mingled with their devotion a brutal licence of rapine, prostitution and drunkenness". "They forgot Constantinople and Jerusalem", says Michaud, "in tumultuous scenes of debauchery, and pillage, violation and murder was everywhere left on the traces of their passage".

The fourth horde of Crusaders which had risen from Western Europe was, according to Mill, "another herd of wild and desperate savages . . . . .The internal multitude hurried on to the south in their usual career of carnage and rapine". But, at last, they were annihilated by the infuriated Hungarian Army which had a foretaste of the madness of earlier Crusaders.

Later the Crusaders met with initial success and conquered a major part of Syria and Palestine, including the Holy city of Jerusalem. But their victories were followed by such brutalities and massacres of innocent Muslims which eclipsed the massacres of Changiz and Hulaku. Mill, a Christian historian, testifies to this massacre of Muslims population on the fall of the Muslim town of Antioch. He writes: "The dignity of age, the helplessness of youth and the beauty of the weaker sex were disregarded by the Latin savages. Houses were no sanctuaries, and the sight of a mosque added, new virulence to cruelty". According to Michaud, "if contemporary account can be credited, all the vices of the infamous Babylon prevailed among the liberators of Scion". The Crusaders laid waste the flourishing towns of Syria, butchered their population in cold blood and burnt to ashes the invaluable treasures of art and learning, including the world famous library of Tripolis (Syria) containing more than three million volumes. "The streets ran with blood until ferocity was tired out", says Mill. "Those who were vigorous or beautiful were reserved for the slave market at Antioch, but the aged and infirm were immolated at the altar of cruelty".

But in the second half of the 12th century A.C., when the Crusaders were in their greatest fury and the Emperors of Germany and France and Richard, the lion-hearted King of England, had taken the field in person for the conquest of the Holy Land, the Crusaders were met by Sultan Salahuddin Ayubi; a great warrior who pushed back the surging wave of Christianity out to engulf the Holy Land. He was not only able to clear the gathering storm but in him the Crusaders met a man of indomitable will and dauntless courage who could accept the challenge of the Christian West.

Salahuddin was born in 1137 A.C. He got his early training under his illustrious father Najmuddin Ayub and his chivalrous uncle Asaduddin Sherkoh, who were the trusted lieutenants of Nooruddin Mahmud, the Monarch of Syria. Asaduddin Sherkoh, a great warrior General was the Commander of the Syrian forces, which had defeated the Crusaders both in Syria and Egypt. Sherkoh entered Egypt in February 1167 A.C., to meet the challenge of the Fatimide Minister Shawer who had allied himself with the French. The marches and counter-marches of gallant Sherkoh and his ultimate victory at Babain over the allied forces, according to Michaud, "Show military capacity of the highest order", Ibn al-Athir writes about it: "Never has history recorded a more extraordinary event than the rout of the Egyptian forces and the French at the littoral, by only a thousand cavaliers".

On January 8, 1169 A.C. Sherkoh arrived in Cairo and was appointed as the Minister and Commander-in-Chief by the Fatimid Caliph. But Sherkoh was not destined to enjoy the fruits of his high office long. He died two months after in 1169 A.C. On his death, his nephew Salahuddin Ayubi became the Prime Minister of Egypt. He soon won the hearts of the people by his liberality and justice and on the death of the Egyptian Caliph became the virtual Ruler of Egypt.

In Syria too, the celebrated Nooruddin Mahmud died in 1174 A.C. and was succeeded by his 11 year old son, Malik-us-Saleh who became a tool in the hands of his interested courtiers, specially Gumushtagin. Salahuddin sent message to Malik-us-Saleh offering his services and devotion. He even continued to keep his name in "Khutaba" (Friday Sermons) and coinage. But all these considerations were of no avail for the young ruler and his ambitious courtiers. This state of affairs once more heartened the Crusaders who were kept down by Nooruddin Mahmud and his capable General Sherkoh. Malik-us-Saleh, on the advice of Gumushtagin retired to Aleppo, leaving Damascus exposed to a Frankish attack. The Crusaders instantly laid siege to the Capital city and raised it only after being paid heavy ransom. This enraged Salahuddin who hurried to Damascus with a small force and took possession of it.

After occupying Damascus, he did not enter the palace of his patron, Nooruddin Mahmud, but stayed in his father's house. The Muslims, on the other hand, were much dismayed by the activities of Malik-us-Saleh and invited him to rule over the area. But Salahuddin continued to rule on behalf of the young Malik-us-Saleh. On the death of Malik-us-Saleh in 1181-82 A.C., the authority of Salahuddin was acknowledged by all the sovereigns of Western Asia.

There was a truce between the Sultan and the Franks in Palestine but, according to the French historian Michaud, "the Mussalmans respected their pledged faith, whilst the Christians gave a signal for a new war". Contrary to the terms of the truce, the Christian Ruler Renaud or Reginald of Chatillon attacked a Muslim caravan passing by his castle, massacred a large number of people and looted their property. The Sultan was now free to act. By a skilful manoeuvre, Salahuddin entrapped the powerful enemy forces near the hill of Hittin in 1187 A.C. and routed them with heavy losses. The Sultan did not allow the Christians to recover and rapidly followed up his victory of Hittin. In a remarkably short time he reoccupied a large number of cities which were in possession of the Christians, including Nablus, Jericho, Ramlah, Caesarea, Arsuf, Jaffa and Beirut. Ascalon, too, submitted after a short siege and was granted generous terms by the kind-hearted Sultan.

The Sultan now turned his attention to Jerusalem which contained more than sixty thousand Crusaders. The Christians could not withstand the onslaught of Sultan's forces and capitulated in 1187. The humanity of the Sultan towards the defeated Christians of Jerusalem procures an unpleasant contrast to the massacre of Muslims in Jerusalem when conquered by the Christians about 90 years before.

According to the French historian Michaud, on the conquest of Jerusalem by the Christians in 1099 A.C., "the Saracens were massacred in the streets and in the houses. Jerusalem had no refuge for the vanquished. Some fled from death by precipitating themselves from the ramparts, others crowded for shelter into the palaces, the towers, and above all in the mosques, where they could not conceal themselves from the pursuit of the Christians. The Crusaders, masters of the Mosque of Umar, where the Saracens defended themselves for sometime, renewed their deplorable scenes which disgraced the conquest of Titus. The infantry and cavalry rushed pell-mell among the fugitives. Amid the most horrid tumult, nothing was heard but the groans and cries of death; the victors trod over heaps of corpses in pursuing those who vainly attempted to escape. Raymond d'Agiles, who was an eye-witness, says, 'that under the portico of the Mosque, the blood was knee-deep, and reached the horses' bridles".

There was a short lull in the act of slaughter when the Crusaders assembled to offer their thanks giving prayer for the victory they achieved. But soon it was renewed with great ferocity. "All the captives", says Michaud, "whom the lassitude of carnage had at first spared, all those who had been saved in the hope of a rich ransom, were butchered in cold blood. The Saracens were forced to throw themselves from the tops of towers and houses; they were burnt alive; they were dragged from their subterranean retreats, they were haled to the public places, and immolated on piles of the dead. Neither the tears of women nor the cries of little children, not the sight of the place where Jesus Christ forgave his executioners, could mollify the victors' passion. . . . . . The carnage lasted for a week. The few who escaped were reduced to horrible servitude".

Another Christian historian, Mill adds: "It was resolved that no pity should be shown to the Mussalmans. The subjugated people were, therefore, dragged into the public places, and slain as victims. Women with children at their breast, girls and boys, all were slaughtered. The squares, the streets and even the un-inhabited places of Jerusalem, were strewn with the dead bodies of men and women, and the mangled limbs of children. No heart melted in compassion, or expanded into benevolence".

These are the graphic account of the massacre of Muslims in Jerusalem about 90 years before the reoccupation of the Holy city by Sultan Salahuddin in which more than seventy thousand Muslims perished.

On the other hand, when the Sultan captured Jerusalem in 1187 A.C. he gave free pardon to the Christians living in the city. Only the combatants were asked to leave the city on a payment of nominal ransom. In most of the cases the Sultan provided the ransom money from his own pocket and even provided them transport. There is a number of weeping Christian women carrying their children in their arms approached the Sultan and said: "You see us on foot, the wives, mothers and daughters of the warriors who are your prisoners; we are quitting for ever this country; they aided us in our lives, in losing them we lose our last hope; if you give them to us, they can alleviate our miseries and we shall not be without support on earth". The Sultan was highly moved with their appeal and set free their men. Those who left the city were allowed to carry all their bag and baggage. The humane and benevolent behaviour of the Sultan with the defeated Christians of Jerusalem provides a striking contrast to the butchery of Muslims in this city at the hands of the Crusaders, 90 years before. The Commanders under the Sultan vied with each other in showing mercy to the defeated Crusaders.

The Christian refugees of Jerusalem were not given refuge by the cities ruled by the Christians. "Many of the Christians who left Jerusalem", says Mill, "went to Antioch but Bohemond not only denied them hospitality, but even stripped them. They marched into the Saracenian country, and were well received". Michaud gives a long account of the Christian inhumanity to the Christian refugees of Jerusalem. Tripoli shut its gates on them and, according to Michaud, "one woman, urged by despair, cast her infant into the sea, cursing the Christians who refused them succour". But the Sultan was very considerate towards the defeated Christians. Respecting their feeling, he did not enter the city of Jerusalem until the Crusaders had left.

From Jerusalem, the Sultan marched upon Tyre, where the ungrateful Crusaders pardoned by Sultan in Jerusalem had organised to meet him. The Sultan captured a number of towns held by the Crusaders on the sea coast, including Laodicea, Jabala, Saihun, Becas, Bozair and Derbersak. The Sultan had set free Guy de Lusignan on promise that he would instantly leave for Europe. But, as soon as this ungrateful Christian Knight got freedom, he broke his pledged word and collecting a large army, laid siege to Ptolemais.

The fall of Jerusalem into the hands of Muslims threw Christendom into violent commotion and reinforcements began to pour in from all parts of Europe. The Emperors of Germany and France as well as Richard, the Lion-hearted, King of England, hurried with large armies to seize the Holy Land from the Muslims. They laid siege to Acre which lasted for several months. In several open combats against the Sultan, the Crusaders were routed with terrible losses.

The Sultan had now to face the combined might of Europe. Incessant reinforcements continued pouring in for the Crusaders and despite their heavy slaughter in combats against the Sultan, their number continued increasing. The besieged Muslims of Acre, who held on so long against the flower of European army and who had been crippled with famine at last capitulated on the solemn promise that none would be killed and that they would pay 2,00,000 pieces of gold to the Chiefs of the Crusaders. There was some delay in the payment of the ransom when the Lion-hearted King of England butchered the helpless Muslims in cold blood within sight of their brethren.

This act of the King of England infuriated the Sultan. He vowed to avenge the blood of innocent Muslims. Along the 150 miles of coastlines, in eleven Homeric battles, the Sultan inflicted heavy losses on the Christian forces.

At last the Lion-hearted King of England sued for peace, which was accepted by the Sultan. He had found facing him a man of indomitable will and boundless energy and had realised the futility of continuing the struggle against such a person. In September 1192 A.C. peace was concluded and the Crusaders left the Holy Land with bag and baggage, bound for their homes in Europe.

"Thus ended the third Crusade", writes Michaud, "in which the combined forces of the West could not gain more than the capture of Acre and the destruction of Ascalon. In it Germany lost one of its greatest Emperors and the flower of its army. More than six lakh Crusaders landed in front of Acre and hardly one lakh returned to their homes. Europe has more reasons to wail on the outcome of this Crusade as in it had participated the best armies of Europe. The flower of Western chivalry which Europe was proud of, had fought in these wars".

The Sultan devoted the rest of his life to public welfare activities and built hospitals, schools, colleges and mosques all over his dominions.

But he was not destined to live long to enjoy the fruits of peace. A few months after he died on March 4, 1193 at Damascus. "The day of his death" says a Muslim writer, "was, for Islam and the Mussalmans, a misfortune such as they never suffered since they were deprived of the first four Caliphs. The palace, the empire, and the world was overwhelmed with grief, the whole city was plunged in sorrow, and followed his bier weeping and crying".

Thus died Sultan Salahuddin, one of the most humane and chivalrous monarchs in the annals of mankind. In him Nature had very harmoniously blended the benevolent and merciful heart of a Muslim with a matchless military genius. The messenger who took the news of his death to Baghdad brought the Sultan's coat of mail, his horse one dinar and 36 dirhams which was all the property he had left. His contemporaries and other historians are unanimous in acknowledging Salahuddin as a tender-hearted, kind, patient, affable person, a friend of the learned and the virtuous whom he treated with utmost respect and beneficence. "In Europe", says Phillip K. Hitti, "he touched the fancy of English minstrels as well as modern novelists and is still considered paragon of chivalry".

# MUHAMMAD, THE CONQUEROR

A breathless Europe in May 1453 watched with amazement a young man of 21 riding his white charger through a gap into the impregnable walls of Constantinople, one of the most beautiful and well-protected cities of the world. This young man was Muhammad II, Seventh Ruler of the Ottoman dynasty. His army which was supported by a strong infantry swept everything before it as it rushed towards the city.

Constantinople had defied repeated attempts to capture it. This historic city that straddles Europe and Asia had been a prize for conquerors ever since mariners founded it, 700 years before Christ. Spread over seven hills like Rome, and overlooking the magnificent Bosphorus, it is the most impressively situated city in the world, protected on one side by the strait of Dardenelles and on the other by the strait of Bosphorus.

The Holy Prophet of Islam had prophesied its conquest by Muslims. It was first invaded during the Caliphate of Ameer Mauawiya, the first Umayyad Caliph. In this campaign the celebrated Companion of the Prophet Hazrat Ayub Ansari lost his life. The ill-fated and chivalrous Ottoman Ruler, Bayazid Yildirim, who had inflicted a memorable defeat on the combined forces of Europe at the gates of Vienna had almost captured it. The Byzantian Emperor had promised to surrender it to him if he would overcome his formidable foe Tamerlane, the great Tatar conqueror. Since Bayazid was defeated by Tamerlane, its capitulation could not be accomplished at that time.

It appeared as if Destiny had ordained that Muhammad II should conquer it, and thus realise the prophecy made by the Prophet of Islam eight centuries ago.

Muhammad II, better known as Muhammad Fateh (conqueror), son of Turkish Emperor Murad II, was born in April 1429. During the lifetime of his father he was posted as Governor of Maghaisa. He ascended the throne in 1451 and died in 1481.

His father's last days became a period of untiring and continued conquest under the leadership of Muhammad II which made possible the enormous expansion of Ottoman Empire during the 16th century.

The young Ottoman Ruler, Muhammad II, speaking five languages, was well versed both in arts of peace and war. He was fully conscious of the formidable task which he had resolved to accomplish—the capture of a strategically situated impregnable city which had defied conquerors for centuries and which, at that time, was defended by the combined forces of the Eastern and Southern European states.

The Sultan set up a foundry at Edirne which started turning out excellent weapons of war, including a huge cannon which fired stone balls weighing more than 1,300 pounds for a mile or more.

In the beginning of 1453, the Turkish troops advanced towards their objective, capturing towns and villages close to the historic city. The Sultan encamped five miles from the city walls and implanted the Turkish standard on the gates of St. Romanus. The memorable siege of Constantinople began on April 6, 1453.

The great cannon hurled stones against the walls and the batteries blasted the fortifications. But the damage done was repaired during the night by the capable defenders.

The Sultan brought another weapon in the battle field. It was a wooden turret, set on wheels which served as a small movable fortress and from its interior the Turkish soldiers discharged their volleys through the loopholes.

The siege had hardly entered the third week when reinforcements for the Byzantine defenders arrived. The barges of Venice were seen on the horizon, leading towards the Byzantine city. The Turkish fleet intercepted the Venetian ships. Ships of the two fleets rammed each other and the sailors also grappled with one another in hand to hand fight.

The Venetian Fleet managed to pass through the city and join the defenders. The Turkish fleet withdrew. It seemed that the Old Turkish proverb proved true once more : "If the earth is the Turks, the sea is the enemy".

The Turkish Sultan now realised that the conquest of the city was impossible unless it was attacked both from the sea and the land. The approach to the city from the seaside was easier but it was blocked by the powerful Venetian and Byzantine fleets.

Muhammad II, thereupon, thought out a bold and courageous plan of sending the ships into the blocked harbour, not by sea but by land. A ten-mile wooden road was laid by fixing together strong wooden planks which were made slippery with the fat of sheep and oxen. Eighty light galleys and brigantines were arranged on rollers which were drawn forward by a chosen team of men supported by horses and oxen. These galleys were manned by selected Turkish warriors.

It was undoubtedly one of the most remarkable and unique plans in the history of naval warfare. The Turkish gallies when let down into the waters of the Golden Horn, took the defenders of the doomed city by surprise.

The next day started the memorable battle in which the Turkish soldiers, galleys and artillery all joined in a thunderous firing on the historic city. The Turkish Sultan, sitting on his white charger, with mace in hand, directed the operations. The cry of *"Allah-o-Akbar"* (God is Great) rent the air and excited the Turks to deeds of valour.

Suddenly a small Turkish column, led by the valiant Hasan, moved forward amidst a shower of stones and fire. Hasan and his few companions started scaling the walls, only to be hurled back by the infuriated defenders. This act of exceptional courage by Hasan, electrified the Turks who surrounded the impregnable walls of the historic city. Ladders were set up all over. Before the defenders could realise what had happened, the Turkish troops were driving them from the summit. The historic city, which defied conquerors for centuries, had at last fallen to the Turks.

Muhammad II entered the historic city followed by his crack army. His first thought was the Byzantine Emperor and he gave orders for a thorough search for him. But, soon he learnt that he was killed by an ambitious soldier. Sultan Muhammad was deeply moved at the death of the last Byzantine Emperor who was given a royal burial.

The next day, the Archbishop of the Greek Church was searched out and brought before the victorious Sultan who received him with all honours and placed in his hands the traditional insignia of office.

Soon the Christian residents of the historic city learnt that they were the subjects of a Ruler who did not make religious distinction among them.

After the fall of Constantinople, the Sultan embarked upon a glorious career of conquest. He obtained success in Serbia and Morea in 1454, and captured Ainos and the island of Lemnos near the Aegean coast. During 1458-59, Serbia was made an Ottoman Province. In 1461 Amasra was taken from the Genoese and Sinub from the last Isfandiyar Oghlu. Trebizond was also captured. The years 1463-64 were mainly occupied by the annexation of Bosnia. A war started with Venice in 1463 which lasted for 17 years. In 1466, the Sultan was successful in Albania and fortified the town of Ilbasan.

The Sultan won the great victory of Erzindjan in 1473 and captured Cilicia in 1474.

The next six years saw the Sultan occupied with the conquest of Europe. He built the fortresses of Sabacs near Belgrade and made incursions into Hungary and Austria. In 1476, he captured Kaffa from the Genoese. In 1476 he was successful in Maldavia. The Tatar Khanate of Crimea offered submission to Ottoman suzerainty. The Sultan's fleet captured Ionian islands in 1479.

He was occupied with his enterprising Asiatic campaign when he died at Takpur Cayiri on May 3, 1481, and was buried in Constantinople.

Muhammad II was a great and humane conqueror. He built many magnificent edifices, including castles on the Dardenelles and other works of naval and military importance. He was an outstanding military administrator as well as a great patron of art and literature.

# YUSUF IBN TASHFIN

In the realm of chivalry. Muslims stand matchless in the world. In the days of their glory Khalid bin Waleed defeated a crack Roman army of 60 thousand soldiers with sixty men only, and during the time of their decline Mustafa Kamal of Turkey in 1923 chased out of Anatolia, a much superior and well-armed Greek army with a few thousand ill-equipped Turks.

During the last quarter of the 11th century A.C., Muslim power in Spain was at its lowest ebb. The country had been split up into small Muslim principalities, governed by rulers who were engaged in mutual disputes. On the other hand, Christian Rulers of Southern France and Northern Spain were united and conspired to wipe out the Muslim power from Spain. Having annexed a few Muslim states, they looked forward to conquering the rest of them.

Realising this danger. Mutamid, the King of Seville, invited Yusuf ibn Tashfin, the Head of a rising Muslim power in North Africa to save the Peninsula from Christian hordes.

Yusuf ibn Tashfin was a capable and valorous head of Almoravides, a religious sect which ruled over a large territory of North-Western Africa.

The Almoravides were originally a religious military brotherhood established in the middle of the 11th century by a pious Muslim in West Africa. The Berbers of the Sahara who had been converted to Islam had joined it in large numbers. Under their spiritual leaders, bearing the title of Marbut or Saints, they conquered vast territories and became a formidable power in North-Western Africa.

In 1061 Yusuf bin Tashfin became the spiritual and political leader of the Almoravides. he was a very gallant and capable ruler, who is recognised as the main builder of the Almoravide Empire. He extended his territories in Central and Western Africa. He founded in 1062, the city of Marakash, which became his and his successors' Capital. The Caliph of Baghdad recognising his services to Islam conferred on him the proud title of *Ameer-ul-Muslimeen* (Commander of the Muslims).

Yusuf ibn Tashfin and his successors acknowledged the authority of the Caliph of Baghdad in spiritual matters. For more than half a century, the Moravide power was supreme in North Africa and Southern Spain.

The Kingdom of Granada was constantly harassed by the Christian kingdoms of the North, specially by Alfonso VI, who styled himself as Emperor. A few Muslim princes had allied themselves with him. His raids into Muslim territories had become regular and reached as far south as Cadiz. He was working under a plan to wipe out Muslims from Spain.

The danger that loomed large obliged Mutamid, the King of Seville to invite Yusuf ibn Tashfin to meet this impending danger to Muslim power in Spain. Yusuf accepted the invitation landed in Spain and marched unopposed towards the North. Enroute he was joined by Mutamid and the forces of other Muslim princes and now their united army which numbered 20 thousand soldiers, marched towards Badajoz in the North. Alfonso VI with 60 thousand seasoned soldiers met the Muslim army at Zallaka. A frightful battle started on October 23, 1086 in which the Muslims inflicted a humiliating defeat on the Christians. The Christian monarch with only 300 horsemen escaped. His large army perished in the battle-field. This brilliant victory of Yusuf ibn Tashfin achieved at a time when Muslim power in Spain was at its nadir once more established the supremacy of Islamic arms. A wave of enthusiasm swept through Muslim Spain and proud Yusuf, not understanding the panegyric of Andaulsian poets expressed in flowery Arabic, returned to Africa according to his promise.

A few years after Yusuf returned to Spain. He wanted to govern Muslim Spain himself rather than leave it to incompetent and pleasure loving Muslim rulers and thus expose this great Muslim country to the raids of Christian hordes. Accordingly, he annexed Southern and Central Spain and incorporated it with the Almoravide Empire. The 'Faqihs' or religious heads exercised great influence under the Almoravide sovereigns.

Yusuf ibn Tashfin proved himself a capable Administrator. He ruled with a firm but just hand. He was great both in peace and war. He was feared, loved and respected.

Yusuf ibn Tashfin died in 1106 A.C. after a glorious reign lasting for about half a century (1061–1106).

# KHAIRUDDIN BARBAROSSA

The great Ottoman Empire which wielded considerable military and political power during the 14–17 centuries A.C., was supreme in the three known continents—Europe, Asia and Africa. Its vast dominions which included the major parts of South—Eastern Europe, West Asia and North Africa, stretched from the gates of Vienna in the West to the wall of China in the East and from Ukraine (USSR) in the North to the source of the Nile in the South.

The Turks were the masters of both land and sea. Their invincible armies stormed the capitals of Hungary and Austria, while their navy commanded by Barbarossa, chased the Genoese and Spanish fleets in the Mediterranean.

The Muslims had mainly been a land power. The Ummayads, the Abbasides, the Fatimides and the Moors of Spain, were, in their days of glory, supreme on land, but had paid less attention towards the development of their naval power. The Turks were the first Muslim nation to realise the importance of naval warfare. Their supremacy over the Mediterranean owes its establishment to the able command of the Barbarossa, who made the Turks the masters of the seas.

A number of stories are told about the origin of the Barbarossa. Yaqub, the father of the celebrated Barbarossa brothers, was probably a Greek Christian who embraced Islam. "In the year 1474", states the author of *"Russo–Turkish War"*, a humble potter in the island of Mitylene—a Greek Christian—had a son born to him who was destined, after becoming a Muhammadan, to re-establish the supremacy of Muslim power on the Southern coast of the Mediterranean. The youth, when twenty, changed his religion and took the name of "Horush". He was popularly known as "Baba Horush" on account of his red beard, and hence on account of this was called Barbarossa by the sailors of the Christian powers for whom he had become the "terror of the seas" *(Russo–Turkish War)*. The author of the *History of the Turkish Rule in Africa*, Captain Walsin Esterhazy also corroborates the above statement and accepts "Barbarossa" (red haired) as the mispronouncement—of the words "Baba Arouj" (Horush). According to the *Encyclopaedia Britannica*, "the contemporary Arab Chronicle published by S. Rang and F. Davis in 1837 says explicitly that Barbarossa was the name given by the Christians to Khairuddin. The founder of the family was Yaqub, a Roumaliot, probably of Albanian blood who settled in Mitylene after its conquest by the Turks. He had four sons, Elias, Arouj, Isaac and Khizr". Arouj and Khizr are called Horush and Khairuddin respectively.

Anyway, it has been established through historical records that the celebrated Barbarossa brothers were born of a Muslim father, who was a convert to Islam.

The Barbarossas came into limelight with the naval exploits of the elder brother in the Mediterranean. He was assisted in his adventures by his later more famous brother Khairuddin. They were a terror for the Christian naval fleets of Genoa and Spain. The elder brother was soon made the Admiral of the Turkish fleet with its Headquarters at Goletta in the Mediterranean. The Turkish naval forces, soon joined by the Moorish adventurers, carried on their marauding expedition against the Spanish Armada.

The Moors who had added a golden chapter to the cultural history of the Mediaeval times and were, in a way, responsible for the renaissance of the Christian West, were at last expelled from Spain. Their expulsion from their homeland forms a very lamentable chapter of Mediaeval history. The downfall of Muslim power in Spain would have led to the conquest of the North African coast too by the rising power of the Spaniards had it not been checked by the ceaseless efforts of the Barbarossas, who enabled the Turks not only to extend their territory to the whole of North African coast up to the shores of the Atlantic but also establish their naval supremacy in the Mediterranean. Attempts were made even to recover the Iberian peninsula.

The Barbaroosa brothers were instrumental in the Ottomans exercising complete control over Morocco, Fez, Algeria, Tunis and Tripolis. The elder brother who commanded the Turkish fleet "was the dismay of the European merchant vessels trading from port in those regions". He assisted the Algerians in turning out the Spaniards from Al-Gezirah. In 1512 he tried to capture Bougel from the Spaniards and in 1514 he seized Jijalli from the Genoese. In 1516 he became a semi-independent Ruler of the North-West African States under the Turkish Emperor. He extended his territories up to Fez. He inflicted several crushing defeats on the powerful Spanish fleet. The Spaniards were greatly alarmed at his growing power and he was killed in 1518 in a fierce engagement with the Spaniards at Rio Salado.

Khairuddin Barbarossa, a man of great talent and ability, succeeded his elder brother. His knowledge of naval strategy soon made him a terror for the rival naval powers in the Mediterranean. He was appointed as the Admiral of the Turkish fleet by Sulaiman, the Mangificent, Emperor of Turkey. In 1519 he was recognised by the Turkish Emperor as the Governor-General of Algeria. He captured Tunis in 1534.

Khairuddin Barborossa soon made Turkey the foremost naval power in the Mediterranean. "From this time", states the author of *"Russo–Turkish War"*, "the Turkish power on the northern coast of Africa was so strongly consolidated that none of the European nations could compete with it".

His sole ambition was the recovery of the lost Iberian peninsula for which he strove till his last. His short term is marked by his incessant efforts to achieve his goal. In this respect he was challenged by the two most powerful naval powers of the time—the Spaniards and the Genoese. Had he lived a few more years he would have certainly fulfilled his ambition. During his lifetime, he had fully established complete Turkish naval supremacy over the Mediterranean. He was a terror for the ports lying on the Northern Mediterranean coasts. He was a constant dread for the enemy ships. He attacked the powerful fleet of Emperor Charles of Spain and seized several coastal towns from his Admiral. He also invaded the coast of Italy. In 922 A.H. a naval battle was fought between France and Spain in which Khairuddin Barbarossa coming to the help of the French captured Corfu island and all islands of the Aegean sea which were in possession of Venice. Thus Turkish domination extended over the Aegean sea and up to the coast of Italy.

In 995 A.H., the Pope made a "holy alliance" with Spain, Hungary and Venice against Turkey, with the sole aim of crushing its naval power in the Mediterranean. Their powerful combined fleet under the celebrated Spanish Admiral Mendoza challenged the Turkish fleet in the Mediterranean. A bloody battle was fought in which the combined enemy fleet had to retreat with heavy losses. Khairuddin Barbarossa won a memorable naval victory. He captured several islands in the Mediterranean.

With the assistance of Khairuddin Barbarossa, the French captured the Spanish port of Niece. In recognition of their valuable assistance, the French gave the port of Toulon to the Turks.

Admiral Barbarossa planned to conquer the Iberian peninsula by capturing Gibraltar. He wanted to enter Spain through the same route which was taken by the Muslim Conqueror, Tariq. With a foothold on Gibraltar, he planned to make a thrust into the heart of the peninsula. But due to his other preoccupations his plan could not materialise for quite a long time. Meanwhile, the Spaniards made full preparations to meet Khairuddin Barbarossa on their soil. Gibraltar, which they had fully fortified.

At last the fateful day arrived. On August 20, 1540, Barbarossa invaded Gibraltar. It was a well fortified town; the Spaniards mustered all their forces to meet the Muslims. They had even recalled Don Bernardio den Mendoza from Sicily to replace Admiral Don Alvaro de Bazon. Barbarossa launched an attack with a fleet of 16 vessels, manned by a thousand sailors and 2,000 fighters. In less than 10 days he gained a foothold on the coast of Gibraltar.

The Spaniards could hardly stand the fierce Turkish onslaught and were forced to shut themselves in the city. They could not face the forces of Barbarossa in the open field.

"The inhabitants, terrified and unable to resist the furious energy of the blood thirsty Corsairs shut themselves in the city" *(History of Gibraltar—Soyer, 1862, London).* But, at last the siege had to be called off due to lack of adequate supplies and land support.

Khairuddin Barbarossa died in 1546. His dream of the conquest of Iberian peninsula could not be realised but he earned an immortal place in the annals of naval warfare as the man who made Turkey the foremost maritime power of his time. His name has been immortalised in the ballads of Don Quixote.

His 14 years of Admiralty of the Turkish fleet added a golden chapter to the annals of Islam. For a pretty long time it had been a practice of the Turkish fleet to fire salvoes as a mark of respect to the memory of Khairuddin Barbarossa while sailing off from the Golden Horn.

# AHMAD SHAH ABDALI

On the assassination of Nadir Shah in 1747, his vast Empire lay crumbling to pieces.

The representatives of the principal Jirgas of Afghanistan assembled at the shrine of Sher-Surkh (Red Lion) at Qandhar to elect a king. Among the aspirants were a number of elderly Chieftains, who commanded much respect and influence. But, despite its eight meetings, the jirga could not come to a unanimous decision. At the 9th meeting Sabir Shah, a universally respected saint proposed the name of a comparatively less known young man, hardly 25 years of age. This was Ahmad Khan, who had been second in command of the Afghan contingent and was Commandant of Nadir Shah's bodyguard. The choice was warmly welcomed by all and Ahmad Khan, a member of a sub-tribe of Abdailis who combined in himself the rare qualities of valour with cool headedness, firmness with kind heartedness and administrative ability with foresight, was assigned the task of guiding the ship of Afghans through the turbulent seas.

The coronation of Ahmad Khan was a simple affair. It was not attended by the usual pomp and pageantry. A spring of wheat was tucked into the turban of the King elect by the celebrated saint Sabir Shah who thereafter, came to be known as Ahmad Shah, the King of Afghans.

Ahmad Shah more than justified his selection. He not only united into a strong nation, the warring Afghan tribes, and governed them under a wise administration but also established a vast Afghan Empire, which on his death in 1773, extended from the Oxus to Oman on one side and from the highlands of Tibet to the shores of the Indian ocean, on the other. Simple and virtuous, courageous and farsighted, Ahmad Shah who emerged at a critical period of Muslim history was the man who changed the history of the subcontinent. It was a time when Muslim India was at its lowest ebb and the dominating Marhatta power was threatening the dwindling Mughal Empire of Delhi and the small Muslim States of Northern India. Ahmad Shah's victory in the Third Battle of Panipat in 1761 over much superior forces and against heavy odds, foiled for ever the dream of Hindu domination over the subcontinent and once more turned the scale in favour of Muslims.

Ahmad Shah Abdali, was a simple, affable democratic ruler, who headed a

Representative Council of Nine who counselled him on all important matters of the State. His just administration and virtuous life had earned for him the nickname of "Ahmad Shah Baba" (Ahmad Shah, the father of Afghans) and he was revered like a saint by his people.

Ahmad Khan was born in 1723 A.C. at Multan. His early life was full of trials and tribulations. His father Zaman Khan, the ruler of Herat, died when Ahmad was very young. His elder brother Zulfiqar ruled over Herat, when Nadir Shah stormed the city. Zulfiqar heroically defended the city for five months, but had to flee due to the intrigues and conspiracies of another Abdali Chieftain.

Zulfiqar, along with his young brother Ahmad, took refuge with the ruler of Qandhar, who, however, imprisoned both. They were exiled to Mazandran in Iran after the fall of Qandhar to Nadir Shah. There Zulfiqar died soon afterwards.

On Nadir Shah's return after his campaigns in Afghanistan, subcontinent and Turkistan, Ahmad Khan, a young lad of 16, offered himself for military service. Nadir Shah, impressed by his youthful personality, offered him an officer's rank in his Afghan Contingent. The young Afghan soon distinguished himself in the Caucasian campaigns with valour and devotion. The great conqueror, Nadir Shah, was so much impressed by him that, according to the author of *"Siraj-ut-Tarikh"*, he used to admit that throughout his long campaigns he had not come across a more gallant and nobler person than Ahmad Khan.

On the assassination of his patron Nadir Shah, Ahmad protected his family from annihilation at the risk of his own life.

Ahmad Khan had become orphan at a very early age. His virtuous mother Zarghuna Bibi to whom he was very much devoted, had played a great part in building his gallant and noble character. She guided him even when he had become a King.

Qandhar was razed by Nadir Shah and when, later on, Ahmad Shah wanted to rebuild it, he had planned to build a moat around it. When Zarghuna Bibi came to know of it, she sent him a letter stating that, "It does not become of you to build a moat, because thereby you betrary the fear that the enemy might come up as far your Capital". On receiving the letter, the obedient son gave up the idea of building a moat.

During Ahmad Shah's Indian campaign a rumour had been set afloat that Abdali had been defeated and made to flee by the Marhattas. On hearing this news, Zarghuna Bibi exclaimed, "It is impossible. Ahmad would die rather turn his back".

Ahmad Shah Abdali, the hero of Panipat, was one of the most gallant and chivalrous monarchs of the 18th century. His courage, military prowess and virility have few parallels in the living history. Few warrior kings have been more chivalrous and at the same time more human. In his account of the *"Kingdom of Caboul"*, Mountstuart Elphinston states: "His (Ahmad Shah Abdali's) military courage and activity are spoken of with admiration both by his nation and the nations with whom he was engaged in war or alliances. He seems to have been naturally disposed to mildness and clemency and though it is impossible to acquire sovereign power and perhaps in Asia to maintain it, without crimes, yet the memory of no Eastern prince is stained with fewer acts of cruelty and injustice. If ever an Asiatic king deserved the gratitude of his country, it was Ahmad Shah, the Pearl of Durranis. In his character, he seems to be cheerful, affable and good natured. He maintained considerable dignity on state occasions but at other times his manners were plain and familiar. He was himself a divine and an author and was always ambitious of the character of a saint".

Unquestionably the unification of the warring and rival tribes of Afghans into a strong nation was a great achievement of Ahmad Shah Abdali, but his greatest achievement was his resounding victory in the Third Battle of Panipat in 1761 against the formidable Marhatta forces, which changed the course of history in the subcontinent. At a time when Muslim India faced its greatest threat in history and the swarming Marhattas were out to overrun the dwindling Mughal Empire and the Muslim States of Northern India, Ahmad Shah Abdali appeared on the Indian scene. With barely sixty thousand soldiers he inflicted a crushing defeat on the Marhatta force of about half a million soldiers, backed by a powerful artillery. After a battle lasting for days, the Marhattas were made to flee, leaving 200 thousand dead on the battle-field and the jewels of their army perished in the encounter. The ignominious defeat suffered by the Marhattas in the Third Battle of Panipat broke the heart of their Supreme Head and frustrated their rising ambition. Their dream of domination over India could not be realised.

His memorable victory at Panipat is a lasting tribute to his chivalry, valour and military genius. He saved Islam in India at a critical juncture of its history. He was requested to accept the throne of Delhi, but he declined the offer stating that his assistance in the battle was not due to any political ambition but the result of his desire to serve Islam. He set an example for all the conquerors of the world by showing exemplary clemency towards the 22,000 prisoners captured on the battle-field. He not only set them free but also gave them two rupees each *plus* clothing. Only Ibrahim Gardi, a mercenary adventurer who commanded the Marhatta artillery and one who proved a traitor to his community was ordered to be shot.

Ahmad Shah Abdali was endowed with unique physical prowess and power of endurance. Once he surprised the Sikh army at Sirhind by covering 135 miles on horseback in less than two days, which may be compared with the lightning marches of Attilla, Changiz, Caesar, Hulaku and Timur.

One aspect of his personality is not much known to the people. He was a Pushto poet of repute and a good writer of Arabic prose and poetry. Being hardly fond of usual princely hobbies of hunting, pleasure making and other frivolities, he devoted his spare time to literary pursuits. It is said that he attended a musical party only once in his lifetime. His poetry bristles with simplicity, sincerity and faith which are characteristics of his personality. His poems speak of virtue, ambition, sacrifice and nationalism.

A number of commentaries are extant on this less known aspect of his life. Muhammad Ghaus has written a 200-page Persian manuscript entitled *"Sharh al-Sharh"* on the Arabic prose and poetry of the great conqueror. The Kabul Academy at the instance of Mr. Daud Khan, at that time Prime Minister of Afghanistan, has published the Pushto Diwan of Ahmad Shah comprising 3,000 couplets, including *ghazals* and quatrains. It has been edited by the celebrated Pushto scholar, Abdul Haiy Habibi. A monograph on the life of the conqueror written by Mir Ghulam Muhammad Ghubar, which was to serve as an introduction to his Pushto Academy, was considered a bit lengthy and has been published separately by the Kabul Academy.

The real greatness of Ahmad Shah Abdali lies in his humane nature. He was great as a conqueror but greater still as a man. Few conquerors in the world possessed so much valour with so much humility. The brighter and more attractive side of his personality lies in his humility, forbearance, affability and above all humanity. He was chivalrous in the true sense of the word—one who combined valour with humanity in himself.

Ahmad Shah Abdali was a democratic ruler. He abhorred the usual pomp and pageantry practised by the monarchs of the world. He led a simple life—never wore a crown and never sat on a throne. He discarded the un-Islamic practice of obeisance in which the visitor used to kiss the floor or even the feet of the ruler.

There are numerous stories relating to his humility and kindness to his subordinates and subjects. The messenger who brought him the message seeking his help for saving Muslim India died in the battle of Panipat. Ahmad Shah Abdali accompanied by his dignitaries visited the house of the poor messenger to offer his personal condolence to his young widow and orphans and entrusted them to the care of the new Mughal Prime Minister.

At another occasion while he was camping a short distance from Qandhar, a sepoy taking advantage of the closeness of his family broke into his house. Instead of welcoming him, the wife of the sepoy rebuked him "How could you dare to come to your family when Ahmad Shah Baba is away from his house?" The sepoy again slipped away into the Imperial army. When Ahmad Shah came to know of the story, he greatly appreciated the spirit of the woman and awarded her a 'Karez', which is still known as 'Ainos Karez'.

With his sympathy and simplicity, magnanimity and affability Ahmad Shah Abdali had endeared himself to his subjects. He was admired not only as a humane and gallant ruler but also recognised as the father of Afghans and a saint.

His death in 1773 A.C. cast a gloom over his vast dominions—nay over the entire Islamic world. He had left behind him a strong nation of Afghans and a vast Empire extending from the banks of Oxus to Oman and from the highlands of Tibet to the shores of the Arabian Sea.

# HISTORIANS, GEOGRAPHERS
# AND EXPLORERS

# TABARI

Baghdad, the metropolis of Abbaside Caliphs and the dreamland of the *Arabian Nights* was the highest seat of learning in the world during the Mediaeval times. It had attracted within its portals some of the greatest minds of the age. There lived on one of its suburbs an old man of Turkish blood with sparse beard and good physique. One evening, a stately procession, followed by a large retinue, stopped at his humble cottage.

Soon after the highest dignitary of the state, the Grand Vizier of the Abbaside Caliphate was brought into the presence of an old man, who was absorbed in his study.

This old man was Tabari, one of the greatest historians of Islam. The Caliph had offered him a handsome pension and sent costly presents in recognition of his contribution to Islamic learning. The celebrated historian refused to accept anything for his services to learning as he did not want to sell his pen.

The advent of Islam paved the way for the growth of historiography in Arabia. Arabs had great attachment for their ancestors and their past. They maintained the lineage of horses and camels even. The abundance of historical data in the Holy Quran provided a "practical incentive for the study of history for the followers of Islam".

The learned discourses of the Holy Prophet of Islam were always punctuated with historical references to the past, which awakened an interest hitherto unknown, for historiography among the adherents of the new faith. History is one of the most copious sections of the Arabic literature.

The German Orientalist Tenfeld collected more than 590 historical works in Arabic written during the first thousand years of the Islamic era. The writing of history commenced during the Umayyad period and was developed during the Abbaside times. The author of *Kashfuz Zunun* gives a long list of 1,300 historical books written in Arabic during the first few centuries of Islam. Only a few historical works of Umayyad period have survived.

The third century of Islamic era is a period of great intellectual attainments. It was in this period that some of the highest intellectual luminaries had risen on the horizon of Islamic learning, whose light guided the later writers in diverse branches of knowledge. Muhammad ibn Jarir Abu Jafar Al-Tabari (838–923 A.C.), was one of them and is today recognised as the father of Islamic History and one of the greatest historians that the world has produced.

Born at Amol in Tabaristan, the mountainous district of Persia, situated alongside the Caspian sea, Tabari is said to have learnt Quran by heart at the age of seven. He received his education at Rayy, Baghdad, Wasit, Basra, Kufa and Fustat (Old Cairo). He made extensive study tours of Persia, Iraq, Syria, Palestine, and Egypt in quest of knowledge and for collecting information for his monumental historical works. After his father's death, he was reduced to great poverty. On one occasion he had to sell the sleeves of his shirt in order to buy bread. Later he was appointed a tutor to the son of the Vizier Obaidullah ibn Yahya. His finances had now improved slightly. He journeyed to Egypt, but soon returned to Baghdad where he remained until his death as a teacher of Tradition and Islamic Law. His life was simple but dignified and was characterised by extreme diligence. According to Yaqut, for forty years Tabari wrote forty pages a day. Yaqut states that Tabari was contemplating to write two books—a history and a commentary of the Holy Quran of 30 thousand leaves (60 thousand pages) each, but his friends dissuaded him that human life would not be sufficient to undertake as well as go through such gigantic works. Hence, he reduced the two books to 1–10 of the original size, i.e. 3,000 leaves each.

Tabari lived for 85 years, died in 933 A.C. and was buried at Baghdad. Among his pupils was Ahmad ibn Kamil, the person to whom Miskawayah owed his guidance in history.

Among his works, the two most outstanding which influenced the later writers are (1) *The Exhaustive Commentary on Quran;* and (2) *Tarikh al-Rasool al Malik* (Annals of Apostles and Kings) which is his universal History. His commentary on Quran comprising about 3,000 leaves is a standard book, having the largest collection of exegetical traditions. "All the books were eclipsed by the annals of Tabari", adds *Encyclopaedia Britannica,.* "whose fame lasts up to the present time. The value of book is very great. The author's selection of tradition is usually happy and most important episodes were treated with most fulness of detail". Several translated and abridged edition of the *Annals* of Tabari have been published. One of these in 13 volumes was published in Lyden. His History *(Annals)* begins with the creation of the world and continues up to 302 A.H. (915 A.C.). This History which is renowned for its details and accuracy was edited by M. J. de Goeje and published in three series consisting of 13 volumes excluding two extra volumes meant for Indices, Introduction and Glossary. The Samanid Minister, Al-Balami had published an abridged Persian Edition of it. This was translated into French by H. Zotenberg.

Tabari's favourite method of presenting narrative is through Isnad. His chief sources of information were the earlier historical works of Ibn Ishaq, Kalbi, Ibn Saad and Moqaffa and Persian translations.

Writing about the *'Annals'* of Tabari, in his *'A History of Muslim Historiography'* Franz Rosenthal states: "Al Tabari's world history was incomparably more important than Al Yaqubi's who soon was all but forgotten. Tabari brought to his work the scrupulousness and indefatigable longwindedness of the theologian, the accuracy and love of order of the scholarly and the insight into political, justice affairs of the practising lawyer politician. All these were qualities which commended enduring and ever-increasing respect in the intellectual circles of orthodox Islam. It was, therefore, only natural that his historical work never ceased to exercise a tremendous influence upon future historians as a model of how history should be written.—The story of Muhammad (P.B.U.H.) follows the *sirah* "pattern".

The Arabic historical composition reached its zenith in Tabari and Masudi, who were pioneers in this branch of learning until the birth of Ibn Khaldun.

His second great work is his *Commentary on the Holy Quran* which comprising about 3,000 pages, is a standard book, having the largest collection of exegetical traditions. It is like *Annals,* known for the same fulness of details. This monumental work of Tabari was published in 30 volumes, excluding extra Index volume at Cairo in 1902-03. The size of this work and spirit of independence pervading it, provided a check to its popularity and wide circulation. This commentary has much influenced well-known scholars like Baghawi and Suyuti. An account of it with brief extracts has been given by O. Loth in the *'Zeitschrift der Deutscher Morgenlendischen Gesellschaft'.* Persian and Turkish translations of the commentary exist in manuscript.

His other works include his voluminous legal work *Ikhtilaf* comprising 3,000 leaves, his *Tahzibul Athar,* dealing with the traditions of the Prophet of Islam and *Al Basit* a juristic treatise. He had projected a third voluminous book, dealing with the traditions of the Companions of the Prophet of Islam, which could not be completed. A list of Tabari's minor works is given in *'Fihrist'.*

This influence of Tabari's historical works and commentary on Quran may be traced in later writers. The well-known historian Miskawayh is indebted for his historical knowledge to Ibn Kamil, the biographer and disciple of Tabari. His *Annals* was the greatest source of information and the most outstanding historical work till the birth of Ibn Khaldun. This was the chief source of guidance for such famous historians as Abul Fida, Ibn Athir, Miskawayah and Ibn Kamil. His annalistic method in the writing of History was followed by Al-Waqidi, Miskawayah, Ibn Athir and Abul Fida. His commentary on Holy Quran was studied and followed by Allama Suyuti and Baghawai. Thus Abu Jafar Al-Tabari, known as 'Livy of Arabs' and the father of Islamic History is one of the greatest historians of the Mediaeval times who paved the way for the gigantic growth of Muslim Historiography in the world.

# AL-MASUDI

The birth of Islam had opened a new vista for the enterprise of the Arabs and their conquests which swept over the three known continents during the early decades of Islamic power, procured a fresh stimulus to their adventurous spirit.

The stories of the famous Arabian Nights, including that of Sindbad the Sailor, give a glimpse of the adventures of those fearless Arabs. It provides a slightly coloured account of the great voyages undertaken by the Arab marines as early as the 1st century A.H., who, being undaunted by the perils en route, roamed about in stormy seas, reaching such distant lands as Ceylon Zanzibar, Maldives, Bering Strait, West Indies, Java and Sumatra.

The innovation of Mariners' compass opened vast oceans for their enterprising voyages. Mostly the European writers have credited the Chinese with the invention of the Mariners' compass, but, according to the famous orientalist George Sarton. "the Arabs were first to make the use of it, a fact which has been admitted by the Chinese themselves". Another well-known orientalist, Phillip K. Hitti, has endorsed the views expressed by George Sarton. According to a statement of Sir R. F. Burton, it even seems that Ibn Majid was venerated in the past on the African Coast as the inventor of the Compass.

Anyway, the practical use of the compass immensely contributed to the undertaking of distant voyages by the Arab sailors, who hitherto confined to coastal strips, now went out to open oceans and roamed about in the Atlantic as well as in the Pacific, circled the African continent and even touched the shores of the New World. The frail boats were replaced by larger sailing ships and the Arabs with the help of the compass and other marine instruments braved the stormy seas. The use of Mariners, compass thus revolutionised the oceanic shipping carried on by the Muslims during the Mediaeval times.

The golden period of Muslim geography, travels and exploration, runs from the 9th to the 14th century A.C., during which a vast amount of travel and geographical literature was produced in the world of Islam which ultimately paved the way for later explorations, and discoveries of the Christian West. Writing in the *"Legacy of Islam"*, J. H. Kramers says: "Europe ought to look upon them (Muslims) as its cultural ancestors in the domain of geographical knowledge, discovery and world trade. The influence which Islam has exercised on our modern civilization in the spheres of action can be seen in the many terms of Arabic origin which are to be found in the vocabulary of trade navigation. The measure of influence can only be proved by studying the historical development of the domain over which our actual geographical knowledge extends.

Among the versatile geniuses of the 10th century A.C., was Al-Masudi, a globe trotter, historian, geographer and physicist, who has left behind invaluable information on travels, history, geography, music and science.

Abul Hasan Ali ibn Husain al-Masudi was born at Baghdad towards the close of 9th century. He was a descendant of Hazrat Abdulla ibn Masud, the celebrated Companion of the Prophet of Islam. He was a Mutazilite Arab who spent the last 10 years of his life in Syria and Egypt. He died at Cairo in 957 A.C.

Masudi was a well-known writer and explorer of the East. He was still young, when he travelled through Persia and stayed in Istakhar for about a year in 915 A.C. Starting from Baghdad, he went to India in 916 A.C. visiting Multan, Mansura, returned to Persia and after touring Kerman went back to India.

Mansura was, in his time the most flourishing town of Western India and was the metropolis of the Muslim State of Sind. In his monumental work *'Muruj uz-Zahab'*, Masudi speaks very highly of this one-time great city. This city, according to him, was named after Mansoor ibn Jamhoor who was the Umayyad Governor of Sind. The city was situated on the bank of river Indus, somewhere near the present Hyderabad. Al-Masudi saw for the first time, eighty elephants in the stable of the Governor.

Mansura, the Capital of the prosperous Arab state, was inhabited by a large population of Syeds, the descendants of Caliph Ali. Long before the Muslim conquest, Masudi found several powerful colonies of converted Muslims in Central India ruled by Hindu Rajas. These converts had embraced Islam due to the missionary work of a number of Muslim saints who had visited Hindu India in the teeth of non-cooperation and stiff opposition. According to Masudi, the Hindu rulers at last yielded to the high character of the Muslim missionaries as well as of their followers and allowed them religious freedom. Some of the Hindu Rajas were so much influenced that they considered Muslims as a token of their good fortune.

Travelling through Cambay, Deccan and Ceylon, he, along with some other merchants, sailed to Indo—China and China. On his return trip, he visited Madagascar, Zanzibar, Oman and arrived in Basra where he settled down for sometime and wrote his great work, *Muruj-uz-Zahab* (Golden Meadows) in which he has narrated his personal experiences of different countries. In an inimitable manner which is enjoyed by the reader.

Masudi also visited the Southern Shore of the Caspian and travelled through Central Asia and Turkistan. He visited Tiberias and described the relics of the Christian Church there. He toured Gujrat in 303 A.H. He found Cham·ir, a port of Gujrat, inhabited by more than ten thousand Arabs and their descendants. He obtained first hand information, when necessary, from Jews, Persians, Indians and Christian Bishops. Leaving Basra and Syria, he returned to Fustat (Old Cairo), where he compiled his voluminous work, *Mirat-uz-Zaman* (Mirror of the Time) in 30 volumes in which he has elaborately dealt with the geography, history and life of the people of countries he had visited.

Masudi, after making an extensive tour of the East, settled down at Basra, where he penned his experiences in his immortal work, *Muruj-uz-Zahab wa Ma'adin-ul-Jawahir* (Meadows of Gold and Mines of Precious Stones). This was completed in 947 A.C. and in 956 A.C. he completed a second edition of this book. Its French translation in 9 volumes was published in Paris in 1861–77. Writing in his *History of the Arabs*, Phillip K. Hitti remarks: "In this encyclopaedic historio-geographical work, the author with catholicity and scientific curiosity, carried his researches beyond the typically Muslim subjects into Indo–Persian, Roman and Jewish History". He had a intimate knowledge of the rise and fall of the Nations which he had incorporated in his monumental work *Muruj-uz-Zahab*. The celebrated orientalist, George Sarton states about this book: "It is remarkable because of the catholicity of its author, who neglected no source of information and of his truly scientific curiosity". In his *Muruj-uz-Zahab* (Golden Meadows) "he tells the rich experiences of his life in the amicable and cheerful manner of a man who had seen various lands, experienced life in all its phases, and who takes pleasure, not only in instructing but also in amusing his reader. Without burdening him with the names of the authorities, without losing himself in long explanation, he delights in giving prominence to that which strikes him as w ⊃nderful, rare, and interesting and to portray people and manners with conciseness and anecdotic skill".

From Basra, he later moved to Fustat (Old Cairo) where he wrote his extensive work, *Kitab Akhbar-uz-Zaman* or *Mirat-uz-Zaman* (Mirror of Times); better known as *"Annals"*, in 30 volumes with a supplement, the *'Kitab-ul-Ausat'*, a chronological sketch of general history. This great work of Masudi was completed in 956 A.C. and is partially preserved.

His earlier work *Muruj-uz-Zahab*, completed the substance of the two parts of *Mirat-uz-Zaman*. His last work, written in the year of his death, is *Kitab-ut-Tanbih wal Ishraf"*. (The book of Indication and Revision), in which he summarised, corrected and completed his earlier works. This book was edited by M. J. Goeje and published in Leiden in 1894 A.C.

History being the favourite subject of the Muslims, they have made invaluable contributions to it and have produced such outstanding Historians as Tabri, Miskawayh, Masudi and Ibn Khaldun. Not only in history but also in almost all branches of learning, the Muslims made lasting contributions during

Mediaeval times. Writing in an *Introduction to the Study of Science,* George Sarton states: "The main task of mankind was accomplished by Muslims. The greatest philosopher, Al Farabi was a Muslim; the greatest Mathematicians, Abul Kamil and Ibrahim ibn Sinan were Muslims : the greatest geographer and encyclopaedist, Masudi was a Muslim; the greatest historian, al Tabari was also a Muslim".

Masudi, known as the "Herodotus and Pliny" of the Arabs, introduced the tropical method of writing history. He revolutionised the writing of history by introducing the critical study of historical events and instead of grouping his events around years he grouped them around dynasties—a treatment later followed and elaborated by Ibn Khaldun. He had a deep knowledge of the rise and fall of the innumerable dynasties of the world which he critically examined in his monumental historio-geographical works detailed above. Masudi was aware of his greatness as a historian. He says, "I have never come across a historian who had dealt with the subject of history in a manner as I have done". A comparison of my historical work with those of my predecessors would convince any reader of the validity of my statement.

He was very broad-minded and was one of the first to make good use of historical anecdotes. He had made an extensive study tour, wandered throughout the Islamic world in quest of first hand information which enabled him to write his great works, *Muruj-uz-Zahab* (Golden Meadows) and *Mirat-uz-Zaman* (Mirror of Times). His other notable work *"Al Tanbih wal Ishraf",* outlines his Theory of Evolution.

Masudi made invaluable contributions to Music and Science. He was a musical theorist of eminence. His *Muruj-uz-Zahab* contains interesting data on the early Arabian music. His other books deal with the music of foreign lands.

His historio-geographical works contain descriptions of the earthquake of 955 A.C., it also deals with the waters of the Dead Sea and other geological discussions. He made the earliest mention of the windmills in Sijistan which were probably the invention of Islamic people.

His immortal historical works were greatly instrumental in moulding the later historical writings. An account of his works is to be found in *de Sacy's Memoirs* and in *Geoje's* Preface to his edition of *Kitab al Tanbih wal Ishraf.* The *Tales of Caliph,* written by C. Field in 1909, is based on Masudi's works.

# IBN KHALDUN

Ibn Khaldun, the talented Muslim philosopher of history and the greatest intellect of his age, is one of the most outstanding thinkers that the world has ever produced. History, before Khaldun, was confined to the simple recording of events, without distinguishing between the probables and improbables.

Being the founder of the science of sociology, Ibn Khaldun had the unique distinction of treating history as a science and supporting his facts with reasoning. "There is nothing in the Christian literature of the Middle Ages" says a celebrated Western critic, "worthy of being compared with it (Khaldun's history) and no Christian historian wrote a version with such clearness and precision on any Muslim state".

Khaldun, whose origin may be traced to Yamanite Arabs of Hadramaut, was born in Tunis on May 27, 1332 A.C., where his family had settled, having migrated from Moorish Spain. Ibn Khaldun had a chequered career during his early life, taking active part in the intriguing power politics of the small North African principalities, enjoying alternately the favour and disfavour of the rulers and at times taking refuge in distant Granada. His revolutionary spirit, being fed up with the dirty politics of those times was obliged to take a short respite of about four years in the suburbs of Tunis, where he completed his immortal 'Prolegomena' in 1377 A.C. Thereafter he shifted to Tunis to finish his masterly work 'Kitab al-Ibar' (World History), where he could get reference books in the Imperial Library. After an eventful, adventurous life in North Africa, the great thinker sailed to Egypt in 1382 A.C.

His fame and outstanding work had preceded him in Egypt and he was warmly welcomed in the literary circles of Cairo where he was invited to deliver lectures at the famous Al Azhar Mosque. He was received by the King of Egypt, who appointed him the Maliki Judge. The intrigues and the rivalries of the Court, soon forced him down and he was appointed on the same post for six times, every time losing it.

Meanwhile, he had a chance of meeting the famous Tamerlane who had invaded Syria and had to make peace with the King of Egypt. The celebrated conqueror was highly impressed with the versatility and eloquence of Ibn Khaldun who, on his return, died in Cairo in 1406 A.C.

Ibn Khaldun has acquired an immortal place in the galaxy of historical philosophers. Before him, history was a mere chronicle of events, recorded in a haphazard manner without caring to distinguish between the real and unreal. Ibn Khaldun stands out quite distinct from the rest of the historians, because he treated history as a science and not merely a narrative. He wrote history in the light of his new method of explanation and reasoning and developed it as a social philosophy. Explaining the art of writing history, Ibn Khaldun says in *'Prolegomena'*: "It is only by an attentive examination and well sustained application that we can discover the truth, and guard ourselves against errors and mistakes. In fact, if we were merely to satisfy ourselves by reproducing the records transmitted by tradition without consulting the rules furnished by experience, the fundamental principles of the art of government, the nature, events, of the particular civilization, or the circumstances which characterise the human society; if we are not to judge of the events which occurred in distant times by those which are occurring under our eyes, if we are not to compare the past with the present, we can hardly escape from falling into errors and losing the way of Truth".

Being the originator of sociology, philosophical history and political economy, his works possess striking originality. *'Kitab-al-Ibar* including *Al Taarif'* is his immortal historical work which contains *'Prolegomena'* as well as his autobiography. He has divided his work in three parts. The first part known as his famous *'Prolegomena'* deals with society, its origin, sovereignty, birth of towns and villages, trades, means of livelihood and sciences. This is the best part of the book where the writer reaches the summits of creativeness, reviewing the diverse subjects like political economy, sociology and history with striking originality and brilliance. Some of the subjects dealt by Ibn Khaldun in *Prolegomena* were dealt with also by his predecessors, but he gave a more logical shape to his theories.

Farabi's statement about the origin of towns and villages is only theoretical, while Khaldun has viewed it from social point of view. According to Ibn Khaldun, the science of *'Al Umran'* (Sociology) did not exist before him. It was only superficially dealt in the *"Politics"* of Aristotle and the celebrated Tunisian might have gone through the commentary written by Ibn Rushd (Averroes) on Aristotlian works. The striking feature of the *Prolegomena,* is its theory of *'Al Asbiah'* which Ibn Khaldun has advanced about the nobility or influence of the lineage of nomadic tribes.

The third chapter dealing with the state and the sovereignty is the best part of the book, where the learned author has propounded his advanced political theories which were later on incorporated in the works of such celebrated political thinkers as Machiavelli and Vico. Like that of Ibn Khaldun, written in stormy times in Italy a century later, Machiavelli's *"Prince"* bears a close resemblance to the *Prolegomena,* and it is just probable that the famous Italian might have borrowed some of his ideas from the works of Ibn Khaldun. "At any rate", says Prof. Gumplowicz, "the priority must be rightly attributed to the

Arab sociologist as regards those counsels which Machiavelli, a century later, gave to the rulers in his *"Prince".* Colosia says, "If the great Florentine instructs us in the art of governing people, he does this as a far-sighted politician, but the learned Tunisian (Ibn Khaldun) was able to penetrate into the social phenomena as a profound economist and philosopher, a fact which urges us to see in his work such far-sightedness and critical art, as was totally unknown to his age".

Ibn Khaldun, whose keenness of observation is equalled by his versatility, sums up the qualities of a ruler in the following words. "The sovereign exists for the good of his people. The necessity of a ruler arises from the fact that human beings have to live together and unless there is someone to maintain order, society would break to pieces".

The second part of *'Kitab-al-Ibar',* which comprises four volumes, namely second, third, fourth and fifth, deals with the history of the Arabs and other Muslims as well as contemporary dynasties, including Syrians, Persians, Saljukids, Turks, Jews, Greeks, Romans and Franks. The real historical work begins with the second volume which deals with Jews, Greeks, Romans and Persians of the pre-Islamic period. The advent of Islam, the life of the Holy Prophet and the history of the Caliphate Rashidia (Four Caliphs) are dealt with in a special supplement to the second volume. The third volume, deals in detail with the Caliphate of Ummayads and Abbasides. The fourth contains the history of Fatimides in Egypt and of Moorish Spain up to the time of the Banu Ahymer dynasty. The fifth volume refers to the rise and fall of Saljuk power, the Crusades and the history of the Mamluk dynasty of Egypt up to the end of 8th century A.H. His sources, in this volume may be traced to the historical works of Ibn Hasham, Masoodi and Tabari.

The third part of his great historical work *'Kitab al-Ibar',* comprising two volumes, namely sixth and seventh, elaborately deals with the history of Berbers and other neighbouring tribes as well as contains the autobiography of the author, known as *'Al Taarif'.* The history of Berbers describes in much detail their origin, greatness, kingdom and dynasties in North Africa. The author having a first hand knowledge of the region and its inhabitants has masterly dealt with the subject matter which is very factual and precise. Ibn Khaldun has minimised the greatness of Arab achievements both in the domains of conquests and scholarship. On the other hand, he has boosted the qualities of Berbers, as he was born in the land of Berbers and he could not help being partial towards them who were ruled by the Arabs since the 1st century A.H. The sixth and the major part of the seventh volume of his book deals with the history of the Berbers.

*Kitab-al-Ibar,* has concluded with several chapters written about the author's own life and is known as *Al-Taarif* (Autobiography). This autobiography, which begins with his birth continues up to 797 A.H. There is another copy of *"Al-Taarif"* preserved in Egypt which relates the events of his life, till a few months before his death. Ibn Khaldun has adopted a more scientific method in the arrangement of autobiography which he has divided into chapters, connected with each other.

Before him autobiographies were usually written in a 'diary form', events having no connection with each other. Ibn Khaldun was the first to write a long systematic autobiography, while shorter autobiographies were written by his predecessors, including Al Khatib and Al Suyuti which were formal, hence insipid. The autobiography written by Ibn Khaldun is a frank confession of deeds and misdeeds of a dynamic personality expressed in a most impressive language. The author has portrayed his career with exceptional frankness and liberty, which has made his autobiography all the more interesting and appealing Moral lapses are not uncommon in great personalities and these, when viewed in the light of their achievements, lose their nasty significance whatsoever. The *Al Taarif* may be favourably compared with the autobiography of Benvenuti Cellini, the celebrated Italian Artist. Both have an air of frankness in them.

It was during the nineteenth century that the translations of his works in various European languages enabled the West to realise the greatness of the historian and appreciate the vigour and the originality of his thought. "Ibn Khaldun", writes D. Boer, "is undoubtedly the first who tried to explain fully the evolution and progress of society, as being caused by certain causes and factors, climate, the means of production, etc., and their effects on the formation of man's mind and sentiment as well as the formation of society. In the march of civilization he perceives an organised internal harmony".

Thus the enlightened West is immensely indebted to the learned Tunisian, for the lead given by him in diverse fields of sociology, historical and political economy which paved the way for later development in these sciences.

# IBN BATUTA

The Arabs were pioneers in the field of explorations and travels during the Middle Ages and had traversed vast tracts of land, crossed impassable deserts, combed inaccessible forests and sailed over endless oceans.

Their ships had touched the shores of the 'New World' five centuries before Columbus, and their ships passing through the Bering Strait had encircled the northern shores of the great land mass now called North America. But the greatest of all the travellers in Islam and one of the greatest of all times was Ibn Batuta who may favourably rank with Marco Polo, Hsien Tsieng, Drake and Magellan.

He was a contemporary of Marco Polo and was 20 years old when Marco died. In his 30 years travel, he covered more than 75,000 miles, a unique record in those times.

His wander lust led him to such far-flung countries as Spain and Indonesia, Central Asia and Central Africa. He chatted with the Caliph and beggars, feasted at palaces and slept at wayside inns, heard tales told by theologians and sailors, traders and pedlars and when he returned home he recorded his varied experiences in vivid memory.

It has now been established that he was the greatest traveller before the invention of steam and had covered the largest number of miles. 'It was estimated (by Sir Henry Yule 1820–89), writes George Sarton, "that he travelled by land and by sea about 75,000 miles, i.e. considerably more than Marco Polo or more than any other traveller before the age of steam and speed. He had visited all the Islamic lands, and in most cases met their rulers, and was recognised before his death as the Muslim traveller par excellence. Moreover, he had visited many non-Muslim countries, such as Caffa, Constantinople, parts of India, Ceylon and China".

Abu Abdullah Muhammad ibn Abdullah ibn Muhammad al-Lawati al-Tanj, widely known as Ibn Batuta, was born at Tangiers (North Africa) on February 24, 1304 A.C.

He came of the Berber Tribe of Lawata. While in India, he was known by the name of Maulana Badr al-Din. His family being well versed in Islamic jurisprudence, produced several Qazis (Judges).

Ibn Batuta, too was given religious and literary education. Prompted by an urge to perform the pilgrimage to Makkah, he left Tangiers on June 14, 1325 A.C. for the Holy cities. He was hardly 21 at that time.

Passing through Tunis and travelling mostly on foot, he felt his loneliness on Eid day in Tunis which moved the young traveller to tears. He returned home in 1349 A.C. but soon afterward set out again for the West. He returned again in 1354 A.C. and was warmly received by the Ruler who entrusted his Secretary to note down the account of his travel. He was later appointed Qazi in his native State and died in 1377-78 A.C.

Considering the difficulties of travels and lack of means of transport in those days, his is a unique record and no explorer or traveller during the Mediaeval times, had traversed so many miles during his lifetime. Starting from Tangier, he arrived in Alexandria on April 15, 1326.

Alexandria, according to him, was a flourishing port and was the important commercial and naval centre in the Eastern Mediterranean. The Sultan of Egypt helped him with presents and money. He set out for Makkah, and passing through Cairo he arrived in Aidhab which was an important port on the Red Sea near Aden. But finding this route infested with brigands he returned to Cairo and went to the Holy cities *via* Gaza, Jerusalem (Palestine) Hamah, Aleppo and Damascus (1326).

He reached Makkah in October, 1326. During the pilgrimage of the Holy cities, he met Muslims who had assembled for performing Hajj from all over the world. This stirred his imagination and produced a yearning in his ambitious heart to see the world.

He gave up the idea of returning home. He crossed the Arabian desert and after visiting Iraq and Iran (Persia) he again returned to Damascus which was once the populous Capital of the Umayyads, but the ravages of Tartar hordes had left deep scars on it. From Damascus he went to Mosul and then to Makkah where he performed his second pilgrimage and stayed there for three years (1328–30).

From there he took a boat for Aden, which was a great commercial port and had a good system of water-supply.

He sailed to Somaliland and thence to East African Coasts, including Zeila and Mombasa. Back to Aden and thence to Oman, Hurmuz (Persian Gulf) and Bahrain island. He performed the third pilgrimage to Makkah in 1332, crossed the Red Sea and travelling through Nubia, Upper Nile, Cairo and Syria, reached Lhadhiqiya, whence he sailed in a Genoese ship to Alaya (Candelor) situated on the Southern Coast of Asia Minor.

He travelled inland of Anatolian peninsula which in 1333 was governed by a number of rival chieftains. He reached Sanub (Sinope), a port on the Black Sea, whence he boarded a Greek ship for Caffa and across the sea of Azov to the steppes of Southern Russia. He arrived in the Court of Sultan Muhammad Uzbeg Khan who ruled over an extensive Empire stretching both in Europe and Asia with its Capital at Serai on the river Volga.

He travelled North to Balghar (54 degree N) in Siberia in order to experience the shortness of summer night and had a desire to travel in the 'Land of Darkness' (extreme North of Russia) but turned back from Balghar due to the inclemency of the weather.

Later he escorted Sultan Uzbeg's Queen, Khatun Pylon to Constantinople where she had gone to see her parents. He writes in his Travelogue : "We entered Constantinople at noon and the bells pealed so that the earth shook with the sound. The Khatun alighted from the horse and kissed the ground before her father and mother, and advancing further kissed the hooves of their horses".

His interview with the Byzantine Emperor was rather peculiar. He was ushered like a captive into the presence of the Byzantine Audronicas III (1328– 41) led by an Indian youth named Sumbul.

The Emperor asked his attendants to "honour him" (Ibn Batuta) and presented him with a horse, saddle and a parasol. Returning to Serai, he took leave of Uzbeg Khan and headed towards Bukhara which was a great centre of learning in the world of Islam. Passing through the arid midwinter steppes and waterless deserts of Northern Persia and Afghanistan, he arrived in Kabul. He met in the Hindu Kush mountains a man, who was said to be 350 years old, and got a new set of teeth after every 100 years.

From Kabul he arrived in Sind which was governed by a Governor of Muhammad Tughlaq whose Headquarters were in Multan. He relates very interesting stories about the life in Sind. He says: "After crossing the river of Sind called Punjab, our way led through a forest of reeds, in which I saw a rhinoceros for the first time. After two days march we reached Janani, a large and fine town on the bank of river Sind. Its people are called 'Samira', whose ancestors established themselves there on the conquest of Sind in the time of Al-Hajjaj (712 A.C.). These people never eat along with anyone, nor may anyone observe them while they are eating and they never marry outside their clan. From Janani we travelled to Siwasitan (Sehwan), a large town outside which was a sandy desert, treeless except for acacia. Nothing is grown here except pumpkins and the food of the inhabitants consists of sorghum and peas of which they make bread. There is a plentiful supply of fish and buffalo milk and they eat a small lizard stuffed with curcuma. When I saw this small animal and then eating it, I took a loathing at it and would not eat it. We entered Siwasitan during the hottest period of summer. The heat was intense".

He was the guest of the Administrator of the town whom he calls a

Governor and who was formerly the Qazi of Herat and had entered the service of the Muslim King of India. He sailed down the river along with the Administrator whose baggage was loaded on 15 ships.

He says: "After 5 days travelling on ship we reached Lahari, a fine town on the coast where the river of Sind discharges itself into the ocean. It possesses a large harbour, visited by men from Yemen, Fars and elsewhere. For this reason its contribution to the Treasury and its revenues are considerable. The Governor told me that the revenue from this town amounted to 60 lakhs per annum. The Governor receives the 1/20 part of this, that being the basis on which the Sultan commits the provinces to the Governors. I rode with Ataul Mulk (Administrator) one day and we came into a plain called Tarna, seven miles from Lahari, where I saw innumerable quantity of statues in the shape of men and animals. We saw the ruins of a house with a chamber hewed out of stones resembling a single block, surmounted by a human figure except that its head was elongated and its mouth on the side of its face and its hand behind its back like a pinioned captive. The place had pools of stinking water and an inscription on one of its walls in Indian characters. Ata-ul-Mulk told me that the historians relate that in this place was a great city whose inhabitants were so depraved that they were turned to stone, and that it is their king who is on the terrace in the house, which is still called the 'King's Palace'. They added that the inscription gives the date of the destruction of the people of that city, which occurred a thousand years ago". (According to Cunningham the ruins were of Debal captured by the Arabs).

Ibn Batuta arrived at Bakkar, a fine city intersected by a channel from the river Sind. In the middle of the channel there was a fine hospice at which travellers were entertained.

Travelling through the large town of Uja (Uch), a commercial centre on the bank of river Indus, he arrived in Multan, the Capital of Sind and the Headquarters of the Principal Amir (Governor). He states: "When the new arrival reaches the town of Multan, which is the capital of Sind, he stays there until an order is received regarding his entry and the degree of hospitality to be extended to him".

At a distance of 10 miles from Multan was the town of Khusrawabad on the confluence of river Ravi and Chenab, where the travellers and their baggage was subjected to rigorous custom inspection. The Imperial Capital of Delhi lay at a distance of 40 days march from Multan.

He passed through Abohar and arrived in Ajudhan. He states, "two days later we reached Ajudhan (Pakpattan) a small town belonging to the pious Sheikh Fariduddin. As I turned to the camp after visiting this personage, I saw the people hurrying out and some of our party along with them. I asked them what was happening and they told me that a Hindu had died, that a fire had to be kindled to burn him and his wife would burn herself alongwith him".

On this first sight of *'Sati'* he was so much ovewhelmed with passion that he had almost fallen down from his horse.

On arrival in Delhi, the capital of Sultan Muhammad Tughlaq, he was appointed the State Qazi and stayed there for eight years. He relates interesting stories about India.

Hindus in those days, drowned themselves in the sacred water of the Ganges in order to gain *Baikunth* (Paradise). Commissioned by Emperor Muhammad Tughlaq, he left Delhi with an embassy to the Emperor of China.

Enroute to Cambay, he was attacked by brigands at Jalali near Aligarh and was made a captive. He was about to be executed when a person implored his safety. He sailed for Calicut from Cambay but his entire treasure was lost due to shipwreck.

Being afraid of the displeasures of the Emperor, he gave up the idea of returning to Delhi and took part in the conquest of Goa, visited Maldives where he was appointed Qazi and married four wives.

In 1344 he visited Ceylon on a pilgrimage to its highest peak, the foot of Adam. He sailed eastward and after 43 days voyage rached Chittagong, Dacca and Sumatra. In Sumatra he stayed for 15 days as the guest of the Sultan. He travelled extensively in the East Indies Islands and visited many ports.

In Malaya he witnessed extreme loyalty of a servant to his master. The servant entered the room with a bared scimitar, spoke a few words, bowed low and with a sweep of his arm cut his own head off.

In Indo—China he came across a woman ruler who spoke the Turkish language and had the ambition to conquer India. He landed at Amoy in China and had the good fortune of sailing to Peking in the luxurious yacht of the Emperor of China.

He also visited Zaitun, the greatest Chinese Harbour in those days.

Returning from China and passing through Sumatra, Malabar, India, Oman Persia, Iraq, he crossed the desert to Palmyra and arrived in Damascus. This city was in those days ravaged by black death. He made fourth pilgrimage to Makkah in 1348. Returning from the Holy cities, he travelled via Jerusalem, Gaza, Cairo, Tunis—took a boat for Morocco, visited Sardinia and arrived in Fez, the Capital of Morocco, on November 8, 1349, after 24 years of travel.

Before finally settling down in his native country, he made two more trips—one across the great Sahara desert of Central Africa and the other to Spain in which he travelled extensively and visited almost all historical places.

In 1352, he left Tunis, crossed the great Sahara desert and reached Timbuktoo. He describes an oasis of Sahara desert where people constructed homes of Rock Salt roofed with camel skins.

In Europe, he visited Spain and earlier visited Eastern Roman Empire and Southern Russia as well as sailed in the Mediterranean and the Black Sea. Hardly was there a Muslim country in the three known continents which Ibn Batuta had not visited. He made several tours of the Arab countries and had performed four pilgrimages of the Holy cities (Makkah and Madina).

In 1354 he returned to Fez after completing his central African trip and finally settled there.

At the behest of Sultan Abu Enan of Morocco, he dictated the story of his travels to Sultan's Secretary Ibn Jauzi, who was an Andalusian Theologian. His record is rich in details and fascinating in description. His account entitled : *Tuhfat al Nuzzarfi Ghara'ib al Amsar wa Aja'ib al Asfar* (Gift to observers, dealing with the curiosities of cities and the wonders of journeys). It was generally known as *Rihlat Ibn Batuta* or *'Rihla'* (Journey).

This was completed by Ibn Jauzi on December 13, 1355 A.C. and the manuscript was transcribed by him in February 1356 A.C. There were several manuscripts of *Rihla,* five of them being in the *'Bibbotheque Nationale* of Paris. One of these, being in Ibn Jauzi's own autograph, was completed in February 1356 A.C.

His immortal travel memoris *Rihla* were translated into several Western and Eastern languages including English, French, Latin, Portuguese, German and Persian.

The account of Ibn Batuta's travels though at times sounds like fiction is generally veracious and honest. Ibn Khaldun had expressed some credulity regarding his account of the life in India but Ibn Batuta was supported by Wazir Faris ibn Wadrar.

The same objections were raised about the travel accounts of Marco Polo as both were relating stories which looked like fiction. But leaving aside a few lapses of memory which is not unnatural in such a vast experiences of travels, his accounts are honest.

His account of Asia Minor reveals the several small states in which the country was divided under the pressure of Mongols. His description of Constantinople is superior in details to those of Christian travellers though he was not conversant with the Greek language.

He speaks highly of the administration of the Muslim kingdom of Delhi.

He was first to give a detailed account of Maldive archipelago and Western Sudan. The Chinese section of his travelogue is full of invaluable details. From historical as well as geographical points of view his account is superior to those of almost all other travellers of the Mediaeval times.

His travel accounts are full of description of the peculiarities of different countries he travelled, which include the rite of *Sati*, the cremation of widows and tricks of *'yogis'* in India. He speaks highly of the postal system of Muslim India.

He also witnessed black death in Damascus in 1348 and mentions the frequency of elephantiasis and hernia in Zafar.

He also gives out of his personal experience the peculiarities of the nature of women belonging to different countries.

Thus, before the advent of steam and speedy means of travelling, Ibn Batuta was the greatest traveller that the world had known.

# SULAIMAN AL-MAHIRI

It is not the flight of imagination of a poet but in reality an expression of truth when Iqbal, the poet of Islam says :—

*Dasht to dasht hai dariya bhi na chhore hamne.*
*Bahr-e-Zulmaat men daura diye ghore hamne.*

We did not spare the desert and even the rivers.
We left loose our horses in the dark ocean (Black Sea).

The Muslim mariners and explorers during the Mediaeval times not only explored the uninhabited and distant parts of the world, turbulent seas and vast deserts, but their ships had even reached the New World (America).

The Mariners' compass played a vital role in crossing vast oceans. The Arab mariners were the first to make use of the compass, which enabled them to brave the dangerous seas.

The Arabs have been greatly responsible for discovering distant lands hitherto unknown to the world. But the real history was hidden from the eyes of people and the Muslim achievements in the field of geographical discoveries had been forgotten.

The literary and intellectual treasures accumulated after centuries of untiring efforts in the field of sciences and arts, geography and travels, in Baghdad and Cordova, had been destroyed by Hulaku Khan, the Mongol and the Christian conquerors of Muslim Spain.

Modern research has now begun to lift the veil from the face of Mediaeval ages and certain strange facts have revealed themselves. One of these is the latest theory about the discovery of the New world (America) by the Arabs.

The spherecity and rotation of the earth has been discussed and proved by the Muslim Geographers of the Mediaeval times. The *Kitab Kalimatul Ain* deals with the rotation of the earth which causes days and nights. According to the famous Muslim historian Ameer Ali, "at the time when Europe believed in the flatness of the earth, and was ready to burn any foolhardy person who thought otherwise, the Arabs taught geography by globes".

The Muslim astronomers, too, have proved that the earth is a sphere and has a shape like a peach. The trigonometrical tables of Khwarizmi were translated by Adelard of Bath, Gerard of Cremona and Roger Bacon, in different Western languages. These theories were incorporated in the well-known book, *Imago Mandi*, published in 1410 A.C. which gave an idea of the new world to Columbus, who thought that there must be some elevated place on the other side of the earth which he set out to discover. This has obliged the celebrated orientalist, J. H. Kramers to admit : "The Islamic geographical theory may claim a share in the discovery of the New World".

But the latest research by a leading South African Anthropologist, Dr. Jefferys, has revealed that the "Arabs, not C. Columbus discovered Ameria. The Arabs scored a beat of nearly 500 years over Columbus".

The Arab Mariners had a very wide knowledge of seas and oceans. The greatest contribution of the Arabs is the discovery that oceans are connected with one another and form a compact oceanic world.

The greatest marine explorers among the Arabs have been Sulaiman al-Mahiri and Ibn Majid.

Sulaiman al-Mahiri lived in the first half of the 16th century A.C. He belonged to the South Arabian tribe, Mahara.

Not much is known about the early life of Sulaiman, He had made an extensive exploration of almost all the great oceans of the world and has incorporated his experience in several treatises written by him during the 1st half of the 16th Century.

The first sea route stated by Sulaiman started from the Indian Ocean and passing through the Pacific Ocean, Bering Strait, Arctic Ocean, Atlantic Ocean entered the Mediterranean through the strait of Gibraltar. The other route started from the Indian Ocean, and passing through the Abysinian Sea, Mozambique Channel and encircling the Cape of Good Hope and then passing through the Atlantic Ocean, it entered the Mediterranean through the strait of Gibraltar. This was the route used by Vasco De Gama.

Sulaiman al-Mahiri wrote five important treatises which contain valuable information about nautical science, stars, planets, sea routes, winds and coastal lands:

The first, *Risala Kiladat al-Shumus wa Stikhraj Kawaid al-Usus,* deals with known years and their use by the world. These include lunar, solar, Byzantine, Coptic and Persian years. The epistle also deals with the science of eras.

The second, *Kitab Tuhfat al-Fuhul,* deals with astronomical and nautical sciences, including the description of spheres and stars, sailing at sea and art of navigation.

The third. *Al Umat al-Mahriya fi Dabt al-Ulum al-Bahriya,* deals with distance of stars at the Equator, names of stars, sea routes along the coast, east and west on cape Camorn, routes leading to Hejaz and to the south coast of Arabia, north-west coast of India, east coast of Africa and India, Malaya, Indo–China and Western China. The treatise also deals with routes to Madagascar and a large number of islands in the Indian and Pacific Oceans including Laccadive, Maldive, Andaman, Ceylon, Nicobar, Sumatra, Java, Formusa, Maluccas, Celebes, Banda, Borneo and Timur.

Chapter V of the same treatise deals with Polar star, latitudes of the ports of Red Sea, eastern coast of Arabia and western coast of India, eastern coast of Africa, Ceylon and the Bay of Bengal.

Chapter VI of the same treatise elaborately deals with monsoons in the Indian ocean and describes in details the two types of monsoons striking against the western and eastern coast of India, Burma and Malaya.

Chapter VII of the same treatise deals in details with voyages to the islands along the Arabian and African coast and to Gujrat, Malabar, Hormuz, Debal, Maldives, Cambay, Goa, Calicut and Malacca. The author also enumerates the ten dangers to be avoided by the sailors.

The fourth treatise, *Kitab al Minhaj al-Fakhir fi Ilm al-Bahr al-Sakhir,* deals with sea routes on the coast of Arabia, Makran, Sind, Gujarat, Kankan, Tulwan, Malabar, Somaliland, East Africa, Bengal, Siam, Malaya, Malacca, Indo–China, Western China and some routes of high seas.

Chapter II of that treatise deals with latitudes of inhabited parts.

Chapter III deals with the coast of large islands, including Madagascar, Sychelles, Laccadives, Maldives, Ceylon, Java, Sumatra, Bande, Moluccas, Formusa, Borneo and Celebes.

Chapter IV of this treatise deals with distances between Arabia and Western India, the Bay of Bengal, East Coast of Africa, and certain ports of Sumatra, Java and Bali.

Chapter VI deals with landings and other landmarks of Western India, the Arabian and East African Coasts.

The fifth treatise, *Kitab Sharh Tuhfat al Fuhulfi Tamhid al Usul,* deals with celestial spheres and stars, routes on the high seas, the altitudes of stars and winds.

Sulaiman al-Mahiri was not only a great explorer, who explored distant and unexplored seas but also a useful writer whose five treatises made a significant contribution to the knowledge of astronomical, nautical and geographical sciences of the Mediaeval times.

# INDEX

# INDEX

7229